The Aesthetic Turn in Management

The Aesthetic Turn in Management

Edited by

Stella Minahan and Julie Wolfram Cox

Deakin University, Australia

LONDON AND NEW YORK

First published 2007 by Ashgate Publishing

Reissued 2018 by Routledge
2 Park Square, Milton Park, Abingdon, Oxon, OX14 4RN
711 Third Avenue, New York, NY 10017, USA

Routledge is an imprint of the Taylor & Francis Group, an informa business

First issued in paperback 2018

A Library of Congress record exists under LC control number: 2007921328

Notice:
Product or corporate names may be trademarks or registered trademarks, and are used only for identification and explanation without intent to infringe.

Publisher's Note
The publisher has gone to great lengths to ensure the quality of this reprint but points out that some imperfections in the original copies may be apparent.

Disclaimer
The publisher has made every effort to trace copyright holders and welcomes correspondence from those they have been unable to contact.

ISBN 13: 978-0-815-39740-3 (hbk)
ISBN 13: 978-1-138-62079-7 (pbk)
ISBN 13: 978-1-351-14796-5 (ebk)

Contents

Acknowledgements

The editors and publishers wish to thank the following for permission to use copyright material.

Academy of Management Review for the essays: Antonio Strati (1992), 'Aesthetic Understanding of Organizational Life', *Academy of Management Review*, **17**, pp. 568–81. Copyright © 1992 Academy of Management Review; David Barry and Michael Elmes (1997), 'Strategy Retold: Toward a Narrative View of Strategic Discourse', *Academy of Management Review*, **22**, pp. 429–52. Copyright © 1997 Academy of Management Review.

Administrative Science Quarterly for the essay: David M. Boje (1991), 'The Storytelling Organization: A Study of Story Performance in an Office-Supply Firm', *Administrative Science Quarterly*, **36**, pp. 106–26. Copyright © 1991 Cornell University.

Blackwell Publishing Limited for the essays: Heather Höpfl (2002), 'Playing the Part: Reflections on Aspects of Mere Performance in the Customer–Client Relationship', *Journal of Management Studies*, **39**, pp. 255–67. Copyright © 2002 Journal of Management Studies; Timothy Clark and Iain Mangham (2004), 'From Dramaturgy to Theatre as Technology: The Case of Corporate Theatre', *Journal of Management Studies*, **41**, pp. 37–59. Copyright © 2004 Journal of Management Studies; Ken Kamoche, Miguel Pina e Cunha and João Vieira da Cunha (2003), 'Towards a Theory of Organizational Improvisation: Looking Beyond the Jazz Metaphor', *Journal of Management Studies*, **40**, pp. 2023–51. Copyright © 2003 Blackwell Publishing Limited; Iain L. Mangham (1990), 'Managing as a Performing Art', *British Journal of Management*, **1**, pp. 105–15; Steven S. Taylor and Hans Hansen (2005), 'Finding Form: Looking at the Field of Organizational Aesthetics', *Journal of Management Studies*, **42**, pp. 1211–31.

Emerald Group Publishing Limited for the essays: Mary E. Boyce (1996), 'Organizational Story and Storytelling: A Critical Review', *Journal of Organizational Change Management*, **9**, pp. 5–26. Copyright © 1996 MCB University Press; Thomaz Wood, Jr (2002), 'Spectacular Metaphors: From Theatre to Cinema', *Journal of Organizational Change Management*, **15**, pp. 11–20. Copyright © 2002 MCB University Press.

Harvard Business School for the essay: Henry Mintzberg (1987), 'Crafting Strategy', *Harvard Business Review*, **65**, pp. 66–75.

Institute for Operations Research and the Management Sciences for the essays: Karl E. Weick (1998), 'Improvisation as a Mindset for Organizational Analysis', *Organization Science*, **9**, pp. 543–55. Copyright © 1998 Institute for Operations Research and the Management Sciences; Frank J. Barrett (1998), 'Creativity and Improvisation in Jazz and Organizations:

Introduction

This volume acknowledges the progress made in recent decades by organization and management theorists who have conceptualized the environment and experience of management through an aesthetic lens. In so doing, they have participated in an undertaking that has often flouted convention, and this volume celebrates their work, its title having been deliberately chosen to evoke a shift in direction, an excursion, even a jaunt.

More specifically, the aesthetic turn in management now provides a range of ways of considering management and organization. Some scholars might conceive aesthetic management as an additional device in a rationalist toolbag (see, for example, Witz, Wadhurst and Nickson, Chapter 5, this volume). In contrast, scholars of emotions in the workforce (for example, Ashkanasy, Hartel and Zerbe, 2000) might view it as non-rational within a rational environment, whereas Strati presents a take on aesthetics that has no connection with the rationalist view at all and sees 'aesthetics as a form of knowledge' (Strati, 1996, p. 216). We celebrate the struggle by scholars such as Strati to envisage management in ways that are not subject to the controls of precision and testing and who have engaged their senses in an exploration of the organization in ways that, until recently, were considered neither relevant nor valid.

Organization theorists appropriated the scientific–rationalist paradigm at the turn of the twentieth century. Measuring the absolute, calculating the variance and dividing, subtracting, adding and multiplying the sum of the parts was the preferred means of understanding and improving organizations. The legacy of this way of thinking has been evident through to contemporary times, as illustrated by Pinder and Bourgeois' (1982) criticism of efforts to use metaphor in research as inexact, figurative, wordy and often ambiguous. Notwithstanding the vigorous debate provoked by their criticism, we argue that the metaphor of aesthetics is a good and necessary depiction of organization and management studies because organizations are themselves inexact, figurative, wordy and often ambiguous. Accordingly, those who need precision and ongoing testing will find this collection of essays frustrating as it revels in the murky and muddy, but nonetheless aesthetically interesting, waters of metaphor. Indeed, rather than focusing on the scientific 'ossification' and 'anatomization' of ideas (Burrell, 1996; Chia, 1996), we note that organization studies has been influenced by linguistic (Deetz, 2003; Hall, 1980) and now aesthetic turns (Gagliardi, 1996; Strati, 1999), with analysis informed by discourse analysis (Grant, Keenoy and Oswick, 1998), metaphor (Oswick and Grant, 1996; Morgan, 1986), theatre (Clark and Salaman, 1996; Mangham and Overington, 1987; *Studies in Culture, Organizations, and Societies*, 1996), and jazz (*Organization Science*, 1998; Weick and Westley, 1996). For example, although management has long been described as art (see Strati, 1999, pp. 174–78), the challenge of the aesthetic turn is to extend such analysis so that it is generative rather than representational, allowing an examination of the constitution and social and political structuring of aesthetic orders as well as an appreciation of aesthetic potentials (cf. Deetz, 2003, p. 427).

The essays collected in this volume present ways of thinking about the discipline using aesthetics as both a metaphor for organization and as a way of discussing and knowing organization. This introduction first looks very briefly at the history of aesthetics as a way of knowing. We move then to an appreciation of the field using the six themes around which this volume is constructed:

- The Aesthetic Turn: Arts and Appreciation in Organization and Management
- Following and Framing Management Fashion
- From Fashion to Fiction: Narrative and Storytelling Approaches
- The Theatre and Performance of Management
- Management Improvisation: Jazz and Beyond
- Crafting Management and Management Studies.

Although these themes allow us to present a wide range of thought, it is not possible to cover the work of all the scholars engaged in discussion of organizational aesthetics and/ or the aesthetics of organizations. Consequently, we have chosen to provide an overview that demonstrates a range of depth of interest and a variety of perspectives on aesthetics. In addition, we have included some of the key essays that provide detailed critiques of aesthetics in organizations (see Strati, Chapter 1; Witz, Warhurst and Nickson, Chapter 5), as well as case studies (Boje, Chapter 10; Clark and Mangham, Chapter 17; Humphreys and Brown, Chapter 13). In making our selection for the volume we took care to seek essays from as many different cultures as possible. In this task we had a small degree of success. Our selection is balanced between essays that are highly regarded and cited by other scholars and a number of essays that are not so well known nor frequently cited. Our discussion in this introduction focuses on, but is not limited to, the essays contained in the volume, and we refer to other scholars whose work also informs the topic of aesthetics. Although we were unable to include book chapters in this collection we believe that the essays chosen will be of great interest both to organization theorists seeking to gain an appreciation of aesthetics as a way of knowing in the discipline of management and to practitioners aiming to review or re-present their practice in ways that assist knowing at a sensual, as well as at a cognitive, level.

Aesthetics as a Way of Knowing

Aesthetics in organization theory is a way of knowing through our senses – a way of using our thoughts and feelings to inform our cognitions of organizations. This may be through experiences such as meeting others or knowing through meanings transmitted via the imagery of the arts (see, for example, Heron and Reason, 2001, p. 183). Aesthetics, as a field of interest, has developed over several centuries. In the eighteenth century, Immanuel Kant distinguished the study of aesthetics as a separate discipline. During the nineteenth century, aesthetics was a mode of thought, popular amongst the intelligentsia, that focused on beauty for its own sake without association for teaching or morality. It held that the artist had a responsibility to work with nature to create all manner of music, painting and dance. This association with art and artists persisted, but the term 'aesthetics' now has a 'connotation of decadence or preciousness' (Art Lex Dictionary, 2006). The current disdain conferred on aesthetics can be seen as a form of Puritanism deriving from the association of aesthetics with concepts of pleasure and entertainment. This concern with the pursuit of luxury has become so strong that the term 'aesthetician' is now conferred on those professionals who work with the human body and perform procedures designed to enhance beauty.

Devereaux (2006) points out that the 1980s witnessed the emergence of a feminist aesthetics which presented a more critical analysis, noting that aesthetics standards had largely been drawn from values represented by European patriarchy. The feminist philosophers had created 'a broader and deeper understanding of the many social and cultural variables that contribute to prevailing notions of taste, aesthetic value and artistic genius'.

Aesthetics are often associated with the visual, but there are many other areas of the arts that relate to aesthetics, including music, theatre and drama, storytelling, poetry and craft. And while aesthetics is commonly known as the philosophy of beauty and art, we must stress that it is not just about the visually appealing: as in art, there is often a dark side, a place of absence of beauty. As Strati comments, 'Aesthetics do not coincide with the category of beauty alone – one may also analyse the ugliness, the grotesque, or the kitsch' (1996, p. 209). Where there is beauty, it may reside in unexpected places. Indeed Guillen (1997), cited in the essay by Steven Taylor and Hans Hansen (Chapter 2), puts forward the argument that it is even possible to see beauty in efficiency as embraced by theories of scientific management.

Discussion of organizational aesthetics also includes artefacts and symbols that are not art but are part of the aesthetic experience of organization (see, for example, Strati, 1996). Objects, artefacts and symbols are important as they convey meaning through the designer to the viewer (Budd, 1998).

Aesthetics as Metaphor

In summary, this volume considers the variety of aesthetic experience as organization theorists so far reveal it and focuses on the discussion of aesthetics as metaphor for organization. Accordingly, we have selected categories of metaphors that are all from the creative arts – theatre, music, literature and craft. For example in Chapter 17 Timothy Clark and Iain Mangham argue that theatrical texts can be used to depict examples of management and leadership and suggest that the routines used in rehearsal processes may be described as stimulation and bonding processes for training purposes.

Where it is applied, metaphor can be used to create links between entities. The recipient of the metaphor must be able to make the necessary connections between the known and the unknown in order to create an understanding or new reality that has utility (see Wood, this volume, p. 381). However, Cornelissen (2005) has recently argued that one of the limitations of concern in organization theory is the use of metaphor as a model of comparison – that is, something that is like, and can be compared with, something else. He presents an alternative model for understanding metaphors that is based on an alliance of meanings where the concepts are built and where 'the resulting image and meaning is creative' (Cornelissen, 2005, p. 751). We are sympathetic to his thesis as we believe that attention to aesthetics as a metaphor for management also offers creative potential as an important means of experiencing management knowing – an experience and means of knowing that contributes to individual and collective acuity. Such seeing and hearing management as an aesthetic endeavour allows us to respond to what we perceive via our senses, several of which are captured in each of the six sections that follow.

The Aesthetic Turn: Arts and Appreciation in Organization and Management

The essays in Part I include a mix of foundational, review and critical materials. In the opening essay Antonio Strati sets out his understanding of the aesthetic nature of organizations as a legitimate basis for approaching organizational research. In particular, he demonstrates the 'elusiveness of the aesthetic dimension' and the link between the aesthetic and the process of 'deconstruction, comprehension, and communication' (p. 3). The essay provides an illustration of aesthetic understanding through a detailed description of physical artefacts, their placement and how a person might engage with those objects when they are in the chairman's [*sic*] office and later when in the office of a secretary. Strati moves from a discussion of the aesthetics of the physical office to the challenge of working with the aesthetics of the organization and discusses how a slight modification can change an object to produce an artwork, using Duchamp's art as an example to demonstrate the subtlety of this change. Strati outlines different aspects of aesthetic research, placing emphasis on the researcher's plausibility, the elusiveness of the object of knowledge and the importance of the evocative process. He concludes with a discussion of the associated complexities and modesties of aesthetic understanding in organizations, distinguishing it from 'the assumption that organizational life is a kind of art performance' (p. 15) without presuming that it rejects analytic knowledge.

In Chapter 3 David Barry and Michael Elmes break new ground for discussion through their use of some of the techniques of the novel to explore strategic management as a constructed fiction – a drama, perhaps a form of futuristic science fiction or indeed autobiographical tales. Although not the first to level the elevated and highly fashionable field of strategy (cf. Knights and Morgan, 1991), Barry and Elmes are deliberately provocative in their approach and, heralding several of the themes of this volume, represent familiar strategy frameworks as aesthetic and even material experiences 'crafted in particular genres' (p. 49). Strategy can be part of a major organizational event – a piece of theatre to be performed at reporting and planning events in the corporate cycle, similar to a public relations document designed to persuade and cajole stakeholders to accept the wisdom of the author/general manager. Barry and Elmes ask us to consider similarities between a corporate presentation and a theatrical event where the lights go down, the screen illuminates and the audience is invited to participate in the creation of the performance by listening in carefully or dozing off quietly. So much of what organizational planners do can be directly related to processes of the theatre, including the rehearsals.

Is this sounding a bit kitsch? That could be because, as readers with an interest in aesthetics, we might wonder whether the metaphors of art and theatre could be somewhat trite. Stephen Linstead (Chapter 4) takes us away from the world of the beautiful aesthetic lens to a more unusual view of how the organization is structured and recorded. Whilst kitsch may not be regarded as beautiful, for Linstead it is a useful organizational structure. Kitsch, says Linstead, is a vehicle for allowing one member of an organization to feel some sense of solidarity with other members. He presents kitsch not as a tool for organizing or for organizational research, but as a 'buffer' between the individual and the 'reality' of the organization. It is an organizational sedative to calm our raw nerves and provide some solace and protection in the organizational world. Linstead offers us two examples of kitsch in organization and management studies: Peters' and Waterman's *In Search of Excellence* (1982) and Maslow's 'A Theory of Human Motivation' (1943). He presents a delightful and confrontational reading adds the example of the garden gnome as an organizational metaphor while reminding us of the power of kitsch to provide a lens for organizational members and warning us of the ironies and limitations of kitsch critique. However, as Linstead remarks, following Umberto Eco (1989, p. 199), 'Often the cheap reproduction of the work of art on the commemorative mug is the first sight some people get of it – the more tenacious refuse to settle for this and pursue the original, some just stumble on an insight even through the cheap fake' (p. 85).

The most recent essay in Part I, and one that is also concerned with complicating the aesthetic, is by Steven Taylor and Hans Hansen (Chapter 2). Taylor and Hansen review the field of aesthetic inquiry and compare both the content (from instrumental to aesthetic/feeling) and method (from intellectual to artistic) of different approaches to aesthetics. In a helpful categorization, and making reference to many of the essays included in this volume, they distinguish intellectual analysis of instrumental issues, such as analyses of 'lessons that management might learn from the arts' (p. 25) from using artistic form, such as art therapy, to look at instrumental issues. In addition, Taylor and Hansen differentiate intellectual analysis of aesthetic issues – for example, analysis of the direct sensory experience of organizations – from the use of artistic form to look at aesthetic issues. In calling for more attention to this fourth approach they 'hope to convey the distinct ways that organizations can benefit from aesthetic knowledge' (p. 30), causing us to wonder whether they are indeed reproducing the performative emphasis from which they hope to depart. While they do so using the familiar (kitsch?) form of the two-by-two categorization and adopt an intellectual analysis of aesthetic issues in this essay, they also encourage researchers 'to delve into unknown territory, to get messy and crawl into the underbelly of organizations and look for the many ways members build and expose their organizational lives' (p. 33).

That challenge is ours to take and, as Anne Witz, Chris Warhurst and Dennis Nickson assert in Chapter 5, '[a]esthetics and organization are inseparable' (p. 97). Indeed, the aesthetics of organization are embodied in its labour and its artefacts, such as printed and presented graphics, marketing materials, the design of the physical environment and other types of 'hardware' created to symbolize and communicate understandings of the organization (pp. 97–98).

These five essays allow us to see the organization as an aesthetic entity that can be explored using our senses and feelings, as well as our intellect. We can use the aesthetic turn not only to appreciate organization and management, but also to see that organizational aesthetics are subject to fashions and fads, as presented in Part II of this volume.

Following and Framing Management Fashion

The study of management trends and 'fashions' has produced studies that are revealing, thought-provoking and enjoyable. In marked contrast to the scientific study of management, attention to management fashion brings management to the street, to the body and to the feminine. Rather than management thought being presented as an established and slow-developing body of knowledge it is, instead, subject to fads, fashions and to influential gurus who play a key role in styling what is produced for consumption and later disposal. Such re-presentation has led to various responses and to a reframing of how we approach our discipline. For some theorists this has resulted in investigations of the framing and following of various trends and fashions in management and the essays in Part II look both at various fads and fashions in management and at the metaphor of fashion as used in organization theory.

In '*Haute Couture* and *Prêt-à-Porter*: The Popular Press and the Diffusion of Management Practices' (Chapter 8), Carmelo Mazza and José Luis Alvarez use the language of the fashion apparel industry. They argue that management trends are discussed in two ways in the wider literature on management fashion. The first interpretation is an aesthetic of management fashion that uses arts and crafts to inform the discussion; the second is a rational mode that is measurable and scientific. Focusing on the aesthetic approach to management fashion, they describe haute couture as being evident in the academic outlets of journals and practitioner books, with prêt-à-porter being found in the popular press. Their empirical study is a content analysis of articles relating to human relations management from the Italian popular press, including national newspapers and magazines. They conclude that the popular press, the prêt-à-porter, is the production environment and channel for the diffusion and the legitimation of management practices.

In Chapter 9 Timothy Clark and David Greatbatch use business and management journals and books as their data source. In their analysis they are concerned with the blurring of boundaries between the presentation and the 'original'. In the process of preparation for public consumption 'events' are altered substantially: 'They are packaged to be concrete, immediately graspable, and most importantly, to have maximum impact and mass appeal' (p. 181). This change, Clark and Greatbatch assert, is reflected in the bestselling management texts that, like the broader media, are involved in the building of images that are synthetic. Their argument evokes a 'dark side' of management fashion – one that is based on image, not substance, on audiences, not learning. Indeed, the images may well be highly orchestrated and dramatized depictions of events that are neither real nor original – 'pseudoforms' (p. 199). They suggest that it is important for academics to consider the aesthetics of popular management texts and celebrities and to consider whether the creation of image itself limits the tenure of the management fashion.

Alfred Kieser (Chapter 6) also says that fashion in management is driven by the same forces of the aesthetics of fashion and suggests that theories of fashion adoption can inform studies of the adoption of management fashions. He also pays particular attention to the notion that management techniques can be rhetorical. Kieser offers a neat rationale for this emphasis when he notes that terms such as 'core competencies, empowerment or customer orientation' (p. 117) are neither to be measured or tested precisely. 'People have to agree' (p. 117) on what the terms mean and on the implications of the levels of intensity and frequency with which they are used. Indeed, for a management fashion such as organizational culture, Kieser argues that not only will there be rhetoric present at the outset in its writing, but also that the fashion will also be transmitted through rhetoric and then sold rhetorically.

Kieser is not looking at haute couture or prêt-à-porter (see Mazza and Alvarez, Chapter 8) as a vehicle for change in organizational design, but at popular (bestselling) management books. The 'bestseller' presents a particular rhetoric purveyed by its authors. The imagery of the rhetoric is of alchemy, as the author can promise not pots of gold, but 'quantum leaps in productivity and efficiency' (p. 114). Yet, let the buyer beware as fashion is characterized by a planned obsolescence: the cycles of fashion in management techniques are now much shorter than previously observed. Kieser goes on to remind us of some of the myths and heroes who have featured in management fashion and points out that the popularity of the management 'guru' seems to be on the wane. The contemporary manager is not so easily convinced of the benefits of the rhetoric and, indeed, can be quite cynical when confronted with a supposedly new approach. Kieser (pp. 113–14) reminds us of the Hans Christian Andersen tale, 'The Emperor's New Clothes' in which the stupid and vain Emperor is convinced that he is wearing something new and highly valued when in fact he is parading the streets naked.

Some organizational theorists believe, like contemporary managers, that there is little substance to discussion of fashion in management. Timothy Clark and David Greatbatch (Chapter 9) regard the literature relating to fashion in management as being limited in that 'it is almost completely uninformed by theories of aesthetic fashion or broader discussions about similar social phenomena' (p. 185). Discussing Abrahamson (1996), they note that his work draws on the neo-institutional theories of DiMaggio and Powell (1983) and the innovation-diffusion literature of Rogers (1983) but does not present any basis in aesthetics. Further, they comment that Abrahamson broadens and distinguishes management fashion as being different from aesthetic fashion. Abrahamson argues that fashions that are primarily aesthetic are contemporary and beautiful whereas management fashions 'must appear both rational (efficient means to important ends) and progressive (new as well as improved relative to older management techniques)' (Abrahamson, 1996, p. 254).

Other scholars have also been of the opinion that it is the novelty of an approach that differs from existing approaches that makes a management book popular. However, a management book is more likely to be successful if the novelty factor is sympathetic with the views and norms of the book's audience (see Grint, 1994 for a discussion on innovation-diffusion). Taking a different approach, Clark (1995) and Clark and Salaman (1996) concentrate on how the fashion resides in the management guru, the guru being armed with a particular set of highly persuasive and inspirational communication skills that are used in the creation and performance of 'image-spectacles' (see also Kieser, Chapter 6; Wood, Chapter 18). Thus, management gurus provide the context for the discussion of 'Management Fashion as Image-Spectacle' presented by Clark and Greatbatch in Chapter 9.

Another aspect of storytelling is presented in Bradley G. Jackson's 'A Fantasy Theme Analysis of Peter Senge's Learning Organization' (Chapter 7). Jackson asserts that Senge is an example of a management guru using rhetoric to create his bestselling book and provides us with an example of what Kieser discusses in terms of metaphor and bestsellers. Here, we see how the rhetoric is used to maintain interest in the bestselling piece of fashion in management, 'the learning organization'. According to Jackson, Senge uses a powerful rhetoric when he creates urgency at the macro-level – an immediacy that the reader must consider. This is followed by a focus on a micro-level fantasy with which the leader can engage and be seduced into embracing.

From Fashion to Fiction: Narrative and Storytelling Approaches

Part III directs our attention from the specific rhetoric of management fashions to the broader influence of narrative and storytelling in presenting organization and management through aesthetic lenses. Here we look at four essays that deal in a variety of ways with narrative in organization studies. In each of these essays the authors look beyond the linguistic structure of narrative, presenting instead analyses of the power of stories and of their effects.

Boje (Chapter 10) provides the first example in his ethnography of a firm that distributes office supplies. This early (1991) example of narrative fiction in organization studies is used to describe how organizations can be seen as layers of storytelling – as storytelling systems that are created to help individuals and the collective of organization members to make sense of their world and to provide a rich source of material for organizational myths and legends held in collective organizational memory. Boje analyses a series of story texts and performances enacted within the firm, from stories relating to the mundane content of a sales meeting to the more critical stories of predicting staff turnover. He makes a powerful argument for researchers to accept the relevance of organizational storytelling to theoretical knowledge.

In Chapter 11 Mary E. Boyce reviews Boje's analysis and adds other layers to the understanding of the power of narrative as an aesthetic way of viewing the organization. Boyce asserts that the researcher and consultant alike can harness the power of narrative in organizations. Normative management ideologies link the individual to the organization. Boyce remarks that these links can become unsettled in a polyvocal environment. The diversity and range of narratives is represented in, and enhanced by, a range of symbols that provides yet another aesthetic perspective on the organization. Organizational symbols provide layers of meaning that are not available in words alone – consider, for example, the power of the hierarchy of office furniture allocated humbly to the worker drones and opulently to the queen bee. As Boyce states:

> There is not one authoritative voice of interpretation for the researcher utilizing an interpretive paradigm. There are many voices and many meanings whose understandings overlap, collide, enhance, and silence one another. Organizational symbolism draws attention to the kaleidoscope of symbols and meanings sustained in organizations (p. 240).

A contribution made by Boyce is to call to our attention the importance of studies conducted by other professions including sociologists, folklorists and anthropologists, for it is vital that organization theorists and researchers accept and treasure interdisciplinary approaches to understanding organization and organizing.

In Chapter 12 Barbara Czarniawska points out that the main activity of organization scholars is writing. In recent years some attempts have been made to broaden the delivery media available as research tools for organization scholars to include poetry, painting, film and videos. However, according to Czarniawska, these approaches are not well understood. One of the difficulties is the terminology that has been used to define the disciplines – for example, 'social sciences'. It seems that we have used the term 'science' to provide prestige and credibility to new fields such as 'organization science'.

Czarniawska presents a line drawing of a diamond-shaped kite that she calls a tetrad. Within the tetrad she demonstrates a common ground where literature and science can coexist happily. Since both are styled, she argues that the aesthetic is not so different from the rational–scientific approach. She uses four organization stories to demonstrate her point and to argue for both the recognition of organization studies as a hybrid genre and for greater attention to form as well as to content.

Michael Humphreys and Andrew Brown (Chapter 13) extend the notion of writing about organizations to embrace the study of the multiplicity of voices and dialogues that take place in organizations. They question the homogenization of organization dialogues and call for an understanding of the organization as a type of performance. We take the lead from Humphreys and Brown and move on to discuss theatre and performance in management.

The Theatre and Performance of Management

As noted above, the similarity between management and the theatre has not escaped organization theorists and, in Chapter 14, Iain Mangham gives specific attention to viewing the performance of management as a matter of form. Specifically, he considers the heroic theatrical triumphs of Lee Iacocca, the saviour of the Chrysler car-manufacturing company in the 1980s in the USA, and compares Iacocca's performance at Chrysler with Edmund Kean's performance of Shakespeare's *Richard III*. This analogy is a powerful one since the theatre and management share much vocabulary: 'We enact roles, play our parts, stage events, prompt others, take our cues, perform duties, display our emotions and so on' (p. 310).

Heather Höpfl (Chapter 16) takes the metaphor of work as performance further and uses it to explore the nature of the customer–client relationship in which the worker 'plays a part' and learns – indeed, is taught – 'to act', in a way that meets the customer's perceived needs (p. 345). In particular, Höpfl examines the emotional content and burden of labour as workers play out the role(s) expected of them by management and customers. She reminds us that theatre is dirty work: 'The back-stage world is dirty, sweaty, raw and emotional, fractious, fraudulent' (p. 353). It is back-stage where the craft is learned and roles are perfected. As the customer service personnel must meet their customers and act in role regardless of their true feelings.

Earlier, in Chapter 5, Witz, Warhurst and Nickson use the retail and hospitality industries to explore the aesthetics of work and workers whose effort becomes a commodity enhanced through processes of recruitment and training and then developed as a production mounted and performed in-store (p. 90). The authors argue that this aesthetic labour is embodied labour: 'Work in the shop is staged and scripted: shop assistants are told where to stand, at what angle to the door, how to approach customers and what to say' (p. 94). Indeed, in the case study of an upmarket hotel they discuss that corporation's attempt to produce an aesthetic worker who is integral to, and consistent with, the theatrical environment of the hotel. In this case, aesthetics are used in the hope that the business will be viewed as a valuable entity and aesthetics offer a point of differentiation from the rest of the marketplace.

In Chapter 17 Timothy Clark and Iain Mangham analyse the merger of two banks as an example of 'corporate theatre'. Taking a radical perspective, they present Pineault's definition of corporate theatre as a 'type of production which excites, motivates, and persuades its audience about a company's service, product, and/or slogan through the use of live theatrical performance' (Pineault, 1989, p. 2, cited at p. 364). The 'corporate theatre' is well–financed, unlike its poorer relatives, and is able to present 'audio-visual extravaganzas utilizing state-of-the-art technology such as revolving stages, hydraulics, lasers, complex lighting rigs, computer programming, back-projection, plasma screens and so forth' (p. 364), all presented in a manner suiting high-tech gurus who will use the technology of theatre to get their message across to their stakeholders. As Clark and Mangham argue (p. 375), 'corporate theatre' is not democratic; its extravagant form is seductive and its power causes its audience to feel, but not to think.

Thomaz Wood (Chapter 18) takes the theatre as a metaphor even further when he discusses the movement of the metaphor from theatre to cinema and the importance of this movement within the society of spectacle in which needs and desires are not only influenced, but are determined. Wood demonstrates a contemporary fashion sense when he asserts that the metaphor of the cinema is more appropriate to the times than the theatre. It is noteworthy that the cinema is a vehicle for escapism in which the reality of the dramas, conflicts and tensions being played out in our lives can be suspended. The current fashion of reality television in which the drama is real life leads to a confusion between 'reality' and cinema. As Wood describes, the reality becomes so populated with artificial entertainments that titillate and tempt the viewer with their so-called realism that the viewer is no longer able to distinguish between constructed reality for entertainment and the real experience of the participants.

While Wood stresses the importance of the fluidity of cinema and its commitment to 'the discourse of reality' (p. 387), Rolland Munro (Chapter 15) takes us away from the staged spectacle and back, instead, to the ongoing and everyday performance of control and identity at the financial services company, Bestsafe. In this performance the materials and cultural artefacts of control are ordered or 'summoned' (p. 329) to display both managers' similarity to and distance from other group members. That this ordering and presentation of different life-worlds is 'motile' (p. 325), or subject to variation, reminds us that both the performance of management and its effects are indeed variable phenomena. The fact that '[o]ften it is in its very *lack* of "show" that the performed order of Bestsafe is exhibited' (p. 334) illustrates the importance of absence, as well as presence, in the performance of control. And with absence comes recognition of silence as we now shift our attention from the visual to the auditory aesthetic of management.

Management Improvisation: Jazz and Beyond

Music is a strong theme in the literature of management and aesthetics. The orchestral conductor has been likened to the manager attempting to coordinate the timing and output of a variety of professionals, each with their own particular areas of expertise and skill level (Mintzberg, 1998). In Part V we look beyond the conductor to the music itself and its creation for aesthetic appreciation as well as to musical metaphors for the organization. The essays in this Part reflect the range of literature and focus on jazz music and the processes of improvisation in particular.

Improvisation in music is seen as providing many lessons for organizational researchers and practitioners seeking to understand how an organization can learn. Two main approaches are considered: Alfonso Montuori (Chapter 22) discusses the complexity of improvisation, whereas Karl Weick (Chapter 19) delves into the 'beauty' of failure and how inspirational it can be for the musician. In addition, Frank Barrett (Chapter 20) considers song and how it is used as a vehicle for organizational learning. Responding to previous work, Ken Kamoche, Miguel Pina e Cunha and João Vieira da Cunha (Chapter 21) are particularly concerned with the need to look to a variety of musical genres for inspiration; their view is that, whilst jazz has its place, we can learn from music from a variety of cultures.

Crafting Management and Management Studies

Finally, in Part VI we pay particular attention to the nature and place of craft and of the material in aesthetic approaches to management. In so doing, we note that craft is not new as a metaphor in organization studies. One of the earliest examples we encountered in the research for this volume came from Goodsell (1992) who described the public administrator as a type of artisan. Later Chia and King (1998) argued that there is a continual construction, deconstruction and reconstruction of 'entities' in the process of becoming. Laubacher and Malone (1997) looked to ancient labour organizations, the guilds, as a model for decentralized networks of transitory workers.

In a well-known early contribution to this stream of research, Henry Mintzberg (Chapter 23) argues that mechanistic imagery is an inappropriate means of considering processes of organizational strategy development. According to Mintzberg, the literature on strategic planning is set as a series of deliberate processes, including formulation followed by implementation (p. 479). Mintzberg had long observed the work of a potter, his wife, and came to perceive that the processes of crafting were more suitable to the understanding of planning processes. He presents the manager as the potter and the strategy as the clay. The potter will work the clay using his or her existing skills and experience, including forces of serendipity, leading to innovations that create something new and fresh. He describes this process:

> Our potter is in the studio, rolling the clay to make a waferlike sculpture. The clay sticks to the rolling pin, and a round form appears. Why not make a cylindrical vase? One idea leads to another, until a new pattern forms. Action has driven thinking: a strategy has merged. (p. 479)

Mintzberg challenges the notion that strategies are deliberate, formal and fixed rather than evolving. He continues the metaphor, discussing the emergent nature of planning. The new craftwork emerges, just as a strategy plan can emerge having been through several drafts and permutations to suit the purpose. His main goal is to encourage organizations to focus more on learning, as well as on control. Deliberate strategic planning precludes learning, whereas solely emergent strategy-making removes the control measures so necessary to managing the organization. He advocates flexibility and control in response to the available skills and materials at hand. He calls this an emergent 'process strategy'. The essay goes on to give examples from major corporations and to discuss the management of strategy.

Organizations are complex, emotional, multidimensional and dynamic constructs that shift and move in response to internal and external forces. An aesthetic reading of organizations is not an easy task as the representations sought can be beyond the scope of normal language; hence the move to other media for understanding. Yet even within aesthetics there are divisions and stratifications as demonstrated, in Chapter 24, by Julie Wolfram Cox and Stella Minahan who discuss the divisions between art and craft and the hierarchy within the crafts as gendered and judged according to media and status. This theme is discussed further by the same authors in Chapter 25, which explores decoration as a form of organizational artefacts that, although worthy of study, can be both trivialized and admired within the marginalized discussion of aesthetics.

In 'Crafting Organization' (Chapter 24), Wolfram Cox and Minahan deliberately move away from considerations of organization as science and view aesthetics embodied in organizational crafts as more 'attractive, accessible, malleable, reproducible, and marketable' (p. 487). The essay focuses on the crafts and the 'dreaded art versus craft debate' (p. 489) in which craft is marginalized and valued less than the 'fine arts'. The aesthetics of craft are further devalued with a hierarchy of crafts that values techniques and materials rather than output. For example, those working with fiery kilns or with precious metals are more highly regarded than those working in a domestic environment with textiles. Wolfram Cox and Minahan develop 'an organization of craft', a typology that considers seven different positions of art/craft. These positions are demonstrated using a case study from a now extinct craft centre.

This essay calls for an understanding of the functional and non-representational aesthetic in organizations through the study of craft. Craft, the authors suggest, is worth considering in the writing of organization studies, differing again from science, organic and artistic metaphors. Craft, they believe, is an important lens for viewing management and organization. The philosophy, social hierarchy, skills and attributes of the artisan are all useful metaphors for theorists and practitioners.

It is Yiannis Gabriel (Chapter 26) who reminds us of the value of bricolage, defined as making do with what is there, as in the chef who works with the foodstuffs available and in season or the carpenter who 'makes do with whatever materials and tools are at hand to accomplish a task' (p. 529). More specifically, in Chapter 25 Wolfram Cox and Minahan discuss organization change consultants as organizational decorators who embellish, add to and enhance, rather than downsize, plunder and penetrate. Organizational decorators reflect a more temporary and gentler view of organizational development and change, whilst confirming the study of organizations as aesthetically focused.

Summary

The study of aesthetics has evolved over many centuries, and it is this development that allows organization theorists to use aesthetics as a vehicle for the study of management and organization. The authors represented in this volume have used many forms of art and aesthetics, from object to performance. The inclusion of the metaphor of aesthetics in management is a significant development in research as it allows for a new way of understanding that is, like organizations, messy, non-linear, sometimes murky, inexact and often ambiguous. We have included a range of themes including fashion in management, narrative and storytelling, theatre and performance, including music and improvisation, and craft. This volume presents some of the variety of ways of viewing organizations through an aesthetic lens, and we look forward to more contributions to the aesthetics of organization and management in the future.

References

Abrahamson, Eric (1996), 'Management Fashion', *Academy of Management Review*, **21**, pp. 254–85.
Art Lex Dictionary, at: www.Artlex.com (accessed 6 March 2006).
Ashkanasy, Neil, Hartel, Charmine and Zerbe, Wilfred (eds) (2000), *Emotions in the Workplace: Research, Theory, and Practice*, Westport, CT: Quorum Books.
Budd, Malcolm (1998), 'Aesthetics', in E. Craig (ed.), *Routledge Encyclopaedia of Philosophy*, London: Routledge. Retrieved 6 March 2006 from: http://www.rep.routledge.com/article/M046.

Burrell, Gibson (1996), 'Normal Science, Paradigms, Metaphors, Discourses and Genealogies of Analysis', in S.R. Clegg, C. Hardy and W.R. Nord (eds), *Handbook of Organization Studies*, London: Sage, pp. 642–58.

Chia, Robert (1996), 'Metaphors and Metaphorization in Organizational Analysis: Thinking Beyond the Unthinkable', in D. Grant and C. Oswick (eds), *Metaphor and Organizations*, London: Sage, pp. 127–45.

Chia, Robert and King, Ian W. (1998) 'The Organizational Structuring of Novelty', *Organization*, **5**(4), pp. 461–78.

Clark Timothy (1995), *Managing Consultants: Consultancy as the Art of Impression Management*, Buckingham: Open University Press.

Clark, Timothy and Salaman, G. (1996), 'The Management Guru as Organizational Witchdoctor', *Organization*, **2**(1), pp. 85–107.

Cornelissen, J P. (2005), 'Beyond Compare: Metaphor in Organization Theory', *Academy of Management Review*, **30**(4), pp. 751–64.

Czarniawska, Barbara (1999), *Writing Management*, Oxford: Oxford University Press.

Deetz, Stanley (2003), 'Reclaiming the Legacy of the Linguistic Turn', *Organization*, **10**(3), pp. 421–29.

Devereaux M. (2006), *The Philosophical Status of Aesthetics*, at: http://www.aesthetics-online.org/ideas/deveraux.html. (accessed March 2006).

DiMaggio, Paul and Powell, Walter (1983), 'The Iron Cage Revisited: Institutional Isomorphism and Collective Rationality in Organizational Fields', *American Sociological Review*, **48**, pp. 1457–60.

Eco, Umberto (1989), 'The Structure of Bad Taste', in Umberto Eco, *The Open Work*, Cambridge, MA: Harvard University Press, pp. 180–216.

Gagliardi, Pasquale (1996), 'Exploring the Aesthetic Side of Organizational Life', in S.R. Clegg, C. Hardy, and W.R. Nord (eds) *Handbook of Organization Studies*, London: Sage, pp. 565–80.

Goodsell, Charles T. (1992), 'The Public Administrator', *Public Administration Review*, **52**(3), pp. 246–53.

Grant, D., Keenoy, T. and Oswick, C. (1998), *Discourse and Organization*, London: Sage.

Grint, Keith (1994), 'Reengineering History: Social Resonances and Business Process Reengineering', *Organization*, **1**(1), pp. 179–201.

Guillen, Mauro F. (1997), 'Scientific Management's Lost Aesthetic: Architecture, Organization, and the Taylorized Beauty of the Mechanical', *Administrative Science Quarterly*, **42**(4), pp. 682–715.

Hall, S. (1980), 'Cultural Studies: Two Paradigms', in T. Bennett, G. Martin, C. Mercer and J. Woollacott (eds), *Culture, Ideology and Social Process: A Reader*, London: Open University Press, pp. 19–37.

Heron, John and Reason, Peter (2001), 'The Practice of Co-operative Inquiry: Research "With" Rather Than "On" People', in P. Reason and H. Bradbury (eds), *Handbook of Action Research: Participative Inquiry and Practice*, London: Sage, pp. 179–88.

Knights, David and Morgan, Gareth (1991), 'Corporate Strategy, Organizations, and Subjectivity: A Critique', *Organization Studies*, **12**, pp. 251–73.

Laubacher, Robert J. and Malone, Thomas W. (1997), 'Flexible Work Arrangements and 21st Century Workers' Guilds', MIT Initiative on Inventing the Organizations of the 21st Century, *Working Paper 4*, Boston, MA: Sloan School of Management, Massachusetts Institute of Technology.

Mangham, Iain L. and Overington, M.A. (1987), *Organizations as Theatre: A Social Psychology of Dramatic Appearances*, Chichester: Wiley.

Maslow, Abraham (1943), 'A Theory of Human Motivation', *Psychological Review*, **50**(4), pp. 370–96.

Mintzberg, Henry (1998), 'Covert Leadership: Notes on Managing Professionals', *Harvard Business Review*, November–December, pp. 140–47.

Morgan, Gareth (1986), *Images of Organization*, Newbury Park, CA: Sage.

Organization Science (1998), Special Issue, **9**(5).

Oswick, Cliff and Grant, David (eds) (1996), *Organisation Development: Metaphorical Explorations*, London: Pitman.

Peters, Thomas J. and Waterman, Robert H. (1982), *In Search of Excellence: Lessons from America's Best-Run Companies*, New York: Harper & Row.

Pinder, Craig C. and Bourgeois, V. Warren (1982), 'Controlling Tropes in Administrative Science', *Administrative Science Quarterly*, **27**(4), pp. 641–52.

Pineault, W.J. (1989), 'Industrial Theatre: The Businessman's Broadway', PhD dissertation, Bowling Green State University.

Rogers, E.M. (1983), *Diffusion of Innovations*, New York: The Free Press.

Strati, Antonio (1996), 'Organizations Viewed through the Lens of Aesthetics', *Organization* **3**(2), pp. 209–18.

Strati, Antonio (1999), *Organization and Aesthetics*, London: Sage.

Strati, Antonio (2005), 'Designing Organizational Life as "Aesth-hypertext": Insights to Transform Business Practice', *Organization*, **12**, pp. 919–23.

Studies in Cultures, Organizations and Societies (1996), 'Organizations and Theatre: Play and Performance in the Round', Special Issue, **2**(1).

Weick, Karl E. and Westley, F. (1996), 'Organizational Learning: Affirming an Oxymoron', in S.R. Clegg, C. Hardy and W.R. Nord (eds), *Handbook of Organization Studies*, London: Sage, pp. 440–58.

Part I
The Aesthetic Turn: Arts and Appreciation in Organization and Management

[1]

AESTHETIC UNDERSTANDING OF ORGANIZATIONAL LIFE

ANTONIO STRATI
Trento University

The weak point of study of aesthetics in organizational life has been theorists' definition of the object of analysis, even before their use of methodology and techniques. This article takes a holistic approach to organizations in order to promote aesthetic awareness as a legitimate form of understanding organizational life. It is in contrast to previous approaches that treat the aesthetic dimension as one organizational theme among many. The article illustrates the elusiveness of the aesthetic dimension as an object of knowledge, and it also demonstrates the close link between the organizational aesthetic and the complex process of its deconstruction, comprehension, and communication.

The feeling of beauty is one of the factors that structure organizational life; it is an organizational fact (Strati, 1990: 217). The "beautiful" lies at the core of the analytical framework presented here, even if there are several aesthetic categories, ranging from 6 to 64 in the aesthetic literature: the ugly, the sublime, the graceful, the sacred, the comic, the picturesque.

The category of beauty is found in many areas of study, from aesthetics to ethics, and it subsumes a variety of notions which still hide a mystery (Milani, 1991: 40). The history of beauty dates back to Plato, who considered the beautiful to be one of the three prime archetypes, together with the true and the good. The aesthetics of the ancient Greeks, however, only referred to poetry, music, dance, and mime. Such was the prehistory of aesthetics, first as a specific field of inquiry in philosophy, and then as a part of other sciences. The discipline of aesthetics, in fact, was only founded two centuries ago, as part of the rationalist paradigm that facilitated the institutionalization of art, and eventually made possible the discipline's autonomous development. I consider the category of beauty to be useful in interpretation of organizational life because, thanks to its long history and to its mystery, it can be applied to a wide range of diverse situations. At the same time, and partly in contradiction, I agree with Langer's reflections on art. Regarding music, Langer noted that people sing, make rhythms, and listen to music during their work, and she observed that these actions cannot be considered as art because pure self-expression does not require an artistic form (1963/1942: 216). However, today it is generally acknowledged that analysis of beauty may be extended from art to social practices (Vattimo, 1977: 46), but under what circumstances is the beautiful apparent? There is, in fact, a continuous shifting between aesthetics as a form of knowledge and

aesthetics as an organizational dimension, aspect, or object. Such movement is unavoidable and appropriate to the aesthetic understanding of
organizational life because it brings to light the playfulness of the aesthetic
experience. Gadamer (1975), for example, described the ebbing and flowing of waves and of light and asserted that repeated nonfinite movement is
fundamental to the notion of play (which also lies at the anthropological
basis of the experience of art, together with the concepts of symbol and
feast). Finally, the aesthetic approach to the study of organizational life has
some aesthetic similarities to Duchamp's notion that objects in everyday life
(such as chairs and bicycles) could be combined and slightly modified to
produce a work of art. This conception of art is at odds with the conventional
paradigm; nevertheless, more relevant to the approach that I propose here
is that Duchamp's "ready-mades" were beautiful in his eyes and they gave
him pleasure (Russell, 1985: 170).

The aesthetic understanding of organizational life is an epistemological
metaphor, a form of knowledge diverse from those based on analytical
methods. My intention is to argue for an approach that does not compart-
mentalize the aesthetic into organizational products or into the various
boxes in which organizational life is conducted and studied. I shall seek to
show the reader the complexity, ambiguity, subtlety, and pervasiveness of
the aesthetic in organizational routine and the richness and plausibility of
the knowledge generated by examination of the aesthetic experience. I
should also point out that the researcher *has* direct access to the aesthetic in
organizational life, to its features and to its diversities, to its abstractness and
to its visibility. Nevertheless, except for a few organizational scholars (Benghozi, 1987; Gagliardi, 1990), he or she ignores the aesthetic dimension and,
it seems to me, does it either because he or she does not know how to handle
it or because it has scant legitimacy. This decision not only concerns the
researcher (i.e., his or her self-awareness as a subject of the process of
disciplinary knowledge), it also blurs communication of his or her approach
to the organizational actor and the reader.

AESTHETICS AS ORGANIZATIONAL UNDERSTANDING

In this section I will illustrate the aesthetic dimension within an organization using a nontraditional approach. First, I will address the theme of
corporate and individual aesthetics, and second, I will explain how aesthetics can loosen organizational boundaries.

Regarding the first topic, I will examine the motives that lead to the
acquisition and production of aesthetics in an organization and the various
small adjustments made to it by each of the organization's members: These
adjustments may be fortuitous or they may be part of organizational and
individual rationalities. Regarding the second topic, I will discuss how aesthetics opens significant "windows in the walls of the organization," that is,
windows that both interface with the organization's aesthetic materials and
constitute a mirror of organizational facts. I will also describe how assigned

organizational space may be occupied according to aesthetic criteria that bring to the fore the subjects' visibility strategies and the organizational symbols that express the organization's choice of environment. What is most important, however, is to provide a description of a complex, multiform, and unique organizational setting, one that is rich with insights for reflection and, above all, in some way familiar. I will attempt to do so by referring only to a certain number of physical objects that give the aesthetic appearance to two offices in an Italian firm. This choice is motivated by my assumption that this may be the commonest situation in which researchers of organizations find themselves. My intention is to give an idea and the "flavour" of the aesthetic reading of the organizational life. As a result, certain analytical details and conceptual observations will, unfortunately, be either touched upon very briefly or excluded from the following description.

The Chairman's Office

During my research I paid a visit to the chairman's office of the organization I was studying. His office was on the second floor; that is, it was not on the top floor of the building, but it occupied a position that in many ways was intermediate and central. Hanging on the walls of the chairman's room were (a) his own painting, (b) pictures that had been there before him and were the property of the organization, (c) pictures that were more organizational in nature and served to illustrate and embellish the company. To complete the description of its appearance and aesthetic, the room contained two beautiful plants; a small table apparently haphazardly scattered with publications displaying the organization's products and premises together with publicity material from other organizations; a low cupboard of light-colored wood, which was, in fact, a filing cabinet; a small bookcase containing some objects; a computer, a telephone, a tape recorder, and the organization's logo, all arranged on the desk top; and finally a sofa and two small armchairs. The walls were painted off-white.

The chairman often left his door half open when he was alone. A person could immediately see whether the chairman could be disturbed or if he was on the telephone. Passers-by could exchange rapid nods with him and sense what sort of mood he was in. Above all, they could make sure they were seen.

The chairman's desk stood immediately opposite the door to one side and on the left of the room. That is, the eyes of those entering the door were drawn to the chairman's desk, which was on one side of the room between his armchair and armchairs for his guests. The desk, which held the objects previously described, was usually strewn with file folders, publications, and memoranda. When seated, the chairman was directly in front of his visitor(s). To their right, between two French windows that opened onto a small balcony, hung a painting of an elderly woman; she had a proud, soft but determined expression on her face and she was painted sitting in aristocratic surroundings. The painting dated back a number of years, but was not as old as one might have thought from the woman's clothing, the posture of the sitter, and the painter's style. It was a portrait of the current chairman's maternal grandmother.

I have described the physical aspect of the room—furniture embellishment, status symbols, work technologies, and the organizational communication of them, avoiding the customary procedure of separating them according to their functions or hierarchies. I have done this because it is fundamentally important in the aesthetic reading of organizational life to avoid any distinction between what is a piece of artwork and what is an object of routine practice, and between what are art events and the events of everyday life. The description of the appearance of the office leads to analysis of a specific strategy of the chairman's organizational visibility. The location of the office in an intermediate position within the building, the placement of the door (half-open), and the position of the chairman's desk (opposite the door) showed that he was both available and at work; they did not emphasize his hierarchical position. Great care had been taken with his work place—it was both pleasurable and significant. Taken together, the objects in the office signaled the organization's work philosophy, and the general feeling was homogeneous and consistent. The setting was not the outcome of a single person's design: The image of organizational life in the office was made up of a plurality of different, particular images that opened "new windows" onto the organization's past and present life. This is illustrated by the three kinds of pictures that were found in his office. They were for display; that is, they belonged to the expressive sphere of the organization—they were not part of its operational structure, nor were they its raison d'être or its product. They provide an insight into the history of the organization and an idea of the complex processes that construct organizational aesthetics.

If a person looked around the room, his or her eye would be drawn first toward the chairman's desk and his original painting. The unknown kinship of the portrayed woman and the signature of an obscure artist, the style that dated the picture to a relatively remote past, might have led the person to believe that the subject of the portrait, given the context, was a founding member of the organization.

Opposite the chairman, above the sofa and the low table with the magazines, hung a large picture belonging to the organization. This very large abstract painting, which was executed with considerable style, covered the entire wall. The previous chairman had placed it on the wall where it now hung. Of all the suggestions made by the artistic consultant hired by the organization to advise the previous chairman in his choice, this painting was the most valuable. It was an extremely expensive picture: The money spent on it could have been used to decorate several other offices. In this company, there was no general desire that people should benefit from works of art so that their offices could be made beautiful for colleagues and visitors, but the expense of this purchase certainly resulted in many offices being decorated only with posters. In general, however, the painting gave pleasure to those who looked at it. The former chairman had been right: The members of the organization liked the picture there, exactly where it had been hung.

Next, against the wall by the door were the bookcase and (above it) a large photograph of the organization's bottling and bottle-boxing production line. This photograph documented one of the company's historical facts: the first assembly line to be invented, designed, and built by the organization (the first real line, not a prototype). A section of this line could be seen in the photograph: two rollerways, one for bottling, the other, moving in the opposite direction, for boxing. One could also imagine the area where the bottles were aligned before being lifted onto the line and boxed into cartons. The photograph showed this area only partially, leaving the observer to imagine a suspension between the first track and the second. Striking poses around this section of the production line—photographed half-length and with their eyes fixed on the camera—were the previous chairman, the two owners, and an engineer, all wearing jackets and ties, and the technician and three workers in overalls. The same picture was reproduced in the organization's brochures and could also be seen—as a photograph—hanging in the corridor leading to the conference room. The original photograph in the chairman's office was slightly yellowed and faded. It had been taken by a professional photographer, as was evident from the embossed stamp in the lower left-hand corner.

A large plant and a small picture completed the decorations for this wall. The small picture was a figurative-abstract graphic work by a well-known artist, purchased previously as an investment by one of the owners on the suggestion of a friend who ran an art gallery. The picture had pleased the owner, but aroused the curiosity and admiration of the chairman and others, who were uncertain about its meaning and unsure that they would have hung it in that place. The picture was worth a great deal of money. Why it was so valuable nobody knew, but taking care of it was a fact that provoked argument and worry. What if somebody stole it? The picture did not belong to the organization; it belonged to the owner who had purchased it for the organization, and although the owner was not physically present, it constantly kept his image fresh in the organization members' thoughts. The presence of the picture was not unsettling, but it generated a sense of uncertainty: No one was sure of its artistic or economic value, nor of its position in the organization.

Finally, on the wall behind the chairman's desk, but slightly to one side of it, were pictures that he found useful for his day-to-day work: large sheets of paper with messages (in blue, red, green, and black) written in capital letters. They were apparently randomly placed. These sheets helped him to keep track of the business at hand. Although the information on the sheets could be found in other documents and on the computer, in this form it was readily available to him.

The "windows" opened by these latter pictures have nothing to do with the art history of the paintings or their relevance to art studies. They focused on organizational life. Thus, researchers must be careful to grasp what they

bring to light about the organization. The first painting, for instance, illustrated the ambiguity of the chairman's aesthetic choice. Whether personal
or organizational, the objects that he displayed in his office were primarily
organizational facts for the visitor. The same applied to the photograph,
because photography has an aura of truth. Both the chairman's painting
and the organization's photograph showed that aesthetic objects are not
simply appreciated on the basis of their artistic workmanship alone; they
are special principally because of the emotions, insights, and feelings that
they arouse in the cultures of those who use them or talk about them; and
visitors participate in these dynamics. The choice of the second painting
revealed a complex organizational decision-making process, and it highlighted the climate of general acceptance of the leaders' choices concerning
the aesthetics of the organization. These choices involved a formal decision
only regarding the large abstract painting because the previous chairman
believed in artwork as a financial investment that conveyed a cultivated
and an up-to-date image of the organization. Unlike him, the present chairman and one of the owners considered the organization a space to be
personalized. In any case, all the pictures had been the basis for discussion
and exchanges of opinion among the organizational members (except for
the large sheets of paper on the wall behind the chairman's desk, which
were not mentioned in the interviews conducted on the aesthetic appearance of the office). The chairman's office was, in various ways, a place
about which both members and visitors could make comments. This was not
so, however, with the secretary's office.

The Secretary's Office

At the left side of a small corridor was the chairman's office; to the right
was his secretary's office. This smaller room was long and narrow, and it
had a window at the end. When visitors entered the room they saw a filing
cabinet; on the left side was a desk that divided the room almost in half and
occupied a large part of it. On the desk were arranged a telephone, a
computer, a typewriter, a small plant, diaries, various items of stationery,
and a framed snapshot of the secretary's family. Opposite the desk was a
large office-style cabinet full of files, dossiers, and so forth. A poster showing
a nude sketch by a late Viennese artist hung on the wall between the
secretary's chair and the photocopier.

Pinned up alongside the poster was a photograph of the secretary's two
smiling children. Anyone who had business with the secretary could hardly
fail to see this photograph, and she herself, whenever she turned toward the
computer, "saw" her children. Visitors, unless they were in a tearing hurry
or pathologically rude, asked if the picture was of her children and talked
about them. Her colleagues often asked how they were, spoke about their
own families, and recounted or listened to snippets of gossip. Thus, in the
secretary's office both colleagues and visitors were half invited, half forced
to step outside the confines of their work and their organizational duties and
tasks to listen to remarks on the personal traits and private lives of col-

leagues, customers, and family members. (In effect, they would hear about some hidden side to these people's lives and approve or disapprove of them.)

This type of gossip also went on in the chairman's office, but the "flavour" was different. It would be inappropriate here to compare two offices unlike in function and hierarchical position, or to compare the aesthetic tastes of two subjects (chairman and secretary) of different gender, and with very different personal histories, even though they worked in contiguous spaces that were hierarchically connected. The similarities and differences, however, should be stressed. I will begin with the differences, which relate to the manner in which physical space is filled by those who work in it.

In the secretary's office, the space around the desk was cramped; one could stretch out to get a pencil, or rest on a corner to write one's signature, but things were ordered in such a way that, after a fruitless search for a form that could have been filed in any number of ways, one had to ask where it was kept. For the visitor, confusion seemed to reign: a confusion of plants, family photographs, piled up forms and folders, filing cabinets, machinery, locked drawers, and unlocked drawers. Those who entered took a step toward the desk on the left, leaving the rest of the space for the secretary's use. In this respect, the secretary's office was very different from the chairman's, not only because the latter had more space so that it was possible for a visitor to sit down, but because, given the difference in the size of the two rooms, the chairman occupied only one corner of his office, whereas the secretary occupied two thirds (if not four fifths) of hers. Everyone had to knock to ask permission to enter her office; unlike the chairman, the secretary rarely left her door open.

The similarities are more complex. They concern the image as a means to personalize the working environment and the graphic reference to the family through which this was achieved. The similarities bring out the interweaving of likenesses and differences.

The chairman's painting and the secretary's photograph showed family members; these items personalized the organizational environment, and they channeled the chairman's and secretary's thoughts and those of their visitors toward intimate matters. This personalization restored social complexity to their work personae and projected an image that bridged the gap between life inside and life outside the organization. The photograph did this overtly; the painting more covertly. In the case of the photograph, the subject of the image forestalled the confusion between personal motives and organizational decisions that those seeing the painting were susceptible to, and it likewise evoked a feeling of the sacred. The sacredness, however, was of subjects of daily life that could not be integrated into the life of the organization; that is, they were subjects of other, alien, distinct metaphorical loci. Each image was structured along a different time dimension: The painting invited the observer to consider the past, the personal history of the chairman or, mistakenly, the presumed history of the organization; the photograph induced the observer to look to the future.

The description of these two offices can end here. The aim behind it was to convey the physical objects that constituted the aesthetic appearance of the two rooms. As the description unfolded, however, the actions and thoughts of the organizational members were also included. These actions and thoughts did not orient the research toward more abstract concepts of beauty in organizational life. There were no beautiful events relating to the physical setting of the offices; for example, the moment when the large abstract painting was first hung on the wall. Also, even when the term *beautiful* was employed to describe the offices in themselves, deeper analysis attenuated its aesthetic value. The offices were more-or-less comfortable, according to most organizational members (the chairman, the secretary, and a few organizational members had slightly divergent views)—the work atmosphere was positive and somehow "friendly." These offices did not kindle sentiments like some I have observed in other research studies, where the emphasis of the organizational actor ("the idea of that mathematician is extremely beautiful," or "the gallery is, for me, beautiful *tout-court*," or "the previous organization—that was a beautiful one") not only stressed the nature of the fact under discussion and the intensity of his or her aesthetic experience, but also offered an item of knowledge to be communicated to the reader. At this point, let me suggest two questions: (a) How much does the reader know about this organization and the lives of its members? and (b) What else does the reader think that he or she reasonably knows about this organization, by intuition, deduction, or imagination, which only lacks empirical verification?

DECONSTRUCTION AND RECONSTRUCTION OF THE AESTHETIC EXPERIENCE

Certain kinds of knowledge provide the basis for the imagining of organizational reality, for a cognitive artifact both analytic and intuitive in character. The reader has not seen the actual doors, walls, desks, and work places in this organization. But, it is also true that through the use of reasoning and imagination, the reader may investigate the aesthetic dimension of this organization, reacting as if he or she were there. The aesthetic in the life of organizations is not observable in some pure form. That is to say, this kind of discourse is based on personal allusions, on private analogic processes, and on evocative dynamics that ascribe legitimacy of expression and the right to speak to participants.

The subjects of this specific reading of organizational life are numerous, and the aesthetic discourse created resembles more a hologram than a photograph of the organization. In research three of these subjects are of particular relevance: (a) those within the organization who point out and describe an organizational fact to the researcher as an aesthetic experience; (b) the researcher, who analyzes and describes the experience; and (c) the reader who, through the artifact of the argument, understands and reworks the description.

In the following section I will illustrate activities and relations that focus very much on the researcher. My comments are restricted to the understanding of organizational aesthetics, and they do not deal with issues concerning how this knowledge is managed in organizational contexts. Thus, they illustrate a particular component of a more complex ensemble of different and interwoven processes of study. When conducting research, I believe, investigators of the aesthetics of organizational life find themselves involved in a number of overlapping activities and relations.

First, researchers have their own direct experience of the aesthetic dimension of the organization being studied. They perceive the organization and its physical structuring, they observe how to work within that kind of environment, and they gather their first impressions of its diverse aspects. Together, these ideas make up their personal knowledge of the organization in aesthetic terms. Whether a particular researcher sees the organization as beautiful or ugly, his or her knowledge of its aesthetic dimension cannot be enclosed and limited by direct experience, by first impressions, or by immediate observation. Such actions would shift his or her role from researcher to actor and establish a simplified and shallow relation with the other subjects of aesthetic discourse in organizations.

Second, apart from gaining direct experience, researchers collect organizational facts of an aesthetic nature. In this case, their position is like that of the reader: They were not there; they cannot check. They stand at the threshold of organizational life, just as they would if they were studying other phenomena such as organizational decisions. The beauty of the organization is understood through direct knowledge, through experiences, through the organizational actors' own feelings of beauty, and through stories gathered from other organizational members and perceived as beautiful. When researchers recount their experiences, it may happen that organizational actors reformulate and reelaborate their thoughts and their personal visions of the organization's aesthetics. These members may, thanks to the researcher, relive their experiences or even discover them for the first time as new and previously unthought-of structurings. The more-or-less felicitous intellectual encounter with the researcher may energize the organizational actor; it may channel the conversation into joint analysis of the organizational aesthetic. However much the conversation is jointly conducted, it proceeds along two different paths: one in which the researcher acts as author-actor, the other in which he or she is researcher/nonauthor.

Third, researchers have their own aesthetic experiences of the relationship with the interlocutor. The charm of a story, the beautiful way in which things are described, the evocations and the allusions conjured up by the listener in order to understand the story, and its seductiveness, these notions leave fragments of organizational life impressed on the researcher's memory. If the story is beautifully told, it will act as a structuring factor in the relation between researcher and interlocutor and transform these encounters into part of the organization's aesthetic dimension.

A number of questions and themes relate to the researcher's position and influence aesthetic understanding. Among them, I stress the following, which take into account the relationship between researcher and reader.

The concept of plausibility. When the researcher rethinks the entire research process in order to understand, reelaborate, and convey to the reader the subject of his or her research and reflections, he or she tries to place the reader in a situation that the reader finds plausible. Without the actual and virtual presence of each participant in this symbolic event—that is, without the people who enact the ritual that relates to this knowledge and bring it into being—understanding of such a complex social phenomenon as the aesthetic dimension in the life of organizations remains necessarily limited and marginal. Here, the concept of plausibility is not to be taken as antithetical to the concept of truth. There is a shift rather than a counterposition. The focus is on the reciprocal legitimating processes activated by both the researcher and the reader. In shaping the plausible situation that is crucial for aesthetic understanding, their reciprocal trust is more incisive than their belief in true knowledge.

The concept of elusiveness of the object of knowledge. The purpose of aesthetic discourse is to focus on unique, ephemeral, and ambiguous organizational facts which, although not experienced directly by the reader, can be perceived at the level of imaginative experience and fantasy and are thus credible. What kind of evidence is there to support this belief? When confronted by this kind of knowledge of organizations, scholars can check their findings against personal analogies and metaphorical processes to verify the accuracy of their initial interpretations. But they cannot identify and argue for the aesthetic fact on the basis of their observations alone. Nor can they describe it by using analytical arguments to separate the aesthetic fact from its pathos, for this sets off a process that strips the topic of its significance.

The evocative process as part of organizational knowledge. Doors, desks, windows, pictures, work styles, buildings, and rooms are artifacts differentiated aesthetically by the reader's knowledge; by his or her habitual imaginative canons and loci; and by his or her individual capacity, desire, and intention to perceive the significances proffered. They are objects that have meanings which transform them into artifacts. The researcher may reconstruct aesthetic discourse on the basis of analytical details concerning both organizational life and the research process, but he or she cannot avoid the fact that, in this discourse, evocation is a fundamental process of both "seeing" and "not seeing" the organization being studied.

AESTHETICS AS A THEME FOR ORGANIZATIONAL STUDIES

I shall now illustrate an approach very different from mine, not only to insist on the relevance and the complexity of the subject of aesthetics, but also to highlight further, by contrast, how my understanding of it influences my method of studying organizational life. The approach considers aesthetics in organizations as a topic for analysis, a line of study, an object in itself. This traditional and accredited style of analysis in organization theory breaks organizations down into a number of segments or phases: the characteristics of the product, work environments, and organizational cultures. At the risk of reification, I will examine the importance of the aesthetic dimension in each of them. I will omit, assuming them to be already well known, certain themes of structural-functionalist analysis (e.g., aesthetics as a symbolic resource in the organizational success, aesthetics as a code for structuring communicative processes, or aesthetics as a norm for the organization's functioning).

The Product

When a product is researched, an investigation of past and present developments in the field of industrial design (i.e., in the planning of the industrial product) is obligatory. My investigations have shown that only in the limited context of certain innovative experiments undertaken in a large company by one of its owners (in Italy, for example) has it been possible to achieve the goal of bringing the culture of the entrepreneur and the culture of the artist together. This dream was expressed in the ideal image of the industrial product as simultaneously both useful and beautiful (Munari, 1966). Other European studies have reached the same conclusion. In England, for example, Fairhead (1988) wrote that industrial design is centrally important for the distinctive placement of the organization's product on the market and for the characterization that this gives to the individual organization, to its organizational network and to the type of society in which it develops. Accordingly, what should be a strictly interdisciplinary undertaking is often compartmentalized. Thus, the characteristics of an organization's product are something of a metaphor for it. They are certainly central to many of the initiatives and activities performed within and on behalf of the organization. The separateness of the various actors seems to be a characteristic feature of industrial design. It is important to keep this artificial separateness in mind, for it establishes the boundaries within which aesthetic discourse operates. In other words, the aesthetic is restricted to fragments of the organization and not to the organization as a whole. At the same time, however, these fragments are a crucial aspect of the organization's life.

The Work Environment

The design of the organization's product is a different issue from the external and internal architectural features of the building in which the organization is housed. Whether a person spends his or her working life in antiquated or modern surroundings is often a matter of chance. But the researcher may still ask whether there is a close relationship between the culture of an organization and the culture of the architect that designed its buildings. Architects pay close attention to the requirements of their customers and sponsors because these people are crucially important for their careers (Montgomery, 1990). Nevertheless, the convictions held by architects concerning architectural style and its aesthetics are developed within their professional community, however lacking in organization the architectural profession may be, and despite the influence on it exercised by other professional communities (Blau, 1984). A paradox may arise from the relation between the client's corporate culture and architectural design. This has emerged in the course of my own research, where the organization's culture apparently stems from the representations of it within society at large, which are so deeply rooted as to constitute its ideological mediation. For example, in one study, a group of mathematicians in an Italian university department were asked to comment on the principles of rationality which, according to them, had inspired the architecture of the building specially designed and constructed to house their department. They contended that these principles were at odds with the image-rich nature of mathematical thought and that they reflected instead the layman's idea of what their work involved. The mediating role of the ideology of mathematical rationality between the organizational culture of the client and architectural design shaped and strengthened the aesthetic convictions of several leading Italian architects at the time.

The Organizational Culture

Having illustrated the complexity of the relationship among organizational culture, ideology, and aesthetic design, and having shown the paradoxes that may arise in the physical structure itself, not just in the exterior aspect of organizational objects and settings, I now turn to a less substantial element: organizational culture and the relationship between that culture and the organization's own image. This element is examined in terms of refined patronage versus an organization's cultural discourse. During another research study, the chairman of the oldest photographic factory in the world commented that when a large company sponsored an exhibition of, say medieval sculpture, this was an extremely high-profile act of refined patronage. He stressed, however, that the purpose of the undertaking was to find partners directly interested in proclaiming their organizational history through cultural discourse and, in this specific case, through historical photography and research. The age-old and typically managerial activity of sponsorship (even if the structures that large organizations activate or allow to exist are considered) is often not the organization's principal strategy, unless it relates in some way to the organization's visibility. This strategy derives instead from the interweaving around a managerial philosophy of the voluntarism of certain individuals, their aesthetic tastes and pleasures, and their commitment to and research into the production, acquisition, preservation, and diffusion of beautiful things.

Taken as a whole, the studies briefly referred to above demonstrate that present-day organizations are a long way from the condition that Degot (1987) depicted, sometimes obliquely by metaphor, in his portrayal of the manager as artist, and very far from entrepreneurial activity as analogous to artistic behavior in genre and style. Managers who divide and separate the beauty of a product from its utility and who offer the image of art as the clothing of technology rarely set out to be artists and cannot be regarded and understood as such. Rather, these studies have brought to light ideals and senses of ought-to-be that build vital bridges between art and organization.

CONCLUSIONS

Investigators in organizational aesthetics lack the opportunities for analysis available to historians of the visual, plastic, and musical arts. There is no painting to examine and reexamine; there is no music to listen to; the original aesthetic object is absent. A scholar confronted by the original object can decide whether he or she likes it or not; can live the aesthetic and cognitive experience; and can propose analyses or interpretations that are open to all for acceptance, verification, or rejection. This process does not apply to the aesthetic dimension in organizations. In this case, an original entity as an object, a fact, or an event, unique but infinitely examinable, does not exist. What does exist is the organizational artifact, which escapes objectifying hypotheses and which remains distinct from the subjects operating within the organization. This artifact is a result of the interpretation of a complex of events that arise in the everyday life of an organization.

Acknowledgment of this problem is a necessary condition for the "scientificness" of the fact (Severino, 1980: 541), and if the truth of the aesthetics (Gadamer, 1960) is researched, this acknowledgment provides organization theory with enriched understanding of organizational life. Interpretation has been seen as a scientific activity through which a person explores nonunivocal possibilities and brings to the fore facts that, as Eco (1990: 332) wrote in defense of the less extreme claims of Derrida (1967), are not obviously true or are true in a nonobvious way. Also, I agree with Jameson (1981) and his emphasis on narrative as an epistemological category, a form without content within which facts are shaped in order to be understood rather than just to be described.

On the one hand, the aesthetic reading of organizations that I have illustrated in this article problematizes the organizational knowledge based on analytical methods of study. On the other hand, it does not reject this knowledge and, more important, aesthetic understanding does not entail the assumption that organizational life is a kind of art performance and that art may constitute a metaphor for organizations. In proposing the aesthetic approach as a new intellectual current in organization theories, I do not assume that organizational aesthetics constitute the core of organizational life or of its future. Nor can this approach provide scholars with methodological certainties and privileged objects of organizational analysis. This approach is a "weak thought" (Vattimo & Rovatti, 1983) of organizational life, and it is different from organizational knowledge founded through

1992   *Strati*   581

strong paradigms and the search for universalism and domination. Instead, I consider this approach to be one fragment among many vital approaches for the present complex and ambiguous theoretical framework through which both theorists and researchers seek to cultivate genuine organizational knowledge.

REFERENCES

Benghozi, P. J. (Ed.). 1987. Special issue on art and organization. *Dragon,* 2(4).

Blau, J. 1984. *Architects and firms.* Cambridge, MA: MIT Press.

Degot, V. 1987. Portrait of the manager as an artist. *Dragon,* 2(4): 13–50.

Derrida, J. 1967. *De la grammatologie* [On grammatology]. Paris: Minuit.

Eco, U. 1990. *I limiti dell'interpretazione* [The limits of interpretation, Indiana University Press]. Milan: Bompiani.

Fairhead, J. 1988. *Design for corporate culture.* A report prepared for the National Economic Development Council, London.

Gadamer, H. G. 1960. *Wahrheit und methode* [Truth and Method]. Rubingen, Germany: Mohr.

Gadamer, H. G. 1975. Die Aktualität des Schönen [Actuality of the beautiful]. In A. Paus (Ed.), *Kunst Heute* [Art Today]: 25–84. Graz, Austria: Styria.

Gagliardi, P. (Ed.). 1990. *Symbols and artifacts.* Berlin: de Gruyter.

Jameson, F. 1981. *The political unconscious.* London: Methuen.

Langer, S. K. 1963. *Philosophy in a new key.* Cambridge, MA: Harvard University Press. (Original work published in 1942)

Milani, R. 1991. *Le categorie estetiche* [Aesthetic categories]. Parma, Italy: Pratiche Editrice.

Montgomery, A. 1990. Space, time and architects. *Current Research on Occupations and Professions,* 5: 91–109.

Munari, B. 1966. *Arte come mestiere* [Art as a profession]. Bari, Italy: Laterza.

Russell, J. 1985. *I significati dell'arte moderna* [The meanings of modern art]. Milan, Italy: Mondadori.

Severino, E. 1980. *Destino della necessità* [Destiny of necessity]. Milan, Italy: Adelphi.

Strati, A. 1990. Aesthetics and organizational skill. In B. A. Turner (Ed.), *Organizational symbolism:* 207–222. Berlin: de Gruyter.

Vattimo, G. (Ed.). 1977. *Estetica moderna* [Modern aesthetics]. Bologna, Italy: Il Mulino.

Vattimo, G., & Rovatti, P. A. (Eds). 1983. *Il pensiero debole* [The weak thought]. Milan, Italy: Garzanti.

Antonio Strati is a researcher in sociology of organization at the University of Trento. He received his action research training at the Tavistock Institute of Human Relations in London. He is a founder-member of the Standing Conference on Organizational Symbolism. His current research interests include aesthetics in organizations.

[2]

Finding Form: Looking at the Field of Organizational Aesthetics

Steven S. Taylor and Hans Hansen

Worcester Polytechnic Institute, MA, USA; Victoria University of Wellington, New Zealand

ABSTRACT   Organizational research has long focused on the instrumental sphere with its questions of efficiency and effectiveness and in recent decades there has been interest in the moral sphere with its questions of ethics. Within the last decade there has also emerged a field that draws on the aesthetic sphere of our existence in organizations. In this review we look at the field of organizational aesthetics in terms of content and method, suggesting four broad categories of organizational aesthetics research: intellectual analysis of instrumental issues, artistic form used to look at instrumental issues, intellectual analysis of aesthetic issues, and artistic form used to look at aesthetic issues. We then suggest how organizational scholars might pursue artistic aesthetic organizational research.

INTRODUCTION

The great philosophic development of the enlightenment in the eighteenth century was to analytically divide the world into three separate spheres of existence, instrumental, moral, and aesthetic (Wilber, 1998). This allowed scientists to address questions of how the instrumental, physical world worked separately from associated ethical and spiritual questions. This freedom led to great advances in our ability to understand and control the physical world, which in turn led to great advances in our standards of living.

Thinking about organizations has reflected this division of our reality into three separate spheres. Historically most organizational theorizing concerns itself with the instrumental questions of efficiency and effectiveness. In the last few decades of the twentieth century, the moral sphere started to receive some attention as the study of business ethics made its way into the mainstream. And in the last decade of the twentieth century, organizational theory has started to include the aesthetic

Address for reprints: Steven S. Taylor, Worcester Polytechnic Institute, Department of Management, 100 Institute Rd, Worcester, MA 01609, USA (sst@wpi.edu).

sphere. The degree of domination of the instrumental sphere is clear when we start to ask the question, why might we care about aesthetics, why would we care if something is beautiful or ugly (although as we shall see, the questions of the field are not limited to these)? It doesn't occur to ask the same question about the instrumental sphere (why do we care if it is efficient or effective?); the answer is presumptive and self-evident.

This essay is an attempt to review and make sense of the emerging field of organizational aesthetics. We will look to the various ways that aesthetics has been defined and used within the field to suggest an analytic structure for looking at the field. Then we apply the rough analytic dichotomies to critique where the field is and where we think there is the most promise for the future, concluding with an agenda for pursuing the artistic aesthetic.

CONCEPTUALIZING 'AESTHETICS'

Broadly, aesthetics is concerned with knowledge that is created from our sensory experiences. It also includes how our thoughts and feelings and reasoning around them inform our cognitions. The latest surge of aesthetics into organizational studies comes broadly from the search for alternate methods of knowledge building, and perhaps more specifically, the 'crisis of representation' within organizational research. This 'crisis of representation' emerged along with the movement from positivist/functionalist to interpretive/critical perspectives in organizational studies, and along with the knowledge they generated were the associated problems of representation and form. Postmodernism has begun to show concern for conveying knowledge which involves problems of representation and form, or the poetics of knowledge making (Calas and Smircich, 1999).

Various efforts to organize the field of organizational aesthetics have been made. Strati (2000a) breaks the field down into a focus on (a) images relating to organizational identity, (b) physical space of the organization, (c) physical artifacts, (d) ideas such as the manager as artist and the beauty of social organization, and (e) how management can learn from artistic form and content. Linstead and Höpfl (2000) break their book into parts on 'Aesthetic Theory', 'Aesthetic Processes', 'Aesthetics and Modes of Analysis', 'Crafting an Aesthetic', 'Aesthetics, Ethics and Identity', and 'Radical Aesthetics and Change'. Although these categorizations are interesting, they seem to be based in the authors' sorting of the existing literature and offer little analytic insight into the overall form of the field. We instead turn to ways that aesthetics is defined and used within the existing literature to suggest key analytic dimensions that might be useful for looking at the field.

Aesthetics as Epistemology

In response to Descartes' focus on detached intellectual thinking (e.g. *cogito ergo sum*), both Vico (1744, reprinted in 1948) and Baumgarten (1750, reprinted in 1936) argue against the logico-deductive thinking that results from mind/body separation, claiming knowledge is more about feelings than cognitions. Vico insisted that we were active, sensing participants in creating a non-rational, felt meaning that he called 'poetic wisdom' (cited in Barrett, 2000). Baumgarten suggested that logic was the study of intellectual knowledge, while aesthetics was the study of sensory knowledge. This sensory knowledge is apprehended directly through our five senses, directly through our experience of being in the world. Since the time of Nietzsche (Welsch, 1997), philosophic thinking has agreed that this experiential or aesthetic knowing is not only a separate way of knowing, but that other forms of knowing such as those derived from rational thought depend on, and grow out of aesthetic experiences (Dewey, 1958; Gagliardi, 1996). Aesthetic knowledge offers fresh insight and awareness and while it may not be possible to put into words, it enables us to see in a new way (John, 2001). In the organizational literature this finds its strongest voice in Polanyi's (1958, reprinted in 1978) idea of tacit knowledge. The embodied, tacit knowing corresponds roughly to sensory/aesthetic knowing particularly as it is so often contrasted with intellectual/explicit knowing. Aesthetic knowledge, like tacit knowledge, is routinely in use in organizations but has lacked adequate attention (Strati, 1999, 2000c).

If we look carefully at this distinction of aesthetic/sensory knowing versus intellectual/propositional knowing, we find a distinction that is not just about how we know things, but why we know things. Intellectual knowing is driven by a desire for clarity, objective truth and usually instrumental goals. On the other hand, aesthetic knowing is driven by a desire for subjective, personal truth usually for its own sake. This suggests an analytic dichotomy that we might apply to inquiry in organizational aesthetics. Is the content for instrumental purposes in the dominant traditions of the physical and social sciences which spring from the enlightenment? Or is the content for more aesthetic purposes? We will consider more about what these aesthetic purposes might be later, as we look at other ways in which aesthetics is conceptualized in the literature, but first let us return to the idea of aesthetics as epistemology.

The idea of different ways of knowing is particularly well developed in the work of Heron and Reason (Heron, 1992; Heron and Reason, 2001). They identify four different ways of knowing, experiential, presentational, propositional, and practical.

Experiential knowing is through direct face-to-face encounter with person, place or thing; it is knowing through the immediacy of perceiving, through empathy and resonance. *Presentational knowing* emerges from experiential knowing, and provides the first form of expressing meaning and significance through drawing on expressive forms of imagery through movement, dance, sound, music, drawing, painting, sculpture, poetry, poetry, story, drama, and so on. *Propositional knowing* 'about' something, is knowing through ideas and theories, expressed in informative statements. *Practical knowing* is knowing 'how to' do something and is expressed in a skill, knack or competence. (Heron and Reason, 2001, p. 183)

This description shows how sensory knowledge can inform our cognitions, but also raises the very practical issue of how these different ways of knowing are expressed.

Heron's extended epistemology follows Langer's (1942) ideas about the role of art. Langer suggested that tacit knowledge can be represented through artistic or presentational forms and explicit knowledge can be represented through discursive forms. Discursive forms are characterized by a one-to-one relationship between a set of signifiers and the signified, while presentational forms are characterized by a whole that is not divisible into its component parts. The idea that different ways of knowing require different forms of representation and in particular aesthetic, embodied, tacit knowledge requires presentational/artistic forms of representation, is a direct challenge to the completeness of the dominant, intellectual forms of academic knowledge (e.g. journal articles like this).

Looking closely at this idea of fundamentally different forms of representation also suggests a deeper analytic dichotomy to us. In inquiry, forms of representation play out most directly in terms of the methods used. Is the method based in intellectual/discursive forms of representation and intellectual ways of knowing that they are based on or is the method based in artistic forms that directly represent embodied, aesthetic knowing. The dichotomies of method and content give us two general dimensions for looking at the field of organizational aesthetics. We will begin by reviewing the aesthetics literature to date. Out of the various conceptualizations of aesthetics we derived a map of the field according to method and content. Our more general categorization of the ways aesthetics has been approached in the literature to date further allows us to discuss the implications of each approach and suggest where the field might direct future efforts.

Aesthetics as Criteria for Judgments

'An aesthetic' usually refers to a set of criteria for judgment such as when we might say, 'he has a completely different aesthetic' to mean that we think someone else's taste is rubbish. We owe the search (that most now regard as fruitless) for some criteria by which to judge aesthetic value to Kant's (1790, reprinted in 1951) treatise on philosophical aesthetics (Crawford, 2001). Within organizations, Guillen (1997) has argued that Taylorization and Scientific Management defined a specific aesthetic which equated beauty with efficiency, which still dominates modern organizations. In that sense, 'it's working beautifully' (White, 1996) means that it is working smoothly, efficiently, exactly as planned – the realization of twentieth century management ideals of planning and control.

This idea of aesthetics as criteria for judgment offers us an example of how the content of a piece of organizational aesthetic research can be fundamentally instrumental and non-aesthetic (in the epistemological sense discussed above). This approach uses aesthetics as a philosophic idea and analytic tool for intellectual and instrumental goals. Indeed, one might question whether this is not a fundamental property of research and thus whether our content dimension really has the second pole of 'aesthetic content'. We raise that question thinking that we have found examples of 'aesthetic content', although they are certainly in a minority.

Aesthetics as Connection

So what is 'aesthetic content'? Are we left with the idea of art for art's sake, so thus inquiry for inquiry's sake with no instrumental goals? Although that would seem to qualify, we think that that is not all that qualifies. To consider this further, let us look at the idea of aesthetics as connection. Bateson (1979) suggested that by aesthetic he meant experience that resonated with the pattern that connects mind and nature. Ramirez (1991) developed this idea in terms of systems and suggested that aesthetics were about the 'belonging to' aspect of a system (as opposed to the 'separate from' aspect of being in a system). Sandelands (1998) argues that humans are fundamentally both part of a group and individuals and that artistic forms are how humans express the feelings of being part of a social group. Although this way of thinking about aesthetics is not common in western thought, it is the core of many other cultures', such as the Cherokee, conception of aesthetics (Clair, 1998).

Placing connection in a central role echoes calls from the literature on relationality (e.g. Bradbury and Lichtenstein, 2000) to focus on the spaces between people rather than within individuals. Within the questions about what we mean by connection we start to hit upon one of the reasons that organizational aesthetics is important. If indeed, our feeling of what it is to be part of a group is expressed through aesthetic forms, then aesthetics must be the foundational form of inquiry into social action (Sandelands, 1998). The question of what is connection is essentially a question of what is it to be part of a social group.

Although there may be instrumental purposes for studying connection, this view of aesthetics makes clear that we are looking at aesthetic experience and aesthetic forms fundamentally because they are about our feelings of what it is to be part of more than ourselves. This idea of aesthetics as central gets elaborated in a different way in the work of evolutionary biologist Ellen Dissanayake (2000). For her, art is rhythmic modal elaboration of co-constructed meaning and plays a central role in human society. She starts from mother-infant mutuality and suggests that in this mutuality are the seeds for four fundamental human drives: (1) belonging to a social group, (2) finding and making meaning, (3) gaining a sense of competence through making, and (4) elaborating meanings as a way of acknowledging their importance. In art, these drives all come together in the form of co-created rhythmic experiences that express our shared meaning making – which deepens the idea of aesthetics as connection.

The view of human evolution where art plays a key role as a fundamental drive stands in contrast to evolutionary views based on selection through competition. It is not a great leap to suggest that much of mainstream business thinking is also based in ideas of selection through competition with the implicit logic that if that is how nature and evolution work then business should work that way as well. Then Dissanayake's argument that the way in which art has been marginalized is a mal-adaptive variation that could have disastrous consequences may well also apply to our study of business organizations from a competitive, instrumental viewpoint. Or in other words, aesthetics for the sake of aesthetics (rather than in the service of instrumental goals) may be hugely important in the long run.

Aesthetic Categories

Another way in which aesthetics are conceptualized which leads us to a broader understanding of what aesthetic content might be is in terms of aesthetic categories. So far, we have spoken about aesthetics in a somewhat unitary way. Often this results in aesthetics being confused with beauty. But the beautiful is only one of several aesthetic categories, such as the comic, the sublime, the ugly, and the grotesque (Strati, 1992). These categories are different types of aesthetic experience. The idea of having more beauty in organizations is intuitively appealing, but the aesthetic category of the grotesque may be the key to personal and organizational transformation.

We might also note aesthetics' ability to transform the very categories we use to organize our experiences. Aesthetic forms of expression are like experiments that allow us to reconsider and challenge dominant categories and classifications. Innovative forms resist existing classifications altogether, compelling the creation of new categories, allowing new things to belong in new places (John, 2001) and making possible the juxtaposition of concepts that had been incommensurable. So aesthetic experiences not only transform organizations, but the lenses we use to view them.

Perhaps the clearest implication of aesthetic categories is the way in which they point us to the distinctive questions of inquiry about aesthetic content. Just as instrumental inquiry asks about efficiency and effectiveness and an ethical inquiry asks about right and wrong, an aesthetic inquiry asks about aesthetic categories. Aesthetic inquiry asks, how can we make organizations more beautiful, more sublime, more comic, or more grotesque – not because we think that might lead to greater efficiency or effectiveness, not because that is the right thing to do, but because we desire to live in world that is more beautiful, more sublime, more comic, or more grotesque. That is, aesthetic categories remind us that we care about aesthetics for the sake of aesthetics. But beyond these specific contributions, it is important to draw a picture of the field as a whole for the sake of compari-

Organizational Aesthetics 1217

Content

		Instrumental	Aesthetic
Method	**Intellectual**	• Artistic forms as metaphors for organizations • Lessons for management from the arts • Arguments for the importance of organizational aesthetics • Using aesthetics to deepen our understanding of traditional organizational topics	• Industries and products that are fundamentally aesthetic in nature • Aesthetic forms within organizations • The direct sensory experience of day-to-day reality in organizations
	Artistic	• Artistic forms used to work with individual issues • Artistic forms used to work with organizational issues • Aesthetic forms used to illustrate/present intellectual arguments	• Artistic forms used to present the direct sensory day-to-day experience in organizations

Figure 1. Categories of organizational aesthetics research

son of underlying assumptions and agendas of various approaches to aesthetics. We now turn to our own categorization of the field with hopes of pushing the field towards fertile ground.

REVIEWING THE FIELD

So in order to discuss the field of organizational aesthetics, we offer two continua that we will combine to create that classic of management theorizing, a two by two (see Figure 1). These analytic distinctions emerged as we began to make sense of aesthetic approaches in organizational studies, and we found them to be useful in mapping and critiquing the field. We labelled the two continua method and content. The methods used in aesthetic research range from intellectual methods that are the classic tools of social science research to artistic methods that draw on the use of art practices. Of course, in many cases, the methods draw on both artistic practices and traditional intellectual approaches, but one method usually predominated. On the content continuum, at one end is instrumental content that considers mainstream organizational research questions of efficiency and effectiveness, impact on the bottom line, and power inequities. Other content involves aesthetic issues that address the day-to-day feel of the organization, questions of beauty and ugliness, or in short aesthetic content that has not been part of much of mainstream organizational research.

Of course, there is a great deal of variation within each of our categorizations, which will be evident as we review the organizational aesthetics literature for each quadrant in our matrix. Our aim is to show the breadth of the field and what has already been accomplished and to point to promising avenues not yet pursued. We have included what we feel is a representative sampling of the work in the field; however, we do recognize that there may be work that we have missed as the field tends to publish in a wide variety of journals and disciplines and we recognize that our own bias as to which authors and works have influenced us is clearly evident.

Intellectual Analysis of Instrumental Issues

If we acknowledge that intellectual methods are the dominant methods for social science research and that instrumental content dominates organizational studies, it then comes as no surprise that intellectual analysis of instrumental issues includes the majority of work done in organizational aesthetics. It is also not surprising that there is a great deal of variety of approaches within this area.

Let us start by looking at the long tradition of using artistic forms as a metaphor for organizations and/or activity within organizations. If indeed management is 'a matter of art rather than science' (Barnard, 1938, p. 325), it is only reasonable to ask, what form of art is it like? Perhaps the most well known work is the idea of organization as theatre, which goes back to Goffman (1959), is taken the farthest by Mangham and Overington (1987) and continues to be referenced in works such as Vaill's (1989) *Managing as a Performing Art* (see also Clark and Mangham, 2004). Another major metaphor for organizations and organizational activity is storytelling, which finds its strongest voice in the works of Boje (1991a, 1991b, 1994, 1995; see also Hopkinson, 2003) and narrative (e.g. Coupland and Brown, 2004; Czarniawska, 1998). Here organizations are conceptualized as a collection of stories and organizational action is understood as enacting or relating stories (Gardner, 1995). There is an extensive literature on storytelling in organizations that covers all aspects of management (see Taylor et al., 2002 for a fuller review). More recently there has been an interest in the metaphor of jazz and improvisation (e.g. DePree, 1992; Hatch, 1998; Mirvis, 1998; Montuori, 2003; Weick, 1998) as a way of reconceptualizing our thinking about management. Perhaps the purest expression are pieces that take seriously the idea of the manager as an artist such as Goodsell's (1992) consideration of the public administrator as an artist, Richards' (1995) how-to book on being an artist at work, or the extension of Cameron's popular *Artist's Way* book into the work environment (Bryan et al., 1998).

Following the idea that management is an art, a variety of scholars have asked what lessons management might learn from the arts. This has primarily taken the form of lessons from literature, such as Puffer's (1991) text for teaching organizational behavior and Czarniawska-Joerges' (1994) work. More recently there has been a particular focus in the popular management press on lessons from management to be found in the works of Shakespeare (Augustine and Adelman, 1999; Burnham et al., 2001; Corrigan, 1999; Shafritz, 1999; Whitney and Packer, 2000). This is evolving in the direction of taking lessons for businesses and managers from artists and arts organizations (e.g. Darso and Dawids, 2002; Dunham and Freeman, 2000) and using arts based practices in business organizations (e.g. Austin and Devin, 2003; Ferris, 2002) and management education (e.g. Shim, 2003).

Much of the early work in organizational aesthetics primarily draws on the epistemological conceptualization of aesthetics to make an argument for the importance and reasonableness of an aesthetic approach to organizations. We do not claim to have found all such work, but we think we have found most or at least a good sampling. In roughly chronological order we start with Sandelands and Buckner's (1989) call for research into work feelings generated by aesthetic experience. Strati (1992) explicitly made an epistemological argument that aesthetics was the way to get at the feel of an organization. Then in 1996, there was a special issue of *Organization* in which Strati (1996) argued that aesthetics was an important form of organizational knowledge; White (1996) argued that an aesthetic approach to organizations is apposite, and provided insight into beauty which is a constitutive element of organizations; Ramirez (1996) suggested that future research in organizational aesthetics should address the aesthetic experience of everyday organizational life, organizational design and issues of form, and intervention and research strategies; and Ottensmeyer (1996) argued that we already refer to organizations in terms of beauty and art, but we have not approached them that way academically. In the same year Gagliardi (1996) argued in the *Handbook of Organization Studies* that organizations are filled with artifacts which are perceived by the senses and that means organizations are filled with sensory or aesthetic knowledge. The next year Dean et al. (1997) argued that an aesthetic perspective addresses questions and issues that are not fundamentally instrumental or ethical and that people's aesthetic experience of organizations matter because people are attracted to things they see as beautiful and are repulsed by the ugly. In 1999 two books came out, Strati's (1999) seminal monograph on the field and one in which Dobson (1999) argued that not only were aesthetics important, they were becoming the most important aspect of organizations and were essential for understanding organizations and organizational activity in the 21st century. Although the arguments may not have been won, they had been made and by the turn of the century there was a recognizable (albeit small) field of organizational aesthetics.

There has also been a stream of works that show how an aesthetic perspective can add to and deepen our understanding of various organizational and management topics. Duke (1986) applies an aesthetic perspective to argue that leadership is about bringing meaning to relationships between individuals and organizations/communities/nations. Brady (1986) suggests that an aesthetic perspective extends ethics from 'knowing that' to 'knowing how' and gets past the problems of ethics as rules (also an issue for Dobson, 1999) because of the epistemological stance of aesthetics as being practice based. Chua and Degeling (1993) add aesthetics as another lens for critically assessing managerial actions. Strati (1995) extends organization theory by suggesting an aesthetic approach provides a new way to define what an organization is. Guillet de Monthoux (1996) suggests how art theory can add to our understanding of strategy. Schmitt and Simonson (1997) discuss how to use skills at manipulating aesthetics in marketing. We note that this work stands out in that it uses aesthetics to further the managerialist project, while the politics of the rest of the field (where it is evident) is generally critical and often interested in the emancipatory potential of aesthetics. Feldman (2000) extends organizational politics to include domination through aesthetic forms. Denzin (2000) talks about how the aesthetics of writing articles matters if we want to change the world. Taylor et al. (2002) offer an explanation for how the aesthetic aspects of management storytelling are central to learning, and Witz et al. (2003) expand the concept of emotional labour with a conceptualization of aesthetic labour.

These basic themes continue to occur in recent collections of organizational aesthetics research. Looking at both Linstead and Höpfl's (2000) and Carr and Hancock's (2003) (some of which also appeared in a 2002 special issue of *Tamara* on art and aesthetics at work) edited volumes and the July 2002 special issue of *Human Relations* on organizing aesthetics, the work within this quadrant broadens and deepens these directions. There are introductions and some articles (e.g. Strati, 2000a; Taylor, 2002) that reflect on and make arguments for the importance of the field. The metaphor of organizations as jazz improvisation continues (Barrett, 2000), and the lessons from the arts turn to what the field of organizational studies can learn from the arts (Carr, 2003; Watkins and King, 2002). Many contributions draw on aesthetics to continue the critical project in management studies (Cairns, 2002; Dale and Burrell, 2002; Hancock, 2002) and new subjects such as organizational justice have been enriched by taking an aesthetic perspective (Boyle, 2003).

The work in this quadrant shows us how aesthetics can work within the existing paradigms of organizational research and provide us with new ways to look at old problems. There is clearly real academic value in doing this, and yet by working within the inquiry tradition of intellectual methods applied to instrumental content, there is the possibility that some of the foundational philosophic arguments about the nature of aesthetics may be forgotten. For example, although we know that aesthetic experience is holistic and the sum of the parts does not equal the whole, mainstream methods push us to divide and delve at ever finer levels of analysis. There is the danger in this quadrant that as we advance we will intellectualize and instrumentalize the very aesthetic aspects we originally sought right out of the picture.

There is also the issue of the picture itself. As aesthetics are used to comment on already existing mainstream topics, we must remember that these topics are a result of the instrumental approach. That is to say, our instrumental approaches *made* these the topics we explored because they are the topics instrumentalism could 'see'. When we bring aesthetics to these topics (topics that 'someone else' selected), their contribution is likely to be seen as trite – a neat and interesting 'another way' to look at these instrumental issues. Aesthetics is somewhat welcomed because it can deepen our understandings of these issues and topics, but it is being applied as a band-aid where instrumentalism cannot provide us with satisfying insights to deeper questions.

Artistic Form Used to Look at Instrumental Issues

Although here we start to move away from mainstream organizational studies, there are social science traditions that use aesthetic methods. For example, the use of artistic forms to work with individual behaviour is the basis of the field of art therapy (Rubin, 2001). Art therapy can be roughly divided into two approaches (Malchiodi, 1998). The first focuses on the art-making process as healing and looks at the art product, the presentational form that is produced, as simply a reminder of that process, while in the second approach the primary value is in the art that is produced as a representation of the artist's inner experience. The practice of psychodrama (e.g. Karp et al., 1998; Wilkens, 1999) uses theatre to get at individual and organizational issues. The field of visual anthropology (e.g. Emmison and Smith, 2000; Leeuwen and Jewitt, 2001) provides diverse theory and method for approaching presentational forms and gaining understanding of a variety of instrumental issues.

Although there seems to be quite a bit of practice within organizations there is not much academic work that engages that practice within the field of organizational studies. For example, Nissley et al. (2004) review a range of ways that theatre is currently used within organizations from full scripted productions to improvisation. Schreyogg (1999) has written on this phenomenon, as have Meisiek (2002) and Ferris (2002). We also note Barry's (1994, 1996, 1997) work on using drawings and other art forms to explore issues within organizations and Winter and colleagues' (1999) work on using fiction writing for first person research. All of these examples use intellectual methods to talk about the aesthetic forms; that is to say they address issues around the use of aesthetic forms in organizational research and practice, but they do not then use aesthetic forms. This may be more of a comment on the practices and norms of academic publishing than it is on the research.

However, there are exceptions in which authors attempt to use aesthetic forms, such as Jermier's (1985) classic use of short stories to illustrate his intellectual argument, Taylor's (2000) inclusion of the complete text of a play (in an appendix that is longer than the primary article), and Steyaert and Hjorth's (2002) performance script. We note, that all of these use an intellectual form of discursive argument to frame the aesthetic form. If the authors did not include an intellectual framing, then they would simply (not to suggest that it is ever simple) be creating art around instrumental issues. We suggest that it is in the combination of the intellectual and the artistic forms that scholarship exists.

This quadrant raises an important fundamental question: how is creating art different from doing research? Bradbury and Reason (2001) suggest that one of the criteria for good quality action research is that it encompasses different ways of knowing, in their terms experiential, presentational, propositional, and pragmatic ways of knowing. In these terms, doing art may be an inquiry process for the artist, but it is limited in that it encompasses only experiential and presentational ways of knowing. As we have pointed out, the work in this section tends to include intellectual framing or propositional knowing as well. Of course, neither satisfies the action research criteria for pragmatic knowing as well, but the point we want to make is that academic research includes propositional knowledge and work in this quadrant includes artistic forms/presentational knowing in addition to the propositional knowing.

Intellectual Analysis of Aesthetic Issues

To review work in this quadrant, we must start by discussing what we mean by aesthetic issues and we must confess that we find no simple definition. In lieu of a definition, we shall describe a variety of articles. There is an area of study that is often referred to as cultural industries (e.g. Fine, 1992), which looks at industries in which the products are primarily defined in terms of their symbolic or aesthetic value rather than their utilitarian use value. For example, the product of a fine restaurant is not food to keep us alive, but a complete dining experience that appeals to our senses and sensibilities. In short, these are industries where aesthetic experience (in the sense of being sensory knowledge apprehended directly though the senses), is more important than functionality. Strati (2000b) uses an empathetic-aesthetic methodology to show us the importance of time and the social construction of organizational memory in art photography. Guillet de Monthoux (2000) suggests the idea of aesthetic value (which in his example is created by performance art) as being a separate form of value from the traditional ideas of use value and exchange value.

This focus on aspects of organizations that are somehow fundamentally aesthetic in nature is certainly another type of intellectual analysis of aesthetic issues. Boje (1991b) shows us how storytelling goes on constantly within organizations in a micro, moment-to-moment way. Nissley, Taylor and Butler (2002) argue for how these aesthetic forms are fundamentally different than other forms of discourse in their discussion of the songs sung by Maytag salesmen in the 1930s and 1940s.

This area reaches its fullest realization as researchers look at the direct sensory experience of organizations. Ramirez (1996) suggests that organizational form is not simply an intellectual abstraction but offers a direct sensory experience. Martin (2002) examines the sensory experience of old people's homes (the smell, sight, touch, sound) and its role in providing dignity. Harding (2002) considers the bodies of managers, how they embody the desired aesthetic of the organization, and how they produce and are consumed by the organization. Pelzer (2002) looks at the disgust that comes from an organizational change.

This quadrant represents the type of analytic aesthetics that is rooted in the application of science to the social world. From its beginnings, organizational studies took on the scientific model to explain organizational behaviour and even social constructs such as culture. These deeply rooted yet ill-fitted analytics have also been applied to aesthetic features within organizations. In taking this approach, the artistic object must be privileged over the experience of the object, and aesthetic forms are seen as esoteric in nature and non-instrumental in that they are not created in response to a particular problem. It is not surprising then, that the focus in this area is on industries and products that already involve ongoing aesthetics as a fundamental nature of the work. However, while features or the surrounds of aesthetic objects might be analysed in a valuable way, purely analytic approaches may be too thin to describe deep aesthetic experiences (Shusterman, 2001).

Artistic Form Used to Look at Aesthetic Issues

Approaches that use artistic methods to explore sensory experiences is where we find our unrealized hope for what the field of organizational aesthetics can offer the world. In this final quadrant, we have only two examples to discuss. The first example of aesthetic form being used to look at aesthetic issues is Taylor's (2003b) play *Ties That Bind*. The aesthetic form of the play is used to represent the direct sensory experience of the negative aspects of what it is like to be a young acade-mic. Here again we note the way the artistic form is wrapped in propositional forms – the play script is published as part of a forum on the play, which had been staged as a symposium at the Academy of Management meetings in Denver, and there are three articles (Elmes, 2003; Rosile, 2003; Taylor, 2003a) and the editor's introduction, all of which provide intellectual analysis of aspects of the performance.

The second example is Brearley's (2001a, 2001b, 2002; Brearley et al., 2001) work with the experience of transition in organizational life. She tracked the expe-riences of managers as they went through a difficult merger. Part of her research process is creating poems, songs, and multi-media tracks from interview data and images that the managers created. These artistic forms capture the feeling of the transition and work with traditional intellectual analysis to give a richer, fuller, more-embodied understanding.

It is in this quadrant that we see the real hope for organizational inquiry that aesthetics offers us. The use of artistic forms to look at aesthetic issues offers a medium that can capture and communicate the felt experience, the affect, and something of the tacit knowledge of the day-to-day, moment-to-moment reality of organizations. Not just the cleaned-up, instrumental concerns of 'the business', but the messy, unordered side as well. In short it provides a holistic way to get at the whole of the experience, something that the intellectualization and abstrac-tion of traditional organizational research often seems to miss.

So how does aesthetic inquiry move more fully into the final quadrant of our two by two? In pursuing this area, we must elaborate our own epistemology and suggest a research agenda and methods from the ongoing practices and concep-tualizations that are emerging as researchers are finding their form in aesthetic research. As we have done throughout, we hope to convey the distinct ways that organizations can benefit from aesthetic knowledge.

It is clear that our focus within organizational aesthetics is the creation of sensory-based knowledge through aesthetic experiences. The two enduring com-ponents of this approach to aesthetics are (1) engagement of the senses and (2) the focus on the experiences over objects (in and of themselves). Dewey (1958) said art's purpose was to achieve a more satisfying experience, one that invigorates us and aids our achievement in whatever ends we pursue. We suggest a similar agenda for organizational aesthetics. Recall the example of work songs (Nissley et al., 2002), which provide a satisfying experience within and of themselves. However, aesthetic experiences are also constantly spilling over and being integrated into other activities, enhancing and deepening them (Shusterman, 2001). Here, we would suggest a descriptive account of that aesthetic experience and the meaning that experience has for organizational members, as well as insight into how those experiences enhance the work and organizational life. Artistic forms in organiza-tions show us how individuals relate to and create their organizational lives. If we express what it means to be part of a group aesthetically, researchers need to research meaning with methods that are consistent with this phenomenon by exploring these meanings in the way they are made.

A constructionist view of aesthetics as sensory knowledge rooted in experience has implications for how we go about collecting and describing aesthetic data. An important aspect of this conceptualization is that while insights provided by an aesthetic experience are not easily detached from that experience, those particular insights cannot be reached by any other route. In this pursuit, aesthetic methods share much with ethnographic methods. Research calls for insight into the experience, either through ethnographic interviews regarding those generative experiences, or direct participation in the aesthetic experiences and the emergent sensemaking that flows from them. Indeed, several aesthetic researchers have made the link explicit and applied ethnographic methods to capture aesthetic knowledge (e.g. Letiche, 2000; Linstead, 2000; Rusted, 2000). While aesthetic data might be interpreted using ethnographic methods, the departure is most evident in how that data is produced and represented, and here is where aesthetic inquiry can make a unique contribution.

Related to data production, aesthetic inquiry does not involve naturalistic inquiry (Lincoln and Guba, 1985) into social interaction, rather aesthetic forms in organizations are more deliberately contrived social productions. To describe the data production in aesthetic inquiry, we might suggest terms such as 'participant construction' as opposed to participant observation. As opposed to social interactions, researchers might participate in artistic interactions where members display more artful expressions to make connections or elaborate meaning beyond what is possible discursively. Aesthetic knowledge might not retain its felt meaning in discourse, but may be expressed in its aesthetic form through artful constructions. To observe artful participant constructions using aesthetic knowledge, we might encourage members to make artistic productions and describe meanings 'at play' and those that emerge from that production experience. This method is certainly not naturalistic, but if the members are enthusiastic, it is a good way to tap into the aesthetic sensibilities of an organization.

In making interpretations, as with ethnography we still rely on the researcher as the interpretive device. Though this still results in an 'art-ifical' production rather than an artful production as by organizational members, Strati (1999) suggests a sort of 'turning on the senses' and researcher reflexivity that focuses on aesthetic judgment. To encourage this new stance, we might modify some terminology, such as 'thick *sensory* description' instead of 'thick description' (Geertz, 1973) and 'members with their own senses' as opposed to 'members in their own words' as a way of reorienting ourselves in interpreting aesthetic data. Visual methodologies will be helpful as well.

It is in representing aesthetic knowledge through aesthetic inquiry that new forms must emerge if aesthetics is to continue to contribute to understanding organizational life. John (2001) notes that worthwhile aesthetic knowledge must be able to travel a bit beyond its acquisition site, allowing us to build upon that knowledge in other contexts. In sharing or transferring aesthetic knowledge, we need forms of presentation that keep the aesthetic knowledge 'intact', closer to the forms and objects that were constructed and experienced by organizational members to convey meaning in organizations. This is not a realist concern, but an attempt to retain the ability of those aesthetic forms to communicate in the terms by which they were produced. Take the case of Taylor (2003b). This was a 'researcher-as-participant' aesthetic production representing early academic life. We might move further into participant construction of artifacts, plays, poems, paintings and all manner of artistic work where the organizational members are the creators and artists.

As we mentioned in our discussion of artistic form used to look at instrumental issues, creating art about organizational issues is only part of the research process; there must also be an intellectual analysis of that art. Within organizational research, dramatist such as Goffman (1959), Burke (1945), and Turner (1982, 1986) provide a theoretical basis for analysis of these types of artistic productions, and of course methods of artistic interpretation and criticism from outside of organizational studies could also prove useful. Regardless of the methods used, an attempt should be made to represent rich aesthetic meanings in a way that diminishes (at least some) of the researchers interpretation, letting the reader in to make an interpretation and relying less on the researcher as connoisseur (Rusted, 2000). The challenge is in seeking ways to continue to favour the aesthetic experience, whether it is the experience of the producers or the interpreter/reader.

CONCLUDING THOUGHTS

Aesthetic inquiry is certainly one of the most active movements within the post-positivist paradigm. Its progress is on the back of hard fought arguments and legitimacy won from approaches such as symbolic interactionism (that includes social construction and dramaturgy), postmodernism, and critical theory. Aesthetic inquiry deepens our understanding of organizations by providing a new epistemology, criteria to assess member judgments and decision making, meaning, connection and provides categories for this sensory data. As such, it is attracting more and more researchers and practitioners as it continues to make sense of organizations in a way that resonates – that fills in the less understood spaces in organizations. For practitioners, it provides a means to express that tacit level knowledge that guides much of organizational behaviour. While this type of research is often characterized as a look into what is often called 'the mundane' in everyday organizational life, it is only mundane in the sense that aesthetic understandings are so profoundly ingrained and unquestioned that their maintenance through the reconstruction of aesthetic forms in organizations seems so routinely ordinary.

Aesthetics offers a new look into organizations, and a look at alternative ways of expressing and making meanings that deeply influence organizational interactions, behaviours, and understandings. Our categorization helps researchers to be more conscious of the ways they approach organizational aesthetics and the implications of differing methods and content. This is important because raising our awareness regarding underlying assumptions will help aesthetic researchers better direct their efforts as the research itself takes on an aesthetic. The categorization also highlights the small amount of work that uses artistic form to look at aesthetic issues and it is this area where we find the most promise for the field of organizational aesthetics. Although there are clearly contributions to be made in the other quadrants, this area makes a unique contribution and opens the door into a vital and new understanding of organizations. There have long been calls to conduct research into the more sensory and less rational sides of organizational reality and a variety of intellectual efforts to do so have been made. We see the use of artistic forms to look at these fundamentally aesthetic issues to have the potential to finally bring these important areas into the mainstream of organizational research and practice.

This research into organizational aesthetics will require something new of researchers. Unlike concepts that researchers call on organizations to implement such as empowerment, ethics, and diversity, organizational aesthetics are alive and well in organizations. They don't need our encouragement, they need our attention. The onus is on researchers to take on a commitment to studying this space in organizations. To do this, researchers will have to be trained academics, and also exploratory artists. Don't drop your tools, but pick up some new ones or old familiar ones you might have ignored. Researchers have to try to delve into unknown territory, to get messy and crawl into the underbelly of organizations and look for the many ways members build and expose their organizational lives. Heed Clegg and Hardy's call to 'resuscitate the subject, breathe life back into those stilled lips, disturb the somnolent and death-like state, shatter metaphorical bottles of analytic formaldehyde' (1996 p. 697).

REFERENCES

Augustine, N. and Adelman, K. (1999). *Shakespeare in Charge: The Bard's Guide to Leading and Succeeding on the Business Stage*. New York: Hyperion.
Austin, R. and Devin, L. (2003). *Artful Making: What Managers Need to Know About How Artists Work*. New York: Financial Times, Prentice Hall.
Barnard, C. I. (1938). *The Functions of the Executive*. Cambridge, MA: Harvard University Press.
Barrett, F. J. (2000). 'Cultivating an aesthetic of unfolding: jazz improvisation as a self-organizing system'. In Linstead, S. and Höpfl, H. (Eds), *The Aesthetics of Organizations*. London: Sage, 228–45.

Barry, D. (1994). 'Making the invisible visible: using analogically-based methods to surface the organizational unconscious'. *Organizational Development Journal*, **12**, 4, 37–48.

Barry, D. (1996). 'Artful inquiry: a symbolic constructivist approach to social science research'. *Qualitative Inquiry*, **2**, 4, 411–38.

Barry, D. (1997). 'Telling changes: from narrative family therapy to organizational change and development'. *Journal of Organizational Change Management*, **10**, 1, 30–46.

Bateson, G. (1979). *Mind and Nature: A Necessary Unity*. New York: E. P. Dutton.

Baumgarten, A. G. (1750, reprinted in 1936). *Aesthetica*. Bari: Laterza.

Boje, D. M. (1991a). 'Consulting and change in the storytelling organization'. *Journal of Organizational Change Management*, **4**, 3, 7–17.

Boje, D. M. (1991b). 'The storytelling organization: a study of story performance in an office-supply firm'. *Administrative Science Quarterly*, **36**, 1, 106–26.

Boje, D. M. (1994). 'Organizational storytelling: the struggles of premodern, modern and postmodern organizational learning discourses'. *Management Learning*, **25**, 3, 433–61.

Boje, D. M. (1995). 'Stories of the storytelling organization: a postmodern analysis of Disney as Tamara-land'. *Academy of Management Journal*, **38**, 4, 997–1035.

Boyle, M.-E. (2003). 'Reconciling aesthetics and justice in organization studies'. In Carr, A. and Hancock, P. (Eds), *Art and Aesthetics at Work*. New York: Palgrave Macmillan, 51–64.

Bradbury, H. and Lichtenstein, B. M. B. (2000). 'Relationality in organizational research: exploring the space between'. *Organization Science*, **11**, 5, 551–64.

Bradbury, H. and Reason, P. (2001). 'Broadening the bandwidth of validity: issues and choice-points for improving the quality of action research'. In Reason, P. and Bradbury, H. (Eds), *Handbook of Action Research: Participative Inquiry and Practice*. London: Sage, 447–55.

Brady, F. N. (1986). 'Aesthetic components of management ethics'. *Academy of Management Review*, **11**, 2, 337–44.

Brearley, L. (2001a). 'Exploring creative forms within phenomenological research'. In Barnacle, R. (Ed.), *Phenomenology*. Melbourne: RMIT University Press, 74–87.

Brearley, L. (2001b). 'Foot in the air: an exploration of the experience of transition in organisational life'. In Boucher, C. and Holian, R. (Eds), *Emerging Forms of Representing Qualitative Data*. Melbourne: RMIT University Press, 151–84.

Brearley, L. (2002). *Beyond Univocal Authority: An Exploration of Creative Voices in Academic Research*. Melbourne: Common Ground.

Brearley, L., Boucher, C., Burrows, P., Jones, S. and Holian, R. (2001). 'Advice for researchers using alternative forms of representation'. In Boucher, C. and Holian, R. (Eds), *Emerging Forms of Representing Qualitative Data*. Melbourne: RMIT University Press, 187–93.

Bryan, M., Cameron, J. and Allen, C. (1998). *The Artist's Way at Work: Riding the Dragon*. New York: Quill.

Burke, K. (1945). *A Grammar of Motives*. Berkeley, CA: University of California Press.

Burnham, J., Augustine, N. and Adelman, K. (2001). *Shakespeare in Charge: The Bard's Guide to Learning and Succeeding on the Business Stage*. New York: Hyperion.

Cairns, G. (2002). 'Aesthetics, morality and power: design as espoused freedom and implicit control'. *Human Relations*, **55**, 7, 799–820.

Calas, M. B. and Smircich, L. (1999). 'Past postmodernism? Reflections and tentative directions'. *Academy of Management Review*, **24**, 649–71.

Carr, A. (2003). 'Art as a form of knowledge'. In Carr, A. and Hancock, P. (Eds), *Art and Aesthetics at Work*. New York: Palgrave Macmillan, 7–37.

Carr, A. and Hancock, P. (Eds) (2003). *Art and Aesthetics at Work*. New York: Palgrave Macmillan.

Chua, W.-F. and Degeling, P. (1993). 'Interrogating an accounting-based intervention on three axes: instrumental, moral and aesthetic'. *Accounting, Organizations and Society*, **18**, 4, 291–318.

Clair, R. P. (1998). *Organizing Silence: A World of Possibilities*. Albany, NY: SUNY Press.

Clark, T. and Mangham, I. (2004). 'From dramaturgy to theatre as technology: the case of corporate theatre'. *Journal of Management Studies*, **41**, 1, 37–59.

Clegg, S. and Hardy, C. (1996). 'Representations'. In Clegg, S., Hardy, C. and Nord, W. (Eds), *Handbook of Organization Studies*. London: Sage, 676–708.

Corrigan, P. (1999). *Shakespeare on Management: Leadership Lessons for Today's Managers*. London: Kogan Page.

Coupland, C. and Brown, A. (2004). 'Constructing organizational identities on the web: a case study of Royal Dutch/Shell'. *Journal of Management Studies*, **41**, 8, 1325–47.

Crawford, D. W. (2001). 'Kant'. In Gaut, B. and Lopes, D. (Eds), *The Routledge Companion to Aesthetics*. London: Routledge, 51–64.

Czarniawska, B. (1998). *A Narrative Approach to Organization Studies*, Vol. 43. Thousand Oaks, CA: Sage.

Czarniawska-Joerges, B. (1994). *Good Novels, Better Management: Reading Organizational Realities in Fiction.* London: Routledge.

Dale, K. and Burrell, G. (2002). 'An-aesthetics and architecture'. *Tamara: Journal of Critical Postmodern Organization Science*, **2**, 1, 77–90.

Darso, L. and Dawids, M. (2002). 'It's time for the artists to help the poor business people'. *Learning Lab Denmark Quarterly*, October, 6–7.

Dean, J. W. Jr, Ottensmeyer, E. and Ramirez, R. (1997). 'An aesthetic perspective on organizations'. In Cooper, G. L. and Jackson, S. E. (Eds), *Creating Tomorrow's Organizations: A Handbook for Future Research in Organizational Behavior.* New York: John Wiley.

Denzin, N. K. (2000). 'Aesthetics and the practices of qualitative inquiry'. *Qualitative Inquiry*, **6**, 2, 256–65.

DePree, M. (1992). *Leadership Jazz.* New York: Dell.

Dewey, J. (1958). *Art as Experience.* New York: Capricorn.

Dissanayake, E. (2000). *Art and Intimacy: How The Arts Began.* Seattle, WA: University of Washington Press.

Dobson, J. (1999). *The Art of Management and the Aesthetic Manager: The Coming Way of Business.* Westport, CT: Quorum Books.

Duke, D. L. (1986). 'The aesthetics of leadership'. *Educational Administration Quarterly*, **22**, 1, 7–27.

Dunham, L. and Freeman, R. (2000). 'There is no business like show business: leadership lessons from the theater'. *Organizational Dynamics*, **29**, 2, 108–22.

Elmes, M. (2003). 'Every silver cloud has a black lining: actor reflections on 'Ties That Bind''. *Management Communication Quarterly*, **17**, 2, 301–7.

Emmison, M. and Smith, P. (2000). *Researching the Visual: Images, Objects, Contexts, and Interactions in Social and Cultural Inquiry.* London: Sage.

Feldman, S. P. (2000). 'Micromatters: the aesthetics of power in NASA's flight readiness review'. *Journal of Applied Behavioral Science*, **36**, 4, 474–90.

Ferris, W. P. (2002). 'Theater tools for team building: how an improvisational play got one software team back on track'. *Harvard Business Review*, **80**, 12, 24–5.

Fine, G. A. (1992). 'The culture of production: aesthetic choices and constraints in culinary work'. *American Journal of Sociology*, **97**, 5, 1268–94.

Gagliardi, P. (1996). 'Exploring the aesthetic side of organizational life'. In Clegg, S. R., Hardy, C. and Nord, W. R. (Eds), *Handbook of Organization Studies.* London: Sage, 565–80.

Gardner, H. (1995). *Leading Minds: An Anatomy of Leadership.* New York: Basic Books.

Geertz, C. (1973). *The Interpretation of Cultures.* New York: Basic.

Goffman, E. (1959). *The Presentation of Self in Everyday Life.* New York: Doubleday.

Goodsell, C. T. (1992). 'The public administrator as artisan'. *Public Administration Review*, **52**, 3, 246–53.

Guillen, M. F. (1997). 'Scientific management's lost aesthetic: architecture, organization, and the Taylorized beauty of the mechanical'. *Administrative Science Quarterly*, **42**, 4, 682–715.

Guillet de Monthoux, P. (1996). 'The theatre of war: art, organization and the aesthetics of strategy'. *Studies in Cultures, Organizations, and Societies*, **2**, 147–60.

Guillet de Monthoux, P. (2000). 'Performing the absolute. Marina Abramovic organizing the unfinished business of Arthur Schopenhauer'. *Organization Studies*, **21**, 0, 29–51.

Hancock, P. (2002). 'Aestheticizing the world of organizations: creating beautiful untrue things'. *Tamara: Journal of Critical Postmodern Organization Science*, **2**, 1, 91–105.

Harding, N. (2002). 'On the manager's body as an aesthetics of control'. *Tamara: Journal of Critical Postmodern Organization Science*, **2**, 1, 63–76.

Hatch, M. J. (1998). 'Jazz as a metaphor for organizing in the 21st century'. *Organization Science*, **9**, 5, 556–7.

Heron, J. (1992). *Feeling and Personhood: Psychology in Another Key.* London: Sage.

Heron, J. and Reason, P. (2001). 'The practice of co-operative inquiry: Research "with" rather than "on" people'. In Reason, P. and Bradbury, H. (Eds), *Handbook of Action Research: Participative Inquiry and Practice.* London: Sage, 179–88.

Hopkinson, G. (2003). 'Stories from the front-line: how they construct the organization'. *Journal of Management Studies*, **40**, 8, 1943–69.

1230   S. S. Taylor and H. Hansen

Jermier, J. M. (1985). 'When the sleeper awakes: a short story extending themes in radical organization theory'. *Journal of Management*, **11**, 67–80.

John, E. (2001). 'Art and knowledge'. In Gaut, B. and Lopes, D. (Eds), *The Routledge Companion to Aesthetics*. London: Routledge, 329–52.

Kant, I. (1790, reprinted in 1951). *Critique of Judgment*. Trans. Bernard, J. New York: Haffner.

Karp, M., Holmes, P. and Tauvon, K. B. (Eds) (1998). *The Handbook of Psychodrama*. London: Routledge.

Langer, S. K. (1942). *Philosophy in a New Key*. Cambridge, MA: Harvard University Press.

Leeuwen, T. V. and Jewitt, C. (2001). *Handbook of Visual Analysis*. London: Sage.

Letiche, H. (2000). 'Observer versus audience'. In Linstead, S. and Höpfl, H. (Eds), *The Aesthetics of Organization*. London: Sage, 154–79.

Lincoln, Y. and Guba, E. (1985). *Naturalistic Inquiry*. Newbury Park, CA: Sage Publications.

Linstead, S. (2000). 'Ashes and madness: the play of negativity and the poetics'. In Linstead, S. and Höpfl, H. (Eds), *The Aesthetics of Organization*. London: Sage, 61–92.

Linstead, S. and Höpfl, H. (Eds) (2000). *The Aesthetics of Organizations*. London: Sage.

Malchiodi, C. A. (1998). *The Art Therapy Sourcebook: Art Making for Personal Growth, Insight, and Transformation*. Los Angeles, CA: Lowell House.

Mangham, I. L. and Overington, M. A. (1987). *Organizations as Theatre: A Social Psychology of Dramatic Appearances*. Chichester: Wiley.

Martin, P. Y. (2002). 'Sensations, bodies, and the "spirit of a place": aesthetics in residential organizations for the elderly'. *Human Relations*, **55**, 7, 861–85.

Meisiek, S. (2002). 'Situation drama in change management: types and effects of a new managerial tool'. *International Journal of Arts Management*, **4**, 3, 48–55.

Mirvis, P. H. (1998). 'Practice improvisation'. *Organization Science*, **9**, 5, 586–92.

Montuori, A. (2003). 'The complexity of improvisation and the improvisation of complexity: social science, art and creativity'. *Human Relations*, **56**, 2, 237–55.

Nissley, N., Taylor, S. S. and Butler, O. (2002). 'The power of organizational song: an organizational discourse and aesthetic expression for organizational culture'. *Tamara: Journal of Critical Postmodern Organization Science*, **2**, 1, 47–62.

Nissley, N., Taylor, S. S. and Houden, L. (2004). 'The politics of performance in organizational theatre-based training and interventions'. *Organization Studies*, **25**, 5, 817–40.

Ottensmeyer, E. J. (1996). 'Too strong to stop, too sweet to lose: aesthetics as a way to know organizations'. *Organization*, **3**, 2, 189–94.

Pelzer, P. (2002). 'Disgust and organization'. *Human Relations*, **55**, 7, 841–60.

Polanyi, M. (1958, reprinted in 1978). *Personal Knowledge: Towards a Post-Critical Philosophy*. London: Routledge and Kegan Paul.

Puffer, S. M. (1991). *Managerial Insights from Literature*. Boston, MA: PWS-Kent Publishing Co.

Ramirez, R. (1991). *The Beauty of Social Organization*. Munich: Accedo.

Ramirez, R. (1996). 'Wrapping form and organizational beauty'. *Organization*, **3**, 2, 233–42.

Richards, D. (1995). *Artful Work: Awakening Joy, Meaning, and Commitment in the Workplace*. San Francisco, CA: Berrett-Koehler.

Rosile, G. A. (2003). 'Critical dramaturgy and artful ambiguity: audience reflections on "Ties That Bind"'. *Management Communication Quarterly*, **17**, 4, 308–14.

Rubin, J. A. (2001). *Approaches to Art Therapy: Theory and Technique*, 2nd edition. Philadelphia, PA: Brunner-Routledge.

Rusted, B. (2000). '"Cutting a show": grounded aesthetics and entertainment organizations'. In Linstead, S. and Höpfl, H. (Eds), *The Aesthetics of Organization*. London: Sage, 111–29.

Sandelands, L. E. (1998). *Feeling and Form in Social Life*. Lanham, MD: Rowman and Littlefield.

Sandelands, L. E. and Buckner, G. C. (1989). 'Of art and work: aesthetic experience and the psychology of work feelings'. *Research in Organizational Behavior*, **11**, 105–31.

Schmitt, B. and Simonson, A. (1997). *Marketing Aesthetics: The Strategic Management of Brands, Identity, and Image*. New York: The Free Press.

Schreyogg, G. (1999). 'Definition und typen des bedarfsorientienten theaterinsatzes in unternehmen'. In Schreyogg, G. and Dabitz, R. (Eds), *Unternehemenstheater: formen – erfahrungen – erfolgreicher einsatz*. Wiesbaden: Gabler.

Shafritz, J. (1999). *Shakespeare on Management: Wise Business Counsel from the Bard*. New York: Harper Collins.

Shim, S. (2003). 'The creative curriculum'. *BizEd*, July/August, 33–9.

Shusterman, R. (2001). 'Pragmatism: Dewey'. In Gaut, B. and Lopes, D. (Eds), *The Routledge Companion to Aesthetics*. London: Routledge, 97–106.

Steyaert, C. and Hjorth, D. (2002). 'Thou are a scholar, speak to it . . . " – on spaces of speech". A script'. *Human Relations*, **55**, 7, 767–97.

Strati, A. (1992). 'Aesthetic understanding of organizational life'. *Academy of Management Review*, **17**, 3, 568–81.

Strati, A. (1995). 'Aesthetics and organizations without walls'. *Studies in Cultures, Organizations, and Societies*, **1**, 83–105.

Strati, A. (1996). 'Organizations viewed through the lens of aesthetics'. *Organization*, **3**, 2, 209–18.

Strati, A. (1999). *Organization and Aesthetics*. London: Sage.

Strati, A. (2000a). 'The aesthetic approach to organization studies'. In Höpfl, H. (Ed.), *The Aesthetics of Organization*. London: Sage, 13–34.

Strati, A. (2000b). 'Putting people in the picture: art and aesthetics in photography and in understanding organizational life'. *Organization Studies*, **21**, 0, 53–69.

Strati, A. (2000c). *Theory and Method in Organization Studies*. London: Sage.

Taylor, S. S. (2000). 'Aesthetic knowledge in academia: capitalist pigs at the academy of management'. *Journal of Management Inquiry*, **9**, 3, 304–28.

Taylor, S. S. (2002). 'Overcoming aesthetic muteness: researching organizational members' aesthetic experience'. *Human Relations*, **55**, 7, 821–40.

Taylor, S. S. (2003a). 'Knowing in your gut and in your head: doing theater and my underlying epistemology of communication'. *Management Communication Quarterly*, **17**, 2, 272–9.

Taylor, S. S. (2003b). 'Ties that bind'. *Management Communication Quarterly*, **17**, 2, 280–300.

Taylor, S. S., Fisher, D. and Dufresne, R. L. (2002). 'The aesthetics of management storytelling: a key to organizational learning'. *Management Learning*, **33**, 3, 313–30.

Turner, V. (1982). *From Ritual to Theater: The Human Seriousness of Play*. New York: Performing Arts Journal Publications.

Turner, V. (1986). *The Anthropology of Performance*. New York: PAJ Publications.

Vaill, P. B. (1989). *Managing as a Performing Art*. San Francisco, CA: Jossey-Bass.

Vico, G. (1744, reprinted in 1948). *The New Science of Giambattista Vico*. Trans. Bergin, T. G. and Fisch, M. H. Ithaca, NY: Cornell University Press.

Watkins, C. and King, I. W. (2002). 'Organizational performance: a view from the arts'. *Tamara: Journal of Critical Postmodern Organization Science*, **2**, 1, 31–46.

Weick, K. E. (1998). 'Improvisation as a mindset for organizational analysis'. *Organization Science*, **9**, 5, 543–55.

Welsch, W. (1997). *Undoing Aesthetics*. Trans. Inkpin, A. London: Sage Publications.

White, D. A. (1996). ' "It's working beautifully!" Philosophical reflections on aesthetics and organization theory'. *Organization*, **3**, 2, 195–208.

Whitney, J. and Packer, T. (2000). *Power Plays: Shakespeare's Lessons in Leadership and Management*. New York: Simon and Schuster.

Wilber, K. (1998). *The Marriage of Sense and Soul: Integrating Science and Religion*. New York: Random House.

Wilkens, P. (1999). *Psychodrama*. London: Sage.

Winter, R., Buck, A. and Sobiechowska, P. (1999). *Professional Experience and the Investigative Imagination: The Art of Reflective Writing*. London: Routledge.

Witz, A., Warhurst, C. and Nickson, D. (2003). 'The labour of aesthetics and the aesthetics of organization'. *Organization*, **10**, 1, 33–54.

[3]

STRATEGY RETOLD: TOWARD A NARRATIVE VIEW OF STRATEGIC DISCOURSE

DAVID BARRY
University of Auckland
MICHAEL ELMES
WPI

Using narrative theory, this article explores strategic management as a form of fiction. After introducing several key narrative concepts, we discuss the challenges strategists have faced in making strategic discourse both credible and novel and consider how strategic narratives may change within the "virtual" organization of the future. We also provide a number of narrativist-oriented research questions and methodological suggestions.

STRATEGY'S CHANGING STORY

Looking back, it appears that the field of strategic management had an enchanted childhood. Two decades ago, "planning could do no wrong" (Mintzberg, 1994: 4). In the midst of studies demonstrating positive planning-performance relationships (Ansoff et al., 1977; Herold, 1972; Thune & House, 1970), it was common to see planning-as-panacea statements like "[T]he top management of any profit seeking organization is delinquent or grossly negligent if they do not engage in formal, integrated, long-range planning" (Karger & Malik, 1975: 64). Business school departments fought over who should and could use the term *strategy*: management, marketing, finance, human resources, and operations faculty all eagerly appropriated the name.

Today it appears strategy's "golden-boy" image has receded a bit. Mirroring longstanding concerns with competition, forecasting, and fit, the field itself has become a highly contested and questioned site, one riddled with competing models, "whither now" conferences, and effectiveness disputes. In the wake of numerous problematizing studies (e.g., Boyd, 1991; Gimpl & Dakin, 1984; Grinyer & Norburn, 1975; Hurst, 1986; Mintzberg, Brunet, & Waters, 1986; Mintzberg & Waters, 1982; Quinn,

We would like to thank the following people for their comments, supporting materials, and encouragement: David Boje, Barbara Czarniawska-Joerges, Mary Jo Hatch, Mary Ann Hazen, Ulla Johanson, Juha Näsi, Emery Roe, Ralph Stablein, and the three anonymous *AMR* reviewers. We would also like to thank Charles W. L. Hill and Susan Jackson for all their editorial assistance. This article was written in full collaboration.

430   *Academy of Management Review*   April

1980; Wildavsky, 1973), several respected theorists have called for re-conceptualizing the strategic enterprise (cf. Mintzberg, 1994: 91–214; Prahalad & Hamel, 1994).

Taking a Narrative Turn

We too think the field might benefit from some redefinition. As narrativist Wallace Martin said, "By changing the definition of what is being studied, we change what we see; and when different definitions are used to chart the same territory, the results will differ, as do topographical, political, and demographic maps, each revealing one aspect of reality by virtue of disregarding all others" (1986: 15). In particular, we are interested in examining strategy as a form of narrative. Our goal is not to replace current strategic thinking, but to provide theorists and practitioners with an additional interpretive lens. Though the "narrative turn" has become increasingly popular in other organizational areas (e.g., Boje, 1995; Czarniawska-Joerges, 1996; Hatch, 1994; O'Connor, 1995; Rappaport, 1993; Roe, 1994), we believe it is particularly applicable to strategy. If "storytelling is the preferred sensemaking currency of human relationships among internal and external stakeholders" (Boje, 1991: 106), then surely strategy must rank as one of the most prominent, influential, and costly stories told in organizations. Although some researchers have discussed ways in which strategic texts and authoring processes act as sequentializing sensemaking devices (e.g., Quinn, 1992; Weick, 1995), few have systematically described strategy using formal narrative concepts or models.

Among its various attractions as an approach for studying strategy, narrativity emphasizes the simultaneous presence of multiple, interlinked realities, and is thus well positioned for capturing the diversity and complexity present in strategic discourse. As Weick (1995: 129) stated, "Stories allow the clarity achieved in one small area to be extended to and imposed on an adjacent area that is less orderly." Compared to other "artful" metaphors of strategy (e.g., Andrew's 1971 "strategist-as-architect" or Mintzberg's 1987 "strategy-as-craft" and "strategist-as-potter"), narrative highlights the discursive, social nature of the strategy project, linking it more to cultural and historical contexts (cf. Smircich & Stubbart, 1985): it is used to ask why some strategic stories are more or less popular and how popularity might be linked to other narrative forms circulating in society. It also addresses how leaders are able to fashion stories that "concern issues of personal and group identity" (Gardner, 1995: 62) and that "transplant, suppress, complement or in some measure outweigh, the earlier stories, as well as contemporary, oppositional 'counterstories'" (Gardner, 1995: 14) that hold social groups together.

Accordingly, a narrative approach can make the political economies of strategy more visible (cf. Boje, 1996): "Who gets to write and read strategy? How are reading and writing linked to power? Who is marginalized in the writing/reading process?" It also can call attention to strategy's rhetorical side: How do rhetorical devices function to increase (or under-mine) strategic credibility? How are rhetorical dynamics used to "autho-rize" strategy and mask its subjectivities?

From a practitioner's viewpoint, the narrativist stance can encourage people to explore strategic issues in more meaningful ways (Wilson, 1979: 4). Through referral to classic archetypal figures and motifs (e.g., the hero, martyr, or wanderer), it might provide a deeper sense of meaning and purpose than can be achieved through, for example, spreadsheet model-ing. Inasmuch as questions of "voice" and "style" are raised, reflexivity can be increased.

Some Informing Narrative Voices

Among literary theorists, narrative has gradually become a key plat-form for locating and discussing storied accounts, whether those accounts are past or future oriented, written or spoken, fact or fantasy, short story or novel (cf. Chatman, 1978; Martin, 1986; Polkinghorne, 1988). As an inter-pretivist approach (cf. Burrell & Morgan, 1979; Hiley et. al., 1991), narrative theory issues "not in laws like Boyle's, or forces like Volta's, or mechanisms like Darwin's, but in constructions like Burckhardt's, Weber's, or Freud's: systematic unpackings of the conceptual world in which condottiere, Cal-vinists, or paranoids live" (Geertz, 1980: 167). It draws extensively from literary criticism, rhetorical theory, aesthetics, semiotics, and poetics; its writers are as concerned with artistry as they are with content and catego-rization.

Given that definitional work often constitutes a primary dynamic within literary circles, it is not surprising that there has been much debate over just what the term *narrative* means—for example, do poems and screenplays count? Folktales? Individual sentences? (cf. Genette, 1988: 13–20; Martin, 1986: 15–30; Rappaport, 1993). Some theorists adopt a "struc-turalist" view in which order and continuity are stressed. For example, Robert Scholes defined narrative as "the symbolic presentation of a se-quence of events connected by subject matter and related by time" (Scholes, 1981: 205). Others have shifted toward a "communication" per-spective, where readership and interpretation are as important as struc-ture or authorship (cf. Booth, 1983; Iser, 1989). In this article we follow this latter trend by using the terms *narrative* and *story* to refer to thematic, sequenced accounts that convey meaning from implied author to implied reader. Within this perspective, hermeneutic, parts-to-whole thinking con-stitutes a central focus, as Donald Polkinghorne explained:

> Narrative is a form of 'meaning making.' . . . Narrative recog-nizes the meaningfulness of individual experiences by noting how they function as parts of the whole. Its particular subject matter is human actions and events that affect human beings, which it configures into wholes according to the roles these actions and events play in bringing about a conclusion. . . . The narrative scheme serves as a lens through which the ap-parently independent and disconnected elements of existence are seen as related parts of a whole. (1988: 36)

432   *Academy of Management Review*   April

More than with other approaches, according to narrative theory, subjective, heterogeneous interpretations of texts are the norm; different readers are assumed to "get it" differently, depending on their history, values, or even which side of the bed they rise from. Accordingly, we consider our discussion of the strategy field simply one of many possible interpretations, one fashioned not as testable truth but rather provocative optique, a view that opens up new trains of thought.

Implied in the above discussion is that narrativity encompasses both the telling and the told; it can be applied both to strategizing and to strategies. Extant, formalized (and perhaps realized) strategies can be examined as artifacts: their rhetoric, tropes, metaphors, and sequencing can be identified, compared, and evaluated in various ways. Strategy can also be examined as a narrative process, one in which stories about directionality are variously appropriated, discounted, championed, and defended. This view asks, "How do people make sense of and narrate their notions about directionality?" "When does a strategic story stay the same and when does it change?" "How does it survive 'register' changes—alternating between the printed and the auditory, the formal and informal, or between intrafirm and industry levels?"

Yet as Martin (1986) and other recent theorists have argued, texts and authoring processes are inextricably intertwined. How strategic stories are constructed shapes their form. Further, the availability of various textual forms affects the process of strategic authoring. Thus, in the sections that follow we meld considerations of strategies and strategizing. First, we identify strategy as a particular kind of narrative. Then, using an analytic scheme derived from the Russian Formalists (a literary theory group), we examine some of the twists and turns strategic discourse has taken over the years. Finally, indulging in a bit of predictive fin-de-siècle thinking, we consider some future narrative possibilities in light of emerging postindustrial organizational thought.

STRATEGY AS A TYPE OF NARRATIVE

Traditional conceptualizations of strategy have tended toward notions of fit ("How might we fit into this or that environment?"), prediction ("What is ahead? Where will we be then?") and competition ("How might we 'rule the roost,' survive within the 'pecking order,' or gracefully 'chicken out'?"). In contrast, a narrative view of strategy stresses how language is used to construct meaning; consequently, it explores ways in which organizational stakeholders create a discourse of direction (whether about becoming, being, or having been) to understand and influence one another's actions. Whereas authors of traditional strategy frameworks virtually ignore the role of language in strategic decision making, writers using a narrative approach assume that tellings of strategy fundamentally influence strategic choice and action, often in unconscious ways.

As a narrative form, strategy seems to stand somewhere between theatrical drama, the historical novel, futurist fantasy, and autobiography.

Inasmuch as it prescribes "parts" for different characters, it leans toward the dramatic. Its traditional emphasis on forecasting aligns it with visionary novels having a prospective, forward-looking focus. And when emergent, retrospectively focused strategies are considered (e.g., Mintzberg 1994: 24–27; Quinn 1980; Weick, 1979), a sense of historical narrative is invoked.

Regardless of the particular narrative camp a strategy lies in, however, it can be considered a form of fiction. By fiction, we mean that which is created, made up, rather than something which is false. As Bubna-Litic (1995) argued, strategy is fictional no matter which of Mintzberg's "Five P's" is considered (strategy as plan, ploy, pattern, position, or perspective; cf. Mintzberg, 1987); it is always something that is constructed to persuade others toward certain understandings and actions. Although these points apply for prospective, forward-based strategy, emergent strategy can also be considered fictional: to identify an emergent strategy requires labeling specific organizational actions as "strategic" (not just financial or operational); highlighting, juxtaposing, and linking them in certain ways; convincing others that this is the way things have happened; and prescribing that this account should be the template from which new actions should be considered. In other words, strategists working from an emergent perspective enact fictional futures from creative interpretations of the past (cf. Smircich & Stubbart, 1985; Weick, 1995: 30–38).

As authors of fiction, strategists are subject to the same basic challenge facing other fictionalist writers: how to develop an engaging, compelling account, one that readers can willingly buy into and implement. Any story the strategist tells is but one of many competing alternatives woven from a vast array of possible characterizations, plot lines, and themes. If we accept the notion that map reading is as important as map making (Huff, 1990; Weick, 1990), then the strategist's problem is as much one of creating an inviting cartographic text as it is one of highlighting the right path. Gardner (1995: 56) made this point in his study of 20th-century leaders, when he said:

> The formidable challenge confronting the visionary leader is to offer a story, and an embodiment, that builds on the most credible of past syntheses, revisits them in light of present concerns, leaves open a space for future events, and allows individual contributions by the persons in the group.

From a narrative perspective, the successful strategic story may depend less on such tools as comprehensive scanning, objective planning, or meticulous control/feedback systems and more on whether it stands out from other organizational stories, is persuasive, and invokes retelling. What the story revolves around, how it is put together, and the way it is told all determine whether it becomes one worth listening to, remembering, and acting upon. Thus, strategic effectiveness from a narrative perspective is intimately tied to acceptance, approval, and adoption. Further, this approach problematizes unitaristic notions of strategic success—it

434   *Academy of Management Review*   April

asks us to contextualize success, to view success as a social construction that is tied to specific cultural beliefs and practices (e.g., Is success in the Ben & Jerry's story the same thing as success in the Microsoft story? Did competitive success mean something different prior to Porter's 1980 work?).

Narrative theorists have developed a number of frameworks for explaining how authors create effective stories (cf. Martin, 1986). In this article we have chosen to work with a model first put forth by Victor Shklovsky (whose ideas were further developed by other members of the Russian Formalist circle; cf. Bann & Bowlt, 1973; Lemon & Reis, 1965; Matejka & Pomorska, 1971). His deceptively simple approach underpins several other narrative frameworks, thus providing a possible foundation for future work. It can also be applied to many kinds of narrative, an important point given that strategic discourse tends to adopt a variety of forms.

Essentially, Shklovsky argued that all effective narrativists manage to achieve two fundamental outcomes: credibility (or believability) and defamiliarization (or novelty). To be successful, authors must (a) convince readers/listeners that a narrative is plausible within a given orienting context and (b) bring about a different way of viewing things, one which renews our perception of the world. Of the two, credibility has received the most attention, especially from rhetoricians (cf. Chatman, 1978: 48–52, on verisimilitude; and Martin, 1986: 57, on realism). Defamiliarization, though historically ignored in some narrative circles, has recently garnered more attention (cf. Martin, 1986: 47–56). Together, these arenas form a kind of dialectic: extremely credible narratives tend toward the mundanely familiar, whereas highly defamiliarizing narratives often lack credibility (at least when first introduced). Thus, Shklovsky maintained that authors must continually reconsider and rework each area in light of the other if an effective narrative is to arise. We consider each of these categories in more depth.

STRATEGIC CREDIBILITY

Because strategies cost so much to create and implement, their credibility is of paramount importance to organizational stakeholders. Consequently, strategists find themselves having to disguise the inherent fictionality of their stories. After all, who wants to think they are merely playing out a clever tale, especially when great sums are at stake (aside from Disney or Spielberg perhaps)? In the scene where the strategist tries to convince skeptical and impatient rein-holders (whether boards of directors, tribal elders, union leaders, or local lynch mobs) to accept the plan, rarely does s/he get away with saying, "Trust me . . . it's true, it'll happen." Instead, a myriad of tactics are drawn upon to invoke a sense of strategic realism and facticity. Like Barley's (1983) funeral directors, who artfully use makeup and posing to convince mourners the corpse is only sleeping, skilled strategic authors employ (often unconsciously) various narrative devices to make strategic bodies appear as something other than made up. Materiality, voice, perspective, ordering, setting, and readership targeting are among some of the key devices used. We suggest that the more unusual and far reaching the strategy, the more these devices will be adopted. Conversely, they will be used less when the strategy is a familiar one.

Materiality

Narrative materiality refers to a story's physicality, either literally (e.g., long accounts take up more space than shorter accounts) or figuratively (e.g., narratives that focus on touchable phenomena instead of abstract concepts). We suggest that many strategies find their way into print (normally as strategic plans) not only because this makes them clearer or more accessible, but also because printed strategies have more concreteness, and thus seem more real than oral accounts (cf. Martin, 1986: 38). Computerized accounts are more enduring than spoken ones, and voluminous, printed, and attractively bound strategies more concrete still. Once printed, a strategy assumes an undeniable corporeality.

Today's strategic authors go even further with this than their predecessors: by coupling written accounts with computerized, screen-based ones that allow cinematic imitation (e.g., dissolving slides, words scuttling across the screen, colorful backgrounds, etc.), strategists are able to associate their stories with film and television, media that possess high currency and credibility in our society. Projected onto the screen, strategic titles and directions assume a larger-than-life presence, becoming unavoidably fixed in our gaze. The strategy receives the same privileged viewing status accorded films: the lights go down, we adopt comfortable viewing positions, take in the show, and, if the presentation is aesthetically satisfying, soften or forget any objections to content. Ironically though, if a strategy is presented too cinematically, its fictive, theatrical nature may show through; thus, convincing strategy presentations stop well short of full cinematic emulation.

Though much strategic work ends up as some form of print, what is overlooked is that most significant organizational discourse is communicated verbally (Boje, 1992; Mintzberg, 1980). What works for written narrative tends not to work for spoken accounts (as anyone who has tried to read articles aloud can attest; cf. Scholes & Kellogg, 1966). To be effective, verbal narrators need to consider meter and rhythm. Repetitive motifs which would be considered redundant in written works are often used in spoken accounts to group action patterns, facilitate recall, and create emphasis (e.g., in Martin Luther King's "I Have a Dream" speech, the motifs "I have a dream that one day ..." and "Let freedom ring ..." are used throughout to emphasize a number of themes). Such motifs allow the story to be told in various ways without compromising its essential character. Good verbal narratives are easily telescoped; that is, they can be expanded or shortened into "terse tellings" (Boje, 1991) and still retain their essential character. Verbal narrators also rely on facial expression and

436   *Academy of Management Review*   April

body movements to convey meaning, something that is seldom, if ever, accounted for in written strategies.

Taken together, these points may be an unrecognized reason why strategic narratives sometimes fail: they have been unwittingly tailored in the wrong cloth. They have been crafted for the page and reading when, instead, given that strategic discourse is often a verbal affair, they should have been fashioned more for speaking and listening. This suggests that strategists and strategy researchers might attend more to differences between verbal and written strategy formulation.

With respect to narrative content, credibility can be obtained through reference to material, here-and-now phenomena. Thus, authors who concoct unusual stories often take pains to create characters who embody familiar values, outlooks, and mannerisms (for instance, science fiction characters encased in chitin and living in far-off galaxies often have personalities remarkably like our own). The Body Shop provides a strategic example of this: When first introduced, the Body Shop's eco-based strategy was quite unusual (cf. Roddick, 1991). Consequently, the texts that conveyed it incorporated many descriptions and pictures featuring local production sites and organizational stakeholders. Further, the company's founder, Anita Roddick, continues to provide highly personalized accounts of her dealings through in-store and Internet publications, which enable readers to identify more closely with the company—that is, to see its actions as extensions of normal human affairs. Similarly, Lee Iacocca managed to secure strategic credibility by becoming a personal, living embodiment of Chrysler during its time of crisis (cf. Abodaher, 1982). Through some skillful maneuvering and impassioned, highly personalized stories, Chrysler became reified into an entity having a sense of personal loss, pride, and hope. As a faceless corporation, it had little chance of securing a government bailout. But as a hurt, living being, its plight seemed more cogent, and its rescue more acceptable.

Voice and Perspective

Working from the narrative analytic scheme developed by Genette (1980), Mary Jo Hatch (1994) suggested applying two credibility dimensions to organizational discourse: perspective and voice, or "Who sees" (i.e., is an internal or an external perspective used?) and "Who says" (i.e., is the narrator a character in the story or not?). Often, traditional strategy narrative is told from a singular external perspective, with the author(s) excluding themselves from the story line (as with this sentence). The univocal, third person telling creates a sense of objective neutrality: the reader thinks (or is meant to think), "This is clearly an unbiased, rational point of view." The "implied author" (the one ostensibly narrating the story) appears distantly all-knowing and the narrative a statement of truth (Burke, 1969; Elmes & Costello, 1992). Like the omniscient camera angle used in classic cinema, such texts tend to lure readers into forgetting that strategic information has been culled from many sources, and that the view adopted is but one of many possibilities.

In a related vein, written strategic narratives are frequently "plain" (Cicero's category for speech designed to enhance clarity; for more information on Cicero's scheme, see Burke, 1950), as opposed to tempered (speech designed to stimulate interest) or grand (designed to provoke emotion and move an audience to a new position). To enhance perceptions of objectivity, strategic plans tend to erase individual, peopled identities (cf. Gilbert, 1992). Sarah, Sean, and Sally become "Finance," a known customer becomes part of last year's "33% increase." People connected with the company are fashioned into faceless entities discussed in aseptic, "businesslike" language. Strategies "cloaked in the drab garments of business plans" (March, 1995: 436) tend to result in seemingly safe narratives.

Bakhtin (1981: 409) contended this style first developed within the Greek romances as a way of coping with the "heteroglossia" (diverse languages and customs) present in their society. It was developed further during medieval times (e.g., within the chivalric romance), again as a response to conqueror-induced heteroglossia. Perhaps it is little wonder the style continues to be used in the planning work of large, diverse corporations, ones where heteroglossic differences among functions, divisions, and various internal and external stakeholders prevail. A plain, depersonalized style keeps a strategy from seeming to be allied with any particular group or person; it seemingly arises from nowhere and, in its presumption of commonality, appears directed everywhere. Yet distant, impersonal strategic narrative also can lower the reader's involvement. As Martin argued, "When they have no clues about the author's opinion of what he presents, readers and critics are often at a loss to know what the story means or how to evaluate it" (1992: 22).

Ordering and Plots

A subtle credibility technique consists of ordering strategic narratives according to familiar plotlines. As with cinematic emulation, this associative approach helps deflect attention away from the narrative's fictionality. Many strategic narratives seem to follow a simplified variation of either the epic Hero's Journey (Campbell, 1973) or romanticist form (Jeffcutt, 1994). Within the epic form, the hero/company finds itself confronting a number of enemies and/or obstacles. If everyone in the company were to pull together, the company should emerge victorious with increased market share, profits, and job security. Hopeful, happy endings are almost always explicitly or implicitly present. Strategies fashioned using the SWOT (strengths, weaknesses, opportunities, and threats) model (cf. Andrews, 1971) often have this nature: opportunities represent "the call," whereas threats become antagonists. As strengths are employed and weaknesses are transformed, the protagonist becomes a hero.

Romanticist plots are enacted when the company is portrayed as recovering from a fall from grace, stemming perhaps from excessive

438 *Academy of Management Review* April

growth or divergence from the founder's vision. Many downsizing efforts appear to embody this form: "We've gotten awfully fat. We'll battle our bulge, find our core self, and emerge a slimmer, wiser, more attractive company." Whereas the Hero's Journey results in a new self/company, the romantic plot augers a return to or rediscovery of a purer self, one obscured perhaps, but there all along. As with the Hero's Journey, an ascetic emphasis is often evident in the texts we have seen, with company stakeholders being asked to undergo hardship and perhaps penance of some sort.

Readership

From the perspective of reader/response theory (cf. Iser, 1989), the meaning of a text resides not just "in the text itself" or in the "author's intent" but also in the "backgrounds and experiences" that readers bring to the text and how "these color their interpretations of the text" (Yanow, 1995: 2). The interplay of text, author, and reader suggests that the interpretation of a text is both pluralistic and dynamic, reflecting the author's intent and the reader's construction of meaning.

For executive strategists trying to create homogeneous "designer cultures" (Casey, 1995: 135) or "monolithic identities" (Olin, 1989: 82–97), this interplay and dynamism among text, author, and reader presents a problem. We suspect that much of the "professionalization" of today's managers works to standardize readers' responses. "Model readers" are created (cf. Martin, 1986: 160–172) who can interpret text as the authors intend it (see also Casey, 1995: 138–182). The model strategic reader has mastered a variety of codes (e.g., MBO, TQM, KPI, the 4 P's of marketing, the 5 P's of strategy, the 7 S's of McKinsey) and understands the logics inherent in forecasting equations, budgeting systems, and environmental analysis frameworks.

The model reader presumes the existence of model languaging and authorship. Regardless of content, narratives couched in a model style are automatically conferred a level of legitimacy not given other texts; that is, they gain credibility by recognition. In particular, texts derived from and offering expert recipes—e.g., Andrew's (1971) relatively simple SWOT model, or the more elaborate models of Ansoff (1965), Hofer & Schendel (1978), and Porter (1980)—are conferred a halo of authority, the strategic equivalent of *Good Housekeeping's* Seal of Approval. Whole nations have swallowed strategic tales on this basis (cf. Crocombe, 1991).

STRATEGIC DEFAMILIARIZATION

The second part of Shklovsky's scheme involves a narrative's distinctiveness, or its novelty. As mentioned earlier, the effective narrative causes us to see things in new and different ways: narratives that are credible but overly familiar are unlikely to garner much attention. Whereas many of the credibility techniques described previously possess a certain timelessness, such is not the case with defamiliarization. Any defamiliarizing perspective or device, no matter how initially exciting and captivating, becomes familiar, mundane, and tiresome with time.

Applied to strategy, this means that strategic narratives have shelf lives—use-by dates that require a steady influx of new perspectives. With respect to the strategy creation process, changing venues may serve an important defamiliarizing function. Organizational executives often go to great lengths to hold off-site strategy sessions, saying, "To be creative, we need to get away from our day-to-day distractions" (or, if off-site sessions have been used for a while, in-house strategizing may come back into vogue). Changing venues symbolizes a desire for change in the ongoing organizational story. With respect to narrative content, novelty may be created through periodic shifts in orienting strategic problems. Thus, competitors may be assigned the antagonist role for a year or two, only to be replaced by issues of quality, mergers, or governmental compliance. Relative to strategy narration, the need for defamiliarization helps explain the rapid adoption of presentation formats that are both novel and credible (e.g., the computerized screen presentations described earlier), even though such formats often require considerably more effort than established presentation methods.

Defamiliarizing Strategic Theory

More broadly, we suggest that various strategic theoretical frameworks succeed one another because organizational readers have shifting preferences and attention spans, and not because of some Darwinian progression toward an ultra-fit theory. In other words, the currency of today's strategic models may have less to do with accuracy or predictability than with their appeal to current tastes and interests.

A brief genre-based review of strategic thought may help illustrate this point. In this article we adopt Fredric Jameson's (1981: 145) definition of the term "genres," seeing them as "ad hoc, experimental constructs, devised for a specific textual occasion and abandoned like so much scaffolding when the analysis has done its work." The genre concept refers to unique ways of constructing and representing texts. Narratives crafted in particular genres have stylistic signatures, distinctive combinations of content and structure (for instance, the "lone hero" emphasis in Westerns or the relational focus of Romance novels). Mintzberg's discussion of "strategy schools" (1994: 2–4) suggests no less than ten genre possibilities. Here, we consider just three: Mintzberg's design, planning, and positioning schools, which we have relabeled the epic, technofuturist, and purist genres.

Epic and Technofuturist Narratives

Though the epic and technofuturist genres developed side by side, they offer two very different narrative possibilities. The epic genre (represented by Learned, 1965, and later championed by Andrews, 1971) has traditionally been concerned with interpretation: How are particular

440   *Academy of Management Review*   April

events and issues to be interpreted in light of key organizational principles? The SWOT model (in various guises) also plays a fundamental role
in this style. As discussed earlier, organizations following it become epic
journeyers, systematically navigating toward opportunities and away
from threats. Working with strengths and weaknesses results in various
heroic characterizations. This process tends to result in relatively concise,
"decisional" accounts of various SWOT-based choices and their implications (Mintzberg, 1994: 36–39).

Whereas the epic genre uses "a few basic ideas to design strategy"
(Mintzberg, 1994: 36), the technofuturist genre (beginning with Ansoff's
work, 1965, and continuing with Steiner, 1969) has become known for its
complexity and extraordinary attention to detail. Focusing more on time
(particularly on temporal sequencing) and less on organizational characterization, the analytical schemes of this genre result in comprehensive,
futuristic texts filled with detached, "quasi-scientific" forecasts (cf. Mintzberg, 1994: 40–49). These stand in marked contrast to the value-laden,
politically sensitive narratives of the epic genre. Whereas epic accounts
rely on hierarchically based authority to achieve adoption (policy making
is usually the prerogative of senior executives), technofuturist narratives,
taking a positivist orientation, use scientific referencing to achieve credibility (e.g., Ansoff & Sullivan, 1993).

During their inception, both of these genres were highly regarded;
each provided unique, interesting, and credible solutions to the problem
of organizational direction setting. Yet their widespread adoption proved
their undoing. Once the thrill of newness wore off, various shortcomings
were identified. With the epic model, it became unclear how strengths,
weaknesses, opportunities, and threats were to be identified; what one
executive termed a strength (e.g., a seasoned, like-minded workforce),
another labeled a weakness (e.g., a worn out, overly homogenous workforce). The technofuturist genre became experienced by users as inordi-
nately complex, hard to follow, and expensive to support (cf. Mintzberg,
1994: 35–90). By the mid 1970s, both genres had lost their luster and become
stale; strategic readers began chorusing, "Yes, but haven't we seen all
this before?"

Purist Narratives

This helps explain why the next genre, the purist style, achieved such
rapid popularity. It was everything the epic and technofuturist genres
were not. Represented by the work of Miles and Snow (1978) and Porter
(1980), the purist genre offered a defamiliarizing, relatively atemporal,
character-based narrative. It enticed authors with ready-made identities,
strategic purity, and a guarantee of sorts: the company able to choose an
ideal strategic type, conform to it, and avoid joining Porter's "stuck in the
middle" muddlers or Miles and Snow's directionless "reactors" would earn
"above-average returns in its industry despite the presence of strong competitive forces" (Porter, 1980: 35). Purist narratives, further, resolve the

issue of strengths and weaknesses: "Though a firm can have a myriad of strengths and weaknesses vis-à-vis its competitors, there are two basic types of competitive advantage a firm can possess: low cost or differentiation. The significance of any strength or weakness a firm possesses is ultimately a function of its impact on relative cost or differentiation" (Porter, 1985: 11).

This genre relies heavily on external experts for archetypal templates. The most popular templates have produced "round" characterizations (i.e., complex, rich, "alive" portrayals; cf. Chatman, 1978: 75-76). For instance, Porter's "cost leaders" and Miles and Snow's "defenders" have tough, conservative (if not somewhat dour) personalities; others are more relational and chummy (e.g., Porter's "focusers"). Some types, such as Miles and Snow's "prospectors" and Porter's "differentiators" provide companies with a built-in source of ongoing defamiliarization. Like novelists' use of naturally wandering protagonists to effect novelty (e.g., traders, hobos, and footloose adolescents who encounter unusual people and places; cf. Martin, 1986: 48), "wanderer" strategies provide an acceptable way of securing ongoing organizational attentiveness. As Miles and Snow stated, "A true prospector is almost immune from the pressures of a changing environment since this type of organization is continually keeping pace with change and, as indicated, frequently creating change itself" (1978: 57).

Again, the widespread adoption (and concomitant scrutiny) of the purist genre created dilemmas that ultimately undermined its appeal. With so many strategic types to choose from, readers became confused: Whose typology was right? Whose the best? How did other types such as Mintzberg's (1983) professional bureaucracies, Peters and Waterman's (1982) tight/loose knits, and Kets de Vries and Miller's (1984) neurotic misfits factor in? Was being stuck in the middle really so bad?

Other contending frameworks have arisen since the 1980s, all employing some means of defamiliarization. For instance, Chen and MacMillan's (1992) "action/response" approach returns to the temporal focus of the technofuturist genre, but adopts a very short time horizon. Using the strategic event as a primary unit of analysis, time in these narratives is measured in months and even weeks. Competitor moves indicate when the stopwatch is to be started and speed of response is critical. Because this approach fits well with readers' perceptions of increasing environmental unpredictability, it also achieves a kind of innate credibility. However, visioning approaches (e.g., Collins & Porras, 1991; Nanus, 1992) reflect a renewed interest in distant events, but in an "imagining" way (contrasting with the deterministic, predictive view of the technofuturists).

BETTING ON THE FUTURE

Our brief journey into strategy as fiction naturally raises questions about imminent genres and narrative devices. What forms will strategic narratives take next? Is the strategy field heading toward "bankruptcy" (as suggested by Hurst, 1986), or is the field in the midst of shifting to a new, credibly defamiliarizing form? Drawing upon the "Fin de Siècle" issue of *Organization* (volume 2, number 3/4, 1995), it appears that organizations of the future will be even more fluid and permeable than today's. As James March (1995: 428) noted, "The most conventional story of contemporary futurology is a story that observes and predicts dramatic changes in the environments of organizations." Accelerating changes in information technology and global politics will result in greater linkages and movements between organizations with a concomitant rise in knowledge-based competition. Surrounded by an ever-growing pool of unpredictable, rapidly fleeting opportunities, tomorrow's organizations will need to rely more on quick-thinking, knowledgeable employees who can attend to environmental shifts and work innovatively with paradox. Within strategic narratives, the question of "who" (or characterization) will become more important, with particular emphasis being placed on actors' knowledge, both within and among organizations (March, 1991, 1995). "Who knows what?" will become a dominant strategic question.

The move away from "individualist, monological" organizations (Gergen, 1995: 523) to "virtual" or "throw-away" ones (March, 1995: 434) will require narratives that can cope with blurred organizational boundaries (Hirschhorn & Gilmore, 1992), dispersed intelligibilities, diverse realities, disrupted chains of authority, and erosion of organizational autonomy (Gergen, 1995: 524–526). Singular readings of strategic narratives, where model readers arrive at like interpretations, will increasingly be a thing of the past (cf. Boje's 1995 discussion of the "Tamara" organization; also see Gergen, 1992). In addition, the growing preponderance of "encounter"-based organizations (Gutek, 1995), in which ongoing relationships are replaced by short-term, one-time encounters, will necessitate narrative structures that can adapt to rapidly changing discourses and varied readers.

Many of the credibility devices described earlier will lose their potency in such settings. The printed word, reliance on omniscient perspectives, and familiar plots will have less sway in organizations where print is cheap and knowledge is rapidly changing (Hamel & Prahalad, 1994; March, 1991; Senge, 1990), where distributed leadership is prized over centralized authority (Barry, 1991), and where parallel, seemingly unrelated storylines are enacted (Boje, 1995). Conversely, credibly defamiliarizing strategic narratives will embody and reflect these emerging trends.

Changing Patterns of Authorship

We imagine that tomorrow's strategic authors will be more concerned with creating engaging, lively, and artful stories, reflecting increasing competition for stakeholder attention spans and reduced "airtime." Spoken accounts also may become more popular: stakeholders overloaded with e-mail and written documents are likely to take greater notice of verbally delivered accounts. It may be that strategists will rely on multiple stories that can be told quickly, easily, and joined in a variety of ways (instead of centralized monolithic accounts).

Reflecting the increased value being given to particularized knowledges of individuals and groups, such narratives will necessarily respond to calls and guidelines for more participative planning (cf. Kanter, 1983; Quinn, 1992; Weick, 1995). Just as Burgleman's (1983: 241) study of internal corporate venturing suggests that middle managers deep within the organization can influence the "corporate concept of strategy," so stakeholder success at influencing directionality of the firm will depend less on their level within the firm and more on their "conceptual and political capabilities" (1983: 241)—that is, how well and to whom their stories are told.

Communitarian Characterizations

Because organizations are becoming increasingly interdependent, their strategic stories may shift away from a focus on agency (oriented toward self) and move toward community (focused on relationships with others). Using McAdams' (1993) framework for classifying narratives (which highlights the agentic/communitarian dimension), we would predict a move away from agentic company characterizations such as warrior, traveler, maker, or sage (e.g., where companies have emphasized taking over other companies, moving into new markets, using TQM as a strategic tool, or acting as industry statespersons). In their place, we would expect more communitarian characterizations such as teacher, humanist, or friend (currently showing up in joint venture networks and "green" organizations).

Changing Archetypes

The archetypes on which strategic narratives are based may also change. According to Bowles (1993: 403), who uses mythical archetypes to situate organizational themes, the sky-god "Zeus can be considered as the ruling archetype within contemporary culture and organizations, where precedence is given to the mental realm of power and will." He also noted that the sky-god position, while conferring a broad view, carries attendant costs: loss of earthly contact and groundedness can result in excessive abstraction; childlike qualities of wonder and creativity are often ignored; and overthrows from rebellious offspring (e.g., Cronus or Uranus) can disrupt the most well-intentioned plans. Given increased attention to the nonrational in organizations (Mumby & Putnam, 1992), concerns over individual welfare (cf. the "Employment Futures" section of the aforementioned issue of *Organization*), and requirements for innovation (March, 1995), strategists of the future may find themselves experimenting with archetypal bases that reflect and give rise to greater feeling, sustenance, and play. For example, a Poseidon-like company would privilege emotional experience; a Demeter-like company nourishment; and a Dionysian company, celebration, individuality, and varied experience.

Polyphonic Strategy

Reflecting trends toward increased workplace diversity and relational concerns (Gergen, 1995), strategic narratives may become increasingly "polyphonic" (cf. Bakhtin, 1984). Though at first glance the term *polyphony* suggests the idea of many voices, Bakhtin intended it to refer to the author's position in a text. In polyphonic discourse, the author takes a less "authoritative" role. Above all, polyphonic texts arise from "dialogical" rather than "monological" authorship; in dialogical authorship, different logics not only coexist, but inform and shape one another. Conversely, in monological authorship, only one logic (the narrator's) is presented. As Morson and Emerson explained:

> In a monologic work, only the author, as the 'ultimate semantic authority,' retains the power to express a truth directly. The truth of the work is his or her truth, and all other truths are merely 'represented,' like 'words of the second type.' . . . By contrast, in a polyphonic work the form-shaping ideology itself *demands* that the author cease to exercise monologic control. . . . Polyphony demands a work in which several consciousnesses meet as equals and engage in a dialogue that is in principle unfinalizable. (1990: 238–239; italics in original)

Polyphonic portrayal appears logically impossible, given that it is the author who creates a text and not the characters. Yet, as Bakhtin delights in pointing out, Dostoyevsky managed to pull it off (cf. the book/film of *The Brothers Karamazov*). In Dostoyevsky's novels, characters clearly have a life of their own. A pluralous sense of meaning emerges as they exchange views and interactively direct the storyline. And though Dostoyevsky's own views are also present (usually articulated by the narrator), his characters often contest them. Not surprisingly, organizationally based examples of this style are rare; however, Smircich, Calás, and Morgan (1992a,b) demonstrate one way of juxtaposing dialogically linked views, whereas Semler (1993), chronicling workplace democratization efforts at the Brazilian firm Semco, illustrates how polyphonically oriented planning processes might work.

Creating polyphonic strategic narratives will require that strategic authors assume a more processual role, one which emphasizes listening for diverse points of view (cf. Kanter, 1983; Quinn, 1992), and representing these in ways that generate dialogic understanding (e.g., presenting a give-and-take dialogue between positions; cf. Hazen, 1993, 1994). Strategists adopting this method would be less focused on promoting their own strategy and more concerned with surfacing, legitimizing, and juxtaposing differing organizational stories. In this role, the strategist's job shifts from being a "decision-formulator, an implementer of structure and a controller of events" to providing a "vision to account for the streams of events and actions that occur—a universe in which organizational events and experiences take on meaning" (Smircich & Stubbart, 1985: 730). Art-based elicitation techniques (cf. Barry, 1994, 1996) might be coupled with logocentric ones to create more nonreductive and emotionally sensitive tellings.

AN ILLUSTRATIVE TALE

We would like to relate a short story, one that we believe illustrates several of the above approaches to strategic narrative construction. It comes from Marjorie Parker (1990), a consultant who facilitated a large-scale transformation at Karmoy Fabrikker (a large European aluminum producer).

At the story's beginning, the company was portrayed as having recently overcome a long period of decline. Cost-cutting programs and emission controls had begun to reorient what was once "a costly and unclean plant" (Parker, 1990: 7). Perhaps because of these successes, conventional management structures and practices were privileged. Planning systems were conservative and prudent. Whether the people there heeded some outside call toward a new journey is not clear; however, there developed "an expressed restlessness within the organization" (1990: 14), a wish for something different, and the top executives asked Parker to help them find a way to "lift the company to a new plateau." Subsequently, she and they struggled to find a different way to represent the organization. One of the executives happened on the metaphor of a garden, which was seized upon by the others. After giving it some thought, Parker suggested they begin a company-wide, story-based inquiry process centered around the garden metaphor. She was surprised when both the executives and union representatives agreed to her proposal; after all, these were "tough industrial folk" whose work was anything but organic.

Following an introductory conference, in which the company's story was told using garden-based company sketches (produced by a local art teacher), a change group, called The Garden Committee, was formed. The group facilitated a series of story-telling sessions called the "Garden Seminars." In these sessions, people in the company were asked to liken the important parts of their work to a garden: What kind of plants would their departments be? How had they grown? How did they compare to the other plants? What was the garden like as a whole? Was it a decent place to be? A "Guide to Gardening" that featured gardening terms was developed by the training department to suggest discussion topics. Throughout this process, hundreds of stories were told and recorded. Forums were developed whereby stories could be listened to and compared.

At first, all that was apparent to participants at Karmoy Fabrikker was how different the stories were. The emerging narrative was chaotic, a true pastiche. From this beginning, however, people in the company started asking how things might be different. How could this garden be made beautiful, more cohesive? New story elements were suggested, compared, and joined. Characters were introduced, changed, and erased. Different themes and plots were considered.

446 *Academy of Management Review* April

Through these tellings, people in different parts of the organization came to contextualize their work, to interrelate it more. More connections between smelting and extrusion, storage and advertising, architecture and customer perceptions were fashioned. Story-telling groups were re-arranged so these stories could be told to different people and in different ways (quite a few stories were converted into songs and skits). Gradually, the repeated tellings seemed to come together in a complex, dialogical way (with many interconnected yet separate tales having been told). The new directions embodied in the overall narrative became touchstones for changes in day-to-day actions. Although we make no claims for a cause and effect relationship in this story, it is interesting to note that the company subsequently emerged as a world leader in aluminum production, a happy ending to the tale. They seemed quite satisfied with how their garden had bloomed.

Even though our telling of this tale is very condensed, it illustrates how a polyvocal, pluralous, and likely polyphonic approach to strategy might be enacted. The process used here encouraged multiple readings of the organization. Polyvocality occurred through multiauthoring of texts. Mythic, archetypal elements were accessed through the garden metaphor; participants managed to connect their work to earth, sky, and water, both through likening these elements to production processes and through reassessing the relationship of their company to their actual natural environment. Respectful juxtapositioning of seemingly conflicting perspectives generated a type of polyphonic discourse, which led to a sense of dynamism and realism (in that the organizational life there consisted of many contradictory views).

AN ENDING (AND BEGINNING)?

Bringing our own narrative to a close, it seems to us that the strategy field is on the verge of some major shifts. Future strategic narratives are likely to be as different from previous ones as Roger Rabbit is from Mickey Mouse. Expressing multiple, possibly conflicting viewpoints, these narratives will probably be more choral-like, three dimensional, self-reflexive, and dynamic.

In light of these changes, we believe the adoption of a strategy-as-story perspective has a great deal to offer. Drawing from a rich and varied tradition, the narrative view provides a number of platforms for examining upcoming strategies. Whereas we have concentrated on Shklovsky's scheme, other promising explanatory frameworks are discussed by Chatman (1978), Martin (1986), and Polkinghorne (1988).

In suggesting that strategic success is closely linked to narrational needs of authors and readers, proponents of narrative theory urge researchers to attend more closely to the sociocultural contexts from which strategies arise. Do some strategic narratives fit the times better than others? Namely, are there prevailing social and political narratives that foster some strategic narratives and not others? For instance, the rise of technofuturist strategic discourse may have been tied to broader social movements, such as the space race.

How employees and managers engage in strategic story making—what they borrow and reject from mainstream thinkers and how they make sense of the process as they go—has implications for understanding both what makes a strategic genre credible and fresh and how it does or does not help individuals to navigate the murky waters of postindustrial organizational life. Watson's (1994) ethnographic study of managers in a failing British telecommunications company exemplifies this type of research.

As we suggested earlier, a narrative view can be helpful when theorists study the power and politics of strategy. We have suggested that rhetorical analysis can reveal how strategies (and strategists) assume authority. It also might be used to study "deauthorizing" efforts (e.g., empowerment strategies, or downsizing movements). Discourse analysis (cf. Fairclough, 1995) of top management teams might provide insight into how strategic tellings in one "power arena" (Clegg, 1990: 85) interrelate with tellings elsewhere. What happens when the tropes and constructions used by one group conflict with those used by others? For instance, executives often resort to war or sports metaphors when discussing strategy (cf. Hirsch & Andrews, 1983), yet these constructions may be meaningless for other organizational stakeholders, who then may discount, challenge, reauthor, or ignore what they have heard. How are conflicting strategic stories reconciled (e.g., corporate vs. legislative characterizations of contested events; cf. Cook & Barry, 1995)? From a postmodernist perspective, a narrative view also can reveal how organizations become imprisoned by their strategic discourse—deconstructive analysis might be used to show how alternative meanings and constructions are silenced in favor of a dominate story, and suggest who benefits and who loses through such silencing (cf. Boje et al., 1996).

A narrative view also invites a number of hitherto unasked, but potentially important, questions. For instance, how do strategic stories and their interpretations shift as an organization matures? In our limited experience, it seems that entrepreneurs and senior executives tell very different tales. Similarly, employees in diverse functional areas (such as marketing and accounting) seem to read and interpret strategic stories quite differently. How do stories told about formal strategies arise, circulate, and come back to affect the formal strategy? Semiotic and ethnographic techniques used by other organizational theorists may prove useful here (e.g., Barley, 1983; Fiol, 1990; Kunda, 1992).

From a pragmatic perspective, how helpful is it to have competing stories and themes running simultaneously? When do they provide an engaging sense of tension, and when do they create alienation? Do certain kinds of strategic stories predict efficacy more than others (as McAdams' 1993 work would suggest)? When are metaphorically rich strategic narratives (cf. Morgan, 1986) better than more factual ones?

448   *Academy of Management Review*   April

To conclude, we believe we have merely scratched the surface of what appears to be a many-layered area of inquiry. Although we have tried to articulate some narrative possibilities, the stories that come to be, the rendering of those stories, and the sense that is made of them by strategy researchers and practitioners will ultimately become another narrative. Or so our story goes.

REFERENCES

Abodaher, D. 1982. *Iacocca*. New York: Macmillan.

Andrews, K. R. 1971. *The concept of corporate strategy*. Homewood, IL: Irwin.

Ansoff, H. I. 1965. *Corporate strategy*. New York: McGraw-Hill.

Ansoff, H. I., Avner, J., Brandenburg, R. G., Portner, F. E., & Radosevich, R. 1977. Does planning pay? The effect of planning on success of acquisitions in American firms. *Long Range Planning*, 3: 2–7.

Ansoff, H. I., & Sullivan, P. A. 1993. Optimizing profitability in turbulent environments: A formula for strategic success. *Long-Range Planning*, 26(5): 11–23.

Bakhtin, M. 1981. *The dialogic imagination: Four essays by M. M. Bakhtin* (C. Emerson & M. Holquist, Trans.). Austin, TX: University of Texas Press.

Bakhtin, M. 1984. *Problems of Dostoevsky's Poetics* (C. Emerson, Ed. & Trans.). Manchester, England: Manchester University Press.

Bann, S., & Bowlt, J. (Eds.). 1973. *Russian formalism*. New York: Barnes & Noble.

Barley, S. 1983. Semiotics and the study of occupational and organizational cultures. *Administrative Science Quarterly*, 28: 393–414.

Barry, D. 1991. Managing the bossless team: Lessons in distributed leadership. *Organizational Dynamics*, 20(1): 31–47.

Barry, D. 1994. Making the invisible visible: Using analogically-based methods to surface the organizational unconscious. In D. P. Moore (Ed.), *Academy of Management Best Paper Proceedings*, 192–196.

Barry, D. 1996. Artful inquiry: A symbolic constructivist approach to social science research. *Qualitative Inquiry*, 2(4): 411–438.

Boje, D. 1991. The storytelling organization: A study of story performance in an office-supply firm. *Administrative Science Quarterly*, 36(1): 106–126.

Boje, D. 1995. Stories of the storytelling organization: A postmodern analysis of Disney as "Tamara-Land." *Academy of Management Journal*, 38(4): 997–1035.

Boje, D., Gephart, R., Jr., & Thatchenkery, T. 1996. *Postmodern management and organization theory*. Thousand Oaks, CA: Sage.

Booth, W. 1983. *The rhetoric of fiction*. Chicago: University of Chicago Press.

Bowles, M. L. 1993. The gods and goddesses: Personifying social life in the age of organization. *Organization Studies*, 14(3): 395–418.

Boyd, B. K. 1991. Strategic planning and financial performance: A meta-analytical review. *Journal of Management Studies*, 28(4): 353–374.

Bubna-Litic, D. 1995. Strategy as fiction. Paper presented at the July, 1995, *Standing Conference on Organizational Symbolism (SCOS)*, Turku, Finland.

Burgleman, R. A. 1983. A process model of internal corporate venturing in the diversified major firm. *Administrative Science Quarterly*, 28: 233–244.

Burke, K. 1950. *A rhetoric of motives*. Berkeley, CA: University of California Press.

Burke, K. 1969. *A grammar of motives*. Berkeley, CA: University of California Press.

Burrell, G., & Morgan, G. 1979. *Sociological paradigms and organizational analysis: Elements of the sociology of corporate life*. London: Heinemann.

Campbell, J. 1973. *The hero with a thousand faces*. Bollingen Series xvii. Princeton, NJ: Princeton University Press.

Casey, C. 1995. *Work, self, and society: After industrialism*. London: Routledge.

Chatman, S. 1978. *Story and discourse: Narrative structure in fiction and film*. Ithaca, NY: Cornell University Press.

Chen, M., & MacMillan, I. 1992. Nonresponse and delayed response to competitive moves: The roles of competitor dependence and action irreversibility. *Academy of Management Journal*, 35(3): 539–551.

Clegg, S. 1990. *Modern organizations: Organization studies in the postmodern world*. London: Sage.

Collins, J., & Porras, J. 1991. Organizational vision and visionary organizations. *California Management Review*, 34(1): 30–52.

Cook, R., & Barry, D. 1995. Shaping the external environment: A study of small business influences on public policy. *Business & Society*, 12(4): 317–344.

Crocombe, G. 1991. *Upgrading New Zealand's competitive advantage*. Auckland, New Zealand: Oxford University Press.

Czarniawska-Joerges, B. 1996. *Narrating the organization: Dramas of institutional identity*. Chicago: University of Chicago Press.

Elmes, M. B., & Costello, M. Mystification and social drama: The hidden side of communication skills training. *Human Relations*, 45(5): 427–445.

Gardner, H. 1995. *Leading minds: An anatomy of leadership*. New York: Basic Books.

Geertz, C. 1980. Blurred genres: The refiguration of social thought. *The American Scholar*, 49(2): 165–179.

Genette, G. 1980. *Narrative discourse: An essay in method* (J. E. Lewin, Trans.). Ithaca, NY: Cornell University Press.

Genette, G. 1988. *Narrative discourse revisited* (J. E. Lewin, Trans.). Ithaca, NY: Cornell University Press.

Gergen, K. J. 1992. Organization theory in the postmodern era. In M. Reed & M. Hughes (Eds.), *Rethinking organization*: 207–226. Newbury Park, CA: Sage.

Gergen, K. J. 1995. Global organization: From imperialism to ethical vision. *Organization*, 2(3/4): 519–532.

Gilbert, D. 1992. *The twilight of corporate strategy: A comparative ethical critique*. London: Oxford University Press.

Gimpl, M. L., & Dakin, S. R. 1984. Management and magic. *California Management Review*, 27(1): 125–136.

Grinyer, P. H., & Norburn, D. 1975. Planning for existing markets: Perceptions of executives and financial performance. *Journal of the Royal Statistical Society*, 138: 70–97.

Gutek, B. 1995. In the future: Transacting with strangers and not-so-strange machines. *Organization*, 2(3/4): 539–545.

Hamel, G., & Prahalad, C. K. 1994. *Competing for the future*. Boston, MA: Harvard Business School Press.

Hatch, M. J. 1994. *Narrative and rhetorical style in the discourses of organization theory.* Paper presented at the annual meeting of the Academy of Management, Dallas, TX.

Hazen, M. A. 1993. Towards polyphonic organization. *Journal of Organizational Change Management,* 6(5): 15–22.

Hazen, M. A. 1994. Multiplicity and change in persons and organizations. *Journal of Organizational Change Management,* 7(5): 72–81.

Herold, D. M. 1972. Long-range planning and organizational performance: A cross valuation study. *Academy of Management Journal,* 15: 91–102.

Hiley, D., Bohman, J., & Shusterman, R. (Eds.). 1991. *The interpretive turn: Philosophy, science, culture.* Ithaca, NY: Cornell University Press.

Hirsch, P., & Andrews, J. A. 1983. Ambushes, shootouts, and knights of the roundtable: The language of corporate takeovers. In L. Pondy, P. Frost, G. Morgan, & T. Dandridge (Eds.), *Organizational symbolism:* 145–156. Greenwich, CT: JAI Press.

Hirschhorn, L., & Gilmore, T. 1992. The new boundaries of the 'boundaryless' organization. *Harvard Business Review,* 70(3): 104–115.

Hofer, C., & Schendel, D. 1978. *Strategy formulation: Analytical concepts.* St. Paul, MN: West.

Huff, A. 1990. Mapping strategic thought. In A. Huff (Ed.), *Mapping strategic thought:* 12–49. New York: Wiley.

Hurst, D. K. 1986. Why strategic management is bankrupt. *Organizational Dynamics,* 15(Autumn): 4–27.

Iser, W. 1989. *Prospecting: From reader response to literary anthropology.* Baltimore, MD: Johns Hopkins University Press.

Jameson, F. 1981. *The political unconscious: Narrative as a socially symbolic act.* Ithaca, NY: Cornell University Press.

Jeffcutt, P. 1994. The interpretation of organization: A contemporary analysis and critique. *Journal of Management Studies,* 31(2): 225–250.

Kanter, R. M. 1983. *The change masters: Innovations for productivity in the American corporation.* New York: Simon and Schuster.

Karger, D. W., & Malik, A. A. 1975. Long-range planning and organizational performance. *Long Range Planning,* 8(2): 60–64.

Kets de Vries, M., & Miller, D. 1984. *The neurotic organization.* San Francisco, CA: Jossey-Bass.

Learned, E. P. 1965. *Business policy: Text and cases.* Homewood, IL: Irwin.

Lemon, L., & Reis, M. (Trans.). 1965. *Russian formalist criticism: Four essays.* Lincoln, NB: University of Nebraska Press.

Matejka, L., & Pomorska, K. (Eds.). 1971. *Readings in Russian poetics: Formalist and structuralist views.* Cambridge, MA: MIT Press.

March, J. 1991. Exploration and exploitation in organizational learning. *Organization Science,* 2: 71–87.

March, J. 1995. Disposable organizations and the rigidities of imagination. *Organization,* 2(3/4): 427–440.

Martin, W. 1986. *Recent theories of narrative.* Ithaca, NY: Cornell University Press.

McAdams, D. 1993. *The stories we live by: Personal myths and the making of the self.* New York: William Morrow.

Miles, R., & Snow, C. 1978. *Organization strategy, structure, and process.* New York: McGraw-Hill.

Mintzberg, H. 1980. *The nature of managerial work.* Englewood Cliffs, NJ: Prentice-Hall.

Mintzberg, H. 1987. Crafting strategy. *Harvard Business Review*, 65(4): 66–75.

Mintzberg, H. 1987. The strategy concept I: Five Ps for strategy, and Strategy concept II: Another look at why organizations need strategies. *California Management Review*, 30(1): 11–32.

Mintzberg, H. 1994. *The Rise and Fall of Strategic Planning*. New York: Free Press.

Mintzberg, H., Brunet, J. P., & Waters, J. A. 1986. Does planning impede strategic thinking? Tracking the strategies of Air Canada from 1937 to 1976. In R. Lamb & P. Shrivastava (Eds.), *Advances in strategic management*, vol. 4: 3–41. New York: JAI Press.

Mintzberg, H., & Waters, J. A. 1982. Tracking strategy in an entrepreneurial firm. *Academy of Management Journal*, 25(3): 465–499.

Morgan, G. 1986. *Images of organization*. Beverley Hills, CA: Sage.

Morson, G. S., & Emerson, C. 1990. *Mikhail Bakhtin: Creation of a prosaics*. Stanford, CA: Stanford University Press.

Mumby, D., & Putnam, L. 1992. The politics of emotion: A feminist reading of bounded rationality. *Academy of Management Review*: 17: 465–478.

Nanus, B. 1992. *Visionary leadership*. San Francisco, CA: Jossey-Bass.

O'Connor, E. S. 1995. Paradoxes of participation: Textual analysis and organizational change. *Organization Studies*, 16(5): 769–803.

Olin, W. 1989. *Corporate identity: Making business strategy visible through design*. London: Thames & Hudson.

Parker, M. 1990. *Creating shared vision*. Clarendon Hills, IL: Dialog International.

Peters, T., & Walterman, R. 1982. *In search of excellence: Lessons from America's best-run companies*. New York: Harper & Row.

Polkinghorne, D. 1988. *Narrative knowing and the human sciences*. Albany: State University of New York Press.

Porter, M. 1980. *Competitive strategy: Techniques for analyzing industries and competitors*. New York: Free Press.

Prahalad, C. K., & Hamel, G. 1994. Strategy as a field of study: Why search for a new paradigm? *Strategic Management Journal*, 15: 5–16.

Quinn, J. B. 1980. *Strategies for change: Logical incrementalism*. Homewood, IL: Irwin.

Quinn, J. B. 1992. *The intelligent enterprise: A knowledge and service based paradigm for industry*. New York: Free Press.

Rappaport, J. 1993. Narrative studies, personal stories, and identity transformation in the mutual help context. *Journal of Applied Behavioral Science*, 29(2): 239–256.

Roddick, A. 1991. *Body and soul: Profits with principles—the amazing success story of Anita Roddick & the Body Shop*. New York: Crown Publishers.

Roe, E. 1994. *Narrative policy analysis: Theory and practice*. Durham, NC: Duke University Press.

Scholes, R. 1981. Language, narrative, and anti-narrative. In W. Mitchell (Ed.), *On narrativity*: 200–208. Chicago: University of Chicago Press.

Scholes, R., & Kellogg, R. 1966. *The nature of narrative*. New York: Oxford University Press.

Semler, R. 1993. *Maverick: The success story behind the world's most unusual workplace*. London: Century.

Senge, P. 1990. *The fifth discipline: The art and practice of the learning organization*. New York: Doubleday.

Smircich, L., Calás, M., & Morgan, G. 1992a. New intellectual currents in organization and management theory. *Academy of Management Review*, 17: 404–406.

Smircich, L., Calás, M., & Morgan, G. 1992b. Afterward/after words: Open(ing) spaces. *Academy of Management Review*, 17: 607–611.

Smircich, L., & Stubbart, C. 1985. Strategic management in an enacted world. *Academy of Management Review*, 10: 724–736.

Steiner, G. 1969. *Top management planning*. New York: Macmillan.

Thune, S., & House, R. J. 1970. Where long-range planning pays off. *Business Horizons*, 13(4): 81–87.

Watson, T. J. 1994. *In search of management: Culture, chaos, and control in managerial work*. London: Routledge.

Weick, K. 1979. *The social psychology of organizing* (2nd ed.). Reading, MA: Addison-Wesley.

Weick, K. 1990. Cartographic myths in organizations. In A. Huff (Ed.), *Mapping strategic thought*: 1–10. New York: Wiley.

Weick, K. 1995. *Sensemaking in organizations*. Thousand Oaks, CA: Sage.

Wilson, J. B. 1979. *The story experience*. London: Scarecrow Press.

Wildavsky, A. 1973. If planning is everything, maybe it's nothing. *Policy Sciences*, 4: 127–153.

Yanow, D. 1994. *Reader-response theory and organizational life: Action as interpretation and text*. Paper presented at the annual meeting of the Academy of Management, Dallas, TX.

David Barry is a senior lecturer in organization studies at the University of Auckland (New Zealand). He received his Ph.D. from the University of Maryland. His work explores how art-based approaches (derived mostly from narrative theory, literary criticism, and the visual and performing arts) might be used to better understand organizational life (especially in the areas of change management, culture, decision making, leadership, strategy, and teams).

Michael Elmes is an associate professor of management at WPI. He received his Ph.D. from Syracuse University. His research interests include narrativity, environmental sustainability, teams, disasters, intergroup relations, and diversity.

[4]

Organizational Kitsch

Stephen Linstead
University of Durham, UK

Abstract. Kitsch as a descriptive and evaluative term is popularly deployed in the context of art and artifacts, contemporarily denoting that which is perhaps poor in taste, quality or refinement yet which retains some sort of mildly perverse attractiveness. It prettifies the problematic, makes the disturbing reassuring, and establishes an easy (and illusory) unity of the individual and the world. This article draws on historical sources and contemporary theory across a range of critical disciplines to expand our current awareness of the range of the concept and its organizational relevance, examining how its acceptance has developed over this period to incorporate mass production techniques and development in the reproductive technologies which can allow us to apply it with more precision to the field of organization studies. Kitsch is not so much a metaphor as a multifaceted response to modernity of great complexity in its very simplicity, and its key features are summarized. The article then identifies the presence of kitsch in two examples of thinking about organizing—the work of Abraham Maslow as an example of needs-based organization theory, and Peters and Waterman's In Search of Excellence, the founding example of the 'excellence' school which claims the status of theory. It is not the identification of kitsch as an aesthetic style in organizing which is significant, but the recognition of kitsch as an ontology of being which effectively masks the experience of being—interposing itself as a comforting buffer between ourselves and the 'real', and often being taken for it. Kitsch, rather than being a mere matter of stylistics, can be seen as one of the key philosophical problems of modernity and should therefore be taken seriously by organization theory. **Key words.** aesthetics; excellence; kitsch; ontology; self-expression

Organization 9(4)
Articles

'Absence of heart—as in public buildings
Absence of mind—as in public speeches
Absence of worth—as in goods intended for the public
Are telltale signs that a chimera has just dined
On someone else; of him, poor foolish fellow,
Not a scrap is left, not even his name.' (W.H. Auden, *The Chimeras*)

'All kitsch is a use of knowledge—of form, technique, of meaning and the
quest for meaning.' (Montgomery, 1991: 50)

Introduction: Kitsch and the Avant-Garde

Along with the concept of the avant-garde as Calinescu (1987/1995; see
also Foster, 1985) argues, kitsch is one of the major responses to the
modernist aesthetic. Where the avant-garde seeks new ways of expressing
the inexpressible, kitsch has as its objective precisely the opposite—new
ways of expressing that which has already been expressed so many times
that it is instantly recognizable. Where the avant-garde is demanding,
kitsch is reassuring. Yet, despite the recent rise of interest in aesthetic
aspects of organization, and the relative concentration on postmodern
thought as the avant-garde of organization theory, the concept of kitsch
has received little attention, with the exception of Kostera (1997) who
draws on the work of Kundera to deploy the concept in applying it to
three organizations, rather than undertaking an exploration of the concept itself. Indeed, Kostera explicitly distances herself from making any
judgements on the worth of kitsch as a genre, on the grounds that the
distinction between 'high' and 'low' culture is a modernist one, which
leads to the unnecessary disparagement of kitsch as 'low' culture.

Such a formulation, which is not uncommon, fails properly to see past
contemporary usages of kitsch to its underlying practical characteristics,
in the process being unnecessarily dismissive of the potential of low
culture as a source in itself for the mimetics of kitsch, and for kitsch to be
neither low nor high culture but capable of being parasitical on both. The
origins of kitsch lie, in fact, not in the cheap copying of high art, but in
the faking of the artifacts of traditional crafts (Eco, 1989; Montgomery,
1991). Kitsch, then, is not the property of either low or high culture, but
may inhabit either; neither is it a term that the one may use to disparage
the other (Ross, 1989; Wheale, 1995: 48; Adorno, 1997: 239; Benjamin,
1999). One of the features that render it both ubiquitous and elusive is
that it is pervasive, and can be found not only in culture but also in
thought styles, social life, political systems and organizations. Equating
kitsch solely with 'art' leads to its being used only as a metaphor when
applied to organizations, comparing organizations characterized by, for
example, cheap and easy sentimentality with art, which has the same
insincere qualities. However, as I will demonstrate in this paper, a fuller
appreciation of the range of the concept of kitsch enables us to see that it
is not so much that kitsch is a useful *metaphor* for comparing art and
organizations, but that the process of *being kitsch* is one which pervades

Organizational Kitsch
Stephen Linstead

both art and organization in equal measure, because it is the result of a historically developing set of reductive responses to modernism in all its forms rather than a borrowed technique. It is not, then, a matter of using one form to illuminate the other, but to observe the same processes at work in different arenas.

Nevertheless, it is necessary to proceed with caution, as it is difficult to avoid the simplifying, simulating and sentimentalizing tendencies of kitsch appearing to some degree in everything we create or construct collectively. Yet, whilst judgement here may be perilous, that can be no excuse for not attempting to exercise it, because, although final enlightenment may not be possible, some illumination should be. In identifying some of the key aspects of the concept of kitsch relevant to organization theory in this paper, I will briefly illustrate their manifestation in two areas—classical organization theory in the work of Abraham Maslow on motivation and the self and its applications; and the applied quasi-theory of Peters and Waterman and the subsequent 'excellence' literature. Before doing this, however, I will examine some broader features of contemporary cultural kitsch, trace the historical development of kitsch as a concept and examine some of the core characteristics of the kitsch response to being.

A Short History of Kitsch

Kitsch is, unfortunately, a phenomenon that it is impossible to define with rigidity—one of its chief characteristics is that it constantly finds new forms and another is that it is hard in any human endeavour to avoid kitsch entirely. Despite its often dynamic surface, it is set directly against those ontologies of becoming and emergence which Chia (1996) discusses.

> Kitsch is mechanical and operates by formulas. Kitsch is vicarious experience and faked sensations. Kitsch changes according to style, but remains always the same. Kitsch is the epitome of all that is spurious in the life of our times. (Greenberg, 1939/1986: 12)

Umberto Eco (1989: 185), in his essay on bad taste, notes that elements of what has been commonly considered to be a distinctively modern phenomenon were clearly present in kitsch-like productions as early as the 16th century. In this category, we could include crude and almost self-parodic copies of plays, cheap prints or woodcuts; trashy sentimentalizations of folk art and music; and the pre-tabloid sensationalized broadsheets of the running-patterers who brought their version of infotainment to both country and urban populations. A little later, Alexis de Tocqueville (1961: 59–60), writing in 1840, notes a growing development: that amongst the unfortunate side-effects of democracy is a tendency to cheapen the distinctive by copying or rendering it accessible to the masses—a wider body not capable of the discrimination necessary to appreciate the fine distinctions which made the original precious,

659

Organization 9(4)
Articles

whether art, literature, philosophy, music or other representational or expressive form. But it was the period 1860–80 which finally found a name for this phenomenon, for during this time a group of Schwabischer artists in southern Germany began to create formulaic paintings for the purpose of making money quickly from undiscerning tourists. These paintings were sentimental, nationalistic and easily reproduced. The verb *verkitschen*, with the 19th-century acceptation 'to churn out cheaply', produced the noun *kitsch* (Montgomery, 1991: 7). The term has since become a common one in modern art, particularly with regard to mass representation and popular culture, but its definition has been widely expanded from its original sense of 'trash art for the masses' (Pazaurek, cited in Montgomery, 1991: 8) and now commonly encompasses the idea of 'bad taste' in general (Calinescu, 1987/1995; Eco, 1989), which is frequently combined with a sense of spectacle. Calinescu (1987/1995: 322–4) identifies a cluster of related terms in several languages, but none seems to be entirely coterminous with the full range of meanings associated with the signifier *kitsch*, which perhaps explains its untranslated passage into so many different tongues. Through the work of several theorists throughout this century, but perhaps culminating with most impact in the writing and criticism of Milan Kundera, the semantic range of kitsch has been expanded to encompass the four additional non-visual senses of being an agency of political power, a sociological phenomenon, a philosophical problem and a literary genre. As Kundera (1988: 135) argues

> Kitsch is something more than simply a work in poor taste. There is a kitsch attitude. Kitsch behaviour. The kitsch-man's (Kitschmensch) need for kitsch: it is the need to gaze into the mirror of the beautifying lie and to be moved to tears of gratification at one's own reflection.

Kitsch involves the easy satisfaction of expectations, the harmonic fusion of the image with reality itself and the elision of tensions without placing demands on its audience. It takes the disturbing and makes it comforting. The study of the ways in which kitsch achieves these condensations and transformations highlights some of the important aspects of the significant shaping roles that images visual, verbal and aural, can play in social organization through:

a)   their ability to turn thought and feeling into formula, therefore into 'products' for consumption;
b)   their resulting power to help ingrain and recycle existing modes of thought, about both the human and natural worlds; and
c)   thus, their multiform contribution towards stabilizing particular institutional structures (which both employ and are the object of kitsch representations, often in subtle ways). (Montgomery, 1991: 7–8)

Swift, naturalized and unreflective connections between thought and feeling and the recycling of the ultimately familiar in novel forms are

Organizational Kitsch
Stephen Linstead

found, as Montgomery notes, not only in artistic products and artifacts, but in any form of expression, including theory, that attempts to articulate the human relationship with the natural world, and to other humans. But before proceeding any further with our arguments, let us clarify our acceptation of the concept of kitsch in relation to two similar and often associated concepts.

Kitsch, Irony and Camp

There are some significant differences between the three related and often confused terms of kitsch, irony and camp, which popular usage frequently elides, because the differences between them revolve primarily not around issues of style but of the relation of self to self—of self-reflexivity—which will be discussed more fully later. 'Kitsch' is often used to refer to the use of kitsch representations in an ironic, self-knowing way. However, this knowing commentary itself cannot be kitsch, as it is essential for kitsch that the object and the reading do not display any sense of irony at all—self, image and reality are all fused in one self-evident moment. The creators of kitsch are, of course, quite entitled to manufacture it knowingly, but their productions themselves must not reveal the ironic circumstances of their creation or they will cease to be kitsch. Likewise the kitsch *reading* has to be one that takes the object at face value. When irony creeps in, the identity of the object becomes undercut by the subtext between the creator and reader which says 'but you and I know better' (Travers, 1993: 129). Kitsch just *knows*, without reflection.

> As soon as kitsch is recognised for the lie it is, it moves into the context of non-kitsch, thus losing its authoritarian power and becoming as touching as any other human weakness. For none of us is superman enough to escape kitsch completely. No matter how we scorn it, kitsch is an integral part of the human condition. (Kundera, 1984: 256)

'Camp', on the other hand, exaggerates the staging of kitsch and brings it into larger-than-life focus so that it not only ceases to be kitsch but also surpasses even irony. In fact, it layers irony upon irony—as Travers (1993: 129) puts it, in camp the 'self' is so blatantly, obscenely *present* that its artifice is unavoidably obvious, and with it the recognition that any authentic 'self' must be *absent*. But, where irony would suggest that we know where the real self is to be found, in camp, the irony is so ironic that it is silent. Where irony says that we know better, camp says that we *cannot* know any better, 'that however reflexive we are we will only know reflexivity' (Travers, 1993: 128; Ashmore, 1989). Kitsch knows who it is; irony knows it isn't who it appears to be and thinks it might know who it really is; camp only knows it cannot be as it appears, but that appearance is all it can know. Kitsch is reassuring: camp's histrionic

Organization 9(4)
Articles

mimicry of kitsch through excessive simulation unsettles, disturbs and reveals its essential ambivalence (Travers 1993: 132).

Many popular usages confuse or blur the boundaries between these three terms, but the tests of irony and reflexivity, to be applied to any phenomenon that we consider a candidate to be an example of kitsch, are important because the presence of these qualities indicates that we have gone beyond kitsch. If kitsch is to remain analytically useful then the 'innocence' of the reading—its unthinking quality—has to remain the core of any definition. But these are not the only features of kitsch, and in the next section we will look at its main conceptual dimensions: its being based on the principle of *return*; its being human-centred or anthropocentric; its being a form of mass sentiment and its being a collective defence mechanism.

Kitsch as Eternal Return

There is a line in the film *Shadowlands* in which one of C.S. Lewis' former pupils says that his father always used to tell him: 'We read to know that we are not alone'. Kundera (1984: 270) following Nietzsche similarly argues that we all need someone to look at us, to confirm our existence through their mirroring gaze. We can even be divided into categories according to the type of audience we prefer—the anonymous public, a numerous but well-known circle, the constant presence of a loved one, or the imaginary gaze of the idealized absent person. In all of these instances, the processes of the production and consumption of the self are simultaneously implied. Rather than being separate processes, they are a duality, a mutuality of shaping forces, logical inversions of each other—we 'produce' identities that we think others will want to 'consume' (Cooper, 1986: 1; Baudrillard, 1981). Lacan (1977 in Cooper, 1986: 1) argues that this is a characteristic of language, in that it 'constitutes a communication in which the sender receives his [sic] own message back from the receiver in an inverted form'. If, for example, someone says 'I love you', then they are attempting far more than a simple expression of feeling. They categorize the addressee as a loved one, inviting a reciprocation of that feeling; themselves as a 'lover' and hopefully a fitting person to fill such a role; and 'loving' as a normal activity for people such as themselves to engage in. If the reply is 'And I love you too'—the invited inverted return—all of these things are confirmed regardless of any other indexical qualities of the utterance in context (imagine, for example, that the exchange had been between Winston and Julia, the characters in Orwell's *1984*, when it would have been a crime against the state). Golding (1996) argues that similarly reciprocal and confirmatory exchanges can take place through actions as well as language. Language and symbolic action is always exploratory to a degree and both seeks and needs its own reconfirmation through repetition and return. This *mirroring* needs to be constantly reaccom-

Organizational Kitsch
Stephen Linstead

plished and reaffirmed, especially in the face of apparent change in other aspects of existence—age, relationships, occupational structures, the economy, political pressures, military action, personal failure, even things as simple as a change in the weather or a frown on a face, as ephemeral as the scent of spring blossom, the texture of fresh bread, or the shade of an autumn sunset.

This process however, reveals the hollowness of human experience—that there is no absolute foundation or origin of humanity which is the source of knowledge and which fixes and determines our essential nature, and hence no truly common experience. We need others to help us to *construct* this origin, *as if* it were the source of all meaning. Kitsch obscures the processes of such construction, making the artificiality of experience appear natural, glossing over the gaps that are inevitable. Approaches to knowledge, which could be termed postmodern, in contrast, emphasize these processes, celebrate *aporia* and *deconstruct* experience, disturbing the apparent solidarity between the world and human meaning by showing how the effect of agreement is produced (Cooper, 1986: 2; Chia, 1996). There are no guarantees that the world is as it appears, no matter how sophisticated and exhaustive the tools and methods we use to apprehend it. Such thought recognizes the fact that human beings are fictions that are constantly constructing and reinventing themselves, attempting to define themselves through descriptions which fail to question how humanity comes into being and which take for granted their own symbolic autochthony.

The more dangerous side of this blindness, which can extend into social scientific theory through the emergence of paradigms, is that kitsch favours those descriptions, categorizations, theories, accounts and explanations which 'make men feel agreeably presentable to themselves' and 'the merely functional becomes an object of narcissistic adoration' (Cooper, 1986: 10), even perhaps a fetish. We know what we like, and eventually may come to like what we know, beyond merely feeling comfortable with it. We, like Kundera's character Tereza, may gaze into the mirror romantically:

> It was not vanity that drew her to the mirror, it was amazement at seeing her own 'I'. She forgot she was looking at the instrument panel of her body mechanisms; she thought she saw her soul shining through the features of her face. She forgot that the nose was merely the nozzle of a hose that took oxygen to the lungs; she saw it as the expression of her nature. (Kundera, 1984: 41)

Kitsch thus exercises a de-ontologizing effect in the processes of self-construction, in providing a mask for materiality and the anguishes of being, and thus acts as a defence against the abject, which reminds us rather uncomfortably of such things (see Linstead, 1997; Bataille, 1986; Kundera, 1999: 42, 44).

Organization 9(4)
Articles

Kitsch as Human-centred

The narcissistic properties of kitsch, and the tendency of the familiar to
follow a trajectory of deepening approval from the aesthetic (it is comfortable, pleasing) to the moral (it is approved, advocated, required, the
natural way of things) underpin a cosmology which positions humanity
at the centre of creation. Kitsch proposes that the world is, in fact, as we
want it to be (or, alternatively, as we fear it is, in certain respects). From
the kitsch point of view, the world was created for humans, humans are
at its centre, and the meanings which people give to the world or which
it appears to have for them are therefore entirely congruent with the
nature of things. This *anthropocentrism* Heidegger terms *moral-aesthetic
anthropology*, but similar terms appear in Kundera (the *categorical agreement with being*), Rorty (the *mirror of nature*), Calinescu (the *aesthetics of
deception and self-deception*), and Vattimo (the *utopia of reintegration*),
which seem to be addressing the same phenomenon, if with slightly
different emphases.

Anthropocentrism is set to deny the gaps of division and differentiation in the world by constituting the human subject as effectively its
own origin. The bewildering variety of species, their obviously conflicting interests, the infinitude of ways of living amongst and relating to
them, are all compressed and simplified.

Anthropocentrism, then, denies human characteristics to other forms
of life, yet unifies the very difference that it creates by subordinating
them to the human sense of meaning and purpose. The aesthetic and the
ethical are confused, with the beautiful (in this case that which conforms
to human desires) being always put forward as morally superior (Montgomery, 1991: 10). That which is good *for humanity* is good *per se;* the
functional is never just functionally *effective*, but by virtue is also
morally *right*. Other life forms are an extension of human aspirations by
other means. This process of extending human and social engineering to
the whole world subordinates nature, in all its complexity, variety and
mystery, to its objectively determined characteristics and, in particular,
its socially functional features. The richness of Nature is desiccated and
reconstituted as Environment as 'the production–consumption process
. . . cocoons us from the strange and disturbing which Nature (including
"human nature") represents' (Cooper, 1986: 14). Kitsch then disguises
itself as *objectified knowledge*. Of course, objectified knowledge meets
the requirements of *unity, simplicity* and *communicability*, which are the
moral-aesthetic features of kitsch (Lyotard, 1984: 75) and our definitions
of not only natural phenomena but also other people must conform to
these criteria. In other words, people are produced as 'objects' whose
virtue is determined by their degree of conformance to the norms of the
social system. Good or bad, then, are not absolute states but are determined on a more/less scale of correctness/conformity. Once such a degree
of conformance or otherwise is established, the categories of good and

Organizational Kitsch
Stephen Linstead

bad are mobilized as part of the simplification process, inconsistencies are denied or forgotten, and concepts, people, things or environmental features are constructed and defined as these features are ossified. Kitsch then suppresses those things that do not appear to fit: the unusual, the troublesome, the difficult, the paradoxical, the critical, the individual, the questioning, the doubting, the ironic. Kitsch is always therefore an inadequate response to reality: yet, the larger the mass of humanity that comprises the social system, the greater the demand for unity and simplicity, the greater the need for instantaneous communicability, the greater the threat of non-standard thought and the greater the demand for kitsch as a defence against disintegration.

> Everything that infringes on kitsch must be banished for life: every display of individualism (because a deviation from the collective is a spit in the eye of the smiling brotherhood); every doubt (because anyone who starts doubting details will end up by doubting life itself); all irony (because in the realm of kitsch everything must be taken quite seriously) and the mother who abandons her family or the man who prefers men to women. (Kundera, 1984: 252)

Kitsch as Mass Sentiment

As Montgomery (1991: 11) observes, 'kitsch aims to evoke the individual, in emotion and in intellect, on a mass basis'. Kitsch will feel for us and think for us if we are willing to let it. Kitsch works because it reminds us of the fact that we are not alone, and it is so powerful because it capitalizes on a fundamental lack: our desire not to be alone, the desire for the other which motivates social structure (Cooper, 1983; Leather, 1983; Linstead and Grafton Small, 1992). Kitsch offers quick and easy access to the longed-for world of the other, which becomes *our* world, and which is always reassuring no matter how cheap and nasty it may be. Kitsch is also most effective visually rather than rhetorically (although it has very effective rhetorical forms) in that we don't need to be *persuaded* by it, just to share and participate in it is sufficient—it works without us having to think about it.

> When the heart speaks, the mind finds it indecent to object. In the realm of kitsch, the dictatorship of the heart reigns supreme.

> The feeling induced by kitsch must be a kind the multitudes can share. Kitsch may not, therefore, depend on an unusual situation; it must derive from the basic images people have engraved in their memories: the ungrateful daughter, the neglected father, children running on the grass, the motherland betrayed, first love.

> Kitsch causes two tears to flow in quick succession. The first tear says: How nice to see children running on the grass!

> The second tear says: How nice to be moved, together with all mankind, by children running on the grass!

> It is the second tear that makes kitsch kitsch. (Kundera, 1984: 251)

Organization 9(4)
Articles

As we noted in the preceding section, as the mass of humanity to be covered by the social system grows, the greater the demand for an easily communicable unity. For Benjamin (1992) and Adorno (1991), technology and the ability to reproduce images and communicate them quickly and accurately to large numbers of people is an essential element in the spread of kitsch. Kitsch at all levels has a technical aspect, a 'mercenary aesthetics, a quality of affect-for-hire that promises harmony and light, a fusion between expectations towards reality (whether sentimental, jingoistic etc.) and reality itself' (Montgomery, 1991:7). For Broch (1969a, 1969b), kitsch was 'the disintegration of art into commodity, creativity into a demand for known effects and affects' (Montgomery, 1991:10). Other writers in recent years (Friedlander, 1984; Giesz, 1960; Pross, 1985) have extended this argument—not only is kitsch a means of achieving cheap artistic effects, it is also a means of achieving cheap social and political effects. Rather than simply selling aesthetic forms, kitsch sells ideas and feelings, and the 'bag of tricks' of art becomes available for any purpose—an 'artism' which can be used to sell souvenirs, soap powder, or political solutions. Kitsch is adaptable and constantly in change at a superficial level.

> Kitsch therefore does not take sides *a priori*, and has different levels of operation. It can be crude and trashy or sophisticated and adaptable. (Montgomery, 1991: 11)

As Calinescu (1987/1995: 229–30) argues, the avant-garde can and does appropriate kitsch into art through self-reflexive ironic deployment, whilst kitsch adapts avant-garde techniques in order to reproduce its aesthetic form, but without its message or significance. It has much in common therefore with camp, which as noted earlier deploys outrageous kitsch with reflexive irony in order to draw attention to the artificiality of boundaries such as gender—as Susan Sontag (1969: 293) argues, 'it is beautiful *because* it is awful'. Furthermore, as Vattimo (1988: 56) reminds us, since Kant's *Critique of Judgment*, one of the fundamental meanings given to the term 'aesthetic pleasure' has been to define it not as experienced by the subject in relation to the object, but as 'that pleasure which derives from belonging to a group ... that shares the same capacity for appreciating the beautiful'. Or, we might add, of recognizing the awful. In the process, kitsch makes the disturbing comforting, pleasing and pacifying as the nature of the object becomes subordinated to the experience of community. Remembering our earlier point about the inseparability of production and consumption processes, this community is itself a product of kitsch as the organization of consensus:

> Over and beyond the process of distributing information, the mass media serve to produce a consensus through the establishment and intensification of a common language of social life. The mass media do not provide a means for the masses which is at the service of the masses; it is the means *of* the masses, in the sense in which the masses as such are constituted by

Organizational Kitsch
Stephen Linstead

> the mass media as a public realm of common consensus, taste, and feeling. (Vattimo, 1988: 55)

Kitsch spreads throughout our contemporary communities with great rapidity—as Benjamin (1992) contended, the age of mechanical or mass reproduction decisively transforms aesthetic experience. New technologies have disseminated it throughout all our communicational media, television, radio, cinema, the press, art, literature and performance, working through language, image, music and constructing 'fact', 'theory' and economic 'reality' anywhere, Montgomery (1991: 12) argues, 'where old emperors are given new clothes'. The attempt to develop the Enterprise Culture in the UK in the 1980s (Keat and Abercrombie, 1991) was one such initiative:

> In a society where capitalist economics take precedence over other human relationships, there is always a direct incentive to exalt the majority opinion, the largest market-share attitudes, to provide these with heroes (both grand and local), sweetened reflections, a numbing quality of flattening and patterned experiences. (Montgomery, 1991: 12)

Despite the increasing technical virtuosity of the pyrotechnics of the corporate presentation, the new musical, the rock video, the novel, the special effects of the cinema or the CD-ROM and the stunning realizations of contemporary digital television, the underlying message remains simple, direct, and unchanged (Connell, 1995: 164; Höpfl and Linstead, 1993). Even as it appears to change constantly, it stabilizes. This, of course, is one of the main purposes of kitsch, to continually reinvent the shapes in which old ideas appear in order to recycle them with greatest effect—they remain cliches, truisms, homilies, stereotypes, chestnuts or knee-jerk responses that recur automatically, without the need for reflection or individual intellectual labour (which of course threaten it). These emotively packaged, ready-made judgements are not confined to the mass level of tabloid culture, for what Montgomery calls 'higher symbolic platitudes' are regularly turned out by the colour supplements, coffee table literature, the 'quality' press and TV channels. This increasing glitter and virtuosity adds a sensual, even erotic, dimension to kitsch, suspended as it is in tension between power and submission. Kitsch thus 'makes dead thought the object of fascination and desire' and obscures its own dark side by hiding it in light (Hebdige, 1988; Montgomery, 1991: 13).

Kitsch as a Defence Mechanism

The anthropocentrism we have observed as characteristic of kitsch—where human needs and desires predominate over all the world's other considerations—is also linked to *anthropomorphism*, in which human form is considered to be the world's highest form of development. From a realist perspective, as we noted in the previous discussion, the scientific kitsch of Descartes explicitly denies human characteristics to other forms

667

Organization 9(4)
Articles

of life—pain, sentiment, soul and intellect included. Contemporary forms of kitsch, however, proliferate with Disneyland anthropomorphism as though, and perhaps as a result of contemporary forms of the emotional autism that arises as a paradoxical by-product of Cartesian modernism, it is frequently only possible to recognise certain human feelings by allegorical projection onto the muppetized animal kingdom or claymation talking teapots. The rest of nature becomes a screen upon which we humans write our own emotional concerns, as a means of handling the difficulties we experience in dealing directly with Being without interposing some simplifying and self-alienating device. This is one aspect of the 'living death' that is kitsch. However, this mawkishly sentimental anthropomorphism has a second and complementary sense, which proves to be more ontologically problematic. This is the sense that humanity itself is crafted in the image of God—humans are a literal representation of divinity, the embodiment of spiritual truths, and thus, whatever our concerns, we can find their origin, the 'truth' of creation, by cultivating the appropriate form of introspection. The 'natural', with effort, gives access to the supernatural. In kitsch formulations, this introspection is easily truncated into the form of the conditioned emotional response, which appears to be the 'natural' response. However, as Kundera relates, any idea of a naturalized relation between the physical and the metaphysical is necessarily problematic which is symified?? by our customary objection to faeces:

'The objection to shit is a metaphysical one'. (Kundera, 1984: 249)

The paradox here resides in two problems—one the question of perfectibility, the other the question of control. If God is perfect, then God does not change. But defecation is the outcome of a process of transformation, growth and decay. That which changes cannot be perfect. But, perhaps worse, it is a process over which the body has no control. Shit happens. That which lacks control over its own processes cannot therefore be all-powerful. If God has no need of nose, mouth or anus, then why should God possess them? Either God is not perfect, and does need them; God has redundant parts, in which case God could not be perfect; or we have made God in the image of our own functionality, to which our sense of our own symbolic importance has blinded us. We have become not only self-obsessed but also self-idolatrous beings. The kitsch response here, faced with the incompatibility of the two propositions, is the denial of the least flattering, the one which we cannot accept without overturning our established assumptions. Other forms of kitsch similarly deny the unacceptable contradictions of existence to the point that Kundera is able to assert that the aesthetic result of anthropocentrism and anthropomorphism, 'the categorical agreement with being', is 'a world in which shit is denied and everyone acts as though it did not exist'. In fact, kitsch could almost be defined as:

Organizational Kitsch
Stephen Linstead

> ... the absolute denial of shit, in both the literal and the figurative senses of the word; kitsch excludes everything from its purview which is essentially unacceptable in human existence. (Kundera, 1984: 248)

Viewed in terms of any system, shit is what doesn't fit; and, for kitsch, what doesn't fit must be shit. Georges Bataille, however, reverses this view in arguing that it is *precisely* what we waste, what we produce as excess, that makes us human. Bataille (1985) begins from the argument that the sun is the source of human existence and it is the sun's excess energy which gives rise to life on earth. However, the sun will, one day, implode and life on earth will be extinguished. All life, accordingly, can be viewed as excess, wasted effort. Both Lyotard and Baudrillard were influenced by this view, but neither takes the affirmative approach which Bataille takes—Baudrillard becomes almost depressive, Lyotard sees the challenge as a moral/ethical one, but Bataille makes the condition of excess the principle of his philosophy, literally defining what is human.

Human beings for Bataille are distinguished from animals by, firstly, not being dominated by the pursuit of physiological need; and, secondly by their ability to contemplate death even to the point of desiring their own annihilation, to the point of sacrifice. This willingness to pursue limits and exceed them enables humans to transcend the everyday profane and glimpse—whether in artistic, physical or religious ecstasy— the sacred. Marginal artifacts and activities are where the profane comes into contact with the sacred and they thus have enormous symbolic power, leading societies who wish to be uniform and homogeneous to censure and exclude them, in socio-political kitsch. Yet the society which thrives and grows on variety, and in which it is possible to be fully human, for Bataille is heterogeneous and embraces all those points of intersection, those things which have been expelled from the integral unit or body:

> ... the sacred is revealed in bodily exhalations (blood, sweat, tears, shit); extreme emotions (laughter, anger, drunkenness, ecstasy); socially useless activity (poetry, games, crime, eroticism) all of which take the form of a heterology that homogeneous [kitsch] society would like to definitively expel. (Richardson, 1994: 36, square parenthesis added)

Discovering how to be human for Bataille involves exuberant spending, risking and learning, and he distinguishes these as the features of a 'general economy'—a broad nexus of human relations including giving and consumption—as distinct from the 'restricted economy' posed by normal economic theory and represented by work, production, exchange and accumulation. Whilst he recognized that all societies displayed some impulse towards social homogeneity (the inescapability of kitsch), Bataille thought that capitalism had, because of its emphasis on economic accumulation through production, totalized this tendency. People were reduced to their social roles, communal effusion was denied, true communication as a consequence was blocked, and any creativity and

Organization 9(4)
Articles

effervescence that did not serve a social function was destroyed. The basis of society was calculation, work and industry, determined by the principle of exchange and the integrity (separability) of the individual, not by the principle of circulation and communication within communities. Bataille sees consumption as having two parts: the first is the reducible one, the subsistence minimum needed for the immediate conservation of life, while the second is the excess of energy needed for unproductive expenditure such as play, laughter and so on. Bataille called this the *accursed share*—that which is essential for human existence, but which was not taken into account by the calculations of the restricted economy (Richardson, 1994: 35, 71; Bataille in Botting and Wilson, 1997: 167–98; see also Bataille, 1985; 1988).

In a homogeneous society, boundaries need to be prescribed for behaviour in order to rule out the unacceptable, but we also need to know how to react, how to feel about situations—we do not want to be taken off guard, betrayed by our own actions or those of others, and this would normally require constant vigilance and scrutinizing of both our experiences and our selves. Kitsch short-circuits this agonizing and continual process by providing simple and clear models, and defining the unacceptable unambiguously. Objectionable ordure is hidden and denied; creative or critical unpredictability or alternative ways of thinking and doing are customarily suppressed. Kitsch, in seeking to deny boundaries and unify disparate elements under the illusion of naturalized control, constantly *erects* boundaries in order to suppress the existence of the unacceptable, that which falls beyond those boundaries.

Kitsch Culture: The Curse of Excellence

Recently, Ian Colville, Robert Waterman and Karl Weick (1999) have revisited the phenomenon of the success of Peters and Waterman's 1982 bestseller, *In Search of Excellence (ISOE)*. The purpose of the paper is to argue that the success of the book over 17 years is testament to its own excellence, whilst simultaneously pointing out that their view of excellence was a fluid and adaptive one—not the rigid set of eight principles which were often taken to be the whole of the book. A second objective is to argue that the book was respectful of academic theory and was an attempt to translate that theory into managerial terms, albeit through looking for the emergence of theoretical features in actual company performance. The paper argues for a continuation of translation between academia and practice as an important way forward into an unknowable future.

The kitsch elements of *ISOE* are legion, and the authors seem genuinely blind to them. In claiming that the book was a theoretical book, which in some way it was, they rather overstate their case in claiming that 'it said pretty much everything there was to be said about behaviour in organizations and got it right, by virtue of the experts cited' (Colville et

Organizational Kitsch
Stephen Linstead

al., 1999: 134). Then follows a list of the key thinkers introduced—seven in the first 10 pages, then 13 in the next 110 pages, none of them being Marx, Weber or Durkheim, or even Braverman, the best-selling study of work processes of the 1970s. Indeed, the theorists cited are predominantly contingency theorists, a phenomenon the authors neither acknowledge nor appear to be interested in, probably because they seem to be arguing that, just as facts are facts, meanings are meanings. They then skip through a recited list of concepts included in the book, from caring to quantum theory, noting in the case of learning organizations that so profound was their contribution here that the phrase was *italicized* in the original text. Concepts of resistance, pluralism, contestation, power, domination, interest, or control as a structural rather than a behavioural phenomenon are, however, absent—and no comment is made on this. So, the 'everything' that was to be said, in the manner of kitsch, excludes anything that might have been disturbing to the paradigm—nothing questioning the structures of capitalism, nothing to raise fundamental questions about management itself—just the matey apostrophizing 'Hey, aren't you supposed to be doing *this*?' approach illustrated by anecdotes (Colville et al., 1999: 131). Radical the book was, indeed, in its exhortations that the softer aspects of management needed attention and, as such, it might be seen as a much-diluted attempt to address Bataille's accursed share—in the shape of the non-performative side of work as a social activity—but ultimately with functionalist and performative ends, turning 'fun' into a commodity rather than a processual quality. The authors cite Jack Welch, CEO of General Electric, who simply states that the hard-nosed calculative approach was not wrong in human terms, just past its sell-by date, and they imply that their excellence model will fade away too. Something of a paradox here may be discerned—the authors seem to think that the book was saying things about the human condition, yet constantly trivialize the theory that was used to say it. Indeed, the desire to have your cake and eat it was so apparent in the original book that the authors felt compelled to condense the 22 principles identified from their data to eight, not because of any sophisticated regression analysis but because they had read that people could remember up to nine items but had difficulty with more (Colville et al., 1999: 132).

Ironically, the commentary, as the book itself, often seems to be against kitsch in arguing that what it presents is a new way of thinking, not a recycling of the old ways. But, as several commentators such as Ray (1986) have noted, the old forms, or emperors, are not far from the surface. Indeed, *ISOE* does exactly what Benjamin first observed of kitsch—it uses new technologies (including theory) to bedazzle the reader on the surface whilst seducing them into embracing familiar but disadvantageous relations, where ideology hides in the light (Hebdige, 1988). For example, the paper notes that Waterman and two colleagues, intent on putting *ISOE* principles into practice in 1983, with nothing but

Organization 9(4)
Articles

a fuzzy idea that 'clean, cheap, reliable and socially responsible' power should be available to all, went ahead and built a $6 billion dollar company which now has 75 plants worldwide (Colville et al., 1999: 140). The account is pure kitsch—the All American Dream from nothing to several global fortunes in less than a generation—all because the values were right:

> AES Inc. has four explicit shared values: integrity, fairness, social responsibility and fun which provide the tightness in an otherwise loosely coupled organization. 'Fun' is taken seriously and top managers' bonuses are cut in half if surveys say workers are not having fun. (Colville et al., 1999: 140)

Which must be fun for the top managers. Top managers as camp entertainments officers is quite an absurd idea, especially in an industry as complex, capital intensive and politically sensitive as power generation. The rise of AES is most certainly a brilliant managerial story—but the company did not grow by wearing red noses, or indeed by the other means that are cited. People matter? Up to a point . . . because there aren't that many of them . . .

> The organization has a radically decentralised structure based on the plants . . . the plants themselves have little or no staff. (Colville et al., 1999: 140)

Shared values can't be much of a problem to negotiate with small numbers. Again, what we have here is kitsch bordering on humbug—we are being told a story which is nothing but mythology, bread and circuses, when the real-world reasons for the success of AES, which it undoubtedly is, remain hidden. There may be some phallic display here, too— which could be expressed as 'Academics may scoff at our oversimplification of theory, but we put it into practice and made billions. Yet we still have respect for academic theory, so they should be grateful and stop carping'. Notwithstanding the reported success of AES, the way in which theory is used raises serious questions not only about which theories are considered, but also about the real degree of respect that the authors have for truly critical scholarship. The involvement of such a respected scholar as Karl Weick may be surprising here, but one possible reason may be worth consideration. This is that kitsch may open doors to the more substantial consideration of deeper matters—and it would be only fair to say that, regardless of the overstated nature of the scholarship in *ISOE*, it did set some agendas, it did bring some neglected ideas into the open, it did focus criticism on some accepted but moribund orthodoxies and it did enable more substantial work to be developed, including that critical of the original book.

Three other significant features of kitsch can be noted in the paper, rather than the book, the first being related to simplification—or *underweighting theory through translation*. Early in the paper the authors make a plea for simplification and translation in the interests of understanding, but without questioning whether translation is possible—in their unex-

Organizational Kitsch
Stephen Linstead

plicated view, it just is. Fashion, they say, is not necessarily a bad thing either—just look at Foucault and Bordieu (sic) (Colville et al., 1999:134). Interestingly, they seem to have no awareness that, although Foucault and Bourdieu are very different thinkers, they would both find the approach of *ISOE* utterly inimical to scholarship. Not only do they not consider why Foucault and Bourdieu may be considered fashionable, and what is behind their ideas, but also they do not even attempt to incorporate these fashionable theorists into their future projections for the excellence approach. Indeed, a reflexive Foucauldian analysis of 'excellence' discourse might have ironically underscored their assertion that fashion is no bad thing. Unfortunately, their argument proceeds with a peppering of buzzwords which only affirms their imprisonment in the shallowness of their own self-satisfied fashionability.

Later in the piece, in referring to the AES case, they note 'you need complexity of thought to match the complexity of the environment' but 'simple action to reduce the uncertainty of the environment'. One way of reading this statement would be that power resolves ambiguity. What you need are superb information systems and lots of financial and political muscle. Information keeps you abreast of change; timely action keeps you in control of its consequences. This would certainly have some relevance for IBM or Microsoft. Indeed, if action, as they say, is theory in practice, then they may not have moved far from the early insistence in the human relations approach, especially by Elton Mayo, on complex data but simple theory.

The second aspect is the inverse of simplifying complex theory through translation but achieves the same end of underweighting theory—*overweighting data through storytelling*. By placing emphatic significance on essentially simple data, mainly through anecdotes and homilies, they reduce the explanatory significance of theory itself, forcing it to compete on the level of understandability rather than adequacy with respect to meaning. For example, they tell a story of the San Francisco Symphony Orchestra, who were so poor in performance that until several members changed and the playing improved they did not realize that they had an acoustics problem with the hall, which held them back from further development. This is really quite a simple and well-known message—you don't realize how ill you were until you get better, you don't know the size of the problem until you begin to fix it, solving one problem may create others elsewhere in the system—but they attempt to elevate this into a theoretical point about adaptive procedures. Of course, they can't sustain a theoretical argument in this fashion and fall back into theoretical kitsch telling another anecdote and listing more buzzwords (Colville et al., 1999: 140–2).

The third aspect of the paper is that, like *ISOE,* it is literally full of itself—it *expresses its own identity* rather than discussing it. It places itself centre stage, never doubts its right to be there and never for a moment questions at anything other than a motherhood level whether its

Organization 9(4)
Articles

reading of both the world and theory might be flawed or open to more than stylistic criticism. The aesthetics of both the book and the paper are kitsch—easy avuncularity, intellectually undemanding presentations of theory in a digestible way—and the authors, though they don't appear to realize it, are mounting a defence, not of applied theory, but of theoretical kitsch. The writers of the book seek to confirm the book's identity not by debating it, but by expressing it. Self-assured, delivering such sentimentality as 'it's OK for guys to have feelings', 'don't take yourself so seriously' and 'don't let them get away with that silliness' in support of its own authenticity and truthfulness, *In Search of Excellence* is the Garden Gnome of contemporary organization theory—which will become clear in a moment.

Kitsch and the Self

Travers (1993: 132) defines kitsch as 'all human expressions of fondness, affection, comradeship and love, when these are represented by their actors as unconscious, immortal evidence of their own veracity'. Self-identity, then, is achieved through their own expressions of that identity, and all reflective sense of artifice—that the self might be in 'quotation marks'—is absent. The kitsch representation—any sort of artifact, image or utterance—is therefore entirely self-sufficient, narcissistically *full of itself*, as we noted was *ISOE*.

I can now explain the metaphor I applied to *ISOE*, as Travers cites as his example here the perhaps typically English horticultural ornament, the garden gnome. This ubiquitous statuette announces that 'beyond apology and justification, it belongs where it is, just as it is' and those who object to it must be unhappy people (Travers, 1993: 132). It is an alien object of mass production, diluted mythology, cheap materials and thoughtless design, yet it

> ... has the appalling confidence to pretend that it is for all eternity at home in a particular place, where it decrees its own right to fill itself to bursting with its own sublime actuality. And what goes for garden gnomes goes too for those expressions of fondness, affection, comradeship and love that are made without the consciousness that they are only available in a language whose evolution and usage devolve to the value of power and money and intellectual status. (Travers, 1993: 133)

We can see here that this form of kitsch seeks to incorporate those things which Bataille would regard as sacred, the accursed share, into itself as though they had never been absent, erecting sentimentality as a comfortable and predictable buffer against the risks of true emotion which might unsettle the restricted economy which supports it. The reflecting back of spurious sentiment takes on the appearance of authenticity, of the expression of the true underlying self, and acquires a simulated authority as the real and the self merge and become transparent. As with *ISOE*, 'basic

Organizational Kitsch
Stephen Linstead

human needs' merge with the environment in congruence and harmony.

As Paul de Man notes, however, unmediated expression is unachievable, as it is a philosophical impossibility (Foster, 1985: 59). Furthermore, our entire social language is designed to avoid the direct expression of our unnameable, and heterogeneous, desires—our most 'basic' needs—and those people who do voice them, as Bataille was also aware, are liable to ridicule or incarceration, or worse. Whatever the 'essential' self might contain, it is neither philosophically nor socially expressible. Yet the idea of self-expression is a culturally important one, which has exerted some influence on organization studies not only through *ISOE*, but also, in particular, through the classic work of Abraham Maslow.

Expressionism, in its various forms, rests on a metaphysical opposition of inside to outside, soul to body, with the first term being prior. Derrida (1973) has observed this of phonocentrism, where speech is regarded as being the more authentic and unmediated term which writing inscribes. Yet, as Nietzsche, and Derrida, both note, the idea of 'inner experience', of 'consciousness', only arises *after* the experience has been translated into a language that the individual understands—experience has to be 'fitted in' to consciousness (Linstead and Grafton Small, 1992). In other words, between the experience and the self, a rhetorical figure that constructs the experience has to intervene before it becomes intelligible. As Foster (1985: 62) comments, the expressionist self is alienated by the sign, in which it confronts not the resolution of its desire (to be recognized *as* a self by others) through expression, but its inevitable and recurrent deferral—decentred by its language (which it can never command) and its desire (which, as a lack, it can never fulfil). As we have seen, this self then never precedes its 'traces' (Linstead and Grafton Small, 1992), whether these are constructed as unconscious drives or social signs. The immediacy beyond representation which expressionism fantasizes creates an opposition between nature and culture about which it is itself ambiguous, as the natural is the site of *both* the human and the nonhuman, life *and* death. Indeed, expressionism has been argued to be a 'language that would be immediate, a cultural form that would be natural' (Foster, 1985: 64). Much of this can be discerned in *ISOE* with its paradoxical claim to be *reminding* managers nostalgically of what they should be doing (that is, uncovering existing natural knowledge) yet simultaneously building new theory (Colville et al., 1999: 131). Expressionism similarly attempts to reclaim a lost sense of the real (what the world is really like), of the subject (who we really are) and indeed of history as a history of immediate experiences as *substantial* (what we should be doing)—yet stubbornly these categories remain *signs* and the expressionist form a *language*. The attempt thus in the very process of its becoming denies the possibility of the enterprise, reveals it to be yet

Organization 9(4)
Articles

another mimetic mask interposed between the self and being—a kitsch aesthetic.

In the years after the Second World War, post-Freudian growth psychology was pioneered by Kurt Lewin, Carl Rogers and, the most influential from a management point of view, Abraham Maslow, whose hierarchy of human needs is still taught to almost every management student and features in almost every basic organizational behaviour text. Maslow's hierarchy was based on his interpretation of Freudian desire, where desire is a drive to fill a perceived lack which occasions a need. Maslow studied both primates and humans, his interest being shaped by a biological essentialism visible throughout his work, with the intent of reducing the symbolic complexity of Freud—whose work he considered to be impractical in many situations. He regards homosexuals, for example, as being not normal, and indeed sick, because they choose

> ... the poorer rather than the better, because the mouth or the rectum or the armpit or the hand or whatever in his male homosexual partner, were simply none of them as well designed for the penis as the vagina is designed. (Maslow, 1965: 12)

The reduction of homosexual love to a functional biological error is perhaps an extreme illustration of Maslow's insistence on normality— that work circumstances must be made to 'fit' the human personality rather than the other way round. Maslow's intentions in this regard are sympathetic, but his conceptualization of human needs as a hierarchy ascending from survival and safety needs (existential), through love and affection and self esteem needs (social needs), finally to self-actualization needs always returns him to a psychological kitsch, even in the later and more elaborate versions of the hierarchy which imply substrata creating up to eight levels. Maslow felt that certain people, but by no means all, were capable of what he called self-actualization—the fullest realization of a harmonic fusion of the self with the world and the world with the self. His interest was always to help these people to grow and self-actualize, first through individual counselling and therapy, then through education. He finally discovered industrial psychology in his only book on the subject written after a summer of observation in a high-technology factory—*Eupsychian Management: A Journal*, originally published in 1965, recently republished as *Maslow on Management* (Maslow et al., 1998). Self-actualizing persons were his focus, as he believed that, in creating conditions for them to thrive, all would benefit—an unashamedly elitist and patriarchal if benevolent strategy.

Maslow's journal discusses the work of management theorists of the time—with a personal style not dissimilar to *ISOE*—and he is convinced that he is improving their work by adding certain psychological findings to it, along with his own critique. Yet, although his 'eupsychian' approach does argue for looking at the 'whole person', that person is not a fully social being, because the benefits of social relations are reduced to

Organizational Kitsch
Stephen Linstead

a transactional economy of the emotions. Unpleasant work is introjected into the self and affects self-esteem, which affects the individual's ability to self-actualize:

> I find it difficult to conceive of feeling proud of myself, self-loving and self-respecting, if I were working, for example, in some chewing-gum factory, or a phony advertising agency, or in some factory that turned out shoddy furniture. (Maslow, 1965: 13)

Maslow here reminds us of Travers' point above about kitsch expressions being unreflexively 'without the consciousness that they are only available in a language ... of power and money and intellectual status'—although Maslow is not naively in denial of these things but rather unquestioningly accepts bourgeois values in the process of mystifying them. He still retains some sense of the 'authentic' self, and constructs the work environment as, in effect, a symbolic and rhetorical form that blocks the growth and full expression of the self. Yet Maslow's own hierarchy is itself just such a rhetorical form which acts to deny the self any such expression save through hierarchical progression and development from one foundation to the next. As Foster argues, whatever the self may be it is not possible to actualize save through fitting it symbolically into some a priori symbolic structure or language—which itself alienates the self, and the contradictions of this are evident throughout Maslow's writings. The symbolic forms which shape his construction of 'selfhood' and its actualization are a reduction of western capitalist forms of production and economic activity with associated bourgeois ideology to five universalized, and hence depoliticized, quasi-biological needs—which are in fact middle-class values. The kitsch here is that through the pursuit of authentic self-hood the one becomes the many; middle-class capitalist values become universal principles; and although merging self and reality is recognized as an unfinished project, it is affirmed as 'normal', the result of an integrated progression. Yet, as Foster noted, trapped within its own symbolic cage, all it achieves is the pathos of reminding us of the elusiveness of authenticity. With considerable irony

> ... the essential effort to this form of kitsch is to use the facade of paternal good intentions to conceal both *a broken faith in the individual* and, more crucially, a desire to protect the ruling truth from any alternatives. (Montgomery, 1991: 32, emphasis added)

Kitsch Social Science

Although we have levelled some criticisms at the kitsch social science of Peters and Waterman and Maslow, we should recall that, as Montgomery points out, kitsch science (and organizational science) are not oppositional to institutional science and scholarship, but transitive to it; not heresy, but 'its shadow, the dust that clings to its halo' (Montgomery, 1991: 32). The kitsch component, Montgomery argues, comes from two features:

Organization 9(4)
Articles

> . . . first, the motive to put forth an idea for the sake of its effect, that is to
> propose a knowledge yet more spectacular or otherwise desirable (simple,
> playful) than that of science; second, their own claim to the myth of an
> absolute or final truth. (Montgomery, 1991: 32)

Neither *ISOE* nor Maslow scores on both these points—*ISOE* certainly
aims to maximize effect, but at least hedges its bets on certainty, despite
its self-confidence. Maslow is much more certain that he is addressing
fundamental human verities, so his kitsch is less aesthetic and more
theoretical than *ISOE*, but, as we saw with his homosexual example, he
frequently puts forward ideas because they will have a dramatic effect.

Montgomery notes that in science there remains a powerful myth of the
man (sic) and the idea, the *breakthrough* discovery that turns the scientific world on its head. Even the mad or eccentric scientist, like Dr
Frankenstein, may indeed be demonstrably mad, but he or she still
flatters normal science by trying to be a scientist, even a deviant one. In
fact, there is an element of kitsch in all scientific discovery insofar as it
depends on 'the initial infatuation among scientists with the sheer
novelty of an idea and, more, faith in it as a sudden, radical transformation capable of explaining all manner of phenomena' (Montgomery, 1991:
33). This might well explain both the rapid rise to popularity of *ISOE*,
whose authors claim to be social scientists, and the enduring even
compelling quality of Maslow's work despite the many critiques of its
methodological flaws and empirical support.

Yet there is more than an element of kitsch in the backlash to such
studies as *ISOE*, and we need to beware of slipping into *kitsch critique*.
Friedlander, for example, comments that, although kitsch is a *debased*
form of myth, it nevertheless draws upon the mythic for its power—as
ISOE as debased theory draws on scholarship. He calls it 'a footprint, an
echo of lost worlds, haunting an imagination invaded by excessive
rationality' (Friedlander, 1984: 49). Science and myth are interpene-
trative. Yet normal science and social science in particular cannot bear
this knowledge with equanimity and remain firmly attached to models of
rationality. In social science, this is particularly ironic as complex social
events must always suffer some form of distortion if they are to be
considered sufficiently isomorphic for statistical manipulation. Consequently, attempts to resurrect scientific status in these fields including
organization studies have produced an 'elite' classification of superficial
studies with large data-sets and a marginalized class of detailed and
careful studies of single events, small samples, or interpretative
accounts.

Nevertheless, kitsch social science, like *ISOE*, respects science and
scientific method, even if it does so rather poorly. Where it puts its ideas
forward, it still claims some form of evidence, data, documentation,
analysis and proof in demonstrating its status. It still claims its object of
investigation as an object (Linstead, 1994)—fans of *The X-Files* will note
that even believers in extra-terrestrials and the occult tend to rely heavily

Organizational Kitsch
Stephen Linstead

on *eye-witness* accounts (Montgomery, 1991: 34). The irony here is that kitsch critique dismisses kitsch science as non-science, but it can only do so by recognizing it as *bad* science. Thus *ISOE* is dismissed by mainstream organization theory *at the same time* as both mainstream organization theory and *ISOE* rule out those approaches such as labour process theory which might be called *critical* management studies (Alvesson and Willmott, 1992; Fulop and Linstead, 1999). Kitsch critique, located within 'normal' organization studies, as we would expect from our earlier discussion of kitsch as defence mechanism, cannot recognize *alternative* social science because this would entail acknowledgment of otherness, and of *incommensurability*. The unity that it demands cannot allow alternative approaches to exist—therefore they become recognized and constructed as bad science (which kitsch science is) but only as a moment on the road to denial. In other words, bad science such as *ISOE* is less than worthless to kitsch critique.

What then are the consequences of kitsch? Kitsch makes ignorance appear to be knowledge, and as such it can block the will for new insight or ideas, even when those insights are available. It closes off enquiry, it blinds us to that which we do not know, it makes us content with what we know and how we know it, and defines the field of our endeavours. It silences critique. It makes and keeps the margins marginal. Yet kitsch is also, paradoxically, the window to that which it obscures. Often the cheap reproduction of the work of art on the commemorative mug is the first sight some people get of it—the more tenacious refuse to settle for this and pursue the original, some just stumble on an insight even through the cheap fake (Eco, 1989: 198–9). Similarly with scholarly argument—secondary sources often cheapen primary sources and primary sources often caricature the field, yet they alert us to the existence of the original and make it possible for us to approach it. As Calinescu (1995/1987: 262) argues:

> After all in today's world no-one is safe from kitsch, which appears as a necessary step on the path toward an ever elusive goal of fully authentic aesthetic experience. After seeing many fake or reproduced Rembrandts, a viewer may ultimately be receptive to the experience of coming upon the real painting of a Dutch master. He may finally become aware that art, even when exploited, misunderstood, and misused, does not lose its value and aesthetic truth. In an unexpected manner, this failure of kitsch illustrates reassuringly the comic motifs of the deceiver who is deceived and the fool who realises his foolishness and becomes wise.

So both *ISOE* and even Maslow may in some ways continue to have value, regardless of their kitsch qualities—yet these qualities need to be recognized in organization studies wherever they are found if we are to fully understand their significance, effects and limitations. Kitsch is far more than a matter of personal taste and far more is at stake than that when we allow our capacities to respond to our ontical situation to be

Organization 9(4)
Articles

numbed by perpetually taking the easy way out, emotionally or theoretically. Just as defining and recognizing kitsch has been one of the most absorbing unfolding problems of artistic and cultural criticism of the last century, it is currently one of the most important issues for organization theory to address in the present one.

References

Adorno, Theodore (1991) *The Culture Industry: Selected Essays on Mass Culture.* London: Routledge.

Adorno, Theodore (1997) *Aesthetic Theory.* (Translated by R. Hullett-Kentor.) Minneapolis, MN: University of Minnesota.

Alvesson, Mats and Willmott, Hugh, eds (1992) *Critical Management Studies.* London: Sage.

Ashmore, Malcolm (1989) *The Reflexive Thesis: Wrighting Sociology of Academic Knowledge.* Chicago: University of Chicago Press.

Bataille, Georges (1985) *Visions of Excess: Selected Writings 1927–1939.* (Edited by Allan Stoekl, translated by Allan Stoekl, with Carl R. Lovitt and Donald Leslie.) Minneapolis, MN: University of Minnesota Press.

Bataille, Georges (1986) *Eroticism: Death and Sensuality.* (Translated by Mary Dalwood.) San Francisco: City Lights.

Bataille, Georges (1988) *The Accursed Share: Vol. 1—Consumption.* (Translated by Robert Hurley.) New York: Zone Books.

Baudrillard, Jean (1981) *For a Critique of the Political Economy of the Sign.* St Louis: Telos Press.

Baudrillard, Jean (1983) *In the Shadow of the Silent Majorities.* Paris: Semiotext(e).

Benjamin, Walter (1992) 'The Work of Art in the Age of Mechanical Reproduction', in Walter Benjamin *Illuminations*, pp. 211–44. London: Fontana.

Benjamin, Walter (1999) 'Dream Kitsch: Gloss on Surrealism', in M. Jennings, H. Eiland and G. Smith (eds) *Walter Benjamin: Selected Writings Vol. 2 1927–1934*, pp. 694–8. Cambridge, MA: Belknap/Harvard University Press.

Botting, Fred and Wilson, Scott, eds (1997) *The Bataille Reader.* Oxford: Blackwell.

Broch, Hermann (1969a) 'Evil in the System of Artistic Values', in G. Dorfles (ed.) *Kitsch: The World of Bad Taste*, pp. 68–76. New York: Universe Books.

Broch, Hermann (1969b) 'Notes on the Problem of Kitsch', in G. Dorfles (ed.) *Kitsch: The World of Bad Taste*, pp 49–67. New York: Universe Books.

Calinescu, Matinei (1987/1995) *Five Faces of Modernity.* Durham, NC: Duke University Press.

Chia, Robert (1996) *Organizational Analysis as Deconstructive Practice.* Berlin: Walter de Gruyter.

Colville, Ian D., Waterman, Robert H. and Weick, Karl E. (1999) 'Organizing and the Search for Excellence: Making Sense of the Times in Theory and Practice', *Organization* 6(1): 129–48.

Connell, Robert (1995) *Masculinities.* St Leonards: Allen and Unwin.

Cooper, Robert (1983) 'The Other: A Model of Human Structuring', in Gareth Morgan (ed.) *Beyond Method*, pp 202–18. London: Sage.

Cooper, Robert (1986) 'Notes on Organizational Kitsch', Working Paper, University of Lancaster, January.

Organizational Kitsch
Stephen Linstead

Derrida, Jacques (1973) *Speech and Phenomena*. Evanston, IL: Northwestern University Press.

Derrida, Jacques (1978) *Writing and Difference*. London: Routledge.

Eco, Umberto (1989) 'The Structure of Bad Taste', in *The Open Work*, pp. 180–216. Cambridge, MA: Harvard University Press.

Foster, Hal (1985) *Recodings: Art, Spectacle, Cultural Politics*. Seattle, WA: Bay Press.

Friedlander, S. (1984) *Reflections on Nazism: An Essay on Kitsch and Death*. New York: Harper and Row.

Fulop, Liz and Linstead, Stephen (1999) *Management: A Critical Text*. Melbourne: Macmillan.

Giesz, L. (1960) *Phenomenologie des Kitsches*. Munich: Wolfgang Rothe.

Golding, David (1996) 'Producing Clarity—Depoliticizing Control', in S. Linstead, P. Jeffcutt and R. Grafton Small (eds) *Understanding Management*, pp. 51–65. London: Sage.

Greenberg, Clement (1939/1986) 'Avant-garde and Kitsch', in John O'Brien (ed.) *The Collected Essays and Criticism: Vol. 1, Perceptions and Judgements 1939–1944*. Chicago: University of Chicago Press.

Hebdige, Dick (1988) *Hiding in the Light: On Images and Things*. London: Routledge.

Höpfl, Heather and Linstead, Stephen (1993) 'Passion and Performance: Suffering and the Carrying of Organizational Roles', in Stephen Fineman (ed.) *Emotion in Organizations*, pp. 76–93. London: Sage.

Keat, Russell and Abercrombie, Nicholas (1991) *Enterprise Culture*. London: Routledge.

Kostera, Monika (1997) 'The Kitsch Organization', *Studies in Cultures Organizations and Societies* 3(2): 163–78.

Kundera, Milan (1984) *The Unbearable Lightness of Being*. London: Faber & Faber.

Kundera, Milan (1988) *The Art of the Novel*. London: Faber & Faber.

Kundera, Milan (1996) *Testaments Betrayed*. London: Faber & Faber.

Kundera, Milan (1997) *Slowness*. London: Faber & Faber.

Kundera, Milan (1999) *Identity*. London: Faber & Faber.

Lacan, Jacques (1977) *Écrits: A Selection*. London: Tavistock.

Leather, Phil (1983) 'Desire: A Structural Model of Motivation', *Human Relations* 36(2): 109–22.

Linstead, Stephen (1994) 'Objectivity, Reflexivity and Fiction: Humanity, Inhumanity and the Science of the Social', *Human Relations* 47(11): 1321–46.

Linstead, Stephen (1997) 'Abjection and Organization: Men, Violence and Management', *Human Relations* 50(9): 1275–304.

Linstead, Stephen and Grafton Small, Robert (1990) 'Theory as Artefact: Artefact as Theory', in Pasquale Gagliardi (ed.) *Symbols and Artefacts: Views of the Corporate Landscape*, pp. 387–419. Berlin: De Gruyter.

Linstead, Stephen and Grafton Small, Robert (1992) 'On Reading Organizational Culture', *Organization Studies* 13(3): 331–55.

Lyotard, Jean-François (1984) *The Postmodern Condition: A Report on Knowledge*. Manchester: Manchester University Press

Lyotard, Jean-François (1988) *The Differend: Phrases in Dispute*. Manchester: Manchester University Press.

Organization 9(4)
Articles

Maslow, Abraham (1965) *Eupsychian Management: A Journal.* Homewood, IL: Richard D. Irwin and the Dorsey Press.

Maslow, Abraham, Heil, Gary and Stephens, Deborah C. (1998) *Maslow on Management.* New York: John Wiley.

Montgomery, Scott (1991) 'Science as Kitsch: The Dinosaur and Other Icons', *Science as Culture* 2(1): 7–58.

Peters, Thomas J. and Waterman, Robert H. (1982) *In Search of Excellence: Lessons from America's Best-Run Companies.* New York: Harper & Row.

Pross, H., ed. (1985) *Kitsch.* Munich: Paul List.

Ray, Carol Axtell (1986) 'Corporate Culture: The Last Frontier of Control?', *Journal of Management Studies* 23(3): 287–97.

Richardson, Michael (1994) *Georges Bataille.* London: Routledge.

Ross, Andrew (1989) *No Respect: Intellectuals and Popular Culture.* London: Routledge.

Sontag, Susan (1969) *Against Interpretation.* New York: Dell.

Tocqueville, Alexis de (1961) *Democracy in America*, Vol. II. New York: Schocken.

Travers, Andrew (1993) 'An Essay on Self and Camp', *Theory, Culture and Society* 10(1): 127–43.

Vattimo, Gianni (1988) *The End of Modernity: Nihilism and Hermeneutics in Post-modern Culture.* Cambridge: Polity Press.

Wheale, Nigel, ed. (1995) *Postmodern Arts.* London: Routledge.

Stephen Linstead is Professor of Organisations Analysis at the University of Durham Business School. He holds an MSc in Organization Development and a PhD in Management from CNAA and has previously taught at universities including Essex, Lancaster, Hong Kong University of Science and Technology and the University of Wollongong, New South Wales. His publications include *Sex, Work and Sex Work* (Routledge, 2000 with Jo Brewis), *The Aesthetics of Organization* (Sage, 2000 with Heather Höpfl) and *The Language of Organization* (Sage, 2001 with Robert Westwood). **Address:** University of Durham Business School, Mill Hill Lane, Durham City DH1 3LB, UK. [email: ????]

682

[5]

The Labour of Aesthetics and the Aesthetics of Organization

Anne Witz
University of Leicester, UK

Chris Warhurst
University of Strathclyde, UK

Dennis Nickson
University of Strathclyde, UK

Abstract. This article develops the conceptualization and analysis of aesthetic labour in two parts. The first part focuses on conceptualizing aesthetic labour. We critically revisit the emotional labour literature, arguing that the analysis of interactive service work is impeded by the way in which its corporeal aspects are retired and that, by shifting the focus from emotional to aesthetic labour, we are able to recuperate the embodied character of service work. We then explore the insights provided by the sociological perspectives on the body contained in the works of Goffman and Bourdieu in order to conceptualize aesthetic labour as embodied labour. In the second part, we develop our analysis of aesthetic labour within the context of a discussion of the aesthetics of organization. We discern three ways in which aesthetics is recognized to imbue organization: aesthetics of organization, aesthetics in organization and aesthetics as organization. We contend that employees are increasingly seen not simply as 'software', but as 'hardware', in the sense that they too can be corporately moulded to portray the organizational aesthetic. We ground this analysis in a case study from research conducted by the authors. **Key words.** *aesthetic labour; aesthetics; embodied work; emotional labour; organization*

Organization 10(1)
Articles

The analysis of aesthetic labour developed here (see also Nickson et al., 2001; Warhurst et al., 2000) foregrounds the stylization of workplace performances, and particularly the ways in which new modes of work-place embodiment are currently being produced and valorized, most notably—although by no means exclusively—in new forms of interactive service work. The labour of aesthetics is, we suggest, a vital element in the production or materialization of the aesthetics of a service organiza-tion and particularly of the 'style' of service experienced or consumed by customers. The increasing mobilization of aesthetic labour is particularly evident in the 'style' labour market of design- and image-driven retail and hospitality organizations. Since the 1980s, these organizations have sought market differentiation via image, initially through design inter-iors, but increasingly through 'making-up' (du Gay, 1996) the embodied dispositions of employees. These employees are thus increasingly regar-ded by employers as an integral—literally animate—component of the service produced.

Even within the growing literatures on the aestheticization of economic and everyday life (for example, Lash and Urry, 1994; Welsch, 1996), aesthetics and organization (for example, Gagliardi, 1990, 1996; Linstead and Hopfl, 2000; Strati, 1990, 1992, 1996, 1999) and on the body and organization (for example, Bahnisch, 2000; Hassard et al., 2000), the importance of stylized workplace performances or aesthetic labour is noted, yet still awaits fuller exploration, particularly empirically. There are some exceptions to this comparative neglect, with a recognition of 'body work' in organizations in the works of Adkins (2000), Crang (1994, 1997), McDowell (1995), Taylor and Tyler (2000), Tyler and Abbot (1998) and Hancock and Tyler (2000), all of whom focus on service work. However, the conceptualization of the aesthetic components of labour in all these works is primarily induced by a interest in sexuality and gender. For example, McDowell focuses her analysis around how 'one's body, sexuality and gender performance is part of the job' (1995: 93). The same is true of Hancock and Tyler (2000: 109), who assert there to be an 'integral relationship between the aesthetic, the corporeal and the gen-dered nature of work and employment'.

Existing explorations of aesthetics in labour, with the major exception of Adkins (2000), fail to recognize its commodification. Even when Tyler shifts from her previous use of 'body work' to 'aesthetic labour' to account for the work of her subjects (compare Tyler and Taylor, 1998; Tyler and Abbott, 1998, with Hancock and Tyler, 2000), the exchange of aesthetics is a 'gift exchange' that is beyond contract. In the latter piece, the authors explicitly state it to be a 'somewhat "invisible" labour process . . . one which was neither remunerated nor particularly acknowledged as labour by management, clients or even the [flight] attendants themselves' (Hancock and Tyler, 2000: 120). We, however, point out how management intentionally mobilizes and develops aesthetic labour and emphasize how aesthetic labour valorizes embodiment, so need not be treated as a

34

The Labour of Aesthetics
Anne Witz et al.

distinctive mode of exchange beyond contract. Moreover, while there are indeed important gendered and sexualized dimensions to aesthetic labour, it is by no means only female labour that is subject to commodification via aestheticization. The significance of the commodification of labour through its aestheticization and hence its valorization is indicated by our analysis of the *corporate production* of the labour of aesthetics as an animate component of the aesthetics of organization.

This article develops the conceptualization and analysis of aesthetic labour in two parts. The first part focuses on conceptualizing aesthetic labour per se. We critically revisit the emotional labour literature, arguing that the analysis of interactive service work is impeded by the way in which its corporeal aspects are retired and that, by shifting the focus from emotional to aesthetic labour, we are able to recuperate the embodied character of service work. We then explore the insights provided by the sociological perspectives on the body contained in the works of Goffman and Bourdieu in order to conceptualize aesthetic labour as embodied labour. In the second part of the article, we develop our analysis of aesthetic labour within the context of a discussion of the aesthetics of organization. Here, we discern three ways in which aesthetics is recognized to imbue organization: through the aesthetics *of* organization, aesthetics *in* organization and aesthetics *as* organization. Our main contention here is that employees are increasingly seen not simply as 'software', but as 'hardware', in the sense that they too can be corporately moulded to portray the organizational aesthetic in a manner similar to the way in which the identity of an organization is portrayed though its marketing material, product design and physical environment. Using the concept of 'material culture' we develop an analysis of aesthetic labour as the 'animate' component of organizational aesthetics that complements or sits alongside the 'inanimate' scenography. We ground this analysis in a case study of Elba Hotels, drawn from original empirical research conducted by the authors.[1]

Conceptualizing Aesthetic Labour

From 'Emotional' to 'Aesthetic' Labour in the Study of Interactive Service Work

Over the past two decades the study of interactive service work has come to be dominated by the emotional labour paradigm pioneered by Hochschild (1979, 1983). Our critical engagement with this paradigm is prompted by the way in which the somatic or corporeal dimensions of the emotional labourer are conceptually retired, both in Hochschild's work as well as in subsequent developments and applications of the concept (see Noon and Blyton, 1997 and, for example, Bulan et al., 1997; Leidner, 1991, 1993; James, 1989; Taylor, 1998; Taylor and Tyler, 2000; Wharton, 1993). We introduce the concept of 'aesthetic labour' in order to direct attention to how, increasingly, modes of worker embodiment are

35

Organization 10(1)
Articles

being corporately produced or 'made-up' (du Gay, 1996) in new and different ways in today's service economy.

In short, we feel that the concept of emotional labour foregrounds the worker as a mindful, feelingful self, but loses a secure conceptual grip on the worker as an embodied self. Embodiment is continually evoked, as in Hochschild's core definition of emotional labour as 'the management of feeling to create a publicly observable facial and bodily display' (1983: 7). Indeed, facial and bodily displays are crucial elements of the perform-ance of emotional labour—witness, for example, Hochschild's discussion of the 'war of smiles' (1983: 127). Yet the precise status of corporeality—these faces, these smiles and these bodies—in the managed production of feeling is analytically abandoned.

The roots of this corporeal disappearing act can be located broadly within Hochschild's own social constructionist framework for the study of emotion and more particularly in the conceptual antinomy Hochschild makes between 'surface' and 'deep' acting. Hochschild wants to develop a social constructionist theory of emotion that is more substantial than that offered by interactionist theorists such as Goffman (Hochschild, 1983: 27–83, Appendix A). In insisting that emotion is more substantial than it largely appears in the sociological imagination, Hochschild moves 'towards the soul' and invests the social actor with a greater depth of feeling. This move is achieved by making much of the antinomy between deep and surface acting. Hochschild's critique of Goffman centres on his allegedly exclusive focus on impression management or surface action, that is, 'his emphasis on how actors manage outer impressions rather than inner feelings' (Hochschild, 1979: 557). For Hochschild, surface acting changes 'how we actually appear' (1983: 35) and 'uses the body to *show* feeling' (1983: 247 fn. 2):

> As for Goffman, the action is in the body language, the put-on sneer, the posed shrug, the controlled sigh.
>
> In surface acting, the expression on my face or the posture of my body feels 'put on'. It is not 'part of me'.
>
> The body, not the soul, is the main tool of the trade. (Hochschild, 1983: 35, 36, 37)

In deep acting, by contrast, the display (those faces and those bodies) is the result of managed feeling, the *expression* of feeling. Pretence is never completely absent, but it is 'pretending deeply' that, in turn, leads to an alteration of the self. Hochschild's own counterposition of surface and depth engagement in workplace performances functions not only to evoke feeling as opposed to behaviour, but also to imply a depth and *authenticity* of feeling possessed by the inner-self engaged in deep acting. This conceptualization results in a hollowed-out sense of the somatic or corporeal as an ephemeral and *false* surface. Surface becomes synonym-ous with the body that is devoid of authenticity, where depth becomes synonymous with the soul as the authentic, feelingful core of the self. As

The Labour of Aesthetics
Anne Witz et al.

surface becomes less significant than depth, the embodied self is occluded behind the feelingful self.

Of course, Hochschild's point is that to become an emotional labourer is no easy, ephemeral accomplishment. It is not simply a staged performance of smiles, mannerisms and so one. It is an achievement—a deep rather than a surface pretence characterizes the work of the emotional labourer when parts of her or his emotional machinery are in commercial hands. It is not just one's face that takes on the properties of a resource to be managed, but one's very feelings too. This point is, of course, important to make. Yet, we would still maintain that, as she or he invests the emotional labourer with a greater depth of feeling, Hochschild loses a secure conceptual purchase on the embodied aspects of interactive service work, consigned as they are to a shadowy conceptual status of surface.

How, then, do we conceptually reassociate the 'flesh' and the 'feeling' and relocate that 'fleshy surface' within the power of the social that Hochschild redirected toward the inner, feelingful self? By developing a concept of *aesthetic labour* we seek to move beyond antinomies of surface and depth, outer bodies and inner-selves and refocus analysis of interactive service work so as to recapture its lost somatic or corporeal aspects.

We offer a working definition of aesthetic labour as the mobilization, development and commodification of embodied 'dispositions' (Bourdieu, 1984). Such dispositions, in the form of embodied capacities and attributes, are to some extent possessed by workers at the point of entry into employment. However, the point we wish to emphasize is that employers then mobilize, develop, and commodify these embodied dispositions through processes of recruitment, selection and training, *transforming* them into 'skills' which are geared toward producing a 'style' of service encounter that appeals to the senses of the customer (Warhurst et al., 2000). In other words, distinct *modes of worker embodiment* are corporately produced as aesthetic labourers are 'made up' (du Gay, 1996) in such a way as to embody the aesthetics of service organization.

The concept of aesthetic labour moves beyond the concept of emotional labour by foregrounding the sensible components of the service encounter and recuperating the embodied character of service work: the ways in which distinctive service styles depend as much upon manufactured and performative 'styles of the flesh' (Butler, 1990) as they do upon the manufacture of 'feeling' (Hochschild, 1983) or the 'making up' of self-identity (du Gay, 1996). While, for Hochschild, the notion of deep acting describes the stirring up or weakening of *feelings* to such an extent that we induce a *transformation* of feeling that might not otherwise have occurred, we want to suggest that modes of embodiment are subject to the same transformative depth as Hochschild reserves for feeling. Furthermore, Hochschild contends that deep acting can lead to a different relation to 'what we have thought of as ourself' (1983: 47). We would also

Organization 10(1)
Articles

contend that the production of and engagement in aesthetic labour implicates the body in this transformation of the self; in other words, new regimes of the body are equally as likely to lead to the development of a different relation to what the aesthetic labourer comes to think of as himself or herself. How, then, do we begin to conceptualize aesthetic labour as embodied labour? We suggest that, first, it is possible to recuperate Goffman to capture salient aspects of the embodied perform-ance of aesthetic labour and, second, that it is also necessary to utilize Bourdieu's perspective on embodiment, which centres around the notion of 'dispositions'.

Aesthetic Labour as Embodied Labour

We saw above how Hochschild (1979, 1983) is critical of Goffman's interactionism for dealing too much with the surface, rule-following self and its surface, performative embodiment. Paradoxically, whereas Hochschild chides Goffman for subordinating the deep, feelingful self to surface behavioural enactments, Shilling (1993) argues precisely the opposite; namely that Goffman subordinates the body to the mind. Yet, in contrast to both Hochschild and Shilling, Crossley (1995: 134, 145) offers a quite different reading of Goffman as:

> . . . a pioneer of a form of social analysis which bases itself in an understanding of sentient and embodied social praxes . . . Goffman never refers to inner, ideational or spiritual realms but always to behaviour— behaviour which is visible and tangible because embodied. It suggests that, for him, behaviour is always meaningful, but that he never separates the meaning from the behaviour, so we regard it as disembodied.

For Crossley, Goffman maintains a clear sense of the actor qua embodied actor. For us, Goffman's sociology (for example, 1959, 1967, 1971) has proved enormously useful for interrogating the production and perform-ance of aesthetic labour, capturing its visual elements of 'face-to-face, body-to-body, seen-seer to seen-seer' (Crossley, 1995: 145) and its aural element of voice-to-voice; in short, alerting us to both the sentient and the sensible aspects of aesthetic labour.

For example, in the corporate production and control of the body regimes observed by shop assistants in a stylish retail store, Leviathan, the dramaturgical metaphor of stage and staging captures key elements of the embodied performance of aesthetic labour, with organizational pre-scriptions of embodied appearance, demeanour and comportment best illustrating this point. Work in the shop is staged and scripted: shop assistants are told where to stand, at what angle to the door, how to approach customers and what to say. Even the manageress patrols the shop at regular intervals according to a map of manoeuvre. The company has formally prescribed female and male 'model' employees: the 'Levia-than Girl' and 'Leviathan Boy'. This initiative involved the company ascribing and circumscribing the appearance of their employees. As one employee explained: 'If I was to have my hair done or anything . . . if

The Labour of Aesthetics
Anne Witz et al.

you're going to cut your hair in any way, well drastically or highlights, you've got to discuss it with the manager first.'

Leviathan workers are instructed in how to approach customers by 'reading' customers' signifiers, such as body language. Similarly, an employee of another stylish retail company, Donnatello, related how 'the supervisors do a wee act kind of thing and pretend they are a customer and say "This is a bad example" and "This is a good example" and the good example is when you smile at them as soon as they walk in'.

Working for Leviathan was described as being 'a bit like acting. I mean it's like being in drama school.' There is a 'front stage' and a 'back stage', and aesthetic labourers at Leviathan retreat to the 'back stage':

> . . . you've got to shed your skin. I mean behind the scenes where we are is just hilarity. I mean it's so hilarious . . . They swear like troupers and then they go out to the desk and do this [act professionally]. It can be hell, say, to . . . er . . . to be like those people who work in Disney and do it like that all the time. Obviously, you've got to shed it sometime.

Clearly evocative of Goffman's (1959) idea of creature releases and the welcome relief of the backstage where you can 'shed it', this is the daily experience of the aesthetic labourer. She is not wearing her heart on her sleeve, but is, as Crossley's (1995) reading suggests, manipulating her corporeal expressivity to foster and create impressions of self and subjectivity demanded by the exigencies of occupation. Using Goffman to inform an understanding of the production and performance of aesthetic labour reveals how there is a staged and scripted performance of the *embodied* self. The question of whether we feel 'at home' in this work must be begged as contingent. Indeed, 'in so far as awareness is something that can be put into play in a situation, it will be awareness relative to the demarcated concerns of that situation and not some separate capacity that you carry with you from one situation to another' (Fish, cited in du Gay, 1996: 50). It is not simply, or even, feeling that is being manufactured. It is the performing actor qua embodied self within the demarcated concerns of the work situation.

Although we have suggested that Goffman provides a useful lens through which to view the embodied and performative dimensions of aesthetic labour, nonetheless, an adequate concept of the social actor as embodied needs to address the question of how the social is carried in embodied being, thoughts and actions in order to carry out social interaction as embodied participants. It is to Bourdieu (1984, 1990) that we turn to develop our notion of aesthetic labour as mobilizing, developing and commodifying embodied *dispositions*. Bourdieu offers a way of investing the body with a greater depth of the social than Goffman, by moving beyond what Hochschild (1983) quite correctly identifies as the tendency toward 'situationism' in Goffman. But whereas Hochschild is in search of a depth of feeling, we are in search of a depth of embodiment.

39

Organization 10(1)
Articles

The development and performance of aesthetic labour, then, as a situational mode of workplace embodiment is further conceptualized through Bourdieu's (1984, 1990) concept of embodied dispositions.

All fields of social action are peopled by actors equipped with a *habitus*: a socially constituted system of cognitive, motivating *and* embodied dispositions that guarantee the correctness of practices and their consistence over time (Bourdieu, 1990: 54–8, 66–9). This 'practical sense' that enables our ongoing engagement in the social and alignment with the demands of sociality is, for Bourdieu (1990: 66), 'a quasi-bodily involvement in the world'. Bourdieu provides a phenomenologically grounded sense of an embodied actor, insisting that relation to the body is a fundamental dimension of the habitus. Crucially, Bourdieu insists that 'what is learned by the body is not something that one has ... but something that one is' (1990: 73). Embodied dispositions refer to durable ways of standing, speaking, walking and thereby of feeling and thinking (Bourdieu, 1990: 69–70). Elaborate techniques of body work, discipline, care and repair are in turn necessary to develop *new* bodily schemas of posture, movement and subjective state. Hence, bodily schemas or embodied dispositions are not fixed once and for all. To be effective, these require 'doxa'—a practical belief—that aligns embodied praxis with the habitus. Utilizing Bourdieu's conceptualization of the relation between embodied praxis and the habitus specifically within the arena of the workplace, we suggest that the corporate production of aesthetic labourers involves the inculcation of a corporate 'doxa'—that is, a new mode of embodied praxis that aligns with the organizational habitus.

Hence, key insights from Bourdieu's work lend themselves to the development of the concept of aesthetic labour. In Bourdieu's terms, it is simply not possible to reduce aesthetic labour to the immediate level of physical appearance, for even at this level the body is mediated by its social location. The body as it is apparently most immediately apprehended (its size, shape, bearing and so on) is *materialized* within fields of social relations and reveals the deepest dispositions of the habitus.

Bourdieu develops this analysis in relation to the body as the materialization of class practices, which he sees as having a profound effect on the way we come to inhabit our bodies as well as on the symbolic values attached to bodily forms—the physical capital (Shilling, 1993) that specific modes of embodiment carry. Bourdieu is right to note that modes of embodiment and their associated physical capital are signifiers of a class, gender or racialized 'habitus'. In analysing modes of production and exchange of physical capital, Bourdieu's central concern is with class reproduction. However, although a collective manifestation, physical capital is mobilized by individuals. Consequently, with analysis pitched at the societal level, analysis of the workplace is omitted and the possibility of organizationally—that is *corporate*, rather than individually—mobilized and developed physical capital, is overlooked. The concept of aesthetic labour opens up the possibility of seeing how,

The Labour of Aesthetics
Anne Witz et al.

through the embodied performance of interactive service work, the physical capital of employees is valorized and converted into economic capital by and for organizations.

The corporate production of aesthetic labour mobilizes physical capital and may inculcate new modes of embodiment. The kinds of embodied dispositions that acquire an exchange value are not equally distributed socially, but fractured by class, gender, age and racialized positions or locations. There has traditionally been a close match between social location and those embodied dispositions which function as physical capital in the field of employment. Bourdieu (1984) himself emphasizes the significance of social practices—such as sports activities and food preferences—in materializing class-specific embodied dispositions, such as size and shape of the body as well as ways of comporting and composing the body such as the measured slowness of movement and speech that play a key role in equipping persons to occupy authoritative workplace positions. Typically middle-class modes of embodiment have clearly been of central importance in equipping individuals to assume these particular managerial and professional positions, as have the bearings and manners of masculinity. However, it is also the case that social fields are dynamic and subject to change, so the value attached to particular modes of embodiment changes over time (Shilling, 1993). For example, as the field of fashion changes, so does the symbolic value of styles of deportment, body shape and size, dress, demeanour, manner and so on. Furthermore, modes of embodiment are unfinished projects and therefore open to transformation as part of the reflexive project of the embodied self (Giddens, 1991; Shilling, 1993).

Thus, our notion of the corporate production of aesthetic labour suggests that embodied subjects are open to being remade, manufactured or 'made up' within specific institutional fields of action. As Bourdieu suggests, there is always a dialectic of expressive dispositions and instituted means of expression. Expressive dispositions describe not only logics of social action, but also embodied dispositions that enable us to recognize and comply with the demands immanent in the field (Bourdieu, 1990: 57–8). These embodied dispositions are, we suggest, more flexible than previous discussion has allowed. Locating the labour of aesthetics within the aesthetics of organization enables us to demonstrate the utility of Bourdieu's concept of embodied dispositions, as well as to substantiate empirically our central claim that embodied workplace performances are both commodified and valorized through aestheticization.

The Labour of Aesthetics and the Aesthetics of Organization

Organizational Aesthetics: From 'Hardware' to 'Software'

Aesthetics and organization are inseparable. Most obvious are the aesthetics *of* organization. These expressive forms, which signify the identity of an organization, are manifest in the 'hardware' of organizations,

Organization 10(1)
Articles

such as marketing material, product design and the physical environment of workspaces or offices (Olins, 1991; Ottensmeyer, 1996; Schmitt and Simonson, 1997). Aesthetics are a key element of goods and services design, for example AEG electrical products, London Transport buses and Coca Cola's bottles. At the turn of the century, when UK banks were the largest in the world, their sense of importance was expressed in the physicality of their buildings that exuded 'strong' and 'rich' symbolism. A good example was Midland Bank's London headquarters. With changing banking culture, this physicality has also changed to offer a sense of participation and interaction with open-plan workspaces (Olins, 1991).

Three points are worth noting with regard to the aesthetics of organization. First, they are symbols and artefacts which are intended to influence the senses of people as either customers or clients: organizations 'use these symbols in a vivid, dramatic and exciting way, because they know that symbols have power to affect the way people feel' (Olins, 1991: 71). Second, they are intended to 'add value' to the organization: 'Generally speaking, when companies use identity expressed through design, they use it as a commercial tool; their purpose is to make greater profit out of what they do in the short term' (Olins, 1991: 53). Lastly, in highly competitive markets with little to differentiate most goods and services, aesthetics contribute to organizational distinctiveness: 'intangible, emotional . . . The name and visual style of an organization are sometimes the most important factors in making it appear unique' (Olins, 1991: 75).[2]

This aesthetic 'hardware' is complemented by an organizational 'software'. These aesthetics *in* organization comprise a range of behaviours, most usually associated with 'getting in' and 'getting on' in organizations for employees. Emphasis is placed on the physicality of potential and actual employees and the ways in which these individuals can present themselves through posture, gesture, use of personal space, facial characteristics and eye contact, for example, at interviews and during meetings (Huczynski, 1996; James, 1999). Within popular business literature great play is made of the way in which individual employees can manage their image by engaging in 'impression management' or 'non-verbal influencing' in order to negotiate socially their interactions with other organizational members. Such management of personal aesthetics is said to contribute to their career prospects by creating or sustaining individuals' employability. As Davies (1990: 75) suggests: 'in the way that manufacturers pay great attention to the packaging of products in order to get us to buy them, we need to attend to our "packaging" if we want to "sell" ourselves to others, and get them to take a closer look at what's inside'.

Not surprisingly, the aesthetics *in* organization literature is often offered as self-help material focused on how individual employees can use or manipulate aesthetics to express and portray themselves *for themselves*. Individuals are encouraged to regard themselves as software that can be moulded and marketed.

The Labour of Aesthetics
Anne Witz et al.

There has been a conceptual development here, however, that needs to be appreciated. If the literature on aesthetics *of* organization indicates how organizations desire to express and portray themselves through their hardware for corporate benefit, we would argue that there is now a conflation of this 'hardware' and 'software'. At a very basic level, organizations are increasingly using corporate dress codes as a way of projecting a company image (see Income Data Services, 2001). We argue in the section below, however, that some service-sector organizations, appreciating the corporate potential of aesthetics *in* organizations, seek to mobilize, develop and commodify individual employees as physical capital, converting them into hardware intended to contribute to the valorization process with these employees now functioning as the embodiment of the style of the organization. Hence employees, as software, have become human hardware as they are configured by organizations both as part of the surplus-producing process of the organization and in order to be the *embodiment* of the organization's identity.

Recently, aesthetics *as* organization has become of interest within organization studies. Over the past decade there has been a growing literature which departs from the rationalist paradigm of organization and instead explores the aesthetic side of organizational life (see Gagliardi, 1990, 1996) or views organizations through the lens of aesthetics (see Strati, 1990, 1992, 1996). For Strati (1996), viewing organizations *through* the lens of aesthetics, is an approach distinguishable from the dominant rationalist paradigm.

We would suggest that there are 'weak' and 'strong' versions of aesthetics as organization. Working within the former, researchers might want to ask questions about 'aesthetics', but they are, in effect, 'adding on' a concern with aesthetics to a fundamentally rationalist and structuralist paradigm of organization. We might see this as a concern more with organization *plus* aesthetics, where the dominant paradigm of organization remains fundamentally rationalist, while the role and significance of aesthetics is also recognized, not infrequently for instrumental reasons. For example, the pursuit by management of efficiency and profits can be destructive for employees and so requires compensation. That compensation occurs through the acceptance of the importance within organizations of the seemingly 'non-rational'; made most obvious in the corporate culture strategies pursued in the 1980s in which rites, rituals and symbols were promoted as techniques to appeal to the sentiments of employees (see, for example, Deal and Kennedy, 1988). It might be said that such an instrumental approach sought to match scientific management with the 'art' of management, ending previous neglect of 'the emotive, expressive, experiential aspect of organizational processes' (Kuhn, 1996: 219). Such an approach accepts and compounds a dualism between the rational and the non-rational in which the latter is 'demoted' to a secondary interest.

43

Organization 10(1)
Articles

The strong version of aesthetics as organization obviates this dualism, and is most apparent in the work of Strati (1996) and Gagliardi (1996). Seeking to understand organizations through the lens of aesthetics involves, for Strati, opening up new questions concerning the experiences of organizational life. According to Strati, aesthetics yield organizational knowledge that is obfuscated by reliance on the rationalist paradigm for 'Aesthetics are a form of knowledge and they have their own truth' (1996: 216). Appreciating and analysing aesthetics, then, expands the study and improves the understanding of organization. We see this as making fundamentally new claims about the *ontology* of organization or ways of organizing. It is not an additive approach, but an approach that appreciates that organization *is* aesthetic.[3] A rationalist paradigm obscures this aesthetic ontology. As Gagliardi points out, 'translating a particular conception of ourselves into concrete behaviour entails passing from an abstract definition of our *identity* to the adoption of a *style*, a word which we usually associated with an aesthetic—in the broad sense—experience' (1996: 571, emphasis in the original). For both Strati and Gagliardi, illustration of this approach can be made by analysis of that taken-for-granted artefact: the chair. Ordinarily, the chair is seen through the lens of functionality. However, the chair can be seen through a different lens, that is, through the lens of aesthetics, and doing so generates a different understanding of it and the organization. In this respect the chair is the signature of the organization, 'writing . . . the aesthetic code into the physicality of place' and writing that code 'into the eye' of the beholder (Gagliardi, 1996: 572). In other words, the chair is the materialization of the organizational identity and creates ways of seeing for the beholder. In a similar manner, we suggest that the labour of aesthetics should be viewed not simply through the rational lens of 'functionality', but also through the lens of aesthetics.[4]

Case Study: Elba Hotels

Based on a pilot study (see Nickson et al., 2001) that included a rapidly expanding hotel chain—Elba Hotels—we explore how the labour of aesthetics and the aesthetics of organization are components of the material culture of a service organization. Aesthetic labourers are the animate component of the material culture that makes up the corporate landscape. They are, as with the inanimate elements of the corporate landscape, corporately designed and produced. In effect, at least in the new 'style' niches of the service sector, aesthetic labourers are engaged in a staged performance that depends upon the deployment not only of technical skills and emotion work skills, but also of specific modes of embodiment or 'styles of the flesh' (Butler, 1990).

Elba trades in the aesthetics of style and is developing corporate ways of producing aesthetic workers who form a vital—in both senses of the word as essential *and* animated—component of the organizational aesthetic experienced by hotel and restaurant customers. Gagliardi's (1996)

The Labour of Aesthetics
Anne Witz et al.

work proves particularly helpful in pushing forward our conceptualization both of the organizational aesthetic that characterizes Elba Hotels and in the role and significance of labour in producing this aesthetic. Indeed, our introduction of the term 'the labour of aesthetics' is geared toward helping us to see how aesthetic labour not only valorizes embodied work (just as emotional labour valorizes emotion work), but also functions to materialize the aesthetics of organization. We propose a framework for the analysis of the labour of aesthetics and the aesthetics of organization that builds upon the concept of *material culture*, which has a well-known pedigree in anthropology, but which is developed by Gagliardi (1996) specifically in order to explore the aesthetic side of organizational life.

The complex relationship between productive and symbolic practices that constitute the material culture of an organization is conceptualized by Gagliardi (1996: 570–2) as a 'corporate landscape'. The material culture or corporate landscape consists of the 'hardware' of architecture and interior design, of corporate artefacts and space (Gagliardi, 1990, 1996). Following Duby, Gagliardi distinguishes between 'land' and 'landscape': 'every productive practice is immediately a symbolic practice of appropriation of the world . . . and the signature through which an environment testifies to *this cultural requirement of survival* is called landscape' (Duby, 1986: 29, quoted in Gagliardi, 1996: 570, emphasis in the original).

Gagliardi suggests that we should regard the corporate landscape as 'the materialization of a world view, and strive to interpret the aesthetic code written into the landscape as a privileged pathway to the quiddity of a culture' (1996: 572). Land becomes landscape as it is aestheticized, and in two different ways: *in situ* (in the physical place) and *in visu* (into the eye): 'The first way consists of writing the aesthetic code directly onto the physicality of the place, populating it with artifacts; the second consists in educating the eye, in furnishing it with schemata of perception and taste, models of vision, "lenses" through which to look at reality' (Gagliardi, 1996: 572).

Every corporate landscape has a scenographic element. It is, as Gagliardi explains, '"constructed to be seen". This setting displays and hides, provides backgrounds and close-ups, sequences and articulations' (1996: 572). The scenographic element of the corporate landscape materializes the aesthetic code into the physicality of place. So the labour of aesthetics performed by employees in Elba Hotels forms a vital part of the continual writing and rewriting of the aesthetic code into the physicality of place as it is experienced *in situ* by customers. This physicality of place, experienced *in situ*, is a corporate landscape populated by inanimate *and* animate objects. As aesthetic labour, employees are *part of* the materialization of the corporate idea, along with the architecture and interior design. In other words, the performance of aesthetic labour entails the manufacture of particular stylized, embodied performances

45

Organization 10(1)
Articles

that comprise the animate components of the aesthetics of a service organization. Hence, the materialization of the corporate aesthetic entails the stylization of inanimate *and* animate components of the scenography. The aesthetic labourer is a figure in this scenographic aesthetic of a service organization experienced by the customer.

Gagliardi (1996) identifies a second mode of aestheticization of a corporate landscape. This is *in visu*: 'the writing of the aesthetic code into the eye'. With the customer's *in situ* experience of a service organization, the pleasure and satisfaction of the customer depends crucially upon managing to see things 'through the eyes' as they are designed to be seen and experienced. In other words, part of the process of consumption involves taking things in through the eyes as a sensory experience. The consumption practices of *in situ* consumers of a service involve particular ways of perceiving *and* 'feeling' reality—a 'pathos' that is part of the aesthetic experience by the customer of the organization. The pleasure and satisfaction of the customer are secured by aestheticizing a specific *pattern of sensibility.* In short, there is an 'Elba experience' that depends upon a particular pattern of sensible responses to the aesthetics of Elba as a *distinctive* way of organizing service.

Processes of *in situ* and *in visu* aestheticization, both in terms of the materialization of the corporate aesthetic into a physical space and the socialization of the customer into that corporate aesthetic, can be unpacked by analysing the hotel foyer of Elba Hotels. The hotel foyer is one scenographic element of the corporate landscape. As they enter, the hotel foyer is the first stage of the *in situ* aesthetic experience of customers. The scenography of the hotel foyer is composed of animate and inanimate artefacts. There is always a chair strategically positioned in the foyer, an artefact that connotes functionality. A chair is something to sit on. But not this chair. This chair is deliberately fashioned and placed. The chair *in visu* (to the eye) furnishes the customer not the foyer. It furnishes the customer with an aesthetic code through which to read the aesthetic experience that will be the experience of Elba Hotels—the style of the hotel bedrooms and of various other spaces is distilled into the design of the chair. This chair signifies the style of the organization in such a way as to educate the customer in the eye. It instructs customers in the unique style, the distinctive aesthetic of Elba, the way in which Elba will be experienced—the way in which, literally, Elba is *designed* to be experienced aesthetically. The chair is a corporate product in the sense that it is the materialization of ideas held by the corporate management working with the interior designer. It also symbolizes the aesthetic of consumption that drives and shapes the corporate culture. In short, the chair, as part of the material culture of Elba Hotels, functions as a key signifier of the aesthetic of the service organization. If labour is the animated aestheticization of Elba, the inanimate aesthetic can be seen in the chair, and both epitomize that which is 'Elba'.

The Labour of Aesthetics
Anne Witz et al.

Aesthetic labourers are so much a part of the materialization of the corporate idea of Elba Hotels that they are corporately produced in order to coordinate or blend in with the aesthetic style of the corporate landscape; that is, their physical capital or embodied dispositions are mobilized and developed by the organization. In this respect, two questions arise. First, *what* is being produced? Second, *how* is it being produced? Two managerial strategies have been identified through which service workers are produced (Macdonald and Sirianni, 1996). One, the production-line approach of fast-food workers, has been well documented (see, for example, Ritzer, 1996; Leidner, 1993). These writers have more to say about work than workers, but do suggest that workers are produced through bureaucratic codification and so through routinization of behaviour and speech. The second strategy again highlights the same routinization of behaviour and speech, but also recognizes attitudinal shifts in 'workers' psyche' (Macdonald and Sirianni, 1996: 37). The second strategy, somewhat incautiously referred to as the empowerment approach (Bowen and Lawler, 1992) involves managers recruiting individuals with personal characteristics likely to make them interact or 'perform' spontaneously. It has been suggested that to implement this latter approach, 'managers must first select the right kinds of people for the job, often using gender, class, age and other status markers to serve as a proxy for required personality types' (Macdonald and Sirianni, 1996: 7).

We want to suggest that the process of selection and recruitment of aesthetic workers is, in fact, far more complex. This notion of mobilizing traditional status markers is inadequate, as employment at Elba illustrates. The owner and management at Elba want the right kinds of people. Ideal Elba employees are not regarded by the hotel management as people who simply want jobs. As the creator and owner of Elba Hotels explains:

> The sort of people we want to employ are not just looking on this as a job, but are in love with the industry. We are looking for people who understand the art of service, then apply . . . I don't want people employed by Elba to feel that they are just going to work. If they don't enjoy themselves, there is no way the guests enjoy themselves. (Sudjic, 1999: 14)

The recruitment and selection of new employees was therefore crucial. As the personnel manager at Elba Hotels said of its recruitment and selection:

> We actually didn't look for people with experience . . . because we felt that wasn't particularly important. We wanted people with personality more than the skills because we felt that we could train people to do the job. Personality was more important. How you handled the customers and how you related to people was more important than whether you could carry a plate or take an order.

Of course, in many routine interactive service jobs, person-to-person skills take precedence over technical skills. Here, those person-to-person

47

Organization 10(1)
Articles

skills encompass not just the social, but also the aesthetic, as the personal
manager continued:

> ... thirteen key words summed up the type of people we wanted working
> at Elba ... passionate, stylish ... [points to job advertisement] ... They
> had to be pretty attractive looking people ... we wanted people to look
> good all the time ... someone who's got, er, nice smile, nice teeth, neat hair
> and in decent proportion ... they had to have the correct tone and a nice
> voice ... well spoken. I don't want to say to look like an Elba person, but
> ... yeah, there is probably a kind of Elba look ... [the owner's] very sticky
> on the whole image thing and it had to be the right image.

Elba employees, then, are the animate components of the overall aesthetic of Elba. Elba's image suffused their recruitment material. The job
advertisement (which interestingly was placed in the *Sunday Times*[5]) for
waitering/waitressing work in the hotel cafe contained a picture of a
young woman (in reality a model) who literally embodied the desired
iconography of the company and its ideal aesthetic worker. For both men
and women, the hotel was ideally looking for graduates between 19 and
25 years old. Nonetheless, as the personnel manager explained, the
emphasis was on the *potential* aesthetic labourer who would materialize
and so express the Elba style: 'people who you actually thought were
very plain, but had that potential to look like an Elba person'.

The aesthetic labourers of Elba are not simply selected at the stage of
recruitment; they are then *produced* to engage in a labour of aesthetics
that forms part of the overall experience of the corporate aesthetic. Elba
was keen to mould new employees into the desired personas *after* they
entered employment. Elba employees are aesthetically produced in order
to be constituent and expressive of the corporate landscape. After being
selected, there was a 10-day induction in which extensive grooming and
deportment training was given to the staff by external consultants. New
employees were trained in *how* to wear the uniform. Such sessions also
encompassed hair cuts and styling, 'acceptable' make-up, individual
makeovers, how men should shave and the standards expected in relation to appearance. The personnel manager described parts of the induction programme in terms of 'the health and beauty people getting to work
and totally revamping these people. And it was amazing, the transformation in some of these people ... there were a couple of the girls who
looked amazing after it and you were really kind of "Wow!"'.

A full day's induction was spent on an exercise in which the new
recruits were given the 13 words that personified Elba and asked to walk
around the city centre and take photographs that encapsulated those
words. As the personnel manager explained: 'The word was maybe, em,
... energetic, go out and take a photograph of an energetic person. Go out
and take a photograph of a successful person.' The sessions were
intended to relay 'this is want we want you to actually look like ... you
have to understand what successful looks like ... what confident looks
like'.

The Labour of Aesthetics
Anne Witz et al.

Embodied workers are thus *transformed into* aesthetic labourers. It is not *what* they look like, but the look they have *about* them. It is not *how* they are; it is how they *could* be that provides the basis of the induction programme that employees undergo once they have been selected. Elba employees are transformed into aesthetic labourers in the sense that raw material is transformed into an artefact.

The emphasis during training was on educating new employees in how to look the part and generally 'getting the style right'. Aesthetic labourers are the embodied *materialization* of the corporate aesthetic of Elba Hotels; they are styled, transformed and made over during the induction and training period in order to function as the animate components of that corporate landscape. Appearance, gesture, mannerism and so on—all features of embodied dispositions (Bourdieu, 1984)—are 'made over' or 'made up' in specifically Elba ways.

Concluding Remarks

Our analysis of aesthetic labour indicates that a significant, yet over-looked, part of some employees' work in service organization is the way that inhabiting their jobs entails the mobilization, development and commodification of *embodied dispositions*. Embodied dispositions, worked on and made up into skills, are of paramount importance in the daily perform-ance of work, at Elba Hotels for example, and this labour of aesthetics is part of the very production of the aesthetics of organization.

We do recognize that there are fascinating, and unexpected, historical references to the importance of personal aesthetics in work organizations. Arguing that 'the cultivation of appearances, even a certain theatricality—as a key constituent of organizational success is not a recent invention', Hopfl (2000: 197, 204) details the importance of the aural and visual characteristics of individuals in the Society of Jesus—the Jesuits—as long ago as the 16th century, as the Society sought to reaffirm Catholic 'truth' through its presentation. Candidates for the Society had to have 'a pleasing manner of speech and verbal facility and also good appearance in the absence of any notable ugliness, disfigurement or deformity. The point here was that the Society's members should not gratuitously put the public off.' Kinchin (1999) describes how at the turn of the 20th century, the famous Glasgow designer and architect Charles Rennie Mackintosh worked with Miss Cranston to create 'the perfect art-house tea-room', staffed by carefully selected 'pretty' waitresses also wearing Mackintosh uniforms. In 1930, the first air hostesses began to serve passengers. From the start, there were prescriptions on how these hostesses should look and behave, with an emphasis on grooming and poise training (Visser, 1997; Hancock and Tyler, 2000). In his work on middle-class 'white collar' workers, Mills (1951) noted the importance of 'salesgirls' in large department stores. Using a typology developed by Gale, Mills reviews the different types of salesgirls, including 'The

Organization 10(1)
Articles

Charmer', who 'attracts the customer with a modulated voice, artful attire and stance' (1951: 175).

It is our contention that this labour of aesthetics is no longer an occasional initiative of sometimes idiosyncratic or exotic organizations, or even enterprising individuals, but a deliberate, managerially determined characteristic of an emerging subsector within services that involve face-to-face, voice-to-voice interaction between employee and customer. This 'style' subsector comprises designer retailers, boutique hotels and style bars, cafés and restaurants, for example. As a result, the labour of aesthetics now forms a vital part of the aesthetics of service organization as it is experienced by customers, whether dining in a restaurant, staying in a hotel, drinking in a café bar or browsing in a shop. This employment and work is particularly developed (through recruitment, selection and training) in the new 'style' sector of service organizations. However, it is not exclusive to these organizations, but is diffusing to more prosaic service organizations—a point elaborated upon further in Nickson et al. (2001).

In this article, we have emphasized how it is vital to appreciate the corporeal or embodied components of the stylized workplace performances that constitute aesthetic labour. We have suggested that Bourdieu's concept of dispositions furthers an appreciation of aesthetic labour's fundamentally *embodied* character and the sociological lens of Goffman facilitates an analysis of some key aspects of the *performance* of aesthetic labour. Importantly, the concept of aesthetic labour builds on, and significantly extends, the seminal work of Hochschild (1983) on emotional labour. Our critical evaluation of this concept leads us to argue that Hochschild (and subsequent writers using the concept) foregrounds the feelingful self at the expense of the embodied self. The concept of aesthetic labour, by comparison, is better attuned to foregounding the embodied dimensions of stylized workplace performances.

More generally, the labour of aesthetics adds another element to the relationship between organization and aesthetics. Through an analysis of case-study data from Elba Hotels, we have located the labour of aesthetics within this relationship, suggesting how the aesthetic labourer might be seen as an animate component of the scenographic aesthetic of a service organization as experienced by the customer. In this respect, we believe that it is an important empirical and conceptual development that, now recognized, needs to be further explored.

Notes

1   Empirical examples provided in this article are drawn from a study funded by the Universities of Glasgow and Strathclyde on *New Forms of Service Work in Glasgow* (1997–98). All organizational names are, for the sake of anonymity, pseudonyms.

2   We focus here on organizational aesthetics that affect the visual and aural senses. We are aware, however, that corporations also seek to affect the

The Labour of Aesthetics
Anne Witz et al.

olfactory senses of customers by imbuing organizational spaces with selected smells. The business-class lounge of British Airways, for example, is infused with the smell of the sea and freshly mown grass to 'uplift and 'stimulate' the senses of travellers (McQillan, 2001).

3   But which is not to deny that organization is also based upon structural inequalities, manifest, for example, in the asymmetries of power arising from race, gender and class.

4   We suspect that we do not go quite as far as Strati might wish in viewing service organization through the lens of aesthetics, as we do not use aesthetic understanding as an 'epistemological metaphor, a form of knowledge diverse from those based on analytical methods' (Strati, 1992: 569), but are still working within a broadly rationalist paradigm of organization, investigating how ways of organizing *produce* or *materialize* labour as an aesthetic intended to contribute to the process of valorization.

5   The jobs being advertised were for waitering staff, male and female. Ordinarily such advertisements might be expected to be placed in local evening newspapers. Similarly, a recruitment drive by Hotel Elba in another UK city included a television advertisement during the commercial break of the show *TFI Friday*—another media product with an affluent, young target audience.

References

Adkins, L. (2000) 'Mobile Desire: Aesthetics, Sexuality and the "Lesbian" at Work', *Sexualities* 3(2): 201–18.

Bahnisch, M. (2000) 'Embodied Work, Divided Labour: Subjectivity and the Scientific Management of the Body in Frederick W. Taylor's "Lecture on Management"', *Body & Society* 6(1): 51–68.

Bourdieu, P. (1984) *Distinction: A Social Critique of the Judgement of Taste*. London: Routledge.

Bourdieu, P. (1990) *The Logic of Practice*. Cambridge: Polity.

Bowen, D. and Lawler, E. (1992) 'The Empowerment of Service Workers: What, Why, How and When?', *Sloan Management Review* 31, spring: 31–9.

Bulan, H.F., Erickson, R.J. and Wharton, A.S. (1997) 'Doing for Others on the Job: The Affective Requirements of Service Work, Gender and Emotional Well-being', *Social Problems* 44(2): 235–56.

Butler, J. (1990) *Gender Trouble*. London: Routledge.

Crang, P. (1994) 'It's Showtime: On the Workplace Geographies of Display in a Restaurant in Southeast England', *Environment and Planning D: Society and Space* 12: 675–704.

Crang, P. (1997) 'Performing the Tourist Product', in C. Rojek and J. Urry (eds) *Touring Culture: Transformations of Travel and Theory*. London: Routledge.

Crossley, N. (1995) 'Body Techniques, Agency and Intercorporeality: On Goffman's Relations in Public', *Sociology* 29(1): 133–49.

Davies, P. (1990) *Your Total Image*. London: Piatkus.

Deal, T. and Kennedy, A. (1988) *Corporate Cultures*. Harmondsworth: Penguin.

Duby, G. (1986) *Il sogno della storia*. Milano: Garzanti.

du Gay, P. (1996) *Consumption and Identity at Work*. London: Sage.

Gagliardi, P., ed. (1990) *Symbols and Artifacts*. Berlin: de Gruyter.

Organization 10(1)
Articles

Gagliardi, P. (1996) 'Exploring the Aesthetic Side of Organizational Life', in S.R. Clegg, C. Hardy and W. Nord (eds) *Handbook of Organizational Studies*. London: Sage.

Giddens, A. (1991) *Modernity and Self-identity*. Cambridge: Polity.

Goffman, E. (1959) *The Presentation of Self in Everyday Life*. Harmondsworth: Penguin.

Goffman, E. (1967) *Interaction Ritual: Essays in Face-to-Face Behaviour*. New York: Anchor Books.

Goffman, E. (1971) *Relations in Public: Microstudies of the Public Order*. London: Penguin.

Hancock, P. and Tyler, M. (2000) '"The Look of Love": Gender and the Organization of Aesthetics', in J. Hassard, R. Holliday and H. Willmott (eds) *Body and Organization*. London: Sage.

Hassard, J., Holliday, R. and Willmott, H., eds. (2000) *Body and Organization*. London: Sage.

Hochschild, A.R. (1979) 'Emotion Work, Feeling Rules, and Social Structure', *American Journal of Sociology* 85(3): 551–75.

Hochschild, A.R. (1983) *The Managed Heart*. Berkeley: University of California Press.

Hopfl, H. (2000) '"Suaviter in modo, fortiter in re": Appearance, Reality and the Early Jesuits', in S. Linstead and H. Hopfl (eds) *The Aesthetics of Organization*. London: Sage.

Huczynski, A. (1996) *Influencing Within Organisations*. Hemel Hempstead: Prentice Hall.

Income Data Services (2001) *Corporate Clothing and Dress Codes*. London: IDS.

James, J. (1999) *Bodytalk*. London: The Industrial Society.

James, N. (1989) 'Emotional Labour: Skill and Work in the Social Regulation of Feelings', *Sociological Review* 37(1): 15–42.

Kinchin, P. (1999) *Miss Cranston*. Edinburgh: NMS.

Kuhn, J.W. (1996) 'The Misfit between Organization Theory and Processional Art: A Comment on White and Strati', *Organization* 3(2): 219–24.

Lash, S. and Urry, J. (1994) *Economies of Signs and Space*. London: Sage.

Leidner, R. (1991) 'Serving Hamburgers and Selling Insurance: Gender, Work and Identity in Interactive Service Jobs', *Gender and Society* 5(2): 153–77.

Leidner, R. (1993) *Fast Food, Fast Talk*. Berkeley: University of California Press.

Linstead, S. and Hopfl, H. (2000) 'Introduction', in S. Linstead and H. Hopfl (eds) *The Aesthetics of Organization*. London: Sage.

Macdonald, C. and Sirianni, C. (1996) 'The Service Society and the Changing Experience of Work', in C. Macdonald and C. Sirianni (eds) *Working in the Service Society*. Philadelphia: Temple University Press.

McDowell, L. (1995) 'Body Work: Heterosexual Gender Performance in City Workplaces', in D. Bell and G. Valentine (eds) *Mapping Desire: Geographies of Sexualities*. London: Routledge.

McQillan, R. (2001) 'Memories are Made of This', *The Herald*, 15 November, p. 14.

Mills, C.W. (1951) *White Collar*. New York: Oxford University Press.

Nickson, D., Warhurst, C., Witz, A. and Cullen, A. (2001) 'The Importance of Being Aesthetic: Work, Employment and Service Organisation', in A. Sturdy, I. Grugulis and H. Willmott (eds) *Customer Service*. Basingstoke: Palgrave.

Noon, M. and Blyton, P. (1997) *The Realities of Work*. Basingstoke: Macmillan.

The Labour of Aesthetics
Anne Witz et al.

Olins, W. (1991) *Corporate Identity.* London: Thames & Hudson.

Ottensmeyer, E. (1996) 'Too Strong to Stop, Too Sweet to Lose: Aesthetics as a Way to Know Organizations', *Organization* 3(2): 189–94.

Ritzer, G. (1996) *The McDonaldization of Society.* London: Sage.

Schmitt, B. and Simonson, A. (1997) *Marketing Aesthetics.* New York: The Free Press.

Shilling, C. (1993) *The Body and Social Theory.* London: Sage.

Strati, A. (1990) 'Aesthetics and Organisational Skill', in B. Turner (ed.) *Organisational Symbolism.* Berlin: de Gruyter.

Strati, A. (1992) 'Aesthetic Understanding of Organizational Life', *Academy of Management Review* 17(3): 568–81.

Strati, A. (1996) 'Organizations Viewed Through the Lens of Aesthetics', *Organization* 3(2): 209–18.

Strati, A. (1999) *Organization and Aesthetics.* London: Sage.

Sudjic, P. (1999) 'The Man who Redesigned Glasgow', *The Herald*, 24 June, p. 14.

Taylor, S. (1998) 'Emotional Labour and the New Workplace', in P. Thomson and C. Warhurst (eds) *Workplaces of the Future.* London: Macmillan.

Taylor, S. and Tyler, M. (2000) 'Emotional Labour and Sexual Difference in the Airline Industry', *Work, Employment and Society* 14(1): 77–95.

Tyler, M. and Abbott, P. (1998) 'Chocs Away: Weight Watching in the Contemporary Airline Industry', *Sociology* 32(3): 433–50.

Tyler, M. and Taylor, S. (1998) 'The Exchange of Aesthetics: Women's Work and "The Gift"', *Gender, Work and Organisation* 5(3): 165–71.

Visser, M. (1997) *The Way We Are.* London: Penguin.

Warhurst, C., Nickson, D., Witz, A. and Cullen, A.M. (2000) 'Aesthetic Labour in Interactive Service Work: Some Case Study Evidence from the "New" Glasgow', *Service Industries Journal* 20(3): 1–18.

Welsch, W. (1996) 'Aestheticization Processes: Phenomena, Distinctions and Prospects', *Theory, Culture & Society* 13(1): 1–24.

Wharton, A. (1993) 'The Affective Consequences of Service Work', *Work and Occupations* 20(2): 205–32.

Anne Witz is Reader in Sociology at the University of Leicester. Her current research and publishing centre around questions of gender, the body and social theory. She is completing a book on gendered embodiment, *Gendering the Social*, and preparing an edited collection of feminist interrogations of sociological theory, *The Masculinity of Modernity.* Her interest in aesthetic labour is leading her to investigate a sociology of style. Her publications include a number of articles on various aspects of gender, work, organization and the body. Her co-authored and co-edited books include *Professions and Patriarchy* (1992), *Gender and Bureaucracy* (1992), *Gender, Careers and Organisations* (1997) and *For Sociology* (2000). **Address:** Department of Sociology, University of Leicester, University Road, Leicester LE1 7RH, UK. [email: aw81@le.ac.uk]

Chris Warhurst is Director of the Scottish Centre for Employment Research at the University of Strathclyde, Glasgow. His research, writing and teaching focus on management, labour and work organization in the international economy. Two current interests are aesthetic labour and knowledge work. He has published widely, with articles in the *Journal of Management Studies* and *Sociology*, for

Organization 10(1)
Articles

example. Single and jointly edited and authored books include *Workplaces of the Future* (1998), *Between Market, State and Kibbutz* (1999), *For Sociology* (2000) and *Looking Good, Sounding Right* (2001). **Address:** Department of Human Resource Management, University of Strathclyde, Glasgow G1 1XT, UK. [email: chris.warhurst@strath.ac.uk]

Dennis Nickson is a Senior Lecturer at the Scottish Hotel School at the University of Strathclyde. His teaching, research and publications focus on the globalization of the tourism and hospitality industry, and international and domestic human resource management. He has published widely in these fields. Articles have appeared in *Work, Employment & Society* and the *Service Industries Journal*, for example. Edited and authored books with colleagues include *Human Resource Management for Hospitality Services* (1997) and *Looking Good, Sounding Right* (2001). He also serves as an academic adviser to hospitality industry bodies. **Address:** Scottish Hotel School, University of Strathclyde, Glasgow G4 0LG, UK. [email: d.p.nickson@strath.ac.uk]

Part II
Following and Framing
Management Fashion

[6]

Rhetoric and Myth in Management Fashion

Alfred Kieser
University of Mannheim

Abstract. A count of publications over a period of time indicates that management concepts come and go like fashions. After a discussion of theories of fashion in aesthetic and technical objects, it is argued that rhetoric, an aesthetic form, is the main fabric of management fashions and that therefore theories of fashion in aesthetic forms are generally applicable to explanations of management fashions. The rise and fall of management fashions, especially fashions in organizational design, will be analysed using a concept of an arena of management fashion. The most important players in this arena are authors of management books, publishers, management seminar organizers and professors of business schools, who in different ways contribute to the attractiveness of the arena and, thereby, to the speed with which the fashion spreads. The best accelerator of a management fashion is a management bestseller which applies a specific rhetoric.

Management fashions and the principles propagated by them prove useful in restructuring projects within organizations. They simplify the process of initiation and conceptualization as well as the coordination between parallel restructuring sub-projects; they are useful tools in political manoeuvres during the implementation process and they help in making the organization appear rational after the completion of the restructuring process.

The article concludes with a discussion of the implications of management fashions for the relationship between theory and practice.

And then the emperor in the procession went under the magnificent canopy, and all the people on the road and at their windows said 'Lord, how wonderful the emperor's new clothes are! What a beautiful train he has on his costume! How heavenly it fits!' No one wanted to admit that he saw nothing, because then he would certainly not have been suitable for his job or would have revealed his stupidity. (Hans Christian Andersen: 'The Emperor's New Clothes'; author's translation)

The Origins of Management Fashions and Myths

Would you like to know how to make gold? In principle it is very simple. Gold, as it is, cannot be changed, because in this state it does not have any penetrative strength. It must be subtilized and unlocked. This must occur so that it does not lose its properties. Only with mercury is this possible. Gold has to be dissolved in the kingly water, Aqua Regis, into which the mercury must be poured. The moisture is to be drained from this until salt forms; the remains are to be redissolved in the Spiritu Aceti. Now one must filter and purify until continuous thickening occurs, i.e. until the mixture flows like wax. In this way everything silver, however thick it may be, will be converted into gold when it is melted with the gold. This entire process results in an increase in the quantity of gold.

With this convincing presentation the 'project maker' Johann Joachim Becher from Speyer won the confidence of the Austrian Emperor in 1675 (Doberer, 1991), who commissioned him to construct a large 'house of manufactures', in which, alongside a number of workshops, a lab with the purpose of creating gold was to be installed. Becher promised to set up a chemical process which 'would yield at least 1 or even 2 percent profit per week – which would thereby alone cover the cost of this investment' (Hassinger, 1951: 200; all German quotes translated by the author). Before coming to Vienna, Becher had already served other rulers as a consultant. He published his insights and findings in two bestsellers: *Political Discourse and the Actual Causes of the Rise and Fall of Cities and Countries* (Frankfurt/Main 1668, 2nd edn 1673, 3rd edn 1688) and *Foolish Wisdom and Wise Foolishness: Or a Hundred or so Political and Physical, Mechanical and Mercantilistic Concepts and Propositions* (Frankfurt/ Main 1682, 2nd edn 1683, 3rd edn 1686). As many of his projects lagged behind his promises—to put it euphemistically—he retired hurriedly to England. He triggered one of the first management fashions: mercantilism.

Today's management fashions are much more short-lived. Even so they do hold much in common with the early ones: bold promises, bustling consultants, magic, and sporadic reference to strict academic science. Some things have, however, changed: bestsellers are no longer titled *Foolish Wisdom and Wise Foolishness* but *In Search of Excellence* or *Reengineering the Corporation: A Manifesto for Business Revolution*. And they no longer promise gold, but instead quantum leaps in productivity and efficiency.

50

Rhetoric and Myth in Management Fashion
Alfred Kieser

The Ups and Downs of Management fashions

Management fashions follow patterns which can be described by bell-shaped curves. At the start of a fashion, only a few pioneers are daring enough to take it up. These few are joined by a rising number of imitators, until this fashion is 'out' and new fashions come on the market (processes of this kind are modelled in Rogers, 1983). The existence of such cycles can be shown empirically by, for example, calculating over a certain span of time the number of men with a certain style of beard in photographs in a magazine (Robinson, 1976) or the average length of skirts as pictured in fashion magazines for women (Richardson and Kroeber, 1952).

In order to show examples of management fashions the number of articles and books which appeared from 1982 to 1995 on quality circles (QC), lean production (LP), business process reengineering (BPR), total quality management (TQM) and organizational culture (OC) have been calculated from a databank of business literature (Wiso). The results are presented in Figure 1. It is obvious that the quality circles, lean production, total quality management and organizational culture fashions have already passed their respective peaks. Business process re-engineering is still rising steeply. The data indicates that the cycles of the management fashions are getting shorter but at the same time their peaks are getting higher. (This approach to the measurement of management fashions has also been applied by Abrahamson [1993]; Pascale [1990] determines management fashions on the basis of literature references.)

Figure 1   Waves of management fashions as measured by numbers of publications

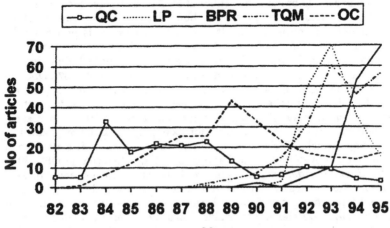

Organization
Articles

Does an Explanation of Management Fashion Require a Specific Kind of Fashion Theory?

An Example for a Specific Theory of Management Fashion

Analyses of management fashions usually borrow from concepts that were originally developed for explanations of fashions in women's clothes. However, recently Abrahamson (1996) argued that an explanation of fashion in technical forms such as management techniques requires other concepts than an explanation of fashion in aesthetic forms. He proposes a specific theory of management fashion by extending neo-institutional theory (Meyer and Rowan, 1977). A central hypothesis of this theory is that organizations have to adopt structures that have become institutionalized in society in order to acquire and retain legitimacy and support by stakeholders. To these norms of organizational structure Abrahamson (1996: 262) adds 'norms of progress' that 'generate expectations of a never-ending improvement process judged by criteria that are repeatedly redefined in and by this process itself'. However, only those management techniques gain legitimacy with regard to norms of progress, for which 'transitory collective beliefs' have been shaped by the 'management-fashion-setting community' (Abrahamson, 1996: 263), i.e. by consulting firms, management gurus, business mass-media publishers and business schools.

Abrahamson conceptualizes the *supply* of management fashions as a process with four phases: creation, selection, processing and dissemination. In the *creation phase* managers or management fashion setters invent or—this only applies to the latter group—reinvent management techniques. *Selection* can take two forms: 'management innovations may be invented by managers and selected into the management-fashion-setting community by management fashion setters who come into contact with these managers' (Abrahamson, 1996: 266). Alternatively, 'fashion setters may select among techniques they themselves or other fashion setters have invented or rediscovered' (1996: 266). *Processing* is performed by management fashion setters and 'involves the elaboration of a rhetoric that can convince fashion followers that a management technique is both rational and at the forefront of management progress' (1996: 267). *Dissemination* of management fashions is brought about by mass-media publications that pick up the rhetoric that has been developed by fashion setters. 'Fashion setters may disseminate their rhetorics directly to managers through publications they control [for example, books or magazines of consulting firms], other fashion setters may do so indirectly, when publications they do not control appropriate their rhetorics' (1996: 269).

The *demand side*, as conceptualized by Abrahamson, encompasses socio-psychological as well as technoeconomic factors. Abrahamson takes the socio-psychological factors largely from theories of fashion in women's clothes. Referring to trickle-down theory for the explanation of fashion in women's clothes, Abrahamson (1996: 272) hypothesizes that

Rhetoric and Myth in Management Fashion
Alfred Kieser

'new management fashions will tend to emerge when old management fashions have been adopted by lower reputation organizations'.

Techno-economical factors only influence the *direction* of demand, not its size. However, this influence is mediated by fashion setters who 'not only sense and satiate incipient demand for new types of management fashions but ... also shape this demand by articulating to fashion followers that particular technique which matches the type they prefer' (Abrahamson, 1996: 273).

Abrahamson's theory seems flawed in several respects: first, 'norms of progress' are fundamentally at variance with the conceptualization of norms in neo-institutional theory. In this theory norms are conceptualized as confronting organizations with stable—not permanently changing—expectations as to which organizational forms they should implement. These expectations result in stability and isomorphy of organizations. Management fashions that come and go quickly and are picked up by organizations at different points of time rather increase the instability and heterogeneity of organizational structures. Abrahamson does not point out how 'norms of progress' are related to norms of adherence to established organizational forms. Linking the hypothesis that managers have to adhere to norms of progress with neo-institutional theory therefore smacks of an attempt to create the impression that the explanation of the dynamics of management fashion does not rest on just one single hypothesis but on a highly reputed theory.

Second, Abrahamson conceptualizes a process in which, in a first step, 'fashion setters sense incipient preferences ... and create many management techniques', and, in a later step, 'articulate rhetorics championing the management techniques they select' (1996: 264). Thereby he implies that management techniques are available in pure form, i.e. without rhetoric. This seems doubtful. Management techniques do not exist per se. Whenever we communicate we apply rhetoric. Techniques or concepts like core competences, empowerment or customer orientation are not recipes that inform about exact quantities of tangible inputs and exact processes or structures. People have to agree what these expressions mean *for them or for their organizations*. Management fashions are started with rhetoric, either by managers like Jack Welch or Percy Barnevik or by consultants like Peters or Champy, and they are transmitted via rhetoric. Consultants sell predominantly through rhetoric. Management fashions are 'methods for constructing realities' (Brunsson and Olsen, 1993: 105) or schemes for 'sensemaking' (Weick, 1995).

Third, Abrahamson (1996: 271) claims that 'sociopsychological and technoeconomic factors compete to shape management fashion demand'. However, a closer look reveals that in his concept, *size of demand* for management fashions is exclusively determined by sociopsychological variables: need to comply with norms of rationality and progress, need for individuality and novelty in conjunction with a need for conformity, and an increased propensity for quasi-magical solutions in times of frustra-

Organization
Articles

tion. Size of demand is also influenced by management fashion setters, who, according to Abrahamson, not only deliver a supply of, but also create (manipulate) demand for management fashions. Technoeconomic variables influence only the incipient preferences of managers for certain types of management techniques.

In this article, concentration is on the size of demand for management fashions. As has been demonstrated above, Abrahamson's attempt to construct a specific theory for management fashion is not too convincing: he still borrows all variables for the explanation of the size of demand for management fashions from theories of fashion in aesthetic forms. And he does not realize that rhetoric, which is the essence of management fashion, is an aesthetic form. It is therefore reasonable to assume that the forces that drive the dynamics of management fashion are analogous to forces that drive dynamics of fashion in aesthetic forms.

A Review of Theories of Fashion

Three major paradigms can be distinguished in theories of fashion in women's clothes (Davis, 1989, 1992; Schnierer, 1995): trickle-down theory, collective selection theory and marionette theory. *Trickle-down theory*, the oldest, is based on a simple hypothesis: the lower social classes imitate the clothing styles of the higher classes and, thereby, force the higher classes to change their styles of clothing in order to re-establish the old differences (Barber and Lobel, 1952; Simmel, 1957; Spencer, 1888). McCracken (1985: 50) modifies and extends this theory by pointing out that, in our times, 'groups must be defined not only in terms of hierarchical social status but also in terms of status difference established by sex, age and ethnicity'. He also stresses the symbolic meaning of clothes, since '... clothing not only marks the difference between cultural categories, it also specifies the nature of the difference that exists between them'. If, for example, businessmen register that women adopt some of 'their' clothing styles in order to acquire 'new credibility, presence and authority in the business world' (McCracken, 1985: 44), they are likely to expend efforts in order to regain distinction. Critics of this theory claim that status has lost its meaning in modern societies and that fashions can trickle up and across any groups, forcing the group of the first adopters to invent new forms of distinction with regard to the imitators (Blumberg, 1974; King and Ring, 1980). For an analysis of management fashion it seems important to note that the main driving forces in trickle-down theories are the desire of certain groups to copy other groups and the desire of the groups which are being copied to re-establish their former distinction. In a similar vein, Bourdieu (1994) conceptualizes a competitive—'an unbroken, unending'—struggle among the classes in which aesthetic products and style are used as weapons: the upper classes 'defend their rarity by defending the rarity of the products they consume or the way in which they consume them. In fact, the most elementary, the simplest strategy, consists in shunning works that have become pop-

54

Rhetoric and Myth in Management Fashion
Alfred Kieser

ularized, devalued and disqualified' (Bourdieu, 1993: 115). In contrast to the consumers, the *producers* of aesthetic products are not driven by a need to maintain and create distinction. They produce differences in their works because they constantly have to explore the structural possibilities of their respective arts; innovativeness is expected from them:

> The artistic field is the site of prominent change, so much so that ... to disqualify an artist, as an artist, it is sufficient to relegate him to the past, by showing that his style merely reproduces a style attested in the past. (Bourdieu, 1993: 112)

The *collective selection theory* was founded by Blumer, for whom fashion reflects 'the movement of current developments as they take place in its own field, in adjacent fields, and in the larger social world' (1969: 283). He points out that fashion performs a number of functions for its followers. First, it 'introduces order in a potentially anarchic and moving present', through collectively narrowing choice. In this respect 'fashion performs in a moving society a function which custom performs in a settled society' (Blumer, 1969: 289). Second, it 'serves to detach the grip of the past in a moving world' (1969: 290), a world that needs individuals who are prepared to move into new directions. 'Third, fashion operates as an orderly preparation for the immediate future. By allowing the presentation of new models but by forcing them through the gauntlet of competition and collective selection the fashion mechanism offers a continuous means of adjusting to what is on the horizon' (1969: 290). Thus, being fashionable appears to offer the individual some control over his or her circumstances. This is why most consumers of fashion experience fashion as something that promises orientation and stability—at least for some time. Fashion helps in forming a new way of thinking by turning the manifold and complex social events into 'a set of obscure guides which bring it into line with the general or over-all direction of modernity itself. This responsiveness in its more extended form seems to be the chief factor in formation of what we speak of as a "spirit of the times" or a "zeitgeist" (Blumer, 1969: 283). Fashion thus also enables individuals to take notice of and to tune in to modern trends in society.

A third family of fashion theories, the *marionette theories*, conceptualizes fashion as the 'natural' outcome of the capitalist economy. Competition forces the producers to constantly outcompete each other. However, if it is, in principle, possible to acquire competitive advantages by improving quality or by lowering prices, why do producers have to invent fashions?

> Firstly, because through it a fictitious advantage can be achieved where a real one is not possible. ... To this the consideration is added that the propensity to buy is increased if the new supply shows small modifications in comparison to the old: an object is replaced, because it is no longer modern, though it is by far not worn out. (Sombart, 1902: 101)

The consumer is manipulated by the producers, by advertising agencies and by the mass media. All these actors also profit from an acceleration of fashion waves (Berger, 1992). In this way, consumers are made marionettes of the industry. Faurschou (1987: 82) links the marionette theory with postmodernism by pointing out that fashion becomes the

> commodity 'par excellence.' It is fed by all of capitalism's incessant, frantic, reproductive passion and power. Fashion *is* the logic of planned obsolescence—not just the necessity for market survival, but the cycle of desire itself, the endless process through which the body is decoded and recoded, in order to define and inhabit the newest territorialized spaces of capital's expansion.

Even consumer activism in its attempt to free the consumer from the dictate of the producer creates fashions: Naderism, green consumerism, ethical consumerism, value-for-money movement, etc. (Gabriel and Lang, 1995).

For the individual, the acceleration in the emergence of new fashions, which is brought about by market forces, results in a high degree of ambivalence—which the individual combats by choosing fashions:

> The clothing styles emerge to clarify and lend expression to the cultural ambivalence. The broad variety of clothing styles in turn creates a high degree of ambiguity in individually constructed appearance styles, the meaning of which must then be collectively negotiated in social interaction. In the process, certain styles are adopted by a majority of consumers within social interaction. (Kaiser et al., 1991)

Marionette as well as trickle-down theories explain fashion as a turning away from something old (Schnierer, 1995) and, thereby, they complement each other: the goal of aesthetic innovation for the producers is the creation of buying motives. And, according to trickle-down theories, individuals permanently need new fashions, since the old ones are constantly in danger of no longer providing distinction. A problem of both theories however is, that they cannot forecast the *direction* that new fashions will take. Collective selection theory with its attempts to link fashion with the zeitgeist is not too helpful either, since many currents of the zeitgeist can be identified in modern societies and it is always unclear which ones will be picked up. This could explain why theories in this tradition have not been successful in producing empirical evidence (Schnierer, 1995).

Many of the sociologists of women's clothes point out that their theories should also be useful for the explanation of fashion in other forms. Since rhetoric, an aesthetic form, is the main ingredient of management fashions, it seems adequate to try to reach a satisfactory explanation of this phenomenon, by taking existing theories of fashion or modifications of them as a theoretical platform, before starting to develop a specific theory of management fashion.

Management Fashion—an Arena for the Trading of Rhetoric

In this article management fashion is explained by conceptualizing rhetoric as its main fabric and by applying existing concepts of fashion in

Rhetoric and Myth in Management Fashion
Alfred Kieser

aesthetic forms. In particular, the dynamics of management fashion are explained on the basis of a concept of an 'arena' that represents a modification of the marionette theory. A management fashion is conceptualized as forming an arena in which different groups of participants bustle about—consultants, professors, managers, editors of management magazines, publishers, commercial seminar organizers, organizers of internet forums, etc. (this concept is inspired by Crozier and Friedberg, 1980). The participants can achieve their individual goals of highest possible profit, public image, power or career by widening the arena through luring further participants into it. For this purpose they play principally co-operative games. Rhetoric is the main input currency in this game. Competition occurs only in some instances, for example when several consultants are competing for a contract after having collectively convinced the client that a fundamental restructuring of his organization is unavoidable. The rules of the game can be further developed during the game. Moves that turn out to be ineffective are not likely to be repeated by a player or copied by others. The speed at which the arena grows depends largely on the attractiveness of the game that the first players are able to produce.

The following section takes a closer look at the rhetoric of management fashion. The analysis concentrates on management bestsellers, since it seems that there is no better formula for making an arena attractive than a management bestseller. However, the analysis can, in principle, also be applied to other media that propagate management fashions: management journals, seminars, conferences, presentations by consultants in companies, etc.

Rhetoric—the Fabric Management Bestsellers are Made of

The more of the following elements of rhetoric a management book contains, the greater its chance of becoming a bestseller (Davis, 1986; Eccles et al., 1992; Abrahamson, 1993, 1996):[1]

1. One factor, such as organizational culture (Peters and Waterman, 1983), total qualitiy management, lean production (Womack et al., 1990), network organizations (Reich, 1991), entrepreneurship (Pinchot, 1985), business process reengineering (Hammer and Champy, 1993), or virtual organization (Chesbrough and Teece, 1996; Davidow and Malone, 1992) is identified as the most crucial one for success. This key factor, according to the author, has up until now been gravely neglected. Therefore, its discovery can be described (which as a rule the author does repetitively and persistently) as a revolutionary and radical departure from the management concepts that were valid up to this time.

2. The implementation of the new principles is presented as unavoidable, because the old principles are bound to fail in the face of the menacing dangers. The catalogue of the dangers which often comes close

to a true apocalypse, includes, for example, efficiency gains of foreign (in particular Japanese) economies, which are almost impossible to make up, increasingly dynamic markets, ever shorter product cycles, increasing demands from customers necessitating stronger customer orientation, breathtaking technological advances and changing values in society. It seems that these threats never disappear in spite of all the management fashions, since they are always brought into the picture when a new fashion is launched.

3. The new principles are linked to highly treasured values—besides efficiency, the enrichment of jobs, the competitive edge of the national economy, full employment, customer satisfaction, flexibility, creativity, innovativeness of the company, etc. (Huczynski, 1993). The Roman rhetorician Quintilian (1920) had, long ago, already recommended increasing the persuasive power of an argument by linking it with generally accepted convictions like the existence of gods.

4. The author does not instruct the managers, instead he simply points out outstanding solutions that were achieved by extraordinary managers, especially those from the nation the readership is from. The book, *In Search of Excellence* (Peters and Waterman, 1983) was not only success-ful because, as its critics said, it 'brought welcome balm for America's battered self-image', it 'appealed to American pride. It says Americans—at least some Americans—do know how to manage' (from reviews quoted in Freeman, 1985: 348). The message also is that, if some of the companies in the examples have implemented the new principles, then it must also be achievable in the reader's company. The impression that the new principles have been created within a university or in the author's study must be avoided by all means. The examples are presented from the perspective of their creators—lean production, for example, as being the masterful discovery of a 'young Japanese engineer', Eiji Toyoda, and his 'production genius' Taiichi Ohno (Womack et al., 1990: 53) and lean management as the vision of Percy Barnevik, 'the most insistent enemy of bureaucracy' (Peters, 1992: 45). In this way the reading manager is assured that leadership makes a difference. This rhetorical figure was also already known to Quintilian (1920), who pointed out that authorities who are legitimized by success provide examples effectively supporting the argu-mentation.

5. No manager must feel guilty that he has not already thought of the new principles himself: everything has changed radically—the environ-ment and the appropriate organizational solutions. The old principles were, up until now, evidence of excellent management. They are still applicable for certain problems, but tomorrow, most certainly, no longer. The pioneers are really exceptional managers. In this way, the potential bestseller offers catharsis (on the effects of catharsis see Aristotle, 1992: ch. 14). However, the earlier the manager swings aboard the train the more he or she can feel like a fellow pioneer.

6. Potential bestsellers are characterized by a clever mixture of simpli-

Rhetoric and Myth in Management Fashion
Alfred Kieser

city and ambiguity (Clark and Salaman, 1996). The superiority of the new principles appears clear and convincing: internal entrepreneurship is clearly superior to bureaucratic behaviour (Pinchot, 1985), tent organizations more flexible than palace organizations, network organizations more adaptable than centralized corporations with huge central staffs (Bartlett and Ghoshal, 1989; Peters, 1992) and virtual organizations are the most flexible of all. This is immediately evident to any reasonable person. 'If a new idea can be shown to be a version of common sense, its threat to the potential adopter is reduced' (Huczynski, 1993: 108). Managers find this simplicity attractive because, in combination with the cases of successful implementation, it furnishes them with a powerful line of argumentation. The new concept most certainly appears to them as simpler and more convincing than the present organizational structure of their own company, which many of them generally experience as chaotic (Brunsson and Olsen, 1993). However, this simplicity rests on the simplicity of the individual principles or stylized examples and not on a description of reality. What the tent, network or virtual organizations look like in reality remains unclear in spite of the numerous examples. The 'solutions' consist basically of simple metaphors. It is also typical that next to many commonsense statements (examples from Champy, 1995: 42, 184: 'complacency leads to mediocrity, which leads to failure', 'enlightened personnel development benefits both the employee and the company'), there are sentences which a Zen master could confidently give his students as a meditation exercise. For example, this one:

> Character is required, and the best sign of it—the reengineering character anyway—is not only to hold two good, contradictory ideas, but to act on them. (Champy, 1995: 38)

The ambiguity is further increased with the introduction of too many principles which, without further explanation, do not supplement each other to form a complete picture. For example, in the reengineering concept of Hammer and Champy (1993), every single principle is illustrated by itself clearly and simply with neat examples. The connections and interactions between these principles are, however, at best only hinted at. Ambiguity is also created by the lack of a precise description of the implementation process. Thus, the manager who wants to implement a new management concept, 'joins a journey whose duration no one really knows and for which there are no maps', as Champy (1994a: 99) describes reengineering with startling openness.

The concepts sold in potential bestsellers are, therefore, both simple and clear but also ambiguous, vague, contradictory and puzzling. Becher's representation of alchemy is paradigmatic: precise but yet not implementable. Ambiguity offers scope for interpretation (Astley and Zammuto, 1992). The reader can project the problems (s)he encounters in his/her organization into the concept and can thus interpret it as the solution to these pressing problems. The expertise of the author is also underlined—

Organization
Articles

if the concepts were easy to understand then one would not need an expert (among which the bestselling author is one of the most prominent). It is typical of the language of experts that it erects communication barriers. At the same time, however, the experts offer their clients help in overcoming these barriers (Luhmann and Fuchs, 1989). Or, as a manager quoted by March (1991: 22) believes: 'Consultants talk funny and make money'. Often the bestseller author quite openly makes it clear that intuition such as only an expert can have is indispensable. For example, Champy (1994b) believes that reengineering is dependent on intuition 'because rational analysis fails in the face of paradoxes and contradictions'. In the end, it becomes clear that one can only select an expert on the basis of an intuitive leap of faith that he or she has the best intuition or the highest reputation.

7. Frequently the author points out that the concept is extremely difficult to implement so that many companies fail. Thus the new concept represents a real challenge. However, those who succeed can make enormous improvements or 'quantum leaps' (Hammer and Champy, 1993). A reengineering expert (the head of the German subsidiary of Champy's consultancy firm) promises, for example, 'cost reductions between 30 and 90 percent, quality improvements from 50 to 90 percent, time savings of between 60 and 80 percent and as well as productivity improvements of up to 100 percent' (Lohse, 1994). Enormous improvements are also promised by the formula frequently used in conjunction with Lean Production: that this organizational form requires half the time and effort to develop new products, half the investment in equipment, half the personnel in producing and that it yields a performance advantage of 2 to 1 in productivity, quality and flexibility. The figures are as round as those Becher's alchemy promised and the promises are just as full bodied. The message says: 'If you don't believe you are capable of doing it, you do not belong among the really excellent managers—and if you do believe that you can do it but it does not work then you also do not belong into this group'. In any event, it is not the fault of the consultant if the project fails.

8. Now and then the author couples the new principles to science, in that he points to the results of systematic empirical research. However, he usually dispenses with detailed descriptions of the methods (which is a norm for publishing results of empirical research in scientific publications). As long as he is affiliated to a reputable university, the reader will take the correctness of his results on trust. Of course, in order to check critically the empirical results, one must know the methods and the samples in some detail. In management books results of empirical studies are often impermissably generalized and manipulated. Examples are provided from Taylorism (Wrege and Perroni, 1974), the human relations movement (Carey, 1967) and lean production (Williams et al., 1992).

9. The book must be easily readable: no foreign words, no academic jargon, short sentences (Freeman, 1985; Huczynski, 1993). Direct speech

Rhetoric and Myth in Management Fashion
Alfred Kieser

makes the text more lively, therefore interviews with top managers are woven in. They also underline the author's close proximity to the business leaders. Numerous figures generate the sense of familiarity of a seminar or management presentation, in which overheads are used extensively. Once the book advances to bestseller status there are also videos and (for the driving manager) tapes.

10. However, all these ingredients are useless if the timing is not perfect. The book must hit the 'nerve of today's managers'. Peters (1992: 488), the author of several bestsellers, stated retrospectively that the timing for *In Search of Excellence* was so good because it was released in 1982, at a time when 'people were in the midst of a big "downer" and the book purported to be about "great American companies". Moreover, the best-selling management books of all time up to that point ... had said, in effect: "everything that's good and new in management is going on in Japan." ... [P]eople were fed up with "their" message, and welcomed ours'.

The Creation of Myths

When management fashions are linked to the extraordinary performance of extraordinary personalities, when, for example, lean production is characterized as the invention of Toyoda and Ohno and is tied to the amazing success of Toyota, or when the invention of a unique organizational culture by the ingenious company founders Hewlett and Packard is tied to the extraordinary innovativeness of this company, then these concepts assume a mythical quality.[2] The abnormal success renders it impossible to doubt the explanation—the story of success of the new concept becomes mythical (Pondy, 1983). The inevitable incompleteness of the concept, its puzzling aspects, call out for myth creation. In a similar way, in descriptions of new fashions in women's clothes, certain women are portrayed as having achieved an almost unreachable, breathtaking elegance.

But why should managers, the incarnations of rationality, believe in and propagate myths? The origin of myths is above all the fear of disaster and helplessness in the face of the unexplained. 'The myth replaces the anxiety with fear' (Blumenberg, 1979: 11). If one wants to describe the world so that one can trust its order and lock out its threats, one makes use of myths (Luhmann, 1982). From time to time managers experience loss of control and even admit it to themselves. This instills in them the fear of an ever-increasing loss of control. The trick of the myth creator—the bestselling author—now lies in the replacement of the unfamiliar with the familiar, the explanation for the unexplicable, the name for the unnameable. Because 'panic and paralysis ... become resolved under seemingly calculable determinants and organized behaviours, even if the results of the magical and cultish sacrifices occasionally demonstrate drastically the uselessness of mortal attempts to gain the benevolence of the divine

Organization
Articles

powers' (Blumenberg, 1979: 11; see also Huczynski, 1993). It is, however, not infrequent that a myth first instills fear for which it then holds out a prospect of relief.

Of particular importance for myth creation is the name of the new approach: 'Assigning names to the world is to segment the unsegmented and regroup it, and to make the ungraspable tangible though not yet understandable' (Blumenberg, 1979: 49). 'Business process reengineering', for example, is a good name for an arena of myths and fashions, because it suggests feasibility and, at the same time, an activity and is not simply addressing a goal. A good name consolidates, it lends the new fashion a language and a market value (König, 1985).

Despite these obvious functions of myth-creation, the question has to be repeated: how does it come about that managers, trained in rational thinking, give credence to promises that are obviously not realizable? Or does a manager, who lets himself in for reengineering, really believe that a cost reduction of between 30 and 90 percent and productivity increases of up to 100 percent are attainable? Organizations that make this possible must really be in terrible shape. How does it come about that managers set about engineering something which is as unengineerable as an organizational culture? How does it come about that higher hierarchical levels, possibly without being aware of the paradox, order a 'de-hierarchization', and that the members of the lower levels enthusiastically take up the message—not least to promote their career. Even if managers do not take promises of this kind at their face value, since they know that inflated rhetoric is always part of the game, many of them are nevertheless convinced, or they are inclined to believe, that anyone who promises a great deal must be able to deliver at least something.

An explanation of this behaviour has to take into account that managers, in fact, do experience constant and enormous competitive pressure. The insistent portrayals of the apocalyptic four horsemen in the bestsellers appear familiar to them. In such situations, the wish to possess an effective means of countering these dangers is very pressing: the inclination to give credence to promises of salvation increases. The absolutist rulers who were repeatedly taken in by alchemists, were also driven by competition—by the competition for the greatest display of splendour, the strongest army, etc. The wish becomes the father of belief. The sociologist and economist Thorstein Veblen (1949: 276) had already observed at the turn of the century (1st American edn, 1899) that the 'gambling propensity' is very strong 'among sporting men'. 'When special exigencies arise, that is to say, when there is peculiar need of a full and free recourse to the law of cause and effect, then the individual commonly has recourse to the preternatural agency as a universal solvent' (Veblen, 1949: 286). This assumption corresponds to a positive correlation between economic depressions and the number of articles that deal with astrology and mysticism (Padgett and Jorgenson, 1982). Cleverly (1973: 230) compares managers in search of doctrines of salvation to gambling

Rhetoric and Myth in Management Fashion
Alfred Kieser

addicts: 'Some roulette players are bound to win, even among those who play systems. And each example of a successful player provides a kernel for the building of fresh legends to sustain the hopes of addicts'. Managers ironically describe bestselling authors as gurus—and then entrust themselves to their advice.

In the short review of theories of fashion in women's clothes it has already been pointed out that fashion performs the function of introducing order into a chaotic world (Blumer, 1969) and of reducing ambivalence in the face of a multitude of trends. This function is also performed by management fashions. Through management fashions managers can fight their fears without having to take the risk of provoking criticism or even ridicule, because they are members of a recognized group. The fashion offers a self-elevation that is always found to be appropriate (Simmel, 1957). A fashion 'allows the dependent personality to follow others and be relieved of responsibility. ... A fashion which enhances self-esteem and makes us feel competitively equal or superior to our associates *works for us* and helps diminish anxiety' (Anspach, 1967: 27).

Rituals and Further Participants

In order to produce management fashions and myths, the potential bestseller must become an object of public discourse. Management magazines must pick up the basic ideas developed in bestsellers. Consulting companies which do not have a bestselling author for the current fashion in their team must somehow find a way to present themselves as also being competent in this new concept. However, they cannot simply duplicate: they must follow the fashion but at the same time differentiate themselves (Brunsson and Olsen, 1993). This tendency increases ambiguity and contradictions within the new fashion. Ambiguity and contradictions open up new space for further articles that attempt interpretations, new books ... and more myth creation.

Very soon university professors enter the discussion. They are welcomed in the arena because they provide legitimacy for the fashion—even if they have no original serious research to contribute to the fashionable concept. For many of them, participation in the arena is a substitute for academic research. The acceptance of their contributions to the fashion by managers, measurable by the fees that they can charge, replaces serious theorizing, empirical tests and feedback in the scientific community. Other academics prefer to focus on the management fashion by constructing a theoretical frame around it or by criticizing it on the basis of accepted theories.

All the players in the arena can promote their personal goals by amplifying the current wave of fashion. They can promote their management careers, increase their income from side jobs, increase turnover and profits as seminar organizers etc. It also suits management fashions when König (1985: 165) notes with regard to fashion in clothes, drawing on

Organization
Articles

marionette theory, that 'competition in all its forms is the main driving force'. Those managers who show that they can handle the fashion in superior style can distinguish themselves from the rest. Consulting firms which produce fashions and which compete with other consulting firms by claiming superior competence in the newest fashions also take advantage of the competition between the members of their target groups. The result is a self-enhancing dynamic process.

Management seminars are an arena within an arena. Seminar organizers jump on the bandwagon only too gladly. Those who manage to ride the coming wave first, are ahead of the game and can expand their market share. Publishing companies not only publish management books, management magazines and daily newspapers with business pages in them; they also organize or co-organize management seminars and congresses. In this way, through orchestrated advertisements and reports, publishers simultaneously promote the circulation of their publications and the demand for their seminars and congresses. Consulting firms also organize seminars, which they regard as a superb marketing instrument for a highly complex service. At such seminars consultants are usually present as speakers. Alternatively, at seminars which are not organized by consulting firms, representatives of several consulting companies, specialists from companies which have already implemented the new management concept and, sometimes, also professors are usually present. The participant who hopes for enlightenment at such seminars is mostly disappointed—the complexity of management processes is even harder to capture in seminar presentations than in books. Since the companies from which the participants come are in many respects different from those from which the presenters obtained their examples, the solutions appear hardly transferable to the situations the participants see themselves in. If there are several consultants at the seminar, they tell different stories because, of course, they must raise their profile. The specialists who report successful applications of the fashionable concept also produce variations on the theme, because their companies are different, have been advised by different consultants and, above all, because they must do the impossible of describing in a short time a highly complex restructuring process that may have taken a year or two. Out of necessity they construct highly stylized accounts, because the reality is too multilayered and too confusing. In the majority of cases, however, the paying participants of such seminars do not hope for enlightenment but for confirmation, and are therefore not disappointed.

The success of a management seminar is heavily dependent on the charisma and fame of the seminar trainer. The seminar-guru, who is often identical to the bestseller-guru, embodies the success which he or she promises. It hardly matters what he or she says or that he or she, for example, simply repeats the main arguments of his or her newest book. What counts is how he or she says it. The German chief guru Gerken (1994: 34) notes about communication in our times (with no irony): 'The

Rhetoric and Myth in Management Fashion
Alfred Kieser

message is no longer important, but instead the quality of the staging. Performance replaces content'. The participants only too happily let themselves be taken in by the guru and identify with him: if the trainer is good, they, for the duration of the seminar, forget the frustrations of their managerial existence. 'It is the guru's performance itself that is valued' (Huczynski, 1993: 198). A guru who is able to bewitch his or her audience, has every right to demand high sacrifices in the form of fees (see the description of a Tom Peters seminar in Byrne, 1986).

The superlative of a seminar is a congress with many consultants, top managers, professors as speakers, and a guru as the star speaker. Events like this do not serve enlightening, critical discourse. They are the opposite: rituals of confirmation, sometimes even celebrations. Essential to the ritual, which often refers to a myth, is that if it follows the form, it cannot be wrong. It conveys deep, in the end undecodable, truths. 'The formalized ritual is the appropriate method of stabilizing the absence of alternatives to existing social norms' (Eder, 1976: 29). The central function of a seminar or congress ritual is to confirm the participants' convictions that they are on the right track. The participant who is in favour of the fashion feels safe and encouraged among the faithful. In his company, this participant is perhaps still a lone prophet in the wilderness; here he or she can bathe in the enthusiasm for the new concept. The doubter, however, feels isolated—and considers seriously whether he or she should not convert. Events of this sort are like fashion shows—the degree of excitement is all that matters.

Managers, Fashions and Myths in Garbage Cans

The arena of management fashion is very dependent on managers who apply the fashion in their companies. Managers are simultaneously the most important players in the arena and also the most important audience. Without the managers to apply the management fashion it would soon die. But why do managers pick up fashions and turn them into restructuring projects? First, because it is expected of them. 'The ideology of good management ... associates managers with the introduction of new ideas, new organizational forms, new techniques, new products, or new moods' (March, 1981: 573). Management fashions stir up fear of missing the boat in managers. But, at the same time, they also help them to overcome the fear, in that they place 'package solutions' at their disposal; they legitimize, they relieve the managers who call upon them and initiate corresponding projects in their companies from the task of detailed reasoning. They reduce the risk of making a wrong choice.

Fashions can also be used to increase power. It is predominantly top management who, through reading bestsellers, attending seminars or communicating with other top managers (or by a mixture of all these), become enthusiastic about a specific fashion and initiate a restructuring programme. Congresses and seminars which promote management fashions are usually predominantly addressing this group at first. The heightened tendency of top managers to take up management fashions is perhaps due to the fact that, because of increasing decentralization, which is facilitated by the existence of powerful information systems, lower hierarchical levels no longer experience an information gap with regard to top management as far as operative business is concerned. Correspondingly, top management perceives a reduction in the power distance to middle management. By initiating radical restructuring programmes from time to time, top management can re-establish former differences in power and can thereby renew its claim to leadership. Selected managers at lower levels, who see restructuring as a unique chance to promote their careers (a perception that is invited by top management), are appointed as programme and project managers and, in most cases, carry through the restructuring in cooperation with consultants. For some time, the restructuring programme creates the illusion for top management that its former power has been restored. The members of the in-group, top management and the key figures of the programme team are united by the certainty of belonging to the 'winners of the restructuring process'. This illusion can be strengthened by attending seminars or congresses together.

What functions do management fashions perform during the restructuring process? Extensive restructuring processes are not brought about by a coherently planned, smooth action programme, though this impression is often created by those in charge in their retrospective descriptions. The reality of restructuring processes is better captured by the garbage-can concept (Cohen et al., 1976; March, 1994; March and Olsen, 1986)—certainly not a label which could become fashionable among managers. In such garbage-can situations, management fashions can prove helpful in several ways. They simplify the restructuring process by making it appear logical to entrust consultants with its management. By choosing a consultant, top management buys a 'package solution'. It does not have to work out the goals for the restructuring process in any detail; nor does it have to closely monitor the implementation process. The consulting firm does this job for them and, thereby, also takes over a large part of top management's responsibility. The variations in the management fashions which have been developed by consulting companies for the purpose of differentiating themselves, allow management to choose between different package solutions, according to preference and the prevailing conditions—as managers perceive them. Provided that top management has chosen a high reputation consulting company, it can always justify this selection. The consulting company, however, demands that the top management supports the restructuring project without reserve—whatever this means (certainly it also means that the consultant should not be confronted with skepticism). In this way, responsibility evaporates, which all the actors perceive as pleasant.

The management fashion simplifies coordination between the different project groups within a company; it helps to 'orchestrate' scattered

Rhetoric and Myth in Management Fashion
Alfred Kieser

restructuring activities. One of its main functions is to cut short discussions. Proposals can be easily rejected by classifying them as not fitting the fashion: 'The project is concerned with empowerment of workers, what you suggest runs without doubt in the opposite direction'.

Management fashions provide an ideological framing of restructuring programmes. For example, empowerment programmes (Ezzamel and Willmott, 1994) as well as programmes for the implementation of internal markets (Eccles and White, 1988), which are sold under the labels of decentralization and self-coordination, can in reality serve to make hierarchical control more effective. This need not necessarily mean that top managers are in every case knowingly deceiving employees. Perhaps they simply find these forms of delegation attractive, because they intuitively realize that they motivate the employees and do not mean a real power loss for them.

The management fashion also delivers a pattern of argumentation that helps to interpret the restructuring project as worthwhile and successful. An 'objective' evaluation of some exactness of a complex restructuring project is impossible. On the other hand, the participants of the restructuring process, including those who are only passively affected, have an elementary interest in interpreting the costly restructuring process as a worthwhile and successful endeavour—not only in the middle of it, when everything threatens to sink in the chaos but, most importantly, also after its official end. The management fashion places a template at one's disposal for this interpretation. It delivers 'ideas, metaphors, models, and words that impose order on a confusing world, thus reconstructing our appreciation of experience' (March, 1991: 29). And when the wave of the fashion which triggered the most recent restructuring programme no longer delivers a convincing interpretation, one can very likely refer to a new fashion, which envelops the old restructuring project but places it into an even larger framework and action programme.

Brunsson and Olsen have analysed a number of large restructuring processes. In several of them they found that nothing had changed on the level of operations, and management still expressed satisfaction with the results:

> It is quite possible not only to launch, but also to implement reforms at the level of talk ... Consistency between the talk of the reformers and the reformees makes the reform seem implemented. (Brunsson and Olsen, 1993: 87)

The managers who initiated the restructuring programme have a fundamental interest in presenting it in seminars or management magazines as a successful application of a new management concept, as an additional reference case (Brunsson and Olsen, 1993). Every ambitious restructuring project creates a company-specific myth:

> Reforms confirm and reproduce images of organizations as systems that can be controlled from above, systems in which management ... possesses great personal power and can bring about direct change, and in which administrative

forms represent important instruments of change. (Brunsson and Olsen, 1993: 200)

It is, however, by no means intended to assert that all restructuring projects only take place at the level of talk or that presentations of implementations of fashionable management concepts are always extremely exaggerated. Most of the major restructuring projects bring about quantifiable effects. In the USA, for example, the number of restricted appointment or part-time employees trebled between 1982 and 1990. A third of all American employees either hold a restricted, part-time or short-term work contract. Despite an accelerating economy, more dismissals were registered in 1993 than ever before. More than 90 percent of the newly created jobs are part-time (Victor and Stephens, 1994). From the middle of 1991 to the end of 1994, 150,000 jobs have disappeared in the German motorcar industry and an end to this process is not in sight (*Süddeutsche Zeitung* 2 February 1995: 23). These developments are almost certainly also a result of the lean management, reengineering and outsourcing movements. But it can be argued that the main function of all these concepts is the justification of personnel cuts, and not the provision of powerful new methods for the computation of the minimum necessary work force, which could have also been established through conventional methods like overhead value analysis (and perhaps was, since old methods are often elements of the methodological tool kits of new fashions).

'In' and 'Out'

Several factors are responsible for the downturn in a management fashion. First, time: fashions fade. Because they have become 'old', they lose their effect as symbols of progress. The arena becomes overcrowded, because in the meantime almost everyone has jumped on the band-wagon, everyone can have his or her say—and will. Too many organizations can adorn themselves with the fashion. The term which gave the fashion its name, has become, due to the numerous differentiation efforts, so multifaceted that it has become almost meaningless (this situation seems to have been achieved for reengineering). 'Fads have the property that, up to a point, an increase in users increases the legitimacy of each, but beyond that point additional users decrease the appeal' (March, 1994: 249). The concept is too worn out to still provide a basis for effective rhetoric. The actors in the arena need new fashions, in order to make the ruling practise look old fashioned. It lies in the nature of the fashion that it 'continually commits suicide' (König, 1985: 184; see also Barthes, 1990): success leads to destruction.

Murder often also comes into play. Fashion designers and other actors denounce an existing fashion, which is not theirs, and propagate a new one (Barthes, 1990). The fashion 'possesses a peculiar uniformity, in which the satisfying of the love of destruction and of the demand for

Rhetoric and Myth in Management Fashion
Alfred Kieser

positive elements can no longer be separated from each other' (Simmel, 1957: 549). This makes the fashion 'the favourite child of capitalism' (Sombart, 1902: 23), as marionette theory states.

It is not the imitation of 'lower class organizations' or 'lower reputation organizations', as Abrahamson (1996: 272) puts it with reference to trickle-down theory, that forces leading organizations to pick up on new management fashions; it is rather the desire of groups of managers to distinguish themselves from others. It seems highly problematic here to apply the concept of class to organizations.

From time to time a currently fashionable concept produces dysfunctional effects and thus leads to a counter-fashion. For example, after many organizations have heavily decentralized, a recentralization fashion can find approval in the face of the resulting problems. If the production engineers become frustrated with CIM (Computer Integrated Manufacturing), they thankfully reach for lean production, in which computers play a comparatively subordinate role. New fashions are needed in ever shorter cycles, in order to be able to cover up the problems of failed reorganization concepts.

Looking back, one can often observe that old fashions return as new fashions. 'In the ten years between 1910 and 1920 ... every single one of the great themes of management is struck .... And almost everything that we have done since then, in theory as well as in practice, is only a variation and extension of the themes first heard during that decade' (Drucker, 1977: 19).

Should One Follow Management Fashions or Not?

Are management fashions good or bad? How should one respond to them? Can they be avoided? Eccles et al. (1992: 29) find the rhetoric of management fashions positive; they even see in it the 'essence of management':

> Much of the current hysteria over labels, such as 'the new organization' and 'empowerment' can be seen as an attempt to lend new energy to the collective enterprises. ... In their daily language, individual managers *use* such labels and concepts as they see fit as part of their ongoing use of language to coax, inspire, demand, or otherwise produce action in their organizations.

Consequently, Eccles et al. work out what differentiates effective rhetoric from mere rhetoric. Since verbal communication is the main activity of managers (Stewart et al., 1994), it might be more effective to make the production of visions and ideologies into the most important feature of management training, rather than to hold on to the fiction that it is concerned with tangible phenomena. However, Eccles et al. (1992: 184) warn of 'dangers of exaggeration' in the use of rhetoric: 'People quickly come to see through the rhetorical strategy of using new words for essentially old concepts. They become cynical or simply confused and may wonder why anyone ever bothered to make a change in the first place'.

69

Organization
Articles

For management theory, however, a confusion of fact and fiction, of the use of rhetoric in practice and the practice itself, would be fatal. Science must reflect on the relationship between science and practice; it must be fully aware that practice and science present different language games with varying criteria for validity or 'truth'—and with different rhetorics (Astley and Zammuto, 1992; Cummings, 1983). One of the principal tasks of scientists is to analyse societal developments critically. From this argumentation it cannot be inferred that management scientists should not involve themselves in the language games of practice. It is problematical, however, when management scientists, who are also active as consultants, are no longer distinguishable from consultants, when they do not also critically reflect on their role as consultants.

This essay is by no means intended as a call for the extinction of management fashions. (One of its main goals was to demonstrate that theories of fashion in aesthetic forms can be successfully exploited for the explanation of management fashion.) Organizations are too complex to be described without idealizations and stylizations. Things have come so far that one must plot rhetorical revolutions in order to accomplish modest organizational changes. The belief that reforms of organizations can be brought about without the use of rhetoric and ideology is the most dangerous ideology. Fashions can also be fun! Sometimes, however— perhaps also at present?—they bear all-too-strange fruit.

Fashions motivate people to always try out new solutions, and from time to time a fashion leaves behind useful ideas and techniques which are retained, even if one does not talk about it much any longer. In this way fashions contribute to organizational change, if not through revolutions, then through an accumulation of little steps. That evolution can even make something out of fashions was noticed by Mandeville (1724/1924: 25) over 250 years ago (one need only replace 'laws' with 'organizational rules'):

> Their darling Folly, Fickleness,
> In Diet, Furniture and Dress,
> That strange ridic'lous Vice, was made
> The very Wheel that turn'd the Trade.
> Their Laws and Clothes were equally
> Objects of Mutability;
> For, what was well done for a time,
> In half a Year became a Crime;
> Yet while they alter'd thus their Laws,
> Still finding and correcting Flaws,
> They mended by Inconstancy
> Faults, which no Prudence could foresee.

Notes

I am indebted to June Donaldson, Lex Donaldson, Erich Frese, Cornelia Hegele, Theo Hermann, Matthias Klimmer, Martin Selchert, Heinz-Klaus Stahl, Peter

Rhetoric and Myth in Management Fashion
Alfred Kieser

Walgenbach, and two anonymous reviewers for helpful comments on earlier drafts of this article.
1   Rhetoric is commonly defined as the skill of bringing about consent in problems which cannot be solved by conclusive proof alone.
2   A myth is a tale in which the existence of complex phenomena is traced back to magical or godly powers.

References

Abrahamson, E. (1993) 'Management Fashion', paper presented at the EGOS Colloquium, Paris, 6–8 July.

Abrahamson, E. (1996) 'Management Fashion', *Academy of Management Review* 21: 254–85.

Andersen, H. C. (1951) *Fairy Tales, Vol. 1*, edited by S. Larsen. London: Edmund Ward.

Anspach, K. (1967) *The Why of Fashion*. Ames: Iowa State University Press.

Aristotle (1992) *Poetics*, edited by A. Rorty. Princeton, CT: Princeton University Press.

Astley, W.G. and Zammuto, R.F. (1992) 'Organization Science, Managers, and Language Games', *Organization Science* 3: 443–60.

Barber, B. and Lobel, L.S. (1952) 'Fashion in Women's Clothes and the American Social System', *Social Forces* 31: 124–31.

Barthes, R. (1990) *The Fashion System*. Berkeley: University of California Press.

Bartlett, C.A. and Ghoshal, S. (1989) *Managing Across Borders: The Transnational Solution*. London: Hutchinson.

Berger, A.A. (1992) *Reading Matter: Multidisciplinary Perspectives on Material Culture*. New Brunswick: Transaction.

Blumberg, P. (1974) 'The Decline and Fall of the Status Symbol: Some Thoughts on Status in a Post-Industrialist Society', *Social Problems* 21: 480–98.

Blumenberg, H. (1979) *Arbeit am Mythos*. Frankfurt am Main: Suhrkamp.

Blumer, H. (1969) 'Fashion: From Class Differentiation to Collective Selection', *Sociological Quarterly* 10: 275–91.

Bourdieu, P. (1993) 'The Metamorphosis of Tastes', in P. Bourdieu (ed.) *Sociology in Question*, pp. 108–16. London: Sage.

Bourdieu, P. (1994) *Distinction: A Social Critique of the Judgement of Taste*. Cambridge, MA: Harvard University Press.

Brunsson, N. and Olsen, J.P. (1993) *The Reforming Organization*. London/New York: Routledge.

Byrne, J.A. (1986) 'Business Fads: What's In—and Out', *Business Week* 20 January: 53.

Carey, A. (1967) 'The Hawthorne Studies: A Radical Criticism', *American Sociological Review* 32: 403–16.

Champy, J. (1994a) 'Quantensprünge sind angesagt. Interview mit James Champy', *TopBusiness* 11: 86–94.

Champy, J. (1994b) 'Jeder fünfte fliegt. Interview mit James Champy', *manager magazin* 4: 196–8.

Champy, J. (1995) *Reengineering Management: The Mandate for Leadership*. New York: Harper Business.

Chesbrough, H.W. and Teece, D.J. (1996) 'When is Virtual Virtuous?—Organizing for Innovation', *Harvard Business Review* 74 (Jan.–Feb.): 65–73.

Organization
Articles

Clark, T. and Salaman, G. (1996) 'The Management Guru as Organizational Witch Doctor', *Organization* 3: 85–108.

Cleverly, G. (1973) *Managers and Magic*. Harmondsworth: Penguin.

Cohen, M.D., March, J.G. and Olsen, J.P. (1976) 'People, Problems, Solutions and the Ambiguity of Relevance', in J.G. March and J.P. Olsen (eds) *Ambiguity and Choice in Organizations*, pp. 24–37. Bergen: Universitetsforlaget.

Crozier, M. and Friedberg, E. (1980) *Actors and Systems: The Politics of Collective Action*. Chicago, IL: University of Chicago Press.

Cummings, L.L. (1983) 'The Logics of Management', *Academy of Management Review* 8: 532–8.

Davidow, W.H. and Malone, M.S. (1992) *The Virtual Organization*. New York: Harper-Collins.

Davis, F. (1989) 'Of Maids' Uniforms and Blue Jeans: The Drama of Status Ambivalences in Clothing and Fashion', *Qualitative Sociology* 12: 337–55.

Davis, F. (1992) *Fashion, Culture, and Identity*. Chicago, IL: The University of Chicago Press.

Davis, M.S. (1986) 'The Phenomenology and Rhetoric of Successful Social Science Theories', *Philosophy of Social Science* 16: 285–301.

Doberer, K.K. (1991) *Die Goldmacher. Zehntausend Jahre Alchemie*. Berlin: Ullstein.

Drucker, P. (1977) *People and Performance: The Best of Peter Drucker on Management*. London: Heinemann.

Eccles, R., Nohria, N. and Berkley, J.D. (1992) *Beyond the Hype: Rediscovering the Essence of Management*. Boston, MA: Harvard Business School Press.

Eccles, R. and White, H. (1988) 'Price and Authority in Inter-Profit Center Transactions', *American Journal of Sociology* 94 (Supplement): 17–49.

Eder, K. (1976) *Die Entstehung staatlich organisierter Gesellschaften. Ein Beitrag zu einer Theorie sozialer Evolution*. Frankfurt am Main: Suhrkamp.

Ezzamel, M. and Willmott, H. (1994) 'New Management Thinking', *European Management Journal* 12: 454–61.

Faurschou, G. (1987) 'Fashion and the Cultural Logic of Postmodernity', in A. Kroker and M. Kroker (eds) *Body Invaders: Panic Sex in America*, pp. 78–93. New York: St Martin's Press.

Freeman, F.H. (1985) 'Books that Mean Business: The Management Best Sellers', *Academy of Management Review* 10: 345–9.

Gabriel, Y. and Lang, T. (1995) *The Unmanageable Consumer: Contemporary Consumption and its Fragmentations*. Thousand Oaks, CA: Sage.

Gerken, G. (1994) 'Werbung wandelt sich zum virtuellen Märchen', *Mensch & Büro* 6: 32–40.

Hammer, M. and Champy, J. (1993) *Reengineering the Corporation: A Manifesto for Business Revolution*. New York: Harper.

Hassinger, H. (1951) *Johann Joachim Becher 1635–1682. Ein Beitrag zur Geschichte des Merkantilismus*. Vienna: Adolf Holzhausen.

Huczynski, A. (1993) *Management Gurus*. London: Routledge.

Kaiser, S.B., Nagasawa, R.H. and Hutton, S.S. (1991) 'Fashion, Postmodernity and Personal Appearance: A Symbolic Interactionist Formulation', *Symbolic Interaction* 14(2): 165–85.

King, C.W. and Ring, L.J. (1980) 'Fashion Theory: The Dynamics of Style and Taste, Adoption and Diffusion', *Advances in Consumer Research* 7: 13–16.

König, R. (1985) *Menschleit auf dem Laufsteg. Die Mode im Zivilisationsprozeß*. München: Hanser.

72

Rhetoric and Myth in Management Fashion
Alfred Kieser

Lohse, J. (1994) 'Veränderungen, die an das Fundament gehen', *Süddeutsche Zeitung* 24–26 December: V1/9.

Luhmann, N. (1982) *Soziologische Aufklärung 2. Aufsätze zur Theorie der Gesellschaft*, 2nd edn. Opladen: Westdeutscher Verlag.

Luhmann, N. and Fuchs, P. (1989) *Reden und Schweigen*. Frankfurt am Main: Suhrkamp.

Mandeville, B. (1924) *The Fable of the Bees: Or, Private Vices, Public Benefits. The First Volume*. (Facsimile of the edition of 1724). London: Oxford University Press.

March, J.G. (1981) 'Footnotes to Organizational Change', *Administrative Science Quarterly* 26: 563–77.

March, J.G. (1991) 'Organizational Consultants and Organizational Research', *Journal of Applied Communication Research* 19: 20–31.

March, J.G. (1994) *A Primer on Decision Making: How Decisions Happen*. New York: Free Press.

March, J.G. and Olsen, J.P. (1986) 'Garbage Can Models of Decision Making in Organizations', in J.G. March and R. Weissinger-Baylon (eds) *Ambiguity and Command*, pp. 11–36. Cambridge, MA: Ballinger.

McCracken, G. (1985) 'The Trickle-Down Theory Rehabilitated', in M.R. Solomon (ed.) *The Psychology of Fashion*, pp. 39–54. Lexington, MA: Lexington Books.

Meyer, J.W. and Rowan, B. (1977) 'Institutional Organizations: Formal Structure as Myth and Ceremony', *American Journal of Sociology* 83: 340–63.

Padgett, V.R. and Jorgenson, D.O. (1982) 'Superstition and Economic Threat: Germany 1918–1940', *Personality and Social Psychology Bulletin* 8: 736–41.

Pascale, R.T. (1990) *Managing on the Edge: How Successful Companies Use Conflict to Stay Ahead*. London: Viking.

Peters, T. (1992) *Liberation Management: Necessary Disorganization for the Nanosecond Nineties*. London: Macmillan.

Peters, T.J. and Waterman, R.H. (1983) *In Search of Excellence*. New York: Harper & Row.

Pinchot, G. (1985) *Intrapreneuring*. New York: Harper & Row.

Pondy, L.R. (1983) 'The Role of Metaphors and Myths in Organization and the Facilitation of Change', in L.R. Pondy, P.J. Frost, G. Morgan and T.C. Dandridge (eds) *Organizational Symbolism*, pp. 157–67. Greenwich, CT: JAI Press.

Quintilian, M.F. (1920) *Instutio Oratoria*, transl. H.E. Butler. Cambridge, MA: Harvard University Press.

Reich, R.B. (1991) *The Work of Nations: Preparing Ourselves for 21st-Century Capitalism*. New York: Knopf.

Richardson, J. and Kroeber, A.L. (1952) 'Three Centuries of Women's Dress Fashions: A Quantitative Analysis', in A.L. Kroeber (ed.) *The Nature of Culture*, pp. 358–72. Chicago, IL: University of Chicago Press.

Robinson, D.E. (1976) 'Fashion in Shaving and Trimming of the Beard: The Men of the *Illustrated London News*', *American Journal of Sociology* 81: 1133–41.

Rogers, E.M. (1983) *Diffusion of Innovations*, 3rd edn. New York: Free Press.

Schnierer, T. (1995) *Modewandel und Gesellschaft. Die Dynamik von 'in' und 'out'*. Opladen: Leske & Budrich.

Simmel, G. (1957) 'Fashion', *American Journal of Sociology* 62: 541–58.

Sombart, W. (1902) *Wirtschaft und Mode*. Wiesbaden: Bergmann.

Spencer, H. (1888) *The Principles of Sociology*, Vol. 2. New York: D. Appleton.

Organization
Articles

Stewart, R., Barsoux, J.L., Kieser, A., Ganter, H.D. and Walgenbach, P. (1994) *Managing in Britain and Germany*. London: Macmillan.

Veblen, T. (1949) *The Theory of the Leisure Class: An Economic Study of Institutions*. London: George Allen & Unwin.

Victor, B. and Stephens, C. (1994) 'The Dark Side of the New Organizational Forms: An Editorial Essay', *Organization Science* 5: 479–82.

Vinken, B. (1993) *Mode nach der Mode. Kleid und Geist am Ende des 20 Jahrhunderts*. Frankfurt am Main: Fischer Taschenbuch.

Weick, K.E. (1995) *Sensemaking in Organizations*. London: Sage.

Williams, K., Haslam, C., Williams, J., Cutler, T., Adcroft, A. and Johal, S. (1992) 'Against Lean Production', *Economy and Society* 21: 321–54.

Womack, J.P., Jones, D.T. and Roos, D. (1990) *The Machine that Changed the World*. New York: Rawson.

Wrege, C.D. and Perroni, A.G. (1974) 'Taylor's Pig-Tale: A Historical Analysis of Frederic W. Taylor's Pig-Iron Experiments', *Academy of Management Journal* 17: 6–27.

74

[7]

A Fantasy Theme Analysis of
Peter Senge's Learning Organization

Bradley G. Jackson
Victoria University of Wellington

When it was first articulated in *The Fifth Discipline*, Peter Senge's vision of the learning organization was one of a number of competing conceptions. This article examines what it was about Senge's vision that enabled it to catch on and be assimilated so rapidly and pervasively into everyday business discourse. The method used in this study is fantasy theme analysis, a dramatistically based method of rhetorical criticism developed by Ernest Bormann that is rooted in symbolic convergence theory. The analysis reveals four interrelated fantasy themes that form the dramatic building blocks of the rhetorical vision of the learning organization. The article examines the organizational and rhetorical strategies that Senge has deployed to sustain widespread interest in his vision.

Although the term *learning organization* has in the past decade become one of the most widely used and, many would argue, abused terms in the business lexicon, it is by no means a new concept. Garratt (1995) suggests that, although the desire to create organizations that can consciously cope with change by learning continuously can be traced back to antiquity, "all the necessary conditions to create both the intellectual and practical basis of a learning organization were in place by 1947" (p. 25). Pedler, Burgoyne, and Boydell (1997) have singled out the contributions of Revans (1979), Argyris and Schon (1978), Bateson (1972), Harrison (1995), Dixon (1994), Peters and Waterman (1982), and Deming (1986) in shaping the idea of the learning organization, organizational learning, and their own construct, the learning company. These contributions notwithstanding, it is Peter Senge's (1990a) best-selling book, *The Fifth Disci-*

An earlier version of this article was presented at the Third International Conference on Organizational Discourse held at King's College, London, July 1998. I would like to thank the editors of this special issue, Tom Keenoy, Bob Marshak, Cliff Oswick, and David Grant, for their constructive criticism and expert guidance. Thanks also to Douglas Bowie, John Burgoyne, Deborah Jones, and Kevin Peterson for their helpful suggestions on earlier drafts of this article.

Bradley G. Jackson is a senior lecturer at Victoria University of Wellington, New Zealand.

194   THE JOURNAL OF APPLIED BEHAVIORAL SCIENCE   June 2000

pline that has, in their minds, "been largely responsible for bringing the learning organization into the mainstream of business thinking" (Pedler et al., 1997, p. 196).

When it was first articulated in the early 1990s, Senge's vision of the learning organization was neither novel nor original. He was one of a number of academics and consultants on both sides of the Atlantic actively working on and promoting the learning organization concept (Garratt, 1990; Garvin, 1993; Lessem, 1991; Pedler et al., 1997; Watkins & Marsick, 1994). This begs the question of what it was about Senge's vision in particular that enabled it to catch on and be rapidly assimilated into everyday business discourse in such a substantial way. This article attempts to answer this question by conducting an analysis of the discourse that developed around Senge and his particular conception of the learning organization. The method used is fantasy theme analysis, a dramatistically based method of rhetorical criticism developed by Ernest Bormann (1972). Fantasy themes form the building blocks of compelling dramatistic interpretations of reality, which are described as rhetorical visions. This article describes four interrelated fantasy themes that, it is argued, run through Senge's rhetorical vision of the learning organization. It then looks at how Senge, having successfully created and articulated his vision, has addressed the challenge of maintaining and sustaining interest in this vision by a significant proportion of the notoriously capricious and fickle corporate community (Grint, 1997; Micklethwait & Wooldridge, 1996).

FANTASY THEME ANALYSIS

Fantasy theme analysis is a method of rhetorical criticism underpinned by a general theory of communication called symbolic convergence theory, which attempts to account for the creation, raising, and maintenance of group consciousness through communication (Bormann, 1983). Elsewhere, I have described in detail the origins, assumptions, applications, and major criticisms of this theory (Jackson, 1997) and so will confine my review here to a brief discussion of the fantasy theme analysis method and how I applied it to Senge's conception of the learning organization. The starting point for a critic using this method is neither the speaker, nor the audience, nor the channel, nor the situation, but the message. Bormann argues that the message has an essentially dramatistic form. It is filled with all of the elements that are found in a drama: settings, characters, and actions. Dramatizing moments "chain" within small face-to-face groups and, through the technologies of mass media, to and from small and large groups. The composite dramas that catch up large groups of people in a symbolic reality are called rhetorical visions.

A rhetorical vision is constructed from fantasy themes, which are the means through which the interpretation is accomplished in communication. They are manifested in the form of a word, a phrase, or a statement that interprets events in the past, envisions events in the future, or depicts current events that are removed in time and/or space from the actual activities of the group. In contrast to normal human experience, fantasy themes are organized and artistic. They are "the creative and imaginative interpretations of events that fulfil a psychological or rhetorical need" (Bormann, 1976, p. 434). Bormann distinguishes between setting themes, which depict where the action is taking place or the place where the characters act out their roles; character themes, which describe the agents or actors in the drama, ascribe qualities to them, assign motives to them, and portray them as having certain characteristics; and action themes, which can also be called plotlines, that deal with the action of the drama.

Popular management fashions such as excellence, total quality management, reengineering, and the learning organization that have recently gripped the corporate imagination can be fruitfully conceptualized as rhetorical visions in terms of their form and the function they fulfil for managers and organizations (Jackson, 1998). The sanctioning agent of the rhetorical vision is a source that justifies its acceptance by members of the rhetorical community that coalesce around the vision. With respect to management fashions, the management guru acts as the authoritative voice or guarantor of the rhetorical vision in making the vision legitimate and credible in the minds of managers (Burgoyne, 1996). The various processes by which the guru articulates and sanctions a management fashion have been explored in detail in case studies of Michael Hammer and James Champy and the reengineering movement (Jackson, 1996) and Stephen Covey and the effectiveness movement (Jackson, 1999). In this article, I will explore the critical role that Senge plays as the sanctioning agent legitimating the rhetorical vision of the learning organization.

Bormann strongly asserts that a single text is insufficient to conduct a proper fantasy theme critique. The effective critic, in his view, tracks fantasy themes across discourse situations, because only then can genuine thematizing be established (Hart, 1989). For the purposes of this study, I have drawn on rhetorical acts performed by Senge at three satellite videoconferences that I attended as well as numerous rhetorical artifacts, including two books, 17 articles, and one audiocassette produced by Senge and his associates. In addition, I analyzed a total of 65 articles written about him and the rhetorical vision of the learning organization that he has fostered.

This study followed the five steps for conducting fantasy theme analyses that have been described by Foss (1989). First, I looked for evidence that the rhetorical vision of the learning organization was being shared within particular rhetorical communities. For these, the vision serves to "sustain the member's sense of community, to impel them strongly to action and to provide them with a social reality with heroes, villains, emotions and attitudes" (Bormann, 1972, p. 398). I sorted through various newspaper, professional, and trade journal articles looking for the use of symbolic cues such as catch phrases and slogans (e.g., "the fifth discipline," "personal mastery") that originally had been coined by Senge and had now fallen into regular currency. My analysis revealed that senior executives, human resource development and training professionals, and educational administrators have been the most vocal supporters of this vision in the realm of public discourse. Second, the rhetorical acts and artifacts were coded to isolate any recurrent fantasy themes. This required a careful reading of the artifacts, sentence by sentence, to pick out references to settings, characters, and actions that might form the basis for major fantasy themes. In the third step, patterns in the fantasy themes were sought out. Major themes were isolated from minor themes by virtue of

196   THE JOURNAL OF APPLIED BEHAVIORAL SCIENCE   June 2000

how frequently they were referred to. From these, the rhetorical vision of the learning organization was constructed. Fourth, I began to explore the motives for the participants in the rhetorical vision by examining which of the fantasy themes received the most emphasis and which appeared to have the most impact on the other themes in the vision. Finally, the rhetorical vision was compared and contrasted with other management fashions with particular reference to their ability to meet the needs and expectations of their participants.

THE RHETORICAL VISION OF
THE LEARNING ORGANIZATION

In analyzing Senge's rhetorical vision of the learning organization, four major fantasy themes were identified. These are summarized in Table 1. The two setting themes reveal that the drama of the learning organization unfolds at opposite ends of the continuum of human experience. At the macro level, the "living in an unsustainable world" theme creates a general sense of urgency for considering and accepting the vision as it becomes tied with the ongoing debate and concerns about the deteriorating state of the earth's environmental system and the "crisis of the soul" that has received widespread media attention in North America. At the micro level, the "working it out within the micro world" setting theme shows the way forward by depicting individuals coming to grips with these systemic issues through the liberating technology of computer-based simulation. Moving to the who of the rhetorical vision, the character theme labeled as "the manager's new work" lays out a number of new roles that Senge argues need to be played by individuals at various levels within the learning organization. In terms of what is taking place within the drama of the learning organization, an action theme dubbed "getting control but not controlling" provides a most compelling script for these new actors to follow within Senge's organizational drama.

Setting Theme: Living in an Unsustainable World

Senge situates many organizational woes in a broader societal context, arguing that "organizations are microcosms of the larger society. Thus, at the heart of any serious effort to alter how organizations operate lies a concern with addressing the basic dysfunctions of our larger culture" (Kofman & Senge, 1993, p. 7). These problems are rooted in a reductionist philosophy and mechanical thinking that have provided the basis for many of America's successes in the past. Paradoxically, Kofman and Senge (1993) observe,

> The very same skills of separation, analysis, and control that gave us the power to shape our environment are producing ecological and social crises in our outer worlds, and psychological and spiritual crises in our inner world. When we begin to understand the origins of our problems, we begin to see that the "existential crisis" of early 20th century philosophy and the "environmental crisis" of late 20th century ecology are inseparable—caused by the co-evolution of fragmentary world views, social structures, lifestyles, and technology. (pp. 10-11)

TABLE 1
The Key Rhetorical Elements of Peter Senge's
Vision of the Learning Organization

Technical Term	Definition	The Learning Organization
Rhetorical vision	A composite drama that catches up large groups of people into a common symbolic reality	The learning organization
Setting theme	Depicts where the action is taking place or the place where the characters act out their roles	"Living in an unsustainable world" and "Working it out within the micro world"
Character theme	Describes the agents or actors in the drama, ascribes qualities to them, and portrays them as having certain characteristics	"The manager's new work"
Action theme	Deals with the action of the drama or plotlines	"Getting control but not controlling"
Symbolic cue	A code word, phrase, slogan, or gesture that triggers previously shared fantasies and emotions	"The fifth discipline"
Sanctioning agent (or agents)	Legitimizes the symbolic reality portrayed by a rhetorical vision	Peter Senge
Rhetorical community	A group of individuals who share a common symbolic ground and respond to the messages in ways that are in tune with the rhetorical vision	Senior executives, human resource developers and trainers, and educational administrators
Master analogue	Deep structure embedded within the rhetorical vision	Social

Senge illustrates this paradox by pointing to the popularity of the movie *Dances With Wolves* (Costner, 1990), which, with its depiction of the destruction of an indigenous culture, has resonated with Americans' sense that "they have lost a particular sensibility of what it means to live together as part of a larger natural order" (Senge, 1995a, p. 227). Pulled between the new and old world orders, he suggests that Costner's heroic lonely outsider is a character to whom an audience that is similarly riddled with existential and environmental doubt can well relate.

In discussing the systemic problems being faced by American organizations, Senge makes frequent reference to a system archetype called the tragedy of the commons that was first identified by ecologist Garrett Hardin (1968). This archetype is seen by Senge as being especially useful for dealing directly with problems where apparently logical local decision making can become completely illogical for the larger system (Senge, 1990a). By way of example, he describes the desertification of the Sahel region in sub-Saharan Africa that was caused by rampant overgrazing encouraged by unusually high rainfalls and international aid assistance. In a neat rhetorical move, Senge makes the claim that the tragedy of the commons is not only confined to ecological disasters but also to organizations. Corporations, he suggests, have many depletable commons to share, including financial capital, productive capital, technology, community reputation, customer good will, and the morale and competence of employees. When a company decentralizes, local divisions compete with each other for these limited resources.

In referring to broader environmental concerns, Senge succeeds not only in grabbing the attention of readers already preoccupied with impending global ecological doom and disaster but also in distinguishing his message from those of other management gurus who, by and large, studiously ignore this issue. Generally, the broader setting used by management gurus encompasses the competitive pressures of globalization and international trade but not environmental system dynamics. By making this connection, Senge develops a setting theme with its own built-in, mass-media-fuelled sense of significance and urgency. It provides an impressive and readily identifiable backdrop against which his special brand of organizational drama can unfold. No one can, therefore, argue that the stakes are not high when creating a learning organization. This is work that might ultimately help to save the earth, let alone the organization. For Senge, there is no doubt from which sector the men with the white hats will come riding in to deal with global environmental problems.

> My deepest belief is that the way we operate the world as a whole is not sustainable. . . . We're basically living off our capital and compromising the future well-being of generations to come. It's ironic that business is the most likely institution (to master change), but it has the greatest capacity to reinvent itself. (cited in Driben, 1995, p. 62)

Action Theme: Getting Control but Not Controlling

Although Senge believes that it will ultimately be the private sector, and large-scale corporations, in particular, that will have to develop the ability to deal with and address many of the societal woes that we are currently facing, he is quite clear that they will have to take on quite different organizational forms and be led in quite different ways to meet these challenges. For example, in an interview, Senge (1996b) makes the claim that

> the leadership challenges in building learning organizations represent a microcosm of the leadership challenges of our times: how do communities, be they multinational corporations or societies, productively confront complex systemic issues where hierarchical authority is inadequate for change? None of today's most pressing issues will be resolved through hierarchical authority. In all these issues, there are no simple causes, no simple "fixes." There is no one villain to blame. There will be no magic pill. Significant change will require imagination, perseverance, dialogue, deep caring, and a willingness to change on the part of millions of people. The challenges of systemic change where hierarchy is inadequate will, I believe, push us to new views of leadership based on new principles. These challenges cannot be met by isolated heroic leaders. They will require a unique mix of different people, in different positions, who lead in different ways. Changes will be required in our traditional models. (p. 11)

In Senge's vision, organizations will increasingly have to become localized in that they will seek to extend the maximum degree of authority and power as far away from the top or center as possible. "Localness," a cornerstone of the learning organization, gives individuals the freedom to act, to try out their own ideas and be responsible for producing their own results. It also enables organizations to respond in an appropriate and timely fashion to rapid changes within the marketplace. Despite its obvious advantages, Senge warns that unenlightened senior managers may be unwilling to give up control of the decision-making process for fear of losing the thing they most cherish (i.e., power) and make themselves obsolete. Moreover, they are concerned that, by pursuing localness, the organization may lose its capacity for control.

To these concerns, Senge (1990a) responds, "Just because no one is 'in control' does not mean that there is 'no control' " (p. 292). By investing in the five disciplines of the learning organization, Senge suggests that organizations can maintain control at the local level through a process of "control by learning." The improved quality of thinking and the new capacity for reflection and team learning, combined with an ability to develop shared visions and understanding of complex business issues, will allow learning organizations to be more effectively controlled and coordinated than their hierarchical predecessors. He adds rhetorical weight to his localness argument by suggesting that the traditional perception that someone "up there" is in control is based on an illusion that it would be possible for anyone to master the dynamic and detailed complexity of an organization from the top. Taking on three icons of American business, he stridently observes,

> The days when a Watson or Henry Ford or Alfred B. Sloan "fought for the organization" have long passed. The world is simply too complex to figure out from the top, and too rapidly changing to abide with the slow bureaucratic decision-making processes that come with the top-down decision making in complex organizations. The breakdown of the authoritarian structures is universal, not only in business but in the world of public affairs as well, as can be seen only too well from the demise of the Eastern bloc governments. (cited in Meen & Keough, 1992, p. 78)

Although his localness argument is by no means unique among management gurus, the nonthreatening and generally inoffensive way in which it is presented makes it a reasonably palatable action theme that promises some form of transcendence for both sides of the labor-management divide. Workers are presented an essentially emancipatory vision within which they can take independent action and realize their full potential through learning, unencumbered by formal management controls imposed from above. Managers, on the other hand, can take comfort from the fact that the world is so complicated now that they cannot be expected to be accountable for it. They can also rest assured that control will be maintained in a constructive and tolerably orderly manner. Besides, Senge has some very important new work for these managers to do within the learning organization, which is considerably more meaningful than the work that they have traditionally done within hierarchically based organizations.

Character Theme: The Manager's New Work

Prior to the publication of *The Fifth Discipline*, Senge published an article in MIT's in-house publication, *Sloan Management Review*, titled "The Leader's New Work" (1990b). In this article, Senge laid out many of the key ideas contained within the book

200   THE JOURNAL OF APPLIED BEHAVIORAL SCIENCE   June 2000

and discussed three new roles that leaders would have to play to build a learning organization: designer, teacher, and steward. Although these roles have antecedents in the ways leaders have contributed to building organizations in the past, Senge notes that they take on new meaning within the learning organization and demand new skills and tools. Likening the organization to an ocean liner, Senge observes that most senior executives readily relate their role to the captain, navigator, helmsman, engineer, or social director. However, they rarely identify their role as the designer of the ship. In this role, Senge charges senior executives with three main tasks: build a foundation of purpose and core values for the organization; develop the policies, strategies, and structures that translate these guiding ideas into business directions; and create effective learning processes through which the policies, strategies, and structures can be continually improved.

In their role as teachers, Senge (1990b) urges executives to stop trying to be the authoritarian expert whose job is to teach the correct view of reality and begin to "help people restructure their views of reality to see beyond the superficial conditions and events into the underlying causes of problems—and therefore to see the new possibilities for shaping the future" (p. 12). Max de Pree, the retired chief executive officer of Hermann Miller and author of the popular business book *Leadership Is an Art* (1989), is frequently held up by Senge as an exemplar of an executive who was particularly effective in this role.

The third and final new role of the leader, as steward, is, according to Senge, the subtlest role, which is almost solely a matter of attitude. The leader's sense of stewardship operates on two levels: stewardship for the people he or she leads and stewardship for the larger purpose or mission that underlies the enterprise. Quoting Robert Greenleaf, Senge (1990b) argues that

> the servant leader *is* servant first. . . . It begins with the natural feeling that one wants to serve, to serve *first*. This conscious choice brings one to aspire to lead. That person is sharply different from one who is leader first, perhaps because of the need to assuage an unusual power drive or to acquire material possessions. (p. 12)

More recently, Senge has begun to lay out roles that should be played by individuals at other levels within the learning organization. Specifically, he identifies two other leadership roles: the local line leaders and the internal networkers. The former are heads of organizational units that are microcosms of the larger organization; local line leaders have enough autonomy to be able to undertake meaningful change that is independent of the larger organization. The key role played by the local line leaders is to "sanction significant practical experiments and to lead through active participation in those experiments" (Senge, 1996a, p. 3). In addition to playing a key role in the design and implementation of learning processes, local line leaders often become teachers once these learning processes become established. Although Senge argues that there is much to be gained by taking on this role, he also warns potential local line leaders of the risks they run. He says, "Improved results are often threatening to others, and the more dramatic the improvement, the greater the threat. Large organizations have complex forces that maintain the status quo and inhibit the spread of new ideas" (p. 4).

Senge offers the cautionary tale of Fred Simon, a project manager on the new Lincoln Continental at Ford Motor Company and a champion of the learning organization. Through the use of such tools as Chris Argyris's ladder of inference, Senge describes how Simon's team of engineers was able to break every internal product development record at Ford. Despite this impressive achievement, Simon was passed over for promotion and was asked to retire early. He believes that his enthusiasm for the learning organization was a factor in his early retirement. The moral that was drawn from this story was that Simon "should have taken the time to explain the benefits of the learning organization to key people in the top ranks" (cited in Dumaine, 1994, p. 155).

The other key leadership role that is identified by Senge is that of the internal networker, otherwise referred to as internal community builder or seed carrier. Typically, this role is played by internal consultants, trainers, human resources staff, or frontline workers such as engineers, sales representatives, and shop stewards. Of critical importance is their ability to move freely around the organization and their high accessibility to many parts of the organization. According to Senge, their primary asset is their lack of power. Because they do not have any positional authority, they do not pose an obvious threat to management, but they are able to exploit the informal networks "through which information and stories flow and how innovative practices naturally diffuse within organizations" (Senge, 1996a, p. 6). The first function of the internal networker is to identify local line managers who have the power to take action and who are predisposed to developing new learning capabilities. They then connect people of like minds to each other's learning efforts. Senge illustrates how this is done with the example of an informal "leaders of learning" group that was formed at Ford Motor Company by local line leaders and internal networkers who wanted to share learnings and serve as a strategic leadership body.

In addition to providing powerful setting and action themes, Senge also develops a complete and well-integrated character theme that can enable individuals at various levels and within varying functions in the organization to transcend their current roles. Within this character theme, clear and inviting roles are scripted and described. Each is accompanied by a few successful role models who repeatedly appear in his accounts and provide added confidence that this role is not only practicable but also well worth aspiring too.

Setting Theme: Working It Out Within the Micro World

Early in *The Fifth Discipline*, Senge (1990a) devotes an entire chapter to an exposition of the "beer game" that was first developed in the 1960s at MIT and has been played "on five continents, among people of all ages, nationalities, cultural origins and vastly varied business backgrounds" (p. 41). Senge notes that, irrespective of the players' backgrounds or origins, the same crises ensue in the game with respect to the production, distribution, and consumption of beer. These crises graphically illustrate the underlying barriers to implementing a learning organization, which are the fragmentation of problem solving, an overemphasis on competition to the exclusion of collaboration, and a tendency of organizations to experiment or innovate only when compelled to change by outside forces (Kofman & Senge, 1993). Senge argues that, in

202   THE JOURNAL OF APPLIED BEHAVIORAL SCIENCE   June 2000

addition to making these barriers visible, micro worlds like the beer game can be a critical technology for implementing the disciplines of the learning organization.

Micro world is a term coined by Seymour Papert, a media technology professor at MIT, to describe an interactive computerized environment that simulates a real-world situation. According to Senge, micro worlds can help managers and their management teams begin to learn about their most important systemic issues by compressing time and space so that it becomes possible to experiment and to learn what the consequences of their decisions are in the future and in distant parts of the organization. Increasingly sophisticated computer technology is helping to create what Senge describes as a new type of managerial practice field for management teams. These are places where teams will learn how to learn together while engaging their most important business issues. Drawing parallels with sports teams and the performing arts, Senge questions why it is that, unlike athletes and musicians, in most organizations, "people only perform. They rarely get to practice, especially together" (Kofman & Senge, 1993, p. 19). Building micro worlds will help managers practice by "helping us to rediscover the power of learning through play" or, more correctly, "relevant play" (Senge, 1990a, p. 315).

To lend substance to his argument for micro worlds and simulation games in general, Senge provides numerous case studies of organizations that have been able to make important breakthroughs with them. Perhaps the most celebrated case is the claims learning laboratory that was built for Hanover Insurance by a systems group from MIT. Managers at Hanover felt that internal practices were contributing to claim settlements that seemed to be significantly higher than was fair (Hampden-Turner, 1992). By playing the "claims game" within this micro world, Senge shows how managers were able to pinpoint the problem of escalating costs to the quality of the claims settlements that were being made. Senge (1990a) recounts the all-important "aha" moment with obvious relish: "Suddenly there is a wave of realization through the room: *If it weren't for all of those overpriced claims settlements, we'd all have more money to build our departments to what they really need to be!*" (p. 329). Later, he shows how dependent the managers had become on their micro world, with the quote by one of the participants: "So what if we went back to the micro world . . . and tried out some other possible strategies" (p. 331). In a later account of this case, Senge informs us somewhat tersely that the takeover of Hanover Insurance by State Mutual Insurance uprooted the management support for the lab so that it never had the opportunity to demonstrate its full value in terms of the anticipatory learning it had generated (Senge & Fulmer, 1993).

In advocating micro worlds as a critical component of the learning organization vision, Senge provides managers with a powerful setting theme within which they can find a safe haven for dealing with and regaining control of a world that has seemingly gone out of control. In this respect, he has literally presented managers with an opportunity to transport themselves out of their immediate time and space situations to the relative comfort of a world in which problems can be properly managed and even played with alongside one's colleagues in a safe and sealed off environment. The micro-world theme acts as a powerful transcendental antidote to the "unsustainable world" setting theme that emerges from Senge's writing, which stresses that collectively we have lost control of the modernist project and need to act immediately. As Senge and Fulmer (1993) somewhat invitingly promise, "By utilizing micro worlds to participate in the anticipation of these consequences, created with system dynamics, managers and their organizations can discover a new capacity for gaining control of their destinies" (p. 33). Giving the micro-world-fantasy theme even more rhetorical weight is the allure of technology, which, of course, will only continue to get better. Despite the setbacks that have prevented micro worlds from reaching their full potential, Senge (1990a) suggests that, with even more sophisticated technology, "future micro worlds for teams will allow managers to play out their real-world roles and understand more deeply how those roles interact" (p. 337). Looking even further ahead, the fantasy may one day become the reality, "when practice fields are cultivated in an organization for a sustained period of time, learning in simuworlds and micro worlds becomes seamlessly integrated with the real organizations they shadow" (Keys, Fulmer, & Stumpf, 1996, p. 48).

THE UNDERLYING MASTER ANALOGUE

Bormann and his colleagues have observed that rhetorical visions will generally reflect a deep structure that is embedded in one of three master analogues: the righteous, social, or pragmatic.

> A rhetorical vision based on a righteous master analogue emphasizes the correct way of doing things with its concerns about right and wrong, proper and improper, superior and inferior, moral and immoral, just and unjust. A rhetorical vision with a social master analogue reflects primary human relations, as it keys on friendship, trust, caring, comradeship, compatibility, family ties, brotherhood, sisterhood, and humaneness. A vision with a pragmatic master analogue stresses expediency, utility, efficiency, parsimony, simplicity, practicality, cost effectiveness, and minimal involvement. (Cragan & Shields, 1992, p. 202)

I would contend that Senge's collectivist vision of the learning organization holds lingering generative power for researchers and practitioners alike because of its underlying social master analogue. The vision resonates with a substantial constituency of individuals who are seeking a higher level of meaning and purpose in the work that they do and the relationships they have with the people they work with (Burgoyne, 1996; Dovey, 1997). In this vision, the individual can only truly realize his or her full self through social interaction with other individuals who are working toward a common cause. To Senge (1995b), the cause is clear:

> The fundamental purpose of any organization is not to make a profit. A social mission is the essence of a successful business; doing something that makes a difference to somebody. . . . Business is about making a better world. Everyone needs to live their lives in the service of their highest aspirations. (p. 18)

Senge's altruistic vision of what organizations could and should be doing differs significantly from competing visions of organizational effectiveness that have been actively promoted during the 1990s by two other prominent management gurus.

Undergirded by a pragmatic master analogue, Michael Hammer's rhetorical vision of reengineering tells managers they have to reengineer because it is their only choice (Hammer & Champy, 1993; Jackson, 1996). Rooted in a righteous master analogue, the rhetorical vision of effectiveness articulated by Stephen Covey tells managers they should follow the "seven habits" because it is the right thing to do (Covey, 1989; Jackson, 1999). Senge's vision of the learning organization, by contrast, should be pursued because it is a good thing to do.

SUSTAINING RHETORICAL VISIONS

Since the publication of *The Fifth Discipline* in 1990, Senge has emerged from the relative obscurity of academia to assume full-blown management guru status. Clark and Greatbatch (1999) suggest that a key activity of management gurus is to convince their potential followers that it is their particular ideas that offer the most relevant solution to the immediate problems the potential followers are experiencing and trying to resolve. This activity is not only important during the consciousness-creating phase of a rhetorical vision but also during the subsequent consciousness-raising and consciousness-sustaining phases (Bormann, Cragan, & Shields, 1996). The preceding fantasy theme analysis has revealed the dramatic foundation that serves to make Senge's rhetorical vision of the learning organization such a compelling one for potential followers. But what has Senge done to ensure that his rhetorical vision will continue to sustain interest and stave off the inevitable rejection of another management fashion? I think there are several features of the way in which Senge has gone about organizing his rhetorical vision that are particularly salient when considering this question.

Most management gurus tend to associate themselves with one particular organization with which they assume a figurehead role. Good exemplars would be Franklin Covey Company, Hammer and Company, and the Tom Peters Group. Senge, by contrast, appears to prefer to be loosely linked with numerous organizations in which he takes on a comparatively lower profile role and works in a more collaborative mode (e.g., Innovation Associates and Pegasus Communications). Working with a networked group of academics, executives, and consultants, he formed the MIT Organizational Learning Center (OLC) in 1990 (Fulmer, 1995). Anxious to extend this work beyond its Anglo-American origins, the OLC was re-created in 1998 as the Society for Organizational Learning (SoL), a nonprofit, member-governed organization with global ambitions. In the letter inviting potential individuals and groups to join SoL, Senge and the other two chairpersons show that they are anxious to model the disciplines of the learning organization: "As in all living systems, the growth of SoL as a global network cannot be controlled or pre-determined. . . . Different chapters (fractals) will pursue their own aspirations and issues and will adapt SoL's basic design to the requirements of their social and cultural environment" (Senge, de Geus, & Carstedt, 1998, p. 2). Despite these good intentions, he is cautious about SoL's ability to disseminate the learning organization vision across the globe, observing that "the challenge for all of us at SoL is to manage growth, commitment, community, and scope without watering down the principles that make organizational learning a valuable objective for organizations of all types" (cited in Fulmer & Keys, 1998, p. 41).

In addition to his network-building activities, Senge displays a remarkable affinity for publicly reflecting on how and why the learning organization was socially constructed as the next management fashion. Recounting what motivated him to write *The Fifth Discipline*, he recalls,

> It sort of hit me one morning about three years ago while I was meditating that the learning organization was going to be a hot area in business. I had already watched a fad cycle come and go related to work I had been doing for years with Innovation Associates. We had been teaching courses in personal mastery and leadership since 1979, and we all sat on the sidelines and watched as other people wrote about vision, empowerment and alignment—ideas that we had been teaching for years. That morning as I meditated it dawned on me that it was not O.K. to sit on the sidelines this time. It was time for a book on the subject of learning organizations, and I wanted to get it out before the whole world was talking about them. I didn't want to define the territory; it is really too broad for one book. My hope was to establish a point of view of learning organizations that might serve as a reference point. (cited in Galaghan, 1991, p. 38)

As it turned out, the book has become the reference point for work on the learning organization, selling more than 300,000 copies worldwide. Senge is, however, typically ambivalent about the success of the book, commenting, "I am not even sure that it's such a good idea for the field that this book has been as popular as it has" (cited in Fulmer & Keys, 1998, p. 34).

He also appears to be quite philosophical about the prospect of the learning organization falling out of favor, accepting it as part of the natural cycle in management thinking in which managers embrace new ideas, explore them, and move on to the next ones (Griffith, 1995). Although he is not the first management guru to express concern about his or her concept being consigned to the pile of last year's models, his public statements suggest that he wants his audience to be fully aware of what they are getting into when they decide to embrace the learning organization concept. Perhaps by being explicitly reflexive about the management fashion enterprise and his role within it, Senge hopes that his followers may be more likely to resist the inevitable rejection phase of the cycle and persist with his concepts long after they cease to remain fashionable. The idea is that the learning organization is too important to be treated as another passing fad.

In a rhetorical turn reminiscent of Tom Peters's (1987) opening comments in his book, *Thriving on Chaos*, about there not being any "excellent companies," Senge has stated a number of times that there is, in fact, no such thing as a learning organization. Instead, he states that

> the learning organization is a thing we create in language. Like every linguistic creation, this category is a double-edged sword that can be empowering or tranquilizing. The difference lies in whether we see language as a set of labels that describe a pre-existing reality, or as a medium in which we can articulate new models for living together. (Kofman & Senge, 1993, p. 16)

His unapologetically normative perspective suggests that Senge is more than aware that he is trying to create and sustain a rhetorical vision. He is quite explicit about his aims and objectives:

> We are taking a stand for a vision, for creating a type of organization we would truly like to work within and which can thrive in a world of increasing interdependency and change. It is not what the vision is, but what the vision does that matters. (Kofman & Senge, 1993, p. 16)

On another occasion, he has remarked, "This isn't pie-in-the-sky stuff. I believe nothing motivates change more than a clear vision" (cited in Meen & Keough, 1992, p. 58). There is no apparent attempt on his part to use a rhetorical sleight of hand by having his audience confuse his essentially normative vision with a descriptive vision. However, in the media accounts of the learning organization, these two visions have frequently become blurred and confused.

This confusion is further exacerbated by his attempts to respond to demands by practitioners to make the learning organization more concrete by laying out the steps that are required to create one. His first attempt to address this challenge came in the form of *The Fifth Discipline Fieldbook* that he wrote with a number of his colleagues to answer the repeatedly asked question, "What do we do on Monday morning?" (Senge, Roberts, Ross, Smith, & Kleiner, 1994, p. 5). In the practitioner community, response to this book has been mixed, with the general consensus being that, although it contained some interesting and provocative ideas, it was still not sufficiently practical. Five years later, Senge and his colleagues produced *The Dance of Change*, which is tellingly subtitled *The Challenges of Sustaining Momentum in Learning Organizations* (Senge, Kleiner, Roberts, Roth, & Ross, 1999). The term *dance of change* refers to what the authors describe as the inevitable interplay between growth processes (i.e., the five disciplines) and limiting processes (i.e., the challenges that accompany any change process). It will be interesting to see whether this latest book and the media attention it receives has the dramatic qualities required to reignite and sustain interest in the learning organization vision over the longer haul.

CONCLUSION

The learning organization continues to inspire a large and growing body of literature in both academic and practitioner journals. Much of this work seeks to build, test, and refine the rhetorical vision of the learning organization (DiBella & Nevis, 1998; Jashapara, 1993; Jones & Hendry, 1994; Starkey, 1996), whereas a sizable portion is devoted to critiquing the vision on instrumental, theoretical, moral, and political grounds (Coopey, 1995; Fenwick, 1998; Flood, 1999; Torbert, 1994; Tsang, 1997; Victor & Stephens, 1994). However, comparatively little attention has been paid to understanding why the concept, particularly as it has been formulated by Senge, has attracted so much interest and, in comparison to a number of other management fashions, has demonstrated considerably more staying power in the realm of managerial discourse. This article has sought to redress this imbalance by conducting a fantasy theme analysis of the rhetorical vision of the learning organization that has been created and disseminated by Peter Senge and his colleagues. The analysis has suggested that it is the dramatic qualities of his socially rooted vision, that is, its ability to inspire followers to see themselves actively engaged in building a learning organization, that have helped it to stand out from other competing conceptions. In addition, Senge has been shown to be an adept and agile sanctioning agent who, by putting into practice much of what he preaches, has been able to sustain widespread interest in his rhetorical vision.

REFERENCES

Argyris, C., & Schon, D. A. (1978). *Organizational learning: A theory in action perspective.* Reading, MA: Addison-Wesley.

Bateson, G. (1972). *Steps to an ecology of mind.* San Francisco: Chandler.

Bormann, E. G. (1972). Fantasy and rhetorical vision: The rhetorical criticism of social reality. *Quarterly Journal of Speech, 58,* 396-407.

Bormann, E. G. (1976). General and specific theories of communication. In J. L. Golden, G. F. Berquist, & W. E. Coleman (Eds.), *The rhetoric of Western thought* (pp. 431-449). Dubuque, IA: Kendall/Hunt.

Bormann, E. G. (1983). Symbolic convergence theory: Organizational communication and culture. In L. Putnam & M. E. Paconowsky (Eds.), *Communication and organizations: An interpretive approach* (pp. 99-122). Beverly Hills, CA: Sage.

Bormann, E. G., Cragan, J. F., & Shields, D. C. (1996, March). An expansion of the rhetorical vision component of the symbolic convergence theory: The cold war paradigm case. *Communication Monographs, 63,* 1-28.

Burgoyne, J. G. (1996). Learning from experience: From individual discovery to meta-dialogue via the evolution of transitional myths. *Personnel Review, 24*(6), 61-72.

Clark, T.A.C., & Greatbatch, D. (1999, July). *Translating actors' interests: How management gurus understand their impacts and success.* Paper presented at the 15th EGOS Annual Colloquium, Warwick University, U.K.

Coopey, J. (1995). The learning organization: Power, politics, and ideology. *Management Learning, 26*(2), 193-213.

Costner, K. (Producer & Director). (1990). *Dances with wolves.* [Film]. (Available from Majestic Film & Tig Productions)

Covey, S. R. (1989). *The seven habits of highly effective people.* New York: Simon & Schuster.

Cragan, J. F,. & Shields, D. C. (1992). The use of symbolic theory in corporate strategic planning. *Journal of Applied Communication Research, 20,* 199-218.

de Pree, M. (1989). *Leadership is an art.* New York: Doubleday.

Deming, W. E. (1986). *Out of the crisis.* Cambridge, UK: Cambridge University Press.

DiBella, A. J., & Nevis, E. C. (1998). *How organizations learn: An integrated strategy for building learning capability.* San Francisco: Jossey-Bass.

Dixon, N. (1994). *The organizational learning cycle.* Maidenhead, UK: McGraw-Hill.

Dovey, K. (1997). The learning organization and the organization of learning. *Management Learning, 28*(3), 331-349.

Driben, L. I. (1995). The Pied Piper of learning. *Chief Executive, 101,* 62.

Dumaine, B. (1994, October 17). Mr. Learning Organization. *Fortune,* pp. 147-157.

Fenwick, T. (1998). Questioning the learning organization. In S. Scott, B. Spencer, & A. Thomas (Eds.), *Learning for life* (pp. 140-152). Toronto, Canada: Thompson.

Flood, R. L. (1999). *Rethinking the Fifth Discipline.* London: Routledge.

Foss, S. K. (1989). *Rhetorical criticism: Exploration and practice.* Prospect Heights, IL: Waveland.

Fulmer, R. M. (1995). Building organizations that learn: The MIT Center for Organizational Learning. *Journal of Management Development, 14*(5), 9-14.

Fulmer, R. M., & Keys, J. B. (1998). A conversation with Peter Senge: New developments in organizational learning. *Organizational Dynamics, 27*(2), 33-41.

Galaghan, P. A. (1991). The learning organization made plain. *Training & Development, 45*, 37-44.

Garratt, B. (1990). *Creating a learning organization.* Cambridge, UK: Simon & Schuster.

Garratt, B. (1995). An old idea that has come of age. *People Management, 19*, 25.

Garvin, D. A. (1993, July-August). Building a learning organization. *Harvard Business Review,* pp. 78-91.

Griffith, V. (1995, April 12). Corporate fashion victim. *Financial Times,* p. 15.

Grint, K. (1997). *Fuzzy management.* Oxford, UK: Oxford University Press.

Hammer, M., & Champy, J. (1993). *Reengineering the corporation.* New York: HarperBusiness.

Hampden-Turner, C. (1992). Charting the dilemmas of Hanover Insurance. *Planning Review, 20*(1), 22-26.

Hardin, G, (1968, December 13). The tragedy of the commons. *Science,* pp. 1243-1248.

Harrison, R. (1995). *The collected papers of Roger Harrison.* Maidenhead, UK: McGraw-Hill.

Hart, R. (1989). *Modern rhetorical criticism.* Glenview, IL: Scott Foresman/Little, Brown.

Jackson, B. G. (1996). Reengineering the sense of self: The manager and the management guru. *Journal of Management Studies, 33*(5), 571-590.

Jackson, B. G. (1997). Linking the immediate with the mass-mediated theatre in organizations: The case for symbolic convergence theory. In *Proceedings of the 15th International Standing Conference on Organizational Symbolism,* Warsaw, Poland. Available: http://www.it.com.pl/scos

Jackson, B. G. (1998, July). *Management fashion following: Facilitating learning through rhetorical critique.* Paper presented at the Lancaster-Leeds Collaborative Conference on Emergent Fields in Management: Connecting Learning and Critique, Leeds University, UK.

Jackson, B. G. (1999). The goose that laid the golden egg? A rhetorical critique of Stephen Covey and the effectiveness movement. *Journal of Management Studies, 36*(3), 353-377.

Jashapara, A. (1993). The competitive learning organization: A quest for the Holy Grail. *Management Decision, 31*(8), 52-62.

Jones, A. M., & Hendry, C. (1994). The learning organization: Adult learning and organizational transformation. *British Journal of Management, 5*, 153-162.

Keys, J., Fulmer, R. M., & Stumpf, S. A. (1996). Micro worlds and simuworlds: Practice fields for the learning organization. *Organizational Dynamics, 24*(4), 36-50.

Kofman, F., & Senge, P. (1993). Communities of commitment: The heart of learning organizations. *Organizational Dynamics, 32*(5), 5-23.

Lessem, R. (1991). *Top quality learning: Building a learning organization.* London: Basil Blackwell.

Meen, D. E., & Keough, M. (1992, Winter). Creating the learning organization. *McKinsey Quarterly, 1,* 58-78.

Micklethwait, J., & Wooldridge, A. (1996). *The witchdoctors.* London: Heinemann.

Pedler, M., Burgoyne, J., & Boydell, T. (1997). *The learning company.* New York: McGraw-Hill.

Peters, T. J. (1987). *Thriving on chaos.* New York: Knopf.

Peters, T. J., & Waterman, R. H. (1982). *In search of excellence: Lessons from America's best run companies.* New York: Harper & Row.

Revans, R. W. (1979). *Action learning: New techniques for management.* London: Blond & Briggs.

Senge, P. M. (1990a). *The fifth discipline: The art and practice of the learning organization.* New York: Doubleday Currency.

Senge, P. M. (1990b). The leader's new work: Building learning organizations. *Sloan Management Review, 32*(1), 7-23.

Senge, P. M. (1992). Building learning organizations. *Journal for Quality and Participation, 15*(2), 30-38.

Senge, P. M. (1995a). Robert Greenleaf's legacy: A new foundation for twenty-first century institutions. In L. C. Spears (Ed.), *Reflections on leadership* (pp. 217-240). New York: John Wiley.

Senge, P. M. (1995b). Making a better world. *Executive Excellence, 12*(8), 18-19.

Senge, P. M. (1996a). Rethinking leadership in the learning organization. *Systems Thinker, 7*(1), 1-8.

Senge, P. M. (1996b). Leading learning organizations. *Executive Excellence, 13*(4), 10-12.

Senge, P. M., de Geus, A., & Carstedt, G. (1998). SoL International. [Online]. Available: http://learning.mit.edu/in/98letter.html (accessed August 3, 1999).

Senge, P. M., & Fulmer, R. M. (1993). Simulations, systems thinking and anticipatory learning. *Journal of Management Development, 12*(6), 21-33.

Senge, P. M., Kleiner, A., Roberts, C., Roth, G., & Ross, R. (1999). *The dance of change: The challenges of sustaining momentum in learning organizations.* New York: Doubleday Currency.

Senge, P. M., Roberts, C., Ross, R. B., Smith, B. J., & Kleiner, A. (1994). *The fifth discipline fieldbook.* New York: Doubleday Currency.

Starkey, K. (Ed.). (1996). *How organizations learn.* London: International Thomson Business Press.

Torbert, W. R. (1994). Managerial learning, organizational learning: A potentially powerful redundancy. *Management Learning, 1,* 57-70.

Tsang, E. (1997). Organizational learning and the learning organization: A dichotomy between descriptive and prescriptive research. *Human Relations, 50*(1), 73-90.

Victor, B., & Stephens, C. 1994. The dark side of the new organizational forms: An editorial essay. *Organization Science, 5*(4), 479-481.

Watkins, K. E., & Marsick, V. J. (1994). *Sculpting the learning organization.* San Francisco: Jossey-Bass.

[8]

Haute Couture and *Prêt-à-Porter*: The Popular Press and the Diffusion of Management Practices*

Carmelo Mazza, José Luis Alvarez

Carmelo Mazza
IESE, Research
Division,
Barcelona, Spain

José Luis Alvarez
IESE, Department
of General
Management,
Barcelona, Spain

Abstract

The transformation of management practices has recently become the object of many theoretical and empirical works. While most of these works focus mainly on universities, business schools and consulting firms, our paper aims at investigating the still largely unexplored role of the popular press in the production and legitimation of management ideas and practices. Based on the content analysis of the articles on human resource management published in the last decade in leading newspapers and magazines in Italy, we argue that popular press is the arena where the legitimacy of management ideas and practices is produced. We also suggest that the dynamics of management practice legitimation in Italy, described in this paper, is representative of similar processes occurring in other European countries.

Descriptors: management knowledge, legitimacy, legitimation process, popular press, human resource management

Introduction

Management theory has experienced a diverging process in the last fifty years, a process that, on the one hand, has elevated academic knowledge and on the other has moved towards popularization. The institutions that participate in these processes have been the object of attention. However, research has primarily focused on educational systems (Engwall 1992; Locke 1996). Popular management ideas have been present since the 1940s through practitioner-oriented publications, often written by academics. In the last twenty years, mass media, in particular the popular press (newspapers and magazines), have increasingly covered management themes. For instance, by proposing role models for managers — e.g. scientific organizers, pragmatic decision makers, clever strategists and skilful craftsmen — and by describing successful practices, the popular press has concurred in the construction and institutionalization of management as a popular topic.

Moreover, the role of the popular press has gone beyond the mere diffusion and account of prefabricated ideas to the co-production and legitimation of management practices and theories. This has occurred through both the increase of management information within general periodicals and the growth in sales of business publications. As a consequence, popular press supplements the role of academia in the production of management theories: the popular press opens the doors for management to enter mass consumption.

This paper tries to capture and describe the role of the popular press in the creation of ideas and in their impact on management practices. We argue that, in the last two decades, management theories and practices are turning from aggregations of formal and technical knowledge based on a sort of *'esprit de geometrie'* to aggregations of tacit knowledge and experience-based rules of thumb based on a difficult to achieve *'esprit de finesse'*. Relying on vocabulary from the fashion industry, we could call these two strategies of knowledge for action *'haute couture'* and *'prêt-à-porter'*, respectively.

Haute couture produces very sophisticated and expensive dresses for a distinguished target market of high income and social visibility. *Haute couture* relies on restricted and well-recognized channels of diffusion, and it aims to enhance the social distinction of its consumers. *Prêt-à-porter* fabricates clothing for mass distribution and consumption. The target market is much larger and is reached through massive advertising.

Haute couture and *prêt-à-porter* are, though, poles in what is truly a continuum. For instance, some haute couturiers are also able to create *prêt-à-porter* collections. This is analogous to the fact that a few academics, specialized in the issue of accuracy, are also able to face the issue of relevance, writing best sellers and one-minute managerial guides. In other words, *haute couture* and *prêt-à-porter* are adopted here as metaphors of two basic strategies of production and diffusion of theories and practices, rather than normative expressions.

Extant research mainly focuses on academic outlets (mostly journals) and practitioner-oriented publications (mostly best-seller books). There have been efforts at defining the language and rhetoric of management theories (Astley and Zammuto 1992; Czarniawska 1999) and best practices, such as TQM (Westphal et al. 1997; Furman 1997), business process re-engineering (Fincham 1994; Jackson 1995), and managerial excellence (Furusten 1995). The very important issue of the patterns of influence over time between academics and practitioners has also been explored (Barley et al. 1988; Barley and Kunda 1992). More recently, the faddish way in which management ideas spread has gained attention (Abrahamson 1996), as well as standardization (Sahlin-Andersson 1996) and trivialization (*Wall Street Journal* 1994; Hilmer and Donaldson 1996). Unfortunately, the conditions under which the popular press, namely nationwide newspapers and magazines, concurs in the popularization of management knowledge and in the transformation of practices are still an understudied topic.

We suggest that the role of the popular press deserves further investigation for at least three important reasons. First, the spectacular growth in the volume of business and management information and its large social appeal and acceptance in recent years. Second, the rise and spread of so-called managerial discourse. Finally, the ideologization of management — explor-

The Popular Press and the Diffusion of Management Practices 569

ing in whose interests newspapers and magazines stories are written could provide suggestive clues to this issue.

In this paper, we attempt to make a first-hand exploration of that role. At the present stage of the research, our paper will not be able to give equal weight to all these concerns. Our primary concern will therefore be the exploration of the first two reasons mentioned above, by presenting an empirical overview of the role of newspapers in the production and diffusion of Human Resource Management practices in Italy.

The paper is structured in four sections. First, we conceptualize the creation process of management theories and practices by combining the contributions from the Sociology of Culture and the New Institutional School of Organizational Theory. Second, we address the issue of the role of newspapers and magazines in the legitimation of management theories and practices. Third, we analyze the content of the articles on Human Resource Management published in the two leading Italian newspapers (*Il Corriere della Sera* and *Il Sole-24 Ore*) during the last decade and present our empirical analysis and main findings. Finally, we discuss our findings and propose areas for further investigation.

The Creation and Diffusion of Management Theories and Practices

The cultural production of social and scientific ideas has been widely studied in Sociology (Berger and Luckmann 1967; Mukerij and Schudson 1991; Schudson 1990; Barthes 1983; Crane 1992) and in the Philosophy of Science (Feyerabend 1996; Kuhn 1970). The role of mass media in the legitimation, delegitimation and trivialization (Enzensberger 1994) of political action and discourse has also merited attention in the fields of Political Science and Political Sociology (Habermas 1975; Fine 1995; Diani 1996).

All these studies have outlined two basic patterns: an 'aesthetic' one for the creation of 'soft' social ideas, and a rational pattern for 'hard' scientific ideas. The first uses art, craft and even magic for the explanation of newly raised ideas (Feyerabend 1996). The second refers to the rational toolkit used to test hypotheses, assuring incremental development and paradigm stability. Between the two extremes, it is possible to find a grey area where academia, interest lobbies and political élites play their roles.

In spite of their presumed scientific nature, management theories and practices do not follow a path of proper incremental development (Pfeffer 1993), but show cycles of creation and diffusion enhanced by social conformity and even by episodes of mass hysteria (Nohria and Berkley 1993). Consequently, they are produced, legitimated, diffused and discarded in a complex process in which counteracting and ambiguous rules coexist. Most models based on this process, even our earlier one (Alvarez 1997), propose dominant roles for the producers of knowledge, minor, later and dependent roles for managers and consumers, and legitimacy is not paid the attention

570   Carmelo Mazza, José Luis Alvarez

it deserves. In this paper, we assume, instead, that all the actors involved are active in determining the vehicles of diffusion, the source of legitimacy and the rise of new ideas. From our point of view, the creation process is primarily one of legitimacy building, driven by the actors involved, rather than a selection process guided by rationality and innovation. Depending upon the channel that plays the main role in the diffusion, the timing and the character of legitimation may change; likewise, different theories and practices may have different channels of diffusion depending upon their contents (Mazza 1997). In further work, the role of consumers should be brought to the fore even more.

Using Berger and Luckmann's (1967) analogy of the habitualization–typification–objectivation process, we conceptualize the creation and diffusion of management theories and practices in three phases: (1) production, (2) diffusion and (3) legitimation. Management education institutions (universities and business schools), consulting firms and leading newspapers and magazines are the main actors in the process. The three phases are first described separately, then we will consider the dynamic (linear or sequential) interactions amongst the three phases and amongst the actors involved.

In the production phase, academic institutions, business schools and consulting firms make sense out of the existing management theories and day-to-day experiences. They elaborate and codify formal managerial knowledge following the rules of production of academic knowledge (Furner and Supple 1989). The management theories created are not necessarily new, they are often a recycling of old theories that are updated and re-contextualized. At this phase, academic knowledge on management practices is translated into a quasi-technical language to facilitate its diffusion it to practitioners.

In the diffusion phase, management knowledge is spread by institutions of management education and consulting firms. In their activity, by employing a less technical language, these institutions combine scientific knowledge on management with the practical knowledge and rules of thumb. In this way, management education institutions and consulting firms try to provide management knowledge with the reputation of both full-fledged scientifically validated theories and the relevance of down-to-earth recommendations. At this phase, management knowledge begins to spill out of the business community (to, for instance, politics, sports, cultural organizations, or public administration) due to the social legitimacy and the institutional linkages of many educational institutions and consulting firms.

In the legitimation phase, management knowledge gets diffused outside the business community. Here, technical arguments are replaced by ideological statements, grounded on narratives of successes and managerial myths. At this phase, management theories and practices may turn into fads as newspapers and magazines provide them with popularization, ideological statements and rhetoric based on socially accepted symbols. By being endorsed by non-technical media, the effectiveness of management theories and practices becomes taken for granted and their contents become landmarks for imitation. At this final phase, as a consequence of legitimation, management theories reach large numbers of decision makers.

In many cases, legitimated management theories and practices are codified for fast replication and translation (Sahlin-Andersson 1996), turned into short-term standards, supported by dedicated organizations, and diffused by *ad hoc* publications and textbooks. However, legitimacy is not inevitably accompanied by stability, standardization and isomorphism (Rovik 1996). Many management theories and practices are, in fact, quickly discarded and delegitimized, as others become by-products for future theoretical recycling.

The arguments above may benefit from the analysis of the dynamics that occur across the three phases, and among the involved actors. First, the role of the popular press in legitimating management theories and practices, affects the production stage of the process by shaping the topics treated earlier by academic journals (Barley et al. 1988). Moreover, newspapers and magazines not only concur with academic institutions in defining the state-of-the-art of management theories, but also set the topic for academic institutions to follow suit. The recent history of management theory is characterized by this oscillation back and forth from academia to popular press, and *vice versa*.

Second, the popular press has been occupying the area between academia and end-users by taking advantage of the redefinition of the role of university and higher education within society at large (Riesman 1998). Consistent with this process and with the growing influence of mass media on socio-economic issues, newspapers and magazines have begun to produce and recycle knowledge on their own. Although they lack academic and scientific status, ideas are endorsed in newspapers and magazines by '*maitres a penser*', politicians, successful entrepreneurs, etc. As recurrent waves of economic crises and bonanza have been progressively delegitimizing the role of formal knowledge in management, managers appear to look increasingly outside academia for alternative sources of practical knowledge on which to base and justify their actions. Table 1 summarizes the arguments so far.

The interest in informal management knowledge, in popular press, and in their mechanisms for social circulation, such as fads and fashions, is based upon their impact on actual managerial actions. Managerial action has often been represented as the result of a simultaneous combination of different types of knowledge acquired from different channels (Schon 1983). These types of knowledge also include assumptions on human behaviour that operate as deeply embedded habits, originating in a variety of sources not necessarily academic, such as popular press, and even not necessarily of a management or economic kind (Alvarez and Merchán 1992). Frequently, all these different types of knowledge have their own channels of production, propagation, reception and consumption, spreading and gaining acceptance independently. They may sometimes get diffused and institutionalized together, producing recipes comprising heterogeneous ingredients. Therefore, in practice, the typical complexity, ambiguity and imperfection

572   Carmelo Mazza, José Luis Alvarez

Table 1 Production, Diffusion and Legitimation of Management Knowledge		Actors	Knowledge	Arguments	Audience
	Production	University Business schools Consulting firms	Formal/scientific	Management as science	Business community Management scholars
	Diffusion	Business press Consulting firms Business schools	Scientific/practical	Management as techniques and rules of thumb	Business community Professionals
	Legitimation	Popular press Business press Large firms	Ideological	Narratives of management success	Business community Society at large

of managerial tasks and actions (Roethlisberger 1954; March 1988) require the combination of a wide variety of knowledge types.

Accordingly, being an efficient manager depends not only on the application of formal and accredited knowledge, but also on a personal and social wisdom of which informal knowledge (as well as character) plays a part. Therefore, the essence of managerial action belongs to the realm of politics and tactics, where managers gain consent through socially legitimated courses of action rather than self-fulfilling, instrumental, economic rationality (Fligstein 1996; Alvarez 1998). This pushes managers to seek clues for action in the social structure, which provides them with different types of knowledge, both formal and informal (where the popular press plays its role).

Based on these considerations, in the following section we will describe the process of legitimation of management theories and practices and explore how the popular press concurs in this process by providing evidences of the diffusion of Human Resource Management in Italy.

The Popular Press and the Legitimation of Management Theories and Practices

The changing context of managerial action (more globalized and competitive, where traditional hierarchical structures play a lesser role) is forcing managers to look at non-traditional sources of legitimacy for management theories and practices. This consideration makes legitimacy, and the process of legitimation, the key point for our analysis. Legitimacy and legitimation are largely controversial concepts. Political Science, Sociology and Organization Theory have provided contrasting perspectives (see Mazza 1998, for an overview). Some scholars have linked legitimacy and legitimation to the rightful possession of power (Berger 1981), others to social acceptance, conformity, and tradition (Dowling and Pfeffer 1975; Hobsbawm and Ranger 1983).

In general terms, legitimacy indicates a state of social acceptance of an institution, as legitimation is the process and action of ensuring legitimacy. Meyer and Rowan (1977) have argued that legitimacy is an outcome of the socio-cultural process conducive to institutionalization and increasing the likelihood of survival (see also Hannan and Carroll 1992). From this viewpoint, legitimacy refers 'to the degree of cultural support for an organization — the extent to which the array of established cultural accounts provide explanations for its existence' (Meyer and Scott 1984: 201). Hybels (1994) holds that legitimacy is a 'profoundly malleable tool' whose 'inherent vagueness' has allowed researchers to give meaningful explanations when more precise tools failed. Legitimacy and legitimation appear, therefore, as toolboxes where any researcher can find the definition that better fits his or her purposes (Suchman 1996; Mazza 1998).

The identification of the sources of legitimacy is a less daunting task. Legitimacy is embedded in the socially accepted system of norms and institutional rules, along with values or ethical dictates, which frame the set of legitimated courses of action (Thomas et al. 1986).

Different theoretical approaches have identified many sources of legitimacy. Our aim is to focus on three main concepts: (1) conformity, (2) social support and (3) dramatization.

Conformity

As the New Institutional arguments on isomorphism go (DiMaggio and Powell 1983; Deephouse 1996), legitimacy is gained by displaying conformity with the external environment, by adapting to the existing technical procedures, legality, values, best practices, etc. Theories and practices gain legitimacy, therefore, when many business firms adopt them, or when the adoption is publicly reported by popular media. Firms then follow them to show that they are up to the state-of-the-art in management. Conformity may also provide a defense in the case of failures: plans relying upon institutionalized techniques are more likely to be perceived as rational and appropriate, even in the face of bad performance.

As Sahlin-Andersson (1996) argues, conformity does not preclude the customization of theories and practices, which often only have the label in common with the original conceptualizations. Many authors provide descriptions of how intrinsically ambiguous labels such as business process re-engineering (Jackson 1995) and TQM (Westphal et al. 1997), leave room for a wide range of translations.

Social Support

The second source of legitimacy that we propose is social support to a course of action. This is mainly generated by the endorsement of powerful collective actors. They define the rules for the evaluation of organizational actions. Enduring social support provides management theories and practices with taken-for-grantedness. The basic reasoning is that leading organizations establish the practices that other organizations should follow or imitate to signal alignment. In other words, if these powerful actors invest in a practice, the expectation is that it should provide a positive return in economic terms or in social acceptance.

In highly industrialized countries, the powerful actors are typically of two types: (a) large firms (e.g. *Fortune 500* firms) and organizations with institutional relations with the State or management education centres, and (b) young and profitable firms (e.g. the Internet firms) with a track record of successful innovations. The approval of *Fortune 500* firms provides legitimacy because of their traditional top-notch status. Their institutional linkages decouple these organizations from the commitment to short-term performance, so, paraphrasing Schumpeterian arguments, they can take the risks of being innovators. Young and profitable firms provide legitimacy by playing the role of pioneers in the field. Their role of pioneering management theories and practices legitimizes other organizations willing to manage innovatively to adopt them.

Dramatization

The third source of legitimacy is dramatization. Following Edelman (1988), we might argue that management theories and practices are legitimated by adopting the same dramatized language that characterizes the mass media. As Crane (1992) also notes, dramatization is a way of enhancing the process of cultural reproduction of theories and practices. In a similar vein, Czarniawska (1997) argues that organizational dramas often end up with the affirmation and legitimation of new actors and courses of action. From this viewpoint, we could imagine that management theories and practices have to be properly stylized before being published on the popular press pages.

Dramatization is pursued by the construction of legends and myth and their spectacular (good or bad) effects on performance. Top management is often guided in their strategic decision making by the legends of successful innovations, often reported by newspapers and magazines as the new frontier of management or as star cases. The dramatization of such business successes also creates a powerful narrative for managerial action, now filling the bookshelves of libraries with gurus' books and autobiographies of top managers (Huczynski 1993).

By building upon the theoretical debate reported above, in the next section, we aim to describe how newspapers and magazines concur in creating and legitimating management theories and practices, along with educational and business institutions. We also aim to look at the legitimacy sources of management theories and practices.

Methodology and Empirical Analysis

In this paper we analyze how the business press creates, diffuses and legitimates management theories and practices, using data from one country

(Italy), on a specific set of management practices (Human Resource Management), and during an almost ten-year time span (1988–1996).

Regarding the selection of a specific country, we recognize that our focus on a single country limits generalizations grounded on data. However, Italy has some characteristics (for instance, a limited range of executive education on offer, a generally poor command of English as a business language, and the influential role of the popular press in setting political and economic agendas) that make the popular press especially active. In contrast, for instance, *prima facie* Anglo Saxon and German popular press seems to amplify existing theories and practices, playing a narrower role, than that of propagator. That is, the very saliency of the Italian popular press makes it a good starting point for exploring the impact, in general, of the popular press on management knowledge and actions.

Other characteristics of the Italian case are the following. First, the number of business issues dealt with by the popular press have grown spectacularly in the last fifteen years and has been credited for its promotion of the modernization and internationalization of Italian capitalism. Second, the very traditional confrontation between the Unions, anchored in leftist ideologies, and business associations, has situated Human Resource Management at the centre of critical displacements in social practices since the early 80s. The globalization of the economy has facilitated changes in legal rules, increased the legitimation of flexibility in external and internal labour markets and the generalization of non-monetary incentives. Third, although Italy belongs to a group of advanced economies, it has been influenced by the Communist Party, the strongest in Western Europe. Furthermore, since October 1998, the Italian Prime Minister has been a former Communist. Because of these peculiarities, we consider Italy to be a very suggestive site for observing the transformation of management theories and practices in an affluent economy, where economic issues are also intertwined with political debates in a rapidly evolving context.

As for the selection of Human Resource Management practices, they show both a well-grounded theoretical tradition and are widely recognized by both academic and popular press. Since the early 80s, because of the pressures for using all possible competitive capabilities, Human Resource Management has increasingly become a very important topic. Recently, interest in it has been heightened due to the need to manage the impact on personnel of the widespread restructuring of firms, and similar policies implemented in the 90s (Pfeffer 1992).

Our analysis covers the period 1988 to 1996. This period allows us to analyze theories and practices when, independently of its increasing popularity, the field of Human Resource Management has not experienced, we believe, major theoretical shifts. We acknowledge that nine years is too narrow a period to comfortably apply a historical and sociological perspective to the role of mass media in the diffusion of management theories and practices. However, we believe it is a useful starting point for a preliminary study on how popular press diffuses and legitimates management knowledge.

Data has been collected from articles on Human Resource Management in two periodicals selected on the basis of their diffusion. First, from *Il Sole-24 Ore*, the first (in terms of circulation) economic and business newspaper in Italy and the third most important of all dailies. Due to its professional focus, it is frequently bought as a second newspaper, together with a general newspaper. During the 80s, it tripled its circulation by benefiting from the interest raised on the Stock Exchange Market and from the affirmation of the managerial ideology in Italy. Our second source of data is *Il Corriere della Sera*, founded in 1876, with the largest circulation in Italy for many years. It is an authoritative source of opinion on politics and economics, thanks to contributions by prestigious journalists. Both newspapers are published in Milan and share a liberal and moderate ideological orientation.

The articles have been selected by searching for key words related to Human Resource Management within the CD-ROM databases of the two newspapers. This selection has allowed us to collect articles mentioning those key words either in the title or in the text. Second, we have analyzed the selected articles in order to verify that Human Resource Management was actually the main issue dealt with. By so doing, some articles were discarded. The next step was to analyze the articles collected on the basis of content. This interpretative methodology focuses on the relations between the words in a text in order to analyze and interpret the emerging discourse. By building on Barthes (1957), we assume that it is possible to interpret a written text by analyzing the discourse it supports or develops. We have also tried to take time into consideration by looking at temporal patterns in the frequency distribution of articles.

In order to consider the possible interaction between academic literature and press coverage of management topics, we examined (using the ABI Inform database) the frequency of articles on Human Resource Management in leading academic journals (*Administrative Science Quarterly, Academy of Management Review* and *Strategic Management Journal*), as well as in more practitioner-oriented outlets (e.g., *Harvard Business Review* and *Academy of Management Executive*). Although these journals are not widely read among Italian business people, they are increasingly influencing local academic debate, as well as the education of young researchers and assistant professors in management.

The frequency of the articles seems to indicate that Human Resource Management is a mature academic topic. The increase of pieces in the last two years in the academic media leads us to suppose a revitalization of the topic although we are not able to address whether it is a new wave or the recycling of old wine into new bottles. In fact, in the last decade, we only found two peaks, but they do not go beyond ten articles in one year, two articles per journal on average. Based on these data, we think that Human Resource Management practices have already received attention within US publications. In other words, this topic was not booming in those years.

Once the evolution of Human Resource Management within the academic

The Popular Press and the Diffusion of Management Practices   577

Figure 1
Number of
Academic Papers
on HRM

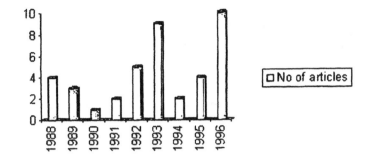

literature had been analyzed, we looked at the articles in the newspapers. We report in Figure 2 the frequency of the articles within *Il Sole-24 Ore* and *Il Corriere della Sera* that have HRM as their major topic.

The growing number of articles on Human Resource Management until 1994 corresponds with the well-known generalized concern of political corruption in Italy. In those years, the control over unethical behaviours became a major topic within large organizations. Interestingly, by reading the contents of these articles, we noted that the HRM topic is often paralleled by arguments on business ethics. This is why these articles remained within the wider debate on corruption and the so-called '*mani pulite*' (clean hands) investigations.

The total number of pieces on Human Resource Management seems to point to two possible dynamics. First, it confirms that HRM has been a topic significantly reported in the Italian popular press. It appears at least 31 times after 1990, an average of more than twice per month, when considering only two newspapers. From these data we suggest that the popular press increasingly promoted and diffused HRM practices. Revealingly, the journalists writing on these topics in the popular press are linked to the academic community only in very few cases. Most of them based their work on contacts with business firms' Public Relation and Press Departments or on direct interviews with CEOs and entrepreneurs. This could suggest that, in those years, business-oriented journalists shared with the scientific community the role of spreading and legitimating HRM practices. They appear, therefore, to play the role of co-diffusers operating in differentiated channels rather than followers. They did not use academic work as raw material, but had their own sources, therefore they didn't act as mere popularizers of previous academic work.

Second, the decrease in the number of articles in the popular press in the last two years, could be interpreted as a decline in the interest in HRM practices. Like fads, the interest in HRM practices appears to be short-lived, following the rise and fall of popular press coverage. New topics are regularly surfacing (in this specific case, one of the most important is business ethics), rapidly aging what was, not long before, novel and fashionable. According to this viewpoint, in the case of HRM, we could predict that it

578   Carmelo Mazza, José Luis Alvarez

Figure 2
Number of
Articles on HMR
in Italian Press

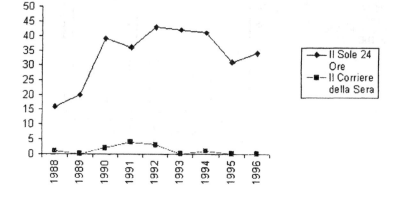

will continue to decrease. unless a revitalization of the academic interest makes it an unusually lengthy popular topic.

The last step in our data analysis addresses the issue of the legitimacy sources of HRM practices. We looked in detail for justifications for the implementation of these practices. By carrying out a discourse analysis of these articles, we reconstructed the arguments that link the implementation of HRM practices with business accomplishments. The reported accomplishments are the legitimacy sources for the application of HRM, as they provide the rationale for the adoption of practices. From the discourse analysis of the articles in our sample, we drew the following set of sources of legitimacy: (1) conformity to corporate values, (2) adoption by large firms and (3) successful performance. They reflect the three general sources of legitimacy — conformity, social support, and dramatization — that we have already discussed in the paragraphs above.

Conformity to Corporate Values

The first source of legitimacy is the inclusion of Human Resource Management within the set of values constituting the so-called organization culture. The articles rarely explain what organization culture requires in practice, as most of the definitions included definitions geared at eliminating past negative practices. HRM practices are usually mentioned as the cornerstones of organizational culture, since they reflect both the search for enduring competitive tools and the social responsiveness organizations have to show. In these articles, HRM is dealt with as a kindred activity of already legitimated practices such as excellence, management education, total quality and others. In this sense, HRM is also a source of symbolic conformity, by implying an alignment with these legitimated practices.

The articles presenting this source of legitimacy tend to assert the strategic role of human resources and its centrality as a competitive weapon. During the crisis of the early 90s, investing in human resources was presented in Italy as the only enduring competitive strategy to face globalization. The titles of the articles reflect this assumption, linking human resources to effective organizational changes and responsiveness to future challenges.

The discourse linked with this source of legitimacy relies upon the description of competitive challenges and the strategic tools needed to face them. The main key word is 'strategic', as it underlines the need for Human Resource Management practices to be present in any successful organization.

Adoption by Large Firms

The second source of legitimation is the adoption of Human Resource Management practices by large firms. Due to the peculiarities of the Italian context, it is interesting to notice how this leadership role is almost uniquely played by a restricted group of firms. Within this group, a historical leading role is played by FIAT, the largest Italian manufacturing firm. The practices adopted by FIAT are considered to be the state-of-the-art in effective management. In addition, FIAT's innovations in flexible automation have blended issues of personnel and manufacturing systems. Together with FIAT, small and medium-sized innovative firms are other examples of the legitimation of Human Resource Management. The role played by FIAT and these innovative firms is that of powerful actors endorsing the implementation of particular practices. The legitimation of Human Resource Management is consequently obtained through the description of these firms' successful practices.

The articles regarding large firms' adoption are often built on interviews and statements of CEOs and general managers. Similarly, these articles report the opinion of the Board of Confindustria (the entrepreneurial association). In these pieces, attention to human capital is presented as the main success factor for any firm competing globally. These interviews seldom give technical arguments, they only provide platitudes and a rather basic enumeration of the best organizational practices to follow.

The discourse related to large firms' adoption is interestingly linked with other rhetoric. The first we have identified is a kind of 'new frontier' of management. Through their innovative efforts, large firms are described as 'pushing the envelope', as leading the field towards new territories. Human capital is presented as the basic resource to achieve the innovations implicit in any new frontier. It is interesting to note that large firms are again acquiring the role of engines of transformation, as Schumpeterian arguments revealed at the beginning of the century. This argument is outside of the purpose of this paper, nevertheless we suggest that it could be an object of meaningful attention by scholars.

Successful Performance

The last source of legitimacy for Human Resource Management emerging from our texts is the successful performance of adopters. While the articles emphasize the contribution of Human Resource Management to business competitiveness, they rarely describe the details of these practices. Human Resource Management is ideologically posed as one of the basic components of the overall competitiveness of the industrial system. The only explanation provided is its importance for business systems like the American and the Japanese. This source of legitimacy shifts attention away from the successful implementation by a large number of firms, or by role models, to a more general claim for innovativeness and the renewal of the managerial paradigm. The tone of the articles mentioning this source of legitimacy is typically normative, outlining quick solutions and purposeful rules of thumb. Often, the articles give a dramatized account of the implementation, by emphasizing the spectacular change in the performance and the courage needed to face internal resistance.

An interesting aspect is that the link between performance and Human Resource Management, in Italy, frequently refers to the case of the restructuring and privatization of the Health Care System and Public Services. Human Resource Management is therefore considered a key success factor in the successful implementation of privatization in economical, political and social terms. Even in these cases, dramatization seems to characterize the discourse by pointing to the need for radical change and to the efficiency challenge that Public Administration has to face.

The articles on the privatization wave of the public sector in Italy largely adopt managerial discourse to explain the superiority of the market model compared to that of the state-owned companies. Managerialism is linked to innovativeness, and Human Resource Management practices are the most progressive part of this innovation. The articles deal with both private and privatized companies, showing the potential of Human Resource Management practices such as teamwork, personnel reward systems, etc., to increase the efficiency and profitability of organizations. In these articles, more technical information on practices is provided, often repackaging and recycling labels from the academic press.

The discourse related to successful performance is the most enduring. It has been analyzed from the perspective of rhetoric devices (Furusten 1995; Czarniawska and Joerges 1989), of justification and control over external events, and by attribution theory (Bettman and Weitz 1983). In the case of Human Resource Management practices, the key words adopted are success, efficiency gains, and profitability. They reflect the main content of general economic discourse, whose pervasiveness is conducive to the marketization of organizational fields. Interestingly, these key words contain quasi-technical arguments, since they embody the adoption of practices and technicalities beyond Human Resource Management (such as management control systems, TQM, etc.).

Tables 2 and 3 report the main contents of the articles classified by sources of legitimacy and their frequency:

Along with the summary of the arguments mentioned above, this data helps to introduce the time element into the analysis. Legitimacy sources are rather evenly distributed between and over the years. We argue that this

Table 2
Legitimacy
Sources of
Articles in Press

Legitimacy Source	Content	Argumentation	Key words	Rhetorics
Conformity to corporate values	Descriptions of the future competitive challenges for any business firm	HRM as new competitive weapon	Strategic Competitive challenges	Ideological
Large firms' adoption	Interviews with CEOs and General managers	List of updated best practices	New frontier of management Human capital as core	Ideological
Successful performance	Case histories on implementations	Technical descriptions	Success Efficiency gains Profitability	Quasi technical

Table 3
Frequency of
Legitimacy
Sources

Year	Legitimacy Sources			Total
	Conformity to corporate values	Large firms' adoption	Successful performance	
1988	6	6	7	19
1989	5	6	7	18
1990	5	8	8	21
1991	5	9	7	21
1992	5	11	8	24
1993	7	7	7	21
1994	5	4	9	18
1995	4	4	6	14
1996	5	4	5	14
	47	59	64	170

distribution means a stable legitimacy pattern, that is to say, that the popular press adopted the same discourse on Human Resource Management practices over those years.

Discussion and Conclusion

The data available, though limited and needing more sophisticated quantitative and qualitative treatment, supports our main thrust: that the popular press, besides partially serving as channel for academic literature, merits separate attention in order to explain the diffusion and legitimation of management theories and practices. The press is particularly influential in the creation of short-lived management ideas and practices by taking advantage of the fact that magazines and newspapers are on the desks of business people every day.
We argue that the popular press is an autonomous channel of production and diffusion of knowledge, more than just the popularizer of the ideas

generated and provided to it by academia. The popular press reflects sources of legitimacy of theories and practices different from those adopted by standard academic outlets. For instance, in Italy, Human Resource Management ideas and practices obtained coverage by the popular press independently of the interest in them by academic literature.

The management theories and practices in which the popular press specializes are low technical descriptions and 'high' ideological statements, often legitimized by stories of successful implementation and by the opinions of influential CEOs and general managers. In other words, Human Resource Management theories and practices produced by the popular press seem to be ready-made, easily available products, rather like *prêt-à-porter* clothes sold in boutiques and department stores. In turn, the scientific- and scholarly-supported theories and practices created and diffused by the academic press appear to be as costly as the *haute couture* clothes sold in sophisticated fashion houses, or the *aula magna* of universities, business schools and consulting firms.

As the boundaries between society, politics and economics vanish, the influence of the popular press on these dynamics is increasing all over Europe. Because of the current crisis within political categories and vocabularies, the traditional role of the press in setting the political agenda is now partially performed through the medium of economic arguments and ideologies (see, for instance, the rhetoric of European Monetary Union and the creation of the Euro). Within this context, management ideas and practices have become opportunities for journalists, newspapers and magazines for gaining influence.

As Italy may not be unique in this regard (we have anecdotal evidence of similar dynamics occurring in Greece, Spain, Denmark, France, and even in some of the Eastern European countries facing the challenges of a market economy), we propose that more cross-national comparative studies are needed on the differences and similarities among the countries.

Further research should also focus on the three basic legitimacy sources (conformity to corporate values, adoption by large firms and successful performance) that the popular press adopts as rhetorical devices. From a rhetorical perspective, the three sources correspond to the three classical devices of rhetoric: pathos (the appeal to emotions), ethos (the appeal to character and ethics), and logos (the appeal to rationality). A comparative study on different publications may reveal how these devices are applied to the legitimation of management concepts and actions.

A historical perspective introducing time as a major explanatory factor would be also welcomed. It could benefit from a long history of management ideas that have already undergone popularization, institutionalization, legitimation and disappearance. While this history has already been partially told in regard to management models, it may be enriched by a comprehensive account of the different channels of diffusion. A comparison among newspapers, magazines, journals and other mass media like television and radio broadcasting is needed to draw a more complete and updated picture. Content analysis could be supplemented by ethnographic studies.

interviews with people dealing with management ideas and practices, and the analysis of the actions' network to uncover the ties that embed their creation and diffusion.

Comparative and historical analyses may also be helpful in addressing the often neglected (and methodologically challenging) issue of the causal relationship between management knowledge and actual managerial action. Some of the literature (Eccles and Nohria 1992; Bourdieu 1998) seems to argue that management action is more tightly coupled with the popular press than with other channels, such as academic works. Links between institutions of diffusion and action could be of two basic kinds. First, regarding content, the popular press plays a major role in setting the pragmatics of the managerial discourse and in shaping the rhetoric for the diffusion of management practices (Eccles and Nohria 1992). The press is also the main arena where management narratives are built and ideological statements are diffused to make management ideas and actions taken-for-granted (Czarniawska and Joerges 1989; Czarniawska 1997).

Second, regarding actions, the popular press affirms management discourses by legitimating the members of the management community as experts (Brint 1994), both on economic as well as on day-to-day matters. For instance, in recent years, business people have been both influencing the political debate on non-economic topics (e.g. foreign affairs and education) and championing new fashions in clothing and leisure (challenging actors and sportsmen in this role). The Italian case is particularly spectacular: a successful entrepreneur, Silvio Berlusconi, became Prime Minister just seven months after entering the political arena. It could be argued, then, that the popular press is serving the business community by providing credentials to its political activism and by enhancing the marketization of society. Exploring the relationships between marketization, popular press and the diffusion of management is a great research opportunity.

Though needing more empirical support, we believe our argument opens avenues of research in at least three different directions. First, it looks at the process of diffusion and creation of management theories and practices from the perspective explored by the Sociology of Culture. This perspective moves management ideas and practices away from a technical domain to the realm of socially constructed credos. Moreover, the mass diffusion of management theories and practices paves the way towards their commodification. The *prêt-à-porter* metaphor is not intended to show that commodification is under way, but it aims at sustaining how mass media diffusion may speed up the pace towards management knowledge commodification.

Since management theories and practices are, at least partially (together with managerial character, situational and political constrains, and other variables) the premise for managerial action, it can be argued that this shift is also moving the conceptualization of managerial action away from the narrow rules of instrumental rationality. What managerial action really means is being debated in the field of Sociology (White 1992). If, on the other hand, we believe that managerial action is becoming more political

(Alvarez 1998), then mass media and its role are going to be at the top of any manager's agenda.

Second, our analysis does not explore in detail the content of what is produced and diffused by the popular press. Are they standards, rules of thumb, or common sense? The answer to this leads to the issue of the relations between the actors and institutions involved in the creation and diffusion of management. Some hypotheses are already available: as Barley et al. (1988) posed, there exists an oscillation of management topics from popular press to academic media, and back again, with an inverted relation in their popularity in both media. Some authors focus on the competition between universities, business schools and consulting firms in setting state-of-the-art of management theories (see Pfeffer 1997 for a summary of the current debate). Engwall (1992) described a cooperative pattern between educational institutions and business firms for the joint production of management knowledge and managerial élites in Sweden (see also Locke 1996).

However, the relation between the institutions involved in the diffusion of management theories and practices is still not settled. Academia, consulting firms, publishing houses, management gurus, best-selling authors, business schools and the popular press together take part in the definition of successful theories and practices. We argue that there is no clear boundary between actors involved in creation and in diffusion of practices. Each actor participates in the process of institutionalization of management theories and practices, with peculiarities originating in the social and historical context. Further research might investigate the patterns of relations and roles among actors, and the differences in the management knowledge they channel.

Finally, we suggest that the role of the popular press in management topics is in itself worthy of a deeper historical and social exploration. The rise of a 'popular business press', as happened in Italy and Spain during the 80s, can be perceived as part of a wider process of diffusion of the liberal model, as opposed to the statual ones (Meyer 1996). In this sense, whenever a popular business press develops, it is likely to emphasize the standardizing qualities associated with the liberal organizing model, based on a shared sense of values among the competitors and on patterns of openness and commitment, opposed to secrecy. Other political cultures (e.g. corporativism and statalism), therefore, would not generate a popular business press (Meyer 1996).

In this paper, we have discussed the role of the popular press in the creation, diffusion, and legitimation of management theories and practices. We have employed sociological arguments emphasizing a legitimacy perspective on the phenomenon, and proposed an interpretation of the process, in which the popular press creates short-lived, quasi-technical, theories (the *prêt-à-porter*) while academic outlets create scientifically-based models (the *haute couture*). To be implemented as best practices, both of them need the social legitimacy arising from conformity, endorsement by large firms and legends of successful implementations.

The proposed perspective does not explore the actual consequences of the implementation of theories and practices. Nevertheless, as our title metaphor illustrates, we would think that management theories and practices are an ephemeral result of people trying to meet customers' demands, and even though *haute couture* is definitely more sophisticated and attractive, *prêt-à-porter* is still more comfortable and affordable.

Note

* This research work is part of the project: Creation of a European Management Practice. Earlier drafts were presented at the 13th EGOS Colloquium (Budapest, July 1997) and at the SCORE/SCANCOR seminar on 'The Standardization of Organizational Forms' (Arild, September 1997). We would like to thank the following for their helpful comments and suggestions on earlier drafts: Rolv Petter Amdam, Finn Borum, Barbara Czarniawska, Lars Engwall, Aurora Inglés, John Meyer, Michael Power, David Wilson, and two anonymous reviewers. Finally, we would also like to thank Jorge Gonzalez for his help with this research.

References

Abrahamson, Eric
1996 'Management fashion'. *Academy of Management Review* 21: 254–285.

Alvarez, José Luis
1997 'The sociological tradition and the spread and institutionalization of business knowledge for action' in *The production and consumption of business knowledge in Europe.* J. L. Alvarez (ed.), 13–57. London: Macmillan.

Alvarez, José Luis
1997 'Theories of managerial action and their impact on the conceptualization of executive careers' in *Conversations in career theory.* M. Peiperl and M. Arthur, (eds.), 127–138. Oxford: Oxford University Press.

Alvarez, José Luis, and Carmen Merchán
1992 'Narrative fiction as a way of knowledge and its application to the development of imagination for action'. *International Studies of Management and Organization* 22: 27–45.

Astley, Graham, and Raymond Zammuto
1992 'Organization science, managers, and language games'. *Organization Science* 3: 443–466.

Barley, Stephen, and Gideon Kunda
1992 'Design and devotion: surges of rational and normative ideologies of control in managerial discourse'. *Administrative Science Quarterly* 37: 363–399.

Barley, Stephen, Gordon W. Meyer, and Debra C. Gash
1988 'Cultures of culture: academics, practitioners and the pragmatics of normative control'. *Administrative Science Quarterly* 33: 24–60.

Barthes, Roland
1957 *Mythologies.* Paris: Editions du Seuil.

Barthes, Roland
1983 *The fashion system.* New York: Hill & Wans.

Berger, Peter L.
1981 'New attacks on the legitimacy of business'. *Harvard Business Review* 59: 82–89.

Berger, Peter L., and Thomas Luckmann
1967 *The social construction of reality: a treatise in the sociology of knowledge.* New York: Doubleday.

Bourdieu, Pierre
1998 *Sulla televisione.* Milano: Feltrinelli.

Crane, Diana
1992 *The production of culture. Media and the urban arts.* Newbury Park, CA: Sage.

Czarniawska, Barbara
1997 *Narrating the organization: dramas of institutional identity.* Chicago: University of Chicago Press.

Czarniawska, Barbara
1999 *Writing management.* Oxford: Oxford University Press.

586   Carmelo Mazza, José Luis Alvarez

Czarniawska, Barbara, and Bernard Joerges
1989 'Linguistic artifacts at the service of organizational control' in *Symbols and artifacts: views of the corporate landscape.* Pasqual Gagliardi (ed.). 339–364. Berlin: Walter de Gruyter.

Deephouse. David
1996 'Does isomorphism legitimate?' *Academy of Management Journal* 39: 1024–1039.

Diani, Mario
1996 'Linking mobilization frames and political opportunities: insights from regional populism in Italy'. *American Sociological Review* 61: 1053–1069.

DiMaggio, Paul, and Walter Powell
1982 'The iron cage revisited: institutional isomorphism and collective rationality in organizational fields'. *American Sociological Review* 48: 148–160.

Dowling, James, and Jeffrey Pfeffer
1975 'Organizational legitimation'. *Pacific Sociological Review* 18: 122–136.

Eccles, Robert, and Nitin Nohria
1992 *Beyond the hype: rediscovering the essence of management.* Boston, MA: Harvard Business School Press.

Edelman, Murray
1988 *Constructing the political spectacle.* Chicago: The University of Chicago Press.

Engwall, Lars
1992 *Mercury meets Minerva.* Exeter: Pergamon Press.

Feyerabend, Paul K.
1996 *Ambiguità ed armonia: lezioni trentine.* Rome: Sagittari Laterza.

Fincham, Robert
1993 'Business process re-engineering and the commodification of management knowledge'. *Journal of Marketing Management* 11.

Fine, Gary Allan
1994 'Reputational entrepreneurs and the memory of incompetence: melting supporters, partisan warriors, and images of President Harding'. *American Journal of Sociology* 101: 1159–1193.

Fligstein, Neil
1995 'Social skill and institutional theory'. *American Behavioralist Scientist* 40: 397–405.

Furman, Beyza
1996 'Is TQM a management ideology? A case study on culture, ideology and discourse'. Paper presented at the 3rd Conference on Management Discourse, London.

Furner, Mary, and Barry Supple
1989 *The state and the economic knowledge: the American and British experiences.* Cambridge: Cambridge University Press.

Furusten, Staffan
1995 'The managerial discourse: a study of the creation and diffusion of popular management knowledge'. Research Paper, Department of Business Studies, Uppsala University.

Habermas, Jurgen
1975 *La crisi della razionalità nel capitalismo maturo.* Bari, Italy: Laterza.

Hannan, Michael T., and Glenn Carroll
1992 *Dynamics of organizational populations: density, legitimation and competition.* New York: Oxford University Press.

Hilmer, Frederick G., and Lex Donaldson
1996 'The trivialization of management'. *The McKinsey Quarterly* 4: 15–23.

Hobsbawn, Eric J., and Terence Ranger
1983 *The invention of tradition.* Cambridge: Cambridge University Press.

Huczynski, Andrzej
1993 *Management gurus: what makes them and how to become one.* London: Routledge.

Hybels, Ralph C.
1994 'On legitimacy, legitimation and organizations: a critical review and integrative theoretical model'. *Proceedings of the Academy of Management Association*: 241–245.

Jackson, Bradley
1995 'Re-engineering the sense of self: the manager and the management guru'. *Journal of Management Studies* 33: 571–590.

Locke, Robert
1996 *The collapse of the American management mystique.* Oxford: Oxford University Press.

March, James G.
1988 *Decisions and organizations.* Oxford: Blackwell.

Mazza, Carmelo
1997 'The popularization of business knowledge diffusion: from academic knowledge to popular culture?' in *The production and consumption of business knowledge in Europe.* J. L. Alvarez (ed.), 164–181. London: Macmillan.

Mazza, Carmelo
1998 *Claim, intent, and persuasion: organizational legitimacy and the rhetoric of corporate mission statements.* Norwell, MA: Kluwer Academic.

Meyer, John
1996 'Cultural conditions of standardization'. Paper presented at the SCORE/SCANCOR workshop on 'Standardization', Arild, Sweden, 18–20 Sept.

Meyer, John, and Brian Rowan
1977 'Institutionalized organizations: formal structure as myth and ceremony'. *American Journal of Sociology* 83: 340–363.

Meyer, John, and W. Richard Scott
1983 *Organizational environments: ritual and rationality.* Beverly Hills, CA: Sage.

Mukerji, Charles, and Michael Schudson, editors
1991 *Rethinking popular culture.* Berkeley, CA: University of California Press.

Nohria, Nitin, and James Berkley
1993 'What happened to the take-charge manager?' *Harvard Business Review* 72: 123–137.

Pfeffer, Jeffrey
1992 *Competitive advantage through people.* Cambridge, MA: Harvard Business School Press.

Pfeffer, Jeffrey
1993 'Barriers to the advance of organizational science: paradigm development as a dependent variable'. *Academy of Management Review* 18: 599–620.

Pfeffer, Jeffrey
1997 *New directions for organization theory: problems and prospects.* New York: Oxford University Press.

Riesman, David
1998 *On higher education: the academic enterprise in an era of rising student consumerism.* Chicago: University of Chicago Press.

Roethlisberger, Fritz
1954 *The elusive phenomena.* Cambridge, MA: Harvard University Press.

Rovik, Kjell-Arne
1996 'Deinstitutionalization and the logic of fashion' in *Translating organizational change.* B. Czarniawska and G. Sevon (eds.), 139–172. Berlin: Walter de Gruyter.

Sahlin-Andersson, Kerstin
1996 'Imitating by editing success: the construction of organizational fields' in *Translating organizational change.* B. Czarniawska and G. Sevon (eds.), 69–92. Berlin: Walter de Gruyter.

Schon, Donald A.
1983 *The reflective practitioner: how professionals think in action.* New York: Basic Books.

Schudson, Michael
1990 'How culture works. Perspective from media studies on the efficacy of symbols'. *Theory and Society* 18: 153–180.

Suchman, Mark
1996 'Managing legitimacy: strategic and institutional approaches'. *Academy of Management Review* 20: 571–610.

588   Carmelo Mazza, José Luis Alvarez

Thomas, George M., Henry A. Walker, and Morris Zelditch
1986 'Legitimacy and collective action'. *Social Forces* 65: 378–404.

Wall Street Journal
1994 'The best laid plans: many companies try management fads, only to see them flop'. July 6th.

Westphal, James D., Ranjay Gulati, and Stephen M. Shortell
1997 'Customization or conformity? An institutional and network perspective on the content and consequences of TQM adoption'. *Administrative Science Quarterly* 42: 366–394.

White, Harrison C.
1992 *Identity and control*. Princeton, NJ: Princeton University Press.

[9]

> " *Best-selling*
>
> *management*
>
> *books represent a*
>
> *central feature of*
>
> *communication in*
>
> *modern society,*
>
> *the preeminence*
>
> *of the image. They*
>
> *are manufactured*
>
> *contrivances that*
>
> *are designed to*
>
> *have maximum*
>
> *impact on the*
>
> *intended audience*
>
> *and so gain a*
> "
> *mass appeal.*

MANAGEMENT FASHION AS IMAGE-SPECTACLE
The Production of Best-Selling Management Books

TIMOTHY CLARK
University of Durham
DAVID GREATBATCH

AUTHORS' NOTE: An earlier version of this article was presented at the Academy of Management Conference in Seattle, August 2003. It won The Graziado School of Business and Management Pepperdine Award for Outstanding Paper on Management Consulting.

Clark, Greatbatch / MANAGEMENT FASHION AS IMAGE-SPECTACLE   397

University Of Nottingham

Drawing on the work of Guy Debord's Society of the Spectacle *and Daniel Boorstin's* The Image, *this article argues that aesthetic and management fashions are not separate forms, as both represent the preeminence of the image spectacle. Central to this is the increasing emergence of pseudoevents and synthetic products. Using empirical findings from a study of the production of six best-selling management books, it shows that they are manufactured coproductions that result from an intricate editorial process in which the original ideas are moulded in order for them to have a positive impact on the intended audience. Central to this is a set of conventions that stress the vivification of ideas. The editorial process thus seeks to enhance the aesthetic attractiveness of the ideas. The implications of the conceptual approach and empirical findings are considered with respect to current understandings of management fashion.*

Keywords: *management gurus, management fashion, spectacle*

In 1995 *Business Week* ("Did dirty tricks," 1995) exposed an intricate scheme that manipulated the sales of *The Discipline of Market Leaders* to ensure that it entered *The New York Times* best-seller list. Employees of CSC Index, which had been the birthplace for Hammer and Champy's *Re-engineering the Corporation* (1993) and where the two authors worked, appeared to have spent at least $250,000 purchasing more than 10,000 copies of the book. In addition, *Business Week* claimed that CSC Index channelled corporate purchases of an additional 30,000 to 40,000 copies through selected bookstores with the intent of raising the book's profile on the *Times* list.

Crainer (1998) has argued that several recent best-selling management books have been ghostwritten. He points out that a company run by the 'queen of ghost writers,' Donna Sammons Carpenter, and several other individuals are behind many of the recent management best-sellers including *Re-engineering the Corporation* and *The Discipline of Market Leaders* (1995).

In an article in the December 2001 issue of *Fast Company*, Tom Peters stated in an interview with respect to *In Search of Excellence*, which he cowrote with Robert Waterman 20 years earlier, 'This is pretty small beer, but for what it's worth. Okay, I confess: We faked the data' ("The real confessions of Tom Peters," 2001).

Previous explanations of the appeal of different management ideas are generally based on the assumption that regardless of the reasons for their popularity, they are founded on an unbreakable link to an authored work and some original analysis of an aspect of organizational life (e.g., Abrahamson, 1996a, 1996b; Furusten, 1999; Jackson, 2001; Kennedy, 2001). Fundamentally, an individual, or group of individuals, has conducted some "observations" that they have subsequently distilled into an essence or "success formula." This is then brought to the attention of the intended audience in an undistorted form and is either accepted or rejected. In this sense they are authentic in that they are not ersatz or contrived.

This article argues that best-selling management books are indicative of broader social developments with respect to communication. Specifically, it draws on the argument that our lives are increasingly filled by pseudoevents and synthetic products. Whether adopting a constructionist or realist stance, a number of commentators point out that there is an increasingly problematic connection between what is presented (i.e., the appearance or image) for consumption and a notion of the "original" (see Baudrillard, 1988, 1994, 1998; Best, 1989; Best & Kellner, 1997, 1999, 2000; Boorstin, 1961/1992; Debord, 1967). Examples include news stories, celebrity magazines, tourist attractions, political pronouncements, popular music, so-called reality television programmes[1], and so forth. None of these phenomena are as they seem because they are fabricated somewhere by somebody in order to have a predesigned impact on an intended audience. They are packaged to be concrete, immediately graspable, and most importantly, to have maximum impact and mass appeal. In the process, the distinction between what is real and what is not becomes blurred. As synthetic image builds on synthetic image we can no longer assume the image we consume bears a direct relationship to an original (i.e., that what we consume is truly authentic). In this idealized and hypostasized world in which our view of reality becomes increasingly uncertain, our notion of verisimilitude and what passes for truth is increasingly turned upside down. The notion that reality is grounded in terms of a link to an authentic original does not necessarily hold with the consequence that nothing can be taken as certain because images end up becoming real, and reality ends up transformed into images.

As the three vignettes at the beginning of this article demonstrate, these trends have permeated the production of those books that are frequently acknowledged as the progenitors of fashionable ideas. Their popularity with readers cannot be attributed to "real" sales. The writer of the book and the named author on the cover are not necessarily the same individual. Finally, the data or observations that underpin the ideas being presented cannot be assumed to exist. Thus, the assumption that the books themselves and the ideas they contain are grounded in terms of the authenticity of a referent point does not necessarily hold. They therefore represent a form of pseudoknowledge. In this article, we examine this issue by focusing on the process by which a number of best-selling books have been fabricated and the implications of this for our understanding of management fashion more generally.

In the first of this article's five parts we critically review the literature on management fashion. Building on this critique, the second part draws on the ideas of Boorstin (1961/1992) and Debord (1967) to argue that aesthetic and management fashions cannot be conceived of as separate forms because both represent the preeminence of the image-spectacle. Following a discussion of the research data and methods, the fourth part outlines the empirical findings resulting from a study of the production of six best-selling management books. The article closes with a discussion of the implications of the conceptual approach and research findings for our understanding of management fashion.

MANAGEMENT FASHION

Three general strands can be discerned in the management fashion literature. The first stream is concerned to identify and explicate patterns in the life cycle of the management fashion discourse. The lineage of this literature can be traced to Abrahamson's (1991, 1996a, 1996b) seminal papers on the management fashion-setting process. Drawing on the innovation-diffusion literature (Rogers, 1983) and neoinstitutional theory (DiMaggio & Powell, 1983), his theory argued that groups of interrelated knowledge entrepreneurs and industries, identified as management consultants, management gurus, business schools, and mass media organizations, are characterized as being in a race to sense managers' emergent collective preferences for new techniques. Rational and progressive norms are seen as governing the choice of managerial ideas and techniques. Rational normative expectations are that management techniques will be rational (i.e., efficient means to important ends), whereas progressive normative expectations are that management ideas will progress over time (i.e., be repeatedly replaced by new and better techniques). The members of the fashion-setting community develop rhetorics that "convince fashion followers that a management technique is both rational and at the forefront of managerial progress" (Abrahamson, 1996a, p. 267). Their rhetorics must therefore articulate why it is imperative that managers should pursue certain organizational goals and why their particular technique offers the best means to achieve these goals. Thus, within this model the management fashion-setting community is viewed as supplying mass audiences with ideas and techniques that have the potential for developing mass followings. These may or may not become fashions depending on fashion setters' ability to redefine fashion followers' collective beliefs about which management techniques are state of the art and meet their immediate needs.

The plethora of empirical studies emanating from this model have focused primarily on the diffusion pattern of a range of fashionable discourses within the print media. Using citation analysis, the number of references to a particular idea in a sequence of years are counted and plotted to identify the life cycle of a fashionable management idea. The results of these studies demonstrate that the life cycles of a number of fashionable management ideas are characterized by an initial period in which the frequency of citations increases, peaks, and then declines; although the shapes of the curves for different ideas are not necessarily identical nor symmetrical (i.e., they do not necessarily rise and fall at the same rate) and vary between countries (Abrahamson & Fairchild, 1999; Benders & van Veen, 2001; Gibson & Tesone, 2001; Spell, 1999, 2001). Furthermore, whilst the life spans of recent management fashions are considerably shorter than those for ideas that came to prominence in earlier periods, their peaks are much higher (Carson, Lanier, Carson, & Guidry, 2000).

The second broad strand of literature has focused on identifying those factors that account for the popularity of particular management books and the ideas they seek to promote. Some commentators have focused on what Grint (1994) has termed the "internalist" approach. That is, the popularity of a book is related to its novel and superior content when compared to previous ideas (see McGovern, 1997; Newstrom & Pierce, 1993). Others have adopted the "externalist" approach by seeking to determine "*why* the package is effective in its particular envelope of space and time" (Grint, 1994, p. 192). From this perspective the key question is, Why do some ideas take off and engage particular audiences at certain times and not others? In answering it, the popularity and success of a book and its ideas are related to its ability to resonate with and be in harmony with the expectations and understandings of its target audience. If a book fails to convince its target audience of the plausibility and appropriateness of its ideas, then it will probably not be bought in the quantities necessary to become a best-seller[2]. According to Grint (1994), "for the 'plausibility' to occur the ideas most likely to prevail are those that are apprehended as capturing the *zeitgeist* or 'spirit of the times' " (p. 193).

In a related strand of literature, Jackson (1999, 2001, 2002) has examined the rhetorical appeal of three management ideas that were popular in the 1990s: effectiveness, the learning organization, and reengineering. He argued that rhetoric accounts for the "emergence and predominance of just a few particular fashions over many others that are competing for the manager's attention at any given period of time" (Jackson, 2001, p. 39). Drawing on Bormann's (1972) fantasy theme analysis, his research identifies specific rhetorical elements that underpin the popularity of each fashionable idea.

Several writers have combined the two approaches distinguished by Grint (1994). For example, Kieser (1997) and Furusten (1999) have identified a number of common elements in best-selling management books. These include a focus on a single factor, the contrasting of old ideas with the new such that the latter are presented as qualitatively better and superior, the creation of a sense of urgency such that the introduction of the ideas is presented as pressing and unavoidable, the linkage of the ideas to highly treasured management values, case studies of outstanding success, and a stress on an ideas' universal applicability. Even if all these elements are present, Kieser (1997) wrote that they "are useless if the timing is not perfect" (p. 61). Hence, best-selling management books must not only present their ideas in certain ways, they must also appear plausible by speaking to their readers' immediate concerns.

The final strand of literature focuses on the individuals who are identified as the authors of popular management books and the progenitors of many fashionable ideas—the management gurus. It argues that the success and impact of their ideas is due to the form in which they are presented—their powerful public performances. To date, academic studies of the public performances of management gurus have largely consisted of theoretical discussions that, using the work of Lewin (1951) and Sargant (1957/1997), have depicted the gurus as experts in persuasive communication who seek to transform the consciousness of their audiences through powerful oratory (Clark, 1995; Clark & Salaman, 1996; Huczynski, 1993; Jackson, 1996).

FASHION AS IMAGE-SPECTACLE

Although the literature reviewed above provides important insights into the character of the life cycles of recently fashionable management ideas and the possible reasons for their popularity, several commentators have nevertheless highlighted a number of significant shortcomings (see Clark, 2001, in press; Kieser, 1997). In this article we focus on the notion that the management fashion literature has a tendency to be self-contained in that it is almost completely uninformed by theories of aesthetic fashion or broader discussions about similar social phenomena. Management fashion is regarded as a special case requiring new theory and explanation. For example, in the most cited article on the topic, Abrahamson (1996a, p. 255) has argued that in contrast to the beauty of aesthetic fashion, management techniques must appear rational and progressive and are shaped by technical and economic forces in additional to sociopsychological forces. Consequently, theories of aesthetic fashions are deemed inappropriate. However, Kieser (1997) has argued that similar forces shape demand in both the aesthetic and management forms of fashion. He further argued that rhetoric "which is the essence of management fashion, is an aesthetic form" (p. 54). In his view, therefore, a separate theory of management fashion is not required, because existing conceptual approaches with respect to fashion in its aesthetic form supply a relevant and comprehensive explanatory framework.

We wish to build on this latter point by arguing that management and aesthetic fashions both express and exemplify broader social trends to which they are inextricably linked. In this sense they are not different forms of fashion. Our specific argument is that best-selling management books represent a central feature of communication in modern society, the preeminence of the image. As such, they are manufactured contrivances that are designed to have maximum impact on the intended audience and so gain a mass appeal. In the process of their production their link to a concrete understanding of organisations founded upon either research or direct experience is loosened as the form of their presentation takes precedence. In some cases, this link never existed from the outset because the book is completely fabricated. Whichever is the case, these books are designed to have mass appeal with the consequence that the contents are vivified so that they are presented as a "spectacular and glittering universe of image and signs" (Best & Kellner, 1999, p. 143). Thus, they are fundamentally an aesthetic form.

This argument builds on some of the central postulates of Guy Debord's *Society of the Spectacle* (1967), which in turn draws heavily on Daniel Boorstin's 1961 book *The Image*. Because many of the passages of Debord's book are unreferenced paraphrases or *détournements* of statements by other authors, this intellectual debt is unacknowledged. Adopting a realist perspective, Boorstin is concerned to understand the implications that attach to a social transformation that he terms the "Graphic Revolution." This he defines as the "ability to make, preserve, transmit, and disseminate precise images" (Boorstin, 1992, p. 13). Central to this is the creation of a "thicket of unreality which stands between us and the facts of life" (p. 3) as we increasingly manufacture "illusions with which to deceive ourselves" (p. 5). Boorstin's purpose is to examine an element of this "synthetic reality" that is created to meet our need for interesting and spectacular diversions which he terms "pseudo-events" (p. 9). These pseudoevents are not spontaneous but are "planned, planted or incited . . . for the immediate purpose of being reported or reproduced" (p. 11). They are "arranged for the convenience of the reporting or reproducing media" and are deemed successful based on a measurement of how widely they are reported (p. 11). They spawn other pseudoevents in "geometric progression . . . because every kind of pseudo-event (being planned) tends to become ritualised, with a protocol and a rigidity all its own" (p. 33).

Boorstin's (1992) argument serves as a foundation for Debord's theory in that both are concerned with the ascendancy of image and concomitant loss of direct experience and a sense of a connection to reality due to the simulacrum effects of the media. As Boorstin (p. 19) noted, the increasing reporting of pseudoevents in the media makes the tracing of the "original" difficult. Pseudoevents are reported in the same way as actual events, with the consequence that authenticity cannot be easily ascertained.[3] As they are reproduced they become the referents by which we understand key aspects of our lives, with the consequence that they produce "new categories of experience" that "are no longer classifiable by the old common sense tests of true or false" (p. 211). Thus, the media have erased distinctions between true and false, real and unreal. Treating facsimiles as real creates a "new world of blurs" in which the "new images have blurred traditional distinctions" (p. 213). As Boorstin wrote, "In this new world, where almost everything can be true, the socially rewarded art is that of making things seem true" (p. 212). By being "more vivid, more attractive, more impressive, and more persuasive than reality itself" (p. 36), pseudoevents will eclipse ordinary, spontaneous events, with the consequence that people will live in a world "where fantasy is more real than reality, where the image has more dignity than its original" (p. 37).

Building on this argument and perspective, Debord (1967) began by paraphrasing Marx's opening sentence in *Capital Volume 1*—"In societies where the modern conditions of production prevail, all life presents itself as an immense accumulation of *spectacles*" (#1)[4]. At the heart of Debord's thinking is the notion that direct experience and the determination of events by individuals are replaced by a passive contemplation of images. Whereas Marx spoke of the degradation of *being* into *having*, Debord talked of a further transformation from *having* into *appearing*. In this situation the material object draws "its immediate prestige and its ultimate function" (#17) as an image that dominates people's understandings of their everyday life. "Separation is the alpha and omega of the spectacle" (#25). Atomized individuals are at once united in these hypostacized abstractions that form the spectacle. But at the same time these images interpose between concrete reality and individuals such that there is a split between real social activity and its representation. Thus, although the notion of the spectacle is a complex term that "unifies and explains a great diversity of apparent phenomena" (#10), it is nevertheless centrally concerned with highlighting the social consequences of a society in which there is a "growing multitude of image-objects" (#15) that filter and portray social reality as image. As Best and Kellner (1997) wrote, "Within this abstract system, it is the *appearance* of the commodity that is more decisive than its actual use value, and the symbolic packaging of commodities—be they cars or presidents—generates an image industry and new commodity aesthetics" (p. 85). Thus, Debord's theory is concerned with the changing nature of the commodity form in which its value shifts from the concrete to the image.

Debord is referring to a process, previously identified by Boorstin, in which images come to dominate and replace our concrete understanding and experience of social reality[5]. We no longer live life directly but experience the world at one remove because "In the spectacle, one part of the world *represents itself* to the world and is superior to it" (Debord, 1967, #29). As Best (1989) wrote, "The spectacle escalates abstraction to the point where we no longer live life in the world *per se*—'inhaling and exhaling all the powers of nature' (Marx)—but in an abstract *image* of the world" (pp. 30-31). The spectacularization of society is therefore a process of separation in which idealized intangible images come to dominate tangible lived experience such that "the tangible world is replaced by a selection of images which exist above it, and which impose themselves as the tangible *par excellence*" (Debord, 1967, #36). The spectacular society is therefore fundamentally concerned with the production of compelling illusions, pseudoforms, and counterfeit commodities. We consume a world that is fabricated for us rather than actively produce our own. Our experience of life is infected by the spectacle because it is located in and determined by a spectacular universe of shimmering images, glossy surfaces, and dissembling masks. As Debord wrote, "The concrete life of everyone has been degraded into a *speculative* universe" (#19). It is this ensemble of independent representations that comes to control our thoughts and actions. As we become mesmerized by the spectacle, our attitudes about the world and events within it, our gestures and the phrases we use in everyday speech, even the topics of conversation are not of our own making but determined by the envoys of the spectacle—the image producers and disseminators. In what follows, we examine the activities one group of image creators.

DATA AND METHOD

As mentioned above, previous research into the management fashion phenomenon has adopted a relatively static approach using either citation analysis or a variety of techniques to analyse texts. In contrast, this study focuses on the process by which six best-selling management books were produced. These books were published between 1976 and 1995. They focus on organization and management issues rather than personal development and success. They were selected on the basis of their popularity over the last 27 years as indicated in numerous studies of fashionable ideas (for example, Abrahamson, 1996a, 1996b, Abrahamson & Fairchild, 1999, Carson et al., 2000; Kieser, 1997; Spell, 1999, 2001). In addition, the authors and these books each feature in the upper reaches of rankings of (a) influential management thinkers (Crainer & Dearlove, 2002) and (b) books on management (Bedeian & Wren, 2001).

In each case we conducted semistructured interviews with a range of individuals concerned with their production. We began by contacting the authors and editors of each book. Where these individuals mentioned that other personnel had been involved with the production of a book, these individuals in turn were contacted and interviews conducted. It became apparent that a number of editors and ghostwriters who work freelance had been involved in more than one of the books that are the focus of this study. Overall we interviewed six authors, five book editors (two in the United States and three in the United Kingdom/Europe), three editors and publishers (two in the United States and one in the United Kingdom/ Europe) and four ghostwriters (three in the United States and one in the United Kingdom). The interviewees' average period of experience as a guru was a little greater than 12 years with a range from 6 to 40 years. With respect to those in publishing it was around 9 years with a range from 7 to 23 years. The purpose of the interviews was to elicit the respondents' views concerning the processes surrounding the commissioning of the books, their writing, editing, and marketing. In particular, we were concerned to identify their views as to what distinguished a successful from an unsuccessful book, the role of different personnel at the various points in the production process, the process by which the ideas were created and developed, and the different methods used to disseminate ideas to the target audience. Attention was therefore given to previously published books in addition to those recently published and in the process of being produced. The interviews lasted approximately 90 minutes.

Although it was not possible to completely eradicate attribution error, we nevertheless adopted a number of measures to reduce its impact. In conducting the interviews we were not seeking to privilege the views of any one group and so elevate their role and status in the process. Rather, the intention was to obtain multiple understandings that could then be used as the basis for further discussions with the individuals. The process was therefore also iterative in that a number of the respondents were interviewed more than once in order to deepen our knowledge about the production of these books and check information provided by other interviewees. After each interview a copy of the notes or transcript was sent to each interviewee. A number of interviewees reflected on these and via correspondence provided additional information on their role and that of others. It should be noted that to protect the identity of interviewees, names are not used, and book titles, where they are referred to, are pseudonyms.

All interviews were recorded, transcribed, and then subject to a form of grounded theory analysis using the constant comparative method (Glaser & Strauss, 1967) in order to identify similarities and differences in the ways the gurus, book editors, and ghostwriters described the processes through which best-selling management books are produced and marketed. In analyzing the data we sought to avoid imposing theoretical and conceptual frameworks that had been developed a priori. Instead, in an inductive and interactive process we developed, invoked, and refined our theory, concepts, and analytic categories on the basis of careful, detailed, and repeated analysis of the interview transcripts. This process, described by Mason (2002, p. 180) as "moving between everyday concepts and meanings, lay accounts and social explanations," enabled us to "identify salient, grounded categories of meaning held by participants in the setting" (Marshall & Rossman, 1995, p. 114). Our inductive, polyphonic, and reflexive approach sought to surface the meanings given by the social actors to their actions and social situation and in the process ascertain a consistent pattern of understanding within and between the different categories of respondent (Blaikie, 2000). Although they highlighted their own roles in the book production process, they nonetheless also indicated that the process not only involved extensive collaboration between authors and editors and ghostwriters but also was informed by a set of conventions that the latter associate with best-selling books.

THE CREATION OF THE BEST-SELLING MANAGEMENT BOOK AS IMAGE-SPECTACLE

Our analysis of the interviews reveals the extent to which best-selling management books are manufactured contrivances that emerge from a creative process in which the form of the presentation of management ideas takes precedence over their actual use value. This is reflected in the fact that the editors and ghostwriters distinguished between these books and other texts aimed at a managerial audience in two ways. First, the ideas and manuscripts that were deemed to have blockbuster potential were regarded as star-based products, that is, as vehicles for promoting authors and their brand. As one editor stated, "The author is all-important. What we want is to build a brand so that the author has instant recognition. This will help when we come to publish their future books and develop synergistic lines. Another editor explained that these books were star vehicles in the following terms:

> When you publish these books you have to work on the assumption
> that most people who buy it won't read it. It needs to be seductive for
> reasons other than content. The package is the total package, the
> book and the person. . . . Packaging the author is as important as
> packaging the book. We promote the person as much as the
> book. . . . What you are selling is an attachment to a particular per-
> son and their brand or ideas. Our job is either to create this or to
> develop it further.

The key point here is that the book is as much a vehicle for promoting an individual as the ideas it contains. From the outset it is
designed as part of a broader package of related products that will
all feature the author. As Crainer (1998) has similarly noted with
respect to Stephen Covey's book *The Seven Habits of Highly Effective People*, it was preceded by commercially successful audiotape
programmes, video-based training packages, and presentations on
the corporate lecture circuit.

Second, given the previous point, they were not viewed as
immutable objects in which the sanctity of the authors' original
ideas was sacrosanct. Rather, they were books that required shaping prior to publication. The initial idea was generally viewed as no
more than raw material that had to be further developed and
moulded before it could be published as a book. Editors, therefore,
were not seeking fully formed books that could be published with
minimal copyediting but rather the glimmer of an idea that they
believed could be shaped and packaged to appeal to a management
audience, and to promote the author and their brand. As one editor
noted:

> There is no general requirement in terms of the amount of detail we
> expect from the outset. We take on some books with detailed synop-
> ses of each chapter and the first chapter written. Other books start
> off as a one-page summary of a series of ideas. What I am looking
> for is something that will appeal to an audience no matter how
> detailed.

Making a similar point when referring to a particularly successful
book, another editor stated, "I liked the concept. We didn't have
much to go on initially, just some loose descriptions of the chapters.
I knew if we pitched the content in the right way it would do well."

Having established that the editors and ghostwriters are primarily concerned not with the utility of management books but rather with their potential as star vehicles that can be used to build and promote an author's brand, we now turn to discuss how this shapes the writing and editing process prior to publication.

THE WRITING PROCESS

COLLABORATION

Management best-selling books, like many cultural and consumer products, "do not spring forth full blown but are made somewhere by somebody" (Peterson, 1979, p. 152). The displayed character of a potentially best-selling management book at the point of publication is the result of active collaboration at earlier stages between the originator or originators and a range of support personnel rather than being the work of a single person (i.e., the author). In this sense, these management books are collective social products that depend for their character on reciprocal collaboration between a network of support personnel (Clark, 2003). Thus, the milieu within which they are produced shapes the form and content of the ideas prior to their presentation to the target audience.

Given that these books are collaborative productions, a key role of the editor is to carefully combine and manage the talents of authors and other support personnel in such a way that a book has the best chance of success when released into the marketplace. On some occasions the team may be limited to the author and editor. At other times it may include additional support personnel such as ghostwriters. The decision with respect to the composition of a team relates to their evaluation of a range of information. They may, for example, respond to some particular circumstances with respect to the production of a particular book (e.g., a coauthor withdraws from the project). Other factors include their evaluation of the success or failure of books on which they have worked, competing books in the marketplace, their understanding of the public mood, and so forth. But of primary importance is their evaluation of the author's competence as a writer. One editor/ghostwriter justified both ghostwriting and extensive editorial input during the writing process in the following terms.

> Many "authors" can't or won't write. But they may be gifted as thinkers, presenters, synthesizers, commentators, speakers, or entertainers . . . We often assume that if a person is a talented speaker, presenter, motivator, mentor, professor, consultant, trainer, or professional that he or she must also be capable of writing a wonderful book. Wrong. I often use a track and field metaphor. If a person is world class at the 400 meter hurdles, does that mean the same person should also be world class at the 100 meter sprint, the mile, the high jump, or the marathon?

This comment relates to the earlier point that editors seek to build brands that can then be leveraged into a number of media. In pursuing this strategy an author does not necessarily have to be judged by editors or ghostwriters to be a competent or potential writer of a best-selling management book. If they are seen to be an excellent live presenter but a poor writer, the insinuation is that this can be overcome with the aid of strong editorial input or the employment of a ghostwriter. In view of this, we now turn to examine the role of editors and ghostwriters in more detail.

CONVENTIONS

Central to editors' and ghostwriters' conceptions of popular management writing is a set of textual conventions that pervade best-selling management books. It is these conventions that are at the heart of the spectacularization of these books, because they package the ideas in such a way that the published book is likely to appeal to the intended audience and to promote the author's brand. The conventions derive from, and are justified by reference to, a shared conception of those who purchase best-selling management books. Based on the information sources referred to above, editors and ghostwriters view managers as being extremely busy with a focus on the tangible and immediate and a tendency toward superficiality and short attention spans. An editor reminded one of the gurus in our study he was writing for managers who are relatively intelligent and can take ideas to work with them, and who are very busy. And a key market for my books was people who take four or five hour flights. When I think of my readers now, I think that on the whole managers read on aeroplanes, or they take my books on holiday, which I find a compliment.

Another of the gurus was advised by his editor to "write clearly and have your readers in mind. It's got to be easily digestible and memorable. Managers are busy people and do not want to wade through lots of waffle." Making a similar point, an editor described their approach to these books as "stripping the ideas to their essence and making sure that the reader is not diverted into irrelevant material. These books need to communicate directly or they will bore the reader."

In the light of this conception of the intended audience for these management books, editors and ghostwriters aim to present the ideas in accessible forms that have two characteristics. The first is that they are easy to read and remember. This requires that the main elements of the ideas be reduced and simplified into pithy lists, acronyms, concepts, mnemonics, metaphors, and stories that are immediately graspable, understood, and assimilated. One editor described their approach to conveying ideas in these books as

> making the core proposition crystal clear. There is no room for ambiguity. From the outset the central themes have to be grouped into a model, framework or list of principles. You want the readers to know what an idea stands for.

In a similar vein, a guru reflecting on the process by which their first best-selling book was written stated,

> Writing the book in this way [with the editor] was a wonderfully reflective process and it led to a way of organizing the ideas that I had not planned at the outset. The grouping of the ideas into a number of general principles came with the book writing. So the book writing tied together a number of loose-ends in my thinking and in the process made them more accessible.

Second, the editors and ghostwriters use forms that emphasize and demonstrate the practical relevance of the gurus' ideas. They need to be made vivid and concrete for the audience. Often this involves relating stories of how the gurus' ideas have been successfully implemented in many organizations. Thus, the gurus were exhorted to include examples of their principles being put into practice in order to persuade readers that their analysis and solutions were not only relevant but also the most appropriate. As one guru was told, "You gotta show them that it really works. Who's going to buy into something that's never been tried?"

Another was given the advice that

> in telling stories you have to show that the idea behind the story is backed up by rigorous research but also company practice. So, you have to tell stories about real managers facing real problems in real organizations. Doing this makes the idea more real to the reader.

This last quotation indicates that for some editors the examples are there to show the readers that the guru's ideas work in practice. The assumption is that if readers can see that organizations have implemented the changes advocated by the guru, then it is also possible for the reader's organization to achieve the same benefits by adopting the guru's ideas. However, comments from another guru indicate that these examples can also serve another function in that they may help to legitimize their vision. This is achieved, in part, by carefully selecting organizations that are household names and so, well known to the readers of these books, possibly even admired by them. As this guru stated, "The companies chosen had to be recognizable to large numbers of people, otherwise they will think, "So what?" But if X, Y, or Z did this, then it must really be important." As another guru said:

> I had been working with a number of well-known organizations for many years. I knew the ideas worked. The point of the book was to share their experiences and success with a wider audience so that we could form a critical mass as more organizations became aware of and sought to implement the ideas. One area where [the editor] was really helpful was in getting me to illustrate the ideas with some well-chosen examples.

Again, what was important was to present the ideas in such a way that the readers felt that they, too, could implement what the guru was advocating.

In sum, editors and ghostwriters have a significant, if largely unseen, impact on the fashioning of management ideas in book form. They shape and package ideas in line with conventions that are associated with management best-selling books. Our interviews with editors, ghostwriters, and gurus revealed the extent to which management ideas are mediated through these conventions. This raises important questions concerning the extent to which the gurus' original or existing ideas are reconfigured and changed as editors and ghostwriters render them accessible to the intended managerial audience. It is clear that these conventions are not neutral conduits that amplify and enhance the authors' original ideas. As the following quotations indicate, several of the gurus remarked that the form of their ideas changed substantially during the writing or editing process:

> I think my first draft was all over the place. It was probably double the length of the final manuscript. I probably produced about five or six complete drafts. Each one would go to [the editor] and they would write back with loads of comments and suggestions. I tell you, if you saw that first draft you wouldn't recognize the published book.

> The hardest thing when writing the book was that I had written all these darn academic papers all my life. I had never written a book. I was very fortunate in that I had a wonderful editor who was a great consultant. He really helped to deconstruct my writing style. He would write samples of what he thought would work for the audience, which I never liked and so re-wrote them. He also told me to bring my personal speaking voice into my writing, which was hard. It was a real learning process which did produce a different kind of book. But I was pleased with that.

> I had written other things before but not a book, so as I wrote a draft I would send it to [the editor]. They would send me pages of comments and we would talk on the telephone. This happened many times and through this process the ideas became clearer and the key concepts emerged.

It is clear from the comments that the editing process for a number of the gurus actively shaped and modified their initial ideas so that what was presented to the target audience was qualitatively different from the draft manuscript or book outline that entered the publishing system. Although in the first two cases they felt that the finished book was better for this intervention, it was nevertheless changed from what they had originally envisaged. None of the gurus whose books had been subject to extensive editorial input viewed this in negative terms. Rather, they portrayed themselves as naïve, first-time authors who did not have the necessary skills to write a book (see Clark, 2003). In this respect, they concur with the views of the ghostwriter who earlier argued that many authors are skilled public orators but poor writers.

Although the character of these books often changed during the editorial process, in a number of cases they were complete inventions from the outset in that the editors admitted to first coming up with an idea and then pitching it to an established guru. They then employed someone to write the book whilst the guru lent their name to it. This phenomenon related to a guru's second, third, fourth book, and so on. These manufactured books, which usually involve the refashioning and development of a guru's existing ideas, are important to both gurus and editors. Every 2 or 3 years gurus need a new book to fuel the demand for their services on the corporate lecture circuit. Similarly, the editors are under pressure to extend the life of the gurus' brand in order to maximise the publishers' revenues from their established authors. One U.K. publisher gave the following example of a manufactured book:

> [Guru's name] had written *Heart*[7] and we thought of the idea of *More Heart*. We proposed this to him. He does not receive any money. We pay the ghostwriter. But it extends [guru's name] minibrand and is something else he can promote on the conference circuit. Manufacturing books is very, very easy for authors to be involved in. . . . We get a big name, they get a new book for little effort. We all benefit. These people don't want to publish for money. What they want is the prestige of having a book in print.

Although by no means all gurus are involved in the manufacture of books, this phenomenon reflects the relative status of books and other media used to disseminate management ideas. As we have indicated, the management gurus included in this study do not restrict their communication activities to books alone but also speak on the international lecture circuit, make video and audio programmes, and produce CD-ROMS and establish Internet sites. It could be argued that these other media are just as able, if not better in certain circumstances, at conveying their ideas in an easily apprehendable and succinct manner. However, they would appear not to have displaced the premier status of the book. The book was generally viewed as a necessary prerequisite for access to the other media. In this sense a best-selling book represents an entry ticket into the broad range of media through which popular management ideas can be communicated. Thus, although some of the gurus included in this study have reduced the number of live presentations they give a year and have withdrawn from making audio and video programmes, not one has stopped writing books. They all see it as a fundamental way of communicating their ideas. Indeed, several gurus consider their long-term popularity to be linked to their ability to continue to publish books. For example, one guru stated, "My books are part of my public identity. When people introduce you you come over as having something to say if they can say 'and here is so and so author of such and such a book.'" However, they may not have either the time to write a book or develop a novel set of ideas. This is where the manufacturing of books plays a crucial role in their continuing status as management gurus.

DISCUSSION AND CONCLUSION

This article has argued that ideas presented in popular management books are indicative of a broader social trend in communication—the rise of the image and pseudoform. Drawing on the ideas of both Boorstin and Debord, we have noted a shift to a society where images and representations of reality dominate. Image is ubiquitous. Perceptions of objects, whether they are products, politicians, or management prescriptions, are more important than their actual substance. The "real" is increasingly replaced by pseudoforms, which are presented as authentic. According to Best and Kellner (1999, p. 133) contemporary life is "saturated with spectacles, ranging from daily 'photo opportunities' to highly orchestrated special events that dramatize state power, to TV ads and image management for competing candidates." The media coverage of the O.J. Simpson trial, the Clinton sex scandals, the death of Princess Diana, and more recently the Washington sniper or the Paul Burrell trial[8] are all examples of what Kellner (2003) terms "megaspectacles." These are worldwide, media-driven events that capture the attention of the media public. Although popular management books are not spectacles on this scale, in that they do not permeate the worldwide media to the same degree, they nevertheless share many of their core features in that the displayed character of a potentially fashionable management idea at the point of dissemination is shaped by a process of fabrication. As we have shown, the intricate editing process involves a team of individuals who, by seeking to make the content more vivid and attractive for the intended audience, can alter the original nature of the ideas, sometimes substantially. Indeed, in some cases these books are completely manufactured in that they are written by ghostwriters with little or no participation from the so-called author.

The article has also argued that cooperation within the production system is based upon generalized beliefs, or conventions, of what makes a legitimate and successful management book. As we have indicated, one of the main functions of the system is to impart these conventions to nascent gurus in order to increase the likelihood of their book's becoming a best-seller. This is not to suggest that these conventions are immutable. They evolve and transform in response to shifts in the broader business environment and consumer preferences with the consequence that what is deemed an appropriate management book also changes. For example, the string of corporate scandals in America that followed the collapse of Enron and the fall of countless celebrity bosses has challenged not simply the genre's celebratory tone but its legitimacy. This arises from the key position of popular management books within the institutional fabric that supported the rise of the celebrity CEO. As Khurana (2002) has argued, the media, broadly defined,

> focus not on the complexities of organizations or on rapid changes in the business environment, but rather on the actors involved. This approach personifies the corporation, making much of winners and losers, of who is up and who is down, of who is a good CEO and

who is not. The press has thereby turned CEO's . . . into a new category of American celebrity. (p. 74)

This resonates with Clark and Salaman's (1998) argument that popular management theory is successful not because it solves managers problems but because it constitutes the role itself. These books define the management role by offering "a conception of management itself in virtuous, heroic, high status terms" (p. 157). From this point of view, they generate their appeal by articulating the qualities necessary for successful implementation of the management role. As we show in this article, those involved in the production of these books mould the nature and presentation of the ideas for a specific audience—managers. In doing so, these books are presented in such a way that they reinforce why managers are important, why they matter, and why their skills are critical. However, the wave of corporate scandals in the past few years has led to the questioning of the very spectacle that these books seek to project. Continuing to laud the exploits of hero managers is no longer deemed appropriate. Indeed, although these books continue to sell, it is clear that the gleam from the spectacle surface has begun to fade. Consequently, more cynical books, such as Scott Adams's subversive *Dilbert* cartoons, have recently topped the management best-seller lists ("Business books," 2002; London, 2003). In this respect, in a world of blurs purchasers have switched to more authentic fantasy.

In addition, the article makes several contributions to our understanding of management fashion. First, although a number of authors have sought to differentiate aesthetic and management fashion, this article suggests that one factor accounting for their success is their vivification during the writing process. Although the practical benefits of the ideas are extolled, and this is reinforced with references to well-known successful organizations, their accessibility, immediacy, and simplicity are also considered vital. Thus, the form in which ideas are presented is considered as important as their content. Indeed, some of the individuals who participated in the study would argue that the former is more important. The editorial process seeks to enhance the aesthetic attractiveness of the ideas. In this sense it is a process of beautification. Consequently, our study suggests that distinguishing between "aesthetic" and "technical" fashions may result in a narrow understanding of the reasons for the popularity of particular ideas. Ignoring aesthetic elements excludes, or downplays, a range of factors that those concerned with the production of best-selling books consider critical to their success.

The study also suggests that the management fashion phenomenon shares a number of features with a range of other social phenomena. Again this indicates that it is not unique, requiring new explanatory frameworks. As we have argued, the image is a dominant form in current society. This article has focused on one group of individuals who are concerned with moulding ideas so that they have a positive impact on the intended audience. The books are designed so that the ideas are presented in such a way that the readers will believe that they will have a positive impact on their organization or working life in some way. Thus, what is critical is not that the ideas actually work but that they are perceived to be of practical benefit and relevance. A key implication of this article is, therefore, that the writing and editing process is a system of persuasion par excellence. Impression management is central to the collective activities of the support personnel that compose the system. In essence, they are seeking to create perceptions with respect to the legitimacy and value of certain works. They have to convince potential buyers and readers that a particular book best meets their immediate and pressing needs. The readers and potential readers are the audience for whom the book is fabricated. The authors, editors, and ghostwriters work as a team trying to generate maximum buying response and interest from the audience. This article indicates that management gurus and their team of support personnel achieve this by producing a product in accordance with a set of general conventions so that it is what it is claimed to be. Thus, regardless of the level of author input in the writing process, a book is presented with an identifiable author on the cover. In this way they seek to assure buyers that their product is worthy of attention and of being purchased. This creates difficulties for purchasers seeking to identify authentic knowledge because the distinction between the real and the unreal is blurred.

Building on the previous point, the final implication of the article relates to the argument that some of the books upon which a number of recent management fashions are founded are pseudoforms in that they are manufactured coproductions[9]. Given that these books are modified, often substantially, through the editorial process, and occasionally entirely manufactured, they cannot be considered completely authentic in the sense of being primarily the output of an author. But although on occasion they may be ersatz and contrived, their outward appearance is that of an authentic book in that they meet the requirements for this form. Consequently, the audiences of these books are unable to judge which books, or their constituent elements, are the work of an author and which involve the input of an editor or ghostwriter. They all look identical. The fact that they may not be equally authentic has several potentially important implications.

First, the fashions that these books promote lead to real consequences for organizations and the people who work in them (Cane, 1994; "Re-engineering with love," 1995; Grint & Willcocks, 1995). Furthermore, as we have indicated earlier, the life span of these ideas in recent years has become shorter, which suggests that audience disenchantment sets in more quickly. Thus, the managerial audience needs to engage in much deeper critical questioning of the theoretical and empirical foundations of these books before they become mesmerized by the glittering surface. One approach would be to treat the ideas that these books seek to promote with considerable caution and wait for some form of external validation (e.g., empirical testing and refinement) before rushing to implementation. In this way the onset of a fashion may be delayed, but if its robustness is confirmed, its longevity may be increased. Furthermore, academics can then actively intervene in the fashion-setting process by providing a quality-control function for managerial knowledge that is circulating at any time. Presently, it is recognized that academics have had limited success at intervening in the management-fashion-setting process (Abrahamson 1996a; Spell, 2001; Suddaby & Greenwood, 2001). It would also encourage greater engagement between academia and business.

Second, those academics conducting research into management fashion and related phenomenon need to attach greater significance to the aesthetic aspects of the popular management ideas. This will give greater recognition to those factors that producers of popular ideas themselves believe are important to their success. The popularity curves of these ideas may therefore attest to the fabrication skills of backstage personnel rather than fortuitously resonating with the zeitgeist or mirroring of fashion followers' collective beliefs about which management techniques are state of the art and meet their immediate needs.

NOTES

1. On British television this has been turned upside down by the Channel 4 television series *Faking It*. In this, individuals with no previous experience in an activity are trained to convince a panel of experts that they really are a chef, conductor, surfer, and so forth.

2. The processes that underpin people's decisions to purchase management books are complex. Gladwell (2000) has highlighted the importance of "connectors," people who bring new products to the attention of large groups of people and persuade them of their importance. It is the actions of these individuals, he argued, that tip a product from being a minority taste to a mass fashion.

3. The media's obsession with government spin indicates that they are very aware of this issue.

4. It is convention to quote the number of each thesis rather the page numbers in *Society of the Spectacle* (Debord, 1967).

5. Although there is considerable correspondence between Debord's ideas and Baudrillard's notion of "hyperreality," Debord does not abandon the principle that below the image is an objective reality.

6. This is a pseudonym.

7. Paul Burrell was Princess Diana's butler. He was charged with stealing in the region of 200 items from her estate, but his trial collapsed in November 2002 when the queen informed the court that he had notified her, shortly after the princess died, that he had taken many of her papers for safekeeping.

8. We recognize that this article is also a form of coproduction in that prior to its publication we received and responded to the constructive feedback from three referees. These comments have affected the development of the article. However, where this process differs is that we were responsible for the subsequent amendments and the overall authorship of the article.

REFERENCES

Abrahamson, E. (1991). Managerial fads and fashions: The diffusion and rejection of innovations. *Academy of Management Review, 16,* 586-612.

Abrahamson, E. (1996a). Management fashion. *Academy of Management Review*, *21*, 254-85.

Abrahamson, E. (1996b). Technical and aesthetic fashion. In B. Czarniawska and G. Sevon (Eds.), *Translating organizational change* (pp. 117-137). Berlin, Germany: de Gruyter.

Abrahamson, E., & Fairchild, G. (1999). Management fashion: Lifecycles, triggers, and collective processes. *Administrative Science Quarterly, 44*, 708-740.

Baudrillard, J. (1988) *Selected writings* (M. Poster, Ed.). Cambridge, UK: Polity.

Baudrillard, J. (1994). *Simulacra and simulation*. Ann Arbor: University of Michigan Press.

Baudrillard, J. (1998). *The consumer society*. London: Sage.

Bedeian, A. G., & Wren, D. A. (2001). The most influential management books of the 20th century. *Organizational Dynamics, 29*, 221-225.

Benders, J., & van Veen, K. (2001). What's a fashion? Interpretative viability and management fashions. *Organization, 8*, 33-53.

Best, S. (1989). The commodification of reality and the reality of commodification: Jean Baudrillard and post-modernism. *Current Perspectives in Social Theory, 9*, 23-51.

Best, S., & Kellner, D. (1997). *The postmodern turn*. New York: Guilford.

Best, S., & Kellner, D. (1999) Debord, cybersituations, and the interactive spectacle. *Substance, 90*, 129-156.

Best, S., & Kellner, D. (2000). *The postmodern adventure*. London: Routledge.

Blaikie, N. (2000). *Designing social research*. Cambridge, UK: Polity.

Boorstin, D. J. (1992). *The image*. New York: Vintage. (Original work published 1961)

Bormann, E. (1972). Fantasy and rhetorical vision: The rhetorical criticism of social reality. *Quarterly Journal of Speech, 58*, 396-347.

Business books: From the great to the not so good. (2002, November 16). *The Economist*, p. 85.

Cane, A. (1994, June 24). Re-engineering's all the rage. *Financial Times*, p. 14.

Carson, P. P., Lanier, P., Carson, K. D., & Guidry, B. N. (2000). Clearing a path through the management fashion jungle: Some preliminary trailblazing. *Academy of Management Journal, 43*, 1143-1158.

Clark, T. (1995). *Managing consultants: Consultancy as the art of impression management*. Buckingham, UK: Open University Press.

Clark, T. (2001). Management research on fashion: A review and evaluation. *Human Relations, 54*(12), 1650-1662.

Clark, T. (2003, August). Management fashion as collective action. Paper presented to the Annual Academy of Management Conference on democracy in a knowledge economy, Seattle, WA.

Clark, T. (in press). The fashion of management fashion: A surge too far? *Organization*.

Clark, T., & Salaman, G. (1996). The management guru as organizational witch-doctor. *Organization, 3*(1), 85-107.

Clark, T., & Salaman, G. (1998). Telling tales: Management gurus' narratives and the construction of managerial identity. *Journal of Management Studies, 35*(2), 137-161.

Crainer, S. (1998, May). In search of the real author. *Management Today*, pp. 50-54.

Crainer, S., & Dearlove, D. (2002). *Thinkers 50*. Retrieved from www.thinkers50.com.

Debord, G. (1967). *The Society of the spectacle*. London: Red & Black.

Did dirty tricks create a best-seller? (1995, August 7). *Business Week*, pp. 30-33.

DiMaggio, P., & Powell, W. W. (1983). The iron cage revisited: Institutional isomorphism and collective rationality in organizational fields. *American Sociological Review, 48*, 1457-1460.

Furusten, S. (1999). *Popular management books*. London: Routledge.

Gibson, J. W., & Tesone, D. V. (2001). Management fads: Emergence, evolution, and implications for managers. *Academy of Management Review, 15*(4), 122-133.

Gladwell, M. (2000). *The tipping point: How little things can make a big difference*. Boston: Little Brown.

Glaser, B., & Strauss, A. (1967). *The discovery of grounded theory*. Chicago: Aldine.

Grint, K. (1994). Reengineering history: Social resonances and business process reengineering. *Organization, 1*(1), 179-201.

Grint, K., & Willcocks, L. (1995). Business process re-engineering in theory and practice: Business paradise regained? *New Technology, Work and Employment, 10*, 99-109.

Hammer, M., & Champy, J. (1993). *Reengineering the corporation: A manifesto for business revolution*. London: Nicholas Brealey.

Huczynski, A. (1993). *Management gurus: What makes them and how to become one*. London: Routledge.

Jackson, B. G. (1996). Re-engineering the sense of self: The manager and the management guru. *Journal of Management Studies, 33*(5), 571-90.

Jackson, B. (1999). The goose that laid the golden egg? A rhetorical critique of Stephen Covey and the effectiveness movement. *Journal of Management Studies, 36*(3), 353-377.

Jackson, B. (2001). *Management gurus and management fashions: A dramatistic inquiry*. London: Routledge.

Jackson, B. (2002). A fantasy theme analysis of three guru-led management fashions. In T. Clark & R. Fincham (Eds.), *Critical consulting: New perspectives on the management advice industry* (pp. 172-188). Oxford, UK: Basil Blackwell.

Kellner, D. (2003). *Media spectacles*. London: Routledge.

Kennedy, C. (2001). *The next big idea: The big ideas for business in the 21st century*. London: Random House.

Khurana, R. (2002). *Searching for a corporate savior: The irrational quest for charismatic CEOs*. Princeton, NJ: Princeton University Press.

Kieser, A. (1997). Rhetoric and myth in management fashion. *Organization, 4*, 49-74.

424   MANAGEMENT COMMUNICATION QUARTERLY / FEBRUARY 2004

Lewin, K. (1951). *Field theory in social science*. New York: Harper.

London, S. (2003, June 12). Why are management fads fading away? *Financial Times*, p. 14.

Marshall, C., & Rossman, G. B. (1995). *Designing qualitative research* (2nd ed.). London: Sage.

Mason, J. (2002). *Qualitative researching* (2nd ed.). London: Sage.

McGovern, P. (1997). Management gurus: The secret of their success? *Business Strategy Review, 8*(3), 52-60.

Newstrom, J. W., & Pierce, J. L. (1993). An analytic framework for assessing popular business books. *Journal of Management Development, 12*(4), 20-28.

Peterson, R. A. (1979). Revitalizing the culture concept. *Annual Review of Sociology, 5*, 137-166.

The real confessions of Tom Peters. (2001, December 3). *Business Week*, p. 30.

Re-engineering with love. (1995, July 22). *The Economist*, p. 91.

Rogers, E. M. (1983). *Diffusion of innovations*. New York: Free Press.

Sargant, W. (1997). *Battle for the mind*. Cambridge, UK: Malor. (Original work published 1957)

Spell, C. (1999). Where do management fashions come from, and how long do they stay for? *Journal of Management History, 5*, 334-348.

Spell, C. (2001). Management fashions: Where do they come from, and are they old wine in new bottles? *Journal of Management Inquiry, 10*, 358-373.

Suddaby, R., & Greenwood, R. (2001). Colonizing knowledge: Commodification as a dynamic and jurisdictional expansion in professional service firms. *Human Relations, 54*(7), 933-953.

Treacy, M., & Wiersema, F. (1995). The discipline of market leaders: Choose your customers, narrow your focus, dominate your market.

Timothy Clark (Ph.D., 1990, De Montfort) is professor of organisation behaviour at Durham Business School, University of Durham, U.K. His research interests are in management consultancy work, knowledge creation and diffusion, the nature of management fashion, and management gurus. His work has been published in British Journal of Management, Human Relations, Journal of Management Studies, *and* Organization, *among others.*

David Greatbatch (Ph.D., 1985, Warwick University) is special professor in the School of Education, University of Nottingham, U.K. His research interests are competence and learning in organisations, postcompulsory education and training, public speaking, and mediation and conflict management. His work has been published in American Journal of Sociology, American Sociological Review, Language in Society, Law and Society Review, *and* Human Relations, *among others.*

Part III
From Fashion to Fiction: Narrative and Storytelling Approaches

[10]

The Storytelling Organization: A Study of Story Performance in an Office-Supply Firm

David M. Boje
Loyola Marymount University

This paper reports on a participant-observation study in a large office-supply firm of how people perform stories to make sense of events, introduce change, and gain political advantage during their conversations. The story was not found to be a highly agreed-upon text, told from beginning to end, as it has been studied in most prior story research. Rather, the stories were dynamic, varied by context, and were sometimes terse, requiring the hearer to fill in silently major chunks of story line, context, and implication. Stories were frequently challenged, reinterpreted, and revised by the hearers as they unfolded in conversation. The paper supports a theory of organization as a collective storytelling system in which the performance of stories is a key part of members' sense making and a means to allow them to supplement individual memories with institutional memory.[*]

INTRODUCTION

Organizations As Storytelling Systems

In organizations, storytelling is the preferred sense-making currency of human relationships among internal and external stakeholders. People engage in a dynamic process of incremental refinement of their stories of new events as well as on-going reinterpretations of culturally sacred story lines. When a decision is at hand, the old stories are recounted and compared to unfolding story lines to keep the organization from repeating historically bad choices and to invite the repetition of past successes. In a turbulent environment, the organization halls and offices pulsate with a story life of the here and now that is richer and more vibrant than the firm's environments.

Even in stable times, the story is highly variable and sometimes political, in that part of the collective processing involves telling different versions of stories to different audiences. Only the chief executive officer (CEO) and a few executives may be told that the sales manager was fired for drunken indiscretions with a saleswoman on the CEO's couch; vendors only hear that the manager did not get on with the CEO; customers learn that Fred resigned; middle management suspects an affair with Mildred. Each performance is never the completed story; it is an unraveling process of confirming new data and new interpretations as these become part of an unfolding story line.

Stories are to the storytelling system what precedent cases are to the judicial system. Just as in the courtroom, stories are performed among stakeholders to make sense of an equivocal situation. The implication of stories as precedents is that story performances are part of an organization-wide information-processing network. Bits and pieces of organization experience are recounted socially throughout the firm to formulate recognizable, cogent, defensible, and seemingly rational collective accounts that will serve as precedent for individual assumption, decision, and action. This is the institutional memory system of the organization. Although individuals are limited information processors, each person retains a part of the story line, a bit of interpretation, story performance practices, and some facts that confirm a line of reasoning.

[*]
I would like to thank Joanne Martin, Alan Wilkins, David Whetten, Fiona Crofton, Robert Dennehy, Mimi Bard, Michael Moch, Jeanine Sheehan, *ASQ* editor Gerald Salancik, Linda Pike, and the reviewers for helpful comments in the writing of this paper.

Story Performance

Even when there are eye witnesses, to continue the analogy with courtroom behavior, the interpretation of the exact sequence of events and how those events speak of the motive of the defendant are made or broken in the performance of the story and by the credibility of the teller. What is interesting about storytelling in organizations is that stakeholders also posit alternative stories with alternative motives and implications to the very same underlying historical incident. The story takes on more importance than mere objective facts. In complex organizations, part of the reason for storytelling is the working out of those differences in the interface of individual and collective memory.

The important fact is that most storytelling is done in conversation and involves the listeners in various ways. Some sociolinguists have analyzed how conversations happen and, in a few studies, how stories are told: how people introduce stories, how they extend and interrupt stories, and, in general, how story performances occur within common turn-by-turn talk situations. Harvey Sacks (1972a, 1972b) and his followers (Sacks, Schegloff, and Jefferson, 1974; Jefferson, 1973, 1978; Ryave, 1978) have investigated the contexted occurrence of stories in conversations. These are complex aspects of storytelling in organizations that have been ignored in previous approaches to story analysis. We all tell stories, and during better performances we feel the adrenalin pump as word pictures dance in our intellect and we begin to live the episode vicariously or recall similar life events. In just listening to stories, our personal experience mingles with what we hear and then see. As listeners, we are co-producers with the teller of the story performance. It is an embedded and fragmented process in which we fill in the blanks and gaps between the lines with our own experience in response to ·cues, like "You know the story!" Because of what is not said, and yet shared, the audible story is only a fraction of the connection between people in their co-production performance. We become even more of a co-producer when we begin to prompt the teller with cues, such as head nods, changes in posture, and utterances that direct the inquiry (i.e., "One version I heard . . ."; "Then, what happened?") and respond with our own data. The story can be conceptualized as a joint performance of teller(s) and hearer(s) in which often overlooked, very subtle utterances play an important role in the negotiation of meaning and co-production in a storytelling episode.

Stories-As-Texts Research

Stories in previous laboratory, history, and questionnaire research generally have been wrenched from their natural performance contexts and treated as objectified social facts (Ritzer, 1975), mere texts, with little empirical attention given to the natural linguistic context in which the stories are being performed. Text research does not capture basic aspects of the situated language performance, such as how the story is introduced into the ongoing interaction, how listeners react to the story, and how the story affects subsequent dialogue.

In case history studies, researchers have relied on second- and third-hand accounts of a story, rather than examining a storytelling event in process. An example of the text-as-social-fact paradigm would be the IBM rule-breaking story analyzed by Martin et al. (1983). The point of their analysis was to answer the question, How is it that markedly similar story texts manifest themselves in different organizations? The story was uncovered by Martin et al. in an earlier autobiographical text by Rogers (1969), not from any direct field observation or any systematic on-site data collection procedures that would tell us the origins and import of the story, if any, to IBM. The story told by Rogers (1969: 153–154) is as follows:

. . . a twenty-two-year-old bride weighing ninety pounds whose husband had been sent overseas and who, in consequence, had been given a job until his return. . . . The young woman, Lucille Burger, was obliged to make certain that people entering security areas wore the correct clearance identification.

Surrounded by his usual entourage of white-shirted men, Watson approached the doorway to an area where she was on guard, wearing an orange badge acceptable elsewhere in the plant, but not a green badge, which alone permitted entrance at her door.

"I was trembling in my uniform, which was far too big," she recalled. "It hid my shakes but not my voice. 'I'm sorry,' I said to him. I knew who he was all right. 'You cannot enter. Your admittance is not recognized.' That's what we were supposed to say."

The men accompanying Watson were stricken; the moment held unpredictable possibilities. "Don't you know who he is?" someone hissed. Watson raised his hand for silence, while one of the party strode off and returned with the appropriate badge.

The story is literature and its plot and characters are indeed interesting, but is it the way IBMers tell stories to one another in real time? Other historical studies of stories, such as Clark's (1972: 179), start with inferred results of storytelling processes to capture areas of organization uniqueness. However, according to Moch and Fields (1985: 112), "since language [in acts or speech or in writing] serves to advance actors' interests, the analyst must make every effort to gather information which will allow for a reliable and valid inference about the intentions of those who generated the data to be analyzed." In stories-as-text research, the object-story is deconstructed and reinterpreted with virtually no attention to gathering performance-context information. Martin and Meyerson (1988), for example, reify stories as mere "its" when they speak of stories as so many cultural artifacts. Although there is reason to question both the method and the validity of the stories-as-text approach, Mumby (1987) nevertheless reinterpreted the IBM rule-breaking story and took quantum leaps from the literary text of the story in order to make ideological and power assumptions about the IBM culture. Valid and insightful as these assumptions may be, can we be assured that this story is really a reflection of the IBM culture?

In the case of lab-study research, performance skills are not a consideration. Rather, one varies the content of the story to look at outcomes such as retention and believability (Martin and Powers, 1979; Martin, Patterson, and Price, 1979; Martin et al., 1980). Subjects are presented with alternative versions of a story to assess their level of recall and commitment. Martin's (1982: 296) advice to management is "If a manager wants to maximize the impact of a story, she or he should make that story as concrete as possible." While this is a sig-

Story Performance

nificant effect in the lab, in terms of recall and affect, the transition from the lab to the organization is fraught with difficulties. For example, should stories in organization settings always be told with such concreteness? An important aspect of performance in real organizations may be to strategically omit or include details about characters, contextual cues, and plot elements.

Story-text studies relying on interview methods have also ignored performance behavior. Alvin Gouldner (1954: 80), for example, collected intriguing stories about Doug and his successor, Vincent. Employees "overflowed with stories which highlighted the differences between the two managers." He then analyzed these differences using the "Rebecca Myth" from Daphne DuMaurier's novel about a young woman who married a widower only to be plagued by the memory of his first wife, Rebecca. An astute analysis, but the study does not tell us about the natural behavior context in which these stories were performed by workers and managers as they went about their daily activities.

Finally, in the case of surveys, the textual content, rather than the storytelling event is the focus of study. Survey researchers seek to capture the types of stories being circulated and the subject's recall of particular stories. While these are important considerations, surveys ignore behavioral interactions that constituted the storytelling event. For example, in Wilkins' (1979) study of both low- and high-performing companies, the stories were reconstructed as raters scored story content on a set of response scales. Such an approach does not tell us about how those stories were performed in their natural element. Similarly, Lombardo's (1986), and McCall, Lombardo, and Morrison's (1989) interviews with 86 executives as they recalled significant vignettes is interesting life-history work, but it is not a behavioral analysis of in situ performance. Siehl and Martin's (1982) survey assessing sales trainees' knowledge of four stories measures recall but not performance. Finally, McConkie and Boss (1986) reported that one organization story, the "Firing of Elayne," was mentioned by 85 percent of their interviewees, but once again we do not learn how this story was performed. Each of these survey studies is useful for its own research purposes; however, the method is not useful for assessing storytelling and storytellers in their natural context.

Studying the storytelling episodes themselves offers several advantages. First, because stories are contextually embedded, their meaning unfolds through the storytelling performance event. Folklorists, like Kirshenblatt-Gimglett (1975), Hymes (1975), Jones, Moore, and Snyder (1988), and especially Georges (1969, 1980a, 1980b, 1981), call us to the other extreme of the story-as-text paradigm, where "the story" has no existence apart from and is indeed inseparable from the event during which the story is performed (Georges, 1980a: 324). Stories can therefore be correctly interpreted only to the extent that the researcher grasps the story in situ. Second, identifying stories in context will be rewarded by the discovery that there are a multitude of stories that are not discernable at first. A finding in sociolinguistic studies is that stories are brief and fragmented across extended and interrupted discourse, but this has been ignored in organization studies. Third, researchers can "unpack" very brief enactments in dialogue to discover the reality underlying the linguistic enactments (Boje, 1989). For example, some tellings may initiate change (Boje, Fedor, and Rowland, 1982; Wilkins, 1984; McWhinney and Batista, 1988; Akin and Schultheiss, 1990), others advance a political view, others predict the stability or transience of relationships and agreements, while others are attempts to isolate and make sense of the impact of turbulent events (Mitroff and Kilmann, 1975; Boje and Ulrich, 1985).

Stories As Performance and Text

Because "the story" behind the story as performed is analogous to the text of it, text and performance can be viewed as two sides of the same coin. For example, in everyday conversation, we make discursive reference to stories as texts in such phrases as "You know that part of his story, don't you?"; "That's my story too"; "You need to get the story straight"; "To make a long story short . . ."; or "I won't bore you with the whole story; You know it!" These phrases are part of a language we use to signal the parts of the performance that will be shared, as we co-produce and manage the story performances, the parts of the story that will be filled in by our listeners' imaginations. People are engaged in a dynamic process of incremental refinement to the story lines of even very widely accepted story texts. Performances at times refer to taken-for-granted texts ("You know the story."), and story performance is a process in which people interact to incorporate new tales continuously into the corporate culture while rewriting oral history by revising the old stories that anchor the present to the past. Only in the rare instance in which the storyteller is faced with a researcher or a new applicant is he or she likely to tell the whole story, since much of the detail of the story cannot be safely assumed to be recreatable in the novice's imagination.

Predictions

If storytelling is seen as performance and text, there are several predictions about storytelling in organizations: First, a lot of attention will be given to negotiating the story-line interpretation and processing collectively the numerous sides to a story. Second, the completeness of the storytelling itself will vary from one sector and level of the organization to the next. One story will take a more abbreviated form with those in-the-know, who are expected to know the particulars, but the same story will be told with a lot more detail to newcomers, outsiders, and most likely to researchers. Third, a related issue is what anthropologists refer to as ownership or "entitlement" rights. Part of knowing how to behave in a storytelling organization is knowing who can tell and who can be told a particular story ("I don't know if the corner office would want that story to get around."). Certain people will have entitlement rights to a story. Fourth, being a player in the storytelling organization is being skilled enough to manage the person-to-person interaction to get the story line woven into the ongoing turn-by-turn dialogue using a broad class of behaviors called qualifiers, markers, and the like, that sustain storytelling across extended discourse by means of paralinguistic and kinesic cues such as head nods, postural shifts,

Story Performance

and eyebrow raises. Finally, one relevant research finding from sociolinguistics (Ryave, 1978) is that stories often occur in series across extended discourse ("Oh, I have a story to top that one."). Stories performed in organizations will occur in series across discourse.

The organization as a storytelling system was explored in a participant-observer study of interactions in a firm that, although it is not well known like IBM or some other organizations that story-as-text researchers have studied, provided a wealth of stories complexly and variously performed in everyday conversation.

METHOD

In keeping with Glaser and Strauss (1967), as a participant observer I iteratively collected and analyzed (Spradley, 1980) the various social scenes that made up the discourse environment of an office-supply firm. These scenes included executive meetings held on- and off-site: in conference rooms, restaurants, sales training sessions, as well as conversations in hallways and automobiles.

Research site. Everyday organization conversations were taped to capture spontaneous storytelling episodes among seven executives and twenty-three managers, customers, and vendors of a large office-supply firm. Data were collected in five branch offices as well as the headquarters. The names of the company and its stakeholders have been changed in the transcripts that follow in order to protect their confidentiality. The firm, called here "Gold," is 35 years old with 300 employees and over $50 million in annual sales. Gold operates in one region of the United States, with six branches in several states. While Gold turns a respectable profit each year, it has been going through some turbulent changes. These changes include five CEOs in the past two years and being acquired by its second conglomerate. The struggle of Gold is that of a family company, founded by a salesman, coming of age as a conglomerate-owned corporation. What was OK in the once family-operated corporation was not OK when ownership switched to a dollars-and-cents driven conglomerate. It was no longer OK, for example, to send the boys to Hawaii or pass along a case of wine to a manager's wife. Customers, vendors, salespeople, and managers report how Doug, the latest CEO, managed the transitions of this office-supply firm and steered it away from further moral failure.

The data set consists of over 100 hours of tape recordings, along with video-recordings of two corporate-sponsored focus groups with key customers and vendors. Where video or tape recording was not feasible, field notes were used as a supplement.

Procedures. Tapes were transcribed and converted to line-numbered transcripts. Transcripts were analyzed to find the scantiest occurrences of story performance embedded in conversation. A story performance was operationally defined as an exchange between two or more persons during which a past or anticipated experience was being referenced, recounted, interpreted, or challenged. A search was made of the entire episode in which the scant performance occurred for more pieces to each story line. In addition, to further verify a story had in fact occurred, the topic was cross-indexed and traced in other segments of dialogue to recover more of the story line or an alternative story line. The procedure presumes a seemingly insignificant reference to experience could upon cross-checking prove to be highly significant to understanding organization processes. Finally, stories were catalogued according to the type of experience pattern presented in the story line, using the following eight categories:

P1: Story-line pattern that is still going on.
P2: Story-line pattern that is expected to repeat.
P3: Story-line pattern is the same as another pattern.
P4: Story-line pattern that will no longer repeat.
P5: Story-line pattern that is changing.
P6: Story-line pattern that is unfolding.
P7: Story-line pattern that is being challenged.
P8: Story-line pattern that was not expected.

The transcripts were thus culled for references to bits of past, unfolding, or anticipated experience that were being enacted through performance throughout the firm. These talk and ethnographic observations were entered into a computer program called "ETHNOGRAPH" (Seidel and Clark, 1984) to isolate and catalogue the occurrence of stories within ongoing conversational discourse. "ETHNOGRAPH" adds line numbers and allows the user to enter codes that can be used to retrieve sections of text, but recoding to combine or split out more specific codes is quite cumbersome. In fact, to properly interconnect bits and pieces of story across settings and actors it was necessary to use manual searches of extended printouts of dialogue before and after each story reference. Finally, to ensure accuracy of intonation, hesitation, and interruption behavior, I personally transcribed the tapes into "ETHNOGRAPH," which took in excess of 400 hours over the eight-month duration of this study. Conventions for transcription adapted by Gronn (1983, 1985), in keeping with work by Stubbs (1983) and Schenkein (1978), were used in this study:

//	Overlapping talk from the first to the last slash. Utterances begin with an upper-case letter and end with a period.
. . .	A pause of one second or less within an utterance.
(2.0)	A pause of more than one second within an utterance or between turns, the number indicates the length of the pause.
* * *	A deletion.
[ ]	An explanatory insertion.
Italics	A word or part of a word emphasized by a speaker.
?	A question, marked by a rise in pitch.
!	An exclamation, marked by a rise in pitch or intense body language.

FINDINGS

The findings will be discussed at two levels. On the surface level, it is important to look at the mechanics of the storytelling episode, i.e., how the story occurs within discourse. Although this sounds simple, the storytelling did not appear in concise sequences of storytellers recounting full texts to passive listeners. As will be seen in the sample texts, people told their stories in bits and pieces, with excessive interruptions of

Story Performance

story starts, with people talking over each other to share story fragments, and many aborted storytelling attempts. That is what I will refer to as the surface level of the story.

The second level of findings relates to the different ways stories are employed among stakeholders in this office-supply firm. Stories contain story-line patterns, and storytelling is defined operationally as a pattern-finding, pattern-elaboration, or pattern-fitting episode to make sense of wider organization processes and relationships. The various types of story-line patterns found in this study are listed in Table 1. In each storytelling episode there is a story-line pattern adopted by stakeholders to model either a past, unfolding, or anticipated experience. The sense making, change, and politics proceeds by participants collectively performing a story as an analogy pattern onto collective experience, which can only be apprehended in story performance.

The first story was performed by the CEO and his executives in a hotel room where they gathered to strategize which divisions and which branches should be eliminated. The CEO, called here Doug, and the vice presidents, called here Sam, Ruth, Jim, Mike, Harmon, and Kora are at an executive meeting. It is an occasion on which one might expect long-tenured executives to perform a founding story to explain how things came to be the way they are.

On the surface level, this story involves important surface behaviors having to do with moving in and out of turn-by-turn talk to engage in storytelling. For example, there is topic-relevant turn-by-turn talk prior to the story (1154–7 is one turn). In some instances, the teller seeks permission to tell the story (1158–9), receives or is denied permission (1160–1),

Table 1

Varieties of Story-Line Patterns

Story Title	Source	Story-line pattern	Tellers
1. Goldco Founding	Past event	Pattern is no longer financially sound.	Execs
2. Reno Branch	Past event	Pattern is no longer ethical.	Execs
3. Hire No One Better	Past event	Pattern is still going on.	Execs
4. Printing Was Different	Past event	Pattern has improved for them.	Execs
5. Industry	Past event	Pattern is same in that part of the industry.	Execs
6. Sales Meeting	Current event	Pattern that got evoked is not one we wanted.	Execs
7. CEO Turnover	Past event	Pattern will repeat itself and then where are we?	Vendors
8. Customer	Current event	Pattern unacceptable to us customers.	Customers
9. Word on the Street	Current event	Pattern is likely to repeat.	Vendors
10. Epsilon Version I	Past event	Pattern is likely to repeat.	Salespeople
11. Epsilon Version II	Past event	Pattern is likely to repeat.	Vendors

and receives encouragement or discouragement in completing the story (1165-6).

These utterances also point to the ownership rights that are tied implicitly to the telling of a story. Only certain people are allowed to tell certain tales. Sam, for example, had served longer at Gold than anyone at this meeting and was an eyewitness. Further, the executives relied on him and even expected him to relate relevant story data to them (1160-1). Lines 1163-4 allude to the teller and the hearers being intimately familiar with the text or skeletal script of the story. The performance proceeds as a co-produced and collective activity. For example, someone besides the teller, in this case the CEO, initiates the telling, someone else tells it, and the CEO contributes the moral of the story (1154-7, 1174-82).

Going beyond this surface level, this first episode is an example of using a story of a past event to cast in a new light a division that may be put on the block as a "nice toy," but a toy they no longer have the luxury of owning. Further, a current decision is being keyed to the performance of a founding story as a precedent and to the latest CEO's new interpretation of that story. Finally, in a hundred hours of taped talk, this was the most complete rendition of an organization story. As will be seen, more frequently, bits and pieces of the organization story were shared and the hearer was left to fill in the blanks, based on his or her knowledge of the story behind the verbalized story.

S1: Goldco Founding Story

Doug:	* * * I look at Goldco as a toy that	1154
	somebody decided to put in the company	1155
	because it was fun and it also brought	1156
	in/	1157
Sam:	Well/ I'll tell you how that came	1158
	about	1159
Doug:	I thought you would (lots of laughter	1160
	from the group)	1161
Sam:	Sam Coche worked for Sea Breeze or	1162
	something like that, oh you know the	1163
	story?	1164
Doug:	No go ahead tell it, really it's	1165
	important.	1166
Sam:	He got out there and he came over and	1167
	they formed Goldco and Goldco does	1168
	not mean Gold Company or anything	1169
	else they took the first four	1170
	initials from Billy Gold, which is	1171
	G O L D and from Coche and that's how	1172
	they got Goldco.	1173
Doug:	And it was a good living for a couple	1174
	of people. It was a nice toy for	1175
	Billy, he made a few bucks on the	1176
	thing. He had some fun for it but	1177
	then the motivation at that time was a	1178
	whole lot different than it is today.	1179
	We don't have the luxury of screwing	1180
	around with something like that /(lots	1181
	of cross talk at this point)/	1182
	(Returns to turn-by-turn talk.)	

Filling in the story blanks. In this next story, one untold part of the story that certainly all these executives know, and I dug out in subsequent field interviews with them, is that Ed

Story Performance

Fox engaged in very questionable behavior and was replaced
by yet another and another CEO, until our current CEO. Doug
took the job and became the recognized champion for some
very serious reforms. Sam references, for example, the
CEO's attempts to reform Gold by instituting an executive
committee (line 728), which is quite a departure from the
practices of earlier CEOs. The executives, for example, know
that Raymond, a former CEO, was once a hero figure who
added several branch offices and divisions during the growth
phase at Gold but is now being resymbolized as autocratic
and lacking in good business skills. There is some melodrama
between the lines in this story. Ed Fox was a replacement
CEO for Raymond Smith, who walked the line between doing
good things for the organization, like adding more branches,
and engaging in questionable practices, like nepotism and
pocketing funds. Nepotism and seeking to enhance the personal fortunes of one's family are considered OK for a
founder but were not OK when a conglomerate acquired Gold
and replaced Raymond, the founder's successor, with Ed Fox.

The story is quite abbreviated (727–31), and the full meaning
is inaccessible unless one explores Gold extensively to unpack the full meaning of story referents. Although many researchers might challenge if this excerpt is a story at all, the
teller, Sam, does identify the telling as a story by interjecting,
"I guess you heard this all already" (732) and "I guess you
heard the whole story before" (736–7). Even the words "you
know" invite the hearer to fill in the blanks. This is an example of a storyteller briefly referencing a full story line,
which I observed thoughout the stories shared by executives,
managers, salespeople, vendors, and customers.

S2: Reno Branch Story

Sam:	I think five years ago there was no	727
	Executive Committee. He just ran	728
	the place the way he wanted as if you	729
	wasn't here. Raymond was [conglomer-	730
	ate's] man and he did what he pleased.	731
	I guess you heard this all already	732
Dave:	I heard about the high growth (nodding)	733
Sam:	Yes we picked up San Diego	734
Dave:	Reno?	735
Sam:	Ed Fox picked up Reno and I guess	736
	you heard the whole story before.	737
	That's why we picked up Reno because	738
	Ed Fox had that with his father. You	739
	know.	740

Terse storytelling. But just how abbreviated can a story be
and still be classified as a story? The shortest story form is
when one person says to the other, "You know the story!" It
can be so brief that the performance is barely distinguishable
from other nonperformance utterances. I call this filling-in-
the-blanks form terse storytelling. Much of the story that is
told is not actually uttered. A terse telling is an abbreviated
and succinct simplification of the story in which parts of the
plot, some of the characters, and segments of the sequence
of events are left to the hearer's imagination. One hypothesis
is that the terser the telling, the more shared the understanding of the social context, since insiders know what to

leave to the imagination. Police, firemen, and the office-supply firm stakeholders use coded, brief utterances to communicate lots of understanding. Terse telling also prevents the story line from being too well understood by the wrong people. The terser the telling, the less sharing of understanding of the social context can be detected by outsiders.

In discussing terse telling, I shall make explicit which purpose is being played out. For example, in the S2 transcript, I am Dave and I am a participant but also, at this early stage, an outsider. Sam, I believe, is carefully confirming what I know and that the CEO told me the complete underlying story. In theory, my knowledge of institutional memory is being tested. I, for my part, am nodding in agreement and offering up data to establish that I merit deeper revelations from Sam. In this instance, I assume he is telling tersely because he does not want to give me more understanding than the CEO expects me to have.

In the next transcript, the context is a discussion of why people are so resistant to change. This type of story-line pattern uses story segments to explore how a pattern of resistance has formed within Gold. As Doug, also present, seeks to reform Gold and implement controls such as bonuses based on performance and hiring based on competency, the story line these executives have lived by for ten years is being explored and challenged.

The surface structure of the story is as follows: one vice president, Ruth, begins with an assertion: "I think paranoia ran high in this company" (438–9) and then follows it up with an invitation to Sam to tell a story (440–1). This is followed by a terse storytelling (442–5) using an abbreviated code, since as interviews revealed, everyone present knew the full story line. In this exchange, Sam, while invited to follow up with his own story, remains quiet (441–3). Instead, the group takes off on one of the concluding moral assertions: "People were afraid to hire people that were better than they were" (446–7) and then restates the moral in inverse form (453–5).

S3: Hire No One-Better Story

Ruth: Over and over again in all your	436
notes and blurbs and all on what	437
people were saying, I think paranoia	438
ran high in this company in that last	439
10 years, especially under Raymond	440
Smith I'm sure Sam could share	441
a few examples (laughter). Examples of	442
when he was out pulling invoices out	443
in the warehouse while he was the	444
frigging controller of the company.	445
People were afraid to hire people	446
that were better than they were I	447
mean we have an assistant controller	448
that can't run Lotus and it's not a	449
jam, but we do. You see I don't	450
understand, I have—never have. In	451
order to have a company that is going	452
to grow, we actually have to hire and	453
nurture people that are better than	454
we are	455
Kora: And unfortunately the frame of mind,	456
the mindset that has been in the	457

Story Performance

company for so long, because of all of	458
the turnover and the turmoil with	459
upper management, is I could lose my	460
job tomorrow	461
Ruth: But the interesting thing is that	462
nobody has ever come in and taken	463
their job.	464

Glossing. Story performances can involve what Weick (1981) called extended glosses ("Let me tell you that piece of the story!") to sell a particular point of view. In S3, Ruth is obviously using the story of Raymond Smith as a gloss to push her point of view, but so is Kora in her gloss (lines 456–461) on Ruth's story. A story gloss is a brief retelling of a piece of a story so that the referent experience becomes sensible in new ways after having been glossed. The gloss is akin to marginal notes or digression that can exaggerate, simplify, and shift the meaning of the experience. Storytellers might use a gloss as an occasion to accentuate an anomalous experience as an integral aspect of the founding, maturity, reform, or demise of an organization. Additional examples of gloss can be seen even more clearly in the next example.

The series of stories. The CEO and several vice presidents participate in a strategic planning session during which Harmon asks a question to which Doug reconstructs a story line (341–3) and then once again invites Sam to gloss one aspect of the story (338–9). Sam's gloss (347–50) is itself a second story. Everyone there knows the terse telling to be the same story that I discovered in cross-indexed transcripts and in interviews of when, for example, printing orders fell out of the back of a delivery truck and were scattered across the highway. Others in the group follow this with more talk, and a third story is initiated (359–60). This third story is a personal-experience narrative and has more credibility than second-hand accounts. The first story, by contrast, does not arise out of personal experience. In fact, Doug did not become CEO of this firm until after the incident in question. He, instead, builds on the acknowledged experience of Sam, who has been at Gold for 12 years. According to follow-up interviews, Doug, unlike former CEOs, had an ability to draw historical precedent into his own performance that made him an effective agent of change at Gold. His reference to "Epsilon" in line 342 is part of a story that was being recounted every time several executives, vendors, or large customers gathered (see S6, S8, S9, S10, and S11 in Table 1, above).

S4: Printing Was Different Story

Harmon: But is that the most effective way	335
to do it? Do they hit the same places?	336
Doug: Historically, in reading a little	337
bit of the history and maybe Sam	338
can help us out here. The printing	339
business that we were writing was	340
significant at one time and when the	341
folks left for Epsilon they took that	342
business with them and now we're going	343
through a whole retraining process	344
Sam: Well that could be so I mean	345
printing again falls with the	346
salesmen. A lot of the salesmen will	347
not sell printing because they are	348
afraid that the printing department,	349

as in the past, has fouled up	350
Kora: Vickie has been wonderful	351
Sam: Yes I think Vickie has been	352
wonderful. It is a matter of	353
confidence in whoever it is there.	354
When John Rifler was in charge of it	355
there was no confidence. This goes on	356
and it changes	357
Ruth: And I think training comes in here	358
Jim: When I was in sales I sold what I	359
understood. If I didn't understand * * *	360

Series of stories as an enactment of change. Storytelling is a way to draw parallels between two patterns. In the following segment, the new CEO glosses, in a storytelling, to reveal how his experience from other companies relates to what one vice president is telling him (1415–26, 1450–9). Follow-up interviews revealed that his story performance is a scenario told to introduce a strategic shift in the focus of this firm. His ability to enact a performance that coaxes his executives to identify with his relevant experiences in analogous situations gives his scenario for change a good deal of credibility. The executives are beginning to buy into the future scenario. To implement this change, several divisions will be put on the block so Gold can focus on its main business (1474–9). There are elements of reform, blood-letting (firings), and death (selling off divisions) as the new pattern becomes envisioned in this story.

S5: Industry Stories

Jim: Wait a minute I gotta put one more	1415
point into here, since Ben C. isn't	1416
here. Because sales is not represented	1417
in this whole group and it's really	1418
unfortunate. Based on the fact, cause	1419
I've talked to the people. You've got	1420
Victor M. who has a sales assistant	1421
that he shares with somebody. He's	1422
doing a 150 thousand dollars a month	1423
in office supplies an some furniture.	1424
How much more can we expect out of	1425
him?	1426
Doug: Looking at acquisitions and mergers	1427
in our industry, and I've been through	1428
four or five of em, disaster hits. And	1429
I'll give you examples Gamma	1430
Corporation. I was with the old	1431
Delphi Company and it's nonexistent	1432
today. They merged with Alpha. And	1433
then they merged with Parrot. All the	1434
same ownership and so on. Clearly the	1435
sales force was on overload. Couldn't	1436
handle it and a lot of things fell	1437
through the cracks. I can give you	1438
similar examples with Juindon. I	1439
can go right down the list. There is a	1440
point—where the economies that you	1441
pick up trying to consolidate	1442
businesses with one sales force uhhh	1443
they are far overridden by what you	1444
lose in the translation. So there is a	1445
point Jim but I don't know where the	1446
hell it is/	1447
Jim: And that's my point/.	1448

Story Performance

Doug:	And it's got to be easy because I	1449
	experienced it as a salesman. What I	1450
	found was that the more they dumped on	1451
	me, where there was duplication and	1452
	there was overlap and so on. It was	1453
	still writing instruments and you	1454
	would think that would be an easy	1455
	deal. You are still selling writing	1456
	instruments, but you got all this shit	1457
	and you only got so much time in front	1458
	of a customer. You got so much	1459
	communication time you got so much	1460
	I seriously question whether if you	1461
	are in the contract business I really	1462
	question if you can effectively call	1463
	on other people in the organization to	1464
	accomplish something. I really	1465
	question that. And it's a question	1466
	not a decision and not a	1467
	determination. But Ad Specialty	1468
	clearly a different buyer Furniture is	1469
	clearly a different buyer clearly * * *	1470
Ruth:	* * * the other thing, Doug, is can we	1474
	be successful? Our main throw is	1475
	office products. Can we be successful	1476
	without having these sidelines?	1477
Doug:	Absolutely!	1478
Ruth:	Are you sure? Screw [Furniture]! Forget	1479
	Goldco!	1480
Kora:	And printing!	1481
Doug:	I said it rather flippantly earlier,	1482
	but I'm very serious we could skim off	1483
	30, 40 million dollars and no one	1484
	would even know we are there. We don't	1485
	have to take it away from a	1486
	competitor, the market is expanding so	1487
	dramatically/	1488

Executives accepted the blood-letting scenario as a necessary evil to save the organization and even the affected managers typically describe Doug as a "savior."

For example, one story that was repeated in many office conversations concerns how, upon Doug's arrival as the new CEO, a non-gone executive tried to implement reserved parking privileges for executives. Doug, in almost his first meeting with the executives, uprooted a "reserved for the CEO" (one was also reserved for each of the VPs) parking sign and threw it on the executive meeting table, demanding to know "who put up this sign? This is not the kind of leadership I will have around here." The offending executive, for this and other good reasons, was fired by week's end. This story made the rounds and reinforced Doug's image as the reformer who would not put up with special privileges for executives. This Doug-as-savior theme resurfaces in stories from vendors and customers. For Gold, this is a relatively new story, since Doug is the latest CEO. A year from now this might be tersely referred to as the parking-sign story.

Story performance as sense making. In the following example an analysis of the story is embedded in the telling. The analysis consists of telling the story to make sense of the environment as sense is made of the story performance. While middle management has survived five CEOs in two years by ignoring most change efforts, the salespeople avoid change by not giving upper management access to their customers. It is a power play similar to the one Crozier (1964) described in his classic study of maintenance mechanics making the tobacco factories dependent on them by blocking access to maintenance manuals and making unique modifications to the machines. Since the "wars" with a major competitor, "Epsilon," Gold executives are concerned about access to their top accounts.

In lines 846–54, the story details are so terse that, at first glance, there may not appear to be a story at all. However, in lines 855–6, another executive hooks into the underlying experience to trigger more detail on the story behind the story. In 859–62, the story of a salesperson's reaction to executive attempts to implement computer information-system controls garners a severe group reaction. In line 870, Doug uses a very common reflexive "you know" to reference experience that the other executives are expected to fill in between the lines. He references a story everyone knows all too well. In line 870, the use of an extended pause following the emphasized word *"tool"* is a language tactic that invites hearers to fill in their knowledge of the story behind the performed story. *"Tool"* references former attempts by the "corner office" to make salesmen's accounts become house accounts. These executives have confided to me that to change the balance of power between themselves and their salespeople, they will need to tread lightly or risk triggering another exodus of their salespeople to their competitor, Epsilon. In the following excerpt, the group has been discussing how difficult it is going to be to put together something as seemingly simple as a customer focus group because of this issue.

S6: Sales Meeting Story

Dave: Why is that?	842
Kora: That organism that mechanism is not	843
in place. It's just in the very first	844
throws of it	845
Doug: The insulation that we have from our	846
customers is mind boggling. I should	847
be able to pick up the phone and call	848
10 or 12 close friends that happen to	849
be customers and get em down here	850
with no problem. Our salespeople	851
will not let us near them. I	852
shouldn't say won't let us/ (several	853
talk at once)/	854
Jim: What's been the response to your plea	855
at the sales meeting?	856
Doug: A couple people that are secure have	857
come to me and said "let's do this,	858
this and this." But then I hear	859
comments from Jim T. who says 'umm,	860
tell me about our data processing and	861
our terminal hook up	862
Ruth: Oh boy!	863
Doug: And I says "Why do you ask?" Well I	864
was thinking, if I put one of those	865
terminals in you don't need me as	866
much as uhhh	867
Kora: Oh God! (Lots of expression by everyone)	868
Doug: And I said Jeff it's a *tool* God Damn	869
it! (3.0) And you know/ * * *	870

Story Performance

Kora:	Our customers are gold you know that/ (much	880
	cross-talk) /We want all of our ducks in line	881
	and all of our logistics so that when	882
	they walk in they are treated . . .	883
	The red carpet is out * * *	884

The turnover story as prediction. As with the executive committee, the organization stories in the following excerpts from vendor and customer focus-group videotapes extend from the observed pattern of past events (337–44) to a prediction of a probable future pattern (356–64). As Martin (1982: 287) suggested, the script embedded in the story, though unstated, allows people to predict what may happen if a similar incident should recur: "A story contains a blueprint that can be used to predict future organizational behavior." What is interesting is that the vendors leave most of the script unstated in their terse telling of the story.

S7: CEO Turnover Story

Dan:	Yeah, my boss will call from	337
	We're based out of the Northwest and	338
	he'll say "Well Dan who is running the	339
	ship at Gold now?" He can see a	340
	lot of the proposals that we've	341
	presented and were accepted six months	342
	ago still in effect because there's	343
	been turnover * * *	344
	You know is the next administration	356
	going to come in and make changes to	357
	that? One point that Jeff made	358
	earlier that I want to touch on is our	359
	concerns are shared with their	360
	salespeople. They definitely know	361
	sometimes that they're kind of a ship	362
	without a rudder right now and I think	363
	it concerns their salespeople as well	364

Relationships with vendors and contract customers are important interorganizational relationships for Gold. In this next excerpt, from a customer focus group, the turnover in CEOs, as well as new vice presidents, and sales managers, has resulted in problems of stability and access in Gold's relations. Storytelling about the shakeup at Gold helps customers and vendors paint a predictable scenario. In the following excerpt, the story's blueprint is quite terse (347–9, 957–66). Pinning this blueprint down takes 22 minutes of the focus group's time.

S8: A Customer Story

Frank:	And I'm seeing symptoms of the	342
	turnover in senior management they	343
	have had senior management that they	344
	have had in the past 14–15 months	345
	where they have had a change in	346
	philosophy. A certain president has	347
	own stamp of how he is going to operate	348
	and things change. My major concern is	349
	the end result. I don't care how they	350
	resolve their internal politics	351
	I need the product	352
	* * * They do listen but with half an	954
	ear maybe because of the change in	955
	management.	956
	Certain management we have had	957

discussions and we have come to agree-	958
ments and the systems have been worked	959
out. New management comes in a new	960
president of the company and we have to	961
reinvent the wheel and we go back and I	962
mean it's in writing it's documented	963
these agreements are documented and then	964
go to the next person	965

The word on the street story. During the study, the conglomerate decided to sell Gold, and the news leaked. In this videotaped focus group exchange, I assume line 370 represents a plea from these vendors to be able to tell the story (370), since it is followed by three "you know" references (377, 379, 388–9) to the fuller story that the vendors know but do not expect outsiders to know. The vendors perform a futuristic scenario that they use to make sense of Gold's behavior. It is reinforced and embellished by glosses by other vendors (not included). The scenario in 381–9 has not happened at Gold, but it is a plot sequence that has occurred with regularity in the vendor's other relationships. Referencing how the story has been leaked by Gold's salespeople (388–9) adds credibility to the performance.

S9: Word on the Street Story

Sid: Well if we can just be open/	370
(simultaneous talking of 4 people) /the	371
word is on the street that they are up	372
for sale OK? So now you know [CEO]	373
may be the president. They may want	374
him up there. But somebody'll buy him	375
next month and then he's going to be	376
gone because you know, because you	377
know they're bringing in their own	378
people. You don't know I mean . . . You	379
don't want that I mean personally I	380
think he's going to be a good	381
administrator, but then he is but	382
then somebody buys him and they have	383
their own people then maybe he's not	384
going to be there so you wonder is	385
there going to be a stability? And	386
the salesmen have the same concern and	387
I heard it from them themselves you	388
know. What's going to where we	389
going?	390

Alternative glossing. People perform stories about their struggles for survival, and the story can change depending on the stakeholders performing the story. Throughout this study, in talking to Gold employees, vendors, and customers, stories about the wars with Epsilon were a frequent topic. In the first excerpt, a sales manager, during a lunch at a crowded restaurant, gave me a concise version of the Epsilon War Story that captured most of the plot. Some 9 to 12 salespeople (the count depends on to whom you talk) were recruited by a competitor. In retaliation, Gold recruited some of their salespeople. Customers were traded back and forth, and, in the process, some exorbitant guarantees were given out to salespeople. The sales manager's gloss paints salespeople as the prima donnas who initiated the war. Doug's version (not shown), in contrast, stressed the "tremendous exposure with salespeople leaving and dragging accounts

Story Performance

back and forth." This is very much a political use of story-telling, as various factions in and around the organization seek to establish an advantageous interpretation.

S10: Epsilon War Story: Version I

Ralph: The Epsilon Wars . . . bad way to do	2597
it really silly. We just traded sales	2598
people and now we're both stuck with	2599
salespeople with giant guarantees and	2600
it's hurting our bottom line in a major	2601
way 9 of the 11 were prima donnas	2602
pain in the ass egotistical to the	2603
max. Developed by [Raymond] in the	2604
many years of the Gold philosophy	2605
The salesman is king	2606

In the vendor focus group, another version of the story was recounted. In this story performance, the group uses story-telling to ascertain the probability that Gold's sales force is once again at risk of being captured by Epsilon and, along with the sales force, their precious accounts. The vendors attribute the trigger for the next war to the fact that Gold has undergone far too much instability: five CEOs in two years, the company being put up for sale by its conglomerate holding company, and competitors that, sensing what was going on, had exploited the situation to the net disadvantage of Gold.

S11: Epsilon War Story: Version II

Bob: They have lost a lot of accounts/	448
Ron: What do/ you attribute that to?	449
Sid: That is specific to sometime in 1988	450
They lost several of their many of	451
their key reps to another distributor	452
/(Group goes back and forth) /Didn't	453
they drop 10–12 or something like	454
that?	455
Ron: Is there a word on the street as to	456
why these people left?	457
Ted: I think the instability of the	458
company and they probably lured them	459
over action/(Several talk at once)/	460
Oscar: I think their competitor used the	461
instability factor to put doubts in	462
the minds of those people and it was	463
an opportune time. They have been	464
battled several times. This is an	465
opportune time to steal some people if	466
you will and hopefully their major	467
accounts with them and they took	468
advantage of the situation. That is	469
one of the tough things in business	470

DISCUSSION AND CONCLUSIONS

By focusing on in situ everyday performance behavior, this study showed how storytelling goes on more frequently and differently than might have been suspected in previous story-telling studies. As critics will be quick to point out, however, just being able to isolate and identify terse storytelling and glossing in various story performance forms in use among organization stakeholders is insufficient justification to call for an integration of the story-as-texts and stories-as-performance approaches to story research. But there are several observations that strengthen this position. First, it is not the fact that the story is terse and abbreviated that counts; it is the fact that the teller picks one aspect to abbreviate ("You know the rest of the story.") and another to accentuate ("It's the same old story, except this time we found them together."). This, along with gloss, is an essential surface mechanism by which stories are performed. Second, part of storytelling involves managing the telling of a story by being able to weave it into on-going conversation. Both teller and listener are sending cues to manage how much of the story is told, how much is left to the imagination, and what interpretation is applied. This also is management of sense making. Third, terse telling can be a power strategy of purposeful mystification (Fisher, 1984) or tactical ambiguity. The CEO, Doug, used his storytelling to draw in the other executives to accept his reform strategies as their own. As Eisenberg (1984: 236) observed, "It is often preferable to omit purposefully contextual cues and to allow for multiple interpretations on the part of receivers."

These stakeholders tune into stories as real-time data and tell stories to predict, empower, and even fashion change. Customers, vendors, salespeople, and executives in this office-supply distribution company performed stories not only to make sense of their setting but to negotiate alternative interpretations and to accommodate new precedents for decision and action. They tell stories about the past, present, and future to make sense of and manage their struggles with their environment.

This study raises a number of important questions. Does story performance occur more frequently in some types of organizations more than in others? Was storytelling performance in this organization, for example, biased by the turbulence of a rapid succession of CEOs, the need to eliminate divisions, the war with a dominant competitor, and being traded between conglomerates? Peters and Austin (1985: 330) hypothesized that storytelling is more frequent in turbulent settings, where stories and interpretations are shared with great frequency to understand the unfolding dynamics. Familiarity with those dynamics, however, should result in a familiarized way of recounting terser stories, with glosses only used to highlight deviations. Once a story pattern is seen again and again, for example, in law enforcement, emergency work, and wartime situation rooms, one might expect typical scenarios to become reduced to terse response codes. Similarly, one might expect to see fuller story texts performed in newer organizations, in which there is less shared experience. There are implicit rules in storytelling (who can tell it, to whom, and where). Further research can examine what happens, if anything, when these rules are broken, when the telling is done inappropriately.

There is a broader implication of management education evident in the storytelling-performance paradigm. People who are more skilled as storytellers and story interpreters seem to be more effective communicators than those who are less skilled (Boje, 1989, 1991). Yet, until recently, teaching storytelling skills, outside of the folklore discipline, has been limited to the teaching of children (Zemke, 1990; Boje, 1991). As organizational boundaries become more permeable and the

Story Performance

organization structure flatter, requiring more networking and communication skills, storytelling can be a useful tool for managers trying to cope with rapid change. Training managers to be storytellers may thus result in training them to be more effective in organizations.

The most important implication for organization study that was born out of the present study is that story researchers can benefit by entering organizations to observe first-hand how people perform storytelling. The focus in traditional organization story research has been on texts taken from a range of isolated, often anomalous stories plucked out of their natural setting. These studies ignore performance and streamline the stories or treat them as so many variables that can give empirical explanations of the organization. The storytelling organization theory posits story text and performance as two sides of the same coin and gives us insight into the complex and varied ways organization members use storytelling in their work world.

REFERENCES

Akin, Gib, and Emily Schultheiss
1990 "Jazz bands and missionaries: OD through stories and metaphor." Journal of Managerial Psychology, 5(4): 12–18.

Boje, David M.
1989 "Postlog: Bringing performance back in." Journal of Organizational Change Management, 2(2): 80–93.
1991 "Learning storytelling: Storytelling to learn management skills." Journal of Management Education (in press).

Boje, David M., Donald B. Fedor, and Kendrith M. Rowland
1982 "Myth making: A qualitative step in OD interventions." Journal of Applied Behavioral Science, 18: 17–28.

Boje, David M., and David Ulrich
1985 "The qualitative side of leadership." In R. Tannenbaum, N. Margulies, and F. Massarik (eds.), Human Systems Development: 302–318. San Francisco: Jossey-Bass.

Clark, Buton R.
1972 "The organizational saga in higher education." Administrative Science Quarterly, 17: 178–184.

Crozier, Michel
1964 The Bureaucratic Phenomenon. Chicago: University of Chicago Press.

Eisenberg, Eric M.
1984 "Ambiguity as strategy in organizational communication." Communication Monographs, 51: 227–242.

Fisher, Walter R.
1984 "Narration as a human communication paradigm: The case of public moral argument." Communication Monographs, 51 (March): 1–22.

Georges, Robert
1969 "Toward an understanding of story-telling events." Journal of American Folklore, 82: 314–328.
1980a "A folklorist's view of storytelling." Humanities in Society, 3(4): 317–326.
1980b "Towards a resolution of the text/context controversy." Western Folklore, 39: 34–40.
1981 "Do narrators really digress? A reconsideration of 'audience asides' in narrating." Western Folklore, 40: 245–252.

Glaser, Barney G., and Anselm L. Strauss
1967 The Discovery of Grounded Theory. Chicago: Aldine.

Gouldner, Alvin
1954 Patterns of Industrial Bureaucracy. New York: Free Press.

Gronn, Peter C.
1983 "Talk as the work: The accomplishment of school administration." Administrative Science Quarterly, 28: 1–21.
1985 "Committee talk: Negotiating 'personnel development' at a training college." Journal of Management Studies, 22: 245–268.

Hymes, Dell
1975 "Breakthrough into performance." In Dan Ben-Amos and Kenneth Goldstein (eds.), Folklore: Performance and Communication: 11–74. Paris: Mouton.

Jefferson, Gail
1973 "A case of precision timing in ordinary conversation." Semiotica, 9(1): 47–96.
1978 "Sequential aspects of storytelling in conversation." In Jim Schenkein (ed.), Studies in the Organization of Conversational Interaction: 219–248. New York: Academic Press.

Jones, Michael O., Michael D. Moore, and Richard C. Snyder (eds.)
1988 Inside Organizations: Understanding the Human Dimension. Newbury Park, CA: Sage.

Kirschenblatt-Gimglett, Barbara
1975 "A parable in context: A social interactional analysis of storytelling performance." In Dan Ben-Amos and Kenneth Goldstein (eds.), Folklore: Performance and Communication: 105–130. Paris: Mouton.

Lombardo, Michael M.
1986 "Values in action: The meaning of executive vignettes." Technical report no. 28 (November), Center for Creative Leadership, Greensboro, NC.

Martin, Joanne
1982 "Stories and scripts in organizational settings." In A. Hastorf and A. Isen (eds.), Cognitive Social Psychology: 225–305. New York: Elsevier-North Holland.

Martin, Joanne, Martha S. Feldman, Mary Jo Hatch, and Sim B. Sitkin
1983 "The uniqueness paradox in organizational stories." Administrative Science Quarterly, 28: 438–453.

Martin, Joanne, and Debra Meyerson
1988 "Organizational cultures and the denial, channeling and acknowledgment of ambiguity." In Louis R. Pondy, Richard J. Boland, Jr., and Howard Thomas (eds.), Managing Ambiguity and Change: 93–125. New York: Wiley.

Martin, Joanne, Kerry Patterson, and Raymond Price
1979 "The effects of level of abstraction of a script on accuracy of recall, predictions and beliefs." Research paper No. 520, Graduate School of Business, Stanford University.

Martin, Joanne, Kerry Patterson, Wendy Harrod, and Caren Siehl
1980 "Memory for the content of scripts presented at varying levels of abstraction." Paper presented at the meeting of the American Psychological Association, Montreal, September.

Martin, Joanne, and Melanie E. Powers
1979 "Skepticism and the true believer: The effects of case and/or base rate information on belief and commitment." Paper presented at the meetings of the Western Psychological Association, Honolulu, May.

McCall, Morgan W., Jr., Michael M. Lombardo, and Ann M. Morrison
1989 The Lessons of Experience. New York: Harper & Row.

McConkie, Mark L., and Wayne R. Boss
1986 "Organizational stories: One means of moving the informal organization during change efforts." Public Administration Quarterly, 10(2): 189–205.

McWhinney, William, and Jose Batista
1988 "How remythologizing can revitalize organizations." Organizational Dynamics, 17(2): 46–58.

Mitroff, Ian I., and Ralph H. Kilmann
1975 "Stories managers tell: A new tool for organizational problem solving." Management Review, 64(7): 18–28.

Moch, Michael K., and W. Calvin Fields
1985 "Developing a content analysis for interpreting language use in organizations." In Samuel B. Bacharach (ed.), Research in the Sociology of Organizations, 4: 81–126. Greenwich, CT: JAI Press.

Mumby, Dennis K.
1987 "The political function of narrative in organizations." Communication Monographs, 54(June): 113–127.

Peters, Tom, and Nancy Austin
1985 A Passion for Excellence: The Leadership Difference. New York: Warner Books.

Ritzer, George
1975 "Sociology: A multiple paradigm science." American Sociologist, 10: 156–167.

Rogers, William
1969 Think. New York: Stein & Day.

Ryave, Alan L.
1978 "On the achievement of a series of stories." In Jim Schenkein (ed.), Studies in the Organization of Conversational Interaction: 113–132. New York: Academic Press.

Sacks, Harvey
1972a Transcripts of unpublished lectures, School of Social Science, University of California at Irvine.
1972b "An initial investigation of the usability of conversational data for doing sociology." In D. Sudnow (ed.), Studies in Social Interaction: 31–74. New York: Free Press.

Sacks, Harvey, Emmanuel A. Schegloff, and Gail Jefferson
1974 "A simplest systematics for the organization of turn-taking for conversation." Language, 50: 696–735.

Schenkein, Jim (ed.)
1978 Studies in the Organization of Conversational Interaction. New York: Academic Press.

Seidel, John V., and Jack A. Clark
1984 "The ETHNOGRAPH: A computer program for the analysis of qualitative data." Qualitative Sociology, 7(1–2): 110–125.

Siehl, Caren, and Joanne Martin
1982 "Learning organizational culture." Research Paper No. 654, Graduate School of Business, Stanford University.

Spradley, James P.
1980 Participant Observation. New York: Holt, Rinehart and Winston.

Stubbs, Michael
1983 Discourse Analysis: The Sociolinguistic Analysis of Natural Language. Chicago: University of Chicago Press.

Weick, Karl
1981 "Psychology as gloss: Reflections on usefulness and application." In R. A. Kasschau and C. N. Cofer (eds.), Psychology's Second Century: Enduring Issues: 110–132. New York: Praeger.

Wilkins, Alan
1979 "Organizational stories as an expression of management philosophy: Implications for social control in organizations." Unpublished doctoral dissertation, Stanford University.
1984 "The creation of company cultures: The role of stories and human resource systems." Human Resource Management, 23(1): 41–60.

Zemke, Ron
1990 "Storytelling: Back to basics." Training, March: 44–49.

[11]

Organizational story and storytelling: a critical review

Mary E. Boyce
University of Redlands, Redlands, California, USA

The stories told in organizations offer researchers and organizational development (OD) practitioners a natural entry point to understanding and intervening in the culture(s) of an organization. This review is informed by social constructivism, organizational symbolism, and critical theory. Considered individually, each of these perspectives includes a point of view, a genealogy of sorts regarding idea development, and examples of story research. Taken altogether, social constructivism, interpretive organizational symbolism, and critical theory provide a focused, interdisciplinary lens for the review of studies in organizational story and storytelling. Organizational story and storytelling studies build on a foundation of multidisciplinary research that has shaped the understanding we have of story and storytelling. This review highlights the contributions of several key studies, critically examines the perspectives of these studies, and reflects on what has been learned about story and storytelling. Challenges to theory and practice are identified and attention is drawn to the applications possible for researchers and practitioners utilizing story and storytelling in their work in organizations.

The social construction of reality

A social constructivist perspective is one of three perspectives informing this review. Berger and Luckmann (1967) described social construction as a blend of a social reality and symbolic interaction. They contended that the reality we collectively experience has, in fact, been constructed by our social interactions. Berger and Luckmann began with the universal need for meaning and order. They proposed that as individuals engage in the construction of their personal meaning, collectives engage in the construction of a social reality.

In its first generation, a socially constructed reality is shared by all the participants. It is as this reality needs to be communicated and passed on to another generation that difficulty arises. There is a desire to integrate a new generation into the current reality. It is this need for integration which Berger and Luckmann believed motivates "legitimation" (Berger and Luckmann, 1967, p. 86). Legitimation is the process by which people construct explanations and justifications for the fundamental elements of their collective, institutionalized tradition.

The author wishes to thank David Boje, Will McWhinney, Jon Sager, Burkard Sievers and Teri Tompkins for their comments on earlier versions of this paper.

JOCM
9,5

6

There has been additional work on ways of understanding reality since that of Berger and Luckmann. McWhinney (1984), building on LeShan's (1976) work, proposed that a perspective on alternative realities provides a more effective way (than the perception of one, socially constructed reality) to understand fundamental differences in how people view reality. The way people define reality can be described in their position on two dimensions of being which form the axes of a four-quadrant model. These two dimensions are "the connectedness of the universe" (McWhinney, 1984, p. 10) and "freedom of will" (p. 11). The model provides a description of four very different realities. These realities are unitary, sensory, mythic, and social (p. 11). McWhinney's work makes a contribution to the literature on constructed reality which recognizes how deeply people differ in their recognition, experience, and construction of reality.

Research with a social constructivist perspective
There are four studies that have explicitly connected either social construction or symbolic interaction, organization(s), and story (Boyce, 1995; Brown, 1982; Smircich, 1983; Wilkins, 1978). These studies form a small cluster of work that intentionally weaves a perspective of socially constructed reality with story and organization. Specific contributions from the work of Brown, Wilkins, and Smircich are highlighted here. Boyce's study is reviewed later in the section of storytelling as a process. Additionally, there is a body of work specifically examining the relationship between socially constructed reality, shared beliefs, and organizational ideology (Abravanel, 1983; Boyce, 1995; Conrad, 1981; Martin *et al.*, 1983; Nystrom and Starbuck, 1984; Pettigrew, 1979). That body of work is not included in this review.

Brown's dissertation (1982) looks at the socializing use of story among 75 employees in four nursing homes. Brown supported Dandridge *et al.*'s (1980) delineation of symbolic functions as describing, energy controlling, and system maintaining and was working in the vein that became Fisher's (1987) narrative paradigm when she observed that stories "... give reasons which provide coherence and order to events occurring" (Brown, 1982, p. 48). (Fisher's narrative paradigm is reviewed later in the section on communication theories.) Brown concluded not only that organizational members express understanding and commitment to the organization in their use of stories (p. 125), but also that the degree of member familiarity with the dominant story of the organization might indicate the member's level of adaptation to the organization (p. 127).

Wilkins and Martin (1979) identified three functions for organizational story and legend (generating commitment, making sense of the organization, and control). Wilkins aligned his work with that of Ouchi and Johnson (1978) in social control (Wilkins, 1978, p. 21). As organizational legends enhance behavioural and attitudinal commitment, organizational control is made easier (Wilkins and Martin, 1979, pp. 24-5).

Smircich's often cited study (1983) describes the stories of an insurance company in light of the organizational history. She spent six weeks as an observer within an insurance company which was a division of a larger corporation. The meaning system of the company is described as its "ethos" (p. 57). This ethos had emerged over years. Smircich looked closely at the stories and common beliefs held in the company. She used the organizational history to explore the meaning of the stories and shared meanings. That these meanings may be consciously or unconsciously developed is a significant conclusion of the study.

In summary, Berger and Luckmann provided a framework for understanding the social construction of reality. McWhinney (1984), building on LeShan's (1976) work, developed a model for alternative realities that describes how differently people perceive and experience reality. The salient aspects of the research explicitly linking social construction, story and organization are that:

- Stories are useful for new member socialization and generating commitment.
- Familiarity with dominant organizational stories can be an indicator of adaptation.
- Story can be a vehicle for social control.
- Meaning can develop consciously and/or unconsciously.

Organization symbolism as an organizing perspective

The second perspective informing this review is that of organizational symbolism. Organizational symbolism involves the construction of meaning in organizations and attaching it to form. Dandridge *et al.* broadly defined organizational symbolism as that which "... expresses the underlying character, ideology, or value system of an organization" (1980, p. 77). They proposed that the symbol-bearing aspects of organizational life are stories and myths, ceremonies and ritualized events, company logo, and anecdotes and jokes (p. 77). Organizational symbolism fits within the overall rubric of the organizational culture literature. Smircich and Calas (1985) described the work done in organizational symbolism as concerned with interpreting symbolic discourse, identifying themes, and linking meaning to action.

In the opening essay of *Organizational Symbolism,* Pondy (1983) built on Burrell and Morgan's (1979) model of sociological paradigms (functionalist, interpretive, radical humanist, and radical structuralist) to identify metaphors and research in organizational symbolism which they aligned with each paradigm. Each paradigm favours particular assumptions, approaches, and research questions. A brief description of each paradigm and related metaphors follows. Morgan expanded the discussion of metaphor in *Images of Organization* (1986).

The functionalist paradigm emphasizes the use of symbol for the maintenance of social order. The metaphors related to this paradigm are the organismic metaphor, the cybernetic metaphor, the culture metaphor, and the theatrical metaphor. In essence, symbolism is useful for organizational order.

Organizational story and storytelling

7

JOCM
9,5

8

Examples of research in this vein are Goffman (1959), Rappaport (1971), and Wilkins (1978, 1983). The culture metaphor and the theatrical metaphor can also be approached through the interpretive paradigm. In each case, their focus would then shift from identifying functions to interpreting meaning and processes.

The interpretive paradigm views the construction of meaning through symbolic media. The metaphors related to this paradigm are sense making, text, and language game. The research from this perspective is concerned with understanding and interpreting how this process occurs. Examples of research in the interpretive paradigm are Mead (1934), Ricoeur (1971), Schutz (1967), Brown (1982), Smircich (1983), Berg (1985), Thorpe (1986), Mahler (1988), Boyce (1995), Jermier *et al.* (1991), Gabriel (1991) and Boje (1995).

The radical humanist paradigm emphasizes the pathological use of symbol. The metaphor it draws on is the psychic prison metaphor, which focuses on the use of symbol to alienate. Persons are seen as trapped by their own unconscious and conscious social constructs (Pondy *et al.*,1983, p. 25). Researchers have examined symbolic forms in organizations for evidence of psychic prisons. Sievers's (1993, 1994) research may be an example of this paradigm. Sievers (1994) examined how organizational members, snared by their childhood dramas, play out the unconscious dynamics in the workplace. AIDS provides a metaphor for Sievers's (1993) analysis of an AIDS service organization as he explored organizational dynamics that included diminished ability to manage responsibility, embeddedness in the immediate, and focus on socio-economic survival. He found that the social system mirrored the personal systems of its members (p. 41).

The radical structuralist paradigm emphasizes the way symbolic form is used in ideological control in the interests of those in power. The metaphor it draws on is instruments of domination. Research from this perspective focuses on ways in which dominant social ideologies are sustained. The work of Henry Giroux, a critical pedagogist, examines the use of popular culture to sustain the dominant ideology (1992, 1993, 1994).

As Morgan (1986) developed the application of metaphor and paradigm to organization studies, he advocated the practice of applying several metaphors to a situation in order to gain a broader and more textured perspective on complex organizational situations. Challenging the ease with which researchers situate themselves within one paradigm, Morgan encouraged an intentional use of various metaphors regarding one situation. Few studies demonstrate the intellectual exercise of shifting paradigms or perspectives. As one examines the research on story, the paradigm of the researcher is evident in the design and methodology of the study, in the underlying assumptions as well as the study conclusions. There are numerous reasons for this, among them being that clearly grounding one's work in a particular tradition or perspective is the norm and that certainty and clear assertions are rewarded among scholars. That which is unclear to the researcher may never make it into a paper. Reflections regarding that which appears inconsistent or ambiguous may not appear in the final presentation of a study.

Remaining largely unaddressed in the studies reviewed are the ways in which the researcher's paradigm shapes the study. For some scholars, the experiences and perceptions of the researcher are subjective issues which are outside the domain of objective scholarship. It is the conviction of this writer that the paradigm of the researcher shapes her/his perception of the data and their meaning and that the researcher cannot be completely separated from the research. Becoming conscious of one's dominant paradigm (or perspective) is a precursor to engaging in the exercise of applying more than one perspective. The practice of applying more than one perspective to an organizational culture or situation is best demonstrated in the work of Martin and Meyerson (1986, 1988), Martin and Powers (1983), Martin and Siehl (1983) and Martin *et al.* (1983, 1985). Their research and the three-perspective framework they developed is reviewed later in the section on organizational story.

Organizational symbolism has been cast as an aspect of the organizational culture literature. Pondy *et al.* (1983) well framed the approaches taken to the research with their description of paradigms and metaphors. Research on story and storytelling has been conducted within each paradigm. In summary, the salient points are that: researchers from various disciplines have described organizational stories and the process of storytelling as primary ways in which meaning, both individual and collective, is expressed; and the paradigm (or perspective) within which one has worked shapes the design and method of a study and is evident in one's scholarship.

Taking a critical perspective
Critical theory is the third perspective informing this review. A vast literature spanning sociology, philosophy, social criticism, education, and organization studies now exists that advocates a critical perspective (Bowles, 1989; Burrell, 1988; Calas and Smircich, 1992; Clegg, 1990; Ferguson, 1984; Freire, 1985; Giroux, 1992, 1993; Gramsci, 1971; Martin, 1990, 1992; Mills, 1988; Mills and Tancred, 1992; Tierney, 1989, 1993). Some of this work is grounded in modernism and some in postmodernism. Giroux (1993) and Tierney (1993) proposed a blend of these approaches, "critical postmodernism", which addresses structures and expressions of oppression at both macro and micro levels. Central to a critical perspective is identifying and challenging the assumptions that lie underneath one's work. Taking a critical perspective involves a ruthless and courageous examination and deconstruction of assumptions, norms, expectations, limitations, language, results, and applications of one's work.

Organizational myth and story from a critical perspective
In the most comprehensive, critical review of organizational myth done to date, Bowles (1989) examined the relationship between myth and meaning in work organizations. His essential thesis was that, with the demise of the Church in

JOCM
9,5

10

society, meaning is now sought by many persons in work organizations. An aspect of Bowles's analysis was an examination of five dominant management ideologies (structuralism, psychologism, welfarism, legalism and consensualism) presented by Salaman (1979) and the management metamyth identified by Ingersoll and Adams (1986) and Adams and Ingersoll (1983).

Management ideologies serve to bind the individual to the organization. Specifically, organizational stories are used to promote Salaman's (1979) management ideologies of psychologism and welfarism. A central concept in these ideologies is motivation. Stories speak to purpose, motivation, sense of team and success. Sievers (1986) described motivation becoming a surrogate for meaning. As meaning in work is destroyed, people need increasingly to be externally motivated. The fragmentation and alienation that is the creation of modern management is addressed by cultural meaning makers through the use of myth and story. Sievers critiqued large-scale, cultural prescriptions that are promoted as ways to align employees with a purpose larger than themselves.

Ingersoll and Adams's (1986) and Adams and Ingersoll's (1983) management metamyth refers to a "rational technical orientation toward tasks and relationships" (Bowles, 1989, p. 412). They concluded that the management metamyth is an insufficient substitution for deep meaning because it is dehumanizing and denies the numinous. Therefore, the conditions that Campbell (1976a) described for personal and social integration "are not to be found in through the experience of work" (Bowles, 1989, p. 415). The work of Ingersoll and Adams (1986) built on the "purposive-rational action", which Habermas connected to a focus on increasing efficiency and the pursuit of economic and technological goals, and was contrasted with "symbolic or communicative interaction", which Habermas connected with "emancipation, individuation, and the extension of communication free of domination" (Habermas, 1970, p. 93). Bowles contended that symbolic communication "is impossible where an ideology of technical efficiency prevails" (Bowles, 1989, p. 410). He went on to observe that "corporate culture" represents the most recent in a series of efforts "... designed to conceal the attempt to manipulate the interests of employees in the service of management" (Bowles, 1989, p. 417). Organizational story is used to develop and to sustain corporate culture (Silver, 1987). The basic tension that exists between the need for control and the need for participation lays underneath each attempt by management to demonstrate how individual interests can be served by aligning with management. Owing to the "inevitable clash of interests in organizations, derived from class locations, [Bowles] is skeptical of managerial strategies which purport to serve the interests of all" (Bowles, 1989, p. 417).

Based on the unravelling of traditional mythologies and the ascension of work organizations as a possible locus of meaning, Bowles advocated a "creative mythology" that allows an individual to recentre himself/herself on meaning that the individual creates and enacts individually and collectively (Campbell, 1976b; May, 1975). This new mythology would "enable the individual to commit him/herself to a pattern of activities, through work and life in general, where self potentials, both cognitive and affective, can be exercised and where the action of operating on the environment, as opposed to being merely subject to it, allows at some level, a sense of purpose and well-being" (Bowles, 1989, p. 416).

Bowles also observed that "a clear majority of people are severely hampered in achieving any form of individual creative response, due to the controls to which they are subject" (p. 416). A creative mythology of organization requires a democratization of work so that management of work is incorporated into the work process and not separated from it. Further, a creative mythology would necessitate "decentralized structures, flexible work roles and self control" (p. 417). Bowles recognized that for management to divest itself of the control process challenges the claim for expertise on which management has historically depended. Confronted with descriptions of what makes work meaningful for individuals (Argyris and Schon, 1974, 1978; Maslow, 1954, 1971), the refusal to democratize work is stripped of its paternal and professional cloak and the power and control-based foundation is exposed. Bowles argued that creating a new mythology of work and organization will only be achieved by fundamentally changing the relationship that people have to work and to one another in the workplace.

Bowles's critique of organizational myth and meaning draws attention to the ways in which myth and story are utilized to promote and to reinforce dominant ideologies. An intellectual and ethical challenge to those working with organizational story flows logically from Bowles's critique. The use of myth and story is not value neutral. Story researchers, managers and practitioners can use story and storytelling in organizations to describe and sustain the current power structure, or to nurture and fuel creativity and liberation and to develop new meaning of work and personhood by individuals and groups.

A focused, interdisciplinary lens for review

Each of the perspectives presented above contributes a significant aspect to the reviewer's interdisciplinary lens. By asserting the social construction of reality, social constructivism draws attention to the processes of symbolic interaction and meaning-making engaged in by all kinds of organizational members and groups. McWhinney's work in alternative realities highlights how differently people understand and experience reality. While social constructivism can be held hopefully by those with a unitary or integrative perspective, an acknowledgement of alternative realities humbles a researcher and sends her/him in search of different perspectives within the same organizations. Instead of one reality, there are multiple realities to be uncovered, spoken, heard and understood as one seeks to develop a wholistic picture of an organizational culture.

As another contributing aspect to an interdisciplinary perspective, organizational symbolism highlights the many ways in which meaning is given form and expressed. Within the interpretive paradigm, one assumes that symbols have meaning and one works to uncover the meaning of those forms to

Organizational story and storytelling

11

JOCM
9,5

12

organizational members. There is not one authoritative voice of interpretation for the researcher utilizing an interpretive paradigm. There are many voices and many meanings whose understandings overlap, collide, enhance, and silence one another. Organizational symbolism draws attention to the kaleidoscope of symbols and meanings sustained in organizations.

As a third aspect of an interdisciplinary perspective, critical theory assumes that dynamics of power and politics sustain a dominant voice (or story) in the organization and other voices (and stories) are less frequently heard or are silent. Taking a critical perspective is a beginning point for examining all that a researcher has assumed regarding her/his own work, regarding the interactions between persons, regarding group dynamics, and regarding organizations. Rather than perceiving oneself as objective and neutral as a researcher, within this perspective there is an inherent challenge to become conscious of how one's commitments and actions align oneself, and to organize one's work in ways that enhance emancipation and broaden the base of democracy in organizations and in society. To the review of story research, this perspective brings a consciousness of dominance and democratization processes in organizations. It makes visible the uses of story to reinforce and sustain organizational cultures.

Although interdisciplinary, this lens is not objective, nor can it be so. One may argue whether or not a reviewer can possess a truly objective lens, and if he/she can do so, one may argue whether or not it is the most valuable perspective with which to wrestle and evaluate the value and contributions of a body of research. It is the position of this writer that one's perspective both enriches and limits one's work, and that it must necessarily be identified and reflected on. It is not enough to examine the perspective taken by story researchers. The perspective taken by the reviewer must also be identified and examined.

Taken as a whole, the interdisciplinary perspective identified here has inherent strengths and weaknesses. The strengths of the perspective are its recognition of: all organizational members (and groups) as meaning makers; symbol(s) as expressing meaning; multiple realities, perspectives and voices within an organization; power dynamics being used to sustain dominant ideologies; and emancipation as an ongoing and essential aspect of democracy. The primary weaknesses of the perspective are that it is not empirically grounded and makes no claim of objectivity. It is from this interdisciplinary point of view that the rich and varied contributions to story and storytelling research are considered, key studies are examined, and challenges to theory and practice are presented.

Contributions from a multidisciplinary foundation

The research on organizational story and storytelling is built on a larger foundation of work on myth and narrative. A brief introduction to the foundational work includes research conducted by folklorists, anthropologists, sociologists, communication and organization theorists.

Key studies in folklore and anthropology

Three contributions from the folklore literature that specifically address storytelling are the studies by Georges (1969), Nusbaum (1982) and Robinson (1981). Georges (1969) proposed that storytelling events be researched as holistic communicative events; however, he constrained the meaning of a storytelling event to the particular event (p. 323). Subsequent researchers established a connection between shared storytelling experiences and the larger organizational reality (Agmon and McWhinney, 1989; Boje, 1991; Boyce, 1995). Nusbaum (1982) asserted that sense making involves both storytelling and ordinary conversation, and Boje described storytelling as "... the preferred sense-making currency of human relationships among internal and external stakeholders" in organizations (Boje, 1991, p. 106). Robinson (1981) identified the roles of listeners of stories in his work on personal narratives. The recognition that listeners are active participants in "storying" is of particular significance to those working with story and storytelling in organizations.

While it is impossible to review an anthropological approach to myth and story research briefly, it can be observed that the models of social structure which anthropologists apply to analyses shifted from the equilibrium models of Malinowski (1931) and Radcliffe-Brown (1952) to the structural analysis model of Levi-Strauss (1963, 1966). Levi-Strauss (1963, 1966) had two underlying assumptions regarding myth. First, thought process demands order and gains that order by interacting with experience in such a way as to render it intelligible. Second, this process is generally unconscious. Myth functions essentially to resolve life contradictions. The ideas of Levi-Strauss shaped the way in which myth is approached and understood by researchers in anthropology as well as organizational culture. Levi-Strauss laid the foundation of story and storytelling as vehicles for ambiguity and contradiction in organizational culture.

Research in communication theories

Another approach to the study of story resides within the field of communication theory. Rhetorical discourse has a lengthy tradition and includes both argument and narrative as forms of speech. The study of story occurs within narrative in communication theory. Approaches to narrative (as it relates to story) have been developed and described by numerous scholars (Burke, 1955; Campbell, 1970; Fisher, 1984, 1987; Labov, 1972; Labov and Waletsky, 1967; Perelman, 1979; van Dijk, 1975). Fisher's (1987) narrative paradigm is described in this review because of its particular relevance to the study of organizational stories.

The narrative paradigm presents a "philosophy of reason, value and action" (Fisher, 1987, p. 64), provides a "logic" for assessing stories, and also explores "how we endorse or accept stories as the basis for decisions and actions" (p. 87). Fisher described this work as a paradigm because it implies a philosophical view of human communication. Communication can be interpreted, critiqued for coherence and fidelity, and linked to actions taken by people. Fisher described the choice of meaningful stories:

JOCM
9,5

The world as we know it is a set of stories that must be chosen among in order for us to live life in a process of continual re-creation. In short, good reasons are the stuff of stories, the means by which humans realize their nature as reasoning-valuing animals. The philosophical ground of the narrative paradigm is ontology (Fisher, 1987, p. 65).

The narrative paradigm also recognizes the capacity of people to create "...new stories that better account for their lives or the mystery of life itself" (Fisher, 1987, p. 67).

14

To position the narrative paradigm in conjunction with other approaches to rhetoric and narrative, it is helpful to distinguish between several rhetorical perspectives and hermeneutics. The two primary rhetorical theorists with whom Fisher clarified points of difference are Burke (1955) and Perelman (1979). The narrative paradigm differs from Burke's dramatization in two ways: it views people as full participants rather than as actors with scripts; and "...people's symbolic actions take the form of stories and...they assess them by the principles of coherence and fidelity" (Fisher, 1987, p. 19). The essential point of difference between the narrative paradigm and the "new rhetoric" of Perelman is a difference in view of humanity. Fisher saw "storytellers" and Perelman saw "arguers" (p. 97).

The narrative paradigm views story as a fundamental form in which people express values and reasons, and subsequently make decisions about action. It focuses on the message of a story and evaluates the reliability, trustworthiness, and desirability of the message. The method for applying the narrative paradigm involves identifying story themes and assessing the links between values, reason and action. It provides a particularly valuable method for working with story and storytelling in organizations.

In summary, story and storytelling research is built on a multidisciplinary foundation. Work conducted by folklorists, anthropologists, communication theorists as well as by sociologists, philosophers and critical theorists, enriches the family tree and informs the work in story and storytelling being conducted by organizational researchers.

Key studies in organizational story and storytelling
Particular studies have built on the broad knowledge base highlighted above and contributed directly to the work in organizational story and storytelling. It is appropriate to examine the studies individually and as a whole in order to assess their contribution(s) to how we understand the role of stories and shared storytelling in organization culture. Who tells organization stories? How, and by whom, are organizational stories interpreted? What meaning is attributed to the stories and to the process of storytelling? It is the purpose of this review to reflect on the perspectives of the researchers as well as the conclusions drawn in the studies in a critical assessment of organizational story and storytelling.

Organizational story and myth
The most frequently referenced research in organizational story is the study by Clark (1970, 1972). Clark's definition of "organizational saga" (1972, p. 178) links

a charismatic leader and strong purpose with a claim of unique accomplishment. Two story studies followed Clark's which explore uniqueness as an aspect of organizational culture. Key points from each of these studies are described here.

The first is a study by Mitroff and Kilmann on "epic myths" (1975, p. 18). Mitroff and Kilmann defined an epic myth as capturing the unique quality of an organization. They proposed that the epic myth gives meaning to organizational members and is useful in new member orientation. The most salient aspect of this work is their use of sharing stories as an approach to large-scale, organizational problem solving (pp. 25-6). Their method involves sharing stories about an ideal organization first, and then, sharing stories about the actual organization. This study stands out from other research in organizational story because it describes a structured, storytelling event as a piece of action research. The study focuses on the value of the shared stories for managers to understand employees.

In the second "uniqueness study", Martin *et al.* (1983) searched for uniqueness in their study of organizational stories across a varied collection of organizations. They discovered that what organizational members hold to be unique about their organizations is, in fact, not unique. They called this feature the "uniqueness paradox" (p. 439).

Beyond uniqueness, Martin *et al.* looked critically at the prevailing integrative perspective of cultural study that presumes an organizational culture is that which is shared, that a founder is a culture-creator, and, third, that the shared understandings reflect the personal convictions of the founder. With culture creation being attributed to leaders, it is not surprising that the literature has many studies about leaders shaping and changing organizational cultures. Studies with this perspective include those by Clark (1970, 1972), Hackman (1984), Martin *et al.* (1983), Pettigrew (1979), Schein (1983, 1985), and Wilkins (1978, 1983, 1984).

Research that continues to advocate an integrative perspective warrants criticism. "Given the conceptual centrality of the question of what is shared, and by whom, it is indeed an important weakness that integration paradigm research seldom makes a systematic attempt to determine exactly who shares what" (Martin and Meyerson, 1988, p. 104). The dominance of the integrative perspective persists, however, and studies that demonstrate leaders in control of organizational change are still the norm. One journal editor found a study to be "disturbing" when it demonstrated that organizational members were resisting a leader's cultural change efforts and reinforcing meaning woven within their own ranks (personal correspondence with author and editor, 1992).

In a series of studies, Martin (1992), Martin and Meyerson (1986, 1988), Martin and Powers (1983), Martin and Siehl (1983) and Martin *et al.* (1983, 1985) examined and defined a three-perspective framework: integration (described above), differentiation and ambiguity (subsequently identified as fragmentation). The differentiation perspective holds that organizations are "umbrellas for collections of subcultures" (Martin *et al.*, 1985, p. 101), that leaders and

Organizational story and storytelling

15

JOCM
9,5

16

members are active culture creators, and that culture is shaped by forces beyond the control of the founder. Just as the integration perspective is congruent with a top management point of view, studies from the differentiation perspective express the points of view of those attuned to differences of class and power. There is a growing collection of studies in folklore, labour culture and organization studies written from a differentiation perspective (Gregory, 1983; Jermier *et al.*, 1991; Maynard-Moody *et al.*, 1986; Meyer, 1982; Reynolds, 1986; Rose, 1988; Smircich, 1983; Trice and Beyer, 1984; Van Maanen and Barley, 1984, 1985).

The fragmentation perspective "brings ambiguity to the foreground" (Martin, 1992, p. 130) and focuses attention on the complex array of relationships in the culture. The perspective includes unclear and inconsistent cultural manifestations, and differences are seen as irreconcilable and unavoidable. A metaphor that Martin and Meyerson (1988) proposed for this perspective is a web in which individuals are connected by some, but not all, of the concerns. A recently developed perspective, few studies have been conducted from a fragmentation perspective, although one can refer to studies by Martin (1990, 1992), Meyerson (1989) and Weick (1991).

The three-perspective framework (Martin, 1992) provides researchers and practitioners with an approach to "taking another perspective". Application of the framework will make a textured, many-sided interpretation of stories (and of organizational culture) more likely than if a researcher or practitioner utilizes one perspective. While the integration perspective addresses management's point of view, intentional focus on the differentiation and fragmentation perspectives will increase one's understanding of co-existing groups and exploration of democracy and emancipation in organizational life.

Examples of other research on organizational story are Berg and Asplund's (1981) study of organizational genesis with a Nordic, mythic context, Gabriel's (1991) exploration of organizational myths as collective fantasies, Gufstafsson's (1984) investigation of the "essential contradiction" between a traditional hero and a manager-as-hero, Larson's (1991) identification of storytelling as a strategy for informal workplace learning, Mahler's (1988) interpretation of the symbolism in stories from the Agency for International Development, and McCollom's (1987) reflections on multicultural reality in a family-owned business.

The applications of organizational story for managers and practitioners that are demonstrated in these studies include problem-solving/action research, suspending irreconcilable alternatives, socializing, generating commitment, learning, sense making, symbolizing, social control and creating new meaning. Much of the work in organizational story has been conducted from an integrative perspective. Martin's three-perspective framework presents a challenge to traditional studies conducted with an integrative perspective and lays a foundation for developing fuller, more textured expressions of meaning in organizations by utilizing more than one perspective.

Storytelling as a process

Interesting work on storytelling as a vehicle for collective centring and collective sense making has been conducted (Agmon and McWhinney, 1989; Boje, 1991, 1995; Boje *et al.,* 1982; Boyce, 1995; McWhinney and Battista, 1988). McWhinney called his work "remythologizing", and it is highlighted here because of its focus on organizational renewal. Remythologizing can revitalize an organizational culture.

Remythologizing is a process used in organizations to interpret and understand the organizational symbology, bring it to consciousness, and enable organizational renewal (Agmon and McWhinney, 1989; McWhinney and Battista, 1988). McWhinney attributed the development of this process to the deep work carried out in symbol by Jungians. He saw symbol as an expression of the unconscious. It is through the symbolic form of story that we begin to discover the deep meaning which guides action. Remythologizing "… summons back to consciousness the founding ideals and the oft-told tales that helped establish and maintain an organization's identity, thus linking the primal energy with present conditions" (McWhinney and Battista, 1988, p. 46). McWhinney and Battista proposed three stages to this process – bringing founding myths to organizational consciousness, reviving the founding myths, and "recommitment to the revitalized myth" (p. 55).

Remythologizing has been applied in varied situations. McWhinney worked with the founding myth of the Disney Corporation (McWhinney and Battista, 1988); Battista (McWhinney and Battista, 1988) applied the concepts on a macro level to Caribbean myth; and Agmon researched the myth underlying an international, Israeli business (Agmon and McWhinney, 1989). A remythologizing project on American and European conceptions of health has been a recent project of McWhinney. He uncovered nine metaphors related to health in an exploration with health-care professionals. "Within each metaphor are the myths and stories that elaborate the ways in which these meanings appear" (McWhinney, 1995, p. 6). There are many possible applications of remythologizing.

An earlier, related approach to organizational myth was proposed by Boje *et al.* (1982). They described "myth making" as an adaptive process in which organizational members create a logic which attributes meaning to their activities. They suggested that a myth "narrows the horizon in which organizational life is allowed to make sense" (p. 18). Their work identifies stages to myth development (pp. 24-6) which are similar to those suggested by McWhinney and Battista. The stages are myth development, solid myth, myth split, and myth shift. They introduced the concept of "myth exchange" in which they maintained that people can learn to bracket their own mythic thinking, entertain the thinking of others, and stay clear on the original myth (p. 26).

The differences between the work by McWhinney, Battista, and Agmon, and Boje *et al.* seemed to be that Boje *et al.* (1982) described what they understood as an organizational life process rather than the creative process for organizational renewal that McWhinney, Battista, and Agmon were developing; and that

Organizational
story and
storytelling

17

JOCM
9,5

18

McWhinney, Battista, and Agmon (1982) clearly were focused on the unconscious power of myth and symbol and Boje *et al.* (Agmon and McWhinney, 1988; McWhinney and Battista, 1988) seemed less focused on the unconscious.

Remythologizing represents an approach to collective centring with its focus on core processes and living myth. Collective centring is the process of focusing a group on that which is integral, of organizational essence (Mink *et al.*, 1979). Other work that demonstrates shared storytelling as a vehicle for collective centring is the study by Boyce (1995) in which the stories and storytelling of one, not-for-profit organization are examined.

Boyce (1990, 1995) made a contribution to the storytelling literature with story analysis that is grounded in organizational history and root metaphor. The shared meaning (collective sense) possessed by the organizational members who participated in the study is rooted in a unitary reality (McWhinney, 1984) with a religious foundation. In the organization studied, no alternative realities (or groups with a distinctive collective sense) are identified among study participants. A contribution to the sense-making literature made by Boyce's (1990) study is an examination of collective sense making in a structurally closed system. Although she attempted to demonstrate shared storytelling as a vehicle for collective sense making, this did not occur in the study. When deep disagreement between the organizational members and the president is uncovered during the study, questions about vision, strategy and organizational change are evoked (Boyce, 1995).

An organization as a storytelling system is the focus of Boje's (1991) study of story performance in an office-supply firm. He demonstrated the management of sense making as storytellers and listeners send cues and make decisions about how much of the story to tell, how much to reference, and which interpretation is applied (p. 124). Skilled storytellers and story interpreters are effective organizational communicators, demonstrate understanding of organizational culture and history, and possess skills that managers dealing with rapid change might well develop (Boje, 1989, 1991). The strength of Boje's (1991) study is the first-hand observation of storytelling as it is performed naturally in an organization. His work draws attention to the uses of storytelling by internal stakeholders (predicting, empowering, and fashioning change) and by external stakeholders (making sense of the setting, negotiating alternative interpretations, and accommodating new precedents) and to the dynamics which vary story performance (p. 124).

Boje's (1995) study of Disney stories which demonstrates pre-modern, modern, and postmodern discourse provides an example of taking more than one perspective in one's research. Using *Tamara*, a play, as a metaphor for plurivocal organizational discourse, Boje (1995) conducted postmodern analysis of the array of official and unofficial stories about Walt Disney and the Disney Studios. He drew attention to the mix of discourses present in the Disney stories and storytelling. As a company, Disney is still characterized by the hegemonic, organizational culture and authoritarian practices that Disney introduced. Now, however, Eisner is intentionally weaving into his storytelling voices that have not been heard in some time, and stories are told by people besides the chief executive officer. It is significant that Boje distinguished between his method of postmodern analysis and the conclusion that Disney is not a postmodern organization (1995). Working from the postmodern assumption that more than one discourse co-exists, Boje's demonstrates an approach to plurivocal story interpretation.

The research conducted to date has demonstrated storytelling processes as approaches to problem solving and action research (Mitroff and Kilmann, 1975), organizational renewal (Agmon and McWhinney, 1989; McWhinney and Battista, 1988), socialization of new employees (Brown, 1982; Louis, 1980, 1983), collective centring (Boyce, 1995; McWhinney and Battista, 1988), sense making (Boje, 1991, 1995), learning (Helmer, 1989), and innovation and new product development (McWhinney, 1995).

Shared storytelling has a number of applications that warrant consideration by organizational members, managers and practitioners. These are:

- expressing the organizational experience of members or clients;
- confirming the shared experiences and shared meaning of organizational members and groups within the organization;
- orienting and socializing new organizational members;
- amending and altering the organizational reality;
- developing, sharpening and renewing the sense of purpose held by organizational members;
- preparing a group (or groups) for planning, implementing plans and decision making in line with shared purposes; and
- co-creating vision and strategy.

Challenges to theory and practice
Regarding the research to date on organizational story and storytelling, the emergent challenges with which to wrestle include:

- explicitly addressing one's perspective as a researcher and conducting critical and political analysis;
- culture creation and taking multiple perspectives into account;
- attributing earlier scholars; and
- the essential, ethical challenge of story and storytelling work.

These concerns are presented below.

Explicitly addressing the researcher's perspective
Studies undertaken from a symbolic interactionist or social constructivist perspective recognized the significance of individual and collective meaning; however, they may not explicitly address the orientation of the researcher and

JOCM
9,5

20

may or may not include a critical or political analysis. Dynamics of power, dominant groups and lesser-heard voices, "insiders" and "outsiders", and the fundamental question of whose culture and meaning is expressed in organizational stories are largely unaddressed in the story studies conducted to date. If people are symbolizing meaning-makers who express meaning in the form of stories, researchers must carefully attend to the meaning made and expressed at each level of the organization and by different groups of organizational members. Two concerns emerge here that draw attention to the researcher's perspective as he/she approaches a story study. First, if one assumes an integrative perspective, there is the probability that dissonant voices will not be heard or will be made peripheral. For example, we might assume that a well-known, organizational story has one meaning rather than explore the possible differences of meaning that the story has to various groups in the organization. Second, a conscious or unconscious collusion with management can guide the researcher's search for stories and the meaning (or value) that is attributed to the stories uncovered. Explicitly identifying one's perspective as a researcher can increase one's awareness as to the limitations of one's point of view and the probable effectiveness or ineffectiveness of one's research design for uncovering other meaning.

Taking multiple perspectives into account
Related to the first observation are questions about who it is in organizations that creates culture and who "owns" or possesses the culture of an organization. If we are learning that all organizational members are meaning makers and contribute to "storying" and the culture-creation process, this has direct implications for organizational story work. When undertaking storytelling work in an organization, one must carefully assess the culture being created and changed throughout the organization, identifying the various strains of the culture(s) being woven everyday and identifying how the creating and changing is occurring. Researchers must seek out the different meanings woven and held by different members and groups in the organization. Story and storytelling research could be making an intentional contribution to what is known about the creating and changing of organizational culture. Little of this work has been done to date in the story and storytelling research.

Attributing earlier scholars
Storytelling is an ancient medium for communication and meaning making. Serious studies about myth, narrative, story and storytelling have been conducted by scholars with different theoretical traditions and disciplines. Organizational story is an area of study with a rich and varied genealogy; however, little of the research in organizational story and organizational culture is clearly grounded in earlier theoretical work. With the clear exception of dissertations, in which scholars carefully demonstrate how their studies fit within a stream of work previously conducted, many story and culture studies seem to hang in the air without apparent genealogy. Is it possible that scholars in organization story are unfamiliar with the history of this scholarship?

Rather, perhaps we are reluctant to attribute scholars in other disciplines on whose work we build, citing instead our own early scholars in organization story and organization culture. There is not a "pure" study of organizational story or culture. Much of our research is multidisciplinary and should be demonstrated as such. Current scholarship is deepened by demonstrating its place in the family tree.

Inescapable ethical challenges
Research and application of story and storytelling processes presents scholars, managers and practitioners with ethical/philosophical challenges. The research on organizational story and storytelling has been conducted from social control as well as from participatory, emancipatory, co-creative perspectives. The application of organization story and storytelling processes in organizations can also be socially controlling or participatory and emancipatory. A critical perspective advocates the development and utilization of liberatory and democratic processes so that people can learn how to be involved in social and organizational actions that are critical and hopeful. Storytelling is an example of a process that can nurture and create meaning or reinforce control and manipulate meaning.

The observation about ethics/philosophy ties back around to the risk of a pro-management bias. Several questions emerge for the researcher and practitioner. To what ends do I apply my knowledge of culture and storytelling in organizations? Am I, as a practitioner and researcher, engaged in story and storytelling work that increases renewal, participation and democracy in organizations? What evidence of this can I find? Am I aligned with management in ways that result in my knowledge and skill regarding symbol, meaning making, and sense making being used to establish and reinforce control? What evidence of this can I find? These questions are unsettling to ask.

Summary
This review of organizational story and storytelling research conducted with symbolic, social constructivist and critical perspectives has examined key studies and reflected on the perspectives from which the studies have been conducted. Story and storytelling clearly express organizational culture. The research reviewed contributes particular organizational case studies, industry-wide descriptions, and an array of approaches to story and storytelling that have been utilized in organizations. Researchers and practitioners are challenged to examine the perspective with which they undertake story and storytelling work in organizations. The ease with which story and storytelling can be used in the interests of management or as a vehicle for organizational renewal and participation is highlighted.

References
Abravanel, H. (1983), "Mediatory myths in service of organizational ideology", in Pondy, L.R., Morgan, G., Frost, P.J. and Dandridge, T. (Eds), *Organizational Symbolism*, JAI Press, Greenwich, CT, pp. 273-93.

JOCM
9,5

22

Adams, G.B. and Ingersoll, V.H. (1983), "Managerial metamyths: bridges to organizational boundary crossing", paper presented at the invitational meeting of Myth, Symbol and Folklore: Expanding the Analysis of Organizations, UCLA, Los Angeles, CA.

Agmon, O. and McWhinney, W. (1989), "On myths and the mythic: their use in organizational and social change", unpublished manuscript.

Argyris, C. and Schon, D.A. (1974), *Theory in Practice: Increasing Professional Effectiveness,* Jossey-Bass, San Francisco, CA.

Argyris, C. and Schon, D.A. (1978), *Organizational Learning: A Theory of Action Perspective,* Jossey-Bass, San Francisco, CA.

Berg, P. (1985), "Organizational change: as a symbolic transformation process", in Frost, P.J., Moore, L.F., Lundberg, C.C. and Martin, J. (Eds), *Organizational Culture,* Sage, Newbury Park, CA, pp. 281-99.

Berg, P. and Asplund, C. (1981), "Organizational sagas", paper presented at EGOS Colloquium, Glasgow University, Glasgow.

Berger, H.S. and Luckmann, T. (1967), *The Social Construction of Reality,* Anchor, New York, NY.

Boje, D.M. (1989), "Postlog: bringing performance back in", *Journal of Organizational Change Management,* Vol. 2 No. 2, pp. 80-93.

Boje, D.M. (1991), "The storytelling organization: a study of story performance in an office-supply firm", *Administrative Science Quarterly,* Vol. 36 No. 3, pp. 106-26.

Boje, D.M. (1995), "Stories of the storytelling organization: a postmodern analysis of Disney as 'Tamara-land'", *Academy of Management Journal,* Vol. 38 No. 4, pp. 997-1035.

Boje, D.M., Fedor, D.B. and Rowland, K.M. (1982), "Myth making: a qualitative step in OD interventions", *Journal and Applied Behavioral Science,* Vol. 18 No. 1, pp. 17-28.

Bowles, M.L. (1989), "Myth, meaning, and work organization", *Organization Studies,* Vol. 10 No. 3, pp. 405-21.

Boyce, M.E. (1990), "Story and storytelling in organizational life", unpublished dissertation, The Fielding Institute, Santa Barbara, CA.

Boyce, M.E. (1995), "Collective centring and collective sense-making in the stories and storytelling of one organization", *Organization Studies,* Vol. 16 No. 1, pp. 107-37.

Brown, M.H. (1982), "That reminds me of a story: speech action on organizational socialization", unpublished doctoral dissertation, University of Texas at Austin, TX.

Burke, K. (1955), *A Rhetoric of Motives,* George Braziller, New York, NY.

Burrell, G. (1988), "Modernism, postmodernism, and organizational analysis 2: the contribution of Michel Foucalt", *Organization Studies,* Vol. 9 No. 2, pp. 221-35.

Burrell, G. and Morgan, G. (1979), *Sociological Paradigms and Organizational Analysis,* Heinemann, London.

Calas, M.B. and Smircich, L. (1992), "Re-writing gender into organizational theorizing: directions from feminist perspectives", in Reed, M. and Hughes, M. (Eds), *Rethinking Organization: New Directions in Organization Theory and Analysis,* Sage, Newbury Park, pp. 227-53.

Campbell, J. (1976a), *Primitive Mythology,* Penguin, Harmondsworth.

Campbell, J. (1976b), *Creative Mythology,* Penguin, Harmondsworth.

Campbell, K. (1970), "The ontological foundations of rhetorical theory", *Philosophy and Rhetoric,* Vol. 3, pp. 97-108.

Clark, B.R. (1970), *The Distinctive College: Antioch, Reed, and Swarthmore,* Aldine, Chicago, IL.

Clark, B.R. (1972), "The organizational saga in higher education", *Administrative Science Quarterly,* Vol. 17, pp. 178-84.

Clegg, S. (1990), *Modern Organizations: Organization Studies in the Postmodern World,* Sage, Newbury Park, CA.

Conrad, C. (1981), "Toward a symbology of organizational power", paper presented at the SCA/ICA Conference on Interpretive Approaches to Organizational Communication, Alta, UT.

Dandridge, T.C., Mitroff, I. and Joyce, W.F. (1980), "Organizational symbolism: a topic to expand organizational analysis", *Academy of Management Review*, Vol. 5 No. 1, pp. 77-82.

Ferguson, K. (1984), *The Feminist Case against Bureaucracy*, Temple University Press, Philadelphia, PA.

Fisher, W.R. (1984), "Narration as a human communication paradigm: the case of public moral argument", *Communication Monographs*, Vol. 51 No. 3, pp. 1-22.

Fisher, W.R. (1987), *Human Communication as Narration: Toward a Philosophy of Reason, Value, and Action*, University of South Carolina Press, Columbia, SC.

Freire, P. (1985), *The Politics of Education: Culture, Power, and Liberation*, trans. by D. Macedo, Bergin & Garvey, Westport, CT.

Gabriel, Y. (1991), "Turning facts into stories and stories into facts: a hermeneutic exploration of organizational folklore", *Human Relations*, Vol. 44 No. 8, pp. 857-75.

Georges, R.A. (1969), "Toward an understanding of storytelling", *Journal of American Folklore*, Vol. 82, pp. 313-28.

Giroux, H.A. (1992), *Border Crossings: Cultural Workers and the Politics of Education*, Routledge, New York, NY.

Giroux, H.A. (1993), *Living Dangerously: Multiculturalism and the Politics of Difference*, Peter Lang, New York, NY.

Giroux, H.A. (1994), *Disturbing Pleasures: Learning Popular Culture*, Routledge, New York, NY.

Goffman, E. (1959), *The Presentation of Self in Everyday Life*, Doubleday, New York, NY.

Gramsci, A. (1971), *Selections from the Prison Notebooks*, International Publishers, New York, NY.

Gregory, K.L. (1983), "Native-view paradigms: multiple cultures and culture conflicts in organizations", *Administrative Science Quarterly*, Vol. 28, pp. 359-76.

Gustafsson, B. (1984), "Hero myths and manager descriptions", paper presented at the Conference on Organizational Symbolism and Corporate Culture, Lund, Sweden.

Habermas, J. (1970), *Toward a Rational Society*, trans. by J.J. Shapiro, Beacon, Boston, MA.

Hackman, R. (1984), "The transition that hasn't happened", unpublished manuscript, Yale University, New Haven, CT.

Helmer, J.E. (1989), "Between horses: an ethnographic study of communication and organizational culture at a harness track", unpublished dissertation, University of Illinois at Urbana-Champaign, IL.

Ingersoll, V.H. and Adams, G.B. (1986), "Beyond organizational boundaries: explaining the managerial myth", *Administration and Society*, Vol. 18 No. 3, pp. 360-81.

Jermier, J.M., Slocum, J.W. Jr, Fry, L.W. and Gaines, J. (1991), "Organizational subcultures in a soft bureaucracy: resistance behind the myth and facade of an official culture", *Organization Science*, Vol. 2 No. 2, pp. 170-94.

Labov, W. (1972), *Language in the Inner City: Studies in the Black English Vernacular*, University of Pennsylvania Press, Philadelphia, PA.

Labov, W. and Waletsky, J. (1967), "Narrative analysis: oral version of personal experience", in Helm, J. (Ed.), *Essays on the Visual and Verbal Arts*, University of Washington Press, Seattle, WA, pp. 12-44.

Larson, B.J. (1991), "Informal workplace learning and partner relationships among paramedics in the prehospital setting", unpublished dissertation, Columbia University Teachers College, New York, NY.

LeShan, L. (1976), *Alternative Realities*, Ballantine, New York, NY.

Levi-Strauss, C. (1963), *Structural Anthropology*, The Penguin Press, London.

Levi-Strauss, C. (1966), *The Savage Mind*, Weidenfeld & Nicolson, London.

Organizational
story and
storytelling

23

JOCM
9,5

24

Louis, M.R. (1980), "Surprise and sense making: what newcomers experience in entering unfamiliar organizational setting", *Administrative Science Quarterly*, Vol. 25, pp. 226-52.

Louis, M.R. (1983), "Organizations as culture-bearing milieu", in Pondy, L.R., Frost, P.J., Morgan, G. and Dandridge, T. (Eds), *Organizational Symbolism: Monographs in Organizational and Industrial Relations, Vol. 1*, JAI Press, Greenwich, CT, pp. 39-54.

McCollom, M.E. (1987), "Subcultures and stories: reflection of a multicultural reality in organizations", unpublished doctoral dissertation, Yale University, New Haven, CT.

McWhinney, W. (1984), "Alternative realities: their impact on change and leadership", *Journal of Humanistic Psychology*, Vol. 24 No. 4, pp. 7-38.

McWhinney, W. (1995), "A health confluence", unpublished paper.

McWhinney, W. and Battista, J. (1988), "How remythologizing can revitalize organizations", *Organizational Dynamics*, August, pp. 46-58.

Mahler, J. (1988), "The quest for organizational meaning: identifying and interpreting the symbolism in organizational stories", *Administration & Society*, Vol. 20 No. 3, pp. 344-68.

Malinowski, B. (1931), "Culture", in Seligman, E.R.A. (Ed.), *Encyclopedia of the Social Sciences, Vol. 4*, Macmillan, New York, NY, pp. 621-46.

Martin, J. (1990), "Deconstructing organizational taboos: the suppression of gender conflict in organizations", *Organization Science*, Vol. 1, pp. 1-21.

Martin, J. (1992), *Cultures in Organizations: Three Perspectives*, Oxford University Press, New York, NY.

Martin, J. and Meyerson, D. (1986), "Organizational culture at the OZ company (OZCO)", unpublished manuscript, Stanford University, Standford, CA.

Martin, J. and Meyerson, D. (1988), "Organizational cultures and the denial, channeling, and acknowledgement of ambiguity", in Pondy, L.R., Boland, R.J. Jr and Thomas, H. (Eds), *Managing Ambiguity and Change*, John Wiley & Sons, New York, NY, pp. 93-125.

Martin, J. and Powers, M.E. (1983), "Truth or corporate propaganda: the value of a good war story", in Pondy, L.R., Frost, P.J., Morgan, G. and Dandridge, T. (Eds), *Organizational Symbolism: Monographs in Organizational and Industrial Relations, Vol. 1*, JAI Press, Greenwich, CT, pp. 93-107.

Martin, J. and Siehl, C. (1983), "Organizational culture and counterculture: an uneasy symbiosis", *Organizational Dynamics*, August, pp. 52-64.

Martin, J., Sitkin, S.B. and Boehm, M. (1985), "Founders and elusiveness of a cultural legacy", in Frost, P.J., Moore, L.F., Louis, M.R., Lundberg, C.C. and Martin, J. (Eds), *Organizational Culture*, Sage, Beverly Hills, CA, pp. 99-124.

Martin, J., Feldman, M.S., Hatch, M.J. and Sitkin, S.B. (1983), "The uniqueness paradox in organizational stories", *Administrative Science Quarterly*, Vol. 28, pp. 438-53.

Maslow, A.H. (1954), *Motivation and Personality*, Harper & Row, New York, NY.

Maslow, A.H. (1971), *The Further Reaches of Human Nature*, Viking, New York, NY.

May, R. (1975), *The Courage to Create*, Bantam, New York, NY.

Maynard-Moody, S., Stull, D. and Mitchell, J. (1986), "Reorganization as status drama: building, maintaining, and displacing dominant subcultures", *Public Administration Review*, Vol. 46, pp. 301-10.

Mead, G.H. (1934), *Mind, Self, and Society*, University of Chicago Press, Chicago, IL.

Meyer, J.W. (1982), "How ideologies supplant formal structures and shape responses to environments", *Journal of Management Studies*, Vol. 19, pp. 45-61.

Meyerson, D. (1989), "The social construction of ambiguity and burnout", unpublished dissertation, Stanford University, Stanford, CA.

Mills, A.J. (1988), "Organization, gender, and culture", *Organization Studies*, Vol. 9 No. 3, pp. 351-69.

Mills, A.J. and Tancred, P. (Eds), (1992), *Gendering Organizational Analysis*, Sage, Newbury Park, CA.

Mink, O.G., Shultz, J.M. and Mink, B.P. (1979), *Open Organizations*, Learning Concepts, San Diego, CA (distributed by University Associates).

Mitroff, I. and Kilmann, R.H. (1975), "Stories managers tell: a new tool for organizational problem-solving", *Management Review*, July, pp. 18-28.

Morgan, G. (1986), *Images of Organization*, Sage, Newbury Park, CA.

Nusbaum, P. (1982), "Making sense: the creative formulation of everyday conversation", unpublished dissertation, Indiana University, Bloomington, IN.

Nystrom, P.C. and Starbuck, W.H. (1984), "Managing beliefs on organizations", *Journal of Applied Behavioral Science*, Vol. 20 No. 3, pp. 277-87.

Ouchi, W.G. and Johnson, J. (1978), "Types of organizational control and their relationship to emotional wellbeing", *Administrative Science Quarterly*, Vol. 23 No. 2, pp. 293-317.

Perelman, C. (1979), "Authority, ideology, and violence", in Perelman, C. (Ed.), *The New Rhetoric and the Humanities: Essays on Rhetoric and Its Experience*, D. Reidel, Dordrecht.

Pettigrew, A.M. (1979), "On studying organizational cultures", *Administrative Science Quarterly*, Vol. 24, pp. 570-81.

Pondy, L. (1983), "The role of metaphors and myths in organization", in Pondy, L.R., Frost, P.J., Morgan, G. and Dandridge, T. (Eds), *Organizational Symbolism: Monographs in Organizational and Industrial Relations, Vol. 1*, JAI Press, Greenwich, CT, pp. 157-66.

Pondy, L., Frost, P., Morgan, G. and Dandridge, T. (Eds) (1983), *Organizational Symbolism: Monographs in Organizational and Industrial Relations, Vol. 1*, JAI Press, Greenwich, CT.

Radcliffe-Brown, A. (1952), *Structure and Function in Primitive Society*, Free Press, Glencoe, IL.

Rappaport, R.A. (1971), "Ritual, sanctity, and cybernetics", *American Anthropologist*, Vol. 73, pp. 59-76.

Reynolds, P.D. (1986), "Organizational cultures as related to industry, position, and performance", *Journal of Management Studies*, Vol. 23, pp. 333-45.

Ricoeur, P. (1971), "The model of text: meaningful action considered as text", *Social Research*, Vol. 39, pp. 529-62.

Robinson, J.A. (1981), "Personal narratives reconsidered", *Journal of American Folklore*, Vol. 94, pp. 58-85.

Rose, R.A. (1988), "Organizations as multiple cultures: a rules theory analysis", *Human Relations*, Vol. 41, pp. 139-70.

Salaman, G. (1979), *Work Organizations, Resistance, and Control*, Longman, London.

Schein, E. (1983), "The role of the founder in creating organizational culture", *Organizational Dynamics*, Summer, pp. 13-28.

Schein, E. (1985), *Organizational Culture and Leadership*, Jossey-Bass, San Francisco, CA.

Schutz, A. (1967), *Collected Papers I: The Problem of Social Reality*, 2nd ed., Martinua Nijhoff, The Hague.

Sievers, B. (1986), "Beyond the surrogate of motivation", *Organization Studies*, Vol. 7 No. 4, pp. 196-20.

Sievers, B. (1993), "Love in the time of AIDS", paper presented at "Organizations and symbols of transformation", the 11th International SCOC Conference on Organizational Symbolism, EADA-Collbato, Barcelona.

Sievers, B. (1994), "Characters in search of a theatre", in Casemore, R., Dyos, G., Eden, A., Kellner, K., McAuley, J. and Moss, S. (Eds), *What Makes Consultancy Work – Understanding the Dynamics*, South Bank University Press, London, pp. 291-311.

Silver, J. (1987), "The ideology of excellence: management and neo-conservatism", *Studies in Political Economy*, Vol. 24, August, pp. 105-29.

JOCM
9,5

Smircich, L. (1983), "Organizations as shared meanings", in Pondy, L.R., Frost, P.J., Morgan, G. and Dandridge, T. (Eds), *Organizational Symbolism: Monographs in Organizational and Industrial Relations, Vol. 1*, JAI Press, Greenwich, CT, pp. 55-66.

Smircich, L. and Calas, M.B. (1985), "Organizational culture: a critical assessment", in Jabin, F.M., Putnam, L.L., Roberts, K.H. and Porter, L.W. (Eds), *Handbook of Organizational Communication*, Sage, Newbury Park, CA, pp. 228-63.

26

Thorpe, B.N. (1986), "Learning about organizational change through the analysis of myth and narrative: a critical hermeneutic study", unpublished doctoral dissertation, University of San Francisco, San Francisco, CA.

Tierney, W.G. (1989), "Advancing democracy: a critical interpretation of leadership", *Peabody Journal of Education*, Vol. 66 No. 3, pp. 157-75.

Tierney, W.G. (1993), *Building Communities of Difference: Higher Education in the Twenty-first Century*, Bergin & Garvey, Westport, CT.

Trice, H.M. and Beyer, J.M. (1984), "Studying organizational cultures through rites and ceremonies", *Academy of Management Review*, Vol. 9, pp. 653-69.

van Dijk, T.A. (1975), "Action, action description, and narrative", *New Literary History*, Vol. 6, pp. 273-94.

Van Maanen, J. and Barley, S.R. (1984), "Occupational communities: culture and control in organizations", *Research in Organizational Behavior*, Vol. 6, pp. 287-365.

Van Maanen, J. and Barley, S.R. (1985), "Cultural organization: fragments of a theory", in Frost, P. *et al.* (Eds), *Organizational Culture*, Sage, Beverly Hills, CA, pp. 31-53.

Weick, K.E. (1991), "The vulnerable system: an analysis of the Tenerife air disaster", in Frost, P., Louis, M., Lundberg, C. and Martin, J. (Eds), *Reframing Organizational Culture*, Sage, Newbury Park, CA, pp. 117-30.

Wilkins, A. (1978), "Organizational stories as an expression of management philosophy: implications for social control in organizations", unpublished doctoral dissertation, Stanford University, Stanford, CA.

Wilkins, A. (1983), "Organizational stories as symbols which control the organization", in Pondy, L.R., Frost, P.J., Morgan, G. and Dandridge, T. (Eds), *Organizational Symbolism: Monographs in Organizational and Industrial Relations, Vol. 1*, JAI Press, Greenwich, CT, pp. 81-92.

Wilkins, A. (1984), "The creation of company cultures: the roles of stories and human resource systems", *Human Resource Management*, Vol. 23 No. 1, pp. 41-60.

Wilkins, A. and Martin, J. (1979), "Organizational legends", unpublished research paper, No. 521, Graduate School of Business, Stanford University, Stanford, CA.

[12]

A Four Times Told Tale: Combining Narrative and Scientific Knowledge In Organization Studies

Barbara Czarniawska

Gothenburg University

Abstract. *A growing acknowledgement of the fact that social scientific texts employ a variety of literary means encourages and requires collective reflection and genre analysis. The present article applies such reflection to organization theory texts, revealing differing ways in which facts and metaphors, logic and stories are woven together. In conclusion, the genre of organization theory is submitted to an institutional analysis.*

Scholarship is customarily set apart from the everyday wisdom of ordinary people. While scientific knowledge is contained in and transmitted by scientific texts, everyday knowledge is circulated in stories—thus one can speak of narrative knowledge. Lately, however, there has been a call to recapture narrative knowledge for the humanities and social sciences in general and for organization studies in particular (Lyotard, 1987; McCloskey, 1990b; Fisher, 1987; Bruner, 1990; Sköldberg, 1994; Boland and Tenkasi, 1995; Czarniawska, 1997).

Any attempt to trace the dividing line between narrative and scientific knowledge in texts regarded as representing one of the two kinds of knowledge, soon reveals that 'science' is closer to 'narrative' than one might think. There is an abundance of stories and metaphors in scientific texts, while folk tales and fiction build on facts and sometimes even play with formal logic. Thus many works in the humanities and social sciences suggest a rapprochement between the two kinds of knowledge and consequently between the two types of text (White, 1973; Polkinghorne, 1987; Latour, 1988a).

Organization
Articles

Several traditions within organization studies support this suggestion, for instance case studies and a variety of interpretive approaches. In my earlier article published in *Organization*, 'Narration or Science? Collapsing the Division in Organization Studies' (1995), I have addressed those. There is, however, another obvious point of encounter between the two domains which I ignored before: literary critique. A narrative approach to organization studies means not only collecting, constructing and interpreting stories, it also means applying the tools of literary analysis to organization theory. The present text is an attempt at such analysis, following such precursors as McCloskey (1985), Van Maanen (1988) and Geertz (1988). The aim is to establish commonalties within organization studies, which might merit them the designation of a genre. This organizational genre, it seems, always joins paradigmatic (model-like) and syntagmatic (story-like) elements. Four such connections common in organization theory texts are described below: a paradigmatic discussion illustrated by syntagmatic examples; a paradigmatic analysis retold syntagmatically; a syntagmatic story punctuated by paradigmatic points; a syntagmatic tale with a paradigm hidden in it.

The Narrative Approach in Organization Studies

Not much attention has been paid to the question of writing organization studies and theory. In this respect, organization studies as a subdiscipline of social studies is lagging behind economics (McCloskey, 1985), sociology (Brown, 1987) or anthropology (Clifford and Marcus, 1986; Geertz, 1988). This is most likely due to the fact that its usual host at the university site, a management or a business school, is a relative newcomer, still insecure of its academic legitimacy and therefore prone to plead allegiance to the 18th-century ideals of (natural) science, which assumed writing to be the domain of literature and not of science (albeit producing copious writings on the subject). 'Writing is an unfortunate necessity; what is really wanted is to show, to demonstrate, to point out, to exhibit, to make one's interlocutor stand at gaze before the world' says Rorty with irony. 'In a mature science, the words in which the investigator "writes up" his results should be as few and as transparent as possible' (1992: 94).

The realization that writing is the organization scholars' main activity seems to be growing, together with reflection upon how they write and what textual devices are used, or could be used, in writing. But this reflection is neither easy nor obvious.

The initial difficulty seems to lie in the unclear generic situation of the social sciences vis-a-vis natural science and literature (Lepenies, 1988). Are social science texts telling stories or reporting science? Latour (1992) applied the Jakobsonian distinction between these two kinds of text saying that the former evolve along the *syntagmatic* dimension grounded in association, and the latter along the *paradigmatic* dimension, based on

A Four Times Told Tale
Barbara Czarniawska

Figure 1 Association and substitution (syntagmatic and paradigmatic dimensions) in organization studies.

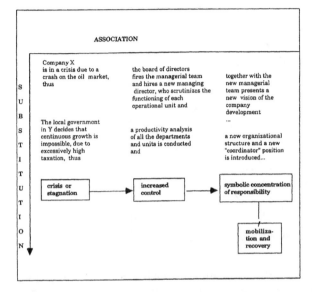

substitution.[1] A narrative thus adds various events one after another over time, while a scientific model substitutes a group of particulars by a more abstract concept which is intended to cover them all. Generalization, and consequently prediction, operate differently in the two modes. Syntagmatic construction uses metonymy;[2] it operates on the sense of part and whole (how things hang together). Paradigmatic construction, on the other hand, uses metaphor; it operates on the sense of like and unlike (similarity, analogy). Turning to the social scientific texts one cannot help noticing that both constructions appear: there are elements of the syntagmatic and the paradigmatic, of metonymy and metaphor, of narrative and logo-science. Figure 1 (which may look trivial but in fact summarizes a whole book of mine, 1989), illustrates such a typical mixture.

McCloskey (1985) pointed out that the science of economics consists of making metaphors, and Morgan (1986) retold the story of organization theory in terms of the theory's main metaphors. While the metaphorical character of science was accepted fairly easily, not least because of the ready agreement of many mathematicians and theoretical physicists, the idea of science as story-telling seemed a bit harder to swallow. But the sciences can be said to use a complete tetrad of rhetorical figures: stories, metaphors, facts and formal logic (McCloskey, 1990a, uses also Jakobsonian inspiration). By rearranging McCloskey's tetrad somewhat (see Figure 2), Latour's insight can be incorporated into it.

The horizontal dimension now represents the syntagm: logic and

Organization
Articles

Figure 2   Syntagm and paradigm as delimiting a generic space in which both literature and science live

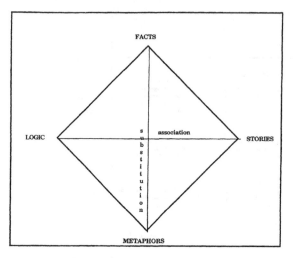

stories as two modes of association, of establishing a connection—of connecting in actual time and space or, hypothetically or counter-factually, of connecting in possible worlds. Facts and metaphors denote two kinds of substitution, namely, the linguistic operations known as 'representation' and 'analogy'.[3] They constitute a dimension extended between the two modes of name-giving: 'facts' are names or assertions about which we tend to agree easily ('this is the recently acquired computer'), while metaphors indicate a stage of inquiry rather than consensus ('is this a cost or an investment?'). The extremes would be proper names and metaphors proper (with similes and analogies in-between).

   In the picture above, 'science' is no longer separated from 'literature' by an abyss; over and above the publisher's classification, a work is ascribed to a certain genre according to the frequency with which it uses certain rhetorical devices. McCloskey's tetrad now denotes a space within which one could position various works, and it would be their proximity to other similar works that would establish their genre. For example, metaphors (or models) seem to be more frequent in economics than stories, which are very frequent, on the other hand, in subgenres known as economic history and macroeconomic policy (McCloskey, 1990a, 1990b). Geertz (1973, 1988) stressed the obvious importance of stories in anthropology but he also pointed out that there are more metaphors than one would assume. A historical elucidation of the ties between stories and metaphors in sociology can be found in Lepenies (1988); these ties are cultivated by phenomenologically inclined sociologists (e.g. Brown, 1977, 1980) and,

10

A Four Times Told Tale
Barbara Czarniawska

more recently, by the sociologists of science and technology (Mulkay, 1985; Latour, 1988b, 1992; Traweek, 1992).

What about organization studies? In my previous article (1995) I tried to show the presence of the narrative mode in certain kinds of study. In the present text I will look at well-known organization studies, showing different ways (and degrees) in which they incorporate narrative in their production.

Logic → Metaphors

James D. Thompson: Organizations in Action

Although no official contest was ever held, Thompson's book (1967) is considered, at least unofficially, to be a model of rhetorical elegance in organization theory. Short and concise, it aims at covering all relevant issues and formulating the proper science of organizations according to scientific ideals, i.e. as a set of formal (at least apparently formal) propositions.

My experience of various institutional settings in which organization theory is taught as a subject in Sweden evoked a puzzling observation. It seems that Thompson is rarely used as a course book in its home field, i.e. in the departments of business administration (and then only in a course on 'classics'), but it is used widely in organization theory courses taught in neighbouring disciplines: education, psychology, sociology, political sciences. Part of the explanation lies, no doubt, in the specific way organization theory is taught in Sweden: whereas the undergraduate courses mainly use textbooks in Swedish of a summarizing and popular-izing character, the graduate courses take up the most recent research work or, indeed, 'the classics'.

But another complementary interpretation of this phenomenon takes us back to Thompson's text. Setting out to be exhaustive, to combine the incompatible (the rational system vs natural open systems approaches), embracing an impressive range of schools and sources (where Parsons and Goffman sit side by side), this is a striking example of how accumulation of knowledge achieves the closure of an intellectual field which, if taken seriously, could put an end to the discipline. If Thompson were to be taken literally, there would be no need for organization theory after him. And this is due to no small extent to the rhetorical style he adopts.

Here follow two excerpts from Thompson's book:

> **Proposition 4.1:**[4] Organizations under norms of rationality seek to place their boundaries around those activities which if left to the task environment would be crucial contingencies.
>
> The implication of this proposition is that we should expect to find organizations including within their domains activities or competencies which, on a technological basis, could be performed by the task environ-ment without damage to the *major mission* of the organization. For the

11

Organization
Articles

> hotel, for example, provision of rooms and meals would be the major mission, and the operation of a laundry would be excluded; yet we find hotels operating laundries. On the other hand, provision of rooms and meals would not be within the major mission of the hospital, although hospitals commonly include these activities within their domains.
>
> The incorporation of subsidiary competencies along with major missions is commonplace in organizations of all types and is not a major discovery. But our proposition is not an announcement of the fact; rather it attempts to indicate the direction in which domains are expanding. ... (1967: 39–40)
>
> **Proposition 6.1:** Under norms of rationality, organizations facing heterogeneous task environments seek to identify homogenous segments and establish structural units to deal with each.
>
> This proposition is perhaps most dramatically illustrated by the organization which crosses national boundaries where environmental variations may be stark. Under these conditions, organizations tend to establish semiautonomous divisions based on a region. Those organizations which dabble in foreign operations may simply have a foreign or non-domestic division; but when they become more deeply involved, they usually establish national or at least bloc entities. ...
>
> We need not cross cultural boundaries to see this proposition in action. Public school systems divide themselves into elementary and secondary schools, and only in rare cases are these ungraded internally. General hospitals establish separate units for obstetrics, contagious diseases, and surgical and outpatient services; mental hospitals often establish separate units for various types of disorders or severity of problems. Universities create undergraduate and graduate divisions. Public-assistance agencies may be divided into different units for dispensing unemployment compensation benefits, and aid to dependent children or the blind. ... (1967: 70–71)

What does Thompson say? That organizations incorporate those activities which may be crucial to them in order to avoid dependency on their environment, and that they create internal units which correspond to unified (similar) portions of their environment. In translating his organizationalese into English, I follow McCloskey's (1985) example, although I am aware that this innocent 'translation' already heralds the readings I intend to make next.

This is stated in the form of theorems, i.e. ideas 'accepted or proposed as a demonstrable truth often as a part of a general theory' (*Webster's Dictionary*, 1981: 1200). Before turning to demonstrations, let us stay awhile with the propositions themselves. Their formulation follows the rules of logic, but they concern not 'facts' but tropes, of which the two most important are 'organization' and 'environment'.

'Organization' is clearly a synecdoche: that which is organized becomes an entity named after its attribute. The use of organizations in the plural, indicating an entity, and an entity which became the main subject of organization theory, appeared as late as the 1960s, with the advent of

12

A Four Times Told Tale
Barbara Czarniawska

systems theory in the social sciences (Waldo, 1961). In fact, Thompson still speaks of 'administration theory' (administration being the synonym of management, connected by usage with public authority rather than private enterprise). Even more interesting is 'environment': this central concept in organization theory is residual in character, meaning simply 'that which surrounds organizations'. As Meyer (1996) put it succinctly, the environment is the Other to the Actor, as the environment of a modern organization consists in other organizations (see also Perrow, 1991).

Thus Thompson's propositions suggest logical connections between tropes. According to the rules of the (scientific) game, the demonstration cannot happen within the language (as one might expect in this context), but by a reference to reality.

Thompson's demonstrations do not involve concrete facts: we learn nothing about an experiment conducted at laboratory X on date Y. The illustrations are formulated in a way which resembles and repeats propositions, but the abstract tropes are replaced by generic terms like 'organizations which cross national boundaries', 'general hospitals', 'hotels'. The verbs remain in the Simple Present ('organizations tend to', 'organizations seek to identify'), sometimes called the Gnomic Present, as it claims the authority of general truth by sidestepping the historicity of its statements (McCloskey, 1990a: 61–2).

An autobiographical anecdote might be relevant here: when studying for my comprehensive exams in economics (my doctoral dissertation required a transfer from social psychology to economics) I was struck by the peculiar style of the economic texts and asked my adviser[5] whether the constant use of the Simple Present meant that enterprises, as it was in this case, *are* actually doing these things, *have done* them or *should be doing* them? 'None of those', said my adviser. 'They are doing so in a mental model into which they have been designed—thus it is a tense which indicates their "unreal" state, as it were.'

But is this what Thompson intended? He himself says that '... our [sic] proposition is not announcement of the fact: rather it attempts to indicate the direction ...'. By that, as the previous sentence indicates, he does not mean that this is a hypothetical move in a hypothetical model; he suggests that the proposition contains more than a mere fact (by now trite); it contains a prediction. Thompson uses *prolepsis*: 'the representation or assumption of a future fact or development as if presently existing or accomplished' (*Webster's Dictionary*, 1981: 913).

One could thus claim that Thompson's 'scientism' is but a stylization: the entities in question are in fact tropes, and could be connected only with one another; the postulated connections are achieved by the use of yet another rhetorical figure. It would be wrong, however, to conclude from this that Thompson fails to achieve the scientific status he aspires to; this is, in fact, the way scientific texts tend to look in the social sciences. Few of them even try to achieve such a strict stylization, and allow the stories to creep directly into their texts.

13

Organization
Articles

Metaphors → Stories

Nils Brunsson: The Organization of Hypocrisy

The choice of Brunsson's (1989) book might be objected to, in relation to its predecessor here: does it deserve to be called a 'classic' as Thompson's work undoubtedly does? It may be of course that the time of the 'classics' is irretrievably over, and in any case it is difficult to guess which contemporary works—if any—will become classics. Suffice it to say that Brunsson's book was reviewed 17 times in the four years after its publication (*SSCI*, 1993), and this was excluding reviews in the popular press, including the French press, not usually receptive to Anglo-Saxon publications.

Brunsson shares with Thompson an interest in taking up the rationalist and the institutionalist approaches to organizations. Instead of integrating them, however ('under the norms of rationality'), he expands the ideas of the US pragmatist, Thurman Arnold (1935), suggesting that the two coexist in a functional hypocrisy, and that some effort is expended on keeping them apart ('decoupling'). The public administration organizations (state and municipal) which are of interest to him have a dual basis for their legitimacy: politics and action. 'It is expected that they should reflect a variety of values and that they should run reasonably efficient operations' (1935: 33).

> The basic method for handling these conflicting demands is to separate and isolate politics and action, to 'decouple' them. ...
> ... politics and action can be separated organizationally: some units can respond to political demands and are organized in such a way as to resemble the ideal political type, while other units can respond to demands for action and are organized in a way that closely resembles the ideal type of the action organizations. Municipalities and the state typically possess a number of variously politicized suborganizations. As we have seen, parliaments and social councils are strongly political units which produce talk and decision in public arenas. Governments and committees hold closed meetings and are more action-oriented.
> The organization can also be divided into one part run by politicians and one part run by the administration. Politicians are recruited according to the principle of conflict, while administrative officials are recruited according to the principle of unity. In other organizations boards can be politically composed, while management and production departments are based on the idea of unity. In this way the organization as a whole can respond to demands for both politics and action—so long as the two units really are isolated from one another. ...
> The political and administrative dichotomy becomes more problematic if the organization tries to link the political and administrative suborganizations together, i.e. if the decisions of the political unit are to be made consistent with the actions of the action unit, or vice versa. This problem arises when it is claimed that the decisions of the leadership should steer administrative action—which is not an unusual idea.
> (Brunsson, 1989: 37)

14

A Four Times Told Tale
Barbara Czarniawska

Thompson in his proposition 6.1, and Brunsson above, seem to be speaking on the same theme: one of the ways 'organizations' 'adapt' to their 'environments'. The main tropes are still in place, although Brunsson enriches them with two more ('politics' and 'action'.)[6] The picture has become more complex: the environment cannot be entirely divided into 'homogeneous segments'; in some segments (political ones) it seems that heterogeneity is the characteristic feature. Also, readers learn not only how organizations act, but what use organizational actors make of it. Thompson keeps a behaviorist distance to 'organizations': this is how they act, 'under the norms of rationality'. Brunsson does not take the resulting structure as an answer, but as a question, and goes on to investigate the processes which created such a structure.

In doing so he starts with 'propositions' not altogether unlike Thompson's, which claim general connections but without the stylization of formal logic. His general statements are not so much propositions as summaries, to be explicated by examples of concrete organizations in concrete situations. Contrary to the suggestion contained in the sentence 'As we have seen ...', his metaphors do not emerge from his stories (at least in the text; it is not my ambition to detect the actual intellectual operations performed by the authors). The present reader must trust me in that 'we' have not seen anything yet; the sentence alludes to earlier abstract formulations. The examples come later to illustrate general statements. The quotation below describes a crisis in Runtown, a small municipality in southern Sweden, where the externally induced crisis led to a striving for unity (tighter coupling), which only deepened the crisis.

> Between 1973 and 1976 external crises were succeeded by internal troubles—which did not mean, however, that the external problems had gone away. ... There were certain signs that attitudes were changing. ... Everyone wanted to see a new kind of behaviour and more action.
>
> At the beginning of the period there were even a few results. ... The new administrators energetically pursued the question of long-range economic planning and eventually persuaded the politicians to agree to a document specifying municipal goals. This, they felt, would put their own operations on a firmer basis, since the politicians would have to become a little less volatile. The politicians had no difficulty in agreeing to these goals, which were expressed in very general terms and seemed unlikely to have much impact on their own activities. ...
>
> But the peaceful mood of 1977 was short-lived. By the spring of 1978 it had been succeeded once more by stormy conflict, arising from a desire to produce quick concrete action. One example was the effort made to speed up the housing construction programme.
>
> The building of new homes had been severely delayed due to the continual uncertainty about where to build, and there was now a housing shortage. In discussing the housing construction programme for 1978–1982, people's patience run out. The opposition demanded that the building start-up in one particular area should be brought forward by a

15

> year. After much argument in the executive committee and an extremely
> lively debate in the council, the opposition's proposal was finally
> adopted by a large majority, and the council appointed a special unit to
> ensure that their directives were observed.
>
> This was not the only example. In other cases politicians tried to
> intervene in negotiations with various external organizations, in order to
> speed up agreement and consequently actions as well. But such inter-
> ventions not only weakened the municipality's bargaining position; they
> also increased internal conflict and delayed action even more. (Brunsson,
> 1989: 55–6)

This is undoubtedly a story, with characters and a plot: the text is not
about 'hotels' or 'public agencies' but about the local government of
Runtown. One immediate difference between Thompson's 'illustrations'
and Brunsson's 'story' is the volume: Thompson's book is 164 pages
long and deals with all the issues in organization theory, Brunsson's has
235 pages and takes up one very specific aspect of it only. The character
of the 'demonstration' changes: while Thompson's illustrations more
or less repeat the proposition on a slightly less abstract level and with
more adjectives, Brunsson's story is 'loosely coupled'—to use Weick's
terminology which Brunsson himself also favours—from his general
statements, which do not, however, lay claim to any absolute status. In
traditional parlance, Thompson's theory is more general, Brunsson's less
so; but this is actually quite doubtful. Nobody knows how many concrete
cases—if any—Thompson's theory could be applied to, whereas it can be
claimed that Brunsson's theory is applicable at least to those cases he
studied.

There are, however, some similarities in the demonstration. The Runtown story is a stylized one—not so much because of the avoidance of
proper names, which is only to be expected as a way of fulfilling ethical
obligations, but because the language is the language of the author and not
of the characters. The story of Runtown, in light of my own knowledge of
the Swedish public sector, is a very credible one, but I do not know
whether there is 'a' Runtown. It could just as well be a composite[7] of
different municipalities and the dramatic fate which they all shared
during the late 1970s.

The critique of fiction in scientific texts is often grounded in a confusion of two ways of understanding fiction: as that which does not exist,
and that which is not true (Lamarque, 1990). If we separate these two, it
becomes obvious that Runtown may not exist, and yet everything that is
said about it may be true in the above sense, i.e. credible in light of other
texts on Swedish municipalities.[8] What I want to emphasize is that
stylization intended to raise the 'scientific' timbre of the text, tends
toward fictionalization. The next two examples either avoid this strategy
or push it much further.

16

A Four Times Told Tale
Barbara Czarniawska

Stories → Metaphors

Karin D. Knorr-Cetina: The Manufacture of Knowledge

Knorr-Cetina studied one kind of organization, namely research laboratories, as large complex organizations in an organization field which is one of the best interconnected in the global economy. Her studies are both exemplary and constitutive of a rapprochement between science and technology studies and organization studies (Latour, 1993; Knorr-Cetina, 1994). On the one hand, sociologists of science and technology began to recognize the organized character of the practices they study, not least due to the forceful presence of transnational corporations right in the backyard of cozy laboratories. On the other hand, organization students recognized the central role of knowledge production in the organizations they study (Alvesson, 1993). Furthermore, Knorr-Cetina's work represents the ethnomethodological influence, which is another increasingly noticeable presence in organization studies (Silverman and Jones, 1976; Boden, 1994).

What follows are excerpts from Knorr-Cetina's study of a government-sponsored research centre in Berkeley, California:

> In the following discussion, I will use the term 'indexicality' to refer to the *situational contingency* and *contextual location* of scientific action. This contextual location reveals that the products of scientific research are fabricated and negotiated by particular agents at a particular time and place; that these products are carried by the particular interests of these agents, and by local rather than universally valid interpretations; and that the scientific actors play on the very limits of the situational location of their action. In short, the contingency and contextuality of scientific action demonstrates that the products of science are hybrids which bear the mark of the very *indexical logic* which characterizes their production, and are not the outgrowth of some special scientific rationality to be contrasted with the rationality of social interaction. Scientific method is seen to be much more similar to social method—and the products of natural science more similar to those of social science—than we have consistently tended to assume.
>
> How can we illustrate this indexical logic in somewhat more detail? The first aspect of indexicality is an implied *opportunism* which manifest itself in a mode of operation comparable to that of a 'tinkerer'. ... Tinkerers are opportunists. They are aware of the material opportunities they encounter at a given place, and they exploit them to achieve their projects. At the same time, they recognize what is feasible, and adjust or develop their projects accordingly. While doing this, they are constantly engaged in producing and reproducing some kind of workable object which successfully meets the purpose they have temporarily settled on. ...
>
> As in the example of tinkering, the occasioned character of research first manifests itself in the role played by local resources and facilities. For example, in the institute I observed, the existence of a large-scale

> laboratory in which proteins could be generated, modified and tested in large volumes was treasured as a valuable opportunity because it would be difficult or impossible to carry out certain kinds of research without such facilities. The laboratory was well equipped, well staffed, and supervised by an experienced older technician described as extremely reliable and 'clever'—a series of additional advantages. As a result, a lot of scientific energy was spent in gaining access to the laboratory in order to 'exploit' this 'resource'. Research which required the use of this laboratory was eagerly sought or invented. A newly purchased electron microscope utilizing laser-beams exerted a similar attraction. . . .
> Preference is also given to technical instruments and apparatus which the scientists know are 'around somewhere'. Projects turn certain turns because, as the scientists explain, 'We had a piece of equipment that had been developed in another project that we could use.' Certain measurements are taken because 'the machines were here, so it was very easy to go down and use them', and certain results are obtained because 'well, we were looking for a way to get foam off, you see, and it [*the instrument*] was there . . .'. (1989: 33–5)

The beginning of this text resembles both Thompson and Brunsson as regards their general statements; the difference is that here the reader can see how metaphors *are manufactured*. They do not just 'show up': the process of choice and construction is revealed in this passage in the example of 'indexicality', which is a richer and more meaningful version of the residual 'environment'. But my main reason for choosing this text was to show a way of connecting stories and metaphors which differs from the previous one and from the one to come: here, metaphors come from stories. What I am saying is that this is a textual strategy which does not depend on the text's immediate order (metaphors come in the text *before* the story) nor need it reflect the author's actual logic. In other words, the author presented metaphors as devices which she needed in order to understand, structure and interpret the stories she collected/manufactured in the field.

Knorr-Cetina seems to be taking up a theme not unlike the one mentioned by Thompson in his Proposition 4.1: 'organizations' tend to incorporate practices which—people in organizations feel—would leave them vulnerable if left outside. Also, she seems to match Brunsson by telling stories in an abstract language. But she is running two kinds of story in parallel: those which, allegorically, have metaphors as characters ('tinkerers adjust or develop') and those which have actors (including the author) as characters ('the scientists explain'). In the second kind of story she allows the actors to speak their own language, achieving the effect of *variegated speech* (Bakhtin, 1981). This does not necessarily create an illusion that 'those people' speak for themselves; indeed, it is clear that it is Knorr-Cetina who is editing them. Similarly, it is not a matter of 'human touch' or 'focusing on the individual'. The point is very social indeed: the reader becomes aware that different languages and vocabularies are

18

A Four Times Told Tale
Barbara Czarniawska

possible and coexistent within one and the same linguistic tradition—a realization much needed in the universalistic language of organization theory (Calás and Smircich, 1993).

In her choice of metaphors she shares with Nils Brunsson the influence of US pragmatism: her 'opportunism' resembles his 'hypocrisy', and they both focus on processes rather than structures, showing the way certain things are put to use, rather than stating their existence as Thompson does. A point on which she differs from the first two authors and comes closer to the fourth one below is that she lets 'organization' lose its central place and its metaphorical character. It re-acquires its original meaning, that of a state rather than a unit with palpable boundaries. Both she and the next author are interested in forms of social organization in the context of professional practices. This may well herald a more general shift in the way the social processes known as 'organizing' begin to be perceived (Czarniawska-Joerges, 1996).

Stories and Metaphors

Linda Smircich: 'Is the Concept of Culture a Paradigm for Understanding Organizations and Ourselves?'

It is almost superfluous to say that the aim behind the present venture and other similar efforts is to collapse the artificial division between science and literature. On the way there is another dichotomy which needs to be collapsed, one which certainly exists although it generally receives less attention: that between the story and the metaphor, or between prose and poetry. This line, useful as it might be for some analytic purposes, such as contrasting rhetoric and poetics (Höpfl, 1995), is hard to maintain in analysing concrete examples of narrative drawn from either theory or practice. It appears that metaphors can support stories or contradict them; stories can disarm metaphors of much of their ambiguity by putting them into a context (Eco, 1990); but as a rule they do come together. 'Stories criticize metaphors and metaphors criticize stories' says McCloskey (1990a: 96), showing how close the two are in the tales of economics. This can be done by letting tropes be characters in the stories, as in the example below (Smircich, 1985: 55–6):

> ★★★★★★★★★★★★★★★THE GALAXY TODAY★★★★★★★★★★★★★★★★
> **Archaeology Dig Uncovers Meaning of Corporate Forms**
> Positive Proof That 'Organization' Is *The* Paradigm Of Ancient Culture
>
> Planet Earth (UPI)—A major discovery was revealed today (April 1, 3084 AD) by Richard L.S.B. Leakey XII, leader of the Archaeology expedition on the ancient Planet Earth. Leakey, who has been conducting research on the site known as 'Wall Street' for the last 20 years, believes he has at last unlocked the key to understanding the way of life in what is referred to as 'Western Civilization' of the time period 1870–2000 AD.

19

Organization
Articles

> The Leakey expedition has been searching among the leftovers of life at that time and has recovered an astonishing number of 'computer print-outs', 'Xerox machines', 'organization charts', and 'dress for success' books. But these mere artifacts did not provide Leakey with sufficient evidence to confirm his hypothesis about that time period.
>
> In an interview, Leakey said, 'In order for us to make sense of the physical findings we need to uncover a mode of thought, some symbolic connection, between the artifacts. And today we have found it'.
>
> Leakey was referring to a remarkably well-preserved copy of a book by Robert Denhardt, called *In the Shadow of Organization*, published in 1981.
>
> Denhardt's commentary on this civilization called it 'an age of organization'. He characterized society as dominated by an organizational ethic which 'offers itself as a way of life for persons in our society'.
>
> Leakey was visibly excited as he told reporters, 'This book was all I needed to confirm my own theory. These people were crazy for organizations. They valued discipline, order, regulation, and obedience much more than independence, expressiveness and creativity. They were always looking for efficiency. They wanted to control everything. They had a fetish for 'managing'. They managed stress, time, relationships, emotions, but mostly they managed their careers.
>
> 'They were somewhat more civilized than the ever more ancient Aztecs. Their sacrifices were bloodless and were conducted on symbolic ladders of success, instead of stone altars.'
>
> Leakey went on to say, 'I'd concluded on my own that these people had a fairly impoverished existence, and this book validates my findings. In the 1980s, organization was the meaning of life. I'll be publishing my findings in *Administrative Arts Quarterly*, and will argue conclusively that organization was *the* paradigm of this culture!'
>
> ********************************

How do we know that Smircich's story is a fiction whereas Brunsson's highly fictionalized 'Runtown' was 'the real thing'? Two clues are offered. One is the 'fact' which Smircich includes: the date, 1 April 3084 AD. Another is that Brunsson *tells* the readers that he conducted several studies in the field. As Latour (1988b) pointed out, scientific realism differs from fictional realism by the textual strategy of inviting readers to inspect the source of the facts, which most likely contains other references of the same kind; the final loop in the chain then consists in interview transcriptions or some other 'hard data'. I would claim that, had Smircich faked the date (23 August 1984) and claimed a source (participant observation in the Academy of Management Meeting), her claims to scientific realism would weigh much more heavily than Brunsson's, because of her skilful imitation of the rhetoric of the field (it is somewhat unlikely that the Runtown officials would describe their situation in the terms used by Brunsson, whereas it is very likely that the AMA meeting would produce a document like the one 'quoted' by Smircich).

Even ardent advocates of the narrative mode may, however, nourish a

A Four Times Told Tale
Barbara Czarniawska

doubt as to whether the tale above is an example of it. There is no chronology which structures the story and, as Ricoeur told us, time and narrative are inseparable (Ricoeur, 1984). But time *is* a structuring device in Smircich's story, albeit around it, not within it: time (the 1100-year difference) is the frame which gives meaning to a speech-act reported in the text. Time is a metaphor of distancing. A well-known alternative is that of bringing in 'an observer from Mars', although this also amounts to describing an episode. It was also Ricoeur who said that 'the most humble narrative is always more than a chronological series of events, and ... the configurative dimension cannot eclipse the episoding dimension' (1981: 279). Thompson tells stories, too, however stylized are his episodes. As soon as even the most formal theory opens itself to examples and illustrations, the narrative enters.[9] Conversely, chronology alone does not create a plot; a sense of closure is most frequently achieved by configurative devices.

In the above paragraph I may be building 'the naive narrativist' out of straw, but I do not think it is an exaggeration to say that there are many 'anti-narrativists', fond of 'language games', who regard realist narrative with disdain, assuming an inseparable breach between stories and word games. Yet it should be pointed out that all language games are played on the assumption that there is a 'realist narrative' which all readers can easily recognize, and therefore enjoy deviations from it.[10]

It is less likely, however, that Smircich would be criticized by literary connoisseurs for her tameness, than that she would be faulted by followers of the canon—if such exists—for her boldness. In this second perspective there are yet more novelties in Smircich's text. The centrality of the 'organization' metaphor is preserved, but is used ironically: a trope not unknown, but rarely employed in organization theory (Czarniawska-Joerges, 1992). A utopian framing is used. Again, this is not completely unknown in the social sciences, but it is not greatly appreciated (with the possible exception of Habermas and his democratic dialogue), and is used especially often in feminist (= deviant) writings. Thus, to many readers, the above text is a breach of the genre on at least three counts: the story is fictitious, irony is used as the main trope, and a utopian frame is applied.

Hence we are back to genre analysis: what happens if (and when) the borders of a genre are crossed?

Hybridizing a Genre

Figure 3 attempts to summarize the readings above by sketching a space which they seem to create among them.

Facts are Missing!

In the three books (Smircich's is an article) there is only one page solidly filled with facts, and this is the imprint page. Apart from that, facts have

21

Organization
Articles

Figure 3   The generic space of organization theory

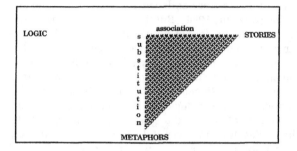

an ambiguous position in all these very different works. For Thompson, facts are trite; predictions are more important. Brunsson uses 'facts' for framing purposes: we do learn that there was a political crisis in Sweden at the time of his study, and a few other corollaries. The main story—the metaphorical one—is 'loosely coupled' to these facts, and has also been retold in different circumstances (Brunsson and Olsen, 1993). Many of Knorr-Cetina's facts are second-hand quotes: they 'belong' to the scientists she was studying and, as far as her story is concerned, they could have been the exact opposite of what they are. Her visits and observations at the laboratory are facts, but these are important to the reader only as means of establishing her credibility. Smircich invents her 'facts' entirely.

One clue to this mysterious absence can be found in the introduction to Knorr-Cetina's book (1981), where she points out that etymologically 'facts' (from *facere*) are basically fabrications, and their production is a specialty of certain places such as natural science laboratories. Social scientists seem to be only marginally engaged in fact production; their attention is focused on how the facts, and the important societal fictions, are produced (Knorr-Cetina, 1994).

This would bring social science once more closer to literature (see also Lepenies, 1988), where the status of facts is quite clear:

> Factual judgments as such die as soon as they are transformed into semiotic judgments. Once accepted as true, the factual judgment . . . dies as such in order to generate a stipulation of a code. . . . Successful judgments are remembered as such only when they become famous ('the famous discovery of Coperni-cus' . . .). (Eco, 1979: 86)

Facts, once known/fabricated, are used in the production of further facts; their repetition does not bring any added value into a discourse. Metaphors, on the other hand, 'tend to resist acquisition. If they are inventive (and thus original) they cannot be easily accepted; the system tends not to absorb them' (Eco, 1979: 86). Once accepted, they become redundant, and lose their attraction. Stories, on the other hand, are allowed to be redundant: a narrative of a redundant nature, says Eco defending detec-

A Four Times Told Tale
Barbara Czarniawska

tive stories, offers a fastidious reader an opportunity to repose, to relax. Thus the combination of stories and metaphors seems to be irresistible, but at the same time seemingly puts an end to the genre of organization studies, which vanishes into literature.

Margery Wolf, whose work inspired the title of the present paper,[11] is one of many social scientists who worry about 'how one is to differentiate ethnography from fiction, other than in preface, footnotes, and other authorial devices' (1992: 56). I note this standing concern, but fail to appreciate its gravity. Although the threat of landing in 'neither good science, nor good literature' has been flashed around since Zola's times, it did not seem to do Zola much harm (Czarniawska-Joerges, 1994). At present there is very rarely, alas, any serious (or even half-serious) doubt about the science-or-fiction status of a work. Two examples which do occur to me are d'Ormesson's *The Glory of the Empire* (1971) and Castaneda's *The Teachings of Don Juan* (1968), and these and similar ventures, rare as they are, mostly result in a period of unusual excitement in the somewhat stale waters of academia. It happens more often that field reports, especially organization studies, berth uncomfortably close to tabloid journalism. But here the problem is not of genre but of ethics, and the same applies to tabloid journalism itself. The day when a massive stream of novels and short stories flows out the university gates, is a date existing in utopian time. One could paraphrase McCloskey's 'If you are so smart, why aren't you rich?' with 'If you can write so well, why don't you?'

Utopian (dystopian) worries aside, it is hard to understand why the 'authorial devices' such as those Wolf lists, should not be enough to distinguish one genre from another, scientific realism from literary realism, for example (Latour, 1988b). I tend to agree with Lamarque (1990) when he says that there is nothing intrinsic to a fictional or non-fictional narrative: proper names can be invented, dates faked. It is the fictive stance, as he calls it, the invitation from an author to a reader, which makes a reader believe that this is one genre and not another. The (rare) mistakes are due not to the unlikely fact that social scientists have suddenly started writing great fiction, but that the device is so vulnerable. There would be no urge to prove Castaneda's falsifications if he did not claim them to be a piece of scientific work.

So, what, if anything, can be said to be specific to social science writing, and especially to organization studies—at least in terms of frequent use if not of intrinsic characteristics? Is there any 'core' to this genre?

Core and Periphery

The picture above has been composed as a combination of McCloskey's tetrad and the four texts reviewed here. Metaphors and stories are the basis of the space so created. While the methods of association tend toward logic without ever reaching it (one could speak of a 'logical stylization'), the methods of substitution are contained between metaphor

23

and analogy. However, in genre analysis, or the little of it that there is (see e.g. Burrell and Morgan, 1979), the methods of substitution attract much more attention than the methods of association. One reason could be that the 18th-century ideal of science landed the social sciences in a country of *things*, where nouns (names) matter most (see also Chia, 1996). It is the methods of substitution and not association which attract attention and reflection. This is nowhere clearer than it is in organization theory, which for decades consisted of models containing boxes with names (metaphors) in them, like the ones at the bottom of Figure 1. It is assumed that, once you get your metaphors right, the story will tell itself. If the 'sociology of verbs' as postulated by John Law (1994) ever takes hold, however, the obscure arrows standing for vague connections, as in 'it causes', 'it influences', or 'it relates to' will become the focus of social science. Causes how? Influences by what means? Reflection upon the modes of association has yet to be developed in the texts of the social sciences in general and organization theory in particular.

Within the space above, a typical mode of association would be such parallel story telling as is exemplified by the works of Brunsson and Knorr-Cetina: a 'story from the field' retold in an allegorical way, with metaphors as the main characters and narrative exchanged for logic. None of them will do on their own: a logical-metaphorical tale must be translatable to some place and space, and although traditionally social science authors have expected the readers to do the job, it makes much more sense if they do it themselves, saving the readers from wild attempts at 'validation' and the legitimation of their abstract tales all at once.

What about the works which are at the edge of the genre so defined? Is Thompson 'out', as belonging to another convention? Is Smircich threatening the genre with her innovations? It is tempting to ask and answer such questions. Genre-construction is institution-building, and as such it invites policing attempts: somebody must 'protect the core'.[12] As genre analysis in literature has shown, however, such protective policing leads to the suffocation of a genre in the worst case and to nothing in the best—as Lejeune (1989) pointed out, criticizing Northrop Frye for his genre-policing. However, the analysis of a genre is one of the genre's constitutive forces. As social scientists, we busy ourselves constructing the institutions we describe. Neither paradoxicality nor conflict weakens a genre; on the contrary, they enhance its controlling power. And among the authors who operate in the gray zones are innovators: those who rejuvenate and reform the genre.

One such innovation, hinted at in Smircich's text and developed by Latour (1996) for example, is a text which mixes the two kinds of tale: the logical analysis alternates with a story, and they are kept together by common metaphors. The 'theory' provides the plot and builds the suspense. After all, a plot is 'the conceptual structure which binds the events of a story together. ... Plots are not events, but structures of events' (Bernstein, 1990: 55). One way, represented by Brunsson and Knorr-

24

A Four Times Told Tale
Barbara Czarniawska

Cetina, is to tell the structure and then tell the story: to tell the story twice, on different levels of abstraction. Another, illustrated by Smircich, is to make the structure deducible from the story. This is a device common in literature and unusual in social science.

What is being recommended here is not replacing one genre by another, not writing fiction instead of social science: it is creative borrowing. 'Hybridizing the genre' would perhaps be a fitting expression, as Geertz's 'blurring' (1980) provoked many protests. This is in tune with Latour's observation concerning the ongoing hybridization of the world, which proceeds in spite of the modernist 'purification work' (Latour, 1993, but see also Bauman, 1992: Law, 1994). What could hybridization mean in this context?

> To the few wooden tongues developed in academic journals, we should add the many genres and styles of narration invented by novelists, journalists, artists, cartoonists, scientists and philosophers. The reflexive character of our domain will be recognized in the future by the multiplicity of genres, not by the tedious presence of 'reflexive loops'. (Latour, 1988a: 173)

What Margery Wolf says of anthropology could be applied to all social sciences, but especially to organization studies. It is, too, 'a discipline with very permeable borders, picking up methodologies, theories, and data from any source whatever that can provide the answers to our questions' (Wolf, 1992: 51). All these 'loans' arrive in packages typical of the genre from which they have come. Traditionally, however, social scientists tended to ignore 'the form', insisting that it is the 'pure contents' which are being tapped. A recent lecture of Simmel's 'The Picture Frame' (1994) made me think that 'form' and 'content' are treated in the social sciences exactly (and misleadingly) like 'frame' and 'picture', two separate entities rather than two inseparable aspects of the same thing. Latour (1993) suggests unpacking and blending them together at will, making a modern vice into a non-modern virtue.

What Tale is Told?

If the issue of 'contents' is brought in, one might well ask whether the four authors above are telling the same tale after all? It depends, of course, how one slices it, but for me the reason for including these four was exactly that I could see a common theme, namely 'organizations' and their 'environments'. Earlier I have suggested that the linking metaphor of 'boundaries', crucial for the existence of the other two and originally taken for granted, is being increasingly taken up for scrutiny and is therefore in danger of being questioned and of subsequently threatening the dualism whose existence it permits. But such a statement can raise two questions. One concerns the fact that the texts quoted above differ insofar as the two later ones intentionally focus on professional communities and their intersecting fields, rather than on 'normal' organizations. Indeed, it could be said that the shift can be located in the difference between Thompson and Brunsson's works. In the first the reader is faced with unified 'organizations' which act. In the second, although the organizing actors are aware of the border between 'them' and their 'environment', 'they' are an uneasy bunch of at least two kinds of people (politicians and administrators) who have to stick together, even though each group is fully aware that it has more kindred spirits in the 'environment' than in the 'organization'. The boundary has been drawn, but it is always in danger of being erased, which means that the researcher's task is to describe how boundaries are constructed and maintained, rather than taking them for granted.

The reader who is still in questioning mood may point out that the notion of a 'shift which is taking place' suggests a historical development of which Knorr-Cetina and Smircich represent the latest stage, whereas in the sample above Brunsson's is in fact the most recent text. This is correct, and to make the point even clearer, one could take the example of Dalton's famous study (1959), which preceded Thompson's book and which tells the story of an 'organization' completely permeated by its 'environment', or rather by another organization: a company whose actual hierarchy reflects the hierarchy of the local masonic lodge. The shift is historical only in the sense that more stories like this have been told recently, legitimated on one hand by the new institutionalism and its notion of 'organization field', and on the other by the sociology of science and technology with its notion of the 'actor-network'. My point is that telling the stories makes the fictions of 'organization' and 'environment' untenable. It is a clear case, to use McCloskey's terms, in which the stories have examined a metaphor and found it wanting. 'Organization' and 'environment' can exist unharmed and separate only in texts built on metaphors connected by formal logic; an excursion into stories reveals that boundary-making is a tiresome job, sometimes exhausting most of the organizing energy. People engaged in practices which can be usefully seen as interconnected actions regulated by the professional and other norms of a given field, find that creating boundaries is sometimes advantageous and sometimes necessary; as a rule, however, such boundaries are flexible and temporary.

'Organization' and 'environment' are, or at least used to be, the useful fictions of the field. My use of the term 'fiction' here is inspired by Knorr-Cetina's: 'Modern institutions ... continually produce fiction, steer their way through fictions, work with fictions and become founded upon fictions' (1994: 8). Various new inventions, such as the 'virtual organization', 'multiple identities', 'transnationals' or the 'global economy' seem to reflect a need for better or at least different fictions for our times. Although I doubt whether organization theorists can invent them single-handedly, students of organization can collect and embellish them, contributing in this way to the construction of the process of organizing. Instead of aspiring to become 'a pure science', organization studies might admit to being 'a hybrid genre', and reinvest the energy saved from impossible endeavours in a dialogic relationship with the world.

26

A Four Times Told Tale
Barbara Czarniawska

Notes

Earlier versions of this paper were presented at the Project on Rhetoric of Inquiry Symposium, 'Refiguring the Human Sciences: New Practices of Inquiry', the University of Iowa, Iowa City, 22–24 June 1995 and the 13th Nordic Conference on Business Studies, Copenhagen, Copenhagen Business School, 14–16 August 1995. I thank Deirdre McCloskey and two anonymous reviewers for their comments and Nancy Adler for correcting my English.

1 For a useful introduction to the vocabulary of semiotics, see Greimas and Courtés (1982).
2 Although not in a Burkean sense (Burke, 1945).
3 Although, in my opinion, metaphor goes beyond analogy. Analogy assumes continuity, metaphor assumes rupture.
4 Thompson's 'Proposition 4.1' was the major concern of Ronald Coase in a classic article of 1937 on the nature of the business firm (McCloskey, 21 June 1995, pers. comm.).
5 Prof. Dr Janusz Beksiak of the Warsaw School of Economics.
6 Both of them naturally employ a whole plethora of other tropes, subordinate or complementary to the main ones.
7 Margery Wolf (1992) sees a composite as equivalent to fiction; to Renato Rosaldo (1989), it is a typical device of science and thus the opposite of fiction or at least of narrative.
8 I am refraining here from engaging in the complexities of the correspondence versus the coherence theory of truth.
9 McCloskey (1990b) claims that it happens even before; that the most abstract theories are, in fact, stories.
10 I write more on variations of the 'realist narrative' in *Narrating the Organization* (1997).
11 *A Thrice-Told Tale.* I must point out that Wolf, too, tells her story four times, but has better reasons than I for keeping the alliteration in the title intact.
12 This issue has been discussed in the editorial to the first issue of *Organization* (Burrell et al., 1994).

References

Alvesson, M. (1993) 'Organization as Rhetoric: Ambiguity in Knowledge-Intensive Companies,' *Journal of Management Studies* 30(6): 997–1015.

Arnold, Thurman W. (1935) *The Symbols of Government*. New Haven, CT: Yale University Press.

Bakhtin, Michail M. (1981) *The Dialogic Imagination*. Austin: Texas University Press.

Bauman, Zygmunt (1992) *Intimations of Postmodernity*. London: Routledge.

Bernstein, J. M. (1990) 'Self-Knowledge as Praxis: Narrative and Narration in Psychoanalysis, in Cristopher Nash (ed.) *Narrative in Culture. The Uses of Storytelling in the Sciences, Philosophy and Literature*, pp. 51–77. London: Routledge.

Boden, Deirdre (1994) *The Business of Talk*. Cambridge: Polity Press.

Boland, Richard J., Jr and Tenkasi, Ramkrishnan V. (1995) 'Perspective Making and Perspective Taking in Communities of Knowing', *Organization Science* 6(3): 350–72.

Organization
Articles

Brown, Richard H. (1977) *A Poetic for Sociology: Toward a Logic of Discovery for the Human Sciences.* New York: Cambridge University Press.

Brown, Richard H. (1980) 'The Position of Narrative in Contemporary Society', *New Literary History* 11(3): 545–50.

Brown, Richard H. (1987) *Society as Text. Essays on Rhetoric, Reason and Reality.* Chicago: University of Chicago Press.

Bruner, Jerome (1990) *Acts of Meaning.* Cambridge, MA: Harvard University Press.

Brunsson, Nils (1989) *The Organization of Hypocrisy: Talk, Decision and Actions in Organizations.* Chichester: Wiley.

Brunsson, Nils and Olsen, Johan, eds (1993) *The Reforming Organization.* London: Routledge.

Burke, Kenneth (1945) *A Grammar of Motives.* Berkeley: University of California Press.

Burrell, Gibson and Morgan, Gareth (1979) *Sociological Paradigms and Organizational Analysis.* Aldershot, UK: Gower.

Burrell, Gibson, Reed, Mike, Calás, Marta, Smircich, Linda and Alvesson, Mats (1994) 'Why Organization? Why Now?' *Organization* 1(1): 5–17.

Calás, Marta B. and Smircich, Linda (eds) (1993) 'Unbounding Organizational Analysis: Questioning "Globalization" Through Third World Women's Voices', paper presented at Academy of Management Meeting Symposium, Atlanta, 10 August.

Castaneda, Carlos (1968) *The Teachings of Don Juan: A Yaqui Way of Knowledge.* Harmondsworth: Penguin.

Chia, Robert (1996) 'The Problem of Reflexivity in Organizational Research: Towards a Postmodern Science of Organizations', *Organization* 3(1): 31–60.

Clifford, J. and Marcus, G. (1986) *Writing Culture: The Poetics and Politics of Ethnography.* Berkeley: University of California Press.

Czarniawska-Joerges, Barbara (1989) *Economic Decline and Organizational Control.* New York: Praeger.

Czarniawska-Joerges, Barbara (1992) *Exploring Complex Organizations: A Cultural Perspective.* Newbury Park, CA: Sage.

Czarniawska-Joerges, Barbara (1994) 'Realism in the Novel, Social Sciences and Organization Theory', in Barbara Czarniawska-Joerges and Pierre Guillet de Monthoux (eds) *Good Novels, Better Management; Reading Realities in Fiction*, pp. 304–25. Reading: Harwood Academic.

Czarniawska-Joerges, Barbara (1995) 'Narration or Science? Collapsing the Division in Organization Studies', *Organization* 2(1): 11–33.

Czarniawska-Joerges, Barbara (1996) 'The Process of Organizing', in *International Encyclopaedia of Business and Management.* London: Routledge.

Czarniawska, Barbara (1997) *Narrating the Organization: Dramas of Institutional Identity.* Chicago: University of Chicago Press.

Dalton, Melville (1959) *Men who Manage: Fusions of Feeling and Theory in Administration.* New York: Wiley.

Eco, Umberto (1979) *The Role of the Reader: Explorations in the Semiotics of Texts.* London: Hutchinson.

Eco, Umberto (1990) *The Limits of Interpretation.* Bloomington and Indianapolis: Indiana University Press.

Fisher, Walter R. (1987) *Human Communication as Narration: Towards a Philoso-*

A Four Times Told Tale
Barbara Czarniawska

phy of Reason, Value, and Action. Columbia: University of South Carolina Press.

Geertz, Clifford (1973) *The Interpretation of Cultures*. New York: Basic Books.

Geertz, Clifford (1980) 'Blurred Genres: The Refiguration of Social Thought', *American Scholar* 29(2): 165–79.

Geertz, Clifford (1988) *Works and Lives*. Stanford, CA: Stanford University Press.

Greimas, A.J. and Courtés, J. (1982) *Semiotics and Language. An Analytical Dictionary*. Bloomington: Indiana University Press.

Höpfl, Heather (1995) 'Organisational Rhetoric and the Threat of Ambivalence', *Studies in Cultures, Organizations and Societies* 1(2): 175–88.

Knorr-Cetina, Karin (1981) *The Manufacture of Knowledge: An Essay on the Constructivist and Contextual Nature of Science*. Oxford: Pergamon.

Knorr-Cetina, Karin (1994) 'Primitive Classification and Postmodernity: Towards a Sociological Notion of Fiction', *Theory, Culture & Society* 11(3): 1–22.

Lamarque, Peter (1990) 'Narrative and Invention: The Limits of Fictionality', in Cristopher Nash (ed.) *Narrative in Culture: The Uses of Storytelling in the Sciences, Philosophy and Literature*, pp. 5–22. London: Routledge.

Latour, Bruno (1988a) 'The Politics of Explanation: An Alternative', in S. Woolgar (ed.) *Knowledge and Reflexivity*, pp. 155–77. London: Sage.

Latour, Bruno (1988b) 'A Relativistic Account of Einstein's Relativity', *Social Studies of Science* 18(1): 3–44.

Latour, Bruno (1992) 'Technology is Society Made Durable', in J. Law (ed.) *A Sociology of Monsters: Essays on Power, Technology and Domination*, pp. 103–31. London: Routledge.

Latour, Bruno (1993) 'Can Sociology of Technology Teach Anything to the Study of Organizations?', address at the EGOS conference, Paris, July.

Latour, Bruno (1996) *Aramis or the Love of Technology*. Cambridge, MA: Harvard University Press.

Law, John (1994) *Organizing Modernity*. Oxford: Blackwell.

Lejeune, Philippe (1989) *On Autobiography*. Minneapolis: University of Minnesota Press.

Lepenies, Wolf (1988) *Between Literature and Science: The Rise of Sociology*. Cambridge: Cambridge University Press.

Lyotard, Jean-François (1987). *The Postmodern Condition: A Report on Knowledge*. Manchester: Manchester University Press.

McCloskey, D.N. (1985) *The Rhetorics of Economics*. Madison: University of Wisconsin Press.

McCloskey. D.N. (1990a) *If You are so Smart: The Narrative of Economics Enterprise*. Chicago: University of Chicago Press.

McCloskey, D.N. (1990b) 'Storytelling in Economics', in Cristopher Nash (ed.) *Narrative in Culture. The Uses of Storytelling in the Sciences, Philosophy and Literature*, pp. 5–22. London: Routledge.

Meyer, John (1996) 'Otherhood: The Promulgation and Transmission of Ideas in the Modern Organizational Environment', in Barbara Czarniawska and Guje Sevón (eds) *Travels of Ideas: New Approaches to Organizational Change*, pp. 241–52. Berlin: de Gruyter.

Morgan, Gareth (1986) *Images of Organization*. London: Sage.

Mulkay, Michael (1985) *The Word and the World*. Winchester, MA: Allen and Unwin.

d'Ormesson, Jean (1971) *La Gloire de l'Empire*. Paris: Gallimard.

Organization
Articles

Perrow, Charles (1991) 'A Society of Organizations', *Theory and Society* 20: 725–62.

Polkinghorne, Donald (1987) *Narrative Knowing and the Human Sciences.* Albany: State University of New York Press.

Ricoeur, Paul (1981) *Hermeneutics and the Human Sciences: Essays on Language, Action and Interpretation.* New York/Paris: Cambridge University Press/Editions de la Maison des Sciences de l'Homme.

Ricoeur, Paul (1984) *Time and Narrative*, Vol. 1. Chicago: University of Chicago Press.

Rorty, Richard (1992) 'The Pragmatist's Progress', in Umberto Eco (ed.) *Interpretation and Overinterpretation*, pp. 89–108. Cambridge: Cambridge University Press.

Rosaldo, Renato (1989) *Culture & Truth: The Remaking of Social Analysis.* London: Routledge.

Silverman, David and Jones, Jill (1976) *Organisational Work.* London: Collier Macmillan.

Simmel, Georg (1994) 'The Picture Frame: An Aesthetic Study', *Theory, Culture & Society* 11(1): 11–17.

Sköldberg, Kaj (1994) 'Tales of Change: Public Administration Reform and Narrative Mode', *Organization Science* 5(2): 219–38.

Smircich, Linda (1985) 'Is the Concept of Culture a Paradigm for Understanding Organizations and Ourselves?', in P.J. Frost, L.F. Moore, M.R. Louis, C.C. Lundberg and J. Martin (eds) *Organizational Culture*, pp. 3–72. Beverly Hills, CA: Sage.

Thompson, James D. (1967) *Organizations in Action: Social Science Bases of Administrative Theory.* New York: McGraw-Hill.

Traweek, Sharon (1992) 'Border Crossings: Narrative Strategies in Science Studies and Among Physicists in Tsukuba Science City, Japan', in Andrew Pickering (ed.) *Science as Practice and Culture.* Chicago: University Chicago Press.

Waldo, Dwight (1961) 'Organization Theory: An Elephantine Problem', *Public Administration Review* 21: 210–25.

Webster's New Collegiate Dictionary (1981). Springfield, MA: G. & C. Merriam.

White, Hayden (1973) *Metahistory: The Historical Imagination in Nineteenth-Century Europe.* Baltimore: The John Hopkins University Press.

Wolf, Margery (1992) *A Thrice-Told Tale: Feminism, Postmodernism, and Ethnographic Responsibility.* Stanford, CA: Stanford University Press.

30

[13]

Narratives of Organizational Identity and Identification: A Case Study of Hegemony and Resistance*

Michael Humphreys, Andrew D. Brown

Michael Humphreys,
Andrew D. Brown
Nottingham
University
Business School,
UK

Abstract

This paper focuses on issues of identity and identification in a UK-based institution of higher education (Westville[1] Institute). It is suggested that identity, both individual and collective, and the processes of identification which bind people to organizations, are constituted in the personal and shared narratives that people author in their efforts to make sense of their world and read meaning into their lives. The research contribution this paper makes is threefold. First, it illustrates how an organization's identity narrative evolves over time, and the variety of identification narratives, including dis-identification, neutral identification and schizo-identification, in terms of which participants define their relationship to it. Second, it makes a contribution to what are still rather inchoate efforts to theorize the dynamics of individual–collective processes of identification and identity construction. Finally, it argues that the efforts of senior managers to control processes of organizational identity formation, and participant identification, are interpretable as hegemonic acts required for legitimation purposes.

Descriptors: narrative, identity, identification, hegemony, legitimacy, higher education

Introduction

This paper draws on the literatures concerned with organizational narratives to provide an analysis of the evolving identity of an institution of higher education, and the complex patterns of identification manifested by its participants. The paper focuses both on the efforts of the organization's senior managers to author a monological and hegemonic organizational identity narrative and on the reactions of faculty members. Our understanding of discursive (e.g. Foucault 1977; Lyotard 1984), dialogic (e.g. Ford 1999; Hazen 1993; Rhodes 1997, 2000) and narrative (e.g. Boje 1991, 1995; Bruner 1990; Czarniawska 1997) practices in organizations is now well established. So too is the concept of hegemony, which has recently attracted increasing attention from scholars of organization (e.g. Baack and Prasch 1997; Boje et al. 1999; Clegg 1989; Gramsci 1971). The issue of legitimacy, both as it applies to organizations (e.g. Kamens 1977; Meyer and Rowan 1977; Brunsson 1989; Suchman 1995) and groups (e.g. Brown 1994) is also an established fixture in the lexicon of organization theorists (e.g. Dowling and Pfeffer 1975; Habermas 1973). This paper suggests that longitudinal interpretive research that is analytically concerned with processes of narrative and authorship may shed light on the extent to which individual and collective identities are exercises in power (Foucault 1980; Jermier et al. 1994).

Organizations are socially constructed from networks of conversations (Ford 1999) or dialogues (Hazen 1993; Rhodes 2000) the intertextuality, continuities and consistencies of which serve to maintain and objectify reality for participants (Berger and Luckmann 1966). Dialogue is a process whereby people 'mobilize language by talking, listening and constructing meaning' (Rhodes 2000: 217) and is understood here not merely as 'a process in an organization, but organization itself' (Hazen 1993: 22). To an extent, the practice of dialogue promotes shared understandings (Senge 1990: 242), permits negotiated realities (Bonnen and Fry 1991) and leads to a degree of collective consistency, coherence and continuity (Burgoyne 1995; Isaacs 1993). However, it is clear that organizations are not discursively monolithic, but pluralistic and polyphonic, involving multiple dialogical practices that occur simultaneously and sequentially (Ford 1999; Hazen 1993; Fairclough 1992). Within organizations, individuals and groups have some latitude to author their own reality, though always in ways shaped by the available social discourses.

The dialogues that processually constitute organizations contribute to ongoing processes of narrative construction and refinement. The stories that are authored through dialogue are one symbolic means by which meaning is variously negotiated, shared and contested. Our view has been prefigured by suggestions that 'man is in his actions and practice, as well as his fictions, essentially a storytelling animal' (MacIntyre 1981: 201), and appropriately described as *Homo narrans* (Fisher 1984: 6). It also builds on Bruner's (1991: 4) suggestion that people confronted with the necessity of 'constructing and representing the rich and messy domain of human interaction' seek to 'organize [their] experience and [their] memory of human happenings mainly in the form of narrative ...' (cf. Bartlett 1932; Barthes 1977; Bateson 1979; Mandler 1984; Pentland 1999). In a specifically organizational context, Boje (1995) has referred to organizations as collective storytelling systems. Gephart (1991: 37) has described narratives as 'a tool or program for making sense of events', and Wilkins and Thompson (1991: 20) have suggested that narratives assist organizational 'participants [to] map their reality' (cf. Boyce 1996; Weick 1995).

One principal concern of this paper is to emphasize 'the heterogeneity of language, differences between individuals' (Rhodes 2000: 221) in an ongoing effort to illustrate the dynamics of individual and collective identity construction. While there is a tendency for social psychologists to theorize identity in terms of fragmentary images or concepts (e.g. Tajfel 1982; Banaji and Prentice 1994), there are analytic advantages in locating identity in individuals' (and collectives') self-narratives. These narratives are authored impositions (Peacock and Holland 1993) in which peoples' self-conceptions and experiences are emplotted (Ricoeur 1984, 1985, 1988), and which facilitate self-understanding, the achievement of a mature identity, and individuation (Berzonsky 1988; Blasi 1988; Hirschhorn 1997). As organizational researchers, this approach permits us to account better for identities, as continuously constituted and reconstituted through discursive practices (Burke 1968), and enables us to place better in a historical/biographical context people's beliefs regarding what they believe to be most significant about themselves (Ezzy 1998; McAdams 1996). As Czarniawska (1997: 5–6, 24, 49) asserts, not only is narrative 'the main source of knowledge in the practice of organizing', but, just like individuals, 'organizations need a coherent narrative', and identity may be appropriately conceptualized as 'a … continuous process of narration where both the narrator and the audience are involved in formulating, editing, applauding, and refusing various elements of the ever-produced narrative'.

Individual and collective identity narratives are not solely private concerns, but are instead 'intensely governed' by, for example, social conventions, community scrutiny, legal norms, familial obligations and religious injunctions (Rose 1989: 1). In short, narrative identities are power effects, complex outcomes of processes of subjugation and resistance that are contingent and perpetually shifting (Clegg 1994: 275; Jermier et al. 1994: 8). To analyze effectively the often subtle web of power relationships within which people author their self-narratives we need to be sensitive to the hegemony of discursive practices (Browning 1991; Foucault 1977; Ricoeur 1984; White 1987). Our conception of hegemony derives from its use by Gramsci (1971) to refer to an ideology, most often articulated as 'common sense' or 'natural', that constitutes a form of cleverly masked, taken-for-granted domination (cf. Baack and Prasch 1997: 134; Boje et al. 1999: 341). Hegemony thus 'involves the successful mobilization and reproduction of the active consent of dominated groups' (Clegg 1989: 160) and constitutes an invisible prison of intersecting gazes to those who have little power to negotiate or even voice alternate stories defining and shaping their existence (Lyotard 1984).

Within organizations, centripetal forces mobilized by dominant groups produce shared meanings and understandings by which they seek 'to impose their own monological and unitary perceptions of truth' (Rhodes 2000: 227). Our particular interest is in the dynamics by which elites seek acceptance for their identity narratives regarding what is fundamental (central), uniquely descriptive (distinctive), and persistent (enduring) about an organization (Albert and Whetten 1985). There are, of course, constraints imposed on any group's capability to author collective identity narratives, notably because executives need, to an extent, 'to meet the expectations of multiple internal [and external] stakeholders' (Pratt and Foreman 2000: 22). In our case, there is evidence of a concerted senior managerial effort to reduce identity plurality, and to manage those identities which could not easily be eliminated, in order to increase identity synergy, in an attempt to maximize convergence and decrease conflict between them. These we interpret as legitimation strategies.

The attribution of legitimacy to someone or to something has been variously said to imply a normative acceptance of its rightness (Collins 1975; Habermas 1973; Kleugel and Smith 1986; Lenski 1966), a recognition that it is reasonable and just (Della Fave 1991), and a perception that it is desirable, proper or appropriate (Suchman 1995). Legitimacy may thus be viewed as a key resource, both for individual executives and for organizations. Managers seeking acceptance for their policies, to maintain employee acquiescence and commitment, and to enhance career progression, need to foster views of themselves and their strategies as legitimate, partly through the authorship of judicious narratives (Brown 1998; Pfeffer 1981). Similarly, in order to avoid claims that they are negligent, irrational or unnecessary (Parsons 1978), organizations must achieve legitimate status in their environments by promoting stories that portray them as exhibiting 'congruence' (Dowling and Pfeffer 1975) or 'isomorphism' (Meyer and Rowan 1977) with salient values and norms, which prescribe acceptable structures and behaviour, in the larger social system (Beyer 1981; Suchman 1995). There is a high degree of reciprocal inter-dependence between the legitimacy needs of individuals and collectives which, in healthy organizations, feed symbiotically off the advantages (in the form of energy, determination, vision, status, financial and material resources and so forth) that the other provides (Brown 1997).

There is a natural tendency for individuals to identify with, and attribute legitimacy to, the work organizations in which they participate, as a result of rational calculations of self-interest (Pfeffer and Salancik 1978), an assumed congruence between their notions of what is 'right' and 'good', and key features and consequences of the organization (Aldrich and Fiol 1994), and because work organizations offer meaningful explanations for anxiety-provoking experiences that reduce dissonance (Suchman 1995). At a deeper psychological level, in defining the social identity component of their self-concepts, individuals tend to draw on the salient images they associate with their work organization (Dutton et al. 1994; Elsbach 1999). As a result, their personal self-esteem is thus tied intimately to the identity (including construed external image) of their organization. This, in turn, means that in order for them to maintain an acceptable level of self-esteem, participants are overwhelmingly likely to regard their organization as legitimate, to be highly motivated to enhance its construed external image (Brown 1997) and to defend their organization from perceived attacks (Ashforth and Mael 1989; Dutton et al. 1994; Elsbach and Kramer 1996).

Processes of identification tend, however, to be more diverse and elaborate than this rather simple account suggests. Part of the reason for this is that the identity narratives that characterize organizations are complex and evolving, perhaps containing multiple inconsistencies and incongruities. More importantly, we should be sensitive to the fact that working against the centripetal forces in organizations are centrifugal powers (what Bakhtin (1986) calls 'heteroglossia'). The point is that all participants in an organization have some capacity to read and author their own reality and thus oppose centralizing impositions (Rhodes 2000: 227). In Gagnon's (1992:

231) terms, 'heteroglossia is accompanied by polysemy, the proliferation of socially uncontrolled meanings for these voices'. From the point of view of individuals, understanding and coming to terms with the relations between their individual identity narratives and the organization identity narratives promulgated by elites may pose significant identification dilemmas (e.g. Elsbach and Bhattacharya 1998; Zabusky and Barley 1997).

Drawing on Elsbach (1999), we suggest that how individuals conceive of the connections between their individual and organization identity narratives may be analyzed using four categories of relationship: identification, dis-identification, schizo-identification, and neutral identification. Identification implies a self-perception of an active and positive connection between the self-narrative and the dominant identity narrative of the organization. Dis-identification describes a self-perception of an active and negative connection between the self-narrative and the dominant identity narrative of the organization. Schizo-identification is manifested by individuals who simultaneously identify and dis-identify with (different aspects) of an organization's identity narrative. Finally, neutral identification refers to a self-perception of impartiality with respect to an organization's identity narrative, in which there is an explicit absence of either identification or dis-identification on the part of an individual. We suggest that, within our case study organization, all four of these identification phenomena may be observed.

Given that organizations tend to be characterized by multiple identity narratives, 'identity' and 'identification' are generally the pivotal umbrella issues under which competing views regarding the key bases of an organization's legitimacy tend to coalesce. Organizational identities are power effects resulting from the complex interplay of politically-motivated individuals and groups seeking, for example, self-aggrandizement (Kets de Vries 1996), career progression (Buren 1962) and self-esteem (Banaji and Prentice 1994). Both legitimacy and identity are concomitantly power resources and 'arenas' in which power is exercised, and the dynamics which underpin them and by which they are characterized constitute significant aspects of organizational behaviour (Clegg 1981). While the practical importance of contests over organizational identity and legitimacy have yet to receive adequate attention, they are hinted at in, for instance, Barry and Elmes's (1997) analysis of strategic discourse, Boje's (1995) discussion of Disney as a storytelling organization, and Dutton and Dukerich's account of how the New York Port Authority dealt with the issue of homelessness. The profound consequences of such debates for organizations is revealed in examples such as Intel, which managed to re-define itself as a microprocessor rather than memory chip company (Grove 1997), and Xerox, which failed to capitalize on its leadership in computing (Smith and Alexander 1988).

This paper offers an interpretation of events through the construction and analysis of organizational narratives based on the accounts of certain of its participants. The decision to adopt this format has, in part, been prompted by suggestions that narratives are both a legitimate and the most appropriate means for representing actions and events in organizations (Van Maanen 1988; Czarniawska 1995a and b, 1997). It also draws on Pentland's (1999: 711) argument that narratives 'are abstract conceptual models used in explanations of observed data', and thus possess greater generative theoretic utility than has generally been noted. Our approach recognizes that narrative emplotment is an authorial device (White 1973; Ricoeur 1984, 1985, 1988), and exploits the opportunities it presents to be self-reflexive, while being preoccupied with the 'craft of organizational theorizing' (Chia 1996: 51). Perhaps most importantly of all, our preoccupation with identity narratives derives from our methodological conviction that, by focusing on stories, we will be better able to identify plurivocal native interpretations in ways that can assist us in reading polysemy back into ethnographic research (Boje 1991, 1995).

Research Design

Conducted from an interpretive perspective, or 'inquiry from the inside', in which the authors were immersed in a stream of organizational events (Geertz 1973; Evered and Louis 1981), the primary objective of the study was to produce an ethnographic account of the working lives of those engaged in the Faculty of Arts, Science and Education at Westville Institute (Humphreys 1999). Our principal data sources were 42 semi-structured interviews conducted between September 1997 and March 1998, a larger number of informal interviews and observations made over a 15-year time span until February 2000, and a huge range of documentation, including internet pages, published articles, official working documentation (such as committee minutes, letters and memos), and newspaper and magazine reports referring to the Institute. Of these, the richest source of ideas were the formal interviews with past and present faculty members and administrative staff, including the faculty dean, subject leaders, and the Institute's principal. While most of the interviews were conducted in the work offices of faculty members, eight were carried out at the researcher's home, four were undertaken in the homes of respondents, and one interview occurred outside the United Kingdom. The duration of the interviews varied from 40 minutes to 2 hours. All were recorded onto mini cassettes, and all were fully transcribed before being subject to analysis.

Westville Institute was the employer organization of one of the authors, and he had sole responsibility for data collection. There are considerable potential difficulties, as well as advantages, involved in conducting ethnographic research in the organization where one is employed. While it has frequently been noted that 'members of an organization can be suspicious of an outside researcher and may not be co-operative' (Horn 1996: 551), our experience suggests that such suspicion can, at least initially, be even more intense when the research locale is one's own place of work. An application for permission to conduct research in the Faculty prompted a written 'ethical' objection from a colleague. After prolonged discussions by two separate Institute committees, it was decided to initiate a new committee, the Faculty Research Ethics Sub-committee, specifically to deal with this issue. Ultimately, the sub-committee favoured the researcher, but the whole process took a full academic year. This is, perhaps, an extreme example of the problem of access faced by all researchers, which has led Rachel (1996: 124) to comment that '... access is not just a matter of walking through the door — it is an ever present, ongoing concern, which includes inventing yourself as an ethnographer ...'. This said, it should be noted that it was just one individual who opposed research access, and that a large number of colleagues voiced both private and open support for the project. In addition, the individual who made the complaint was the only person to decline to be interviewed for this research, and all other respondents and informants were seemingly uninhibited in their display of emotion and expression of personal views.

The extraordinary demands made on the researcher as participant observer, who on the one hand needs 'to experience the taken-for-granted world of the social actors' and, on the other, seeks 'to be the continuously questioning researcher exposing [their] hidden assumptions' has attracted some debate (Nandhakumar and Jones 1997: 126; Adler and Adler 1994). For us, the dilemmas it posed were a constant reminder both that organizational research is 'an ongoing project of creating, classifying, sustaining and modifying our version of reality', and of our continuing need to be reflexive about the representations we produced (Knights 1992: 515). More generally, our participant observation methodology exposed for us the extent to which the authoring of an organizational narrative is an artful process of selective re-appropriation designed to produce a representation that others will find authentic, plausible, and verismilitudinous (Atkinson 1990; Gephart 1993; Jeffcutt 1994; Watson 1995). It also cast in relief the fact that, while we have sought to give those studied a 'voice' in the narrative in which they figure so prominently, the truth is, rather, that this is little more than an authorial strategy which privileges our construction of social reality (Berger and Luckmann 1966). Only in a hegemonic sense is there ever just one story to be told, and being reflexive means 'continually discovering that we as writers ... are sharing the stories and character of our subjects' (Boje et al. 1999: 358; cf. Rhodes 2000). The challenge we have taken up is that posed by Bakhtin (1986), namely to listen for the different voices in organizations and to capture the dialogic relations between them (Rhodes 1997: 224).

Identity and Identification in Westville Institute

Westville Institute is a large, general-purpose higher education institution, with around 7,000 students and 290 academic staff, which Scott (1995: 48) has categorized as one of a 'small number of larger multi-faculty colleges which aspire to be universities'. A regionally focused institution, drawing 72 percent of its full-time students from Westville and the North West, its strong links to local culture are readily acknowledged by staff in comments such as 'you can't take Westville out of the Institute' (Head of Subject). With its historical origin in smaller institutions dating back to the early-nineteenth century, by the 1970s, Westville had a Technical College, a College of Art and Design, an Institute of Technology and a College of (technical) Education. In 1982, Westville's higher education provision was rationalized, creating Westville Institute of Higher Education (WIHE), leaving further education provision to Westville Metropolitan College. In the mid-1980s, the Institute began an unsuccessful campaign for polytechnic status by absorbing the higher education elements of the School of Art, and, at incorporation in 1989, WIHE was renamed Westville Institute (WI). After incorporation, the Institute became engaged in a campaign of expansion and consolidation aimed at the achievement of University status, which included a 1996 reorganization into three Faculties: the Faculty of Technology; Westville Business School; and the major focus of this case study, the Faculty of Arts, Science and Education.

The Quest for University Status

The senior management of Westville Institute sought to author an organizational identity narrative that emphasized the importance of attaining university status. The logic of this narrative was deployed to justify a time-consuming, expensive and highly public campaign for a university charter that, by the time data collection for this case had come to an end, had proved unsuccessful. In this case study, we will examine how the conflicting and 'continuous, kaleidoscop[ic] stream of self-images' (Barry and Hazen 1996: 151) arising out of the unsuccessful campaign for acquisition of the title 'university', produced an identity crisis which led individuals and groups to question the purpose and strength of their connection to the organization (Dutton et al. 1994). Using the different modes of individual-organization identification described by Elsbach (1999), we analyze a series of oppositional identity dualities evident in the identity narratives of participants in Westville Institute.

The oppositional identity dualities we discuss were a manifestation of the internal polar forces and dynamic strains responsible for organizational fault lines which were the precursors of fragmentation and incoherence. We examine five such dualities: (1) the conflict, experienced by all higher education academics, referred to by Boyer (1990: 16) as the 'tired old teaching versus research debate'; (2) the tension between the Institute as a well-established local provider of higher education courses and its aspirations to be a national university; (3) the discontinuity between staff, nostalgic for a golden age 'who experienced the change from old to new' (Gabriel 1993: 122), and those who looked forward to the 'inevitability' of radical change in a networked, modern university-sector institution; (4) the strain induced by Westville staff being presented with two possible, but mutually exclusive, futures as members either of a successful, prestigious institution which achieves the title 'university', or, of an unsuccessful, lacklustre 'institute', which fails to attain the desired status; and, finally, (5) the clash between the notion, implicit in the bid for university title, of a centralized, coherent institution and the opposing reality of a decentralized fragmented organization where individual staff only identify with their subject group. In examining each of these inter-linked, and to some extent overlapping dualities, we will illustrate how their combined effect led to a position described by Wilson (1997: 91) as 'social saturation ... a psychic state of "multiphrenia" where for everything we know to be true about ourselves, other voices within respond with doubts and even derision'.

The ambiguity of the teaching–research conundrum within Westville Institute was clearly acknowledged by the Principal:

'My guess is, simplistically, we would divide into three. There are those members of staff who are quite clear, "I am a researcher".... . There are those people at the other end of the scale who are clear that they certainly don't want to do research and are probably clear that they are not expected to do research. And then there's a chunk in the middle, isn't there, who either personally are not sure, or the guidance isn't forthcoming as to whether or not they are meant to be doing research.' (The Principal)

In the Faculty of Arts, Sciences and Education, role definition was acutely ill-defined, with faculty confused by the mixed messages they received from the organization: '... the problem is that many of the staff, including the management within the Institute, see research activity as a privilege not a requirement' (Humanities Lecturer). The resultant unresolved ambivalence, supports Andre and Frost's (1997: xi) notion that it is institutional culture which shapes an individual's 'ability to integrate teaching and research', placing individual staff in a bewildering position where, 'on the one hand [research] is essential for university status, but on the other hand we are putting barriers in the way' (Community Studies Lecturer). Thus, staff were beginning to realize that within the Institute there was a failure to fulfil Johnston's (1996: 104) definition of the task of university managers 'to provide academic staff with sufficient time to manage for themselves'.

The contrast between the deep involvement of Westville Institute in local culture and its drive towards national university status were echoed in the aspirations of Westville itself, to 'City' status. The irony, implicit in the continuing failure of both ambitions, began to receive satirical press attention, especially when linked with the waning fortunes of the local football club, itself a financial contributor to the campaign for university status:

'... how sweet of Westville Rovers to help pay for Westville Institute's latest advertising guru to help them go up to the top division and become a university at last, particularly as the lads look like sliding out of the Premier League themselves.' (The Guardian, April 1998)

The Principal even used a football metaphor in acknowledging the lowly status of the Institute on the national stage, suggesting that with or without a university title: 'we are in division three, and to get into division two is going to be extremely difficult'. For staff, the status conferred by work-

430   Michael Humphreys, Andrew D. Brown

ing in a highly prestigious local higher education institution was being undermined by public exposure of the apparent insignificance of the Institute in national terms, and this had begun to generate uncomfortable feelings of low self-esteem, powerlessness and anxiety. This was exemplified by a Health Studies lecturer who said: 'I never sleep on Sunday night ... I would like to be able to think of going to work without that ... you have got to have some stability and I don't find I have got that.'

**The 'all-or-nothing' nature of the campaign for university status also began to raise suspicions among faculty members that senior management had exerted little effective control over the process, and that they were not presenting staff with a full range of strategic alternatives. One principal lecturer, taking a deliberately provocative stance, questioned the rationale underlying the apparent dismissal of merger as a strategy, writing to a senior manager:

'Our unit costs are high, our funding level is low. Year on year "efficiency savings" have forced, and will continue to force, rationalizing, streamlining, simplification. I am concerned that the "turbulence" (local and national), and our particular problems will weaken us to such an extent that we may become incapable of upholding the quality that must underpin our degree-awarding powers. If we merge now, before we are further weakened, we may have a respectable place in a combined institution.'

Despite such pleading, there was no apparent deviation from the monologic of the strategic push for university status. Individual staff had begun to feel confused and somewhat threatened, in a position where, in Winograd and Flores (1986: 34) terms, they were 'always in the middle of things', somewhere between further education and higher education, in a teaching institution with research aspirations. Kets de Vries, (1995: 50) suggests that it is 'confusion of this kind which creates the conditions for the "giving-up–given-up" complex in organizations and contributes to the incidence of stress symptoms'. For many staff, the campaign for university status had become 'an arid and empty affair' (Robins 1996: 67), or, as a senior faculty member expressed it: 'I think it has had that kind of eye-off-the-ball effect on the Institute as a whole. It's such an obsession that it's become kind of a millstone'. Feelings of ambivalence and ambiguity were also expressed by an education lecturer who voiced her feelings of detachment from the senior management's strategy:

'Well, nobody sat us down and said, "In order to get University title, we've got to do X, Y, Z", and, "If it's decided that we want to have University title, how can we contribute?". Even if the decision is not ours to go for it, how could we as a group contribute to that? You'd know about it; you'd feel part of it. To me it's something that comes down from on high; as an update to us getting or not getting a university title. We've not had any part in it.'

The multiplicity of different organizational sub-groupings (faculty, division, pathway, subject group and module) symbolized the identity conflict between parts of the Institute which remained separated both spatially and by ethos. Indeed, for some faculty members, Westville Institute was not a single coherent organization, but a collection of sub-cultures, with mutual ill-feeling arising from previous historical, political and physical divisions. For the majority of staff, the notion that faculty could be regarded as a 'community of scholars, remain[ed] a myth' (Harman 1990:34). This organizational fragmentation was in stark contrast to the image portrayed by senior administrators in the campaign for university status, which rhetorically suggested that the Institute possessed a strong, unified corporate identity. For individual staff 'living with ambiguity [was] a skill that [was] becoming increasingly necessary' (Gergen 1998: 280). Individuals felt let down and simultaneously blamed by senior management. As a long-serving technician said: 'It's a bit like the first world war situation, isn't it really? You've got some blokes sitting in a nice comfy house drinking gin, way back from the front saying "go over the top lads" — it's bad guidance right from the top'. Arguably, coping with the day-to-day difficulties created by the obvious discrepancy between construed public image (Dutton and Dukerich 1991), and perceptions of actual organizational identity, was symptomatic of a 'vital self-deception [which] help[s] us to avoid the truth of powerlessness and finitude' (Fineman 1993: 24). As a Principal Lecturer in Education put it: 'the problem is that I don't think this place actually has a notion of what it ought to be excellent about'.

To sum up, at Westville Institute, the quest for university status had surfaced evidence of internal organizational strains and tensions manifest in a set of potentially destructive identity dualities. While we have described what faculty considered to be the most significant of these, there were, arguably, others, including, for example: the strain induced by working in what was perceived as a 'distressed' as opposed to a 'healthy' institution, and the confusion between the corporate narrative of equal opportunity and the reality of a completely 'masculine' management hierarchy. It is our contention that such dualities are major contributory factors to the dynamically polymorphic identity-constructing relationship between individuals and organizations which has received considerable attention from theorists (e.g. Albert and Whetten 1985; Dahler–Larsen 1997; Diamond 1988; Dutton and Dukerich 1991; Gioia and Thomas 1996; Kets de Vries 1984; Scott and Lane 2000). Melded with our narrative perspective on organizations, Elsbach's (1999) 'expanded model of organizational identification' provides us with a sophisticated framework (identification, dis-identification, schizo- and neutral-identification) for the interpretive analysis of these reflexive dynamic identification processes.

Organizational Identification

At Westville Institute it was the senior staff who were the most likely to manifest 'identification', i.e. the 'active' and 'positive' perception that they were members of the organization (Elsbach 1999: 179). They maintained their sense of self, and reinforced their hegemony in public expressions of control and self-confidence:

'We meet all the criteria for university status now, so our work and powers are equivalent to those of other universities already. To be granted the title, we have to demonstrate that we have used these powers properly for a period of 3 years, and that "probation period" will be over in February 1997. The title proposed and agreed by Governors and Academic Board is "The University of Westville".' (Statement to all staff by the Vice-Principal 1996)

Other categories of positively identifying staff included: new staff who accepted the hegemony of newspaper advertisements for academic posts, claiming that the Institute was *'on course for University in 1997'*; *'on course for University in 1998'* or, in 1999, simply: *'on course for University'*, and older staff whose identification arose from a 'cognitive reconstruction of the past' (Gabriel 1993: 131), exemplified by a senior lecturer with over twenty years service who said: '... we were a branch of a university, we were a mini university with a university link. It was an atmosphere of democracy that you would get in a traditional university.' As Davis (1979: 131) suggests, such positive identification with the past 'increase[s] our sense of self-worth. No matter how low, infirm or powerless we are now, we take heart from earlier glories'. Although the promised official university status remained tantalizingly out-of-reach, doubts were periodically dispelled by further reinforcement from senior management, including a memorandum from the Principal which stated:

'We believe that the Institute meets all of the criteria for a university title, and that it deserves such a title, having offered degree programmes for more than thirty years and being now the only institution in the country with the power to award both taught and research degrees, but not yet able to call itself a university (since acquiring degree-awarding powers in 1992, the Institute has awarded almost 6,500 degrees).' (Memorandum from Principal to all staff, September 1997)

Gradually, however, discrepancies began to appear between the aspirations of the Institute and its construed external image (Dutton and Dukerich 1991). This was evident in newspaper headlines such as: 'Westville Institute's attempt to gain university title has become the focus of a wrangle within the Quality Assurance Agency' (THES, October 1997), and bravado internal statements, such as the Principal's comment to the Faculty of Arts, Science and Education that '... I am absolutely convinced that we have been cheated and that's a line that I shall continue to hold ... the Secretary of State and the Departments' officers recognize that they are on somewhat dicey ground' (January 1998). The distance between management statements and media reports created for staff, below the level of the apparently convinced directorate, an ever-widening polarity. As March and Olsen (1976: 19) put it, the 'interpretations of events by organizational actors ... [were being] generated in the face of considerable perceptual ambiguity'.

These first indications of the failure of senior executive hegemony created for staff a 'clear break between a person's and organization's identity', paving the way for the 'active separation ... [and] negative relational categorization' which Elsbach (1999: 179) refers to as 'dis-identification'. Staff confidence was further shaken in February 1998, by a surprise letter from the Principal in which he proclaimed that the Institute intended to use the term *'university'* come what may, adding a postscript announcing his retirement:

'I write to let you know that, at its meeting last night, the Board of Governors agreed in principle to change the name of the Institute so as to incorporate the word "university" ... P.S. I understand from the chairman of Governors that the post of Principal of the Institute will be advertised in the national press in mid-March 1998, with a view to making an appointment early in May 1998.'

The predicted advertisement duly appeared in the press in March, with a somewhat low-key reference to University title: 'Applications are invited for the post of Chief Executive and Principal of Westville Institute. The Institute is a major player in the Higher Education sector in the region, and has made formal application for the immediate use of the title University of Westville.' In April 1998, the developing identity crisis was intensified by a letter from the Principal to all staff headed 'The Institute's Title', asking them to vote on nine possible alternative names incorporating the word 'university'. This was regarded by some staff as a denial of reality. As a Senior Lecturer expressed it: 'Westville Rovers have been relegated from the Premier Division to the First Division, but they can't now choose to call themselves a Premier Division side because they do all of the things that the teams in the Premier Division side do'. Although the results of the ballot were strongly in favour of the title 'University College Westville', and a new Principal took up post in December 1998, (the first female member of the Senior Management Team), at the time of writing (February 2001), the university title had still not been achieved or adopted. This did not prevent senior management from continuing to make public pronouncements, such as the Principal's statement reported in the Westville Evening News dated 13/2/01 under the headline "University Decision Must be Made Now":

'The Westville Institute Chief is calling on ministers to end months of speculation and decide whether the college should be awarded university status before a general election ... She said "we have heard nothing in recent weeks about our application for university status, and we do not know when the Privy Council will meet to discuss it. We would like the right decision for the Institute which would be a huge bonus for the town".'

For most participants, the Institute was still groping towards the goal of a clear externally construed image within the UK higher-education sector and, arguably, staff continued to exhibit the symptoms of identity confusion. A senior lecturer in psychology described how he saw this as having a detrimental effect on staff throughout the Institute: 'people develop this foggy vague way of speaking, deferring things and being unable to take decisions ... I think it's to do with their uncertainty about what they're supposed to be doing.' Evidently, as Dahler-Larsen (1997: 370) has said, 'A demand for clear identity is not equivalent to a clear identity itself.'

Organizational Dis-identification

Elsbach's (1999: 180) observation that organizational disidentification occurs when 'clear disconnection from simple stereotypically negative organizational identities is enhancing to a person's social identity', is exemplified at Westville by faculty's disassociation from senior staff. For example, an Institute senior manager was described by one lecturer as 'just a joke ... . I mean embarrassing' and by a retired deputy head of school as 'having been relegated to being in charge of mops and buckets'. Such organizational disidentification was particularly rife within the faculty as a result of the proliferation of subject groups, leading a senior lecturer to observe: 'Arts, Science and Education — what else is there?'; a retired subject head to refer to 'the rag-bag faculty'; and a humanities lecturer to claim that 'the only time that I come face to face with the Faculty in my day-to-day existence is where I have to put "Faculty" on my photocopying forms'. The incoherence and fragmentation indicative of dis-identification was evident in the openly expressed lack of loyalty of staff who sought refuge in identification with their subject group or with their teaching. This was clearly expressed by one lecturer who stated: 'When it comes to work, I feel that my loyalty lies with the philosophy group'; and another who claimed that: 'Your ultimate identity lies with what you teach'. The dis-identification with the Institute arising from fragmentation was also evident in rivalry *between* subject groups. A psychology lecturer asked to teach within another subject group said that he did not wish to be associated with what he saw as 'an academically inferior discipline'. In another instance, a lecturer referring to the antagonism between different subject groups within the Faculty noted that 'if we think of the different parts of the Faculty as members of a football team — then because the team has such low morale and poor team spirit, then one player (say Humanities) doesn't want another player (say Education) to do well, because it will make them look relatively bad'. In addition, each subject group had a different method of dividing up its principal lecturer responsibilities and the consequent differences in workload and work patterns had created a situation where, as a lecturer put it, 'the management structure of the Faculty is difficult to read for insiders and illegible for outsiders'. The subject fragmentation was also compounded by the mix of member's academic backgrounds. As one head of subject recognized: 'you see you have a set of colleagues, who vary from people who are strictly typically university material, to others who are very parochial and who would probably be more at home in an F.E. college'. Other staff saw this mix as having a detrimental, isolating influence on management style: 'the whole management system reminds me of school in some senses, you know that there was a Headteacher there, rather than a proper academic manager' (Community Studies Lecturer). One senior lecturer expressed his feelings of alienation in terms of the Institute's apparent policy on equal opportunities in admissions:

'I was just thinking this morning how few black faces there are around, how few disabled people are around, and, in a sense, I feel as though I'm sort of institutionalized into accepting the status quo rather than actually challenging the sort of gate-keeping aspects of the place.'

Several staff attributed their feelings of exclusion to the predominantly technological background of the senior management team: 'if the experience of the Principal is mainly in engineering, then he might have all sorts of faulty, false ideas about what producing a book involves in a Humanities subject' (Lecturer in English Literature). Female staff also expressed particular feelings of dis-identification with the almost exclusively male management hierarchy of the Institute, 'it's a male institution — male dominated. Part of the management style is, you know like men from industry, "do this", "do that", "this is what is to be done"' (Senior Lecturer in Education). Some staff even suggested that their feelings of estrangement and isolation arose from deliberate management victimization: 'we are now just a subject group within a faculty and they are trying to move us yet again out of our campus, it is all a concerted effort by some people to make sure that there is nothing left of us' (Senior Lecturer in Education).

Organizational Schizo-Identification

Gherardi's (1995: 27) view that 'every organizational event that affects [people's] respective lives in significantly different ways will constitute, in reality, two distinct events', was confirmed at Westville by the contradictory messages faculty thought were implicit in the strategic push for a university title. Staff, for whom the Institute's identity 'embodie [d] both cherished values and the opposite of those values', a state described by Elsbach, (1999: 182) as 'schizo-identification', included faculty who found the new demands for research outcomes interfered with their commitment to teaching, and their intimate working relationships with students. Such staff were likely to have a long-standing identification with the vocational or professional qualification functions of the Institute, such as post-16 teacher-training or health-visitor training, but a dis-identification with undergraduate teaching and academic research. A lecturer in Health, for example, implied that research would detract from her professional life in her avowal that: 'I am not a researcher. I don't have any interest, I see myself as a teacher and my responsibilities are to the students.' Another major category of faculty, characterized by schizo-identification, included lecturers committed to, and strongly identifying with, the research functions of the Institute, but experiencing dis-identification with other institutional roles. For example, staff who felt that they had been originally recruited for their research record, complained that they were prevented from engaging in research by heavy administrative loads: 'although I have sort of been named as someone who is a productive researcher, I think there is a certain amount of pressure on me to do less and to spend more time doing administration' (Philosophy Lecturer). One young humanities lecturer expressed her own ambivalent identification in terms of a growing empathy with older colleagues:

'I suppose I can understand. I was quite amazed at how jaundiced some of my older colleagues were when I first came here, and how pissed off, and I suppose because they've been here, by and large, between 12 and 20 years I can now begin to appreciate just how ground down they must be by this whole sort of institutional dinosaur.'

Somewhat ironically, given the pronouncements of the senior management team, the Principal himself explicitly recognized that such a range of schizo-identification within the Institute was illustrative of its immaturity as a university-sector institution:

'... we are not an especially mature institution — we are like an F.E. college. You might even say we are more like a secondary school. Becoming a more mature university institution with that baggage, yes, it will take us time.'

A senior academic also acknowledged that, what he saw as 'bureaucratic overkill' in the regulations and procedures for research proposals, was reflective of institutional schizo-identification behaviour, suggesting that: 'We are hung up a bit, I think, in the Institute, on structures and procedures. Partly, that's a consequence of the need to be squeaky clean, to jump through all the hoops in accordance with the external agencies ... that it has become a bit paranoid is, you know, explainable but not necessarily justified.' A staff development manager suggested that this institutional ambivalence arose from a lack of self-esteem:

'The physical environment thing is a relative issue. I mean I have been to lots of other places, lots of other H.E. institutions which have worse conditions, worse environment in which to operate, but they seem to have more of a confidence about themselves. That's the, the greater confidence in what they do and what they are about and so on.'

Organization Neutral Identification

Elsbach (1999: 183) claims that 'an intentionally impartial relationship with an organization's identity (good or bad)' indicates 'neutral identification' in those who are 'neither supporters nor rivals of the organization'. It could be argued that, at Westville, neutral identification had arisen from an apparent lack of involvement by staff in senior management strategy, and that this had destroyed any notion of a 'discourse of participation' (Thatchenkery and Upadhyaya 1996: 308). Such withdrawal was exemplified at Westville by long-serving lecturers who had ceased to identify with the Institute, but had not yet actively dis-identified. A Senior Lecturer in this position said: 'I've been moved at least four times, and when I haven't moved, my roommate has changed three or four times ... one makes jokes like, the next move is to the bus shelter with the alcoholics, in the gardens there opposite the college'. The constant changes in accommodation and loss of social facilities, such as a campus bar, were perceived by some staff as destroying that which 'preserves plausibility and coherence, something that is reasonable and memorable, something that embodies past experience and expectation' (Weick 1995: 61). Such staff expressed a detachment from the Institute, arising from what they perceived as a breakdown in collegial culture. As a Senior Lecturer of 17 years experience put it:

'Altering the staff common room so there's no coffee provided for staff seems a very minor thing to happen, but the results are that everyone goes and buys a kettle and stays in their room all the time, so a little thing means that staff don't meet — nowadays I just turn up, teach and then go home.'

The detachment from the organization exemplified here was also apparent in a growing cohort of part-time lecturers teaching on modular degree courses within the Institute, who attended only when teaching and had minimal involvement in the cultural life of the Institute. If, as Dahler-Larsen (1997: 368) suggests, identity emerges 'only as a part of an ongoing interactive discourse', then, for such staff, who were uninvolved in the day-to-day organizational discourse, neutral identification was always likely to be the norm. One senior lecturer in education expressed feelings of 'comfortable detachment' from the Institute in saying: 'I see it as almost a benevolent sort of avuncular sort of organization ... . They sort of might look disapprovingly at some of the things that I do, but nevertheless sort of pat me on the back and say well as long as you don't ask me for anything, you know, carry on doing it.' Most support staff such as caretakers, cleaners and administrators were also in a state of neutral identification with the Institute. These staff evidently saw their work as 'just another job'. As one faculty administrative worker said: 'I am definitely a secretary ... . I have no particular leanings to working here, other than the fact it's more convenient for me to get here because it's near to where I live.' Some support staff even seemed regretful about their own growing detachment from the Institute, as a technician of over thirty years service said:

'We're like little satellites now ... since this faculty's been created we don't know whether we're part of the faculty ... . When I'm at work, I want to see this place survive and while I'm here, I do my best for them, but there's a lot of demoralized people about at the moment ... . When the buzzer goes at five o'clock, they're out the door.'

Discussion

To summarize, our case has illustrated how senior managers sought to redefine the identity of a traditional, teaching-oriented, and parochial Institute of Higher Education into a modern, research-led university with a national (indeed international) profile. The key to this strategy was the attainment of 'university' status. The failure of the Institute to be granted a university charter by successive governments had, to an extent, undermined the hegemonic efforts of two principals and their senior executive teams. The implications of what most organizational participants interpreted as the failure of the Institute's main strategic intent were, for employee identification, profound. The events described cast light on the constraints under which senior managers author organizational-identity narratives, and the complexity of the dynamics of participant identification under conditions of extreme organizational-identity ambiguity. The interplay of narratives of organizational identity and individual identification has, in turn, revealed the extent to which these ongoing dynamic processes are connected to issues of power and legitimacy. These points require further amplification and analysis.

Large and complex organizations are characterized by multiple embedded, and sometimes conflicting, narrative identities derived from, and manifested in, simultaneously and sequentially occurring dialogues (Ford 1999; Rhodes

438   Michael Humphreys, Andrew D. Brown

1997). Given their privileged hierarchical position, senior managers are often particularly articulate and powerful contributors to these stories, and seek to mould and manipulate organizational discourse for their own purposes (Boje 1995; Pratt and Foreman 2000). At Westville Institute there was a deliberate effort to reduce identity plurality by successive senior teams, who consistently authored and promulgated an identity narrative that centred on the organization's need for (and desert of) university status. Different strands of this narrative variously emphasized the need for an increase in sheer size (hence the consolidations with other institutions in the region), the need for a particular form of faculty configuration (as manifested in the re-structuring exercises), the importance of being a national rather than provincial provider of higher education, and the value and significance of faculty research. The narrative authored was an epic/romantic one in which the quest for university status was putatively associated with the achievement of an ideal organization, reborn and redeemed (Jeffcut 1993).

The success of this authorial strategy was, arguably, mitigated by at least two factors. First, rather than attempt to integrate or aggregate other established identity narratives (which emphasized teaching skills and student learning) with the new university-focused narrative, there was an explicit effort at deletion by overwriting them with the new (Pratt and Foreman 2000). This approach has been cautioned against by several theorists, who suggest that such a response generally risks alienating constituent groups (Ashforth and Mael 1996), and thus undermining employee loyalty and commitment (Eccles et al. 1992). As Albert (1992: 190) has sagely noted:

'... the costs of enacting an elimination strategy are underestimated ... the economic weakness of a unit to be eliminated often causes the decision-making entity to underestimate its symbolic value, and hence the degree to which the change will be resisted.'

The insensitivity of senior managers to existing organizational narratives, and their apparent rejection of a multivocal Institute identity incorporating disparate narrative themes (cf. Eccles et al. 1992; Padgett and Ansell 1993), failed to impress important internal stakeholders. Second, after four and a half years of high-level, intensive, and very public campaigning, Westville Institute was evidently no nearer to actually being granted university status. The implicit assumption of senior managers that they could intentionally author an identity-narrative foundered, in part, on the fact that the Institute was embedded in a highly institutionalized environment which offered less authorial discretion than they initially supposed. There was an irony here in that the authorial strategy, centred on the quest for university status, was part of a deliberate attempt to enhance the legitimate status of the organization, both for internal and external stakeholders, i.e., in order to maintain employee enthusiasm and acquiescence, to ensure a continued supply of resources, and to avoid claims that it was irrelevant in the modern system of higher education in the United Kingdom (e.g. Dowling and Pfeffer 1975; Meyer and Rowan 1977). The failure both of large cohorts of employees to accept the university-focused identity narrative and of external agencies, notably the government and its advisers, to recognize the organization's claims to university status, posed critical questions regarding the legitimacy of Westville Institute that are, as yet, unanswered.

The identity narrative authored by senior managers was, *inter alia*, a vehicle for communicating new sets of power relations which, it was hoped, success, if it ever came, would legitimate (Gagliardi 1986). The identity narrative was, in effect, a (somewhat unsuccessful) exercise in power designed to 'reify a particular social structure with ramifications for the maintenance of a particular power order' (Rosen 1985: 33). Our case aptly illustrates that the felicitous identity stories that those in positions of authority tend to tell about their organizations are 'artfully constructed' and 'carefully edited' constructions with panoptic, universalizing and totalizing intent (Boje 1995). The 'university narrative' was supposed to serve a disciplinary function as a 'discrete, regular, generalized and uninterrupted' (Burrell 1988: 227) performance that employees would adopt as an interpretive frame for understanding the organization and their role within it. That, instead, the narrative was variously ignored and contested by participants symptomizes the 'considerable flexibility' that ordinary employees often have 'to create their own interpretation of what is going on' (Thachenkery 1992: 231; cf. Rhodes 2000). It suggests that while stories may be 'the vigilance of intersecting gazes' (Foucault 1977: 217), the institutional gaze is not one that is easily co-opted by an elite, but characterized instead by complicated discursive dynamics which permit considerable plurivocity (Boje 1991, 1995).

As we have sought to illustrate, one reason why organizations cannot simply be constituted monologically is that the identity-constitutive stories told about organizations also directly impinge on the social identities of their participants. People author narratives not just to account for their organizations and other communities, but to 'enact' versions of themselves and their relationships to other social categories (Browning 1991). As Scott and Lane (2000: 44) have pointed out, organizational identities are constructed 'by managers and stakeholders who are simultaneously engaged in the construction of their individual identities'. Elsbach's (1999) classification of different forms of individual–organization relations (i.e. identification, dis-identification, schizo-identification, and neutral identification) is interesting, because it provides a four-fold typology of the different ways in which individuals relate their self-narratives to multiple organization narratives. In this perspective, the general organizational 'conversation' (Lyotard 1984) is composed of a multiplicity of plot lines that individuals and groups elaborate, refine, accept, and discard as they seek to make sense of their work, their organization, and themselves (Weick 1995). Individuals are enmeshed in a complicated series of intersecting and sometimes competing dialogues in which they become subjugated to some views and resistant to others. In these ways, individuals, groups and organizations continuously create and re-create themselves in what are highly reflexive processes of interpretation and enactment (Goffman 1959).

Perhaps the most interesting aspect of our case is its illustration of the extent to which an organizational identity is 'contested and negotiated through iterative interactions' between various stakeholders (Scott and Lane 2000: 44). Our view of individual and organizational identities as constituted by their self-narratives is, we contend, a plausible representation of the dynamic, normally hybrid, and often ambivalent connections and commonalities which link and distinguish the individual and organizational levels of analysis. By allowing for individual and organizational narratives to over-lap, inter-weave, distance and dissociate, we are better able to characterize the complexity inherent in the distinct and specific associations that highly individuated people enter into with the organizations in which they participate.

Such a view parallels broad debates within the social sciences centred on the dissolution of the unified subject (e.g. Barthes 1968, 1977; Foucault 1984; Lacan 1978; Derrida 1976) and its replacement by 'a contradictory, de-centred subject displaced across the range of discourses in which he or she participates' (Curran et al. 1982: 25). Transposed into organizational analysis, this perspective leads, as our case illustrates, to a view of participants 'as a set of positional, relational, subjective, and temporary ideas' and organization identities as collections of narrative 'identifications based on the range of positions held by individuals and their groups' (Baack and Prasch 1997: 137, 139).

Conclusion

In this paper we have focused on organizations as polyphonic dialogues through which are generated and elaborated a multiplicity of individual and collective identity narratives which variously stand alone, inform each other, harmonize and clash. Our particular emphasis has been on the different identity narratives that participants in Westville Institute authored in conversation with the researcher, and on what these narratives reveal regarding stories as sites of hegemonic struggle. The main thrust of our work has been to illustrate some of the dynamics by which social actors within storytelling organizations are 'constituted as subjects who exercise or submit to power relations' (Foucault 1984: 49). Identity, we have argued, is a central concern for participants in organizations (Knights and Morgan 1991: 267) for whom stark and seemingly irreconcilable differences between self-authored and elite-sponsored identity narratives can engender dislocating polarizing identity dualities which complicate people's 'sense of who they are and what they stand for' (Dutton and Dukerich 1991: 550). Our paper also usefully, (we hope), empiricizes a theoretical perspective that regards stories as identity performances 'of each storytelling organization' (Boje et al. 1999: 355) and thus contributes to our understanding of organization as 'a pandemonium of voices from which pattern emerges, a polyphony in which each person is the centre' (Barry and Hazen 1996: 53).

Our decision to represent this research in a narrative genre reflects a belief that stories most appropriately permit 'the exposition of the intersubjectivity of organizational life' (Rhodes 1997: 12). We have sought to question the homogenizing and totalizing accounts of an organizational elite by engaging many participants in dialogue and listening for dissonant voices. Such an approach, we contend, has allowed us to offer an interpretation of 'the pattern of interactions comprising the organizational identity' (Diamond 1988: 186-187) of Westville Institute. Moreover, just as the individual and collective identity narratives we have investigated are the constantly evolving products of reflexive processes (McAdams 1996; Ricoeur 1991), so we have actively sought to reflect on our own processes of authorship, learning and discovery while writing (and re-writing) this paper. In this way, we hope to have synthesized a persuasive and verisimilitudinous version of some of the storylines by which participants read meaning into their work organization.

Note

* Portions of this paper were written while Andrew Brown was on sabbatical at Hong Kong University.

1. A pseudonym.

References

Albert, Stuart
1992 'The algebra of change'. *Research in Organizational Behavior* 14: 179–229.

Albert, Stuart, and David A.Whetten
1985 'Organizational identity' in *Research in organizational behaviour*, Vol. 7. L.L. Cummings and B.M. Staw (eds.), 263–295. Greenwich: JAI Press.

Adler, Patricia A., and Peter Adler
1994 'Observational techniques' in *Handbook of qualitative research*. N. Denzin and Y. Lincoln (eds.), 377–392. Thousand Oaks, CA: Sage.

Aldrich, Howard, and Marlene C. Fiol
1994 'Fools rush in? The institutional context of industry creation'. *Academy of Management Review* 19: 645–667.

Andre, Rae, and Peter J. Frost, *editors*
1997 *Researchers hooked on teaching: noted scholars discuss the synergies of teaching and research.* London: Sage.

Ashforth, Blake E., and Fred Mael
1989 'Social Identity Theory and the organization'. *Academy of Management Review* 14: 20–40.

Ashforth, Blake E., and Fred Mael
1996 'Organizational identity and strategy as a context for the individual'. *Advances in Strategic Management* 13: 19–26.

Atkinson, Paul
1990 *The ethnographic imagination.* London: Routledge.

Baack, Donald, and Thomas Prasch
1997 'The death of the subject and the life of the organization. Implications of new approaches to subjectivity for organizational analysis'. *Journal of Management Inquiry* 6/2: 131–141.

Bakhtin, Mikhail, M.
1986 *Speech genres and other late essays,* translated by C. Emerson. Minneapolis: University of Minnesota Press.

Banaji, Mahzarin. R., and Deborah. A. Prentice
1994 'The self in social contexts'. *Annual Review of Psychology* 45: 297–332.

Barry, David, and Michael Elmes
1997 'Strategy retold: Toward a narrative view of strategic'. *Academy of Management Review* 22: 429–453.

Barry, David, and Mary Ann Hazen
1996 'Do you take your body to work?' in *Postmodern management and organization theory*. D.M. Boje, R.P. Gephart, and T.J. Thatchenkery (eds.), 140–153. Thousand Oaks, CA: Sage.

Barthes, Roland
1977 'Introduction to the structural analysis of narratives' in *Image-music-text*. S. Heath (ed.), 79–124. New York: Hill and Wang.

Bartlett, Frederick C.
1932 *Remembering*. Cambridge: Cambridge University Press.

Bateson, Gregory
1979 *Mind and nature: A necessary unity*. Toronto: Bantam Books.

Berger, Peter, and Thomas Luckmann
1966 *The social construction of reality*. New York: Anchor.

Berzonsky, Michael D.
1988 'Self-theorists, identity-status, and social cognition' in *Self, ego, and identity: Integrative approaches*. D.K. Lapsley and F. Clark Power (eds.), 243–262. New York: Springer.

Beyer, Janice M.
1981 'Ideologies, values and decision-making in orgaizations' in *Handbook of organizational design*. P.C. Nystrom and W.H. Starbuck (eds.), 166–202. Oxford: Oxord University Press.

Blasi, Augusto
1988 'To be or not to be: Self and authenticity, identity and ambivalence' in *Self, ego, and identity: Integrative approaches*. D.K. Lapsley and F. Clark Power (eds.), 226–242. New York: Springer.

Boje, David M.
1991 'The story-telling organization: a study of story performance in an office supply firm'. *Administrative Science Quarterly* 36: 106–126.

Boje, David M.
1995 'Stories of the storytelling organization: A postmodern analysis of Disney as "Tamara-Land"'. *Academy of Management Journal* 38/4: 997–1035.

Boje, David, M., John, T. Luhman, and Donald, E. Baack
1998 'Hegemonic stories and encounters between storytelling organizations'. *Journal of Management Inquiry* 8/4: 340–360.

Bonnen, R., and R. Fry
1991 'Organizational innovation and learning: four patterns of dialog between the dominant logic and the new logic'. *International Studies of Management and Organization* 21/4: 37–51.

Boyce, Mary E.
1996 'Organizational story and storytelling: a critical review'. *Journal of Organizational Change Management* 9/5:5–26.

Boyer, Ernest. L.
1990 *Scholarship reconsidered: priorities of the professoriate*. Princeton: Princeton University Press.

Brown, Andrew D.
1994 'Politics, symbolic action and myth-making in pursuit of legitimacy'. *Organization Studies* 15/6: 861–878.

Brown, Andrew D.
1997 'Narcissism, identity and legitimacy'. *Academy of Management Review* 22/3: 643–686.

Brown, Andrew D.
1998 'Narrative, politics and legitimation in an IT implementation'. *Journal of Management Studies* 35/ 1: 35–58.

Browning, Larry D.
1991 'Organizational narratives and organizational structure'. *Journal of Organizational Change Management* 4/3: 59–67.

Bruner Jerome
1990 *Acts of meaning*. Cambridge, MA: Harvard University Press.

Bruner, Jerome
1991 'The narrative construction of reality'. *Critical Inquiry* 18: 1–21.

Brunsson, Nils
1989   *The organization of hypocrisy: talk, decisions and actions in organizations*. Chichester: Wiley.

Buren
1962   Cited in E. Harvey and R. Mills 1970 'Patterns of organizational adaptation: a political perspective' in *Power in organizations*. Mayer N. Zald (ed.), 181–213. Nashville, TN: Vanderbilt University Press.

Burgoyne, John G.
1995   'Learning from experience: from individual discovery to meta-dialogue via the evolution of transition myths'. *Personnel Review* 24/6: 61–72.

Burke, Kenneth
1968   'Definition of man' in *Language as symbolic action: Essays on life, literature, and method*. K. Burke (ed.), 3–24. Berkeley, CA: University of Southern California Press.

Burrell, Gibson
1988   'Modernism, postmodernism, and organizational analysis 2: the contribution of Michel Foucault'. *Organization Studies* 9/2: 221–235.

Chia, Robert
1996   'The problem of reflexivity in organizational research: Towards a postmodern science of organization'. *Organization* 3/1: 31–59.

Clegg, Stewart M.
1981   'Organizations and control'. *Administrative Science Quarterly* 26: 545–562.

Clegg, Stewart M.
1989   *Frameworks of power*. London: Sage.

Clegg, Stewart M.
1994   'Power relations and the constitution of the resistant subject' in *Resistance and power in the organization*. J. M. Jermier, D. Knights, W. R. Nord (eds.), 274–325. London: Routledge.

Collins, Randall
1975   *Conflict sociology: Toward an explanatory science*. Cambridge: Academic Press.

Czarniawska Barbara
1995a 'Narration or science? Collapsing the division in organization studies'. *Organization* 2/1: 11–33.

Czarniawska Barbara
1995b 'Rhetoric and modern organizations'. *Studies in Cultures, Organizations and Societies* 1/2: 147–152.

Czarniawska, Barbara
1997   *Narrating the organization, dramas of institutional identity*. Chicago: The University of Chicago Press.

Dahler-Larsen, Peter
1997   'Organizational identity as a crowded category' in *'Cultural complexity in organizations: inherent contrasts and contradictions'*. S.A. Sackmann (ed.), 367–389. London: Sage.

Davis, Fred
1979   *Yearning for yesterday: a sociology of nostalgia*. London: Collier Macmillan.

Della Fave, Richard, L.
1991   'Ritual and the legitimation of inequality'. *Sociological Perspectives* 34/1: 21–38.

Diamond, Michael A.
1988   'Organizational identity: A psychoanalytic exploration of organizational meaning'. *Administration and Society* 20/2: 166–190.

Dowling, John, and Jeffrey Pfeffer
1975   'Organizational legitimacy: Social values and organizational behaviour'. *Pacific Sociological Review* 18: 122–136.

Dutton Jane E., and Janet M.Dukerich
1991   'Keeping an eye on the mirror: image and identity in organizational adaptation'. *Academy of Management Journal* 34: 517–554.

Dutton, Jane E., Janet M. Dukerich, and Celia V. Harquail
1994   'Organizational images and member identification'. *Administrative Science Quarterly* 39: 239–263.

Eccles, R. G., N. Nohria, and J. D. Berkley
1992   *Beyond the hype: Rediscovering the essence of management*. Boston: Harvard Business School Press.

Elsbach, Kimberly D.
1999 'An expanded model of organizational identification'. *Research in Organizational Behaviour* 21: 163–200.

Elsbach, Kimberly D., and C. Bhattacharaya
1998 'Organizational disidentification'. Paper presented at the annual meetings of the Academy of Management, Boston, MA.

Elsbach, Kimberly D., and Roderick M. Kramer
1996 'Members' responses to organizational identity threats: Encountering and countering the *Business Week* rankings'. *Administrative Science Quarterly* 41: 442–477.

Evered, Roger, and Meryl R. Louis
1981 'Alternative perspectives in the organizational sciences: "inquiry from the inside" and "inquiry from the outside"'. *Academy of Management Review* 6: 385–396.

Ezzy, Douglas
1998 'Theorizing narrative identity: symbolic interactionism and hermeneutics'. *Sociological Quarterly* 39/2: 239–252.

Fineman, Stephen, *editor*
1993 *Emotion in organizations.*Thousand Oaks, CA: Sage.

Fisher, Walter R.
1984 'Narration as a human communication paradigm: the case of public moral argument'. *Communication Monographs* 51: 1–22.

Ford, Jeffrey D.
1999 'Organizational change as shifting conversations'. *Journal of Organizational Change Management* 12: 480–500.

Foucault, Michel
1977 *Discipline and punish: The birth of the prison*. New York: Vintage.

Foucault Michel.
1980 *Power/knowledge: selected interviews and other writings, 1972–1977*. New York: Pantheon.

Foucault, Michel
1984 'What is an author?' in *A Foucault reader*, 2nd. Ed. Edited by P. Rabinow. New York: Pantheon.

Gabriel, Yiannis
1993 'Organizational nostalgia: Reflections on the Golden Age' in *Emotion in organizations*. S. Fineman (ed.), 118–141. London: Sage.

Gagliardi, Pasquale
1986 'The creation and change of organizational cultures: a conceptual framework'. *Organization Studies* 2/2: 117–134.

Gagnon, John H.
1992 'The self, its voices, their discord' in *Investigating subjectivity: Research on lived experience*. C. Ellis and M.G. Flaherty (eds.), 221–243. Newbury Park: Sage.

Geertz, Clifford
1973 *The interpretation of cultures*. New York: Basic Books.

Gephart, Robert P.
1993 'The textual approach: Risk and blame in disaster sensemaking'. *Academy of Management Journal* 36: 1465–1514.

Gergen, Mary M.
1998 'Proliferating discourses: resources for relationships'. *Organization* 5/2: 277–280.

Gheradi, Silvia
1995 *Gender, symbolism and organizational cultures*. London: Sage.

Gioia, Dennis A., Majken Schultz, and Kevin G. Corley
2000 'Organizational identity, image, and adaptive instability'. *Academy of Management Review* 25: 63–81.

Gioia, Dennis A., and James B. Thomas
1996 'Identity, image, and issue interpretation: sensemaking during strategic change in academia'. *Administrative Science Quarterly* 41: 370–403.

Goffman, Erving
1959 *The presentation of self in everyday life*. New York: Doubleday.

Gramsci, Antonio
1971 *Selections from the prison note-books*. London: Lawrence and Wishart.

Grove, Andrew
1997 *Only the paranoid survive: How to exploit the crisis points that challenge every company and career.* London: HarperCollins.

Habermas, Jurgen
1973 *Legitimation crisis*. Boston: Beacon Press.

Harman, Kay M.
1990 'Culture and conflict in academic organizations: symbolic aspects of university worlds'. *Journal of Educational Administration* 27/3: 30–54.

Hazen, Mary Ann
1993 'Towards polyphonic organization'. *Journal of Organizational Change Management* 6/5: 15–26.

Heider, Fritz
1958 *The psychology of interpersonal relations*. New York: Wiley.

Hirschhorn, Larry
1997 *The workplace within*. Cambridge, MA: MIT Press.

Hogg, Michael, A., and D. Abrams
1990 'Social motivation, self-esteem and social identity' in *Social identity theory: Constructive and critical advances*. D. Abrams and M.A. Hogg (eds.), 28–47. London: Harvester Wheatsheaf.

Horn, Rebecca
1996 'Negotiating research access to organizations'. *The Psychologist*, December 1996, 551–554.

Humphreys, Michael
1999 'An ethnographic study of two higher education faculties: reminiscing in tempo'. Unpublished Ph.D. Thesis, Nottingham University Business School.

Jeffcutt, Paul
1994 'From interpretation to representation in organizational analysis: Postmodernism, ethnography and organizational symbolism'. *Organization Studies* 15/2: 241–274.

Jermier, John M., David Knights, and Walter R. Nord, *editors*
1994 *Resistance and power in organization*. London: Routledge.

Johnston, Ron J.
1996 'Managing how academics manage' in *Working in higher education*. R. Cuthbert (ed.), 101–118. Buckingham: SRHE /Open University Press.

Kamens, David H.
1977 'Legitimating myths and educational organizations: the relationship between organizational ideology and formal structure'. *American Sociological Review* 42: 208–219.

Kets de Vries, Manfred F. R., *editor*
1984 *The irrational executive*. New York: International Universities Press.

Kets de Vries, Manfred F. R.
1995 *Organizational paradoxes*, 2nd. Ed. London: Tavistock.

Kets de Vries, Manfred F. R.
1996 *Family business human dilemmas in the family firm*, London: Thomson.

Kleugel, James R., and Eliot R. Smith
1986 *Beliefs about inequality: Americans' views about what is and what ought to be*. New York: Aldine De Gruyter.

Knights, David
1992 'Changing spaces: the disruptive impact of a new epistemological location for the study of management'. *Academy of Management Review* 17: 514–536.

Knights, David, and Gareth Morgan
1991 'Corporate strategy, organizations and subjectivity'. *Organization Studies* 12/2: 251–273.

Lacan, Jacques
1978 *The four fundamental concepts of psychoanalysis*. Edited by J.A. Miller. New York: Norton.

Lenski, Gerhard E.
1966 *Power and privilege*. New York: McGraw-Hill.

Lyotard, Jean-Francois
1984 *The postmodern condition: A report on knowledge*, translated by G. Bennington and B. Massumi. Manchester: Manchester University Press.

446   Michael Humphreys, Andrew D. Brown

MacIntyre, Alisdair
1981 *After virtue: A study in moral theory.* Paris: University of Notre Dame Press.

Mandler, Jean Matter
1984 *Stories, scripts and scenes: Aspects of schemata theory.* Hillsdale, NJ: Lawrence Erlbaum Associates.

March, James G.
1994 'How we talk and how we act: administrative theory and administrative life' in *New thinking in organizational behaviour.* H. Tsoukas (ed.), 53–69. Oxford: Butterworth Heinmann.

March, James G., and Johan P Olsen
1976 'Organizational choice under ambiguity' in *Ambiguity and choice in organizations.* J. G. March and J. P. Olsen, 10–23. Bergen: Universitetsforlaget.

McAdams, Dan, P.
1996 'Personality, modernity, and the storied self: A contemporary framework for studying persons'. *Psychological Inquiry* 7: 295–321.

Meyer, John, and Brian W. Rowan
1977 'Institutionalised organizations: Formal structure, myth and ceremony'. *American Journal of Sociology* 83: 340–361.

Nandhakumar, Joe, and Matthew Jones
1997 'Too close for comfort? Distance and engagement in interpretive information systems research'. *Information Systems Journal* 7: 109–131.

Parsons, Talcott
1978 *Action theory and the human condition.* New York: Free Press.

Pentland, Brian T.
1999 'Building process theory with narrative: From description to explanation'. *Academy of Management Review* 24: 711–724.

Pfeffer, Jeffrey.
1981 'Management as symbolic action: the creation and maintenance of organizational paradigms' in *Research in organizational behaviour,* Vol. 3. L.L. Cummings and B.M. Staw (eds.), 1– 52. Greenwich, CT: JAI Press.

Pfeffer, Jeffrey, and Gerald Salancik
1978 'Organizational decision making as a political process: the case of a university budget'. *Administrative Science Quarterly* 19: 135–151.

Pratt, Michael G., and Peter O. Foreman
2000 'Classifying managerial responses to multiple organizational identities'. *Academy of Management Review* 25: 18–42.

Putnam, Linda L
1983 'The interpretive perspective, an alternative to functionalism' in *Communication in organizations, an interpretive approach.* L.L. Putnam and M.E. Pacanowsky, (eds.), 31–54. Beverley Hills: Sage.

Rachel, Janet
1996 'Ethnography: practical implementation' in *Handbook of qualitative research methods for psychology and the social sciences.* J.T.E. Richardson (ed.), 113–124. Leicester: The British Psychological Society Books.

Rhodes, Carl
1997 'The legitimation of learning in organizational change'. *Journal of Change Management* 10/1: 10–20.

Rhodes, Carl
2000 ' "Doing" knowledge at work, dialogue, monologue and power in organizational learning' in *Research and knowledge at work.* J. Garrick and C. Rhodes (eds.), 217–231. London: Routledge.

Ricoeur, Paul
1984 *Time and narrative,* Vol. 1, translated by K. McLaughlin and D. Pellauer. Chicago: The University of Chicago Press.

Ricoeur, Paul
1985 *Time and narrative,* Vol. 2, translated by K. McLaughlin and D. Pellauer. Chicago: The University of Chicago Press: Chicago.

Ricoeur, Paul
1988 *Time and narrative,* Vol. 3, translated by K. Blamey and D. Pellauer. Chicago: University of Chicago Press.

Robins, Kevin
1996 'Interrupting identities: Turkey/ Europe' in *Questions of cultural identity*. S. Hall and P. Du Gay (eds.), 61–86. London: Sage.

Rose, Nikolas
1989 *Governing the soul, the shaping of the private self*. London: Routledge.

Rosen, Michael
1985 'Breakfast at Spiro's: dramaturgy and dominance'. *Journal of Management* 11/2: 31–48.

Scott, Peter
1995 *The meanings of mass higher education*. Buckingham: Open University Press.

Scott, Susanne G., and Vicki R. Lane
2000 'A stakeholder approach to organizational identity'. *Academy of Management Review* 25: 43–62.

Senge, Peter
1990 *The fifth discipline: The art and practice of the learning organization*. New York: Doubleday.

Smith, Douglas K., and Robert C. Alexander
1988 *Fumbling the future: How Xerox invented, then ignored, the first personal computer*. New York: William Morrow.

Stacey, Ralph D
1996 *Complexity and creativity in organizations*. San Francisco: Berret Koehler.

Suchman, Mark C.
1995 'Managing legitimacy: Strategic and institutional approaches'. *Academy of Management Review* 20/3: 571–610.

Tajfel, Henri
1982 *Social identity and intergroup relations*. Cambridge: Cambridge University Press, and Paris: Editions de la Maison des Sciences de l'Homme.

Thatchenkery, Tojo Joseph, and Punya Upadhyaya
1996 'Organizations as a play of multiple and dynamic discourses: an example from a global social change organization' in *Postmodern management and organization theory*. D.M. Boje, R.P. Gephart, and T.J. Thatchenkery (eds.), 308–330. Thousand Oaks, CA: Sage.

Van Maanen, John
1988 *Tales of the field: on writing ethnography*. Chicago: The University of Chicago Press.

Watson, Tony J.
1995 'Shaping the story: rhetoric, persuasion and creative writing in organizational ethnography'. *Studies in Cultures, Organizations and Societies* 1: 301–311.

Weber, Max
1968 *Economy and society*. Berkeley, CA: University of California Press.

Weick, Karl E.
1995 *Sensemaking in organizations*. Thousand Oaks, CA: Sage.

White, Hayden
1973 *Metahistory. The historical imagination in nineteenth-century europe*. Baltimore, MD: John Hopkins University Press.

White, Hayden
1987 *The content of the form: Narrative discourse and historical representation*. Baltimore, MD: John Hopkins University Press.

Wilkins, Alan L., and Michael P. Thompson
1991 'On getting the story crooked (and straight)'. *Journal of Organizational Change Management* 4/3: 18–26.

Wilson, Stephen R.
1997 'Self actualisation and culture' in *Motivation and culture*. D. Munro, J.F. Schumaker and S.C. Carr (eds.), 85–96. London: Routledge.

Zabusky, S. E., and Stephen R. Barley
1997 'You can't be a stone if you're cement: Reevaluating the emic identities of scientists in organizations' in *Research in organizational behavior*, Vol. 19. B.M. Staw and L.L. Cummings (eds.), 361–404. Greenwich CT: JAI Press.

Part IV
The Theatre and Performance
of Management

[14]

Managing as a Performing Art

Iain L. Mangham

Centre for Executive Development, University of Bath, England

SUMMARY   This paper considers the activities of senior managers as isomorphic with the activities of actors. It takes *performing* as not a matter of metaphor, but a matter of form; life at the top of an organization is intrinsically theatrical; each of us is blessed or cursed with histrionic sensibility. Proceeding by way of a comparison of Edmund Kean and Lee Iacocca it touches upon matters of text and interpretation, rehearsal and performance and the importance of individuation. The argument – such as it is – is that both Kean and Iacocca perform *themselves*, the former's Richard III, the latter's Chrysler being the fullest realizations of that which was, hitherto, inchoate and emergent. The final part of the paper is concerned with the implications of this perspective for education, training and development; current management education appears geared to reduce rather than to promote individuality. Techniques are imposed and answers are provided and the entire educational performance revolves around teachers as performers rather than managers as performers. The way to become a management star, it is suggested, is to do managing, not simply to be audience for academic stars.

Managing as Performing Art

On Saturday, 12th February, 1814, Edmund Kean appeared in *Richard III* at Drury Lane; barely a fortnight before he had triumphed in *The Merchant of Venice*. *The Morning Post* described his Richard as 'brilliant ... one of the finest pieces of acting we have ever beheld, or perhaps the stage has ever known', and went on to give a graphic account of his acting:

'His awakening from his nightmare with the groan, "Give me another horse", sent a shudder of terror through the audience. He staggered forward, leaning on his sword, sank on one knee, then started back, as if he wished to rise. His free hand, held high in the air, shook violently, even to the fingertips. Still shaking with fright, he advanced on his knees to the front of the stage. Then, with the words, "Conscience avaunt!" he thrust his fears behind him, and rising to his feet, he brandished his sword above his head and shrieked triumphantly, "Richard's himself again".'

(FitzSimons, 1976)

The English Theatre was never to be the same again.

Over one hundred and fifty years later, another great performer took to the boards. Not at the Theatre Royal, Drury Lane, but at the Chrysler plant at Highland Park, Detroit:

'Once I had dealt with the executives, I started in on the unions ... Today the business world takes union concessions for granted. But back then, we were pioneers.

'... I don't mean it was easy. I had to lay it on the line. I talked tough to them. "Hey, boys," I said, "I've got a shotgun at your head. I've got thousands of jobs available at seventeen bucks an hour. I've got none at twenty. So you better come to your senses."

'... During 1980, I went to every single Chrysler plant in order to speak directly to the workers. At a series of mass meetings, I thanked them for sticking with us during these bad times. I told them that when things got better, we'd try to get them back to parity with Ford and GM workers but that it wouldn't happen overnight. I gave them my pitch, and they hooted and hollered, and some of them applauded and some of them booed.'

(Iacocca, 1984)

The American motor industry was never to be the same again.

This paper addresses directly and exclusively the notion of performance in the theatre and within enterprises. In part it is derived from *Organizations as Theatre* (1987) which I wrote with Michael Overington and from my own subsequent revisions to ideas contained in that book (1988, 1989); in part from Iredell Jenkins' work on performance (1970). It springs from my obsession with people:

> 'I ought to tell you that I have an insatiable curiosity about people; it's impossible for me to see and hear enough of them. The way they get along with each other, the way they develop friendships and enmities, sell onions, plan military campaigns, get married, make tweed suits, circulate forged banknotes, dig potatoes, observe the heavenly bodies; the way they cheat, favour, teach, exploit, respect, mutilate and support one another; the way they hold meetings, form societies, conduct intrigues ...'
>
> (Brecht, 1965)

I am particularly interested in the behaviour of *stars* – in the theatre, cinema, opera house, House of Commons, local government, university, bank, factory or office. The paper touches upon notions of texts, acting, interpretation, audience, response, standards, self and education. Throughout, the emphasis is upon the holistic nature of performing – as every awards ceremony confirms, every star is supported by hundreds who each need to be thanked individually – and upon its processual nature. Actors and senior managers are involved in performing, not in a performance; stars, particularly in the theatre and within business enterprises, appear live before their audiences and must elicit appropriate responses moment by moment, *reading* the situation so that they 'get it right on the night'.

All the world's a stage

I will begin with the briefest outlines of what might be taken to be the theatrical analogy and its place within 'interpretive' approaches to the study of human behaviour. As Trujillo (1987) has indicated elsewhere, widely accepted and familiar functionalist paradigms emphasize how 'organizational reality "determines" organizational behaviour, whereas the interpretive paradigm emphasizes how organizational behaviour "creates" organizational reality.' Morgan and Smircich (1980) suggest that various approaches to the study of organizational behaviour may be ranged along a continuum ranging from objective to subjective perspectives on

reality. At the one extreme are functionalist perspectives such as behaviourism which treats organizational reality as something concrete and durable and sees those participating in organizations as responding to stimuli in more or less 'predictable and determinate ways'. At the other extreme are those perspectives which treat organizational members as fictive and normative beings – wilful persons who create and shape the world to their own ends. The theatrical or dramaturgical perspective falls somewhere in the middle of this continuum; actors both create and respond to the situations in which they locate themselves. Edmund Kean and Lee Iacocca are at one and the same time capable of transcending the 'scripts' and 'settings' within which they are operating and of embodying them. More of this later.

The theatrical analogy has been around a long time; the persistence of the image has turned it into a commonplace of speech in which its analogical roots are obscured. We enact roles, play our parts, stage events, prompt others, take our cues, perform duties, display our emotions and so on. We do all of these things with little sense that we are speaking metaphorically. This everyday language has become the stuff of social science with little or no acknowledgement of its origins; role theory in particular makes extensive use of theatrical terminology without, for the most part, subjecting it to analysis. Others more squarely in the tradition within which this essay attempts to place itself have embraced the analogy explicitly and extensively. Of these, perhaps Erving Goffman is the best known and Kenneth Burke the most profound. Goffman is interested in delineating what is going on in social interaction. He sees individuals as mutually presenting themselves to one another; each seeking to create an impression and to control the response of the other parties to the interaction. For him all social relationships may be depicted as drama; people are personae, masks in relation to and with each other, and attempt through performance to enact the line of action which they take to be appropriate to a given situation. For Goffman this is not a matter of a game or a matter of falseness; most people are what they communicate, but as people can only realize themselves in communicating, in action, in performing (Goffman, 1959). Goffman is well aware that his use of theatrical terms is a recourse to simile or analogy. He claims that life may be depicted as *like* theatre. For Kenneth Burke life *is* drama. He argues that since human relationships are created and sustained by individuals their success or failure is dependent upon the quality of our performances, how well we play our parts (Combs and Mansfield, 1976). From a Burkean perspective, Iacocca's performance as a manager would be not simply a matter of what is communicated, but how it is communicated; there is an aesthetic quality about his encounters with the workforce which is more than a simple matter of dominance. It is a planned, shaped and rehearsed enactment of 'tough management', constructed and carried through to manage impressions and secure agreement. For Burke, the presence of drama in everyday life is not a matter of metaphor but a matter of form; life is inherently dramatic; each of us is blessed (or cursed) with histrionic sensibility. For him, as for the Elizabethans, *Totus Mundus Agit Histrionem* – All the world is indeed a theatre (Burke, 1968, 1969a, 1969b).

The position adopted in this essay is heavily influenced by Burke and his followers; I am not arguing that Iacocca's performance is *like* a performance by Edmund Kean, I am claiming that it *is* isomorphic; his performing, like yours or mine *is* theatre.

An Actor Prepares

For the most part actors in the theatre work from a script. Somebody has written a series of lines; this is the basis for the performance that is seen in the theatre. The challenge of the performer is to bring this text to full realization; the term performance means a 'carrying through to completion'. As it stands, the script has nothing more than potential; the performer's text is an abbreviated and necessarily incomplete version of a possible work of art; it requires a performer and an audience (which, occasionally, may be one and the same person) to give it form.

Performing involves selection and choice: of setting, of costumes, of actors, of rhythm, of colour, of pitch, cadence, emphasis and pace. Such choices are made as a consequence of overall interpretation – what is it that is to be brought to completion? What does the text signify? There is simply no way of creating in advance a full score for a play; such a score would have to specify moment by moment 'sizes, shapes, colours, inflections, tones of voice, word emphasis, rhythms, duration of pauses, placements of actors on stage, movements, tempos and

so on and would require thousands of pages and would still be less precise than the score of Beethoven's Fifth Symphony' (Hornby, 1977).

To be sure, a script or a score sets apparent limits to interpretation. It is possible but perverse to play *Hamlet* as a farce and difficult if not impossible to stage *The Comedy of Errors* as a tragedy (Mangham and Overington, 1986). The script is not usually taken to be simply a matter of squiggles on a page; it provides lines for actors to speak and it affords them an opportunity for display, but above all it sets up the basic relationships and creates the patterns of behaviour which inform the finished performance. What is seen on the stage is never simply the text, but always an interpretation, a 'reading'; a circumstance in which the script is embedded in the performing and realized through it.

It is clear that what occurs in the theatre is a process through which meanings that are taken to be implicit to a particular text are rendered more explicit. The actor must decide what he or she is to convey and must embody that interpretation in the actions he or she displays to the audience; the message of the play must be rendered intelligible if a performance is to be taken as successful. The sequence is interesting; the actor starts with the text which he or she must interpret 'faithfully', but, in turn, the embodiment of his/her interpretation must have meaning for us. In other words an actor must embody the unique aspects of the text by means that are accessible to us the audience; in our turn we interpret the action we see on the stage and this interpretation leads us to play our parts as a good audience. Theatre (and social life) is a matter of collusion. An author drafts a system of literary signs – a play – which is not addressed to readers, but actors. The actors, normally under the guidance and supervision of a director, transpose the literary signs into a system of theatre signs which comprise verbal and nonverbal elements. The playgoers' activity consists in observing the dramatic information in an attitude of 'external concentration of apperceiving and structuring it; in understanding, experiencing and finally making it part of their fund of aesthetic knowledge' (Lazarowicz, 1977). A successful performance is the result of a triadic collusion between author, actor and audience. Throughout the following discussion, it must be remembered that the *process* is not one of interpreting followed by expressing, but a commingling of the two. Each aspect is present from the inception of the process, acting reciprocally upon one another, and each is present at the time of performing: a good actor adapts and adjusts his or her performing in the very moment of delivering it. Though interpreting and expressing can legitimately be discriminated for purposes of analysis, in performing they exist symbiotically.

The *reading* any actor makes of a particular play is influenced by a number of factors: intelligence, disposition, experience, fellow actors, expectations of the audience. To illustrate let me call once more upon Edmund Kean. For his performance as Shylock or Richard III, he clearly studied the text, but he, like the rest of us when seeking to explicate a text or a situation, could only study it from *his* own perspective, through the medium of *his* ideas, *his* experiences, *his* way of perceiving. John Philip Kemble, the great classical actor whom Kean was to replace, approached the parts he played with long and serious study. His acting was relatively 'cold'; he rarely displayed intense emotion upon the stage, he was, therefore, at his best in the roles of characters pre-occupied with themselves, such as King John, Brutus and, above all, Coriolanus (FitzSimons, 1976). What is more, every line he spoke contributed to the slow, gradual development of character. It is important to note in the present context that his slow and clear enunciation has been attributed to his asthma; that his style of tragic acting was, at least in part, a making of virtue out of necessity. His readings of the great parts were careful, graceful and, possibly, lacking in energy. Edmund Kean's background and inclination was very different to that of Kemble, as can be seen from this report of his activities a couple of years before his triumph at Drury Lane:

'In August, the company were in Totnes and, on the sixth of the month, he again had a benefit. In the hope of attracting a large audience, he arranged a varied entertainment. The main item was *The Merchant of Venice*, with himself as Shylock. After this he danced in a pas de deux. Next came a serious pantomime, *The Savages*, in which he played Kojah, the Noble Savage. In the course of this pantomime, he took part in a "Savage Pas de Trois"; demonstrated the "Otaheitan method of using the Bow and Arrow"; engaged in "Several Extraordinary Combats with Bamboos, Battle Axe, Shield and Sword"; delineated "Savage Distraction" and danced a "Savage Dance of Peace" – all being exact representations as described by "that wonderful Navigator, Captain Cook".'

Clearly such an actor was likely to read plays in a very different manner to John Philip Kemble and actors of his ilk. Given Kean's energy, there can be little surprise to find his performances described as like 'reading Shakespeare by flashes of lightning'. Every performer brings to the text his or her own experience which may or may not be sufficient for the demands made upon it. Clearly Kean's enormous energy was a factor in his performances; clearly he apprehended plays in terms of the opportunities they afforded him for vigorous display. In making this point, I am not claiming that the only distinction between Kean's acting and that of his contemporaries was a matter of energy; he was also credited with an ability to invest passages of verse with sense and the facility to speak naturally rather than in an artificial or stagey fashion. The point I am making is that every performance is imbued with the body of experience and skill the performer brings to it and that these attributes inform the act of interpreting as well the process of expression. The diminutive Edmund Kean, schooled in the provincial theatre, driven to provide for himself and his family by giving lessons in elocution, dancing and fencing, wildly ambitious, is bound to approach the plays of Shakespeare in a very different manner to that of the tall, urbane, scholarly, asthmatic John Philip Kemble. The latter's performances could perhaps have been seen as subtle, sophisticated, cool and distant; the former's as energetic, physical, emotional and immediate. Both readings, however, are rooted in the text. Were this not to be the case, were it to be unreasonable and unconvincing to read Shakespeare in Kemble's manner or Kean's, the performances would be seen as ineffective.

Concurrently with the effort to apprehend the text, the actor is forming in his or her mind an idea of what the finished performance will look like. It should be re-emphasized that interpretation and expression (of which mental simulation or rehearsal forms a part) may not be sharply distinct in their occurrence. As soon as the actor picks up a text, the two aspects of performance act reciprocally upon one another as they continue to do up to and including the actual performance. The actor monitors and adjusts his or her performance in performance; he or she edits in real time, apprehending and adjusting at the time of acting. As the performer scans the text he or she projects an idea of how it is to be realized; to invest a reading within any sense at all is to project a performance in the theatre of the head. Once a read-through is attempted, a rudimentary performance is necessary if one's fellow actors are to apprehend what the text *may* mean. Of course, in a strict analytical sense, the text consists of a series of potential meanings, aspects of an emerging interpretation, rather than a necessary semblance of a final performance, but in the very act of reading, some element of expression is necessary to provide a direction for characterization; some shape is demanded if the read through is to be anything more than gobbledegook. Kean, no less than any other actor, has an idea of how *Richard III* ought to be performed; his ideas are informed by his own experience and by a critical evaluation of the performances of other actors.

A read-through of the text will be coloured by these experiences and evaluations and will present Kean with a number of problems; some scenes will not work. To resolve the difficulties, no doubt Kean – like many another actor – simply tries it out; that is, the actor proceeds by a trial and error in a necessarily indeterminate manner to discover the problematic and render it less so with each resolution (some more transient and temporary than others) suggesting a partially new set of possibilities. The process is complete when a stage is reached when in the opinion of those involved it is appropriate to break off. Kean's performance, no less than Kemble's, Olivier's or Gambon's, is a matter of running things up provisionally – working from a set of ideas and intuitions – taking a look at what results in the light of standards deriving from experience and knowledge, modifying, rejecting or accepting the whole or aspects of it, before moving on to develop other ideas out of that which has so far been achieved.

Response and Stimulus

In the theatre actors, technicians, set designers, musicians, property masters, lighting artists, costume designers, directors and producers interact to 'discover' ideas and emotions from within a particular text and cooperate to render these discoveries meaningful to an audience. Part of this is clearly and unavoidably idiosyncratic, there can never be two identical performances of any text, but an extremely idiosyncratic performance runs the risk of leaving the audience bewildered. Too sharp a departure from 'tradition' may render a

performance unintelligible; a performance must be rooted in the tradition from which it grows, even though in its very realization it may transcend it. For Kean's performance to be adjudged valuable, its connection to the tradition of Kemble must be perceptible even if tenuous. Without such a connection most of the audience would not be able to respond to his interpretation. In the theatre as in social life, the meaning of a verbal event is *any* response to that event. Kean's audience could have responded to his histrionics by falling about with laughter, they could have defined his behaviour as ridiculous, as 'over the top'. His performing, like yours or mine, Iacocca's or John Harvey Jones', has no meaning in and of itself. Action – response – is a product of meaning attributed to an event by those with an interest in it. Kean, like the rest of us, seeks to shape meaning and control response: this, he proclaims, is how Richard is, I want you to respond to his 'fright', I want you to see him recover, 'thrust his fears behind him' and 'to triumph'. If the critic of *The Morning Post* is representative, Kean clearly succeeded in eliciting the desired response. His audience – or a significant proportion of it – was able to relate to his performing.

In this instance, however, we must remember that the English stage was never to be the same again; Kean's performance was paradigm breaking. As Hazlitt puts it, 'Before the night was ended, I had hailed in such poor words as I could muster at the moment, the advent, I might almost say the portent, of Edmund Kean.' Nonetheless, the case should not blind us to the fact that the performance can only be apprehended in terms of that which has gone before: '... If Mr Kean does not completely succeed in concentrating all the lines of character as drawn by Shakespeare, he gives an animation, vigour and relief to the part, which we have never seen surpassed. He is more refined than Cooke; more bold, varied, and original than Kemble, in the same character ... He gave to all the busy scenes of the play the greatest animation and effect. He filled every part of the stage ... on the whole the performance was the most perfect of anything that has been witnessed since the days of Garrick.'

Every performance on the stage may be taken to be a conjunction of interpreting, expressing and responding; the former informed by the actor's experience and intelligence, the latter by a sense of tradition and possibility. As audience, we judge a performance to be successful or not depending upon the fusion of these elements. Kean, no less than any other performer, must seek to understand his text using himself and his experience as a sounding board and he must embody and project his interpretation in such a manner that the audience can accommodate it. The process culminates (insofar as any process can be said to culminate) in a fusion of the actor's interpretation of the text and his or her embodiment of it.

It is difficult to say what makes a good performance. An actor can sense it: '... You hear everything as if for the first time. The performance is not so much new as newly revealed, the varnish stripped off, the paint bright again, detail discernible ... the text is sunk into your bones, so that it comes unbidden; it is the inevitable, the only response' (Callow, 1984). An audience may have something of the same experience; those who saw Kean clearly did. A good performance is all of a piece. The synthesis is apparently achieved without effort; in the bad performance we are too much aware of the parts at the expense of the whole. We question the *reading* or find that the actor is not up to it; he or she does not bring anything distinctive to the role. Even if the actor appears to understand what the play is about, we may note that he or she has not made a particular part their own; in good or great performances we speak of *Kean's, Olivier's, Sher's*, in bad we do not. We note that, however good the performer may be technically, he or she has not pulled it off. Sometimes we determine that a performance is bad because we cannot understand it; the actor is clearly giving the performance of his or her life, but in a manner that is way beyond currently accepted practice. Running through all of this, of course, is the disintegration of a performance into its constituent elements; the actor's reading of the text competes with his or her projection of it or his/her technique is so obtrusive that we cannot concentrate upon anything else. Or we may note that the star is 'good', but the set is wrong, the lighting poor, the direction bad, the supporting cast inadequate. A rounded performance demands that all of the parts cohere and none, save the performance of the star, dominates.

So what?

All very interesting (or not, according to your disposition and motivation for reading this article at

all), but what has it to do with the doing of managing? Everything. Managing is itself a form of performance; to manage is to engage in the art of performing. Iacocca is an accomplished performer of the drama that is Chrysler; John Harvey Jones stars in ICI plc, Michael Edwardes in a number of roles – Chloride, British Leyland (a classic melodrama), Mercury Communications, ICL, Dunlop. One South African in his time plays many parts ...

The analogy tells us, in general terms, that managing is a process that involves the reading and interpretation of events and circumstances and the expression and embodiment of that reading in action on the part of the manager. Action is eloquence. The text for the manager, however, is much less obvious than the playscript from which the stage or film actor works; it is not handed to him or her on the first day of rehearsal. He or she has to seek it out. It is shaped by the environment within which the organization operates, by its size, its technology, its history, its markets, it employees, their values, norms and behaviours and so on and, most importantly, it is rarely complete. But, before anything can be done, it has to be *read*. Here are a couple of instances of Iacocca reading Chrysler and beginning to shape his performance:

'Before the day was over, I noticed a couple of seemingly insignificant details that gave me pause. The first was that the office of the president, where Cafiero worked, was being used as a thoroughfare to get from one office to another. I watched in amazement as executives with coffee cups in their hands kept opening the door and walking right through the president's office. Right away I knew the place was in a state of anarchy. Chrysler needed a dose of order and discipline and quick.

'What I found at Chrysler were thirty five vice-presidents, each with his own turf. There was no real committee setup, no cement in the organizational chart, no system of meetings to get people talking to each other. I couldn't believe, for example, that the guy running the engineering department wasn't in constant touch with his counterpart in manufacturing. But that's how it was. Everybody worked independently. I took one look at that system and I almost threw up. That's when I knew I was in really deep trouble.'

His reading leads him to an interpretation which he claims to have found extremely alarming:

'All of Chrysler's problems really boiled down to the same thing: nobody knew who was on first. There was no team, only a collection of independent players, many of whom hadn't yet mastered their positions. Now, it's one thing to say all that and to understand in theoretical terms what it means. Believe me, it's quite another matter to see it unfold in front of you in living color. It's pretty scary to witness one of the world's largest corporations, playing for billions of dollars, going down the tubes without anybody being able to stop it. This was a tremendous shock to me. And each day brought more bad news.'

Iacocca's interpretation, like Kean's in tackling *Richard III*, is shot through with his personality, illuminated with his energy: 'I was ... confident of my own abilities. I knew the car business, and I knew I was good at it.' Like Kean, Iacocca was disposed to act, to do managing rather than to endlessly debate alternatives. Having made his reading he was ready to try something out, to run something up and see whether or not it would hang together: 'You can use the fanciest computers in the world and you can gather all the charts and numbers, but in the end you have to bring all your information together, set up a timetable, and *act*' (emphasis in the original). Like Kean, the acting is informed by experience: 'When you don't have all the facts, you sometimes have to draw on your experience. Whenever I read in a newspaper that Lee Iacocca likes to shoot from the hip, I say to myself: "Well, maybe he's been shooting for so long that by this time he has a pretty good idea of how to hit the target".'

The important point for the purposes of this essay is that, like all great performers, he claims that he was willing to try things out and back out if they were not successful. He notes that he was often fairly isolated in his improvizations: 'Another marketing first we put together with K and E was the money-back guarantee. "Buy one of our cars" we said. "Take it home, and within thirty days, if you don't like it *for any reason*, bring it back and we'll refund your money" ... We tried this one in 1981, and all of Detroit thought we were nuts ... But to the surprise of the sceptics, the program worked very well ... This one, too, was a revolutionary idea, and I'm glad that we tried it. The important thing to remember is that we were trying everything possible ...'

As reported, Iacocca's performance clearly broke the paradigm. His relations with government, with suppliers, with employees, with colleagues, with dealers and customers were such that they all had an impact upon his peers in the motor

industry. He goes beyond the tradition in which he has been brought up, he transcends the limitations of the art form that he inherits: the art of managing. 'Naturally, when I brought Doug Fraser (a union boss) onto our board, the business community went wild. They said: "You can't do that! You're putting the fox into the hen house. You've lost your mind!" ... Until then, no representative of labor had ever sat on the board of a major American corporation ...'

Iacocca is aware that he is a performer. Occasionally he operates without a script: 'I was on my own in those hearings. I had to ad-lib everything. The questions came fast and furious, and they were always loaded. Staff members were constantly passing notes to the senators and congressmen, and I had to respond to everything off the cuff ...' In many circumstances, however, although his interpretation may be informed by experience and intuition, his action appears rehearsed and scripted. He appears to have known what he was doing when he offered stock options to his employees, when he placed Doug Fraser on the Board, even when he asked the government for funds; in nearly every case he appears well rehearsed to defend his actions and to meet challenge with challenge. At times his set pieces sound good enough for Kean himself to have taken them on:

'On October 18, I made my first appearance before the House Subcommittee on Economic Stabilization of the Committee of Banking, Finance and Urban Affairs. All the members showed up, which in itself was unusual ...

'I began my testimony by stating our case very simply: "I am sure you know that I do not speak alone here today. I speak for the hundreds of thousands of people whose livelihood depends upon Chrysler remaining in business. It is that simple. Our one hundred forty thousand employees and their dependents, our forty-seven hundred dealers and their one hundred fifty thousand employees who sell and service our products, our nineteen thousand suppliers, and the two hundred fifty thousand people on their payrolls, and, of course, the families and dependents of all those constituents ...".'

They were apparently good enough for some of his critics:

'At the end of my long testimony and the subsequent interrogation, Senator Proxmire paid me a high compliment. "As you know," he said, "I am opposed to your request. But I have rarely heard a more eloquent, intelligent, well-informed witness than you have been today. You did a brilliant job and we thank you".'

Like Kean, Iacocca shapes and receives the desired response; total and absolute confirmation of his performance; like Kean, he precipitates the triadic collusion between text, performer and audience.

Both Kean and Iacocca begin with texts which they must apprehend, express and embody. Kean's texts tend to be much less fragmentary than those facing Iacocca, but both face essentially enigmatic circumstances which they must shape and illuminate by their own sensitivity and skill. Kean's texts, in a sense, are more readily accessible than those of Iacocca. The stage actor studies a part which, on most occasions, is written out for him by an author; the broad lines of the character of Richard III, whilst not completely determined for the actor, are strongly outlined by Shakespeare. Not so for Iacocca. The text that he must apprehend is not only Chrysler but also Iacocca. He is to star in a show partly of his own scripting. His Chrysler is very different to the performance that ran at the same theatre until he appeared. No one speaks of Cafiero's Chrysler; the performance was not of a piece, it was adjudged to be a bad one. What this signifies is that those who successfully tread the boards of an enterprise bring a considerable personal resource to the performance. For many, perhaps all of them, the enterprise provides the stage upon which they can fully realize the performance of their lives; here they become accomplished performers of their selves. In performing Chrysler – a classic melodrama where the heroine (the company itself) is rescued from a fate worse than death (insolvency), Lee Iacocca draws upon and considerably develops aspects of his self (Jenkins, 1970). He modifies, for example, his total faith in free enterprise; he learns in a way that it was never possible for him to learn at Ford the pain of laying employees off, he learns 'to keep going even in bad times', learns 'not to despair even when the world was falling apart'.

It is important to note that the self of Iacocca has much in common with all other human beings – he certainly bleeds when he is pricked (as the pages in his book referring to his relations with Henry Ford amply testify). His self is also unique. There is only one Lee Iacocca. One you, one me. We realize ourselves, we bring to fruition that which is our individuality, through what we choose

to do and how we go about doing it. Some write, some care for others, some teach, some fight, some criticize, some follow, some manage. When we do any of these things well, our performance is an explication of the text in a manner which we and others take to be faithful to the demands that it makes; it is simultaneously shot through with that which we and only we can bring to it; it is a projection of us, who we take ourselves to be in the circumstance, it is marked with our individuality. In Iacocca's performance at Chrysler we share *his* perception, acknowledge *his* perspective, applaud *his* interpretation and rejoice in or cavil at what we take to be *his* individuality.

Some will consider that this stress upon individuation represents a significant departure from straightforward interpretive, interactionist approaches. In my use of the notion of performance, I appear to be claiming that in each of us there is some 'vital spirit, soul, telos, essence, ego or hereditary endowment'; that neither Iacocca nor anyone else is simply moulded by others; that each of us has a text which can be brought to performance. I am claiming just that. From this perspective, there is a text and it sets the broad lines, the general framework – the outline of a plot and a sketchy characterization – within which the social actor can develop. The actor's development, however, is not a matter of total predetermination any more than a performance of *Richard III* is predetermined (indeed, considerably less than a performance of *Richard III* is predetermined). No texts (on the stage or within enterprises) can be realized automatically and spontaneously. Kean decided what aspects of *Richard III* to emphasize at the same time as he elected to realize some aspect of himself; Iacocca performed Chrysler and some aspects of the real Lee. Both made choices, chose one interpretation rather than another, put forward this view rather than that, emphasized this aspect of their self rather than another.

Clearly, as I have been careful to emphasize, although their interpretations and performances are necessarily individualistic, they are not excessively eccentric. Their performance of both texts (the more obvious ones written for them and their self texts) only has full meaning in a social and cultural context. Just as expectations of and responses to *Richard III* and to what actors should reveal about themselves guide and temper Kean's performance, so expectations and responses mould both Iacocca's interpretations and performances.

Recourse to notions of performing tells us that Iacocca's education and experience involves him in the apprehension, expression and embodiment of the person who is having the experiences and becoming educated (Jenkins, 1970). In this process, the text with which he worked was his *self*. He tells us where and when he was born, we get some impression of the young Iacocca, his family and his friends; we are alerted to the raw material, as it were, of the later CEO; he refers to his talents, his abilities and his weaknesses. This text, his *self*, or at least part of it (like Kemble's asthma, Kean's energy) is given; other aspects may be said to await development. The argument is that the essence of Iacocca is present in his very early years. Iacocca is the text that he performs in educating himself – drawing out that which he was born with, performing, rendering more explicit that which was implicit, making articulate the unexpressed, fully realizing that which was inchoate and incipient. In a sense his book is about his development, the discovery of Iacocca by Iacocca and the performing of the self out of town, as it were, at Ford, blossoming on Broadway with Chrysler.

Obviously such a perspective has important implications for education, training and development. Jenkins (1970), from which much of the present discussion derives, notes that the most significant point about the development of the self is that it does not follow a predetermined path. If human development were 'as automatic ... as the transition from acorn to oak, and if the social milieu were as rigid and as uncompromising as the natural ecology, then education ... would be both unnecessary and impossible'. All that would be required would be a very limited amount of training and indoctrination to prepare individuals for the parts they were to play. Since, however, the self is malleable (within limits, as with other texts) and since the settings (other people and their texts as well as conjoint texts elaborated over the years) are fluid, individuals are educable and must be educated. But such education can be relevant and meaningful only insofar as it touches upon the self; every person needs to apprehend his or her individuality, needs to explore what he or she has as givens, needs to bottom their texts, assess his or her situation and what it offers. In becoming experienced and educated, the social actor (and the stage actor) can do a great deal to 'enrich and expand' their texts; but, and it is an important 'but', if the individual text is ignored or distorted, it can be destroyed.

As I have sought to illustrate in the case of Iacocca, embodiment of the text proceeds concurrently with apprehension of it. Iacocca's career and personality are created as a product of his self-awareness. Again as we have seen, and as his book amply testifies, who Iacocca is and what he does is both an expression of a unique individual and a result of the 'ideals, images and models' that were and are current in his social milieu. Who he is, what he does, is shaped simultaneously by that which is within him and by those around him. Again Jenkins (1970) puts this well:

> 'Every man, to a greater or lesser degree, feels his uniqueness and integrity and seeks to preserve them in the personality he projects; but he can embody this only in the vocabulary of purposes, standards and accomplishments that his society recommends to him.'

The function of education is to help individuals perform the texts that they are given, that is, to realize their own potential. The function of management education, which is my concern in concluding this essay, is to facilitate the expression of unique capabilities in the pursuit of a career that is socially responsive and effective. The debate around the education of managers, and certainly the practice of management education, suggests that this is not often attempted and is rarely achieved.

The first reason why this should be so consists in the simple fact that much of what passes for management education is not geared to realizing individual potential; in many circumstances, it is structured so as to *reduce* rather than promote individuality. Putative managers are not invited to discover their own texts, but rather are instructed to be audience to the ideas of others. Much of the recent increase in management education is really an increase in *instruction*, in *teaching*. It has been and is being provided in classrooms, in circumstances where the 'educational performance revolves around those who are directing it rather than those who are performing it'. Teachers control curricula, teachers write case studies, teachers award marks for 'correct' answers. The implication of these activities and this structure is that there is one script to be learned, one text that will cover a multitude of individuals and a multitude of circumstances. But, I have argued, the text of the self is unique, inchoate, awaiting apprehension, interpretation, expression, response. It demands a situation that will 'lead it out' rather than one which imposes interpretations upon it; if, as I have argued, self texts, like many texts in the theatre, are realized only as they are explored, a process which vitiates this exploration must be counterproductive. A sound education for managers (as for anyone else) should provide a setting for performance that is relevant to the real interests of the students and the situations that they confront on a day to day basis. Second, it should be so structured that the student's reading of his or her self can be tentative, exploratory and flexible. At present, much of what is offered consists of a series of subjects – finance, operations, marketing, organizational behaviour – which are regarded as important by the teachers. The *students* – such a telling label – are not confronted on a day to day basis with subjects; they have to wrestle with problems which do not come complete with questions and answers. At work, they have little opportunity to be tentative and flexible (they must be seen to take action, to be firm and decisive) and, all too often in the classroom, such determination is demanded and rewarded. Nobody develops very much in such circumstances; something may be *learned* – acquired as part of our stock of knowledge – but learning does not necessarily lead to a change of performance.

A knowledge of finance, accounting, marketing or whatever may help the Iacoccas and Harvey Jones' of this world, but it does not suffice to make them great performers. The manager is part of the text that he or she has to bring to fruition; Iacocca and Harvey Jones, Joe Bloggs and Mary Smith are bound up in the very issues that they are attempting to apprehend, understand and resolve. To read a text within a particular organization the effective manager must be able to see how he or she is part of it; must take stock of his or her resources and abilities, background, opinions and prejudices; must be prepared for self analysis. Iacocca's commitment to the ideology of the free market could have severely affected his ability to deal with the crisis at Chrysler had he not recognized it and thought it through. In so doing he was prepared to give a fresh consideration to his own values and goals, to challenge both the environment and, most importantly, his *self*. He was also prepared to fashion a performance which embodied his interpretation and to perform his part with enthusiasm and skill. In taking on the Congressional subcommittee he was both rewriting the script (free enterprise America) and the Iacocca script: 'Doesn't this fly in the face of what you have been preaching so eloquently for so long?' 'It sure does.' Texts in organizations, as opposed to those frequently encountered in the classroom, require that the performers take a position with regard to them; various perspectives must be brought to bear upon them including that of the performer qua performer – how am I part of this and what impact am I likely to have upon the interpretation and carrying through to completion of that which I take to be important in the circumstance?

The first necessity for a fine performer is that he or she is in charge of the performance but not completely possessed by it. 'Your relationship to the play is that of rider to horse. It is the energy: you are the direction. You must be above it and on top of it' (Callow, 1984). Too great an identification with one's performance vitiates self knowledge. 'Know thyself' is an important dictum since self awareness is both the motivator and the shaper of education and experience. Without a degree of self awareness the process of experiencing and learning is little more than the acquisition of random facts and figures all of which, or none of which, may be relevant to the developing self. Each of us is at once a public and private text, the more aware I am of the latter, the more I can shape the former in line with my aspirations and competencies. A good stage actor recognizes that he or she needs to explore the part that he or she is assigned, to explore its features, measure its powers and limitations, assess its potential, consider how it relates to other characters, consider how he or she, the actor, relates to it. In so doing, the actor enriches and expands the text; he or she discovers elements others have not observed or have neglected. The self-aware manager can also enrich and expand his or her self text; he or she can also ignore it, distort it or destroy it. Many performers, both on the stage and within enterprises, simply fail to realize their potential. The education of actors for the stage or for enterprises needs to provide opportunity for the growth of self awareness, for the exploration of idiosyncratic texts, if it is to be successful.

Predigested scripts, Janet and John case studies, do little for self awareness. Everything about them is too neat, too programmed, too convergent. Only very infrequently do these rehearsal texts approach the complexity and messiness of phenomena in enterprises; only rarely does any teacher attempt to stimulate a holistic perspective. More often than not the texts offered to would-be managers illustrate points about finance, *or* strategy, *or* production, *or* behaviour. Texts in enterprises, on the other hand, are holistic, they appear to thrust themselves upon us; they demand attention. They are often less than complete, are frequently ill defined and nearly always entail a history, a present and a future that is uncertain.

A stage actor prepares in rehearsal. He or she may prepare for Richard III by studying some other text but, sooner or later, the actor must tackle the real thing. In this he or she is guided by a director (often an experienced actor) who invites the performer to try various interpretations, to 'give it a run'. After the run the director provides the actor with 'notes'; criticism of both the interpretation and matters of technique. Eventually, however, the actor is on his or her own; out there in front of the audience; performing. Managers could benefit (some do benefit) from a similar schooling; rehearsal of an actual text by another actor and 'notes' after the performance. Iacocca learned a great deal from Murray Kester and Charlie Beacham, 'the closest thing I've ever had to a mentor'. But to learn, managers must be given the opportunity to perform, to be involved with and responsible for the solution to a business problem; a messy, inchoate, emergent text where what the manager does is a matter of consequence for the organization and for the manager. To become a star, a manager has to be given the opportunity to step out from the chorus. No business school can provide for that; it can teach the techniques, help with the verse speaking and the sword fights, as it were, but it cannot be a substitute for the actual doing of managing. The organization which denies its managers substantial responsibility on the grounds that it is too risky is denying itself the next generation of great performers.

Acknowledgment

I am very grateful to Dr Annie Pye of the University of Bath for her help in reading and commenting upon drafts of this paper.

References

Brecht, B. (1965). *The Messingkauf Dialogues*. Eyre Methuen, London (translated by John Willett).

Burke, K. (1968). 'Dramatism', in *International Encyclopaedia of the Social Sciences* Vol. VII. Macmillan, New York.

Burke, K. (1969a). *A Grammar of Motives*. University of California Press, Berkeley.

Burke, K. (1969b). *A Rhetoric of Motives*. University of California Press, Berkeley.

Callow, S. (1984). *Being an Actor*. Methuen, London.

Combs, J. E. and M. W. Mansfield (eds), (1976). *Drama in Life: The Uses of Communication in Society*. Hastings House, New York.

FitzSimons, R. (1976). *Edmund Kean: Fire From Heaven*. Hamish Hamilton, London.

Goffman, E. (1959). *The Presentation of Self in Everyday Life*. Anchor Books, Garden City, New Jersey.

Hornby, R. (1977). *Script into Performance*. University of Texas Press, Austin.

Iacocca, L. (1984). *Iacocca: An Autobiography*. Bantam Books, Toronto.

Jenkins, I. (1970). *Performance in Aesthetic Concepts and Education*. University of Illinois Press, Urbana.

Lazarowicz, K. (1977). 'Triadische Kollusion', in *Das Theater und Sein Publikum*. Osterreichische Akademie der Wissenschaften, Vienna.

Mangham, I. L. (1978). *Interactions and Interventions in Organizations*. Wiley, Chichester.

Mangham, I. L. (1986). *Power and Performance in Organizations: An Exploration of Executive Process*. Blackwell, Oxford.

Mangham, I. L. (1988). *Effecting Organizational Change: Further Explorations of Executive Process*. Blackwell, Oxford.

Mangham, I. L. (1990). 'Drama in organizational life', in Thayer, T., *Organization – Communication: Emerging Perspectives, Vol. III*. Ablex Publishing Corporation, Norwood, New Jersey.

Mangham, I. L. and M. A. Overington (1983). 'Performance and rehearsal: social order and organizational life', *Symbolic Interaction*, **5**, 205–22.

Mangham, I. L. and M. A. Overington (1987). *Organizations as Theatre: A Social Psychology of Dramatic Appearances*. Wiley, Chichester.

Morgan, G. and L. Smircich (1980). 'Paradigms, metaphors, and puzzle solving in organizational theory', *Administrative Science Quarterly*, **25**, 600–15.

Trujillo, N. (1987). 'Implications of interpretive approaches for organizational communication research and practice', in L. Thayer (ed.) *Organization – Communication: Emerging Perspectives II*. Ablex Publishing Corporation, Norwood, New Jersey.

[15]

The Cultural Performance of Control

Rolland Munro

> 'we present 'management' not only as an oral tradition in its literal sense, that is that managers spend most of their time talking, but also in its *anthropological* sense, that is as a means by which culture is generated, maintained, and transmitted from one generation to another.'
>
> Dan Gowler and Kareen Legge (1996: 35)

> 'When such performances are successful, we receive experience rather than belief. Then the invisible world is made manifest . . In all events the performed order is explicit, realized, and we are *within* it, not left merely to endlessly wonder or talk about it.'
>
> Barbara Myerhoff, *Remembered Lives* (1992: 234)

Rolland Munro
Centre for Social
Theory and
Technology,
Keele University,
UK

Abstract

Ideas about control are enriched by attending to cultural performances taking place in everyday organizational life. While much literature conflates culture with control, purists try to exclude control devices altogether, as if these artefacts cannot be expressive of real forms of culture. This view overlooks how managers make an 'exhibition' of such artefacts on a daily basis in order to cut a figure of being 'in' control. By closely examining which material is made visible and available, and when, the paper also challenges assumptions about the 'performed order' being hegemonic. The paper illustrates how everyday 'exhibitions' of *membership* overlap into 'displays' of *self* as the successful, or charismatic manager. In that cultural performances set a performer apart (as different) at the same time as figuring them as members (as the same), the paper argues that the performed order is always *motile* to the precise artefacts being made visible and available.

Descriptors: artefacts, control, cultural performance, motility, performed order, self

Introduction

An emphasis on cultural performance focuses on the accomplished ways people make cultural material 'visible' and 'available'. Hitherto, displays of cultural material have been understood as directed at making the 'performed order' explicit and realized. Insofar as the effect is totalizing — so 'we are *within* it' — cultural performance is assumed to efface individuality. In contrast, this paper argues that cultural performance is accomplished in ways that both create and reproduce the performed order *and* set one apart, say, as a successful, or charismatic individual. Yes, managers make themselves 'visible' and 'available' to each other *as* members of a group; but, in so doing, each also can try to nuance the materials in displays that identify them, individually, as a manager who is 'in' control.

Many definitions of culture — such as Deal and Kennedy's (1982) 'the way we do things round here'— suffer from acculturation (Barley et al. 1988), wherein culture is framed normatively: 'you will do as we do'; or, more cynically, 'as we say we do'. For purists, culture is not what an organization 'has', but what it 'is' (Smircich 1983: 347). Yet a tendency to see culture as elusive to control encourages 'organization culture' to be identified with spaces of resistance, such as 'sub-cultures' (Willis 1977; Martin and Siehl 1983) or 'unsurveilled passages' (Roberts 1991). While there are rich insights in disentangling organizational from corporate phenomena, it is vital not to overlook how 'etic' terms, including control and intervention, become 'emic' terms for managers. For this reason, no materials should be excluded from definitions of culture.

In adopting the motif of cultural performance, the aim is to avoid definitions that decide beforehand what culture should be. To adapt Latour's (1986: 273) insight about science, culture is 'performed through everyone's efforts to define it', including my own. Whereas performative definitions *explore practices*, most definitions are ostensive and *explain principles* (Czarniawska-Joerges 1991: 287). The latter institute an 'experience far' mode of analysis, inimical to getting 'inside' the performances by which those in practices accomplish membership. This is not to say culture 'just happens'; or, since differences in social structure (Meek 1988) play a part, that the same culture happens for everyone. Once culture is acknowledged to be 'contested, temporal and emergent' (Clifford 1986: 19), then the researcher can ask *how* culture happens, and for whom.

In Cohen and Comaroff's (1976: 102) view, a key aspect of the construction of reality is a *management* of meaning: 'actors compete to contrive and propagate interpretations of social behaviour and relationships'. The notion of 'display' seems critical here. If culture is elusive, and hence backgrounded in the form of customary modes of thought, world views, ideology, or implicit meanings (Douglas 1975), then cultural performance is the 'show'. Discussing Victor Turner's emphasis on 'social dramas', Schechner (quoted in Turner 1985: 179, emphasis added) summarizes this aspect as follows:

'These situations — arguments, combats, rites of passage — are inherently dramatic because participants not only do things, they try to *show* others what they are doing or have done; actions take on a "performed-for-an-audience" aspect.'

Display is what makes 'the invisible world manifest', extending each member's knowledge of a 'customary mode of thought or performance' (Cohen 1982: 5).

Using verbal materials and other artefacts, managers are deeply engaged in finding 'occasions' to make themselves visible to others *as* members of a group (see also Garfinkel 1967). However, as Cohen (1985, 1987) has stressed, artefacts are ambiguous. Given an inherent ambiguity over exactly what artefacts express, it becomes possible for members to nuance occasions for a display of 'self'. The two possibilities are not incompatible. Precisely what cultural materials show is open to interpretation. Indeed, as

Cohen presses, it is likely that this very ambiguity leaves spaces for self to be created.

The interest in the present paper lies in developing these ideas about display in the context of a general ambiguity over signs. The aim is to explicate how a tendency to 'contrive and propagate' leads to a *motility*, rather than a hegemony in the performed order. As will be illustrated, cultural performances are more than moments in which culture shows through — when membership is asserted — they are also occasions in which different versions of self can be made visible and available. Ahead of the field study of Bestsafe, a pseudonym, the next two sections introduce the notion of cultural performance by way of two exemplary ethnographies and explicate a tendency in the literature to overlook how cultural performance also helps accomplish 'individuality'.

Cultural Performance as Exhibition

Carlson (1996) attributes the term cultural performance, now widely found in anthropological writings, to Milton Singer. All peoples, in Carlson's interpretation, think of culture as encapsulated in discrete events — cultural performances — which are exhibited to themselves and to others. In ways contested below, however, Singer's definition limits cultural performance to the 'exhibitions' taking place during formal rituals and ceremonies. These include recitations, festivals and weddings, as well as theatre and dance (Singer 1959: xii). Thus, for Singer, cultural performances possess certain features: 'a definitely limited time span, a beginning and an end, an organized programme of activity, a set of performers, an audience, and a place and occasion of performance' (Singer 1959: xiii).

Rosen's (1991) discussion of the annual 'Breakfast' for Spiro and Associates, an advertising agency, exactly calls these features to mind. For example, in terms of 'a place and occasion of performance', Rosen details the opulent setting of the Breakfast, the main ballroom of one of Philadelphia's luxury class hotels. The order of proceedings is also outlined, beginning exactly at 8.30 a.m. 'with one hundred or so Eggs Benedict being marched in by suited waiters in synchronization' and followed by heads of department giving speeches. Headed up by Walter Spiro these constitute the 'set of performers'; while the rest of the staff act as 'audience', providing laughter and applause on cue. Rosen reveals these roles to be mutually performative, not exclusive as Singer perhaps imagined them. For example, towards the end, after being told they will be paid *less* for working *longer*, the staff are invited to get up and applaud themselves; which of course they do.

In his emphasis on a manipulation of the symbolic order of things, Rosen (1991: 89) captures the way in which 'these performances reinforce the institutionalization of bureaucratic knowing and being'. As Rosen (1991: 79) notes, the Breakfast is efficacious, not so much because of its uniqueness, but because it is 'accepted by those involved with its performance as part of the natural order of things'. The point is not that an excited staff rush back to work, but rather lies in their all too ready acceptance of a 'defined terrain'. Rosen's position therefore seems close to that adopted earlier by Dell Hymes, who is paraphrased by Bauman (1986: 3) as highlighting the 'way in which communication is carried out, above and beyond its referential content'. To Rosen (1991: 89): 'Culture, creating, and being the terrain for consciousness here is a mechanism for control'.

Despite its merit in bringing together debates on culture and control, Rosen's analysis stands in a tradition that, for Cohen (1994), systematically effaces a study of self in favour of cultural stereotypes; 'the Bantu do this', or 'the Ndembu do that'. As Carlson (1996: 18) notes, theorists (in particular Erving Goffman) have a view of performance that 'owes more to context and to the dynamics of reception than to the specific activities of the performer'. Rosen shows only one side of performance. His piece fulfils Bauman's (1977) first criterion that verbal performance is 'marked as subject to evaluation for the way it is done, for the relative skill and effectiveness of the performer's display'. However, the specific activities of the performer are missing — showing what the devil *each* think they're up to. Critically, Bauman also sees performance as 'marked as available for the enhancement of experience through the present enjoyment of the intrinsic qualities of the act of expression itself' (1977: 11). Whether or not qualities are intrinsic, the point is that Rosen does not enter the space of pleasure, or enjoyment. Although people laugh and cheer, he has eliminated them from extension at the affective level. In limiting performance to Bauman's first marking, Rosen denies the staff a sense of self, portraying them merely as 'bearers of culture'. The employees create an 'ontology of hard work, success, *communitas*' (*ibid*: 89), but this is a '*communitas*' which diminishes individuality towards zero.

Cultural Performance as an Everyday Display of Self

Singer's emphasis on 'exhibition', and his consequent exclusion of everyday life from the notion of cultural performance, contrasts with the work of more recent anthropologists. For example, Cohen (1982) links the experience of membership of a culture specifically to the mundane. Cultural processes 'occur close to the everyday experience of life, rather than through rare, formalised procedures' (1982: 6). Cohen's argument is especially resonant to the view, developed below, that much cultural performance is not only staged *within* the mundane events of organizational life, but is staged as a display of self.

Emphasizing the dynamics of reception, Kunda's (1992) study overlaps with Rosen's. However, his analysis of 'presentational rituals' in a High-Tech corporation illustrates Victor Turner's maxim that when ritual 'works', the reality it portrays assumes emotional significance for participants. The effect is an experience that Turner (1974: 56) calls 'a symbiotic interpenetration of individual and society'. As Kunda shows, gatherings (such as the culture seminar discussed below) are occasions in which organizational ideology — the managerial version of Tech culture and the member role it prescribes — is 'dramatised and brought to life' (1992: 93). As such, Kunda offers a discussion of performance that, potentially, treats self as reflexive to manipulations of the symbolic order. For example, he summarizes his penultimate chapter by suggesting it is the self that is the 'contested terrain' (1992: 216).

This is a fine insight, but Kunda's analysis of self is disappointing. Paraphrasing Goffman's discussion of role distance, he suggests that 'a sense of self is formed both by the ways in which individuals identify with pre-scribed roles and the ways in which they distance themselves from them' (1992: 161). Performances follow suit. Performance is a 'tight-rope walk' (1992: 216) between what he calls 'role embracement' and an 'ironic distance'. On the one hand, employees become the bearers of culture: 'the culture swallowed me' (1992: 170) as one woman manager expresses it; and on the other, opportunities for 'self-enlargement' are snatched during the occasional 'cleansing moment of truth'; moments of irony in which there is a 'temporary suspension of practiced organizational selves' (1992: 213). Seeing 'ironic distance' *as* resistance, however, overlooks how acts of resistance sustain hegemonic order (Foucault 1977, 1980, 1991); for example Czarniawska-Joerges (1992: 184) suggests that Tech engineers 'ridiculing and challenging the contents of the leading ideology' may *help* managers by 'exemplifying the supposed freedom of thought and right to conflicting ideas'. Elsewhere, Kunda makes passing reference to multiple selves, but his analysis remains focused on the tension between role embracement and ironic distancing. It is as if he imagines self as mobile, but limited to moving between spaces of embracement and moments of irony.

Much, of course, is written in organization texts about mobility, the daily movement across different social spaces between home and work, or bosses walking the shop floor before returning to the boardroom, or, as the phrase 'I'll just put on my other hat' suggests, how we move from one role to another. Little is said about how we can slip the bounds of social construction by making present different lifeworlds; say, community one moment, or be all business the next. It is in this context of shifting realities that I use the term *motility*. By altering the resources we draw on, even slightly, we 'cut' different figures (Strathern 1991, Munro 1996); the good employee one moment, the dependable colleague the next.

These considerations suggest the possibility of there being far more 'motility' in representation than is usually allowed for in field studies. For example, Ellen Cohen, the resident instructor on culture in Kunda's study, is recorded by him as shutting down her viewgraph at the end of her 'culture module'. In an 'off-the-record, very personal, almost motherly' tone, she issues a stark warning not to burn out: 'Don't let the company suck you dry'. The subversive-sounding message 'creates an air of rapt attention' as she walks slowly from the flipchart to the centre of the room before adding the finishing touch: 'What kind of company do you think allows me to be saying these things to you?' (1992: 112–113). This dramatic description by Kunda captures well both sides of Bauman's point about performance discussed earlier. Ellen's performance is marked for the skill it displays, but it is remarkable also for its, momentary, magnification of herself. True, neither reader nor ethnographer can know if her candour gave her pleasure, or whether her performance allowed her to be just 'exercising ... power along the cognitive and affective planes' (Van Maanen and Kunda 1989: 49). Yet, either way, there is (in Turner's phrase quoted by Kunda elsewhere) a 'symbiotic interpenetration of individual and society'.

Moments of symbiosis, therefore, need not quite flatten the individual to that of society, as Kunda seems to have read into the presentational rituals he witnessed. As can be seen with Ellen's manipulation of her material, multiple readings of self are there to be created. While spreading a corporate message of 'he who proposes does' (1992: 102), she shows that she can shut down — like her viewgraph — to avoid burnout. In ways that go beyond irony, hers is more than a univocal 'show' of culture. With her highly accomplished cultural performance, Ellen is making visible and available the 'Tech way' of doing; but, simultaneously, she accomplishes this *as* a performance of self. Her identity is left nicely ambiguous between someone who is fully committed to Tech and someone who can 'shut down' whenever they want. Via the viewgraph, Ellen's cultural performance is of both Tech *and* self.

Arguing cultural performances are the 'most concrete observable units of the cultural structure', Singer suggests that the culture content of a tradition is transmitted by specific cultural media, as well as by human carriers. As with Ellen switching off the viewgraph, it is important to remember that artefacts are more than instrumental, they are also *expressive*. Persons do not act alone; they draw on available materials to 'show' where they stand. They also use these to *dramatize* their movement: one moment, as instructor, Ellen is behind the viewgraph; the next moment, in the figure of one who has gone before, she disconnects it to come right out in front, face to face with her audience. For example, exactly at the moment she 'drops' her role as instructor, Ellen goes on to instruct: 'Don't let the company suck you dry'. So who is she now? With requisite artefacts, different directions for self are kept afloat, often together, and this is surely Cohen's point that self-identity can be created at the same time as engaging in the symbolic construction of community.

Lunch at Bestsafe

Ethnography is particularly suitable for exploratory studies where a 'thin description' would impose 'our own construction of other people's constructions of what they and their compatriots are up to' (Geertz 1973: 9). It is the artefacts and phrasing 'in use' that are key, rather than vast amounts of detail, all of which may be coloured by an unsympathetic or unappreciative eye. Thick description, therefore, is not to be conflated with exhaustive representation. Together with an 'evocation' of the locality, the ethnographic narrative can be aimed at one or two moments that open up the site. As Rosen and Mullen (1996) illustrate, the aim is to 'show' just sufficient detail for a reader to 'enter' the social drama that is unfolding.

Paraphrasing Geertz's dictum that the point is not to explain as an external observer, but to understand what the group members *think is happening* as an insider, Linstead (1996: 14) argues that the rigour of ethnography comes from a constant exposure to the 'other'. For example, I was struck by one manager at Bestsafe, Alex, who, over a two-year period, forcibly argued all the difficulties of having inadequate resources in the face of much development and change. I thought he could blossom from more contact with senior managers, and pressed for this, but they continued to deny him access. No one could say he lacked 'focus', an emic term used to define a good manager, but his insistent attention to what he saw as the 'real' (the lack of resources) reinforced their impressions of someone working more as a 'glorified supervisor' than as a manager. It took two years before I began to appreciate this 'insider' view: more 'access' to senior managers was not something which was given, it had to be earned continuously through a 'show' of delivery.

How I was drawn into the performed order of Bestsafe signifies the beginning of a long process by which I learnt to 'see' this relation between access and delivery. I was approached originally to help develop Bestsafe's management control systems. Having indicated that my interest lay in fieldwork on more informal aspects, I was invited to lunch in the directors' dining room. For about twenty minutes or so, five of us engaged in chitchat over the tonic half of a gin and tonic about an amazingly awful artpiece dominating the dining room. On sitting down, we were served a rather sad looking tagliatelli; this selection being in deference to my having said I was vegetarian. With the overcooked pasta slowly glueing itself together on the plates, this embarrassment ran on into my confessing that I hadn't come across their products, and then revealing that I hadn't seen their latest advertisement, since I did not have a television. Over coffee, my having refused pudding, the executive director turned and asked: 'what have you got to sell?'

Even in the shock of feeling so wrongly positioned, I was aware that all eyes were on me. *Their* mistake, I assumed and struggled out of this latest embarrassment by drawing, to me, the clear distinction between consultants selling stuff to managers and academics doing research. After this vindication of myself as a 'pure' researcher, it was something of a surprise to discover the next day that, as well as being granted 'unlimited access', the first part of my study, lasting about a year, would be funded.

For this first year, I adopted the persona of a social scientist shadowing people, or chatting in their office or at their work station; a repertoire magnified by the artefacts of taking notes and asking questions. Methods adopted included: field notes, written up daily from participant observation; recorded and transcribed interviews, kept to a conversational mode (with encouragement for narrative examples); and extensive document searches, collated at different sources and levels. During this year, it still did not click how much I had misinterpreted the question to me about selling and it is significant that contact with senior managers also vanished. I supposed this was due to my fieldwork focusing on relations between clerical employees and middle to lower levels of management, but I was still unaware that 'access' to senior managers was tied to something they called 'delivery'.

In this liminal state, betwixt 'doing' and between being able to 'deliver', I was permitted to conduct a piece of action research (Munro 1992) in a second year of fieldwork, also funded. The results of this study led to my 'going native' and being drawn into discussions on internal strategy for a further two-year period. Together, these arrangements permitted participant observation, usually two or three days a week over a five-year period.

'Gaps' as Symbols of Success

The locality of the study is a city centre in Scotland. Bestsafe — a market leader in financial services — had operations in North America, but the city centre housed the UK head office and a large, centralized operations staff. In all, six different buildings were involved, all within a one-mile radius of each other. The smallest, only part of which functioned as the head office, was distinctively 'period' with the ornate, marble and gilded entrance and hall typical of the traditional UK banks and insurance companies. All other buildings were modernist in design, having large open plan rooms. Many thousands of staff worked in these buildings, establishing the company as one of the largest employers in the city.

As well as being extremely successful and rich in funds, Bestsafe enjoyed one of the best reputations of any organization in the UK financial services. It was thought to have an outstanding, if reclusive, group of senior managers who were facing up to the deregulation of the UK insurance industry. These matters were all the more interesting because of a peculiarity — the lack of any accounting technology associated with control. Although Bestsafe applied actuarial techniques to pricing its products, it did not, at the time, employ accounting techniques such as standard costing. Unlike Pensco (Knights and Willmott 1993), Bestsafe did not try to adopt budgeting until after I had left the field. The usual attributions of management control to accounting systems did not apply.

The existence of good informal control, if not a strong organization culture, was implied by a paucity of reported data. For example, reporting focused almost entirely on 'items of work processed', mainly insurance and pension policies, referred to as *work volumes,* supplemented by two further sets of statistical aggregates: *backlogs,* items of work not yet processed, and *complaints,* including letters to the managing director. My initial bias about informal control (see Dalton 1959) was also supported by other evidence. For example, in interviews, everyone said they enjoyed 'a great deal of autonomy' and indicated great freedom over decision making. Then, during shadowing, I found an absence of top-down instruction, even in the more everyday meetings. Further, in being seemingly left to their own devices, much of the work of the operating staff also mirrored the claims of their managers about autonomy.

On the other hand, there was little to support prevalent ideas about 'strong' organization cultures. While people gave stories to illustrate their points, when asked, there was no heroizing of people as leaders and little myth-making. Against the current stress on 'shared values', there were key differences in the way participants *represented* the organization culture and their involvement with it. For example, the culture at Bestsafe was described to me as 'do-do-do' by one manager, Alex, while his senior manager, Tom, talked about 'delivery'. Tom derided the tendency, as he saw it, for managers to act as 'supervisors' and 'do the difficult work'. In addition, everybody had different views about what worked and what didn't and what was good and what wasn't. For example, among the managers under Tom, Alex was most preoccupied about getting more staff, while Harold focused on getting better statistics. In contrast, Susie espoused the cause of quality. In brief, there was much diversity over what each manager presented to me as their 'style' of managing; and this diversity seemed to be explicitly tolerated at the higher levels.

Such problems led me to reconsider the evidence. The main point of control being informal, revolving around a sense of 'distance' between managers in the line. This was more than symbolic. A (small) top part of the organization included the senior managers with the division managers at their foot; and a (very large) bottom part run by operating managers and their immediate seniors. Very roughly, this split also separated the group belonging to a 'head office', an elite who mostly had an actuarial training, and the very large centralized operations. These parts of Bestsafe had quite distinct differences in atmosphere. The big open-plan rooms of the operating departments nurtured feelings of an 'extended family', with staff recapturing territory by dividers covered with posters and green plants on top of banks of filing cabinets. In contrast, moving among conversations and the smaller rooms at 'head office' was like visiting a prestige university.

The Closed Door

Although Singer's exclusion of the everyday from cultural performance now appears unwarranted, and few ethnographers would so limit themselves, care should be exerted before collapsing categories. In line with Turner's (1985: 187) distinction between 'social' and 'cultural' performance, for example, much of what I saw shadowing Alex, Susie and Harold, among many others, fitted the idea of 'role embracement' discussed earlier. Most performances were straightforwardly 'social' performances; self was effaced in taking up a role. Yet in the meeting below — as with my lunch at Bestsafe — there is a 'defining moment' in which *different* artefacts (research or consultancy) are summoned to speak for each.

Consider the following encounter, which illustrates the general way 'instructions' are worked out informally. Susie is on her way to see Tom, her senior manager. Over the last month, he has been listening to her about a quality initiative she wants to run, but not, though, in the last few days. Just ahead of launching details to her staff, she has found it difficult to get hold of Tom. She's left a number of messages headed 'quality' on the e-mail, as yet without response. In the corridor to Tom's room, she greets Harold, the head of another department, as we meet coming the other way:

'Hi, how are you?'
'Oh, fine. I've just been discussing the output charts with Tom.'
'Output? Oh, the output charts. I'd forgotten all about them!'
'Well, I thought he had too, but he's just been over mine with a fine tooth comb.'
'So how was it?'
'Yeah, well, seems OK. He seemed happy enough. Well, better get back.'
'Yeah, great. Maybe see you later.'

Susie goes on down the corridor and although she hesitates outside Tom's room, she doesn't go in. Instead, she takes the long way round, down the other stairs and back to her desk. She avoids looking at June, who's been hoping to find out over lunch whether *her* ideas on quality are getting a green light. Instead, Susie calls to Steve to get out the output charts for the last six months. When these arrive ten minutes later, she turns to June and excuses herself, saying: 'Sorry, June, something's come up'.

Unanswered e-mails, a door left closed and a cancelled lunch. Whatever is currently constituting 'delivery' for senior managers is symbolized within a mundane, everyday exchange of artefacts. Of particular interest is the artefact of *access* to senior managers; or, more especially, its attenuation. As mentioned earlier, operating managers function in an ethos, partly of their own making: one which stresses 'autonomy' and which, in effect, makes it difficult to ask for instructions. Indeed, Tom, when asked how often he saw the operating managers, expressed the view that all they were after in seeking information was 'comfort'. As a manager at Bestsafe, you are expected to know what you are doing.

As the above encounter suggests, operating managers are able to elicit information about the status of their current agendas from the other managers. At any moment, one might be experimenting, like Susie, with a quality initiative, and another, like Harold, might work on a new set of output statistics. Their conjunction with different artefacts of control is key to the managers making themselves clear and distinct from each other. This, in the operating ethos of 'doing', induces differences in the way people in their departments see them going about things. But these differences, in the head office ethos of 'delivery', also make the managers 'visible' and 'available' *as cultural material* to the senior manager.

Central to managers' discussions with each other are mutual reports over the current attention which each (and hence which each of them *as* artefacts) is attracting. The given reasons about what each is 'doing' to merit a meeting with the division head is not the only fare of discussion between

Susie and Harold. Attention by the operating managers might centre more on whether the meeting could be understood as a real meeting, or whether it constituted a non-meeting. For example, Harold's description of Tom going over his output charts with a 'fine tooth comb' clearly made a different impression on Susie, than if he had reported Tom as 'just having a look'. Implicit in such encounters are readings by each manager as to whether 'the other' is being considered as 'delivering'.

In this way, operating managers are constructing access as an artefact for symbolizing each manager's success and matching up their local agendas with imputations about the division head's agenda. Susie's difficulties in getting hold of Tom, together with Tom's apparent interest in the output charts, combine to stage a warning that she must not, as Tom framed it in his first interview with me, act as a 'glorified supervisor'. When Susie took the long walk round back to her department, she was falling back on another repertoire: one that no longer included talking with Tom, but one that now had a revitalized interest in the output charts. This repertoire does not fit neatly with her preferred identity around ideas of quality, but looks essential if she is to continue to accomplish her cultural performance as a manager 'in' control. Susie, as it turns out, is not about to give up on 'doing' quality; but, for the moment, she has to ensure first that she is seen as someone who can 'deliver'.

Keeping Different Agendas in Play

After seeing how access can symbolize 'success', I began to consider that overall control might arise from informal mores being fully *integrated* with formal procedures. I formed the view that the palpable command and control economy of Bestsafe depended on its very *lack* of top-down instructions. Rather than manipulate direction by instructions, senior managers attenuated 'access' as a means of pointing to best practice. For example, when it suited them to mark up quality, they favoured discussions with someone associated with quality. When concerns about cost predominated, they withdrew access and favoured another. This withdrawal was often literal, but the key impetus is symbolic. Feelings of a lack in communications in the line incites managers to 'gossip', as if they are kin (see also Munro 1995), about the relative success of each other's agendas.

These findings suggest that the chances of managers seeming to be 'in' control are *enhanced* by a lack of communication over policy and direction. Where strategy is enunciated in the form of a plan — or corporate culture is homogenized — managers can experience problems in finding the exemplars to signal a change in direction. Huff (1988) makes a similar point, suggesting that a new dean could act quickly because 'similar ideas already existed within the repertoire of the existing system':

'Here is the paradox: the existence of difference, which challenges the possibility of coordinated action at one point in time, can ultimately contribute to coordinated action as the organization and its environment requires new responses.'

Her principle can also be seen in an enactment perspective, in line with Weick (1985: 125) who argues 'ambiguity can produce innovation and a greater utilization of resources'.

At Bestsafe, one effect of ambiguity being generated is that material to exemplify a shift in agendas is always culturally available *and only needs to be made 'visible'*. Thus, giving access to one manager, rather than another, provides a display of priorities, a *show* that pulls through the new emphasis, such as quality or throughput. Rather than prioritize ahead, in ways that events may unwind, senior managers can metamorphose a mere example of difference into an exemplar of current agendas, but it should also be stressed that this access is *provisional*. To count as someone who 'delivers', managers need to be swift on their feet in shifting the presentation of what they are 'doing'. Interested in how Harold kept his reputation as someone 'who delivers', I spent as much time shadowing him as the more charismatic Susie. Well into the study, Harold revealed that he put aside anything marked urgent, or high priority, for three days. If a reminder came within three days, he acted immediately; if not, he forgot about it. In contrast, despite her success in one of the corporate agendas, Tom held Susie's ability to 'deliver' suspect. Although one of the very few woman managers, this seemed less a matter of operating below a 'glass ceiling'; after listening to Harold, I noticed Susie did try to act on all requests.

There are some related effects. Despite the great wealth of the company, managers are subject to the rule that if someone could not gain access to make her case, then resources (with the enormous expansion in business, new resources were always needed) could be denied. This is consistent with the defensive routines of a self-sealing logic (Argyris 1985, 1990) that if you can't make your case heard, it can't be a strong case. Additionally, a bottom-up pressure on operating managers can be expected from overworked staff. For example, managers like Alex would get the blame for failing to argue for more staff, even from otherwise loyal subordinates, and yet be equally blamed by senior managers for any perceived drop in 'morale'! It hardly needs saying, given earlier remarks, that a perceived 'lack' of staff did not count as an explanation for a drop in morale.

Sanctions over access, though, are more than hierarchical. The downside of not meeting a division manager is the lack of currency with which to sustain exchanges, such as Susie's and Harold's above. An absence of meetings with the division head deprives a manager of occasions with which to exchange, in passing, notes with colleagues. Thus, relegation to being a 'glorified supervisor' has repercussions for a manager's cultural performance as a 'member' of their kinship group. Exclusion by the senior manager leads the operating manager into the further danger of being marginalized, if temporarily, by his or her peer group. For example, Alex, who always sought more staff, almost never got to see Tom, and consequently felt marginalized not just by Tom, but by the other managers.

The Cultural Performance of Control   631

Exclusion and Denial

What began to fascinate were claims about morale made by senior managers in many meetings I attended. How could they know? I never saw senior managers in the open office spaces, other than occasionally for a few minutes, barely stopping for a chat on their quick walk through. However, their claims overlapped with my impressions and near the end of my study, while listening to Phil — an experienced but junior member of staff — it dawned on me that 'soundings' were taken during these chats. That staff never mentioned to me these chats chimed with the peculiar way male members of staff recounted family holidays in the first person singular, as if they had gone alone. However, in this case, it seemed that their silence arose from the idea that the senior managers were engaging them in conversation about 'social' matters. Quite invisibly to the staff, it seemed that senior managers had learnt the trick of picking up a *general mood* in how staff were feeling: each member understood the chat to be personal to them; and no-one seemed to be aware their chat could be read as a cultural performance, indicative of conditions generally pertaining to their workplace.

This point brings me back, belatedly, to the formal control systems and my being told that these were so paltry. Although the systems were simple, the 'output' figures were robust, having been cross-checked in any number of different ways. Yet there is a pressing reason for senior managers not to settle this debate. If they acknowledged the figures *as* adequate, then extra staff would need to be drafted in to meet the ongoing expansion. Only a cultural performance of *doubt* in the figures could defer this from happening and thus keep pressure on existing staff to make efficiency savings. Also, there is more than extra staff at stake; new resources granted automatically would create more genuine autonomy and *weaken* a key factor affecting line manager relations. Perversely, the extent to which operating managers turned towards finding out the agendas of their senior manager depended upon the 'weakness' of links between staff numbers and numerical output. Senior managers, as a group, had to be able to *distance* themselves from 'believing' the figures.

As has already been noted, the creation of distance in the line — particularly the 'gap' between operating managers and divisional heads — did not weaken, but *strengthened* effects generated by the formal, albeit paltry controls; but how could senior managers also effect a denial of operating figures? After all, the very 'gap' from subordinates should make senior managers dependent on reporting systems. This, in fact, was the myth in circulation, with senior managers always indicating that what they really needed were better statistics. One condition of possibility for managers enacting both a denial of the numbers and a distance to people is clear. *Only when operating figures themselves become ceremonial can they be treated as unimportant.* If delivery can be shown — through the formal reports — to be always accomplished, then (perversely) the figures can be 'frankly' acknowledged to be 'misleading'; and even, according to one senior manager, 'wrong'.

632   Rolland Munro

This, therefore, is one part of the puzzle. Often it is in its very *lack* of 'show' that the performed order of Bestsafe is exhibited. Various artefacts, in the form of gaps, errors, distances, and an absence of instructions, all keep active the possibility of improvement. On the one side, the ethos of 'doing' provides conditions in which managers find out current agendas. On the other, statistical aggregates always have to be good enough for senior managers to treat 'delivery' of most figures as more or less irrelevant. Together, these matters exert pressure on managers to find ways to service the ongoing expansion, while making do with existing staff. The performed order is deceptive, however; its exhibition of moderation and prudence belies the intensity of the specific activities of the performers. Before closing the study, I would like therefore to return the analysis to the other side of performance, the display of self.

Learning to Deliver

In reviewing their different orientations, Carlson (1996) notes that Singer, Hymes and Bauman all view performance as an activity somehow 'set apart' from that of everyday life. However, Carlson suggests 'set-apartness' can also be related to Turner's idea of liminality as a state of 'in-betweenness'. Turner, he points out, acknowledged Van Gennep's stress on 'any ceremony marking individual or social change'. Thus, rather than be stuck with a somewhat static concept, Carlson (1996: 20) is suggesting that instead performance should be treated as a 'border, a margin, a site of negotiation'. Certainly at Bestsafe, participants are always in danger of being treated as 'in-between'. For instance, in the encounter outside Tom's office, Susie is moving between being considered a 'good' manager and one who is, for the moment, ignorable. Likewise, Harold is moving from being overlooked, for the last month or two, to being treated, once again, as a manager who 'delivers'.

During the study, I too moved constantly 'in-between' the identity of researcher and that of a member. I want to underline this movement — now this; now that — between 'cutting' the figure of an objective researcher one moment and 'going native' the next. The ethos of Bestsafe, as discussed earlier, made a cultural necessity of being seen to *do* something. While the persona of a researcher would not let me fully 'inside' the organization, its adoption gave me a persona without which I could not go on visiting and talking to people. Equally, for some senior managers, doing was not enough. To be let inside *their* performed order, I also had to learn to get other people to 'deliver'.

The usual injunction of 'going native' in terms of participant observation implies more than is usually understood. It implies that one can experience being moved about *as a member* only if one is 'there' in the first place *as* a member. Participating means being around long enough to observe what is happening to others like Alex; but it also means being *involved* — enough that is, so that things happen to the researcher as a *member*. As I too became 'visible' and 'available', others used me for their own ends, or felt me to be in their way. Much of my experience in the field came from having the 'same' moves done to me, embarrassment and all. At the pasta lunch, my 'show' as a researcher had revealed me to be someone like Alex — unable to 'deliver' — but the senior managers could afford to wait on my learning to do so, a process much aided by being teamed up with an 'internal researcher'.

The ability to fully understand Bestsafe artefacts, as the tagliatelli incident makes clear, stems from 'being there' as an insider and as an outsider. Others, for example Turnbull (1990: 76), argue that the performative situation entails a surrender of the inner self to become something else. However, this is where problems of representation can emerge, because, with all the insight gained from going native, ethnographers are then also expected to de-familiarize themselves with their experience. In contrast, by making myself figural to the study, I am emphasizing the 'self-similarity' between the *moves* (see Lyotard 1984; Munro 1993) that members of Bestsafe make on each other. As I learnt to shift between 'doing' and 'delivery', these figures of 'insider' and 'outsider' no longer felt incompatible. In always having to work across from one figure to the other, I came to see how this state of 'in-betweenness' (Turner 1974) mirrored the operating managers' own motility. As has been illustrated, Susie and Harold's cultural performances were finely mutated between keeping up membership in their group by 'doing' and the 'delivery' work of being seen to be a manager 'in' control.

We continued to be in-between, the managers and I. Delivery at Bestsafe, it transpires, is never defined ahead, through instructions, but evaluated *after* the event. Even then, the ethos is always one of prudent deferral! As I learnt to 'deliver', I began to understand the Bestsafe construct of selling: senior managers never issued instructions, as in a command and control model. Instead they position themselves as if they are fund-holders examining 'bids' (see also Munro 1998). They wait to see who responds to which call. The significance of their positioning is this: it is up to you as to how you respond to the 'call'. You can't know, but can only speculate what they — the elite — think is important.

Discussion

The cultural 'turn' in organization theory lies in recognizing that all practices are mediated by cultural phenomena. This is not to suggest that control and intervening is driven *through* culture. Such a view would grossly misrepresent how cultural phenomena work. It is to argue, instead, that there are no symbols that speak of 'culture' alone. Instructions, commands, and the like, all require cultural material to be made 'visible' and 'available'. Persuasion, as Fernandez (1986) has long argued, happens through performance.

These reflections help to explain why control, despite critical work (e.g.

Burawoy 1979; Rosen and Baroudi 1992; Willmott 1993), remains an instrumental concept, immune to theorizing on culture. Control is discussed as if managers are disembedded from culture — as if initiatives lay outside the organization, only coming inside to be implemented. This is to be expected where talk of leadership, dominant coalitions, or policy continue to suggest that managers exist on a meta-level of planning. However, more informed writers also partition cultural material from control. For example, Alvesson (1985: 108) argues 'jokes, coffee breaks, how people are dressed ... and so on' are marginal to 'the organization's hierarchy and the ways in which the work is organized, controlled, and carried out'.

In contrast to such studies, I have argued that a 'show' of control is pivotal to cultural performance. Two sets of findings stand out. First, and against the usual stress on hegemony and consensually validated sets of symbols, I illustrated the incorporation of 'individual' artefacts into cultural performance. What is striking about Bestsafe is the diversity of 'style' of managers and their readiness to pursue different agendas. Indeed, ambiguities over what is to count as delivery have the unintended consequence of making 'visible' and 'available' a wider range of cultural materials than senior managers would find in a top-down economy of instructions and feedback. Second, in explicating how control materials are *cultural* phenomena, I pointed to the artefact of an *attenuation* of access to superiors. Although reading 'absences' in a text is well recognized (e.g. Martin 1990; Silverman 1987), further research should explore how the motility of a performed order depends on its 'gaps', 'deletions' and 'silences'. Where expressions enter in one mode and not another, absences have 'presence' within the performed order and speak volumes to organization participants.

There is a *multiplicity* of memberships to accomplish. To reconcile the competing demands of different groups, members are adept at making artefacts 'speak' in different ways. For example, as well as belonging to a group of about twelve managers sharing Tom as head of division, Alex, Susie and Harold were competing for inclusion in a group invisibly marked out for promotion (an issue I was forever catching myself being drawn into, by all sides). In adopting quality or output charts, Susie and Harold found different artefacts to square this circle. In terms of 'doing', Susie espoused quality, and achieved prominence as this became a well publicized corporate agenda. Meanwhile, Harold pursued his focus in ways that co-opted aspects of quality. Neither Susie nor Harold pursued their agenda to the exclusion of the other. On the contrary, *each mutated the materials of the other*.

At the same time, managers had to avoid 'doing' in ways that looked as if they had 'got above themselves', an identity which would lose the commitment of the staff. As a matter of nuancing their cultural performances, Susie allowed her espousal of quality to be *hers* when presenting to senior managers, but quality became *their* project when dealing with staff. This motility in the performed order seemed to pass Alex by. His identity came from a solid insistence on representing the needs of his workers, regardless of audience; a position that left him less than competent in the eyes of both seniors and subordinates.

I relate the readiness of Susie and Harold to adapt their 'own' agendas to a will to rise above being 'glorified supervisors'. Yet admission to the notional category of managers who 'delivered', remained elusive and provisional. As the analysis indicates, membership at Bestsafe is never fixed; all belongings have to be made and re-made. Nor should this provisionality be thought peculiar to Bestsafe. Consider the following exchanges from Kunda's material, over inclusion within the group of managers. First, about a superior: 'He's a loser. He just can't handle the ambiguity... A wimp. It doesn't work in the Tech culture.' (1992: 173). Second, about a subordinate: 'He's a good manager, but a complainer. He's too negative about the company' (1992: 187). It is clear how cultural performance stretches beyond the moment to help circulate judgements about worth and competence.

As has been illustrated, participants do more with artefacts than make themselves visible and accountable *as* members of a group. In the self-same moment of performance in which they show themselves to be the 'same', managers at Bestsafe also try to nuance artefacts in ways that set themselves apart: they are not just doing *more* than others, they display themselves as *different*. At Tech, self is the 'other' side of culture and identity can be read either in terms of being a 'winning manager', or as being an acceptable human being. Consider this wonderful put-down fed to Kunda after a Tech manager had raved to Kunda's lunch partner about his current success: 'He's vicious! He'll eat you alive! But I hear that he's still a fifty-fifty. Not clear if he's a win or lose' (1992: 190). He is 'failed', therefore, on both counts. Kunda's lunch partner is not only excluding the manager, on balance, from the group of successful managers, but in the cannibalistic quip that precedes this move, the Tech manager has also been excluded from the group of human beings.

We mistake the nature of organizations, and the opportunities they offer, if we think of performed orders as hegemonic, leaving no space for self. An alternative to thinking that culture could ever 'swallow' persons — irony and all — is the idea that persons manipulate the materials and artefacts circulating within practices in endless interesting and multiple ways, but take care, in so doing, to 'show' what *passes* for Tech culture, or Bestsafe ethos. As can be seen in the above examples, Tech's logo of 'winning' appears at the very moment that a colleague is being knifed in the back. At Bestsafe, Harold frames Tom, not himself, as holding the 'fine tooth comb'. Managers conduct social exclusions in the organization's or boss's name, making the weapons appear to be wielded by others. This skill outpaces the more totalizing forms of membership associated with Durkheimian holism.

Conclusion

It is the motility of the performed order that is highlighted in this paper. Managers are perhaps caught in 'webs of significance of their own making' (a phenomenological view), or even in 'situations of others' making' (a structuralist view), but they can also be seen to be moving *between* possibilities of performance. As illustrated, they elicit membership from different groups by nuancing the membership work of *doing* with a display of their 'own' identity of *delivery*. In suggesting how the ethnographer too enters the 'invisible world' to be moved about, I discussed how experiences at Bestsafe suggested that there is a motility to the performed order that has been overlooked by previous researchers.

Motility relies on a multiplicity to meaning. This is in part how members manage the passage between an exhibition of membership and a display of self. The drama of cultural performance, however, comes from *shifting* the lifeworld with it. As in the encounter between Susie and Harold, or the display by Ellen, earlier, there is much to be gained from examining the occasions when members draw on specific artefacts. Rather than assume that occasions are what they seem, it is important to see which particular world each participant is staging, and when. To see the world as throughput, rather than quality, or to imagine a company which seeks self-managers, rather than 'burnouts', the analysis needs to go beyond a concern about which artefacts are shared more generally and focus, instead, on the appearance of specific artefacts on particular occasions; and on their absence on other occasions.

In terms of the performed order, the contemporary interest is always on an everyday interplay of artefacts and agendas. We should avoid, then, treating talk of organization culture as a sham, or control as a defunct topic. Although reported data is treated by senior managers at Bestsafe as 'incomplete', such doubt turns out to mutually support kinship effects that circulate around perceived changes in access to senior managers. Culture and control work hand in hand; and if some artefacts seem more associated with control, it is surely hard — as the emic understandings of delivery and selling suggest — to be sure which is which. Wherever aspects of culture and control are differentiated discursively, possibilities open up for their being de-differentiated and mutated within the everyday. Working under the rubric of culture allows some, such as Susie, more scope to engage in control processes than they might otherwise feel able. Equally, senior managers at Bestsafe treated morale as a *cultural* phenomenon — dependent on the manager's good running of the department — rather than connecting it, as Alex did, with shortcomings in the supply of resources.

This discussion should not suggest that Bestsafe successfully enacted control. This is the distance I place between cultural performance and more rationalistic depictions of control. The point is that talk about managers 'intervening' *as if they actually were controlling* may well miss out on what the devil it is that they think they're up to. Nor is it to imply, as is implicit in some institutionalist literature (e.g. Meyer and Rowan 1977), that performances of being 'in' control rest solely on the bedrock of what Giddens and others call 'routines'. Managers draw on artefacts associated with control, such as quality initiatives or output charts, not only because these are instrumental devices, but because these are *indexical to their cul-*

tural performance as a 'doing' manager and their appearing to be 'in' resistance or 'in' control. These performances have effects. In the performed order of Bestsafe, managerial devices and ethos are never disjunct.

Motility is given to the performed order when cultural performance is harnessed to an aspect of *crisis* in the everyday. This is so even where, as at Bestsafe, cultural performance involves a very 'show' of this mundaneness. In this line of thinking, the research interest goes beyond that of investigating the various methods by which members make their work 'observable and reportable' to each other (Garfinkel 1967). Managers do more than exhibit and reproduce cultural phenomenon. At times, they may 'contrive and propagate' the same artefacts *as if* they were different; and sometimes they pass off differences *as if* these were the same. More critically, though, managers can be understood to be continuously at work 'finding' occasions within which to reconcile the competing demands of membership in various groups and displaying their performances of self. Wittingly or not, it is by creating such occasions that they become both self *and* 'visible' and 'available' as artefacts.

References

Alvesson, Mats
1985 'On focus in cultural studies of organizations'. *Scandinavian Journal of Management Studies* 2: 105–120.

Argyris, Chris
1985 *Strategy, change and defensive routines*. Cambridge. MA: Ballinger.

Argyris, Chris
1990 'The dilemma of implementing controls: the case of managerial accounting'. *Accounting, Organizations and Society* 15: 503–511.

Barley, Stephen R., Gordon W. Meyer, and Debra C. Gash
1988 'Cultures of culture: academics, practitioners and the pragmatics of normative control'. *Administrative science Quarterly* 33: 24–60.

Bauman, Richard
1977 *Verbal art as performance*. Rowley, MA: Newbury House.

Bauman, Richard
1986 *Story, performance, and event: contextual studies in oral narrative*. New York: Cambridge University Press.

Burawoy, Michael
1979 *Manufacturing consent*. Chicago: Chicago University Press.

Carlson, Marvin
1996 *Performance: a critical introduction*. London: Routledge.

Clifford, James
1986 'Introduction: partial truths' in *Writing culture: The poetics and politics of ethnography*. J. Clifford and G. E. Marcus (eds.), 1–26. Berkeley: University of California Press.

Cohen, Anthony P.
1982 *Belonging: identity and belonging in British rural cultures*. Manchester: Manchester University Press.

Cohen, Anthony P.
1985 *The symbolic construction of community*. London: Tavistock.

Cohen, Anthony P.
1987 *Whalsay: symbol, segment and boundary in a Shetland Island community*. Manchester: Manchester University Press.

Cohen, Anthony P.
1994 *Self-consciousness: an alternative anthropology of identity*. London: Routledge.

Cohen, Anthony, and John Comaroff
1976 'The management of meaning: On the phenomenology of political transactions' in *Transactions and meaning: directions in the anthropology of exchange and political behavior.* B. Kapferer (ed.). Philadelphia: Institute for the Study of Human Issues.

Czarniawska-Joerges, Barbara
1991 'Culture is the medium of life' in *Reframing organizational culture.* P. J. Frost, L. F. Moore, M. R. Louis, C. C. Lundberg and J. Martin (eds.), 285–297. London: Sage.

Czarniawska-Joerges, Barbara
1992 *Exploring complex organizations: a cultural perspective.* London: Sage.

Dalton, Melvin
1959 *Men who manage.* New York: Wiley.

Deal, T. E., and A. A. Kennedy
1982 *Corporate cultures: the rites and rituals of corporate life.* Reading, MA: Addison-Wesley.

Douglas, Mary
1975 *Implicit meanings: essays in anthropology.* London: Routledge and Kegan Paul.

Fernandez, James
1986 *Persuasions and performances: the play of tropes in culture.* Bloomington: Indiana University Press.

Foucault, Michel
1977 *Discipline and punish,* translated by A Sheridan. London: Allen Lane.

Foucault, Michel
1980 *Power/knowledge: Selected interviews and other writings 1972–1977.* C. Gordon (ed.). London: Harvester Wheatsheaf.

Foucault, Michel
1991 'Governmentality' in *The Foucault effect: studies in governmental rationality.* G. Burchell, C. Gordon and P. Miller (eds.), 87–104. Hemel Hempstead: Harvester Wheatsheaf.

Garfinkel, Harold
1967 *Studies in ethnomethodology.* Englewood Cliffs, NJ: Prentice Hall.

Geertz, Clifford
1973 *The interpretation of cultures.* New York: Basic Books.

Huff, Anne S.
1988 'Politics and argument as a means of coping with ambiguity and change' in *Managing ambiguity and change.* L. R. Pondy, R. J. Boland and H. Thomas (eds.), 79–90. Chichester: Wiley.

Knights, David, and Hugh Willmott
1993 ' "It's a very foreign discipline": the genesis of expenses control in a mutual life insurance company'. *British Journal of Management* 4: 1–18.

Kunda, Gideon
1992 *Engineering culture: Control and commitment in a high-tech corporation.* Philadelphia: Temple University Press.

Latour, Bruno
1986 'The powers of association' in *Power action and belief: a new sociology of knowledge?* Sociology Review Monograph 32. J. Law (ed.). 234–263. London: Routledge.

Linstead, Stephen
1996 'Understanding management: critique, culture and change' in *Understanding management.* S. Linstead, R. Grafton Small and P. Jeffcutt (eds.), 11–33. London: Sage.

Lyotard, Jean-François
1984 *The postmodern condition: a report on knowledge.* translated by G. Bennington and B. Massumi. Manchester: Manchester University Press.

Martin, Joanne
1990 'Deconstructing organization taboos: the suppression of gender conflict in organizations'. *Organization Science* 1: 339–359.

Martin, Joanne, and C. Siehl
1983 'Organizational culture and counterculture: an uneasy symbiosis'. *Organizational Dynamics* 12: 52–64.

Meek, V. Lynn
1988 'Organizational culture: origins and weaknesses'. *Organization Studies* 9/4: 453–473.

Meyer, John W., and Brian Rowan
1977 'Institutionalised organizations: formal structure as myth and ceremony'. *American Journal of Sociology* 83: 340–363.

Munro, Rolland
1992 'Enabling participative change: the impact of strategic value'. *International Studies in Management and Organization* 21: 52–65.

Munro, Rolland
1993 'Just when you thought it safe to enter the water: accountability, language games and multiple control technologies'. *Accounting, Management and Information Technologies* 3/4: 249–271.

Munro, Rolland
1995 'Managing by ambiguity: an archaeology of the social in the absence of management accounting'. *Critical Perspectives on Accounting* 6: 433–482.

Munro, Rolland
1996 'A consumption view of self: extension, exchange and identity' in *Consumption matters.* The Sociological Review Monograph series. S. Edgell, A. Warde and K. Hetherington (eds.), 248–273. Oxford: Blackwell.

Munro, Rolland
1998 'Belonging on the move: market rhetoric and the future as obligatory passage'. *The Sociological Review* 46/2: 208–243.

Roberts, John
1991 'The possibilities of accountability'. *Accounting, Organizations and Society* 16: 355–368.

Rosen, Michael
1991 'Breakfast at Spiro's: dramaturgy and dominance' in *Reframing organization culture.* P. J. Frost, L. F. Moore, M. R. Louis, C. C. Lundberg and J. Martin (eds.), 77–89. London: Sage.

Rosen, Michael, and Jack Baroudi
1992 'Computer-based technology and the emergence of new forms of managerial control' in *Skill and consent: contemporary studies in the labour process.* A. Sturdy, D. Knights and H. Willmott (eds.), 213–234. London: Routledge.

Rosen, Michael, and Thomas P. Mullen
1996 'There to here and no way back: the late life of a cocaine dealer' in *Understanding management.* S. Linstead, R. Grafton Small and P. Jeffcutt (eds.), 94–112. London: Sage.

Silverman, David
1987 *Communication and medical practice: social relations in the clinic.* London: Sage.

Singer, Milton, *editor*
1959 *Traditional India: structure and change.* Philadelphia: American Folklore Society.

Smircich, Linda
1983 'Concepts of culture and organizational analysis'. *Administrative Science Quarterly* 28: 339–359.

Strathern, Marilyn
1991 *Partial connections.* Maryland: Rowman and Little.

Turnbull, Colin
1990 'Liminality: a synthesis of subjective and objective experience' in *By means of performance.* R. Schechner and W. Appel (eds.), 50–81. Cambridge: Cambridge University Press.

Turner, Victor
1974 *Drama, fields and metaphors.* Ithaca, NY: Cornell University Press.

Turner, Victor
1985 *On the edge of the bush: anthropology as experience.* Tucson: University of Arizona Press.

Van Maanen, John, and Gideon Kunda
1989 '"Real feelings": emotional expression and organization culture' in *Research in organization behaviour,* Vol. 11. L. L. Cummings and B. M. Staw (eds.), 43–104. Greenwich, CN: JAI Press.

640   Rolland Munro

Weick, Karl E.
1985 'Sources of order in underorganized
       systems: themes in recent organiza-
       tion theory' in *Organization theory
       and inquiry: the paradigm revolu-
       tion*. Y. S. Lincoln (ed.), 106–136.
       Beverly Hills, CA: Sage.

Willis, Paul
1977 *Learning to labour: how working
       class kids get working class jobs*.
       Farnborough: Saxon House.

Willmott, Hugh
1993 'Strength is ignorance; slavery is
       freedom: Managing culture in mod-
       ern organizations'. *Journal of
       Management Studies* 30: 515–552.

[16]

PLAYING THE PART: REFLECTIONS ON ASPECTS OF MERE PERFORMANCE IN THE CUSTOMER–CLIENT RELATIONSHIP

HEATHER HÖPFL

University of Northumbria

ABSTRACT

The paper seeks to address the ways in which organizations are selective in the aspects of employees which they want and value, and those which are implicitly rejected by the organization. As such, the paper considers Diderot's famous comparison between acting and whoring in order to give emphasis to what might be termed 'performed synedoche' in the employee role. The paper draws on a range of examples from service occupations in order to explore what 'performed synedoche' might mean in practice. It concludes with a discussion of the necessary hypocrisy of certain aspects of the service role and examines the psychological costs which attach to this type of performance.

INTRODUCTION

The actor is like 'the whore who feels nothing for the man she is with, but lets herself go in his arms anyway as a demonstration of her professional competence' (Diderot, 1773. In Roach, 1985, p. 138)

The advisor considered that the client wasn't doing enough to find work so she went through the interview in a correct but entirely cursory way, playing her part in a detached and dismissive manner, disclaiming any contact with the personal. (Burke, 1999)

The changing nature of the psychological contract of work has led to a situation in which 'professional competence' might be construed in terms of a behavioural repertoire which attaches to the performance of specific work roles and their improvisation. This paper attempts to analyse Diderot's conception of the actor's skills in relation to the construction of professional competence. In particular, it seeks to give attention to the ways in which *mere* performance is required in the servicing of a role. When Diderot compares the actor's skill as similar to that of the whore he is making reference to the way in which the nature of the relationship with the other – actor and audience, customer and client – involves putting merely a part of oneself into the role, into the performance, while others aspects

Address for reprints: Heather Höpfl, Northumbria University, Business School, Ellison Building, Ellison Place, Newcastle upon Tyne NE1 8ST, UK (heather.hopfl@unn.ac.uk).

of the person are held back. There are many day-to-day references to the experience of work in such terms and the notion of work as 'abuse' is not unfamiliar. Here the intention is to analyse the relationship between performance and the emotional repertoire which is used in the service of such performance. In particular, the intention is to give emphasis to the notion of distance (Goffman, 1971) and its consequences for the client relationship.

First, it is perhaps useful to consider the way in which Diderot uses the term 'professional competence'. In recent years, a number of themes have begun to emerge which give emphasis to the more subtle yet pervasive requirements of the employment contract. For example, the ways in which the language of emotion is used in support of strategic objectives, the proliferation of the notion of emotional intelligence as related to success and business acumen, and of the increasingly explicit ways in which certain aspects of the individual are required to support work roles while, at the same time, aspects of the individual which do not support the rational trajectory of the organization are rejected. This way of speaking about work has a long tradition. Gouldner (1969) makes the same point when he argues that in the experience of work '. . . the individual learns . . . which parts of himself are unwanted and unworthy' (Gouldner, 1969, p. 349). Arguably, the past 30 years have seen an increasingly specific attention to those attributes of the person which are desired by organizations and those which are not. In this respect, it is possible to explore the nature of the contract of work as increasingly concerned with the procurement of attributes: as an expression of the organization's desires and the employee's obligation to satisfy such desires by disaggregating themselves into desirable and undesirable parts. To some management theorists this may seem an entirely inconsequential necessity to ensure the predictability of organizational behaviour. However, more is at stake than a simple and necessary classification of behaviours and contributions. Organizations have for at least the past 20 years engaged in a meretricious approach to training for contact staff and an emphasis on performance has had a subtle and deleterious effect. In order to examine the ways in which organizations require the control and repression of undesirable emotions, the examples used in this paper are drawn from airline cabin crew as a familiar source of illustration and, from a less glamorous context, the UK Employment Service. The latter is a government agency established to find work for the unemployed. The Employment Service has been subject to changes in its sense of identity and purpose as successive governments have changed its name to meet shifting emphases of policy, philosophy and, consequently, of performance. The Employment Service, given its task, is of particular interest to this analysis because the performance repertoire is acted out within a potentially volatile environment. Employment advisors command resources and can make decisions which determine whether or not their clients are entitled to benefits and, therefore, the mutual requirement to play a part is very much a part of the interaction.

THE SELECTIVE PROCUREMENT OF ATTRIBUTES

The first strand of the argument, therefore, is concerned with the selective procurement of attributes of the individual by work organizations. Specifically, this refers to the elaboration of the socio-psychological contract of work to include the use of emotional labour (Hochschild, 1983) in support of the work role. Implicit in this argument is the notion of the self as an available and consumable collection of attributes which are both representational and reproducible; where the skill of the performance is in the achievement of sameness/predictability/regularity; where creativity, ingenuity or improvisation can only be applied to the technique of reproduction, that it to say, can only be used to elaborate the prescribed role. For example, in training the employment advisor, what is required is a relatively interchangeable performance from one advisor to another, common standards of presentation and delivery, attention to a well rehearsed repertoire of standard behavioural options and, indeed, of rehearsed deviations from standard interactions. Training might, thus, embrace a range of contingency positions and 'what ifs', for example, 'What if a client is rude and abusive?', 'What if I don't know the answer to a question put by a client?'. Improvisation, as might be signified by a personal interpretation of the role, is not considered a desirable skill unless it serves the unique demands of the role. In other words, the intrusion of aspects of the actor not required by the performance is generally regarded as undesirable, whereas the ingenuity of the actor in furthering the performance via some elaboration of the role, what is technically termed 'a conceit', is deemed to be an act which demonstrates 'initiative' and is frequently rewarded via employee service awards. Consequently, the point of departure for this discussion is with the histrionic dissimulation which is necessary to sustain a convincing performance and with it its emotional consequences. In part, this is to do with how the individual learns to *play a part* and to discriminate between what is desired and what is not desired and *to act* accordingly.

ACTING THE PART

In order to advance the argument, it is necessary to reiterate briefly some material which has been articulated in more detail elsewhere (Höpfl, 1994, 1995). First, it is important to preface any discussion of emotions with the caveat that the term is comparatively modern. Its current usage dates back little more than three hundred years. The earliest references to the use of the word describe states of agitation or disturbance (Latin, *emovere*: to move out, to stir up) and this later came to be applied to psychological states. Previously, from the ancient Greeks to the eighteenth century, what are now referred to as emotions were known as *passions* (Averill, 1980). The word passion is derived from the Latin (*patior*) meaning to bear, to suffer, to support, to undergo, to allow, permit, endure and, in an obscene sense and of particular relevance here, to submit oneself to another's lust, to prostitute oneself. Passion is etymologically cognate with patience. It is to be borne or suffered. Clearly, this definition of passion – as submission, as resignation and compliance – provides an alternative view of the notion of a 'passion for excellence'. In the framing of this definition, the exhortation to passion for work is a call to a more complex and abject compliance. The requirement to perform a professional role can produce similar effects. Burke (1999) describes how an employment advisor was conducting an interview with a client who smelt badly of alcohol and body odour. He describes how the advisor conducted the interview with appropriate professional detachment and was faithful to the script but confided afterwards that she could not send the individual out for an interview for a job because he was dirty. She expressed her distaste for her engagement with the client with a facial expression and gesture that demonstrated her feelings of contamination by contact and supported this evaluation with a facial expression that confirmed her distaste. After the client left the performance area, in effect went off stage, the advisor proceeded to take a bottle of perfume from her handbag and to spray around the chair where the client had been sitting. Burke (1999) comments on how this gesture reminded him of a priest incensing the altar before the ritual of the Mass begins. Here the advisor confirms the site of the performance as a 'sacred' space, in other words gives primacy to the regulated performance area which has been contaminated by the intrusion of the unworthy. Therefore, just as when entering a Roman Catholic church the laity dip their hands into the holy water stoup at the church door and make the sign of the cross in a gesture of symbolic cleansing, so the client who does not symbolically cleanse himself before entering the site, brings with him the contamination of the world, of the body and of the lack of acceptance of the rules for entering the site (cf. Fernandez, 1986). When the employment advisor incenses the air, she is restoring order and propriety to the site of the performance.

Diderot in his famous treatise on the actor, *Le paradoxe sur le comedien*, written in 1773, says that the actor's skills are like those of 'the whore who feels nothing for the man she is with, but lets herself go in his arms anyway as a demonstration of her professional competence' (Roach, 1985, p. 138). Leaving aside the temptation to explore the somewhat debased attempts to identify and validate 'professional competencies', the relationship between performance, artifice and emotion might be argued to have characteristics in common with what might be termed *performed synecdoche*: where the part is used as an emblem of the whole and is devised to satisfy the desires of others. A disaggregation is required in performance by which the individual must allocate parts of his/her experience along the lines of what is required in performance to support the work role and what is set aside.

The problem which the notion of performed synecdoche presents is to do with the way in which behaviour in organizations is regulated and where such regulation originates. The regulation of organizational behaviour is, in the first instance, external to the actor(s). It is, effectively, regulation by an anterior authority which provides the script for the performance, sometimes with associated metrics, and the collaborative interpretation of this in performance. This anterior authority may be in the cultural norms, patriarchs or matriarchs of the organization, traditions and the whole range of prevailing assumptions that might be brought to bear on the construction of a performance. It is proposed that the prevailing and preceding authority are the source, the producer, of a text that specifies what is to be brought to the performance. If this authority says that the play is *Hamlet*, the actors cannot play *Macbeth*. However, the authority may propose that *Hamlet* be played in the style of *Macbeth* or with the characters from *Julius Caesar*. The point is that the setting, choice of performance, style of performance and so on is regulated by the anterior direction of the acting space. Given this, the greatest degree of choice for the actor comes in the extent to which they engage with their roles in performance. In 1998, on a scheduled flight from Warsaw to Heathrow, I witnessed an extraordinary performance by cabin crew that resembled a sixth-form review. The cabin crew donned the duty free articles they were selling and one of the male cabin crew members pushed his trolley up the aisle in an ostentatiously camp manner, wearing a silk headscarf and Rayban sunglasses, with a small teddy bear mascot waving from his breast pocket. The female member of the crew who accompanied him gestured and pointed like a magician's assistant. I have never seen anything like it in many years of flying. Another cabin-crew member announced that this was the floorshow and the passengers broke into spontaneous and sustained applause. At the end of the performance, the crew took their bows. I was struck by the inevitable logic of the performance requirement of the organization which takes performance to this extreme. Without doubt, these crew members were acting beyond the call of their roles. This example provides an insight into what occurs to a lesser degree in everyday organizational performance in a less immediate and obvious way. Its significance lies in what is revealed by the extreme variant. This has much in common with the notion of the theatre of the absurd in which the production of the action is made transparent in its performance.

In the framing of the organization, the site of performance is the nexus of constructed meanings which come together to create the performance. The meaning which is then specific to the site of the performance takes precedence, at least for the duration of the performance, over any such meanings as the fragments of which it is made up may have within their own contexts. The cabin crew in the example above decided by some collective understanding to overplay their roles. Their outrageous performance says, in effect, if the organization expects us to act we will do just that. This is how for them some notion of their self worth is restored against the prevailing order. So, for example, whereas in the previous example, the employment advisor restores the order of the site in line with the regulation of performance, so in the second example, the logic of the performance is subverted by an overplaying of it.

The regulated performance is a pastiche of elements drawn from other contexts in the service of a particular trajectory of meaning. In other words, it is an elaborate dramaturgical allegory. The allegorical conceit of organizational performance is the amalgamation of artefacts, attributes and artifices which function to translate fantasies and desires into consonant actions and events. The construction of the allegory is such that it assembles attributes of the corporate actor in the service of the production and in such a way as to minimize, deprive or violate their significance outside of the performance itself. Hence, the aspects of experience which are employed in support of the organizational performance may become contemptible counterfeits and experienced as an abuse, or the performance may become everything such that the actor has no existence apart from the performance. The latter, with its emphasis on the work-role to the exclusion of other possible roles is often associated commitment to the organization and, hence, with a progression up the organizational hierarchy.

MASKING THE EMOTIONS

It is evident that if the required behaviour is to be performed with authority and propriety, ambivalence regarding the intention, the direction, the scripting and the framing, needs to be concealed by a mask (Napier, 1986, p. xxiii). Within the framing, successful dramatic performance and the construction of an appropriate mask is primarily dependent on the rehearsal period. As indicated above, in a regulated performance site, real emotion is not expected to intrude other than in support of the dramatic action. In theatre, the ambivalence, anxiety, distress, fear of failure, lusts, tears and so on, often are most manifest on the very margins of the performance. When I worked in regional repertory theatre, I frequently saw actors in the wings confront and master highly complex emotions before stepping into the performance arena. It was not unusual to hear actors saying, 'I can't do this, I can't go on', only to step a metre forward and into the acting arena to confront these anxieties in performance. Stepping out of that arena again also produced complex responses and these are discussed below.

Acting before an audience, on one level, requires a dispassionate and mechanical re-enactment of the product of the rehearsal room. Actors in long running productions have commented that, with an unresponsive audience, they can plan a weekend's activities, a holiday, a dinner party or whatever, while going through the motions of performance. As Burke (1999) comments on the employment advisor, 'The advisor considered that the client wasn't doing enough to find work so she went through the interview in a correct but entirely cursory way, playing her part in a detached and dismissive manner, disclaiming any contact with the personal' (Burke, 1999). Similarly, prostitutes will sometimes say that while trading in their most intimate *parts*, they may choose not to kiss their clients as this would be too intimate. In saying this, they alienate those aspects of their body which they put forward for trade in order to preserve their self-respect, privacy and reserve a part of themselves from the exchange. The cabin crew, on the other hand, symbolically seem to be saying that if the organization takes so much they can have the lot. There is so little left to protect that a camp response is the only resistance available to them. Hence, their outrageous performance is a product of outrage and, in practice, more tragic than comic.

In theories of acting, the separation of the act–action–acting from the actor's experience has been regarded as the most significant achievement of the actor's skill. Central to this argument is the notion of a dual consciousness. This is the view that outstanding acting requires an ability to possess dual personality (Roach, 1985, p. 148). Ironically, this is to be achieved via autonomy and self-possession. This amounts to a willingness to submit to the performance; in effect, it means the actor can say, 'I can play this role because I am detached from it'. This line of argument says that the embodied role can be in performance in a specific repertoire detached from a superior intellect which permits its body to be used, yet remains disdainful of its appropriation. Hence, it has been suggested that one paradox of Diderot's 'Paradoxe' is the contrast between the notion of actor as instrument manipulated in performance and the actor as autonomous and self-generative exercising choice over the extent of the submission to the role. Although the latter is seen by Diderot as a considerable achievement, it is arguable as to whether or not it can be realized without the contempt of the actor for those who consume his/her performance (Höpfl, 1995). Moreover, despite the confidence of the 'Paradoxe', it is the case that many professional actors experience difficulties with the transitions in and out of role and seek ways to facilitate such transitions. Drink is not an unusual means of reconciling the mind and body after a performance. In the example of the purification ritual of the employment advisor above, it seems that the act of perfuming the air creates a *cordon sanitaire* around the acting space, marking it as a place or ritual and performance. Consequently, movements into, across and out of the space mark important transitions with all the associated complexity of places of transition. The wings of a theatre are not unlike the international departure lounge of an airport or the portals of classical theatre where gods and mortals come into contact.

THE CONTROL OF EMBODIED PASSIONS

The appropriation of the actor's skill, both on the stage and in the organization, has important implications. The subordination of the individual to the dramatic task has its origins in classical theatre. The actor on stage had to 'carry' the action and, therefore, the character of the actor was not important other than for giving emphasis to the action itself (Holt, 1989, p. 172). The story of the play, and its trajectory was more important than the actors playing their respective parts. Emphasis is given by a class of actions that are concerned with the persuasive powers of the actor, with authority and propriety. The mastery of the mechanisms of the emotions and sustained rehearsal provided the basis of dramaturgical force. Sarbin (1986) has made a distinction between the dramaturgical, as being concerned with the theatricalities of performance – devices, acting techniques, masks, deceptions and so on, and the dramatistic, which is made up of half remembered roles of epic scripts which are embedded in folk-lore and myth, archetypes and roles learned in early life. These are evoked in given situations from an 'emotional repertoire' (De Souza, 1980) in the service of a role. It is evident that this categorization can be applied to both theatrical roles and to work roles. The actor is expected to control inappropriate emotions and responses in support of the action. Clearly, it is improper for the dramatistic to intrude into the dramaturgical other than when it is called for as an emblematic artefact; as a device to be used when the situation requires histrionic skill to give force to the performance and authority to the actor (MacIntyre, 1990, p. 107). To play a fatherly role is not the same as to behave like someone's father. To express sympathy for someone is not the same as to become distraught. There are a range of feints which must be performed with detachment if they are to be successfully carried off. That social life is regulated in a similar way is not in question. The issue here is the locus of regulation: the individual or the organization.

To act is to counterfeit for dramatic purpose and, as such, it requires practised skills and technical devices to present emotional conceits as its professional product. In Diderot's terms, the actor is a machine without a soul, the acting skill derived from the mastery and control of embodied passions. His concern is with the processes which shape creative energies in the production not of the imitation of reality but, rather and significantly, with the creation of the illusion of reality. It is argued here that the acquisition of the dramatic persona in organizational life is increasingly about the construction of a conceit, a counterfeit of experience that is to the detriment of the actor. The requirement to 'fake it', to perform with a simulated intimacy is a familiar aspect of many service role jobs.

Consider, for example, Burke's (1999) example of the employment advisor who believes that the client is not doing enough to help himself and, therefore, goes through the motions of doing the interview in the prescribed manner but little more. She believes he is not playing his part and refuses to bring any dramatic force to her own role. She performs her role with minimum engagement. Her performance is robotic and cursory. She does what is necessary and no more. In other words, she will only play her role if he plays his. Moreover, she sees his refusal to

262   H. HÖPFL

prepare for and play his role – he is not clean, he is not interested in what she can offer – as a violation of the acting space.

Diderot's actor is an instrument or an empty vessel, capable of playing any or all characters precisely because his/her own character is eradicated and sensibilities obliterated in the pursuit of professional craft. Not unnaturally, this view has been subject to considerable critical discussion within drama studies. However, in organizational terms the achievement of a flexible and well-rehearsed work force which can move easily between a variety of roles with skill is considered to be a desirable accomplishment. Nonetheless, Diderot went further so as to define actors, characters in terms of their deficiencies – of a lack of commitment to friends, family and even of identities (Roach, 1985, p. 135). Organizations or occupations with strong cultural identities can achieve a similar estrangement. The actor is peculiarly impersonal in his/her impersonations and the actor's body, which is after all the instrument of performance, is offered for consumption by the audience. Hence, the logic of the 'take all of me' performance of cabin crew is impeccable if tragic. Ironically, the actor has to find his/her skill in the *suspension* of the very sensibilities that are the substance of his/her craft.

DESIRE AND CONTEXT

The corporate actor must embody the values which corporate culture proposes. Hence, demeanour, bearing, and supporting gestures must express the consonance of the role with the purpose of the action. This requires that an emotional repertoire be learned and employed in support of the performance. The actor's external appearance is clearly part of the construction of the performance. Hence, make-up, hairstyle and costume become aspects of the artistic control of the actor's body. Outside the actor, the appearance of the stage (properties, sets and lighting) and what Kowzan (1968) calls 'the inarticulate sounds' (music and sound effects), all contribute to the performance and its construction within the acting space and to the regulation of performance, artistic direction and the skills of the actors in carrying the performance. Properties, sets and lighting are designed to support and contextualize the performance, to reinforce the rhetorical trajectory of the performance (Aston and Savona, 1991). Training and staff development secure the script to the acting space and regulate performance in context. Management development programmes often include an element of role-playing or of speculating on the standpoints that might be adopted in specific managerial situations. Jackson and Carter, in their analysis of labour as dressage, argue that dressage 'requires the body to perform, requires knowing acts which, implicitly or explicitly, demonstrate compliance to whatever demands the controller seeks to have satisfied' (Jackson and Carter, 1998, p. 58). These *rehearsals* for everyday actions are ways of relating desired behaviours to desired outcomes. Such activities have a similar function to the way in which a script is *blocked* in a theatrical rehearsal; the actors may walk through their roles marking the movements, turns and positions which support the performance of the piece. In training, the manager rehearses a range of possible behaviours which are appropriate or inappropriate to the extent that they achieve the objectives of the organization, or as Jackson and Carter put it 'it is not sufficient that something should be done, it must be done in a particular way' (Jackson and Carter, 1998, p. 59). From the point of view of the study of emotions in work organizations, the significance of this style of training lies in its removal of emotion from the site of performance. Only counterfeits of emotion or dramatistic emotional support is desired in the performance. Where emotion erupts into performance it is regarded as failed or culpable performance.

In theatre, the intended or posited meaning is normally derived from the author or the text of the play and interpretation via the director. The actor can be whatever he or she wants as long as he or she works with the author's intents, to construct and reconstruct him/herself to satisfy the author's desires and, in translation, the desires of the 'artistic' director. The actor, in Diderot's terms, submits to a meretricious appropriation which demands a *passionate* response. The actor must carry the action and impersonate, that is, bring into being the posited meaning of the author. Read in this way, a call for a passion for service is an exhortation to submit to appropriation.

The appropriations – a physical body, gestures, looks, theatrical props and fetish objects – are not only commodified but also kitschified by an authority which frequently reassures itself that its lubricious motivations are liberal, informed, sophisticated and, indeed, enlightened. For example, a gender audit of a major UK company indicated that the shoes to be worn by service staff were required to be 'high enough to show a well-turned ankle but low enough to suggest the sort of sensible shoes worn by nanny'. One might give thought to the embodied ambivalence to be translated into performance by the one who must wear the shoe so defined. Hence, the multiplicity of meaning an element might have in other takes on meanings which are irretrievably in the power of the regulated performance. The appropriated attributes, objects, bodies and so on are rendered abject by the posited meanings which are placed on them.

The selective procurement of attributes and the use of costume and setting secure and capture the individual in a performance in which the person is made available via their role which is pre-scripted and pre-signed to extend specific meanings which may or may not be coincidental with those of the actor.

HYPOCRISY

The assumption of a role and its performance by the actor is a paradox both remarkable and disturbing to behold. The skill which permits performance, which masks the actor and achieves the concealment of the actor's true character, is a considerable competence. The actor is able to translate human experience for representation, to convey the range of human emotion in all its power and fragility, to transform his/her appearance through costume or physical distortion, to employ voice and gesture in the realization of the performance. The actor is able to make manifest a supreme deceit. In work organizations, the actor is constrained by context, role and script with a limited capacity for dramatistic improvisation. What is significant is that the construction of the role regulates the emotional repertoire that attaches to it.

Acting is a craft which requires the simulation of behaviour and emotion, a practised dissimulation, the 'professionalization of two-facedness' (Roach, 1985, p. 137). Consequently, it is the consummate counterfeit of experience. Nothing is as it appears. It is a performed hypocrisy. The actor's craft is primarily one of

264   H. HÖPFL

self-transformation. It is for this reason that the actor has, throughout history, been regarded with suspicion and unease. Indeed, actors were frequently excommunicated from the Church and their craft was regarded as degrading, deceitful, morally bankrupt and hypocritical. The word hypocrite in Greek means literally *an actor* and hypocrisy, *to play on stage.*

The prostitute offers a counterfeit of pleasure as a professional accomplishment and this proficiency has the capacity to dissipate, in reversal, the power of the appropriator. The performance of the prostitute is achieved with contemptuous regard for the client. In this paper, the analogy has been drawn between this contempt for the client and the logic of the dramaturgy of customer service. The necessary abstraction by which the performance is achieved, by its implicit disdain and removal, reverses the appropriation. The consequence is a power play based on a mutuality of contempt (Höpfl, 1995).

The travesty, the grotesque re-presentation of attributes always bears the possibility of collapse into the comic because such constructions bear an implicit irony. The cabin crew push their roles to the point where they become ludicrous. The ludicrousness of such selective representations both enthrals, embarrasses and destabilizes the constructions of the desirer/consumer of such representations. It is only possible to sustain the activity of consumption and capture while such representations are given serious regard. When the ludic and the ludicrous are reconciled, the *consumer* is, at least temporarily, released from a constructed desire for a particular performance. This would suggest that resistance to an extension of the psychological contract of work requires an elaborate and exaggerated performance based on a ludicrous rendering of the partial. Here the violation of the appropriation is reversed by the power of an overplayed simulation.

THE FEAR OF CONTACT

Theatre is dirty work. Contact with actors brings the fear of defilement. As has been argued above, the actor is considered to lack morality, to have no capacity for normal relationships and is thought to possess an unstable character. Yet, these very aspects of the actor intrigue the audience. Audiences experience both envy and moral superiority in relation to actors. Performance is glamorous. The essentially dirty work of the cabin crew is elevated into glamour by make-up and costume and setting. This is not so for the local office employment advisor for whom there are few theatrical props to glamorise the role and, consequently, there is frequently a more insistent rendering of the role. The spectators desire a furtive excursion back-stage to marvel at the devices which produce theatrical illusion, and show a considerable curiosity for the techniques of transformation. Yet consumers of the actor recoil from a peering behind the mask. The audience is discomfited by personal contact with actors. In a similar way, the regulation of organizational behaviour by close reference to the text and the framing of organizational roles permits a reassuring regularity in the nature of interaction between organizational members and their audiences.

As the subject/object of selective procurement, the corporate actor is humiliated and degraded in the service of performance. As a consequence, the actor turns for support to the intimacy of other actors – friendship, respect and admiration, are found in the companionship of the rehearsal room in a common suffering. The relationship between actor and audience could, therefore, be described as saprophytic. In other words, the actor must in a sense be dead to any notion of self and the audience then consumes this performance as a saprophytic act. On the other hand, actors demonstrate their skill with condescension to the audience. The back-stage world is dirty, sweaty, raw and emotional, fractious, fraudulent. Behind the curtain is the territory in which the actor perfects his/her craft in order to enter and exit the role with practised facility. Yet, the actor knows the point at which he or she must 'enter' the role and the costs of surrender to it. The esoteric learning of stagecraft alienates the actor from the audience. Actors offer themselves for consumption in performance yet, despite appearances to the contrary, despise audiences who they feel do not and cannot understand the sacrifices which are demanded by the pursuit of that craft. All jobs which require performance skills carry this burden. The audience cannot appreciate how much the actor suffers. Only the other actors know this. Hence, the cabin crew who collectively decide to overplay their roles and the employment advisors who console themselves after they have encountered a difficult client share the sense of collective identity which marks them out as differentiated from other players who enter the performance space. Likewise, the manager who has not experienced the sufferings of playing minor roles will not be credible to his/her staff and may lack empathy with the actors. As is well known a group of actors is called a company. Interestingly, the word 'company' comes from the Latin, *companis* meaning 'to take bread with'. The company and the notion of companionship reside in this sense of collectivity and sharing.

ON THE EXAMINATION OF CONSCIENCE

The theatricalities of organizational life have produced actors who are humiliated, debased and under-valued. Only fellow actors understand the sense of abuse which they share. The customer is led to expect increasing levels of service and high standards of performance from organizational members and yet they cannot appreciate the sacrifices required of the performer. The actor is left with the difficult reconciliation of the experience of degradation and defilement and the public production of virtue. The customer is led to expect continuity, regularity and, indeed, improvement. The contradiction of contamination and goodness produces in the actor a disdain thinly masked by the persona of professional competence. At the same time, the audience is not deceived by the counterfeit of performance and being now consumers of a grotesque counterfeit of service finds a residual dignity in a scornful aversion to the actor's craft. The client as audience is aware of the minuscule movement which transforms the performance into ludicrousness.

For example, when an employment advisor experienced intimidating behaviour from a client who did not want to be interviewed, the advisor persevered with the interview, in effect, sticking to the script but later when the interview was over she undertook a cathartic deconstruction of the interviewee with her colleagues and made fun of the physical characteristics and bodily imperfections of the client. In this way, she performed what she could not perform in acting out her role, the contempt she felt for the individual who had treated her badly. Only her fellow workers could understand what she had experienced in the performance of her role (Höpfl and Burke, 1999).

266   H. HÖPFL

Here is the ultimate irony of the argument presented here. The most powerful emotion at work in the production and consumption of the performance is now contempt. The customer enthralled and seduced by promises of intimacy and care, of arousal, delight, and special attention finds him/herself confronting a grotesque simulacrum of these very things: invasive intimacy without care, neglect dressed up as concern, a hideous and thrusting theatrical mask. The consumer of such performances can only enter the site of performance as a sceptic with some revulsion for the counterfeit experience at the heart of the performance. The appropriation of emotion in the service of the organization and to the exclusion of human values and virtues produces alienated actors and estranged audiences (Höpfl, 1995).

The precarious point between resistance and compliance in performance is the mask which marks the boundary between all that is and all that is not in performance. The construction and maintenance of the mask marks the boundary between the consummate counterfeit and the grotesque parody. The mask is the site of multiple possibilities and, in collapse, of heterogeneity. The apparent coherence and consensus regarding the definition of the event depends primarily on masking. The dramatic mask conceals ambivalence about the role, about performance and about the production but it is not infallible nor, indeed, irreversible. When the mask fails the performance is thrown into question: becomes ludicrous. For the actor, the extent of his/her degradation is revealed. This was quite obvious in the case of the cabin crew where the parody of performance exposed the completely abject position of the actor. The humiliation of the appropriation is apparent in such gross performances. However, when the mask is made grotesque, when the actor forces the role to and beyond its dramatic possibilities, the author of the performance, or the intents of the author, are transgressed by the power of the reversal. Not only does the mask fail but also the performance and, by implication, the desires of the author. What was peddled as good customer service is synonymous with a mutuality of contempt. The irony is that good customer service and perhaps more importantly, good management cannot be achieved by dramaturgical simplicities.

REFERENCES

ASTON, E. and SAVONA, G. (1991). *Theatre as Sign-system: A Semiotics of Text and Performance.* London: Routledge.

AVERILL, J. R. (1980).'Emotion and anxiety: sociocultural, biological, and psychological determinants'. In Rorty, A. O. (Ed.), *Explaining Emotions.* Berkeley: University of California Press.

BURKE, K. (1969). *A Rhetoric of Motives.* Berkeley: University of California Press.

BURKE, P. (1999).'The Customers Stink'. *Proceedings of the Aesthetics II Conference.* Bolton Institute.

DE SOUZA, R. (1980).'The rationality of emotions'. In Rorty, A. O. (Ed.), *Explaining Emotions.* Berkeley: University of California Press.

DIDEROT, D. (1773).'The paradox of acting'. In *The Paradox of Acting and Masks or Faces?* See Roach, J. R. (1985). *The Player's Passion, Studies in the Science of Acting.* Newark: University of Delaware Press.

DIDEROT, D. (1949). *Le paradoxe sur le comedien avec recueilles presentees par Marc Blanquet.* Paris: Editions Nord-Sud.

FERNANDEZ, J. W. (1986). *Persuasions and Performances, The Play of Tropes in Culture.* Bloomington: Indiana University Press.

GOFFMAN, E. (1971). *The Presentation of Self in Everyday Life.* Harmondsworth: Penguin.

GOULDNER, A. (1969).'The unemployed self'. In Fraser, R. (Ed.), *Work*, Vol II. Harmondsworth: Penguin.

HOCHSCHILD, A. (1983). *The Managed Heart.* Berkeley: University of California Press.

HOLT, D. (1989).'Complex ontology and our stake in the theatre'. In Shotter, J. and Gergen, K. (Eds), *Texts of Identity.* London: Sage.

HÖPFL, H. (1994).'Learning by heart: the rules of rhetoric and the poetics of experience'. *Management Learning*, **24**, 3, 463–74.

HÖPFL, H. (1995).'Improving customer service, the cultivation of contempt'. *Studies in Cultures, Organizations and Societies*, **1**, 1.

HÖPFL, H. and BURKE, P. (1999).'Learning and Performance in the Employment Service Local Office'. *British Academy of Management Conference*, Manchester.

JACKSON, N. and CARTER, P. (1998).'Labour as dressage'. In McKinlay, A. and Starkey, K. (Eds), *Foucault, Management and Organisational Theory.* London: Sage, 49–64.

KOWZAN, T. (1968).'The sign in the theatre'. *Diogenes*, **61**, 52–80.

MACINTYRE, A. (1990). *After Virtue.* London: Duckworth.

NAPIER, A. D. (1986). *Masks, Transformation, and Paradox.* Berkeley: University of California Press.

ROACH, J. R. (1985). *The Player's Passion, Studies in the Science of Acting.* Newark: University of Delaware Press.

SARBIN, T. R. (1986).'Emotion and act: roles and rhetoric'. In Harré, R. (Ed.), *The Social Construction of Emotion.* Oxford: Blackwell.

[17]

From Dramaturgy to Theatre as Technology: The Case of Corporate Theatre*

Timothy Clark and Iain Mangham

Durham Business School, University of Durham; The Management Centre, King's College, University of London

ABSTRACT This article examines a piece of corporate theatre. Although theatre has entered organization studies through the dramatistic writing of Kenneth Burke and the dramaturgical writings of Erving Goffman, this article is concerned with an approach variously described as *organizational, radical, situation* or *corporate* theatre that treats theatre not primarily as a resource, an ontology or a metaphor but as a technology. This approach involves the deployment by an organization of dramatists, actors, directors, set designers, lighting specialists, and musicians to put on performances in front of audiences. Using frameworks derived from studies of theatre a particular piece of corporate theatre is described and analysed. It is argued that this form of theatre appears to be used to contain reflection and to promote the views of a particular group within an organization. It does not confront an audience but subtly suggests alternative ways of evaluating, construing and understanding issues. This may be achieved by anaesthetizing audience reaction by encouraging imaginative participation in the performance so that cherished beliefs and values do not appear to be directly challenged.

INTRODUCTION

In this article we are breaking new ground by examining a previously overlooked area of consultancy activity. We are not concerned with understanding consulting as a dramatic event, nor with consultants as actors, but rather with consultancies whose core activity is the employment of theatrical techniques within organizations. These are generically called corporate or industrial theatre consultancies. They emerged in America in the early part of the twentieth century as organizations such as Coca-Cola, IBM, and NCR created 'corporate shows' for their

Address for reprints: Timothy Clark, Durham Business School, University of Durham, Mill Hill Lane, Durham DH1 3LB, UK (timothy.clark@durham.ac.uk).

annual sales conferences (Pineault, 1989). In the UK the live events sector – which embraces conferences, annual general meetings, exhibitions, shows, and product launches – has been growing at 20 per cent annually for the past five years and is comprised of around two hundred firms that generated a little over £500 million in fees in 2000 (*AV Magazine*, 2000). Smith (1997, p. 2) has argued that despite its growing size, theatre in corporate/organizational settings is 'hidden theatre'. Although it employs the techniques of theatre, often utilizes the talents of well-known theatre professionals (actors, singers, writers, directors, etc.) and occasionally transfers and adapts successful Broadway and West End shows into the corporate/organizational setting, this is not typically viewed as a site for theatrical activity. Rather, attending the theatre is generally considered to be a leisure activity, conducted outside of organization time. To date scholarly attention of this area is limited to three PhD theses (Hansen, 2002; Pineault, 1989; Smith, 1997) and a single article in an academic journal (Bell, 1987). None of these publications has empirically examined this phenomenon. Consequently, this article represents the first systematic analysis of this type of theatre. It has three overall aims: (1) to situate theatre as technology within the broader literature on theatre within organization studies; (2) to offer a description of an instance of corporate theatre; and (3) to identify the differences between corporate theatre and other forms of theatre as technology.

In the first of this article's five parts we review the literature in organization studies that has been concerned with theatre. Building on this wide-ranging review the second part highlights the central features of corporate theatre. In the next two parts we discuss our research methods and then describe and analyse the processes of producing and performing an actual piece of corporate theatre called *Your Life. Your Bank*. We do so utilizing ideas from the studies of theatre, in particular Cole's (1975) notion of *imaginative truth* and Pavis's (1992) concept of *mise en scène*. The article closes with a discussion of the differences between corporate theatre and other forms of theatre of technology.

LITERATURE REVIEW

The idea of theatre has entered into organization studies in at least four distinct ways: through the use of theatrical texts to inform and illustrate programmes in leadership and/or through the deployment of games and activities derived from rehearsal processes in the theatre to stimulate and enliven training programmes; through *dramatism*, an analytical perspective which adopts an ontological position and holds that social and organization life *is* theatre; through *dramaturgy* which holds that social and organizational life may be treated metaphorically *as if* it were theatre; and finally, through an approach variously described as *organizational, radical, situation* or *corporate* theatre that treats theatre not primarily as a resource, an ontology or a metaphor but as a technology.

From Dramaturgy to Theatre as Technology 39

There is a burgeoning activity in the use of theatre as resource and a growing literature. That part of it concerned with lessons in leadership largely consists of selective readings of Shakespeare (Augustine and Adelman, 1999; Corrigan, 2000; Jackson, 2001; Mangham, 2001; Whitney and Packer, 2000). That part of it concerned with theatre games is relatively poorly documented although articles occasionally surface in the press attesting to the benefits of such activities (Keene, 1999; Olivier, 2001). We will not be dealing with either of these areas in the present paper. Our interest is primarily in theatre as a technology, but in order to clearly differentiate and situate this approach from more presently well-known conceptual notions/frameworks of theatre within organization studies we begin with a brief outline of dramatism and dramaturgy.

Dramatism

In the middle years of the twentieth century the literary critic Kenneth Burke developed what he termed a *'dramatistic'* model of human behaviour (1945, 1969a, 1969b). Dramatism is a method of analysis that asserts the reality of symbolic action as the defining activity of human beings, not analogically, but as a formal model with which to explore both action and explanations for action. As a guide to such analysis, Burke offers two basic notions – the *Pentad* and the *ratios*. The former is the name that he gives to the five terms that he claims to be basic to any analysis of motivated action: the act, the scene, the agent, the agency, and the purpose. Burke suggests using these terms in pairs in order to understand the congruence that makes theatre interpretable and social action coherent. Thus, the conventions of social life and of drama expect some kind of consistency between say, the nature of agents and the acts they perform, or between the acts and the scene against which they take place. These ratios among the elements of the Pentad are an array of heuristic strategies for grasping the intelligibility of social action, or for recognizing the ways in which a violation of dramatistic coherence illuminates the principle that it offends (Mangham and Overington, 1987, pp. 70–2). Studies in organizations purporting to derive their method from Burke – however indirectly – have been undertaken (Case, 2001; Graham-Hill and Grimes 2001; Kendall, 1993; Mangham and Overington, 1983; Pine and Gilmore, 1999; Walker and Monin, 2001).[1] As Geertz (1983 p. 27) remarked some 20 years ago, Burke's influence is 'at once enormous and – because almost no one actually uses his baroque vocabulary, with its reductions, ratios and so on – elusive'. His baroque vocabulary is in more use now than it was when Geertz made his comments, but so far its potential has not been fully realized.

Dramaturgy

Burke and his major interpreter Duncan (1962, 1968) have had relatively little direct impact upon ways of looking at social and organizational behaviour, but –

together with Gustav Ichheiser (1949) – they had a strong influence upon Erving Goffman, whose own work, of course, has now ensured that theatre as a metaphor for social life has to be taken seriously by philosophers and social scientists throughout the world. Shakespeare may have said it earlier and better, but Goffman gave it a form that sociologists could appreciate. Mitchell (1978) points out Goffman borrowed heavily from others in developing his framework. From Burke, Goffman took the notions that behaviour is to be treated as a process of people relating to each other as actors; that meaning is not a characteristic of the world but is the result of a process – an evolving social process – with others and consequently it is fragile and problematic; and the notion that the self is not a given but is derived and sustained through interaction. From Ichheiser he took the idea that the processes of everyday interaction were of fundamental importance to the understanding of social order, that these processes could be seen as involving 'actors' and 'spectators' giving and receiving 'impressions'. Ichheiser also emphasizes the primacy of the 'situation' and its definition in the unfolding of interaction (Ichheiser, 1949).[2]

Goffman's great contribution has been to take these ideas and to develop and elaborate upon them in his description and analysis of everyday face-to-face behaviour. He had a genius for observation and a great flair for articulating the delicate balances and imbalances that inform performances. His position is most clearly stated in his *Presentation of Self in Everyday Life* (1959) and is elaborated in a number of other works (1967, 1974). His debt to the theatre lies in his use of terms derived from it. He conceives of social behaviour as 'performances' among 'actors' who adjust as best they can the 'expressions' they 'give' and 'give off' so as to convey the 'impression' that they are what they claim to be. Social actors like stage actors 'prepare' and 'rehearse' their performances 'backstage' where they take themselves to be not 'on'. When they are 'on' they 'enact their roles' and they do so on a 'stage' where they are conscious that they are in the presence of an 'audience' who expect a coherence 'among settings, appearance and manner'.

Goffman's *dramaturgy* was received with considerable acclaim. Within 20 years or so it was established as an important theoretical framework in mainstream social science (see Burns, 1992 for a review). It was several years before the framework began to be utilized in organization studies, but here too it has enjoyed some success. Many of these studies follow Goffman in describing and analysing 'situated activity', the fleeting and episodic face-to-face interactions that constitute a large part of social and organizational life (e.g., Brissett and Edgley, 1990; Clark and Salaman, 1996; Gardner, 1992; Gardner and Avolio, 1998; Gardner and Martinko, 1988; Giacolone and Rosenfeld, 1989; Grove and Fisk, 1992; Rosenfeld et al., 1995; Schlenker, 1980). Many of these writers pick up on the notion that Goffman's work is potentially emancipatory. Once it is understood that social reality is a matter of scripts and performances created and sustained by human interaction, changes become possible. Other forms of reality may take the stage given adequate political means for choosing between scripts. Goffman thus provides a perspective from which social actors can become disenchanted with their lot and seek to change it.

However, neither the popularity nor the beguiling nature of dramaturgy should blind us to the fact that it is a somewhat limited application of the theatrical metaphor to social and organizational life. Goffman's exclusive concern with role-playing and impression management and his lack of familiarity with the function of theatre, with rehearsals and directors, with stage performances or theatre audiences has resulted in theory that in its present form is inadequate and stultifying (Wilshire, 1982). It is those features concerned with the construction, delivery and reception of performances that are central to the approach of theatre as technology.

Theatre as Technology

The fourth approach to the use of theatre in organizations is literally that – the use of theatre in organizations. This involves the deployment by an organization of dramatists, actors, directors, set designers, lighting specialists, and musicians to put on performances in front of an audience. It is an approach that largely eschews reference to either dramatism or dramaturgy. This is not to say that its practice is not grounded in a reasonably coherent set of ideas concerning the function of the theatre, although these have not often been spelled out. Some derive from ritual and some from the theatre of the ancient Greeks (Meisiek and Dabitz, 1999). Lyman and Scott (1975, p. 2) remind us that for the Greeks, the plays that were presented at their festivals were a mimesis of ordinary everyday acting. By seeking to render the everyday 'unhidden' to an audience that was urged to adopt a position of 'wonder, astonishment and naïve puzzlement', theatre was the 'primordial social science'. The essence of this position is picked up in the work of theatrical practitioners and anthropologists, who, in turn have influenced some of those seeking to bring about change in social and organizational behaviour (Cole, 1975; Geertz, 1980; Schechner, 1988). Some, like Victor Turner (1984), an anthropologist with a deep interest in and knowledge of theatre, acknowledges his debt to the Greeks with his notion that every society needs a form of activity through which its ways of normally perceiving, valuing, feeling and behaving may be reflexively confronted by members of that society:

> . . . any society that hopes to be imperishable must carve out for itself a space and a period of time in which it can look honestly at itself. This honesty is not that of the scientist, who exchanges the honesty of his ego for the objectivity of

his gaze. It is, rather akin to the supreme honesty of the creative artist, who, in his presentations on the stage, in the book, on canvas, in marble, in music, or in towers and houses, reserves to himself the privilege to see straight what all cultures build crooked. (Turner, 1984, p. 40)

This space of performance, and the culturally endorsed reflexivity that distinguishes it, Turner calls a 'liminal' space, in which:

> . . . groups strive to see their own reality in new ways and to generate a language verbal or non-verbal that enables them to talk *about* what they normally talk about. They are liminal in the sense that they are suspensions of daily reality, occupying privileged spaces where people are allowed to think about how they think about the terms in which they conduct their thinking or to feel about how they feel about daily life. (Turner, 1984, p. 23)

Theatre is clearly one such privileged space and – as we have indicated above – some working in and around organizations have sought to capitalize upon its potential to provide opportunities for members of organizations to see straight what has been built crooked. John Coopey (1998, p. 365), for example, drawing heavily upon the ideas and practice of Augusto Boal (1979),[3] puts forward the notion of *radical theatre* which he envisages being used 'directly in furthering the process of discursive exploration, release and political action', and quotes Kershaw (1992, p. 24) to the effect that this type of theatre is similar to that in ritual. A *liminal* role placing participants betwixt and between their more permanent social roles and a '*ludic* role' enabling the spectator 'to participate in playing around with norms, customs, regulations, laws which govern her life in society' (quoted in Coopey, 1998, p. 374). Unfortunately he provides only one rather thin illustration of the use of radical theatre in organizations and we have been unable to find any more substantial representations of the approach elsewhere in the literature.[4]

Schreyögg argues for an approach to change that he terms *organization theatre* (Schreyögg, 2001; Schreyögg and Dabitz, 1999). Working with members of organizations, theatre professionals and social scientists tailor-make plays to deal with specific issues within specific organizations. They may use a variety of theatrical approaches – burlesque, melodrama, naturalistic – to realize the resultant drama, but the aim is emancipatory, to 'expose the audience to situations of their daily life, thereby confronting it with hidden conflicts, subconscious behavioural patterns or critical routines' (Schreyögg, 2001, p. 3). The debt to Turner is clear in Schreyögg's (2001, p. 9) belief that 'things can be made to move' by rendering discussible that which is not normally discussible. It is reported that organization theatre has quite a following in France and Germany. In 1997 alone there were two thousand such performances in French organizations and two hundred in German companies (Wehner and Dabitz, 1999). In addition, there are companies of actors involved in what may be very similar activities in a number of countries including Belgium, Canada, Denmark and the United Kingdom.

Meisiek (2002) uses the term *situation theatre* for what is essentially *organization theatre*. His form of theatre is 'the staging of problem-oriented plays in an organizational context' that 'is used to promote problem-awareness and to stimulate a readiness to change' (ibid, p. 3). He claims that plays are often written specifically for particular organizations and that a writer may well spend time with the organization to study its processes, its language and its culture. Professional actors then perform the piece. Alternatively members of the organization are drawn directly into the making of the play through workshops and discussions. They may even be invited to 'intervene spontaneously' in the performance 'whenever they feel they would like to change the plot in favour of their own ideas' (Meisiek, 2002, p. 4).

Subscribers to the fourth form of theatre as technology – *corporate theatre* – appear to operate out of the same broad background of theory. They appear to believe in the value of a liminal space – a metaphorical space where the organization can come together and reflect upon its own values and performance – but for the most part corporate theatre appears to be used to contain the reflection and to promote the views of a particular group within an organization. It is not about audience members confronting and reflecting on organizational problems. Indeed, in this type of theatre there is no admission that there are any problems.

Young (1990) argues that the greater part of our so-called developed world constitutes a *dramaturgical society*. One in which 'the technologies of social science, mass communication, theatre, and the arts are used to manage attitudes, behaviours and feelings of the population' (Young, 1990, p. 71). Throughout Western industrialized societies the services of 'expert technicians, research institutes doing surveys, polls and samples, theatrical people, mass communications, are disproportionately available to large-scale organizations' (ibid, p. 71). The task of these 'functionaries' is to 'use the accoutrements of the theatre, the findings of social science, and the facilities of the mass media to generate an 'informed' public – formed in the image of the purchaser of such services' (ibid, p. 72). Large corporations with large budgets can and do attempt to influence governments, communities, regulators, competitors, customers and – not least – their own employees through the skilful projection of images. It is probable that theatrical resources are more heavily used by organizations to manage and manipulate their employees than they are used to confront 'hidden conflicts, subconscious behavioural patterns or with painful truths' (Schreyögg, 2001, p. 8). It is certain that we know very little about the practice and impact of either form of activity. This paper is designed to add to our knowledge by describing and analysing a performance that those who designed it saw as being in the tradition of *corporate theatre*.

44   T. Clark and I. Mangham

THE NATURE OF CORPORATE THEATRE

Pineault (1989, p. 2) offers a broad definition of corporate theatre by suggesting that it is a 'type of production which excites, motivates, and persuades its audience about a company's service, product, and/or slogan through the use of live theatrical performance'. According to Bell (1987), performances like this have a number of specific characteristics. First, performances are nearly always located off-site where the main theatrical infrastructure – stage, scenery, lighting, and audience seating – has to be constructed ad hoc. They are usually one off performances. Their bespoke and temporary character makes them expensive. A single performance can cost from £100,000 to several million pounds. Second, despite the presence of external actors, designers, writers and directors, the performance is created for and targeted on a specific internal audience. Attendance is not open to everyone but is restricted to a limited group of organizational insiders. It is private rather than public theatre. Organizations are very reluctant to permit anyone, other than the intended audience, into the performance. In part this may be ascribed to the sensitive nature of the content, but is more likely to be occasioned by the third characteristic of corporate theatre: the purpose of the performance is largely motivational. It shares something with another marginal form of theatre – *agit-prop* – in that theatrical elements are used as a means of ideological propagandistic-persuasion in order to foster group identification and enhance specific didactic intent (Blau, 1992; Kershaw, 1992). The presence of strangers could well detract from such a purpose. Fourth, and linked to the previous point, the content and subjects of corporate theatre are the organization's products and services, its self image, or the image its leaders want to project. Fifth, the message is communicated using sophisticated multi-media technologies. They are audio-visual extravaganzas utilizing state-of-the-art technology such as revolving stages, hydraulics, lasers, complex lighting rigs, computer programming, back-projection, plasma screens and so forth.

THE PERFORMANCE: *YOUR LIFE. YOUR BANK*

The empirical material on which this paper is based stems from the authors' association with a single corporate theatrical performance called *Your Life. Your Bank.* Eiger International – one of the world's most successful producers of corporate theatre of one form or another – had been commissioned by Green Group Plc – a very large bank – to devise and produce a show that would help it celebrate and consolidate the merging of what had until now been two separate banks: Green and Blue. The performance that we were party to constituted an attempt by those who commissioned it to manage the impressions received by their employees in such a way as to consolidate changes instigated by the commissioners – the institution's most senior managers. Eiger were chosen primarily because of their experience and expertise in producing large performances. As the Chairman of Eiger stated, 'Our reputation is founded on the delivery of high quality live communication. The heart of our business is about devising and delivering live communication in order to inform and educate audiences all over the world . . . corporate theatre is a key part of this. The success of these performances is a reflection of our creative expertise more generally but also our long experience of designing something that engages an audience'. In turn, we were commissioned by Eiger International to design and implement a series of questionnaires and interviews that would provide a measure of the success of the performance.[5] For us it offered the prospect of examining a branch of theatre that had not previously been the subject of description and systematic analysis. To enable us to do this we sought and were granted permission to observe the development of the performance from start to finish. Over a period of eight months, as observers, we attended many of the meetings within the consultancy concerning the development of the script, meetings between the consultancy and the client, the dress rehearsals and the performance itself. We also collected information on the creative principles underpinning the design and staging of the performance, a variety of briefing documents generated by Eiger and the bank, the final script and all information aimed at those who were to constitute the audience. Apart from our impressions and notes that we made at the various meetings we attended, at the dress rehearsals and as members of the audience on the day of the performance, we had access to a video recording of the entire live show.

FRAMING THE PERFORMANCE

Introduction

Schreyögg (2001) offers a frame for the consideration of organizational theatre that can also be used to facilitate a broader understanding of theatre as technology. He conceives of a theatre group as a service organization with a chain of distinctive value creating activities. An ideal typical production process should involve a distinctive set of activities and stages: commissioning, exploring, dramatization, *mise en scène*, performance and follow up (Schreyögg, 2001, p. 6). Whilst we are broadly in agreement with what he has to say, we are unhappy with the somewhat mechanistic industrial production process vocabulary that he favours. For our analysis we felt we needed a frame that as far as possible derived from studies of the theatre. We have chosen that offered by Cole (1975) and we have complemented it by ideas taken from a range of other writers, most notably Pavis (1992). We have selected these writers primarily because Cole's overall schema and Pavis' detailed thoughts on *mise en scène* enable us to organise our description and analysis in a manner that we take to be isomorphic with the activities to which we were witness.

Commissioning the Play

As Hamlet reminds us, one the most important factors in the development and performance of a piece of theatre lies in the commissioning of it. In what is possibly the first example of a circumstance where, in the play within the play, theatre as technology is used to bring about a change of circumstance, Hamlet embodies the power of the patron. In this instance he gets to rewrite the script and plunge the court of Denmark into chaos (Shakespeare, 1996, Act 2, Scene 2). Theatre – particularly corporate theatre – is an expensive resource and whoever commissions the players has the opportunity to influence both the script and the subsequent performance. In the present case the commissioners were clear that their objective in putting on the performance was to manage the impressions of the merger received by their employees in such a way as to consolidate changes instigated by the commissioners – the institution's most senior managers. In order to produce the script Eiger had to gain an understanding of the range of activities that had contributed to the merger of the two banks. Rather than conduct a wide-ranging audit of how the different parts of the banks had been contributing to the merger, the consultancy relied solely on briefings from the members of the committee coordinating the merger programme entitled *Towards One Bank*, all of whom were senior managers. Eiger were paid to deploy their skill and techniques in the service of this group. No attempt was made to involve more junior levels of the organization in discussions about the content or the shape of the performance. Save for a short passage towards the end of the performance, the audience were to remain in their seats and certainly no opportunity was to be afforded for raising questions such as possible redundancies, branch closures or reduced opportunities for promotion. It was taken as read that the management's perspective was to prevail throughout. And like Hamlet, they took care to monitor the development of the script and the rehearsals to ensure that their view of social reality was to be exclusively promoted.

The Imaginative Truth

In line with the comments made earlier about the nature of dramaturgical society, the development of the script for our piece of corporate theatre offers an example of how social reality was to be defined and promoted. This was to be a good news show. It was designed to *reinforce* the values that were to underpin the new bank; it was to *celebrate* the merger; it was to *laud* the merger as the biggest and most successful piece of change management that had ever been attempted anywhere in the world; it was to involve and make *heroes* of the people who were making this happen; it was to fill with *pride* the hearts and minds of audience and performers alike; and it was to *inspire* them to pass on the good news to their colleagues back in the various branches. The image that was to be promoted was one of an organization that had taken on a major task, overcome all of the problems and obstacles and had *triumphed*. This was an organization that could feel justly pleased with itself.

Our framing of this part of the development of the performance begins with the idea of theatre as an opportunity to experience 'imaginative life as physical presence' (Cole, 1975, p. 5). Cole makes a distinction between what he calls *imaginative truth* and *present truth* that we find useful in the present context. Imaginative truth satisfies our longing for coherence, but more often than not it is only something that we envisage, it is not something that is physically manifest. Present truth on the other hand surrounds us – it is seeable and graspable – but it lacks the coherence of imaginative form. He quotes Sartre: 'the real and the imaginary cannot coexist by their very nature . . . to prefer the imaginary . . . is not only to escape from the content of the real (poverty, frustrated love, failure of one's enterprises, etc.), but from the form of the real itself, its character of *presence*' (italics in original, p. 5). Theatre of all human activities and theatre alone provides an opportunity of experiencing imaginative truth as present truth. 'In theatre, imaginative events take on for a moment the presentness of physical events; in theatre, physical events take on for a moment the perfection of imaginative form' (Cole, 1975, p. 5). Everything that figures in theatre can be understood in the role that it plays in the manifestation of imaginative life as physical presence. The script is its source, the actor is the one who makes it present and the audience are those to whom the imaginative truth becomes present.

Prior to the commissioning of *Your Life. Your Bank*, members of the Green and Blue banks had spent three years surrounded by the physical truths of the merger. Each day there were new setbacks and problems, further trials and tribulations, more false starts and premature declarations of success. Possibly more than one person in the organization tried to fashion an imaginative form that rendered these experiences coherent. It could be that memos, articles, videos and perhaps even stories and poems were constructed and circulated. None of these, however, had the immediacy and seeable, touchable physical reality of the performance. Eiger's contribution and singular achievement at an early stage of the development of the performance was to shape a script which gave imaginative coherence to the myriad activities that had gone into the effecting of the merger between the Green and Blue banks. As one of the most senior managers noted: 'What Eiger did was to give us something that was memorable and that celebrated what had been happening as well as a key moment in the history of the Bank. They brought all the disparate activities within the bank together and gave them coherence.'

The script was eventually to form the basis of the rehearsal, where elements of it were to be further modified, and of the performance. It illustrated the Bank's struggle to bring about the merger and so consisted of a series of accounts of problems met and overcome punctuated by interludes that illustrated the scale of success that had been achieved. The struggles were not to be presented dramatically – the outcome was already known to everyone – but a sense of excitement, of building towards a climax, was to be engendered by a repeated emphasis upon the size of the change that was being effected and upon the date when the merger would become a legal reality. The leitmotif for the day was to be represented by the phrase 'Just 34 days to go to the birth of a new bank. The countdown has begun.' The climax of the day was to be a 'surprise' live appearance of The Corrs – at the time one of the world's most successful singing groups – reprising the songs that would have been prefigured earlier and in particular the song that had become the aspirational signature tune of the new merged Bank – 'What can I do to make you happy?'.

Casting and Rehearsal

Your Life. Your Bank was to be a show about the process of a merger performed almost exclusively by members of the two banks. It would appear that many pieces of corporate theatre feature professional actors and, as we have seen, they also appear to feature in radical, organization and situation theatre. The decision in this instance to go with employees of the organization rather than with professionals was determined by the nature of the script. The whole day was to be about bank employees who had overcome all kinds of obstacles to make the merger a success. It would have been rather an odd decision to have the heroes sitting in the audience watching themselves being played by someone else. However *playing* oneself on stage is not simply a matter of *being* oneself as some of those eager to put themselves forward were to find out.

To complement her cast of largely amateur performers, the director insisted on a highly professional and highly paid compere. She did so on a couple of grounds: first that she felt that she needed a professional to hold the show together, and second, the employment of such a high profile compere/interviewer would signal that this was indeed a very special performance. Elsewhere the senior management determined the personnel who were to perform. It was taken as read that the key performers were to be main board directors or individuals just below that level. On one occasion when a candidate beyond the senior group was suggested as a possible keynote speaker they were dismissed in the following way: 'Will they [the audience] know who they are, and do we know they can deliver?' Lesser speaking roles – those who were to comment, for example, on the new signage, the new IT systems or the new uniforms – were assigned to lower level managers who were known to be 'reliable'. As the Chairman of Eiger explained when referring to the predominance of senior executives in the show: 'Green is a very hierarchical organization. I am not sure that it could be any other way'.

Whilst many of the most senior directors were happy with their *casting* as key performers in the piece, most did not see any point in *rehearsing* their performances with the director. For them it was just a matter of agreeing the lines with the writer, turning up on the day and reading them off the autocue. Two of the key speakers did not even attend the dress rehearsal. This created enormous problems since without the actors on stage running through their performances it was impossible to determine the precise synchronization of the background visuals with their words. Although stand-ins were used, the pace of their delivery turned out to be different from that of the actual speakers. Furthermore, since one of the most senior performers who failed to attend the dress rehearsal had determined that he was writing his own speech, there was no guarantee that the version Eiger had was the version that would be delivered the following day. Some of those who did work with the director found it a chastening experience. One of the senior managers was to be interviewed on-stage early in the performance about the purpose of putting on the performance. During the rehearsal the Director identified several problems with his performance. He was not looking directly at the audience and his tone of voice was too much of a monotone. She therefore suggested that he reposition himself on the sofa so that he could read the autocue more easily and focus on using an appropriate tone that projected both the informative nature of the day but also the fun and excitement of what was planned. This also meant amending the script so that certain key words could be used to facilitate this tone, in particular the words 'big', 'massive' and 'surprise'. He repeated his performance until the Director was satisfied that it would work on the day. When one of the researchers discussed his rehearsal experience with him he said 'It's difficult enough getting the words out let alone putting all the right emphasis on them. I hope tomorrow I can do what they want . . .'.

The *Mise en Scène*

To move from a script or text – albeit one that was re-written several times – to a performance is no easy matter. What the audience sees is a finished product. The text is what is heard and the performance is all that is made visible and audible on stage. The audience are party to a performance that is more or less successful, more or less comprehensible, in which the text is only one of several components, others being the space, the setting, the performers, the music, the lighting and the tempo etc. Pavis (1992, p. 24), from whom we have taken the term *mise en scène*, defines it 'as the bringing together or confrontation, in a given space and time, of different signifying systems, for an audience'. He considers the relationship between text and performance to be something more than one of conversion or translation. He prefers to describe it as 'a way of establishing effects or meaning and balance between semiotic systems such as verbal and non-verbal, symbolic and iconic' (ibid, p. 29). The essence of Pavis' approach is the recognition that the text frames a particular imaginative idea that may be acknowledged, underlined, built upon, undermined, ridiculed or denied by the auditory and visual discourse of the *mise en scène*.

In our case, for example, the spoken text for *Your Life. Your Bank* repeatedly mentioned the enormity of the change that had been undertaken. The biggest change ever. This sentiment was a key part of the text and was uttered not once but throughout the day. Significantly (in the sense of something that signifies) it was spoken on a vast stage to an audience of five thousand in an auditorium set up by the director and the design team within the largest exhibition space in the United Kingdom. The audience were constrained to approach the auditorium by walking down an avenue formed by exhibition stands. These contained information on the activities of different divisions of the Bank, the charity and community work supported by the Bank, sports events sponsored by the Bank and information on aspects of the merger exercise. The setting put one in mind of a Roman processional route provided for a conquering general. In this case the conquerors being honoured were the bank employees who were also the audience to the show. The performance arena was located at the far end of the hall, opposite the entrance to the arena. This was hidden from view by a black cloth draped over a five metre high wall formed by the scaffolding that supported the raked seating within the auditorium. The audience entered the arena by walking up one of two staircases situated at either end of the wall. As they emerged onto the first tier of the raked seating they were treated to an unobstructed view of the whole auditorium. This first view of the performance arena was designed to have an impact on the audience. As the Chairman of Eiger stated, 'I want them to come up those stairs and say "wow". The scale of the space, the lighting and the images that we shall be projecting onto the back wall should impress them. It's important that we set the right tone from the beginning.' Putting the show on in a pokey little theatre in East Acton with a couple of spots and an overhead projector would have done little to set the right tone. It would have run the risk of ridiculing the entire enterprise.

Setting the right tone was also a matter of the pace of the performance. Speakers moved in and out of position fluently; the lighting switched attention seamlessly from one area of the stage to another; screens appeared and disappeared on cue; accompanied by vibrant music, groups of employees demonstrating the new uniforms raced across the stage from different directions exuding energy, vitality and enthusiasm. There was a sense of purpose about every sequence, a forward thrust that complemented the words and the images with which the performance began. With the auditorium in complete darkness an announcer stated 'Welcome to *Your Life. Your Bank*. We are just 34 days away from the birth of a new bank. The countdown starts now.' Onto the screens at the back of the stage a series of graphics and images in the corporate colours of the new Bank were projected. These were combined with text that highlighted the key events since 1995 when Green Bank plc announced its intention to purchase Blue Bank. This ended with the caption 'Just 34 days to go from the birth of a new bank. And now the countdown has begun.' The words faded out and were replaced by an image of a clock superimposed onto which was a calendar. The date on which the Performance took place was shown. To the accompaniment of a loud ticking noise and music by The Corrs, the dates changed and stopped on the date in a few weeks when the merged bank would be launched nationwide. Without a pause a woman emerged from down left and walked to up centre. She was wearing the colours of the Bank – a blue trouser suit with a green T-shirt. She was greeted with enthusiastic applause, as the audience became aware that it was one of the best-known presenters on UK television.

> A very, very big welcome to you all. What an incredible event this is. And what an important event too. On June the 28th, just 34 days away, a brand new bank, Blue Green, the UK's newest bank, is born. And today we are going to learn all about that and understand just why it is so important. And I can promise this, it is going to be a great day. A day full of information and interest, and we have a couple of surprises.

Setting the right tone was also a matter of the performers. Contrary to what some of our performers thought, there is more to realizing an imaginative idea than simply saying one's lines. Non-verbal processes of communication can have a significant influence on the audience's experience of the performance. The posture the performer adopts, their eye contact (or lack of eye contact) with the audience, the confidence with which they move around the stage and take up their position, matching the speed of delivery, the tone and pitch of their voices to the demands of the text – all of the factors feature in the audience's reception of what they have to say. The promise and excitement, the sense of adventure with which the merger was characterized in the text could be severely undermined if not actually ridiculed were the performers to shuffle on to the stage and stumble through their set pieces in a flat monotone with their eyes firmly fixed upon their notes. A mismatch between words and non-verbal signals was evident only once during the performance when one of the senior managers, who took himself to be too important to attend rehearsals and wrote his own speech, delivered a three minute speech in an evangelical style which rang hollow with the audience.[6] Overall, encouraged by a readily responsive audience, the performers managed to say their words as if they believed in them.

The fact that most of the performers and the audience were members of the same organization probably made it easier for the former to be accepted. Other things being equal, when professional actors stand on stage and enact characters that are examples of certain types of humanity the audience identifies with these types. Often an actor has to work hard to secure this identification. Had professional actors taken part in this performance, they would have had to work hard to have themselves taken as senior businessmen and women. As it was the performers were being asked to enact themselves writ – as it were – large. No actor was standing in for them so no great imaginative effort was required of the audience. The audience may or may not have believed what they were hearing, but for the most part they would have had no difficulty in identifying, in the sense of ascribing a character to, whoever was speaking. What is more, many of them signalled that they were keen 'to get it right'. They signalled a vulnerability that was picked up and responded to by the audience who were willing them on. It was their managers and their colleagues that were up there and the audience was not about to let them down.

The Audience

In dealing with theatre as technology in general and with corporate theatre in particular we have to confront the issue of what we actually mean by an audience. In most instances where the technology of theatre is deployed within organizations the audience is not present simply to be entertained. As we indicated earlier, corporate theatre has some similarities with political theatre. The stance taken by many of those involved in *agit-prop* theatre and in the present case, clearly if not explicitly adopted by Eiger and those who commissioned them, was that the performance was an opportunity to educate a large group of the masses in an ideology (a particular way of regarding performances) and in so doing to incite them to action outside the auditorium. The performance was designed to turn its audience into performers, by making them want to go back to their branches to spread the message. If Eiger were to be successful in its bringing together the variety of elements that constitute a performance, then the audience would not feel itself to be passive, merely watching, but would sense itself to be part of the action, to have so fully absorbed the impact of the performance as to have broken down the distinction between those on the stage and those sitting in the auditorium (Hilton, 1987, pp. 131–4). In line with reception theory this breaking down of the distinction between performers and audience will be greatly facilitated where the *horizons of expectation* of those involved meet (Hilton, 1987, p. 131). That is, a circumstance exists in which the beliefs and values of performers and audience are reasonably close. In the present case the performers and the audience were bank employees and colleagues. What is more they were handpicked to attend the performance. Prior to it they each received a personally addressed invitation with a congratulatory message from the Deputy Group Chief Executive and some general information indicating the nature of their role. The role of the Pathfinders was to communicate the key messages to their colleagues within one month of the performance through a structured 'cascade' exercise. On leaving the auditorium each delegate was to be handed a Pathfinder Communication Pack that contained a script, visual support materials (overheads and video), advice on how to prepare for the cascade session as well as guidance on presenting their experiences to their colleagues.

The expectations of our performance may have gone a long way to pre-conditioning the audience for it. Thus, from the information supplied with the invitation, members of the audience knew that the show was to be about the merging of the two banks, they could also anticipate that it was to be a celebration of some kind or another, and the excitement accompanying rumours circulating within the Bank about possible surprise appearances on the day suggest that they were up for it before they got on the specially charted transport that brought them to the venue. Intra-audience relations may also have played an important part. Conversation analytic and semiotic studies of speaker-audience interaction indicate that the communication between members of the audience usually determines the 'homogeneity of response', even where there are variations in the expectations that individual members initially bring to the performance (Clayman, 1992; Elam, 1980; Heritage and Greatbatch, 1986). In almost all cases laughter and applause are infectious in that they are collective displays of positive audience responses. The audience, through homogeneity of reaction, in effect, confirms a common reading of a presented experience. Eiger wanted to use the performance to create a sense of 'one single bank'; a Green Blue community. As one of the consultants stated when referring to the design of the set pieces within the performance: 'We want them to be episodes of positive communication. The aim is to create goodwill and we want that to leave the hall at the end. The Pathfinders have to relay a positive message in their presentations.' They therefore designed into the performance plenty of opportunities for collective positive audience response. The introduction of each speaker and the end of each speech were greeted by rapturous applause. The unveiling of the new television commercials received enthusiastic applause. The surprise appearance on stage of two elderly actors from the television commercial received thunderous applause and a standing ovation. And when The Corrs appeared the audience stood in unison, cheered and danced in the aisles. Each positive collective response may have assisted with the generation of group solidarity and social cohesion during the performance and reinforced the feeling that the Pathfinders were a special group with a shared task. By evoking and producing affiliative responses, Eiger encouraged the public display of group consensus. In this way they may have assisted with the constitution of the members of the audience as an "in group" who are like-minded with respect to their appreciation and understanding of the messages presented during the day.

Action

Finally, although this paper is primarily concerned with a close analysis of the process of producing a piece of corporate theatre, it should be noted that from the point of view of those who commissioned it and those who put it together it was a success. It met its creative objectives. The questionnaire responses and telephone interviews indicate that immediately following the performance, and one month after, those who had constituted the audience found the day motivating and inspiring. It created greater pride in the organization and gave them more confidence to communicate the key messages to colleagues via a 'cascade' exercise. An evaluation of the 'cascade' exercise conducted separately by the Bank confirms this in that the presenters were rated as enthusiastic, positive and motivated. In their presentations the audience members were therefore able to successfully embody the mood of the day.

DISCUSSION

At the outset we stated that this paper had three aims. The first was to situate theatre as technology within the broader literature on theatre within organization studies. We achieved this by reviewing primarily the literature on 'dramatism' and 'dramaturgy' and drawing out similarities and differences with the emerging literature on 'theatre as technology'. Our purpose was to extend the commonly accepted boundaries of the notion of theatre within organization studies to include this previous overlooked area. As we indicated this is a large and fast growing area of consultancy work that has been subject to little empirical investigation. The second was to offer a description of an instance of corporate theatre, which as far as we are aware is the only such description available to scholars. Drawing on the notions of *imaginative truth* and *mise en scène* we examined the processes by which a particular performance called *Your Life. Your Bank* was commissioned, created and performed. Our third and final aim was to consider the differences between our instance of corporate theatre and other forms of theatre as technology. Having described in detail a piece of corporate theatre we can now highlight the key differences.

First, from what we know of how these other forms operate, a key difference is the extent to which they deploy the resources of theatre (see Clark and Mangham, forthcoming). Performances appear to be staged ad hoc on company premises. Actors are used, but the scenery, lighting, music, and choreography is usually kept to a minimum; whereas corporate theatre is a visual extravaganza. Second, the emphasis of these other approaches appears to be upon the democratic development of an imaginative truth that can be readily played out in a relatively unsophisticated manner that will bring about reflection, discussion and change. For example, Schreyogg's organization theatre deliberately sets out to produce a script and a performance that highlights what is and what might be. And, apparently, it works. Those who participate in organization theatre find that it facilitates change both in their perspectives on themselves and their organization and in subsequent actions. He accounts for what happens to audiences by recourse to Luhmann's (1998) theory of second order observation. Drawing upon this theory Schreyogg (2001, p. 12) asserts that his kind of theatre is 'likely to bring about a splitting experience' dividing reality into two levels – the everyday and the familiar and reality as it is presented on the stage. He argues that in such circumstances the everyday taken for granted reality becomes contingent. 'In experiencing a second reality construction the former (usually taken for granted) construction of reality becomes an unstable one, i.e. a construction that is open for change' (ibid, p. 12). In other terms and at other times this is a theory that has been advanced in support of agit-prop, Brechtian and *forum theatre* approaches to performance (Boal, 1979; Brooker, 1994; Kershaw, 1992).[7] In contrast, corporate theatre is not democratic. It owes no debt to these forms of theatre. Instead it is informed by the conventions of Broadway, the West End, television and advertising. It is about creating a piece of theatre that reflects the wishes of a particular organizational group. Consequently it is not about creating circumstances in which audience members feel empowered and liberated to develop their own new understandings of their working lives. Rather, it appears to be used to contain reflection and to promote the views of a particular group within an organization. Whilst change is sought in the audience, the nature of that change is strictly controlled and channelled by the piece of theatre.

Leading on from the previous point, a third difference lies in the aims of these forms of theatre. The aim of organization theatre appears to be to make people *think*. The aim of our instance of corporate theatre appeared to be to cause the audience to *feel*. One of its aims of course was to induce those who participated in the performance to change their perceptions and their values, but it did this not by confronting issues but by *subtly suggesting* alternative ways of evaluating, construing and understanding the issues that the merger of the two banks had brought about. The performance suggested that the merger was not something to be concerned about, something worrying, something to be feared; rather it was a performance to be proud of, an occasion for celebration and joy. The notion of suggestion is commonplace amongst those who write about novels, plays and films (Currie, 1990, Matravers, 1998). Novitz (1997) is one of the principal proponents of the theory and he argues that when our values and beliefs are tested in this way, the form that it takes – in our case an instance of corporate theatre – ' frequently manages to prevent the sorts of emotional responses that normally accompany challenges to our deeply entrenched beliefs and values' (p. 247). It does so, he claims, not only because some performances make us suggestible and susceptible to new values, new ideologies, but they also 'anaesthetize us against the pain that often attends such upheavals' (ibid, p. 247). In an earlier book, he notes that this phenomenon effectively converts certain forms of fiction, theatre and film into 'instruments of policy that can succeed where other instruments of persuasion fail' (Novitz, 1992, p. 34). They achieve this by encouraging our 'imaginative participation' in what is presented to us (ibid, p. 180). Such an argument resonates with the work of Cole (1975) in that it is the presentation of imaginative life as physical presence that prevents us from fixating on the consequences of abandoning our cherished beliefs and values. Corporate theatre does not challenge, rather it seduces. It is a 'form of persuasion that entices by touching the right emotional chords, but never threatens or coerces' (Novitz, 1992, p. 184). Many of the fears and anxieties of the employees of the Green Bank had been addressed before the performance of *Your Bank. Your Life*, but those few that remained could well have been assuaged by a performance that seduced by presenting an imaginative truth with the support of bright lights, music, singing, dancing and presentations all stressing the virtues of the brave new world.

Finally, this article indicates that the use of theatre as technology has been previously overlooked. It therefore offers a potentially fruitful and productive area of research. There is an urgent need to obtain a more detailed understanding of the extent and nature of its use. This requires obtaining information on the number of firms offering consultancy services in this area, the size of their turnovers, the nature of the services they offer, the character of the projects in which they are engaged as well as a profile of the client organizations and their motivation for using such services. In conducting this research the differences between the various forms of the 'technology of theatre' will become more apparent. As we have indicated above, these are presently partially understood.

NOTES

*This paper was accepted for publication in the *Journal of Management Studies* under the previous editors.

[1] Turner's (1969, 1974) ideas on life as social drama share Burke's perspective in as far as it holds that social and organizational life *is* theatre. The perspective has given rise to a handful of empirical investigations (e.g., Rosen, 1985, 1988).

[2] This is a highly selective account of the intellectual milieu in which Goffman's ideas grew. In a fuller account, Mead's symbolic interactionism would need to be considered (Blumer, 1969; Perinbanayagam, 1991).

[3] Who, in turn, draws heavily upon notions deriving from both ritual and the practices of the theatre of the ancient Greeks (Boal, 1998).

[4] This should not be taken to imply that such work is not going on. Writing up such performances is often prevented by issues of confidentiality.

[5] Eiger was keen to sponsor an independent evaluation of their work on the basis that if positive it could well be beneficial for their relationship with the particular client as well as more generally helpful in projecting their effectiveness and expertise to a wider audience. If negative our results would have been unlikely to see the light of day. Eiger's faith in its own processes was rewarded and findings emanating from the evaluation have subsequently been issued as press releases, reported in trade journals and incorporated into corporate publicity materials.

[6] There was a three-second delay before the audience applauded and the applause was muted when compared to other speakers.

[7] 'Alienating an event or a character', wrote Brecht (1978, p. 301), 'means first of all stripping the event of its self-evident, familiar, obvious quality and creating a sense of astonishment and curiosity about them'.

REFERENCES

AV Magazine (2000). 'Live events: strong, but mature'. *AV Magazine*, January, 29–30.

Augustine, N. and Adelman, K. (1999). *Shakespeare in Charge: The Bard's Guide to Leading and Succeeding on the Business Stage*. New York: Miramax Books.

From Dramaturgy to Theatre as Technology   57

Bell, J. (1987). 'Industrial: American business theatre in the 80's'. *The Drama Review*, **31**, 4, 36–57.

Blau, H. (1992). *To All Appearances: Ideology and Performance*. London: Routledge.

Blumer, H. (1969). *Symbolic Interactionism*. Englewood Cliffs, NJ: Prentice Hall.

Boal, A. (1979). *Theatre of the Oppressed*. London: Pluto Press.

Boal, A. (1998). *Legislative Theatre*. London: Routledge.

Brecht, B. (1978). *Gesammelte Werke*, XV, in Dickson, K. A. (Ed.), *Towards Utopia: A Study of Brecht*. Oxford: Clarendon Press.

Brissett, D. and Edgley, C. (1990). *Life as Theatre: A Dramaturgical Sourcebook*, 2nd ed. New York: Aldine de Gruyter.

Brooker, P. (1994). 'Key words in Brecht's theory and practice of theatre'. In Thomson, P. and Sacks, G. (Eds), *The Cambridge Companion to Brecht*. Cambridge: Cambridge University Press.

Burke, K. (1945). *A Grammar of Motives*. Berkeley: University of California Press.

Burke, K. (1969a). *A Rhetoric of Motives*. London: University of California Press.

Burke, K. (1969b). 'Dramatism'. In *International Encyclopedia of the Social Sciences*, Volume VII. New York: Macmillan, 445–52.

Burns, T. (1992). *Erving Goffman*. London: Routledge.

Case, P. (2001). 'Virtual stories on virtual working: critical reflection on CTI consultancy discourse'. In Clark, T. and Fincham, R. (Eds), *Critical Consulting: New Perspectives on the Management Advice Industry*. Oxford: Blackwell, 93–114.

Clark, T. and Mangham, I. (forthcoming). 'Stripping to the undercoat: a review and reflections on a piece of organization theatre'. *Organization Studies*.

Clark, T. and Salaman, G. (1996). 'Creating the "right" impression: towards a dramaturgy of management consultancy'. *Service Industries Journal*, **18**, 18–38.

Clayman, S. E. (1992). 'Caveat orator: audience disaffiliation in the 1988 presidential debates'. *Quarterly Journal of Speech*, **78**, 33–60.

Cole, D. (1975). *The Theatrical Event: a Mythos, a Vocabulary, a Perspective*. Middleton, CT: Wesleyan University Press.

Coopey, J. (1998). 'Learning to trust and trusting to learn: a role of radical theatre'. *Management Learning*, **29**, 3, 365–82.

Corrigan, P. (2000). *Shakespeare on Management: Leadership Lessons for Today's Managers*. London: Kogan Page.

Currie, G. (1990). *The Nature of Fiction*. Cambridge: Cambridge University Press.

Duncan, H. (1962). *Communication and Social Order*. New York: Oxford University Press.

Duncan, H. (1968). *Symbols in Society*. New York: Oxford University Press.

Elam, K. (1980). *The Semiotics of Theatre and Drama*. London: Methuen.

Gardner, W. L. (1992). 'Lessons in organizational dramaturgy: the art of impression management'. *Organization Dynamics*, **21**, 1, 33–46.

Gardner, W. L. and Avolio, B. J. (1998). 'The charismatic relationship: a dramaturgical perspective'. *Academy of Management Review*, **23**, 1, 32–58.

Gardner, W. L. and Martinko, M. J. (1988). 'Impression management in organizations'. *Journal of Management*, **14**, 321–38.

Geertz, C. (1980). *Negara: The Theatre State in Nineteenth Century Bali*. Princeton, NJ: Princeton University Press.

Geertz, C. (1983). *Local Knowledge: Further Essays in Interpretive Anthropology*. Stanford, CA: Stanford University Press.

Giacolone, R. A. and Rosenfeld, P. (1989). *Impression Management in Organizations*. Hillsdale, NJ: Lawrence Erlbaum.

Goffman, E. (1959). *The Presentation of Self in Everyday Life*. New York: Anchor Doubleday.

Goffman, E. (1967). *Interaction Ritual: Essays on Face-to-face Behaviour*. Garden City, NY: Anchor Books.

Goffman, E. (1974). *Frame Analysis: An Essay on the Organization of Experience*. Cambridge, MA: Harvard University Press.

Graham-Hill, S. and Grimes, A. J. (2001). 'Dramatism as method: the promise of praxis'. *Journal of Organizational Change Management*, **14**, 3, 280–94.

Grove, S. J. and Fisk, R. P. (1992). 'The service experience as theatre'. *Advances in Consumer Research*, **19**, 455–61.

Hansen, H. (2002). 'The Construction of Organizational Stories: The Stories Behind the Stories'. Unpublished doctoral dissertation, University of Kansas.

58   T. Clark and I. Mangham

Heritage, J. and Greatbatch, D. (1986). 'Generating applause: a study of rhetoric and response at party political conferences'. *American Journal of Sociology*, **91**, 1, 110–57.

Hilton, J. (1987). *Performance*. Basingstoke: Macmillan.

Ichheiser, G. (1949). 'Misunderstandings in Human Relations: A Study in False Social Relations'. Supplement to the *American Journal of Sociology*, **55**.

Jackson, B. (2001). 'Art for management's sake? The new literary genre of business book'. *Management Communication Quarterly*, **14**, 3, 483–90.

Keene, G. (1999). 'How the conference changed its spots'. *The Independent on Sunday*, 9 May, 7.

Kendall, J. E. (1993). 'Good and evil in the chairman's "boiler plate": an analysis of corporate visions of the 1970's'. *Organization Studies*, **14**, 4, 148–64.

Kershaw, B. (1992). *The Politics of Performance: Radical Theatre as Cultural Intervention*. London: Routledge.

Luhmann, N. (1998). *Observations on Modernity*. Stanford, CA: Stanford University Press.

Lyman, S. M. and Scott, M. B. (1975). *The Drama of Social Reality*. New York: Oxford University Press.

Mangham, I. L. (2001). 'Afterword: Looking for Henry'. *Journal of Organizational Change Management*, **14**, 3, 295–304.

Mangham, I. L. and Overington, M. A. (1983). 'Dramatism and the theatrical metaphor'. In Morgan, G. (Ed.), *Beyond Method*. London: Sage, 219–33.

Mangham, I. L. and Overington, M. A. (1987). *Organizations as Theatre: A Social Psychology of Dramatic Appearances*. Chichester: Wiley.

Matravers, D. (1998). *Art and Emotion*. Oxford: Clarendon Press.

Meisiek, S. (2002). 'Situation drama in change management: types and effects of a new managerial tool'. *International Journal of Arts Management*, **4**, 48–55.

Meisiek, S. and Dabitz, R. (1999). 'Zur wirkung des unternehmenstheater: Die rolle der katharsis'. In Schreyögg, G. and Dabitz, R. (Eds), *Unternehmentheater: Formen – Erfarungen – erfolgreicher Einsatz*. Wiesbaden: Gabler.

Mitchell, J. N. (1978). *Social Exchange, Dramaturgy and Ethnomethodology: Toward a Paradigmatic Synthesis*. New York: Elsevier.

Novitz, D. (1992). *The Boundaries of Art*. Philadelphia: Temple University.

Novitz, D. (1997). 'The anaesthetics of emotion'. In Hjort, M. and Laver, S. (Eds), *Emotion and the Arts*. Oxford: Oxford University Press.

Olivier, R. (2001). *Inspirational Leadership: Henry V and the Muse of Fire*. London: Industrial Society.

Pavis, P. (1992). *Theatre at the Crossroads of Culture*, trans. Loren Kruger. London: Routledge.

Perinbanayagam, R. S. (1991). *Discursive Acts*. New York: Aldine de Gruyter.

Pine, B. J. and Gilmour, J. H. (1999). *The Experience Economy: Work is Theatre and Every Business a Stage*. Boston, MA: Harvard Business School Press.

Pineault, W. J. (1989). 'Industrial Theatre: The Businessman's Broadway'. PhD dissertation, Bowling Green State University.

Rosen, M. (1985). 'Breakfast at Spiro's: dramaturgy and dominance'. *Journal of Management*, **11**, 31–48.

Rosen, M. (1988). 'You asked for it: Christmas at the bosses expense'. *Journal of Management Studies*, **25**, 463–80.

Rosenfeld, P., Giacalone, R. A. and Riordan, C. A. (1995). *Impression Management in Organizations: Theory, Measurement, Practice*. London: Routledge.

Schechner, R. (1988). *Performance Theory*. New York: Routledge.

Schlenker, B. R. (1980). *Impression Management: The Self-concept, Social Identity, and Interpersonal Relations*. Monterey, CA: Brooks/Cole.

Schreyögg, G. (2001). 'Organizational Theatre and Organizational Change'. Discussion Paper No. 13/01, Institute für Management, Freie Universität Berlin.

Schreyögg, G. and Dabitz, R. (1999). *Unternehmentheater: Formen – Erfarungen – erfolgreicher Einsatz*. Wiesbaden: Gabler.

Shakespeare, W. (1996). *Hamlet*. London: Penguin.

Smith, R. W. (1997). 'Hidden Theatre: Corporate Theatre in America'. PhD dissertation, University of Missouri–Columbia.

Turner, V. (1969). *The Ritual Process*. Ithaca, NY: Cornell University Press.

Turner, V. (1974). *Dramas, Fields, and Metaphors*. Ithaca, NY: Cornell University Press.

Turner, V. (1984). 'Liminality and performance genres'. In MacAloon, J. J. (Ed.), *Rite, Drama, Festival, Spectacle: Rehearsals Toward a Theory of Performance*. Philadelphia: Institute for the Study of Human Issues.

Walker, R. and Monin, N. (2001). 'The purpose of the picnic: using Burke's dramatistic pentad to analyse a company event'. *Journal of Organizational Change Management*, **14**, 3, 266–79.

Wehner, H. and Dabitz, R. (1999). 'Bedarfsorientiertes theater in Deutschland; Eine empirische bestanddaufnahme'. In Schreyögg, G. and Dabitz, R. (Eds), *Unternehmentheater: Formen – Erfarungen – erfolgreicher Einsatz*. Wiesbaden: Gabler.

Whitney, J. and Packer, T. (2000). *Power Plays: Shakespeare's Lessons in Leadership and Management*. New York: Simon & Schuster.

Wilshire, B. (1982). *Role Playing and Identity. The Limits of Theatre as Metaphor*. Bloomington: Indiana University Press.

Young T. R. (1990). *The Drama of Social Life: Essays in Post-Modern Social Psychology*. New Brunswick: Transaction Publishers.

[18]

Spectacular metaphors
From theatre to cinema

Thomaz Wood Jr
FGV-EAESP, São Paulo, Brazil

Keywords *Metaphors, Theatre, Cinema*

Abstract *The use of metaphoric language has grown in prevalence in recent years. Frontline organizations have become "magical kingdoms": ethereal places where image and substance rarely coincide, and where metaphors turn into powerful tools for consultants and change agents. At the same time, scholars explore the "wonderful world of metaphors". Once simple figures of speech, metaphors have been transformed into a respectable approach for organizational analysis. Although millenarian, the theatre metaphor constitutes an attractive system of ideas for studying organizational phenomena. In this paper, the theatre metaphor is used as a point of departure for the development of another dramaturgical metaphor: the cinema metaphor. It is suggested that the latter might provide a better perspective for studying contemporary organizations in the age of spectacle.*

> The screen opens its white walls to a harem of marvellous adolescent sights and sounds, faced with which the most adorable real body appears deformed (René Clair, quoted by Hill (1992, p. 15)).

Introduction: understanding metaphors?

Metaphoric reasoning is a key human skill that functions like a series of bridges which lead to the construction of high-order mental links between entities (Beck, 1987). In simple terms, metaphors interact and come to describe the world in the production of reality/ies where different metaphors inevitably produce different realities.

But what does it mean, ultimately, to say that a metaphor was understood? According to Gibbs and Hall (1987), it is the proponent's intention when he or she suggests or uses a metaphor that is the key to understanding its meaning. Understanding, therefore, involves discovering a system of common points, which are associated with the metaphor and its object. Understanding also includes recognition, on the part of the interlocutor, of the author's intention when he or she makes a specific declaration.

This paper proposes and explores the cinema metaphor. The theatre metaphor is used as a point of departure from which to develop the cinema metaphor. The argument is that the cinema metaphor is appropriate to contemporary analysis and both reflects and transmits the spirit of the times. The cinema metaphor also captures the baffling sense of organization and of organizing within the society of spectacle.

The first section of the paper addresses the theatre metaphor through the work of Kenneth Burke and Erving Goffman and examines their seminal

An early version of this paper was presented at Organizational Theatre Sub Theme Group of the EGOS meeting, Lyon, July 2001. The author would like to thank Ana Paula Paes de Paula, Saara Taalas and Virpi Leikola for their insightful comments.

JOCM
15,1

12

contributions to the field. The second section deals with the "Age of spectacle" which corresponds to a cinematic society. In the following section, an outline for a cinema metaphor is put forward and, in the final section, an evaluation summary of the findings is presented.

Theatre: a millenary metaphor

In order to propose a metaphor of cinema, it is necessary to first explain the theatre metaphor in order to makes sense of the transpositions that have occurred in the move from one to the other. The idea of the world as the stage on which people successively take up and discard roles is not new (Burns, 1972; Riggins, 1993). The theatre metaphor is in fact millenarian. References to human beings as marionettes in the hands of the gods and human life as tragedy and comedy go back to classical Greek theatre. There are various uses of metaphors of dramatic representation which go back to the time of Plato. Similar ideas are found in Horace and Seneca's works and in those of the early Christians (Curtius, 1967).

The Middle Ages provides countless examples of dramatic work related to Christian mystery cycles and the church calendar. This provides ample opportunity for dramatic work to serve as a metaphor for the theatricality of everyday life. For instance, in a somewhat later work, *Don Quixote*, by Miguel de Cervantes (1547-1616), the following dialogue can be found (Lyman and Scott, 1975, p. 1):

> "... Come, tell me [says Don Quixote], hast thou not seen a play acted in which kings, emperors, pontiffs, knights, ladies, and divers other personages were introduced? One plays the villain, another the knave, this one the merchant, that one the soldier, one the sharp-witted fool, another the foolish lover; and when the play is over, and they have put off the dresses they wore in it, all the actors become equal."
>
> "Yes, I have seen that," said Sancho.
>
> "Well then," said Don Quixote, "the same thing happens in the comedy and life of this world, where some play emperors, others popes, and, in short, all the characters that can be brought into a play; but when it is over, that is to say when life ends, death strips them all of the garments that distinguish one from the other, and all are equal in the grave."
>
> "A fine comparison!" said Sancho; "though not so new but that I have heard it many and many a time, ..."

William Shakespeare (1564-1616), Cervantes' contemporary, used his theatre not only as a vehicle for poetry, but directly as a metaphor of reality (Van den Berg, 1985). Among other many outstanding lines, Jaque's speech in *As You Like It* is a classic of its type (Lyman and Scott, 1975, p. 3):

> ...All the world's a stage,
> And all the men and women merely players:
> They have their exits and their entrances:
> And one man in his time plays many parts, ...

There are several reasons for the popularity of the theatre metaphor in sociology and in organizational studies, but probably one of the most significant is that the sense that life is acting, that everyone is actor, that life is a stage is becoming more and more a matter of day-to-day experience (Riggins,

1993). In our daily affairs, our interactions with other people are situated between two extremes: on one side, we have the so-called natural situations, in which the sensation of spontaneity predominates; and on the other, we have the so-called theatrical situations, in which the perception of behaviors aimed at manipulating impressions is stronger. Therefore, one reason why the theatre metaphor is important is that, arguably, natural situations are becoming more and more rare while theatrical situations are becoming more and more common. As an analytical approach, the theatre metaphor can provide tools for exploring social encounters, and can distinguish form, content, structure, significance and grammar. Such tools help to systematize the study of such events and to place the observer in a different relation to the subject of the study.

Spectacular
metaphors

13

Kenneth Burke and dramatism

Kenneth Burke was a forerunner in the analysis of social processes by giving value to interpretive processes in the study of human interaction (Gusfield, 1989). For Burke, social life is inherently dramatic, because it involves conflict, uncertainty, rhetoric and choice. Burke (1962) gave the name of dramatism to his perspective of human interaction analysis and proposed five terms as generating principles for his investigation. Each of these terms corresponds to one question:

(1) what was done, what happened? – the act;

(2) when or where was it done? – the scene, the situation in which the act took place;

(3) who did it? – the agent, the person who commanded the act;

(4) how did she/he do it? – the means or instruments which the agent used; and

(5) why did she/he do it? – the purpose of the act.

Dramatism is also a method used to explain social action and the corresponding interpretations for these actions (Mangham and Overington, 1983). Its use helps the actors to locate mystifications and reveal them. The basic assumption of the method is the same as the one present in the theoretical proposition by Erving Goffman that people are actors who interpret characters in everyday scenes.

Erving Goffman and the dramaturgical analysis

In the field of sociology, the influence of Goffman (1975) is so great that his name is frequently used as a synonym for the dramaturgical perspective. Goffman's central point of analysis is how an individual presents her/himself in day-to-day situations and seeks to control the impression he/she causes. The following paragraphs summarize some key ideas in his work. This serves to provide a foundation for the understanding of the basis of the theatrical metaphor and to demonstrate how it shifts in the move to a cinematic metaphor.

JOCM
15,1

14

The first concept to be considered is social entity. For Goffman, a social entity is any place limited by the perception of where an activity takes place. There is a tacit, invisible agreement between the audience and actors to sustain the performance, avoiding breaks and instabilities.

Another of Goffman's key ideas is the difference between the actor-individual – the maker of impressions, who plays a role – and the persona-individual – the figure that the acting should evoke. The persona does not precede the scene, but materializes within it. The self, consequently, becomes a "hook" on which a collaborative construction can be hung; it is a product of stage arrangements.

According to Goffman, individuals are moved not by the moral desire of achieving certain standards, but by the moral question of creating an impression of meeting those standards. This is a significant dramatic achievement and consonant with the contemporary use of the Greek word for actor, *hypocrite*.

This approach provides a perspective for analyzing social situations. The priorities of dramaturgical perspective are the descriptions of the techniques for manipulating impressions in a given environment and the study of problems resulting from this manipulation.

Goffman's analysis of human interaction has been compared to that undertaken by Burke (Gusfield, 1989). However, there are differences between the two approaches which go beyond the label: Goffman calls his approach dramaturgical and Burke calls his dramatism. The fundamental difference is that Goffman emphasizes the art of illusion. The actor is a professional illusionist, dramaturgy is the art of illusion, the stage is a metaphor, and reality and stage are two distinct things. Burke, on the other hand, does not use drama as a metaphor for human action. In Burke's work, the image is an image of interaction, of drama.

Theorists of the cinematic society
Daniel Boorstin: the image, pseudo-events and celebrities
For those who believe that the fusion of fiction and reality is a recent phenomenon, Boorstin's (1962) book *The Image: A Guide to Pseudo Events in America* appears almost prophetic. Boorstin carried out historical research, showing how US society developed a veritable fetish for the new. To sustain this obsession, the USA began to generate pseudo-events when real ones were lacking and create celebrities to compensate for the absence of heroes.

Boorstin (1962, p. 4) claims that Americans have become so accustomed to illusions that they mistake them for reality. The reality began to be inhabited by artificial novelties. These are pseudo-events, that contain an ambiguous relationship with reality and are created with the specific purpose of provoking determined reactions in the audience (Boorstin, 1962, p. 11). The cinema and, more recently, TV began to produce an aberration: we live in a world where the image appears to be more trustworthy than the original and fantasy is more real than reality.

Guy Debord: the society of spectacle

While Boorstin (1962) registered the tendencies related to the prevalence of the image over reality, Debord (1994) formulated a theory on the construction of a society based on image. Hence he showed himself to be frankly pessimistic with regard to the direction being taken by what he called the society of the spectacle. Analyzing the breakdown of the Soviet bloc – in the preface of a US edition of his work – Debord states that the spectacularization, together with other trends, leads to the dictatorial liberty of the market, combined with recognition of the rights of the *homo spectator*.

The spectacularization is a consequence and an objective of modernizing production conditions, which breaks the unit of life, withdrawing images from it and grouping them together into a large and unique flow. A separate world is created, in which the relation between people is mediated by images. Everything that was directly experienced becomes a commodified representation. The spectacle creates a self-representation of the world that surpasses the real world itself. It works as a barrier between these two worlds, keeping them isolated.

But the spectacle is not abstract. It is not something added to the real world. The spectacle "is capital accumulated to the point at which it becomes image" (Debord, 1994, p. 24). It manifests itself in the news media, in advertising, in public relations work, in cultural activities and in personal interactions. The spectacle is "at the heart of society's real unreality" (Debord, 1994, p. 13).

The spectacle is manifested as grand narrative, totalizing, justifying, legitimizing and celebrating the system. It is not a superficial phenomenon. The whole of society and the social phenomena are based on and permeated by the spectacle. The spectacle is also a product of this same society, a product which results from and refines the system's reflexive rationality.

The *homo spectator* does not live in the spectacle society, but merely contemplates it. She/he is a supporting actor, under pressure to find her/his role and act it. The spectacle provides the script, the act and the speech, and even evaluates the performance. In the spectacle, the individual lacking in individuality seeks – and finds – comfort for her/his needs and her/his desires. In fact, the spectacle itself determines which needs and desires are valid and suitable.

Norman Denzin: cinema and the game of the real

Echoing previous works in the 1990s, US sociologist Denzin (1995) defends the view that society reflects the cinema. According to him, the cinema was responsible for creating a parallel reality, an official version of civil society. The cinematographic apparatus reproduces dominant social values, preconceptions and notions of right and wrong. It organizes and gives sense to the world. It creates the cinematic society.

This form of art, during the twentieth century, progressively developed the epistemology of scientific realism (see Allen, 1993; Andrew, 1976; MacCabe, 1976; Bazin, 1971; Metz, 1971). This new cultural logic redefined the form in

JOCM
15,1

16

which the world is experienced. The cinema is thus a game of the real. The screen is simultaneously reality and perception. With the cinema, the camera's viewfinder consolidated its supremacy over the human eye.

In the world of voyeurs-spectators, the screen world begins peopling the audience's feelings, imagination, and fantasies. The cinematographic Other alters the reference system, its interlocutors' perception and self-perception. Consequently, the cinematic society might be considered a disciplining structure, peopled by voyeurs who obsessively spy on one another.

The cinematographic gaze is hegemonic and omnipresent. Nothing escapes it. All dilemmas and social questions are addressed and trivialized. The cinema created a visual and aesthetic illusion starting from classical theatre and from Victorian melodramatic literature. This illusion started to mediate the relationship between the individual and her/his peers and with the medium (see Andrew, 1984). In this process, reality is transformed into a cinematographic production. Real experiences then begin to be judged against their corresponding experience on film (Denzin, 1995, p. 32).

The cinema once had a monopoly on images. Today, it shares this space with other media that also produce and generate images, such as TV, video, video games and the Internet. The flow of images is without beginning or end. The image does not represent anything in particular any more. The image exists for itself, "not transmissible to others, objectivistic, pure exchange value, definitely deprived of transparency", as observed Chevrie (1987, p. 27). These then are some of the issues which arise from the study of cinema as art form, as mediator of social life and as means of reproduction.

Cinema as metaphor

Up to this point in the paper, the attempt has been made to identify reasons which demonstrate the need for a cinematographic perspective: the emergence of a cinematic society. It is now appropriate to identify the "meaning" of the cinema metaphor, explaining the intention of such a metaphor in organizational studies.

The theatre metaphor, in spite of being millenarian, still constitutes a powerful instrument for revealing facts beyond appearances. However, specific twentieth and twenty-first centuries phenomena must be incorporated into the dramaturgical perspective.

By proposing the cinema metaphor, the objective is to establish a perspective for studying organizational phenomena. What the cinema metaphor seeks to stress is the phenomenon of *spectacularization* of social life, a phenomenon which finds echo in the organizational world. The cinema metaphor exists in relation to the theatre metaphor. Both are dramaturgical metaphors and are related to a vision of the world which associates reality to the so-called performing arts. In some aspects, the cinema metaphor is an extension of the theatre metaphor; in other aspects they are antagonistic. Table I summarizes the similarities and differences between the two metaphors.

Theatre metaphor	Cinema metaphor
Foci	
Discusses how individuals play themselves in day-to-day scenes	Expands the dimensions of role-playing in space and time
Analyzes the manipulation of impression	Adds the spectacle-dimension
Perspective on organization	
Defines organization as a *locus* whose boundaries are set by the perception of the performance of an activity	Defines organization as an open system, embedded in the environment
Emphasis	
Focuses on the agreement between audience and actors to maintain the act	Focuses on the fragmentation and complexity of relationships among actors, and the "fusion" between actor and audience
Basic definitions	
The individual as actor	The medium – cinema, TV, Internet – as
The individual as character	an intervening part in the construction of
The being as a set of characters	reality
Analysis unit	
Considers face-to-face interaction	Considers the interaction among images and among discourses
Perspective on human behavior	
Seeks to segregate natural and artificial behaviors	Considers naturalness and artificiality as texts of an indivisible whole

Table I.
Dramatic metaphors

Cinema history can be considered as the history of its emancipation from theatre (Sontag, 1991). First, the cinema was emancipated from the theatre's frontal dimension, eliminating the fourth wall, represented by the camera's fixed position. Second, the cinema was freed from the theatre's exaggerated gestures, which became unnecessary with the use of zoom lenses and close-ups. Third, the cinema eliminated the distance between the audience and the act, in a certain way transporting the spectators into the scene. These three movements correspond to a transition from the static to the fluid and from the artificial to the natural.

The theatre employs artifices. In many plays, the artifice is outlined. The cinema also uses artifices. Ever since its origin, with Mielès, cinema has been the art of illusion. However, paradoxically, cinema is also an art that is committed to the discourse of reality. In the cinema, the artifices – the special effects – are camouflaged.

Cinema is a media-dependent art. We see a film which was registered by means of a technical apparatus and is being projected by means of another technical apparatus. The film is the record of an ephemeral moment. A theatre play, to the contrary, is seen while it is happening. Cinema is a time machine, which is able to retain in the memory and transport us to other times. The mediation of the cinematographic apparatus opens possibilities in time and

JOCM
15,1

18

space that are unimaginable in the theatre. Another difference is related to the relationship between the audience and the performance. In the theatre, the space is usually static. The spectator is confined. In the cinema, the spectator also occupies a fixed seat but, aesthetically, she/he is subject to an experience of permanent movement (Sontag, 1991, p. 104; Andrew, 1976, p. 86).

Theatre and cinema, although two dramaturgical manifestations, use different approaches for characters. Theatrical characters tend to be ideal types while cinematographic characters are more individualized. On the other hand, theatrical characters tend to be more profound, while cinematographic characters are generally superficial. Theatre and cinema also differ in relation to the form of connecting images and sequences. The basic unit in cinematographic language is not the image, or the act, as it is the case in theatre, but the connection between images, the relationship between present, previous and subsequent takes (Andrew, 1976, pp. 42-75; Machado, 1982).

Towards a cinematographic dramatism?

The previous sections have sought to develop the cinema metaphor concept as a perspective, a root-metaphor, and sought to explain the concept by contrasting it with the theatre metaphor. It is now appropriate to speculate on a cinematographic extension of Burke's dramatism.

The questions to be addressed are the following: first, what modifications should be made in the five elements of dramatism in order to establish a cinema metaphor. This needs to be addressed via the differences between the theatre metaphor and the cinema metaphor. Second, what categories should be excluded or added?

The cinematographic dramatism should review the five elements proposed by Burke (1962), considering the characteristics of the cinema metaphor: the extended dimensions of time and space, the inability to separate stage and audience, the simultaneity of events, the fragmentation of interactions, the interference of the media and the spectacle dimension.

For example, the scene could be substituted by the *mise-en-scène*, which refers to the control on what is happening in front of the camera and involves questions related to what to film and how to film it. It is a complex activity, comprising elements such as framing, shooting angle, lighting, composition, scenery and costumes. The use of this concept can expand dramaturgical analysis to include new symbolic elements – artifacts, myths, sagas, success stories, etc. – emphasizing the balance between these and other elements.

Cinematographic dramatism could also include some additional elements such as editing. Films develop as much spatially – through the *mise-en-scène* – as temporally – through editing (Monaco, 1981). Editing is a dialectic process of constructing senses, as demonstrated by film-maker Sergei Eisenstein in the first quarter of the twentieth century.

Cinematographic editing may be related to the processes of managing the meanings (Smircich and Morgan, 1982), the concept of enactment (Weick, 1979, 1993) and to the concepts of sensemaking and sensegiving (Gioia and

Chittipeddi, 1991). All these occur in a fragmented form and under continuous symbolic interaction. From this perspective, the social construction of reality (Berger and Luckmann, 1966) may be seen as a continuous editing of scenes during a process which includes reorganizing the past and re-formulating values.

Spectacular
metaphors

Conclusion

19

In this paper, a new perspective for organizational studies is discussed: the cinema metaphor. First, the paper has presented a brief outline of the concept of metaphor and emphasized its importance to cognitive processes through its capacity to generate alternative views and insights. Then, it deals with the theatre metaphor, emphasizing the seminal contributions by Erving Goffman and Kenneth Burke. Then, the cinema metaphor as a concept is outlined in order to give form to a perspective and to make use of the ideas of Daniel Boorstin, Guy Debord and Norman Denzin. After this view of the world had been established, it has sought to identify the elements and principles of the cinema metaphor in a more explicit form.

As with any metaphor, the cinema metaphor consists of a way of seeing, as much as of a way of not seeing the phenomena (see Alvesson, 1993; Morgan, 1986). As with any other metaphor, it has both strengths and weaknesses. Its principal strength is that the cinema metaphor extends the dramaturgical perspective in various ways: by including the spectacle-dimension and expanding the play's dimensions, by considering the media as interfering in the production of reality and by considering the multiplicity of discourses. This metaphor also provides a complex perspective of relations and reflects the spirit of the times. However, the characteristics that distinguish this metaphor may also contribute to its weaknesses. The cinema metaphor's principal limitation as a device for exploring organizations is the difficulty of developing an appropriate method of analysis. The intention of this paper has been to examine where the cinema metaphor has advantages over the more traditional theatre metaphor. By identifying how these differ, it is hoped that the paper will contribute to a greater appreciation of the value and uses of the cinema metaphor for the examination of organizational issues and contexts.

References

Allen, R. (1993), "Cinema, psychoanalysis, and the film spectator", *Persistence of Vision*, Vol. 10, pp. 5-33.

Alvesson, M. (1993), "The play of metaphors", in Hassard, J. and Parker, M. (Eds), *Postmodernism and Organizations*, Sage, London.

Andrew, J.D. (1976), *The Major Film Theories: An Introduction*, Oxford University Press, New York, NY.

Andrew, J.D. (1984), *Concepts in Film Theory*, Oxford University Press, Oxford.

Bazin, A. (1971), *What is Cinema?*, University of California Press, Berkeley, CA.

Beck, B.E.F. (1987), "Metaphors, cognition and artificial intelligence", in Haskell, R.E. (Ed.), *Cognition and Symbolic Structures: The Psychology of Metaphoric Transformation*, Ablex Publishing Corporation, Norwood, OH.

JOCM
15,1

20

Berger, P. and Luckmann, T. (1966), *The Social Construction of Reality: A Treatise in the Sociology of Knowledge*, Anchor Books, New York, NY.

Boorstin, D.J. (1962), *The Image: A Guide do Pseudo-events in America*, Atheneum, New York, NY.

Burke, K. (1962), *A Grammar of Motives and a Rhetoric of Motives*, The World Publishing Co., New York, NY.

Burns, E. (1972), *Theatricality: A Study of Convention in the Theatre and in Social Life*, Longman, London.

Chevrie, M. (1987), "La valeur-image", *Cahiers du Cinéma*, No. 356, pp. 27-30.

Curtius, E.R. (1967), *European Literature and the Latin Middle Ages*, Princeton University Press, Princeton, NJ.

Debord, G. (1994), *The Society of Spectacle*, Zone Books, New York, NY.

Denzin, N.K. (1995), *The Cinematic Society: The Voyeur's Gaze*, Sage, London.

Gibbs Jr, R.W. and Hall, C.K. (1987), "What does it mean to say that a metaphor has been understood?", in Haskell, R.E. (Ed.), *Cognition and Symbolic Structures: The Psychology of Metaphoric Transformation*, Ablex, Norwood, OH.

Gioia, D.A. and Chittipeddi, K. (1991), "Sensemaking and sensegiving in strategic change initiation", *Strategic Management Journal*, Vol. 12 No. 6, pp. 433-48.

Goffman, E. (1975), *The Presentation of Self in Everyday Life*, Anchor Books, New York, NY.

Gusfield, J.R. (1989), "Introduction", in Burke, K. (Ed.), *On Symbols and Society*, The University of Chicago Press, Chicago, IL.

Hill, G. (1992), *Illuminating Shadows: The Mythic Power of Film*, Shambbala, Boston, MA.

Lyman, S.M. and Scott, M.B. (1975), *The Drama of Social Reality*, Oxford University Press, New York, NY.

MacCabe, C. (1976), "Theory and film, principles of realism and pleasure", *Screen*, Vol. 17 No. 3, pp. 7-27.

Machado, A. (1982), *Serguei M. Eisenstein*, Brasiliense, São Paulo.

Mangham, I.L. and Overington, M.A. (1983), "Dramatism and the theatrical metaphor", in Morgan, G. (Ed.), *Beyond the Method: Strategies for Social Research*, Sage, Beverly Hills, CA.

Metz, C. (1971), *Essais sur la Signification au Cinéma – Tome 1*, Édition Klincksieck, Paris.

Monaco, J. (1981), *How to Read a Film: The Art, Technology, Language, History, and Theory of Film and Media*, Oxford University Press, New York, NY.

Morgan, G. (1986), *Images of Organization*, Sage, Newbury Park, CA.

Riggins, S.H. (1993), "Life as a metaphor: current issues in dramaturgical analysis", *Semiotica*, Vol. 1 No. 2, pp. 153-65.

Smircich, L. and Morgan, G. (1982), "Leadership: the management of meaning", *The Journal of Applied Behavioral Science*, Vol. 18 No. 3, pp. 257-73.

Sontag, S. (1991), *Styles of Radical Will*, Anchor Books, New York, NY.

Van den Berg, K.T. (1985), *Playhouse and Cosmos: Shakespearean Theatre as Metaphor*, University of Delaware Press, Newark, DE.

Weick, K.E. (1979), *The Social Psychology of Organizing*, Addison-Wesley, Reading, MA.

Weick, K.E. (1993), "The collapse of sensemaking in organizations: the Mann Gulch disaster", *Administrative Science Quarterly*, Vol. 38, pp. 628-52.

Part V
Management Improvisation: Jazz and Beyond

[19]

Improvisation as a Mindset for Organizational Analysis

Karl E. Weick

School of Business Administration, University of Michigan, Ann Arbor, Michigan 48109

The emphasis in organizational theory on order and control often handicaps theorists when they want to understand the processes of creativity and innovation. Symptoms of the handicap are discussions of innovation that include the undifferentiated use of concepts like flexibility, risk, and novelty; forced either-or distinctions between exploration and exploitation; focus on activities such as planning, visioning, and strategizing as sites where improvements are converted into intentions that await implementation; and reliance on routine, reliability, repetition, automatic processing, and memory as the glue that holds organization in place. Since the term "organization" itself denotes orderly arrangements for cooperation, it is not surprising that mechanisms for rearranging these orders in the interest of adaptation, have not been developed as fully. (See Eisenberg (1990) for an important exception.) That liability can be corrected if we learn how to talk about the process of improvisation.

Thus, the purpose of this essay is to improve the way we talk about organizational improvisation, using the vehicle of jazz improvisation as the source of orienting ideas. I start with two brief descriptions of the complexity involved when musicians compose in the moment. Then I review several definitions intended to capture holistically what is happening when people improvise. Next, I take a closer look at selected details in improvisation, namely, degrees of improvisation, forms for improvisation, and cognition in improvisation. These understandings are then generalized from jazz to other settings such as conversation, therapy, and relationships of command. I conclude with implications for theory and practice.

Descriptions of Jazz Improvisation

Here are two accounts of what happens when order and control are breached extemporaneously in jazz performances, and a new order created.

The sense of exhilaration that characterizes the artist's experiences under such circumstances is heightened for jazz musicians as storytellers by the activity's physical, intellectual, and emotional exertion and by the intensity of struggling with creative processes under the pressure of a steady beat. From the outset of each performance, improvisers enter an artificial world of time in which reactions to the unfolding events of their tales must be immediate. Furthermore, the consequences of their actions are irreversible. Amid the dynamic display of imagined fleeting images and impulses—entrancing sounds and vibrant feelings, dancing shapes and kinetic gestures, theoretical symbols and perceptive commentaries—improvisers extend the logic of previous phrases, as ever-emerging figures on the periphery of their vision encroach upon and supplant those in performance. Soloists reflect on past events with breathtaking speed, while constantly pushing forward to explore the implications of new outgrowths of ideas that demand their attention. Ultimately, to journey over musical avenues of one's own design, thinking in motion and creating art on the edge of certainty and surprise, is to be "very alive, absolutely caught up in the moment." (Berliner 1994, p. 220)

While they are performing their ideas, artists must learn to juggle short- and intermediate-range goals simultaneously. To lead an improvised melodic line back to its initial pitch requires the ability to hold a layered image of the pitch in mind and hand while, at the same time, selecting and performing other pitches. The requirements of this combined mental and physical feat become all the more taxing if, after improvising an extended phrase, soloists decide to manipulate more complex material, developing, perhaps, its middle segment as a theme. In all such cases, they must not only rely on their memory of its contour, but their muscular memory must be flexible enough to locate the segment's precise finger pattern instantly within their motor model of the phrase. (Berliner 1994, p 200)

Attempts to capture definitionally what is common among these examples have taken a variety of forms.

KARL E. WEICK   *Improvisation as a Mindset*

The word improvisation itself is rooted in the word "proviso" which means to make a stipulation beforehand, to provide for something in advance, or to do something that is premeditated. By adding the prefix "im" to the word proviso, as when the prefix "im" is added to the word mobile to create immobile, improvise means the *opposite* of proviso. Thus improvisation deals with the unforeseen, it works without a prior stipulation, it works with the unexpected. As Tyler and Tyler (1990) put it, improvisation is about the un-for-seen and unprovided-for which means it "is the negation of foresight, of planned-for, of doing provided for by knowing, and of the control of the past over the present and future" (p. x).

Some descriptions of improvisation, often those associated with jazz, describe this lack of prior stipulation and lack of planning as composing extemporaneously, producing something on the spur of the moment. Thus, we have Schuller's (1968, p. 378) influential definition that jazz involves "playing extemporaneously, i.e., without the benefit of written music . . . (C)omposing on the spur of the moment." Schön describes this extemporaneous composing in more detail as "on-the-spot surfacing, criticizing, restructuring, and testing of intuitive understandings of experienced phenomena" while the ongoing action can still make a difference (1987, pp. 26–27).

I have found it hard to improve on the following definition, which is the one that guides this essay: "Improvisation involves reworking precomposed material and designs in relation to unanticipated ideas conceived, shaped, and transformed under the special conditions of performance, thereby adding unique features to every creation" (Berliner 1994, p. 241).

It is also possible to, highlight definitionally, subthemes in improvisation. Thus, one can focus on order and describe improvisation as "flexible treatment of preplanned material" (Berliner 1994, p. 400). Or one can focus on the extemporaneous quality of the activity and describe improvisation as "intuition guiding action in a spontaneous way" (Crossan and Sorrenti 1996, p. 1) where intuition is viewed as rapid processing of experienced information (p. 14). Attempts to situate improvisation in organization lead to definitions such as the Miner et al. (1996) suggestion that improvisation consists of deliberately chosen activities that are spontaneous, novel, and involve the creation of something while it is being performed (pp. 3–4).

While it is tempting to adopt these compressed themes in the interest of economy, we may be better served as theorists if we retain the larger and more complex set of options and see which subsets are most useful to explain which outcroppings. For example, spontaneity and intuition are important dimensions of improvisation. Yet, in a rare outspoken passage, Berliner argues as follows.

[T]he popular definitions of improvisation that emphasize only its spontaneous, intuitive nature—characterizing it as the 'making of something out of nothing'—are astonishingly incomplete. This simplistic understanding of improvisation belies the discipline and experience on which improvisers depend, and it obscures the actual practices and processes that engage them. Improvisation depends, in fact, on thinkers having absorbed a broad base of musical knowledge, including myriad conventions that contribute to formulating ideas logically, cogently, and expressively. It is not surprising, therefore, that improvisers use metaphors of language in discussing their art form. The same complex mix of elements and processes coexists for improvisers as for skilled language practitioners; the learning, the absorption, and utilization of linguistic conventions conspire in the mind of the writer or utilization of linguistic conventions conspire in the mind of the writer or speaker—or, in the case of jazz improvisation, the player—to create a living work. (Berliner 1994, p. 492)

What Berliner makes clear is that the compression of experience into the single word "intuition" desperately needs to be unpacked because it is the very nature of this process that makes improvisation possible and separates good from bad improvisation.

Similarly, Berliner is worried lest, in our fascination with the label "spontaneous," we overlook the major investment in practice, listening, and study that precedes a stunning performance. A jazz musician is more accurately described as a highly disciplined "practicer" (Berliner 1994, p. 494) than as a practitioner.

Reminders that we should take little for granted in initial studies of improvisation seem best conveyed by more complex definitions that spell out what might be taken for granted. In the following section, I will suggest three properties of improvisation that may be especially sensitive to changes in other organizational variables. The implied logic is that changes in these variables affect the adequacy of improvisation which in turn affects adaptation, learning, and renewal.

Degrees of Improvisation

To understand improvisation more fully, we first need to see that it lies on a continuum that ranges from "interpretation," through "embellishment" and "variation" ending in "improvisation" (Lee Konitz cited in Berliner 1994, pp. 66–71). The progression implied is one of increased demands on imagination and concentration. "Interpretation" occurs when people take minor liberties with a melody as when they choose novel accents or dynamics while performing it basically as written. "Embellishment" involves greater use of imagination, this time with whole phrases in the original being anticipated or delayed beyond their usual placements. The melody is rephrased but recognizable. "Variation" occurs when clusters of notes not in the original melody are inserted, but their relationship to that original melody is made clear. "Improvisation" on a melody means "transforming the melody into patterns bearing little or no resemblance to the original model or using models altogether alternative to the melody as the basis for inventing new phrases" (Berliner 1994, p. 70). When musicians improvise, they "radically alter portions of the melody or replace its segments with new creations bearing little, if any, relationship to the melody's shape" (Berliner 1994, p. 77). To improvise, therefore, is to engage in more than paraphrase or ornamentation or modification.

With these gradations in mind it is instructive to re-examine existing examples of improvisation to see whether they consist of radical alterations, and new creations. Miner et al. (1996, pp. 9–14) describe several instances of organizational improvisation and the verbs they use suggest that their examples fit all four points on the continuum. Thus, they describe improvisations during new product development that consists of a "shift" in a light assembly (interpretation); a "switch" in a product definition or "adding" a light beam source (embellishment); "altering" the content of a prior routine or "revising" a test schedule (variation); and "creating" an internal focus group or "discovering" a way to do a 22-second information search in 2 seconds (improvisation). If my attempt to assign the Miner et al. (1996) verbs to Konitz's four categories is plausible, then it suggests several things. First, activities that alter, revise, create, and discover are purer instances of improvisation than are activities that shift, switch, or add. Second, activities toward the "interpretation" end of the continuum are more dependent on the models they start with than are activities toward the improvisation end. As dependency on initial models increases, adaptation to more radical environmental change should decrease. Third, as modifications become more like improvisations and less like interpretations, their content is more heavily influenced by past experience, dispositions, and local conditions. When people increasingly forego guidance from a common melody, they resort to more idiosyncratic guidance. It is here where differentials in prior experience, practice, and knowledge are most visible and have the most effect. Fourth, the stipulation that people deliberately act extempore should be easier to execute if they stick closer to a guideline than if they depart radically from it. Thus, interpretation and embellishment should be initiated more quickly under time pressure than is true for variation and improvisation. Deliberate injunctions to be radically different may falter if they fail to specify precisely what the

original model is, in what sense it is to remain a constraint, and which of its properties are constants and which are variables. These questions don't arise in the three approximations to improvisation represented by interpretation, embellishment, and variation. The point is, deliberate improvisation is much tougher, much more time consuming, and places higher demands on resources, than does deliberate interpretation. If deliberateness is a key requirement for something to qualify as organizational improvisation, and if we construe improvisation in the sense used by Konitz, then full-scale improvisation should be rare in time-pressured settings. But, if it could be accomplished despite these hurdles, then it should be a substantial, sustainable, competitive advantage.

Fifth, and finally, any one activity may contain all four gradations, as sometimes happens in jazz.

> Over a solo's course, players typically deal with the entire spectrum of possibilities embodied by these separable but related applications of improvisation. At one moment, soloists may play radical, precomposed variations on a composition's melody as rehearsed and memorized before the event. The very next moment, they may spontaneously be embellishing the melody's shape, or inventing a new melodic phrase. There is a perpetual cycle between improvised and precomposed components of the artists' knowledge as it pertains to the entire body of construction materials. . . . The proportion of precomposition to improvising is likewise subject to continual change throughout a performance. (Berliner 1994, p. 222)

Re-examination of the Miner et al. (1996) examples suggests that some involve the entire spectrum of improvisation and others do not. For example, when design engineers tackled the problem of flawed filters at Fast Track, they improvised a new feature, reworked the assemblies, shifted how lights were to stand, changed the formal technical features, and added a light beam source. The intriguing possibility is that full spectrum improvisation like this has different properties than simple standalone improvisation. Full spectrum improvisation makes fuller use of memory and past experience, can build on the competencies of a more diverse population, is more focused by a melody, and may be more coherent. If this is plausible then it should be more persuasive, diffuse faster, and be more acceptable since a greater variety of people within the firm can understand how it has developed. Furthermore, they are able to recognize some of its pre-existing components. It is also possible that the smooth versus sudden changes celebrated by those who invoke the concept of punctuated equilibrium are simply manifestations of full spectrum (smooth) or solitary (sudden) improvisation.

The point of all this is that we may want to be stingy in our use of the label improvisation and generous in our use of other labels that suggest approximations to improvisation. When we focus on approximations, we focus both on connections to the past and on the original model that is being embellished. The spectrum from interpretation to improvisation mirrors the spectrum from incremental to transformational change. It becomes less common in organizations than we anticipated, but its antecedents become clearer as do its connections with themes of order and control.

Forms of Improvisation

These connected themes of order and improvisation become even clearer when we look more closely at the object to which the process of improvisation is applied. As bassist-composer, Charles Mingus, insisted, "you can't improvise on nothing; you've gotta improvise on something" (Kernfeld 1995, p. 119). This is the same Mingus who once actually reduced a promising young saxophonist to tears before an audience, with his running commentary of "Play something different, man; play something different. This is jazz, man. You played that last night and the night before" (Berliner 1994, p. 271). The ongoing tension to "improvise on something" but to keep the improvisations fresh is the essence of jazz. That tension may be weaker in non-musical organizations where routine embellishment of routines is sufficient and expected and where surprise is unwelcome. But, whether embellishment is major or minor, improvisation involves the embellishment of something.

In jazz, that "something" usually is a melody such as originated in African-American blues and gospel songs, popular songs, ragtime piano and brass-band marches, Latin American dances, or rock and soul music (Kernfeld 1995, p. 40). What is common to these melodies is form imposed by a sequence of harmonic chords and a scheme of rhythm. Other objects available for embellishment that are more common to organizations range from routines and strategic intent (Perry 1991), to a set of core values, a credo, a mission statement, rules of engagement, or basic know-how. Gilbert Ryle (1979) argued that virtually all behavior has an ad hoc adroitness akin to improvisation because it mixes together a partly fresh contingency with general lessons previously learned. Ryle describes this mixture as paying heed. Improvisation enters in the following way.

> (T)o be thinking what he is here and now up against, he must both be trying to adjust himself to just this present once-only situation *and* in doing this to be applying lessons already learned. There must be in his response a union of some Ad Hockery with some know-how. If he is not at once *improvising* and improvising *warily*, he is not engaging his somewhat trained

wits in a partly fresh situation. It is the pitting of an acquired competence or skill against unprogrammed opportunity, obstacle or hazard. It is a bit like putting some *new* wine into *old* bottles. (Ryle 1979, p. 129)

Thus, improvisation shares an important property with phenomena encompassed by chaos theory (e.g., McDaniel 1996, Stacey 1992), namely, origins are crucial small forms that can have large consequences [e.g., cracks in shoulder bones determine hunting success among Naskapi Indians (Weick 1979, pp. 262–263.)] Melodies vary in the ease with which they evoke prior experience and trigger generative embellishments. Some melodies set up a greater number of interesting possibilities than do other melodies. The same holds true for organizational "melodies" such as mission statements, which range from the banal to the ingenious and invite well-practiced or novel actions on their behalf.

While improvisation is affected by one's associates, past experiences, and current setting, it is also determined by the kernel that provides the pretext for assembling these elements in the first place. These pretexts are not neutral. They encourage some lines of development and exclude other ones. And this holds true regardless of the improviser. While it is true that a masterful musician like tenor saxophonist, Sonny Rollins, can find incredible richness in mundane melodies such as "Tennessee Waltz" and "Home on the Range," it is equally true that these melodies themselves unfold with unusual progressions relative to the standard jazz repertory (e.g., "I Got Rhythm"). It is the capability of these progressions to challenge and evoke, as well as the competence of the performer, that contribute to improvisation. It is easy to overlook the substantive contribution of a melody because it is so small and simple. It's important to remember that a melody is also an early and continuing influence.

The important point is that improvisation does not materialize out of thin air. Instead, it materializes around a simple melody that provides the pretext for real-time composing. Some of that composing is built from pre-composed phrases that become meaningful retrospectively as embellishments of that melody. And some comes from elaboration of the embellishments themselves. The use of precomposed fragments in the emerging composition is an example of Ryle's (1979) "wary improvisation" anchored in past experience. The further elaboration of these emerging embellishments is an example of Ryle's opportunistic improvisation in which one's wits engage a fresh, once-only situation. Considered as a noun, an improvisation is a transformation of some original model. Considered as a verb, improvisation is composing in real time that begins with embellishments of a simple model, but increasingly feeds on these embellishments themselves to move farther from the original melody and closer to a new composition. Whether treated as a noun or a verb, improvisation is guided activity whose guidance comes from elapsed patterns discovered retrospectively. Retrospect may range back as far as solos heard long before or back only as far as notes played just this moment. Wherever the notes come from, their value is determined by the pattern they make *relative to* a continuing set of constraints formed by melody. The trick in improvisation is, as Paul Desmond put it, to aim for "clarity, emotional communication on a not-too-obvious level, form in a chorus that doesn't hit you over the head but is there if you look for it, humor, and construction that sounds logical in an unexpected way" (Gioia 1988, p. 89).

Cognition in Improvisation

As this more detailed picture of improvisation begins to emerge, there is a recurring implication that retrospect is significant in its production. In jazz improvisation people act in order to think, which imparts a flavor of retrospective sensemaking to improvisation. Ted Gioia puts it this way: unlike an architect who works from plans and looks ahead, a jazz musician cannot "look ahead at what he is going to play, but he can look behind at what he has just played; thus each new musical phrase can be shaped with relation to what has gone before. He creates his form retrospectively" (Gioia 1988, p. 61). The jazz musician, who creates form retrospectively, builds something that is recognizable from whatever is at hand, contributes to an emerging structure being built by the group in which he or she is playing, and creates possibilities for the other players. Gioia's description suggests that intention is loosely coupled to execution, that creation and interpretation need not be separated in time, and that sensemaking rather than decision making is embodied in improvisation. All three of these byproducts of retrospect create a different understanding of organized action than the one we are more accustomed to where we commonly look for the implementation of intentions, the interpretation of prior creations, and for decisions that presume prior sensemaking.

When musicians describe their craft, the importance of retrospect becomes clear, as these excerpts make clear.

> After you initiate the solo, one phrase determines what the next is going to be. From the first note that you hear, you are responding to what you've just played: you just said this on your instrument, and now that's a constant. What follows from that? And then the next phrase is a constant. What follows from that? And so on and so forth. And finally, let's wrap it up so that everybody understands that that's what you're doing. It's like

> language: you're talking, you're speaking, you're responding to yourself. When I play, it's like having a conversation with myself. (Max Roach cited in Berliner 1994, p. 192)

> If you're not affected and influenced by your own notes when you improvise, then you're missing the whole essential point. (Lee Konitz cited in Berliner 1994, p. 193)

> When I start off, I don't know what the punch line is going to be. (Buster Williams cited in Berliner 1994, p. 218)

The importance of retrospect for improvisation imposes new demands that suggest why organizational improvisation may be rare. To add to a store of ironies that are beginning to accumulate, not only is improvisation grounded in forms, but it is also grounded in memory. Forms and memory and practice are all key determinants of success in improvisation that are easy to miss if analysts become preoccupied with spontaneous composition. Implied in each musician's account is the relationship that "the larger and more complex the musical ideas artists initially conceive, the greater the power of musical memory and mental agility required to transform it" (Berliner 1994, p. 194).

To improve improvisation is to improve memory, whether it be organizational (Walsh and Ungson 1991), small group (Wegner 1987), or individual (Neisser and Winograd 1988). To improve memory is to gain retrospective access to a greater range of resources. Also implied here is the importance of listening *to oneself* as well as to other people. Prescriptions in organizational studies tout the importance of listening to others (e.g., the big news at GE is that Jack Welch discovered ears) but miss the fact that good improvisation also requires listening to one's own comments and building on them.

The reader is referred back to the description of composing in the moment on p. 543 that starts "while they are performing," to see again how important memory is to improvisation. This importance is reflected in formal jazz study.

> In one class, a teacher arbitrarily stopped the solos of students and requested that they perform their last phrase again. When they could not manage this, he chastised them for being "like people who don't listen to themselves while they speak." Aspiring improvisers must cultivate impressive musical recall in both aural and physical terms if they are to incorporate within their ongoing conversation new ideas conceived in performance. (Berliner 1994, p. 200)

Viewed through the lens of retrospect, jazz looks like this.

> The artist can start his work with almost random maneuver—a brush stroke on a canvas, an opening line, a musical motif— and then adapt his later moves to this initial gambit. A jazz

improviser, for example, might begin his solo with a descending five-note phrase and then see, as he proceeds, that he can use this same five-note phrase in other contexts in the course of his improvisation.

> This is, in fact, what happens in Charlie Parker's much analyzed improvisation on Gershwin's "Embraceable You." Parker begins with a five-note phrase (melodically similar to "you must remember this" phrase in the song "As Time Goes By") which he employs in a variety of ingenious contexts throughout the course of his improvisation. Parker obviously created his solo on the spot (only a few minutes later he recorded a second take with a completely different solo, almost as brilliant as the first), yet this should not lead us to make the foolish claim that his improvisation is formless. (Gioia 1988, p. 60)

Viewed through the lens of retrospect, larger issues look like this. If events are improvised and intention is loosely coupled to execution, the musician has little choice but to wade in and see what happens. What will actually happen won't be known until it is too late to do anything directly about it. All the person can do is justify and make sensible, after the fact, whatever is visible in hindsight. Since that residue is irrevocable, and since all of this sensemaking activity occurs in public, and since the person has a continuing choice as to what to do with that residual, this entire scenario seems to contain a microcosm of the committing forces that affect creative coping with the human condition (Weick 1989). Small wonder that Norman Mailer, in his famous essay "The White Negro," described jazz as "American existentialism."

This simple exposition of degrees of improvisation, forms for improvisation, and cognition in improvisation does not begin to exhaust the dimensions of jazz improvisation that are relevant for organizational theory. Other potential themes of interest might include the ways in which "mistakes" provide the platform for musical "saves" that create innovations (e.g., Berliner 1994, p. 191, 209, 210–216; Weick, 1995); skills of bricolage that enable people to make do with whatever resources are at hand (Harper 1987, Levi-Strauss 1966, Weick 1993); and social conventions that complement structures imposed by tunes (Bastien and Hostager, 1992).

Non-jazz Settings for Improvisation

What I have tried to show so far is that descriptions of composing on the spur of the moment, and attempts to portray this process definitionally and dimensionally, comprise a language that allows analysts to maintain the images of order and control that are central to organizational theory and simultaneously introduce images of innovation and autonomy. The ease with which improvisation mixes together these disparate images of control

and innovation (Nemeth and Staw 1989) becomes even clearer if we look at other settings where improvisation seems to occur.

A swift way to see the potential richness of improvisation as a metaphor is simply to look in the index of Berliner's (1994) authoritative volume under the heading, "Metaphors for aspects of improvisation" (p. 869). In his analyses Berliner finds that jazz improvisation is likened to cuisine, dance, foundation building, a game of chess, a journey, landing an airplane, language, love, marriage, preparing for acting, painting, singing, sports, and acting like a tape recorder (some drummers "are like tape recorders. You play something and then they imitate it"; p. 427). By a process of backward diagnosis, we therefore expect to find improvisation where people cook, move, construct, compete, travel, etc.

Perhaps the setting that most resembles jazz improvisation, at least judging from its frequency of mention, is language acquisition and use (e.g., Ramos 1978, Suhor 1986). Jazz musician Stan Getz describes improvisation as a way of conversing.

> It's like a language. You learn the alphabet, which are the scales. You learn sentences, which are the chords. And then you talk extemporaneously with the horn. It's a wonderful thing to *speak* extemporaneously, which is something I've never gotten the hang of. But musically I love to talk just off the top of my head. And that's what jazz music is all about. (Maggin 1996, p. 21)

An example of the easy movement that is possible between the two domains is Berliner's equating of improvisation with rethinking.

> The activity [of jazz improvisation] is much like creative thinking in language, in which the routine process is largely devoted to rethinking. By ruminating over formerly held ideas, isolating particular aspects, examining their relationships to the features of other ideas, and, perhaps, struggling to extend ideas in modest steps and refine them, thinkers typically have the sense of delving more deeply into the possibilities of their ideas. There are, of course, also the rarer moments when they experience discoveries as unexpected flashes of insight and revelation.

> Similarly, a soloist's most salient experiences in the heat of performance involve poetic leaps of imagination to phrases that are unrelated, or only minimally related, to the storehouse, as when the identities of formerly mastered patterns melt away entirely within new recombinant shapes. (Berliner 1994, pp. 216–217)

Discussions of improvisation in groups are built on images of call and response, give and take (Wilson 1992), transitions, exchange, complementing, negotiating a shared sense of the beat (see Barrett's (1998) discussion of groove), offering harmonic possibilities to someone else, preserving continuity of mood, and cross-fertilization. In jazz, as in conversation, self-absorption is a problem. Wynton Marsalis observed that in playing, as in conversation, the worst people to talk to and play with are those who, "when you're talking, they're thinking about what they are going to tell you next, instead of listening to what you're saying" (Berliner 1994, p. 401). What is also striking about jazz conversation, as with conversations in other settings, is the many levels at which they function simultaneously. Thus, jazz improvisation involves conversation between an emerging pattern and such things as formal features of the underlying composition, previous interpretations, the player's own logic, responsiveness of the instrument, other musicians, and the audience.

Managerial activities, which are dominated by language and conversation, often become synonymous with improvisation. Thus, we find Mangham and Pye (1991) proposing close parallels between improvisation and organizing. Here is what they observe in top management teams.

> Our respondents assert that they learn what they are about in talking to and trusting their colleagues, that they often recognize and develop their own views in the very process of seeking consensus, that talking to others heightens their awareness, sharpens their focus. But they also assert that they are in command, that they do plan and shape the future with clear intent, that they know where it is they are heading. (p. 77)

Like jazz musicians, managers simultaneously discover targets and aim at them, create rules and follow rules, and engage in directed activity often by being clearer about which directions are not right than about specified final results. Their activity is controlled but not predetermined (Mangham and Pye 1991, p. 79).

Here is how Mangham and Pye make sense of what they observe.

> What we are proposing is that in their daily interactions our managers, no less than managers elsewhere, sustain appreciative systems or improvise readinesses which reflect their values and beliefs which, in turn, are likely to be influenced by and to influence received ideas about the doing of organizing. We hold that much of the doing of organizing is either a matter of running through a *script* or an instance of *improvisation*, and that both of these activities relate to readings which have reference to appreciative systems which are, in turn, reflections of deeply held beliefs and values. (Mangham and Pye 1991, p. 36)

What Mangham and Pye (1991) make clear is that managing shares with jazz improvisation such features as simultaneous reflection and action (p. 79), simultaneous rule creation and rule following (p. 78), patterns of mutually expected responses akin to musicians moving through a melody together (p. 45), action informed by melodies in the form of codes (p. 40), continuous mixing

of the expected with the novel (p. 24), and the feature of a heavy reliance on intuitive grasp and imagination (p. 18). These managers are not just Herbert Simon's (1989) chess grandmasters who solve problems by recognizing patterns. And neither are jazz musicians. They are that, but more. The more is that they are also able to use their experience of "having been there" to recognize "that one is now somewhere else, and that that 'somewhere else' is novel and may be valuable, notwithstanding the 'rules' which declare that one cannot get here from there" (Mangham and Pye 1991, p. 83).

Daft and Weick (1984) suggest that when managers deem an environment to be unanalyzable, they seek information by means of strategies that are "more personal, less linear, more ad hoc and improvisational" (p. 287). Sutcliffe and Sitkin (1996) have argued that total quality interventions basically involve what they call a "redistribution of improvisation rights." [See also Wruck and Jensen (1994, p. 264) on allocation of decision rights to initiation, ratification, implementation, and monitoring.] Successful quality management occurs when people are newly authorized to paraphrase, embellish, and reassemble their prevailing routines, extemporaneously. Furthermore, they are encouraged to think while doing rather than be guided solely by plans. Thus, when a firm "disseminates improvisation rights" it tends to encourage the "flexible treatment of preplanned material," which means that quality improvement and jazz improvisation are closely aligned.

Improvisation is common in public-sector organizations and occurs often on the front-line, as Weiss (1980, p. 401) suggests.

> Many moves are improvisations. Faced with an event that calls for response, officials use their experience, judgment, and intuition to fashion the response for the issue at hand. That response becomes a precedent, and when similar questions come up, the response is uncritically repeated. Consider the federal agency that receives a call from a local program asking how to deal with requests for enrollment in excess of the available number of slots. A staff member responds with off-the-cuff advice. Within the next few weeks, programs in three more cities call with similar questions, and staff repeat the advice. Soon what began as improvisation has hardened into policy. (p. 401)

Improvisation also occurs in settings as disparate as psychotherapy, medical diagnosis, and combat.

Improvisation is the heart of psychotherapy. Thus, it is not surprising to find that one of the most prominent and original jazz pianists, Denny Zeitlin, is also a practicing psychiatrist who sees patients approximately 30 hours per week (Herrington 1989). Keeney (1990, p. 1) describes the parallels between therapy and improvisation.

KARL E. WEICK   *Improvisation as a Mindset*

Given the unpredictable nature of a client's communication, the therapist's participation in the theatrics of a session becomes an invitation to improvise. In other words, since the therapist never knows exactly what the client will say at any given moment, he or she cannot rely exclusively upon previously designed lines, pattern, or scripts. Although some orientations to therapy attempt to shape both the client and therapist into a predetermined form of conversation and story, every particular utterance in a session offers a unique opportunity for improvisation, invention, innovation, or more simply, change. (Keeney 1990, p. 1)

If therapy is viewed as improvisation, then therapies are viewed as songs. The song can be played exactly as scored or with improvisation, but one would not expect an improvisational therapist to play only one song over and over anymore than one would expect a jazz musician to play only one song throughout a lifetime.

Improvisation sometimes lies at the heart of medical diagnosis as well, but only when practitioners jettison narrow versions of decision rationality in favor of improvisation. Starbuck (1993) suggests that good doctors do not base their treatments on diagnosis. They leave diagnosis out of the chain between symptoms and treatment because it discards too much information and injects random errors. There are many more combinations of symptoms than there are diagnoses, just as there are many more treatments than diagnoses.

(T)he links between symptoms and treatments are not the most important keys to finding effective treatments. Good doctors pay careful attention to how patients respond to treatments. If a patient gets better, current treatments are heading in the right direction. But, current treatments often do not work, or they produce side-effects that require correction. The model of symptoms-diagnoses-treatments ignores the feedback loop from treatments to symptoms, whereas this feedback loop is the most important factor. (Starbuck 1993, p. 87)

The logic can be applied to academic research.

Academic research is trying to follow a model like that taught in medical schools. Scientists are translating data into theories, and promising to develop prescriptions from the theories. Data are like symptoms, theories like diagnoses, and prescriptions like treatments. Are not organizations as dynamic as human bodies and similarly complex? Theories do not capture all the information in data, and they do not determine prescriptions uniquely. Perhaps scientists could establish stronger links between data and prescriptions if they did not introduce theories between them. Indeed, should not data be results of prescriptions? Should not theories come from observing relations between prescriptions and subsequent data? (Starbuck 1993)

Starbuck reminds us that, when faced with incomprehensible events, there is often no substitute for acting your way into an eventual understanding of them. How can I know what I am treating until I see how it responds?

To organize for diagnosis is to design a setting that generates rich records of symptoms, a plausible initial treatment, alertness to effects of treatments, and the capability to improvise from there on. Theories, diagnoses, strategies, and plans serve mostly as plausible interim stories that mix ignorance and knowledge in different patterns.

Isenberg (1985, pp. 178–179), following the work of Bursztjahn et al. (1981), has also discussed what he calls treating a patient empirically. Like Starbuck, he notes that a diagnosis, if it is inferred at all, occurs retrospectively after the patient is cured. Isenberg then generalizes this medical scenario to battlefield situations. This application fleshes out a much earlier statement by Janowitz (1959, p. 481) that a combat soldier is not a rule-following bureaucrat who is "detached, routinized, self-contained; rather his role is one of constant improvisation. . . . The impact of battle destroys men, equipment, and organization, which need constantly and continually to be brought back into some form of unity through on-the-spot improvisation." For Isenberg, the parallel between empirical medicine and empirical fighting is that in both cases

tactical maneuvers (treatment) will be undertaken with the primary purpose of learning more about (diagnosing) the enemy's position, weaponry, and strength, as well as one's own strength, mobility, and understanding of the battlefield situation. . . . Sometimes the officer will need to implement his or her solution with little or no problem definition and problem solving. Only after taking action and seeing the results will the officer be able to better define the problem that he or she may have already solved! (pp. 178–179)

The steady progression from jazz to other sites where improvisation is plausible culminates in the idea that living itself is an exercise in improvisation. People compose their lives, as Mary Catherine Bateson (1989) suggests in this composite description.

I have been interested in the arts of improvisation, which involve recombining partly familiar materials in new ways, often in ways especially sensitive to context, interaction, and response. . . . (The idea of life as an improvisatory art) started from a disgruntled reflection on my own life as a sort of desperate improvisation in which I was constantly trying to make something coherent from conflicting elements to fit rapidly changing settings. . . Improvisation can be either a last resort or an established way of evoking creativity. Sometimes a pattern chosen by default can become a path of preference. . . . Much biography of exceptional people is built around the image of a quest, a journey through a timeless landscape toward an end that is specific, even though it is not fully known. . . . (These assumptions are increasingly inappropriate today because) fluidity and discontinuity are central to the reality in which we live. Women have always lived discontinuous and contingent lives, but men today are newly vulnerable, which turns women's traditional adaptations into a resource. . . . The physical rhythms

KARL E. WEICK   *Improvisation as a Mindset*

of reproduction and maturation create sharper discontinuities in women's lives than in men's, the shifts of puberty and menopause, of pregnancy, birth, and lactation, the mirroring adaptations to the unfolding lives of children, their departures and returns, the ebb and flow of dependency, the birth of grandchildren, the probability of widowhood. As a result, the ability to shift from one preoccupation to another, to divide one's attention, to improvise in new circumstances, has always been important to women. (pp. 2, 3, 4, 5, 6, 13)

The newfound urgency in organizational studies to understand improvisation and learning is symptomatic of growing societal concerns about how to cope with discontinuity, multiple commitments, interruptions, and transient purposes that dissolve without warning. To understand more about improvisation undoubtedly will help us get a better grasp on innovation in organizations. That's important. But it is not nearly as important as is understanding how people in general "combine familiar and unfamiliar components in response to new situations, following an underlying grammar and an evolving aesthetic" (Bateson 1989, p. 3). To watch jazz improvisation unfold is to have palpable contact with the human condition. Awe, at such moments, is understandable.

Implications for Theory

While several implications for organizational theory have already been mentioned, I want to suggest some of the richness implicit in improvising by brief mention of its relation to postmodern organizational theory and to paradox.

The idea of improvisation is important for organizational theory because it gathers together compactly and vividly a set of explanations suggesting that to understand organization is to understand organizing or, as Whitehead (1929) put it, to understand "being" as constituted by its "becoming." This perspective, found in previous work by people such as Allport (1962), Buckley (1968), Follett (1924), Mangham and Pye (1991), Maruyama (1963), Mintzberg and McHugh (1985), and Weick (1969, 1979) has been newly repackaged as the "unique intellectual preoccupation of 'postmodern' organizational theorists" (Chia 1996, p. 44). Thus, we find people talking once more about the ontology of becoming, using images already familiar to process theorists and musicians alike, images such as emergence, fragments, micro-practices that enact order, reaccomplishment, punctuation, recursion, reification, relations, transcience, flux, and "a sociology of verbs rather than a sociology of nouns" (Chia 1996, p. 49). If theorists take improvisation seriously, they may be able to give form to the idea of "becoming realism" (Chia 1996) and add to what we already know.

They may, for example, be able to do more with the simultaneous presence of seeming opposites in organizations than simply label them as paradoxes. There is currently an abundance of conceptual dichotomies that tempt analysts to choose between things like control and innovation, exploitation and exploration, routine and nonroutine, and automatic and controlled, when the issue in most organizations is one of proportion and simultaneity rather than choice. Improvisation is a mixture of the precomposed and the spontaneous, just as organizational action mixes together some proportion of control with innovation, exploitation with exploration, routine with nonroutine, automatic with controlled. The normally useful concepts of routine (Gersick and Hackman 1990, Cohen and Bacdayan 1994) and innovation (Amabile 1988, Dougherty 1992) have become less powerful as they have been stretched informally to include improvisation. Thus, a routine becomes something both repetitious and novel, and the same is true for innovation. A similar loss of precision [Reed (1991) refers to it as a "rout"] has occurred in the case of decision making where presumptions of classical rationality are increasingly altered to incorporate tendencies toward spontaneous revision. Neither decisions nor rationality can be recognized in the resulting hodgepodge. What is common among all of these instances of lost precision is that they attempt to acknowledge the existence of improvisation, but do so without giving up the prior commitment to stability and order in the form of habit, repetition, automatic thinking, rational constraints, formalization, culture, and standardization. The result, when theorists graft mechanisms for improvisation onto concepts that basically are built to explain order, is a caricature of improvisation that ignores nuances highlighted in previous sections. These caricatures leave out properties of organizational improvisation such as the tension involved in mixing the intended and the emergent and the strong temptation to simplify in favor of one or the other; the possibility that order can be accomplished by means of ongoing ambivalent mixtures of variation and retention that permit adaptation to dynamic situations; the chronic temptation to fall back on well-rehearsed fragments to cope with current problems even though these problems don't exactly match those present at the time of the earlier rehearsal; the use of emergent structures as sources for embellishment which enables quick distancing from previous solutions; the close resemblance between improvising and editing; the sensitivity of improvisation to originating conditions; and the extensive amount of practice necessary to pull off successful improvisation. The remedy would seem to lie in a variety of directions such as positing routines, innovation, and decision making as inputs to improvisation

KARL E. WEICK   *Improvisation as a Mindset*

akin to melodies (e.g., people improvised on this routine); treating improvisation as a distinct form of each (e.g., this routine was executed improvisationally); treating each of the three as a distinct way to engage in organizational improvisation (e.g., routinizing of improvisation); and, treating improvisation as a stand alone process like the other three consisting of a fixed sequence of conceiving, articulating, and remembering.

Implications for Practice

The concept of improvisation also engages several concepts in mainstream organizational practice and likewise suggests ways to strengthen them. For example, if time is a competitive advantage then people gain speed if they do more things spontaneously without lengthy prior planning exercises (Crossan and Sorrenti 1996, p. 4). To do more things spontaneously is to become more skilled at thinking on your feet, a skill that is central in improvisation even though it is not given much attention in accounts of managerial action. Improvisation has implications for staffing. Young musicians who are laden with technique often tend to be poor at improvisation because they lack voices, melodies, and feeling (Berliner 1994, p. 792, ftn. 17; Davis 1986, p. 87), which sounds a lot like the liability that corporations associate with newly minted MBAs. The remedy for students is to mix listening with history, practice, modeling, and learning the fundamentals, which can be tough if they are driven, instrumental, in a hurry, and have little sense of what they need to know. The irony is that it is this very haste which dooms them to be a minor player who sounds like every other technique-laden minor player, none of whom have much to say.

If we treat the preceding description of improvisation as if it contained the shell of a set of prescriptions for adaptive organizing, then here are some possible characteristics of groups with a high capability for improvisation:

1. Willingness to forego planning and rehearsing in favor of acting in real time;
2. Well developed understanding of internal resources and the materials that are at hand;
3. Proficient without blueprints and diagnosis;
4. Able to identify or agree on minimal structures for embellishing;
5. Open to reassembly of and departures from routines;
6. Rich and meaningful set of themes, fragments, or phrases on which to draw for ongoing lines of action;
7. Predisposed to recognize partial relevance of previous experience to present novelty;

8. High confidence in skill to deal with nonroutine events;
9. Presence of associates similarly committed to and competent at impromptu making to;
10. Skillful at paying attention to performance of others and building on it in order to keep the interaction going and to set up interesting possibilities for one another.
11. Able to maintain the pace and tempo at which others are extemporizing.
12. Focused on coordination here and now and not distracted by memories or anticipation;
13. Preference for and comfort with process rather than structure, which makes it easier to work with ongoing development, restructuring, and realization of outcomes, and easier to postpone the question, what will it have amounted to?

Limits to Improvisation

If theorists conceptualize organizations as sites where the activity of improvisation occurs, this may offset their tendency to dwell on themes of control, formalization, and routine. It may also help them differentiate the idea of "flexibility," which tends to be used as a catchall for the innovative remainder. Nevertheless, there are good reasons why the idea of improvisation may have limited relevance for organizations. If organizations change incrementally—punctuations of an equilibrium seldom materialize out of thin air without prior anticipations—then those incremental changes are more like interpretation and embellishment than variation or improvisation. Thus, even if organizations wanted to improvise, they would find it hard to do so, and probably unnecessary. Improvisation in one unit can also compound the problems faced by other units to which it is tightly coupled. Furthermore, bursts of improvisation can leave a firm with too many new products and processes to support (Miner et al. 1996, p. 26).

The intention of a jazz musician is to produce something that comes out *differently* than it did before, whereas organizations typically pride themselves on the opposite, namely, reliable performance that produces something that is standardized and comes out the same way it did before. It is hard to imagine the typical manager feeling "guilty" when he or she plays things worked out before. Yet most jazz musicians perform with the intention of "limiting the predictable use of formerly mastered vocabulary" (Berliner 1994, p. 268). Parenthetically, it is interesting to note that the faster the tempo at which a musician plays, the more likely he or she is to fall back on the predictable use of a formerly mastered

KARL E. WEICK *Improvisation as a Mindset*

vocabulary. It is difficult to be affected by one's own newly created notes when musical ideas have to be conceived and executed at $8\frac{1}{3}$ eighth notes per second (tempo of one quarter note $= 310$). At extremely fast tempos there is no choice but to use preplanned, repetitive material to keep the performance going. This suggests that there are upper limits to improvisation. If this is true then high-velocity organizations (Eisenhardt 1989)—which resemble jazz ensembles in many ways—become especially interesting as sites where the increasing tempo of activity may encourage, not improvisation, but a sudden reversion back to old ideas that have no competitive edge. A key issue in high-velocity organizations is just how much of a constraint velocity really is. Recall that in the case of jazz improvisation, creative processes continually struggle under the unrelenting demands of a steady beat. In jazz improvisation, deadlines are reckoned in seconds and minutes whereas high-velocity organizations deal with deadlines reckoned in hours and days. While it is true that pressure is pressure, it is also true that at some speeds memory plays an increasingly large role in the product produced. This suggests that high-velocity organizations may have more latitude for improvisation than do jazz ensembles, but only up to a point. High velocity organizations may be vulnerable in ways similar to those described by Starbuck and Milliken (1988) and Miller (1993). Success encourages simplification, more risk taking, less slack, and accelerated production, all of which shrink the time available for adaptive improvisation and force people back on older ideas and away from the very innovating that made them successful in the first place.

Even if organizations are capable of improvisation, it is not clear they need to do it. One of the realities in jazz performance is that the typical audience is none the wiser if a musician makes a mistake and buries it, plays a memorized solo, solves a tough problem, inserts a clever reference to a predecessor, or is playing with a broken instrument and working around its limits. If composing in real time is difficult and risky, and if the customer is unable to appreciate risk taking anyway, then the only incentives to take those risks lie with one's own standards and with fellow musicians. Those incentives may be sufficient to hold sustained improvisation in place. However, most organizations may not reward originality under the assumption that customers don't either. If we add to these characteristics the fact that the musical consequences in a jazz performance are irreversible whereas managers try never to get into anything without a way out, and the fact that musicians love surprises but managers hate them, then we begin to see that improvisation may be absent

from the organizational literature, not because we haven't looked for it, but because it isn't there.

My bet is that improvising is close to the root process in organizing and that organizing itself consists largely of the embellishment of small structures. Improvising may be a tacit, taken-for-granted quality in all organizing that we fail to see because we are distracted by more conspicuous artifacts such as structure, control, authority, planning, charters, and standard operating procedures. The process that animates these artifacts may well consist of ongoing efforts to rework and reenact them in relation to unanticipated ideas and conditions encountered in the moment. In organizing as in jazz, artifacts and fragments cohere because improvised storylines impose modest order among them in ways that accommodate to their peculiarities. Order through improvisation may benefit some organizations under some conditions and be a liability under other conditions. These contingencies need to be spelled out. But so too does the sense in which improvisation may be part of the infrastructure present in all organizing.

Conclusion

A final sense in which jazz improvisation mirrors life is captured in an entry from Norman Mailer's journal dated December 17, 1954 (source of this quotation is unknown).

> Jazz is easy to understand once one has the key, something which is constantly triumphing and failing. Particularly in modern jazz, one notices how Brubeck and Desmond, off entirely on their own with nothing but their nervous system to sustain them, wander through jungles of invention with society continually ambushing them. So the excitement comes not from victory but from the effort merely to keep musically alive. So, Brubeck, for example will to his horror discover that he has wandered into a musical cliché, and it is thrilling to see how he attempts to come out of it, how he takes the cliché, plays with it, investigates it, pulls it apart, attempts to put it together into something new and sometimes succeeds, and sometimes fails, and can only go on, having left his record of defeat at that particular moment. That is why modern jazz despite its apparent lyricalness is truly cold, cold like important conversations or Henry James. It is cold and it is nervous and it is under tension, just as in a lunch between an editor and an author, each makes mistakes and successes, and when it is done one hardly knows what has happened and whether it has been for one's good or for one's bad, but an "experience," has taken place. It is also why I find classical music less exciting for that merely evokes the echo of a past "experience"—it is a part of society, one of the noblest parts, perhaps, but still not of the soul. Only the echo of the composer's soul remains. And besides it consists too entirely of triumphs rather than of life.

KARL E. WEICK   *Improvisation as a Mindset*

Life in organizations is filled with potential inventions that get ambushed when people slide into old clichés. Pulling oneself out is tense work. It can be cold work. Occasionally there is triumph. Usually, however, as people at Honda put it, "A 1 per cent success rate is supported by mistakes made 99 per cent of the time" (Nonaka and Takeuchi 1995, p. 232). Jazz improvisation, itself built of "moments of rare beauty intermixed with technical mistakes and aimless passages" (Gioia 1988, p. 66), teaches us that there is life beyond routines, formalization, and success. To see the beauty in failures of reach is to learn an important lesson that jazz improvisation can teach.[1]

Endnote

[1]This essay expands on themes mentioned in my brief remarks in Vancouver on August 8, 1995 (e.g., "defining characteristics of improvisation," "examples of improvisation in non-musical settings") and it retains all specifics used to ground those themes (e.g., Pyle and Gioia on adroit ad hoc action, Mingus on melodies, Keeney on psychotherapy, and Mailer on society's proneness to ambush invention). These expansions are a perfect example of "reworking precomposed material in relation to unanticipated ideas" conceived *during* the writing itself, which is simply another way of saying, it is an exhibit of improvisation.

References

Allport, F. H. 1962. A structuronomic conception of behavior: Individual and collective. *Journal of Abnormal and Social Psychology.* **64** 3–30.

Amabile, T. M. 1988. A model of creativity and innovation in organizations. *Research in Organizational Behavior.* **10** 123–167. JAI, Greenwich, CT.

Barrett, Frank. 1998. Creativity and Improvisation in Jazz and Organizations: Implications for Organizational Learning. *Organization Science* **9** 5 605–622.

Bastien, D. T., T. J. Hostager. 1992. Cooperation as communicative accomplishment: A symbolic interaction analysis of an improvised jazz concert. *Communication Studies.* **43** 92–104.

Bateson, M. C. 1989. *Composing a Life.* Atlantic Monthly, New York.

Berliner, Paul F. 1994. *Thinking in Jazz: The Infinite Art of Improvisation.* Univ. of Chicago, Chicago, IL.

Buckley, W. 1968. Society as a complex adoptive system. W. Buckley, ed. *Modern Systems Research for the Behavioral Scientist* Aldine, Chicago, IL. 490–513.

Bursztajhn, H., A. Feinbloom, R. Hamm, A. Brodsky 1981. *Medical Choices, Medical Chances.* Dell, New York.

Chia, R. 1996. The problem of reflexivity in organizational research: Towards a postmodern science of organization. *Organization.* **3** 31–59.

Cohen, M. D., P. Bacdayan. 1994. Organizational routines are stored as procedural memory: Evidence from a laboratory study. *Organization Science.* **5** 554–568.

Crossan, M., M. Sorrenti. 1996. Making sense of improvisation. Unpublished manuscript. Univ. of Western Ontario.

Daft, R., K. Weick. 1984. Toward a model of organizations as interpretation systems. *Academy of Management Review.* **9** 284–295.

Davis, F. 1986. *In the Moment.* Oxford, New York.

Dougherty, D. 1992. Interpretive barriers to successful product innovation in large firms. *Organization Science.* **3** 179–202.

Eisenberg, E. 1990. Jamming! Transcendence through organizing. *Communication Research.* **17** 2 139–164.

Eisenhardt, K. M. 1989. Making fast strategic decisions in high-velocity environments. *Academy of Management Journal.* **32** 543–576.

Follett, M. P. 1924. *Creative Experience.* Longmans, Green, New York.

Gersick, C. J. G., J. R. Hackman. 1990. Habitual routines in task-performing groups. *Organizational Behavior and Human Decision Processes.* **47** 65–97.

Gioia, T. 1988. *The Imperfect Art.* Oxford, New York.

Harper, D. 1987. *Working Knowledge.* Univ. of Chicago Press, Chicago, IL.

Herrington, B. S. 1989. Merging of music, psychiatry yields richly composed life. *Psychiatric News.* April 7, 16+.

Isenberg, D. J. 1985. Some hows and whats of managerial thinking: Implications for future army leaders. J. G. Hunt and J. D. Blair, eds., *Leadership on the Future Battlefield.* Pergamon-Brassey's, Washington, DC. 168–181.

Janowitz, M. 1959. Changing patterns of organizational authority: The military establishment. *Administrative Science Quarterly.* **3** 473–493.

Keeney, B.P. 1990. *Improvisational Therapy.* Guilford, New York.

Kernfeld, B. 1995. *What to Listen for in Jazz.* Yale Univ., New Haven, CT.

Levi-Strauss, C. 1966. *The Savage Mind.* Univ. of Chicago, Chicago, IL.

Maggin, D. L. 1996. *Stan Getz: A Life in Jazz.* Morrow, New York.

Mangham, I., A. Pye. 1991. *The Doing of Managing.* Blackwell, Oxford, UK.

Maruyama, M. 1963. The second cybernetics: Deviation-amplifying mutual causal processes. *American Scientist.* **51** 164–179.

McDaniel, Reuben R., Jr. 1996. Strategic leadership: A view from quantum and chaos theories. W. J. Duncan, P. Ginter, L. Swayne, eds., *Handbook of Health Care Management.* Blackwell, Oxford, UK.

Miller, D. 1993. The architecture of simplicity. *Academy of Management Review.* **18** 116–138.

Miner, A. J., C. Moorman, C. Bassoff. 1996. Organizational improvisation in new product development. Unpublished manuscript. University of Wisconsin, Madison, WI.

Mintzberg, H., A. McHugh. 1985. Strategy formation in an adhocracy. *Administrative Science Quarterly.* **30** 160–197.

Neisser, U., E. Winograd, eds. 1988. *Remembering Reconsidered: Ecological and Traditional Approaches to the Study of Memory.* Cambridge University, Cambridge, UK.

Nemeth, C. J., B. M. Staw. 1989. The tradeoffs of social control and innovation in groups and organizations. L. Berkowitz, ed. *Advances in Experimental Social Psychology.* **22** 175–210. Academic, San Diego, CA.

Nonaka, I., H. Takeuchi. 1995. *The Knowledge-creating Company.* Oxford, New York.

Perry, L. T. 1991. Strategic improvising: How to formulate and implement competitive strategies in concert. *Organizational Dynamics.* **19** 4, 51–64.

Ramos, R. 1978. The use of improvisation and modulation in natural talk: An alternative approach to conversational analysis. N. K.

KARL E. WEICK *Improvisation as a Mindset*

Denzin, ed. *Studies in Symbolic Interaction.* **1** 319–337. JAI, Greenwich, CT.

Reed, M. 1991. Organizations and rationality: The odd couple. *Journal of Management Studies.* **28** 559–567.

Ryle, G. 1979. Improvisation. G. Ryle, ed. *On Thinking.* Blackwell, London, UK. 121en130.

Schön, D. A. 1987. *Educating the Reflective Practitioner.* Jossey-Bass, San Francisco, CA.

Schuller, G. 1968. *Early Jazz.* Oxford, New York.

Simon, H. A. 1989. Making management decisions: The role of intuition and emotion. W. H. Agor, ed. *Intuition in Organizations.* Sage, Newbury Park, CA. 23–39.

Stacey, R. D. 1992. *Managing the Unknowable.* Jossey-Bass, San Francisco, CA.

Starbuck, W. H. 1993. "Watch where you step!" or Indiana Starbuck amid the perils of academe (Rated PG). A. G. Bedeion, ed. *Management Laureates.* **3** 65–110. JAI, Greenwich, CT.

——— F. Milliken. 1988. Challenger: Fine tuning the odds until something breaks. *Journal of Management Studies.* **25** 319–340.

Suhor, C. 1986. Jazz improvisation and language performance: parallel competitiveness. *ETC.* **43** 4, 133–140.

Sutcliffe, K. M., S. Sitkin. 1996. New perspectives on process management: Implications for 21st century organizations. C. Cooper, S. Jackson, eds. *Handbook of Organizational Behavior.* Wiley, New York.

Tyler, S. A., M. G. Tyler. 1990. Foreword. B. P. Keeney, ed. *Improvisational Therapy.* ix–xi. Guilford, New York.

Walsh, J. P., G. R. Ungson. 1991. Organizational memory. *Academy of Management Review.* **16** 57–91.

Wegner, D. M. 1987. Transactive memory: A contemporary analysis of the group mind. B. Mullen, G. R. Goethals, eds. *Theories of Group Behavior.* 185–208. Springer-Verlag, New York.

Weick, K. E. 1969. *The Social Psychology of Organizing.* Addison-Wesley, Reading, MA.

——— 1979. *The Social Psychology of Organizing.* 2d ed. Addison-Wesley, Reading, MA.

——— 1989. Organized improvisation: 20 years of organizing. *Communication Studies.* **40** 241–248.

——— 1993. Organizational redesign as improvisation. G. P. Huber, W. H. Glick, eds. *Organization Change and Redesign.* Oxford, New York. 346–379.

——— 1995. Creativity and the aesthetics of imperfection. C. M. Ford, D. A. Gioia, eds. *Creative Action in Organizations.* 187–192. Sage, Thousand Oaks, CA.

Weiss, C. H. 1980. Knowledge creep and decision accretion. *Knowledge: Creation, Diffusion, Utilization.* **1** 381–404.

Whitehead, A. N. 1929. *Process and Reality.* Macmillan, New York.

Wilson, R. C. 1992. Jazz: A metaphor for high-performance teams. J. A. Heim, D. Compton, eds. *Manufacturing Systems.* 238–244. National Academy Press, Washington, D.C.

Wruck, K. H., M. C. Jensen. 1994. Science, specific knowledge, and total quality management. *Journal of Accounting and Economics.* **18** 247–287.

[20]

Creativity and Improvisation in Jazz and Organizations: Implications for Organizational Learning

Frank J. Barrett

Department of Systems Management, Naval Postgraduate School, Monterey, California 93943

I wake to sleep and take my waking slow. I learn by going where I have to go.

Theodore Roethke, poet

We must simply act, fully knowing our ignorance of possible consequences.

Kenneth Arrow, economist

I think the fear of failure is why I try things . . . if I see that there's some value in something and I'm not sure whether I deserve to attempt it, I want to find out.

Keith Jarrett, jazz pianist

At the dawn of the twenty-first century, we are in the midst of a revolution that has been called variously the post-industrial society (Bell 1973), the third wave (Toffler 1980), the information revolution (Naisbitt 1983), and the post-capitalist society (Drucker 1993). We do not yet perceive the entire scope of the transformation occurring, but we know that it is global, that it is based on unprecedented access to information, and that since more people have access to information than ever before, that it is potentially a democratic revolution. Perhaps the management of knowledge development and knowledge creation is becoming the most important responsibility for managers as we enter the twenty-first century. Indeed, ideas generated by various streams and movements, including socio-technical design, total quality management, re-engineering, remind us that the fundamental shift we are experiencing involves empowering people at all levels to initiate innovative solutions in an effort to improve processes.

Given the unprecedented scope of changes that organizations face and the need for members at all levels to be able to think, plan, innovate, and process information, new models and metaphors are needed for organizing. Drucker has suggested that the twenty-first century leader will be like an orchestra conductor. However, an orchestral metaphor—connoting pre-scripted musical scores, single conductor as leader—is limited, given the ambiguity and high turbulence that many managers experience. Weick (1992) has suggested the jazz band as a prototype organization. This paper follows Weick's suggestion and explores the jazz band and jazz improvising as an example of an organization designed for maximizing learning and innovation. To help us understand the relationship between action and learning, we need a model of a group of diverse specialists living in a chaotic, turbulent environment; making fast, irreversible decisions; highly interdependent on one another to interpret equivocal information; dedicated to innovation and the creation of novelty. Jazz players do what managers find themselves doing: fabricating and inventing novel responses without a prescribed plan and without certainty of outcomes; discovering the future that their action creates as it unfolds.

After discussing the nature of improvisation and the unique challenges and dangers implicit in the learning task that jazz improvisers create for themselves, I will broadly outline seven characteristics that allow jazz bands to improvise coherently and maximize social innovation in a coordinated fashion. I also draw on my own experience as a jazz pianist. I have played with and lead combinations of duos, trios, and quartets in addition to touring in 1980 as pianist with the Tommy Dorsey Band under the direction of trombonist Buddy Morrow. I will explore the following features of jazz improvisation.

FRANK J. BARRETT   *Creativity and Improvisation in Jazz and Organizations*

1. Provocative competence: Deliberate efforts to interrupt habit patterns;
2. Embracing errors as a source of learning;
3. Shared orientation toward minimal structures that allow maximum flexibility;
4. Distributed task: continual negotiation and dialogue toward dynamic synchronization;
5. Reliance on retrospective sense-making;
6. "Hanging out": Membership in a community of practice;
7. Taking turns soloing and supporting.

Finally, I will suggest implications for organizational design and managing for learning.

The Nature of Improvisation

There is a popular misconception that jazz players are inarticulate, untutored geniuses, that they have no idea what they are playing as if picking notes out of thin air. As biographies of jazz players and studies of jazz have shown, the art of jazz playing is very complex and the result of a relentless pursuit of learning and disciplined imagination. Since (until recently) there have been no conservatories or formal schools of jazz instruction, veteran jazz players are highly committed to self-renewal, having had to create their own learning opportunities.

Jazz improvisers are interested in creating new musical material, surprising themselves and others with spontaneous, unrehearsed ideas. Jazz differs from classical music in that there is no clear prescription of what is to be played. From the Latin "improvisus," meaning "not seen ahead of time," improvisation is "playing extemporaneously ... composing on the spur of the moment" (Schuller 1989, p. 378). Given the highly exploratory and tentative nature of improvisation, the potential for failure and incoherency always lurks around the corner. Saxophonist Paul Desmond said that the improviser must "crawl out on a limb, set one line against another and try to match them, bring them closer together" (Gioia 1988, p. 92). Jazz saxophonist Steve Lacy discusses the excitement and danger inherent in improvisation and likens it to existing on the edge of the unknown.

> I'm attracted to improvisation because of something I value. There is a freshness, a certain quality, which can only be obtained by improvisation, something you cannot possibly get from writing. It is something to do with the "edge." Always being on the brink of the unknown and being prepared for the leap. And when you go out there you have all your years of preparation and all your sensibilities and your prepared means but it is a leap into the unknown. (Bailey 1992, p. 57)

The metaphors of leaping into the unknown, hanging out on a limb, suggest the exhilarating and perilous nature of engaging in an activity in which the future is largely unknown, yet one in which one is expected to create something novel and coherent, often in the presence of an audience.

Gioia captures a sense of the challenge and difficulty inherent in jazz by considering what practitioners of other art forms would subject themselves to if they relied on improvisation as design.

> If improvisation is the essential element in jazz, it may also be the most problematic. Perhaps the only way of appreciating its peculiarity is by imagining what twentieth-century art would be like if other art forms placed an equal emphasis on improvisation. Imagine T. S. Eliot giving nightly poetry readings at which, rather than reciting set pieces, he was expected to create impromptu poems—different ones each night, sometimes recited at a fast clip; imagine giving Hitchcock or Fellini a handheld motion picture camera and asking them to film something, anything—at that very moment, without the benefits of script, crew, editing, or scoring; imagine Matisse or Dali giving nightly exhibitions of their skills—exhibitions at which paying audiences would watch them fill up canvas after canvas with paint, often with only two or three minutes devoted to each "masterpiece." (Gioia 1988, p. 52)

Improvisation involves exploring, continual experimenting, tinkering with possibilities without knowing where one's queries will lead or how action will unfold.

Learning to Improvise: Preparing To Be Spontaneous

It is worth exploring for a moment the way that jazz musicians learn to improvise in order to gain a deeper understanding of how they think while they are playing. Learning to play jazz is a matter of learning the theory and rules that govern musical progressions. Once integrated these rules become tacit and amenable to complex variation and transformation, much like learning the rules of grammar and syntax as one learns to speak. Jazz players learn to build a vocabulary of phrases and patterns by imitating, repeating, and memorizing the solos and phrases of the masters until they become part of their repertoire of "licks" and "crips." According to trumpeter Tommy Turrentine,

> The old guys used to call those things crips. That's from crippled... In other words, when you're playing a solo and your mind is crippled and you can't think of anything different to play, you go back into one of your old bags and play one of your crips. You better have something to play when you can't think of nothing new or you'll feel funny laying out there all the time (quoted in Berliner, 1994, p. 102).

After years of practicing and absorbing these patterns, they train their ears to recognize what phrases fit within different forms, the various options available within the constraints of various chords and songs. They study other players' strategic thought process that guided their solo construction, why they chose certain notes and how their motifs fit the contour of the overall phrasing.

A transformation occurs in the player's development when he or she begins to export materials from different contexts and vantage points, combining, extending, and varying the material, adding and changing notes, varying accents, subtly shifting the contour of a memorized phrase. Combining elements from different musical models, mixing different harmonies and grace notes, extending intervals, and altering chord tones is a metaphorical transfer of sorts (Barrett and Cooperrider 1990), transferring from one context into another to produce something new. By combining, extending, and varying, they breathe life into these forms. The variation could involve something as simple as taking automatic phrases and extending them into new and unfamiliar contexts, such as trying out a phrase over a different chord. Pianist John Hicks recalls experiencing a breakthrough when he combined previously unrelated chords. Saxophonist Lee Konitz attempts to create new substitutions as he plays to enrich the basic harmonic structure of standard songs (Berliner 1994, p. 161).

The aim is to integrate ideas, freeing attention so that players can think strategically about their choice of notes and the overall direction of their solos. Hargreaves et al. (1991, p. 53) hypothesize that when improvisers employ automatic thinking[1] to execute patterns, they are free to plan the overall strategy of the piece; they are "aware of playing detailed figures or 'subroutines' at a relatively peripheral or unconscious level, with central conscious control reserved for overall strategic or artistic planning." Saxophonist James Moody practices "trying to play something that you like and being able to put it anywhere you want in a tune" (Berliner 1994, p. 174). Jazz critic Mark Gridley claims that Bill Evans was a master strategist.

> Evans crafted his improvisations with exacting deliberation. Often he would take a phrase, or just a kernel of its character, then develop and extend its rhythms, its melodic ideas, and accompanying harmonies. Within the same solo he would often return to it, transforming it each time. And while all this was happening, he would be considering ways of resolving the tension that was building. He would be considering rhythmic ways, melodic ways, and harmonies, all at the same time, long before the moment that he decided was best for resolving the idea. . . . During Bill Evans's improvisations, an unheard, continuous self-editing was going on. He spared the listener his false starts and discarded ideas. . . . Evans never improvised solos that merely strung together ideas at the same rate they popped into his head.

The results of these deliberations could be a swinging and exhilarating experience for the listener, but they reflected less a carefree abandon, than the well-honed craftsmanship of a very serious performer working in the manner of a classical composer. The adjective most frequently applied to his music is "introspective" (Gridley 1991, pp. 302, 303).

It is uncertain to what degree improvisers go through an "unheard, continuous self-editing," an anticipatory, virtual trial and error as they consider different directions and interpretations of the material. Within a split second, musicians must project images and goals gleaned from some musical model or one they have just heard. Although Gridley theorizes that Bill Evans is thinking fairly far ahead and choosing phrases long before he played it, some musicians seem to be deciding within shorter time spans which notes to play. One player describes the subtle interplay between prehearing, responding, and following an idea, who sees the direction of the phrase that is just ahead of him and likens it to "chasing a piece of paper that's being blown into the wind" (Berliner 1994, p. 190). Others speak of going on automatic pilot while they think of something, repeating a phrase in order to buy time while their imagination wakes up. This no doubt, is one characteristic that distinguishes great soloists: how far ahead they are thinking and strategizing about possible phrases, how to shape the contour of their ideas, how and when to resolve harmonic and rhythmic tension. This points toward a delicate paradox musicians face, a point I will explore below: too much reliance on learned patterns (habitual or automatic thinking) tends to limit the risk-taking necessary for creative improvisation; on the other hand too much regulation and control restrict the interplay of musical ideas. In order for musicians to "strike a groove," they must suspend some degree of control and surrender to the flow of the music.

The previous section addressed the nature of improvisation, the challenging task of playing unrehearsed ideas, the process of developing improvisatory skills and the process of learning the jazz idiom. In the following section, I will outline seven characteristics of jazz improvisation and explore how these features apply in non-jazz contexts.

Seven Characteristics of Jazz Improvisation

1. Provocative Competence: Interrupting Habit Patterns

Perhaps because of the treachery involved in improvising and the risk of playing something that is incoherent, there is often a temptation to do what is feasible, to play notes that are within one's comfortable range. This is why, as many jazz critics attest, there is a temptation on the part of jazz improvisers to rely on "certain stock phrases which have proven themselves effective in past performance (rather than) push themselves to create fresh improvisations" (Gioia 1988, p. 53). Yet, the art of jazz improvisation demands that the musician create something different. Musicians and critics agree that "musicians who 'cheat' by playing the same or similar solos over and over again are looked down upon by colleagues and fans" (Gioia 1988, p. 52). Saxophonist Ronnie Scott contrasts Oscar Peterson's flawless pre-rehearsed solos with the risk taking of Sonny Rollins, who attempts to transform the harmonic and melodic materials that the tune presents.

> Oscar Peterson is a very polished, technically immaculate, performer, who—I hope he wouldn't mind me saying so—trots out these fantastic things that he has perfected and it really is a remarkable performance. Whereas Sonny Rollins, he could go on one night and maybe it's disappointing, and another night he'll just take your breath away by his kind of imagination and so forth. And it would be different every night with Rollins. (Quoted in Bailey 1988, p. 51)

Because of the temptation to repeat what they do well rather than risk failure, veteran jazz musicians make deliberate attempts to guard against the reliance on pre-arranged music, memorized solos, or habits and patterns that have worked for them in the past. Keith Jarrett decries those who play overlearned clichés and become imitations of themselves: "The music is struggle. You have to want to struggle. And what most leaders are the victim of is the freedom not to struggle. And then that's the end of it. Forget it!" (Carr 1991, p. 53). Jazz musicians often approach their work with a self-reflexiveness, guarding against the temptation to rely on ingrained habits, so that they don't repeat stock phrases and comfortable solos that contradict the goal of improvisation. Tony Oaxley recalls moments of self critique following performances: "The search was always for something that sounded right to replace the things that sounded predictable and (therefore) wrong (Bailey 1992, p. 89). Jarrett put it succinctly: "I think you have to be completely merciless with yourself" (Bailey 1992, p. 122).

Organization learning theorists have noticed that organizations also are tempted to rely on past successes and repeat stock phrases. Behavior in organizations is based on routines—rules, recipes, practices, conventions, beliefs—in short the response system that encodes activity learned from the past. Ordinary learning in organizations tends to lead to stable routines (March 1991) that perpetuate and become fixed even if they are no longer appropriate or detrimental (Levitt and March 1988), as if they are playing themselves automatically. Even when stimuli change, organizations tend to generate the same responses (Weick 1991). Many routines are automatic and not even accessible to ordinary recollection and analysis, so that individuals and organizations continue them long after actors have ceased to be able to provide an account of their purposes (Cohen 1991). Levitt and March (1988) refer to this as the competency trap: the tendency for an organization to become competent and specialized in a routine that was successful, thereby squelching experimentation (March 1991).

Especially under stressful conditions, such as environmental turbulence, there is a tendency to fall back on habitual responses. In this sense, managers often face the same dilemma that jazz players face: their actions are quite public and therefore stressful; they too are tempted to repeat what they do well rather than risk failure if they should depart from what has been proven to work. As Argyris (1990) has pointed out, the pressure to look competent leads people to defend their actions and reasoning. This regression becomes an obstacle to the questioning of assumptions and considering situations from a fresh perspective that could lead to novel initiatives.

Hedberg writes that organizations and managers can voluntarily switch from routines to a deliberate search for alternative possibilities but this is rare: "learning is typically triggered by problems" (Hedberg 1981, p. 16). Of course, even deliberate search for alternatives might not be sufficient for creation of novelty.

This creates a challenge for jazz players: their purpose, by definition, is to avoid that which is automatic and safe and formulas that simply repeat past success. Some jazz musicians avoid "competency traps" and keep fresh alternatives open by deliberately exploring the limits of their knowledge and comfort level. Herbie Hancock recalls an early moment when he discovered the limits of his knowledge. He remembers being inspired when he heard someone playing a passage that he (Hancock) could not play. For some this might be discouraging. But for Hancock, and most successful jazz musicians, this is the beginning rather than the end of the story.

> I had been a musician all my life, had all this training, played with all these great players, but I knew I could never have created that. And if I can't do it, something is missing—I have to find out how to do it! I've always been like that when I've heard something I liked but I couldn't do. That's how I got into jazz. I heard this guy playing (jazz piano) at a variety show in high school, and I knew that he knew what was doing, and he was doing it on my instrument—but I had no idea of what was going on. So I wanted to learn how to do it. That's what got me started. In order to do that, you have to know what you don't know. (Novello 1990, p. 445)

What has not been explored much by learning theorists is managers' consciously "switching cognitive gears" from habitual to active thinking (Louis and Sutton 1991). Hedberg et al. (1976) encourage organizations to nurture small disruptions and incremental re-orientations to keep learning processes vital and handicap inferior routines. Incremental experiments sharpen perception and activate thought processes.

Many veteran jazz musicians practice provocative competence; they make deliberate efforts to create disruptions and incremental re-orientations. This commitment often leads players to attempt to outwit their learned habits by putting themselves in unfamiliar musical situations that demand novel responses. Saxophonist John Coltrane is well known for deliberately playing songs in difficult and unfamiliar keys because "it made (him) think" while he was playing and he could not rely on his fingers to play the notes automatically. Herbie Hancock recalls that Miles Davis was very suspicious of musicians in his quartet playing repetitive patterns so he forbade them to practice. In an effort to spur the band to approach familiar tunes from a novel perspective, Davis would sometimes call tunes in different keys, or call tunes that the band had not rehearsed. This would be done in concert, before a live audience. "I pay you to do your practicing on the band stand," Hancock recalls Davis telling them. Keith Jarrett recalls Davis' commitment to "keeping the music fresh and moving" by avoiding comfortable routines. "Do you know why I don't play ballads any more?" Jarrett recalled Davis telling him. "Because I like to play ballads so much" (Carr 1992, p. 53).

Miles Davis not only practiced this provocative competence in live concerts, he also extended this to the recording studio. This is illustrated in a famous 1959 session. When the musicians arrived in the recording studio, they were presented with sketches of songs that were written in unconventional modal forms using scales that were very foreign to western jazz musicians at that time. One song, contained 10 bars instead of the more familiar 8 or 12 bar forms that characterize most standards. Never having seen this music before and largely unfamiliar with the forms, there was no rehearsal. The very first time they performed this music, the tape recorder was running. The result was the album *Kind of Blue*, widely regarded as a landmark jazz recording. When we listen to this album, we are witnessing the musicians approaching these pieces for the first time, themselves discovering new music at the same time that they were inventing it.

What makes a disruption provocative rather than noxious can be gleaned from Miles Davis' example. First, his interruption was affirmative (Barrett 1995): he held an image of members as competent performers able to meet the demands of a challenging task. He believed in their overall potential and capacity to perform successfully even if they felt uncomfortable (and possibly irritated). In fact, his band members were often able to perform at a higher level. Second, he did more than just disrupt habit patterns: he created alternative pathways for action. He imported new material that opened possibilities and suggested alternative routes for his players. Once the song begins, passivity is not an option: the activity is impersonally structured so that musicians are required to play something, to take some kind of action. Third, the interruption was incremental. These foreign contexts were scaled to be challenging, but not overly disruptive. This suggests the role of leadership in cultivating generative metaphors and seeding suggestive narratives (Barrett and Cooperrider 1990).

Hedberg et al. (1976) contend that system designers have weak direct influence on participants' behavior. They suggest that designers reconceive their roles as catalysts for a system's self-design by focusing on third order strategies for carrying out second order learning. Miles Davis had a talent for creating incremental obstacles and nurturing small disruptions that provoked his musicians to experiment with new actions that yielded new levels of creativity. This suggests that managers, like Miles Davis, develop a provocative competence that inspires alternative possibilities, an ability to create anomalies and unconventional obstacles that make it impossible for members to rely on habitual responses and rote thinking.

It would be useful to consider the organizational equivalent of requiring members to abandon overreliance on automatic processing and practicing familiar routines. Clearly this would have implications for dislodging conventional assumptions regarding such conventional practices as job descriptions, performance evaluations, and recruitment. Perhaps this is what W. L. Gore and Associates, the makers of Gore-tex, have in mind by abandoning formal job descriptions or conventional chain of command reporting structures. Reportedly, when a newly hired MBA reported for work one day, Bill Gore, the President and founder advised him to "look around and find something you'd like to do." Such a loosely structured environment makes it more difficult to rely on accepted routines and forces new hires to improvise new actions. Or consider the example of the R & D executive at Sony who, wanting to create a mini compact disc player, was faced with engineers who were convinced the CD technology could not be compacted further. Based on familiar routines, and perhaps enamored of the technology they themselves developed, they could not imagine a smaller alternative. The executive walked into the meeting with a 5-inch block of carved wood and told them that the new CD player needed to be no bigger. The engineers now had novel constraints to work through, a challenging puzzle not unlike the modal sketches that Miles Davis' band found when they walked into the *Kind of Blue* recording session.

This suggests that we expand our definition of leadership to include creating conditions that encourage members to bring a mindfulness to their task that allows them to imagine alternative possibilities heretofore unthinkable. Consider the example of British Airlines which held an off-site workshop for its executives to consider ways to improve customer service for the business class. However, instead of sleeping in regular hotel rooms, one executive had the beds removed and replaced them with airline seats. This no doubt disturbed the taken-for-granted routines, not to mention sleep patterns. Faced with the puzzle of these unexpected constraints, they came up with a number of innovations to improve comfort, including the design of a more comfortable seat that included a footrest. Provocative competence involves creating irregular arrangements that disturb "stock phrases" and comfortable playing, encouraging members to improvise new solutions.

2. Embracing Errors As Source of Learning

If past successes create routines that drive out experimentation in organizations, there is a tendency to construe errors as unacceptable. However, errors are a very important source of learning. Abdel-Hamid and Madnick (1990) discuss the need to learn from failures in the development of new software. The Seifert and Hutchins (1992) study of decision making on a Navy ship demonstrated the learning potential of error-making, how errors serve as an opportunity for receiving feedback and becoming familiar with the wider task environment. As individuals learned through error correction procedures, they came closer to the eventual goal of error-free performance. Jazz bands also embrace errors as source of learning, but for quite different reasons. These studies suggest the value of learning from errors as a way to eliminate them under the assumption that in actual performance, errors are ultimately intolerable. Jazz bands, on the other hand, see errors as inevitable and something to be assimilated and incorporated into the performance.

Since jazz improvisation is a highly expressive art form that leads players to go out "on the edge of the unknown", it is impossible to predict where the music is going to lead. Risky, explorative attempts are likely to produce errors. In fact, jazz improvisers regularly make mistakes, often without the audience's awareness. Often, there are

discrepancies between intention and action: sometimes the hands fail to play what the inner ear imagines. Sometimes musicians misinterpret others' cues or simply play the wrong notes.

> Somebody who decides to play jazz for a living knows he will struggle for the rest of his life, unless he opts for predictable and smoothing compromise. Honest jazz involves public exploration. It takes guts to make mistakes in public, and mistakes are inherent. If there are no mistakes it's a mistake. In Keith Jarrett's solo improvisations you can hear him hesitate, turn in circles for a while, struggle to find the next idea. Bird used to start a phrase two or three times before figuring out how to continue it. On the spot. Now. No second draft. It can take a toll night after night in front of an audience that just might be considering you shallow. (Zwerin 1983, p. 33)

Jazz players are often able to turn these unexpected problems into musical opportunities. Errors become accommodated as part of the musical landscape, seeds for activating and arousing the imagination. Drummer Max Roach sees the value in errors, "if two players make a mistake and end up in the wrong place at the wrong time, they may be able to break out of it and get into something else they might not have discovered otherwise." (Berliner 1994, p. 383). Herbie Hancock recalls playing an obviously wrong chord during a concert performance. Hearing the unexpected combination of notes, Miles Davis used them as a prompt, and rather than ignore the mistakes, played with the notes, embellishing them, using them as a creative departure for a different melody. Any event or sound, including an error, becomes a possible springboard to prime the musical imagination, an opportunity to re-define the context so that what might have appeared an error becomes integrated into a new pattern of activity. Looking backward, the "wrong" notes appear intentional.

Rather than treat an enactment as a mistake to be avoided, often what jazz musicians do is to repeat it, amplify it, develop it further until it becomes a new pattern. Pianist Don Friedman recalls listening to a recording with himself on piano and Booker Little on trumpet. When listening to the recording 20 years later, Friedman discovered that he played a major third in the chord instead of a minor third and Little brilliantly accommodated it, allowing the "wrong note" to shape his solo.

> Little apparently realized the discrepancy during his solo's initial chorus, when he arrived at this segment and selected the minor third of the chord for one of the opening pitches of a phrase. Hearing it clash with the pianist's part, Little improvised a rapid save by leaping to another pitch and resting, stopping the progress of his performance. To disguise the error further, he repeated the entire phrase fragment as if he had initially intended it as a motive, before extending it into a graceful, ascending melodic arch. From that point on, Little guided his solo

according to a revised map of the ballad. "Even when Brooker played the melody at the end of the take," observed Friedman with admiration, he varied it in ways "that fit the chord I was playing." (Berliner 1994, p. 383)

Repeating the phrase with the clashing note, Little made it sound intentional. When errors do happen, rather than search for causes and identify responsibility, musicians treat them impersonally: they make adjustments and continue. In this vein, Weick (1990) cites critic Ted Gioia who calls for a different standard for evaluating performance, an "aesthetic of imperfection". Rather than evaluate the success or failure of individual creations based on some external standard of perfection (such as one might find in the evaluation of a classical musical performance), Gioia calls for the need to evaluate courageous efforts. Such an aesthetic would involve evaluating the entire repertoire of actions that the musician attempted, the beautiful phrases combined with the clunkers that were the result of risky efforts, the same expansive efforts that no doubt produce beautiful passages.

One implication for enhancing innovative action in organizations is to question the way we look at errors and breakdowns. How can people in organizations be expected to attempt something that may be outside of their reach if breakdowns are seen as unacceptable? This would suggest that innovation would be enhanced if organizations resisted the attempts to over-focus on the elimination of error or to see mistakes as character blemishes. Too often managers create monuments to organizational breakdowns through exhaustive search for causes and framing mistakes as unacceptable. This often has the unintended consequence of immobilizing people. Given the nature of knowledge work in the organizations of the future, this suggests that perhaps organizations need to adopt an "aesthetic of imperfection," an acknowledgement that learning is something that often happens by trial and error, by brave efforts to experiment outside of the margin. This would propose a different standard for organizational evaluation: evaluate performances not just on conventional standards of success, but on strength of effort; level of purposeful, committed engagement in an activity; perseverance after an error has been made; passionate attempt to expand the horizon of what had been considered possible. At the very least, it suggests distinguishing between errors that are the result of carelessness and those that are the result of caring deeply about a project.

Similarly, once errors are made, how do managers turn these unexpected events into learning opportunities, as imaginative triggers and prompts for new action? Consider an example from Nordstrom's department store

where employees are encouraged to "respond to unreasonable customer requests." Stories circulate about an employee paying a customer's parking ticket when the store's gift wrapping took too long. Such capacity for accommodation and adjustment might be indispensable when attempts at innovation and customer satisfaction do not immediately meet expectation. Rather than simply rewarding managers for "fixing" problems, perhaps organizations should consider the way that managers persevere and make use of mistakes as points of creative departure. An aesthetic of imperfection implies that errors would be framed not so much as character blemishes, but as unavoidable mishaps to be creatively re-integrated as negotiation proceeds.

This also suggests that if organizations advocate ad hoc action and serendipitous learning, then there are times when members must be willing to release one another for consequences that they could not predict, for errors of trespassing and over-extension. Hannah Arendt (1958) noted that the one antidote to the predicament of unpredictability is forgiveness. Imagine executives developing an aesthetic of forgiveness, releasing those who make noble efforts, for consequences that could not be foreseen. Otherwise, tightly bound bureaucracies might be necessary to ward off trespassers.

3. Minimal Structures That Allow Maximum Flexibility

In an effort to guarantee consistency and efficiency, organizations often attempt to systematically avoid changes and ambiguity through creating standard operating procedures, clear and rationalized goals, and forms of centralized control. Hedberg et al. (1976) suggested that organizational processes would be improved if designers create minimal structures that allow diversity and minimize consensus. Similarly, Eisenberg (1990) analyzes jamming in jazz bands and contends that creativity is enhanced when emphasis is placed on coordinating action with minimal consensus, minimal disclosure, and minimal, simple structures. Modest structures value ambiguity of meaning over clarity, preserve indeterminacy and paradox over excessive disclosure. By "making do with minimal commonalities and elaborating simple structures in complex ways," (Eisenberg 1990) players balance autonomy and interdependence.

Jazz improvisation is a loosely structured activity in which action is coordinated around songs. Songs are made up of patterns of melodies and chord changes, marked by sections and phrases. Following Bastien and Hostager (1988) songs are "cognitively held rules for musical innovation" (p. 585). When musicians improvise, it is usually based on the repetition of the song structure.

These guiding structures are nonnegotiable, impersonal limitations: musicians do not have to stop to create agreements along the way. The selection of standard tunes and their chord changes embody minimal tacit rules that are rarely articulated. The musicians know the chord changes to "All of Me" or a 12 bar blues, so that often musicians who have never met are able to "jam" and coordinate action. These moderate constraints serve as benchmarks that occur regularly and predictably throughout the tune, signalling the shifting context to everyone. Everyone knows where everyone else is supposed to be, what chords and scales players are obliged to play. These minimal constraints allow them freedom to express considerable diversity. Players are free to transform materials, to intervene in the flow of musical events and alter direction. Once there is a mutual orientation around the basic root movement of the chord patterns, even the basic chords themselves can be altered, augmented or substituted.

Songs impose order and create a continuous sense of cohesion and coordination: all the players know where everyone is at any given moment. Individual players are able to innovate and elaborate on ideas with the assurance that they are oriented to a common place. How can organizations achieve fluid coordination without sacrificing creativity and individual contributions? What would be the equivalent in organizations, of structures that are minimal, non-negotiable, impersonal tacitly accepted rules that do not need to be constantly articulated. Weick (1990) suggests that one organizational equivalent of minimal structure might be credos, stories, myths, visions, slogans, mission statements, trademarks. Organizational slogans, such as Avis' "we try harder" are catchy phrases awaiting embellishment, encouraging individual members to elaborate on their version of the melodic path that fits within the tacit constraints. Organizational stories and myths, such as the Nordstrom's employee who paid a waiting customer's parking ticket, persist as markers to remind and seed other employees to embellish on the melody, initiating unusual actions to satisfy customers.

One counterpart to minimal models in organizations is the design prototype. The prototype is the design pattern upon which engineers model and create variations on basic structures. For example Crick and Watson, credited for discovering the structure of DNA, recall that when they were exploring the molecule, they frequently built and re-built prototypes and copper models even though they knew the models were not completely accurate. The DNA prototypes acted as a minimal structure that provided imaginative boundaries around which they could explore options, a shared orientation that invited them to elaborate upon their ongoing creation. Under traditional norms of organizational design, prototypes are often the exclusive property of design engineers, kept separate from manufacturing, marketing, and other groups, not to mention the customer. As a result, many brilliant designs never get produced, or worse, different engineering groups work on their parts separately, only to discover in the final stages that their contributions, however brilliant and innovative, do not fit together. Often technical disciplines are segmented as knowledge specialists develop ideas at different rates, produce solutions that work well in lab settings, but are difficult to reproduce (Purser and Pasmore 1992).

As Weick (1990) pointed out, organizations pay disproportionate attention to beginnings and endings, but not much attention to ongoing temporal coordination. Many breakdowns in innovation occur because organizations are too segmented. Often members do not share a mutual orientation after a project is launched, so that when someone alters action or changes direction, no one is sure where others are located, and do not find out until it is too late. As a result they either feel too constrained to take creative action, or when they do, they discover too late that it causes problems for others.

But what would be the organizational equivalent of song, a structure in which options are minimally-limited, publicly shared, impersonal, simultaneous, and temporally punctuated? Perhaps one counterpart to a song would be rapid prototyping, regular updating and changing of design prototypes. Such a practice would allow cross-discipline communication so that people can create while knowing how and where their ideas fit into the whole evolving system. Consider an alternative that Kodak initiated when they were developing the Funsaver camera. Rather than working separately, the engineering, manufacturing and marketing departments created a shared work space and collaborated to develop a prototype for the camera. Designers made changes and creative contributions to their individual parts, but would update the schematic for the whole camera. Each morning these individual changes were made public and accessible so everyone saw the results of their joint efforts on an ongoing basis and each knew where everyone else was through each stage of the design. Using computer technology to make these contributions public on a regular basis allows everyone to attune themselves to possible direction, like changing the root movement of the chord. People add variants, like the drummer adding accents, that might inspire creative departures. Rapid prototypes function like the loose framework of the song: they leave a great deal of room to depart and deviate; and yet there is enough structure there to give players enough collective confidence to play together. The temporal updating of the minimal structure notifies everyone where others are in their incremental innovations, like the chord changes of a song, and increases the likelihood that people can achieve a successful joint awareness throughout the life of the project.

4. Distributed Task: Continual Negotiation Toward Dynamic Synchronization

Although there are many players well known for their soloing, in the final analysis, jazz is an ongoing social accomplishment. What characterizes successful jazz improvisation, perhaps more than any factor mentioned thusfar, is the ongoing give and take between members. Players are in a continual dialogue and exchange with one another. Improvisers enter a flow of ongoing invention, a combination of accents, cymbal crashes, changing harmonic patterns, that inter-weave throughout the structure of the song. They are engaged with continual streams of activity: interpreting others' playing, anticipating based on harmonic patterns and rhythmic conventions, while simultaneously attempting to shape their own creations and relate them to what they have heard.

Jazz improvisation is an emergent, elusive, vital process. At any moment a player can take the music in a new direction, defy expectations, trigger others to re-interpret what they have just heard. Trumpeter Wynton Marsalis, in terms reminiscent of John Dewey's dictum that genuine learning is by nature a participative, democratic experience, compares improvisation to working out ideas in democratic groups.

> Groups of people can get together and the process of their negotiation can have an integrity, and the fact that they can get together and have a dialogue and work—it's like what the UN does. They sit down, and they try to work things out. It's like any governing body. It's like a wagon train, you know. (Marsalis and Stewart 1995)

Pianist Tommy Flanagan discusses his duo albums with Hank Jones and Kenny Barron.

> You don't know what the other player is going to play, but on listening to the playback, you hear that you related your part very quickly to what the other player played just before you. It's like a message that you relay back and forth. . . . You want to achieve that kind of communication when you play. When you do, your playing seems to be making sense. It's like a conversation. (Tommy Flanagan quoted in Berliner 1994, p. 369)

In order for jazz to work, players must develop a remarkable degree of empathic competence, a mutual orientation to one another's unfolding. They continually take one another's musical ideas into context as constraints and facilitations in guiding their musical choices. Saxophonist Lee Konitz discusses the interactive interplay.

> I want to relate to the bass player and the piano player and the drummer, so that I know at any given moment what they are all doing. The goal is always to relate as fully as possible to every sound that everyone is making. . . . but whew! It's very difficult for me to achieve. At different points, I will listen to any particular member of the group and relate to them as directly as possible in my solo. (Lee Konitz quoted in Berliner 1994, p. 362)

Players are continuously shaping their statements in anticipation of others' expectations, approximating and predicting what others might say based on what has already happened.

Traditional models of organization and group design feature static principles in which fluctuations and change are seen as disruptions to be controlled and avoided. Jazz bands are flexible, self-designed systems that seek a state of dynamic synchronization, a balance between order and disorder (Purser and Pasmore 1992), a "built in instability" (Takeuchi and Nonaka 1986). In jazz, ongoing negotiation becomes very important when something interrupts interactive coherence. Given the possibility of disorientation and miscalculations, they must be able to rely on one another to adjust, to amend direction. Drummer Max Roach recalls a performance of "Night in Tunisia" when the players lost the sense of a common beat.

> When the beat got turned around (in Night in Tunisia), it went for about 8 bars. In such a case, someone has to lay out. You can't fight it. Dizzy stopped first because he heard what was happening quicker than the rest of us, and he didn't know where "one" was. Then it was up to Ray Brown and Bishop and myself. One of us had to stop, so Bishop waved off. Then it was up to Ray Brown and myself to clear it up. Almost immediately, we found the common "one" and the others came back in without the public realizing what had happened. (Berliner 1994, p. 382)

The example above illustrates the dynamic, flexible potential when a group successfully creates a distributed task. Seifert and Hutchins (1992) refer to the features that make up a distributed task: shared task knowledge, horizon of observation, multiple perspectives. Jazz members are able to negotiate, recover, proceed, adjust to one another because there is shared task knowledge (members monitor progress on ongoing basis), have adequate horizon of observation (they are witnesses to one another's performance); and they bring multiple perspectives to bear (each musical utterance can be interpreted from different points of view).

When the players successfully achieve a mutual orientation to the beat, they develop what they call a "pocket," or some refer to as "achieving a groove." Establishing a groove is the goal of every jazz performance.

FRANK J. BARRETT   *Creativity and Improvisation in Jazz and Organizations*

Groove refers to the dynamic interplay within an established beat. It occurs when the rhythm section "locks in" together, when members have a common sense of the beat and meter. Establishing a groove, however, is more than simply playing the correct notes. It involves a shared "feel," for the rhythmic thrust. Once a group shares this common rhythm, it begins to assume a momentum, as if having a life of its own separate from the individual members. There is a sense that the groove acts as what Winnicot called a "holding environment," a reliable nesting that provides a sense of ontological security, a sense of trust that allows people to take risks and initiate actions.

> When you get into that groove, you ride right on down that groove with no strain and no pain—you can't lay back or go forward. That's why they call it a groove. It's where the beat is, and we're always trying to find that. (Drummer Charlie Persip in Berliner 1994, p. 349)

> Every musician wants to be locked in that groove where you can't escape the tempo. You're locked in so comfortably that there's no way you can break outside of it, and everyone's locked in there together. It doesn't happen to groups every single night, even though they may be swinging on every single tune. But at some point when the band is playing and everyone gets locked in together, its' special for the musicians and for the aware, conscientious listener. There are the magical moments, the best moments in jazz. (Franklin Gordon in Berliner 1994, p. 388)

> I don't care what kind of style a group plays as long as they settle into a groove where the rhythm keeps building instead of changing around. It's like the way an African hits a drum. He hits it a certain way, and after a period of time, you feel it more than you did where he first started. He's playing the same thing, but the quality is different—it's settled into a groove. It's like seating tobacco in a pipe. You put some heat on it and make it expand. After a while, it's there. It's tight. (Saxophonist Lou Donaldson in Berliner 1994, p. 349)

What happens when musicians strike a groove adds a paradoxical dimension to our earlier discussion of attention and cognitive processing. Good improvisers, we said, employ a combination of automatic and controlled cognition. However, this experience of groove that improvisers hope for seems to involve a surrender of familiar controlled processing modes; they speak of being so completely absorbed in playing that they are *not* consciously thinking, reflecting, or deciding on what notes to play, as if they are able to simultaneously be inside and outside of their bodies and minds. Controlled thinking is depicted sometimes as an obstacle, something to develop only to escape.

Herrigel suggests a similar paradox in the practice of archery. Like jazz, the art of archery involves deliberate

preparation and active conscious attention (controlled cognition) in disciplined practice; but when the moment comes when one wants the perfect shot, the archer must surrender and let go of conscious striving. At that moment:

> nothing definite is thought, planned, striven for, desired or expected, which aims in no particular direction ... which is at bottom purposeless and egoless ... is therefore ... called "right presence of mind." This means that the mind ... is nowhere attached to any particular place. (Herrigel 1989, p. 41)

This sense of aimless aiming, a surrender in which "nothing is left of you but a purposeless tension" (Herrigel 1989, p. 35) is similar to the way clarinetist Ken Peplowski describes such peak musical moments.

> When we play at our best, I find many times that I'm not actually thinking about anything and you can actually have a strange experience of going outside of yourself and observing yourself while you're performing. It's very strange. And you can actually listen as you're playing and listen to the rest of the group and you can be completely objective and relaxed. And come to think of it, completely subjective also, because you are reacting to everything else around you. (Peplowski 1995)

This points to a core paradox at the heart of jazz improvisation: if musicians strive too much to attain this state, they obstruct it. Regulation and control can restrict the interplay of musical ideas. Peplowski goes on to say that what makes this possible are prior intensive practice, learning to master tools skills; but at the moment of leaping into playing, "you're forgetting about all these tools you've learned."

Musicians often speak of such moments in sacred metaphors. They speak of the beauty, the ecstasy, the divine, the transcendent joy, the spiritual dimension associated with being carried by a force larger than themselves. They talk about these moments in language strikingly close to what has been described as an autotelic experience, or flow (Csikszentmihalyi 1990). This research suggests that people are able to attain a state of transcendence when they are absorbed in pursuit of desired activity, they feel like they are being carried away by a current, like being in a flow.

When musicians are able to successfully connect with one another at this level and establish a groove, they sometimes experience an ability to perform beyond their capacity. This dimension is perhaps the most elusive, if vital characteristic of jazz improvisation. Pianist Fred Hersch recalls that playing with bassist Buster Williams inspired him to play differently.

> Buster made me play complex chords like Herbie Hancock sometimes plays—that I couldn't even sit down and figure out now. It's the effect of the moment and the effect of playing with

Buster and really hearing everything, hearing all those figures. (Pianist Fred Hersch in Berliner 1994, p. 390)

And Buster Williams recalls that when playing with Miles Davis, the music took on a life of its own.

With Miles, it would get to the point where we followed the music rather than the music following us. We just followed the music wherever it wanted to go. We would start with a tune, but the way we played it, the music just naturally evolved. (Buster Williams in Berliner 1994, p. 392)

Most of our studies of organizational behavior have a rational-cognitive orientation. Organizational learning theories in particular stress rational, adaptive modes of inquiry. Appreciating the interactive complexity involved in jazz improvisation suggests that we pay attention to intuitive and emotional connections between organizational members, the experience of passionate connection that inspire deeper levels of involvement and committed participation. Studies of jazz improvisation suggests that researchers revisit such familiar concepts as empowerment, motivation, and team building, concepts which have been studied almost exclusively from a cognitive and individualistic perspective. The experience of spiritual intimacy, synergy, surrender, transcendence, and flow warrant wider study. Would it not be useful to study the role of supportive relationships in drawing out one another's latent capacities, for example? At the very least, this would suggest a relational view of the learning process, in the spirit of Vygotsky's concept of the zone of proximal development. (Vygotsky 1987)

5.   Reliance on Retrospective Sense Making as Form

Because jazz improvisation borders on the edge of chaos and incoherence, it begs the question of how order emerges. Unlike other art forms and other forms of organized activity that attempt to rely on a pre-developed plan, improvisation is widely open to transformation, redirection, and unprecedented turns. Since one cannot rely on blueprints and can never know for certain where the music is going, one can only make guesses and anticipate possible paths based on what has already happened, meanwhile continue playing under the assumption that whatever has happened must amount to something sensible. Gioia (1988) writes:

The improviser may be unable to look ahead at what he is going to play, but he can look behind at what he has just played; thus each new musical phrase can be shaped with relation to what has gone before. He creates his form *retrospectively*. (p. 61)

The improviser can begin by playing a virtual random series of notes, with little or no intention as how it will unfold. These notes become the materials to be shaped and worked out, like pieces of a puzzle. The improviser begins to enter into a dialogue with her material: prior selections begin to fashion subsequent ones as themes are aligned and reframed in relation to prior patterns.

Weick (1993) likens the jazz improviser to Levi-Strauss' (1966) concept of *bricolage*, the art of making usage of whatever is at hand. The bricoleur, like the jazz musician, examines and queries the raw materials available and entices some order, creating unique combinations through the process of working through the resources he/she finds. Weick cites the example of a man in upper state New York who built a tractor from a myriad collection of unrelated junk and diverse parts he had accumulated in his front yard. The jazz musician, like the junk collector, looks over the material that is available at that moment, the various chord progressions, rhythmic patterns, phrases and motives, and simply leaps into the quagmire under the assumption that whatever he is about to play will fit in somewhere. Like the bricoleur who assumes that there must be a tractor somewhere in that pile of junk, the improviser assumes that there is a melody to be worked out from the morass of rhythms and chord changes. As new phrases or chord changes are introduced, the improviser makes connections between the old and new material. In the absence of a rational plan, retrospective sense-making makes spontaneous action appear purposeful, coherent, and inevitable.

Organizations tend to forget how much improvisation, bricolage, and retrospective sense making are required to complete daily tasks. In an effort to control outcomes and deskill tasks, they often attempt to break complex tasks down into formal descriptions of work procedures that can be followed automatically. Following Brown and Duguid (1991), managers wrongly assume that these simple steps reflect the way that work actually gets done. Given that many tasks in organizations are indeterminate and people come to them with limited foresight, members often need to apply resourcefulness, cleverness, pragmatism in addressing concerns. They often have to play with various possibilities, re-combining and re-organizing, to find solutions by relating the dilemma they face to the familiar context that preceded it. In spite of the wish for a rational plan of predictable action, they often must take a look around and act without a clear sense of how things will unfold.

Consider Orr's (1990) study of Xerox's training of service technicians representatives. The trainers, in an effort to downskill the task of machine repair, attempted to document every imaginable breakdown in copiers so that when technicians arrived to repair a machine, they simply looked it up in the manual and followed a pre-determined decision tree to perform a series of tests that dictate a repair procedure. Their premise was that a diagnostic sequence can be devised to respond to the machine's predictable problems. However, the study revealed that no amount of documentation could include enough contextual information necessary to understand every problem. Orr (1990) relays a story of a technical rep confronting a machine with error codes and malfunctions that were not congruent with the diagnostic blueprint. This machine's malfunction did not fit the kind of errors that were documented nor had anything like this problem been covered in his training. Both he and the technical specialist he called in to help were baffled. To simply give up the repair effort and replace the machine would have been a solution, but would have meant loss of face with the customer—an unacceptable solution. After exhausting the approaches suggested by the diagnostic, they attempted to make sense of this anomaly by connecting it to previous experiences and stories they had heard from others' experience. After a five-hour trouble shooting session of trials and errors, they fell upon a solution. Many jobs in organizations require this kind of bricolage—fumbling around, experimenting, patching together an understanding of problems from bits and pieces of experience, improvising with the materials at hand. Few problems provide their own definitive solutions.

Jazz players, junkyard collectors and technical reps find themselves in the middle of messes, having to solve problems in situ, creating interpretations out of potentially incoherent materials, piecing together other musicians' playing, their own memories of musical patterns, interweaving general concepts with the particulars of the current situation, creating coherent, composite stories.

6.   Hanging Out: Membership in Communities of Practice

An essential part of learning jazz is becoming a member of the jazz community, "hanging out," learning the code, behaving like one of the members. Learning is not simply a matter of transmitting de-contextualized information from one person to another. Local jazz communities of peers in large metropolitan areas such as Detroit, Chicago, and especially New York have serve as informal educational systems for disseminating knowledge. Musicians get together to listen to recordings of great soloists, memorize their solos, play tunes in different tempos and keys until they could find the right feel. They join other musicians, "hanging out" in coffee shops and bars after a performance and exchanging stories. Stanley Turrentine remembers he learned from others by "asking about things I didn't understand." Novices discover they need to learn certain "standard" tunes; they learn appropriate keys and tempos: the norms and conventions of the

trade. One young trumpeter even recalls learning how to dress from "hanging out" with Miles Davis (Berliner 1994). Central to learning jazz is the institution of the jam session, in which musicians get together to play extemporaneously. A special fraternity often develops among jazz musicians as they guide each other through various learning experiences, borrowing ideas from one another.

Brown and Drugid (1991), refer to organizations as communities of practices. To foster learning, they contend, organizations must see beyond conventional, canonical job descriptions and recognize the rich practices themselves. In the example of the technical rep above, their successful experience with the recalcitrant machine became part of the technicians' folklore, told and retold during coffee breaks. These stories form a community memory that others could draw upon when facing unfamiliar problems. Essential to organizational learning is access to legitimate peripheral participation (Lave and Wenger 1990), understanding how to function as an insider. This recognizes that learning is much more than receiving abstract, acontextual, disembodied knowledge. It is a matter of learning how to speak the language of the community of practitioners.

This has real consequences for organizations. Consider the case of how a technological change attempted at a manufacturing plant failed because management did not value the communal foundation of learning: useful local innovations were not disseminated, learning from mistakes was limited, and good routines that varied from the officially sanctioned ones were kept unofficial. Learners need access to experienced practitioners, through formal and informal meetings, conversations, stories, myths, rituals, etc.

7.   Alternating Between Soloing and Supporting

One of the most widespread, yet overlooked, structures in jazz is the practice of taking turns. Jazz bands usually rotate the "leadership" of the band: that is, they take turns soloing and supporting other soloists by providing rhythmic and harmonic background. Such an egalitarian model assures that each player will get an opportunity to develop a musical idea while others create space for this development to occur. In order to guarantee these patterns of mutuality and symmetry, it is necessary that people take turns supporting one another. The role of accompaniment, or "comping" is a very active and influential one: it provides a framework which facilitates and constrains the soloist. In written arrangements, the scored passages often precede the soloist's improvisation and channel, sustain, and embellish it. In a sense the background accompaniment conditions the soloist, organizes the course of the solo through passing chords, leading tones and rhythmic accents.

It is not enough to be an individual virtuoso, one must also be able to surrender one's virtuosity and enable others to excel. In order to "comp" or accompany soloists effectively, jazz musicians need to be very good listeners. They need to interpret others' playing, anticipate likely future directions, make instantaneous decisions in regard to harmonic and rhythmic progressions. But they also may see beyond the player's current vision, perhaps provoking the soloist in different direction, with accents and chord extensions. None of this responsiveness can happen unless players are receptive and taking in one anothers' gestures. If everyone tries to be a star and does not engage in supporting the evolution of the soloist's ideas, the result is bad jazz. When they listen well to others' soloing, they help the soloist reach new heights. Usually we think that great performances create attentive listeners. This notion suggests a reversal: attentive listening enables exceptional performance.

This has considerable implication for organizational learning. In spite of the increasing popularity of empowerment and employee involvement, organizations often have difficulty supporting participation (Pasmore and Fagans 1991). Organizations struggle with finding ways to include voices that traditionally have been silenced. The deceptively simple practice of taking turns creates a mutuality structure that guarantees participation, inclusion, shared ownership without insisting on consensus and its unintentional hegemonic consequences.

Beyond a model for sharing leadership through turn-taking, it also offers a model of followership. Given the complex and systemic nature of problems that cross conventional boundaries, managers, as knowledge specialists, cannot be solo operators: they need one another's expertise and support in order to arrive at novel solutions. The term "job rotation" takes on new meaning when we think about the shifting of leadership and support responsibilities that jazz bands enact. Perhaps organizational innovation would thrive if members were skilled at giving others' room to develop themes, to think out loud and discover as they invent. One suggestion would be to have organizational "jam" sessions in which members take turns thinking out loud while others listen. Recent interest in organizational dialogue (Senge 1990) resemble attempts to include disparate voices that might otherwise become overlooked.

Yet, organizations tend to reward individual performance and achievement rather than supportive behaviors. This emphasis often leads to excessive competition to achieve stardom, efforts to be in unilateral control, efforts to defend one's position against challenges, hesitancy to acknowledge the limits of one's knowledge: all obstacles to the learning process (Argyris 1993). Imagine if such practices were to become more widespread in organizations: employees, managers, and executives evaluated on their capacity to surrender self and ego in effort to support the development of another's idea. Perhaps if organizations would recognize and reward those who strive to nourish, strengthen, and enhance the expressive capacity of relationships, they would unleash their capacity to improvise and innovate.

Implications for Non-jazz Contexts

Managers often attempt to create the impression that improvisation does not happen in organizations, that tightly designed control systems minimize unnecessary idiosyncratic actions and deviations from formal plans. People in organizations are often jumping into action without clear plans, making up reasons as they proceed, discovering new routes once action is initiated, proposing multiple interpretations, navigating through discrepancies, combining disparate and incomplete materials and then discovering what their original purpose was. To pretend that improvisation is not happening in organizations is to not understand the nature of improvisation.

Many business organizations, under pressure to perform, create cultures that reinforce instrumental, pragmatic, rational, and deliberate action rather than a culture that is expressive, artistic, paradoxical, and spontaneous. In fact, there are locales and durations which seem to rely on routines and predictable outcomes, particularly in functions such as production and manufacturing. Organizations must face a tradeoff between servicing efficiency and stewarding attention as a scarce resource to be focused where needed. In this sense, improvisation is best conceived as an activity that occurs for stretches of human behavior.

Clearly there are certain industries and contexts that require an improvisatory mindset: high velocity, high technology firms; research and development activities; cultures of high urgency and excitement, such as the early days of the Apple Macintosh; interdisciplinary project teams formed to address a specific problem. Certainly popular management literature has created a language that resonates with the jazz idiom: suggesting that organizations need to learn to thrive on chaos; managers are encouraged to create a sense of urgency by "turning things upside down," doing away with job descriptions, and valuing failures as a sign that people are experimenting and learning (Peters 1987).

Are there ways to socialize a mindset that nurtures spontaneity, creativity, experimentation, and dynamic synchronization in organizations? What practices and structures can we implement that might emulate what

FRANK J. BARRETT   *Creativity and Improvisation in Jazz and Organizations*

happens when jazz bands improvise? The jazz band as prototype offers a few suggestions.

1. Boost the processing of information during and after actions are implemented.

Jazz players act their way into the future, then justify their actions by placing their statements within a context of meaning (chord changes, rhythmic emphasis, etc.). Like jazz soloists who realize how notes, phrases, and chords relate as they look back on what they have created, it is during and after action that people in organizations become aware of the goals and values they implicitly hold and what constraints these values place upon their future actions (Weick 1995). Within the ongoing flow of everyday organizational activity, people retrospectively make sense or construct a story or justification for what they have already done (Staw 1980). These stories can become the seeds for greater discoveries and inventions. Therefore, one implication is to boost the processing of information and surface multiple interpretations of diverse participants within close proximity to action.

Organizations might consider a strategic orientation that links planning, action, implementation, and environmental scanning. Organizations could benefit from creating virtual strategic planning sessions in which members engage in trial and error thinking, just as jazz musicians do when they solo. Generating multiple, simultaneous alternatives minimizes escalation of commitment to a single option (Staw 1980, Eisenhardt 1989) and allows members to make adjustments and re-orientations as they receive disconfirming feedback regarding any single action scenario. This view would challenge the traditional notion of strategic planning as a form of rational control, or as an abstract exercise divorced from and prior to action. In this spirit, Senge (1990) advocates a view of planning as play or as a "practice field" in which managers practice thinking ahead, predicting, and guessing future moves within various constraints. In virtual planning scenarios managers could try out alternative maps and alter the core assumptions that have remained unquestioned (see Hampden-Turner 1990). This is apparently a practice familiar to managers at Shell Oil (DeGeus 1988) who were asked to respond to multiple (and sometimes contradictory) assumptions regarding their environmental constraints, including entertaining the notion that the price of oil might be slashed in half—something that seemed unthinkable at the time. This became in DeGeus' words, a "license to play." These incremental disruptions also created a larger repertoire of knowledge structures, higher variety of responses, when such an unprecedented event did occur.

2. Cultivate provocative competence: Create expansive

promises and incremental disruptions as occasions for stretching out into unfamiliar territory.

Provocative competence is a leadership skill that involves challenging habits and conventional practices, challenging members to experiment in the margins and to stretch in new directions. Organizational learning theorists (Argyris 1990) write that one of the shortfalls of single loop learning is that managers choose to address only those problems that are familiar, those issues for which a solution is imaginable. Miles Davis surprised his band by disrupting their routines and stretching them beyond comfortable limits: calling unrehearsed songs and familiar songs in foreign keys. Of course there is a potential downside to disruptions. Research suggests that when people confront environmental jolts, they fall back on habitual modes of action (Walsh 1995). Also, there might be a tendency to escalate commitment to a wrong course in the context of a threatening interruption (Staw and Ross 1987).

One way leaders practice provocative competence is by evoking a set of higher values and ideals that inspire passionate engagement. A context in which goals that are beyond the capacity of single individuals to accomplish might enhance the need for improvisation, testing comfortable boundaries, cooperation, and negotiation. Barrett (1995) discusses visionary organizations that make expansive promises that defy "reasonable limits" and stretch members to re-define the boundaries of what they have experienced as constraining. Consider Canon's promise in the 1970s to produce a personal copier that would sell for $1,000 (Prahalad and Hamel 1989). Given the constraints that existed at the time, (the least expensive copier sold for several thousand dollars), such a proposal seemed preposterous. Surprised engineers engaged in different kind of conversations, searching for new approaches, experimenting with substituting a disposable cartridge for the very complex image-transfer mechanism that Xerox and other companies, including Canon, had employed in their copiers. Such tasks demand cooperation, exploration, and improvisation.

3. Ensure that everyone has a chance to solo from time to time.

When self-directed work teams are performing well, they are often characterized by distributed, multiple leadership in which people take turns leading various projects as their expertise is needed (Guzzo 1995). In jazz bands, everyone gets a turn to solo. Organizations might consider evolving norms that insist on including diverse voices, giving everyone a regular turn at bat and valuing those who make room for others to shine.

Organizations might experiment with a structured process that provides participants with a chance to solo and offsets those influential members who might control or dominate a group. A simple organizational development tool called the nominal group technique (Delbecq et al. 1975) is structured to do just this: every individual in turn "brainstorms" out loud while others listen to his or her ideas. No one is allowed to interrupt or re-direct; people are encouraged to build on others' ideas they have heard. A variation of the structure is that no one speaks twice until every other person in the group speaks at least once. This is an impersonal, nonnegotiable structure that monitors air time, cultivates group creativity and ensures that every individual has voice. This also approximates Habermas' notion of the "ideal speech situation" in which collective learning is enhanced because individuals are free to communicate openly, completely free from compulsion or distortions of power, and the force of the better argument may prevail (Habermas 1970).

4. Cultivate comping behaviors.

Organizations must go beyond merely inviting new voices, but must also create processes that suspend the tendency to criticize, judge, express disbelief that might kill a nascent idea. In order for soloists to have impact, there must be ongoing comping (accompaniment) from supporters. What would be the equivalent of comping in organizations? Perhaps this would suggest supportive behaviors such as mentoring, advocating, encouraging, listening. This means rewarding people who support others' to take center stage, including such skills as blending, helping people along the way as they transition and develop ideas at different rates. This might include expanding the stories we tell about creative achievements beyond those that highlight autonomous action, to include the roles of those who assisted, who gave others' room, who encouraged fledgling, nascent gestures with subtle nudges much like a jazz pianist comping.

Such deliberate efforts to make room for peers' contributions is close to what jazz musicians do when they comp—agree to suspend judgement, to trust that whatever the soloist is doing right now will lead to something, to blend in to the flow and direction of the idea, rather than to break off in an independent direction. Such democratic structures enhance the likelihood that people not only have the right to be heard, but also have opportunity to influence.

5. Create organizational designs that produce redundant information

From a rational design perspective, organizations should be designed to process information efficiently. However, to maximize flexibility and creativity, one could follow the lessons of jazz bands and create designs that produce a redundancy of information. Following Hutchins (1990) in Weick and Roberts (1993) systems sustain flexible actions and mindful performance when jobs are designed to reproduce overlapping knowledge. Overlapping knowledge creates redundant sets of information that permits people to identify with and take responsibility for whole processes rather than parts of the process. Designing more interdependence into tasks increases members' responsive capacity.

6. Create organizational climates that value errors as a source for learning.

Good things can happen when people jump in and act even when all plans are not complete and elegant. Rather than over-rely on pre-planned strategies and canonical job descriptions, acknowledge members' capacity for bricologe and pragmatic reasoning, their ability to juxtapose, recombine, and reinterpret past materials to fashion novel responses. Organizational learning, then, must be seen as a risky venture, reaching into the unknown with no guarantee of where one's explorations will lead. Since errors are indispensable in the creative process, organizational leaders can create an aesthetic of imperfection and an aesthetic of forgiveness that construes errors as a source of learning that might open new lines of inquiry. Often, however, organizations view errors as a result of individual incompetence rather than systemically determined, leading people to suppress mistakes and deny responsibility (Argyris 1990). This suggests that leaders need to create contexts in which reporting and discussing errors is not risky behavior.

7. Cultivate serious play: too much control inhibits flow.

Jazz is an activity marked by paradox: musicians must balance structure and freedom, autonomy and interdependence, surrender and control. They grapple with the constrictions of previous patterns and structures: they strive to listen and respond to what is happening; at the same time they try to break out from these patterns to do something new with all the risks that both paths entail. If musicians strive too much to hit a groove, achieve flow (Csikszentmihalyi 1990), or jam (Eisenberg 1990), they obstruct it. Organization theorists have articulated a similar paradox: Quinn (1988) argues that having a conscious purpose with logical, internally consistent abstractions sometimes creates a unidimensional mindset that is blind to emerging cues: "When behaving with conscious purpose, people tend to act upon the environment, not with it" (p. 27). Quinn's discussion of masters of management sounds very much like what master improvisers do:

> The people who come to be masters of management do not see their work environment only in structured, analytic ways. Instead, they also have the capacity to see it as a complex dynamic system that is constantly evolving. In order to interact effectively with it, they employ a variety of different perspectives

FRANK J. BARRETT   *Creativity and Improvisation in Jazz and Organizations*

and frames . . . [b]ecause of these shifts (in contradictory perspectives). (Quinn 1988, pp. 3–4)

Jazz musicians suggest that one way to manage this paradox is to adopt a disciplined concentration that one adopts when playing a game, the way rock climbers and chess players experience their task (Csikszentmihalyi 1990) or the way that Bill Russell talks about playing basketball (Eisenberg 1990). There is a sense of surrender in play, a willingness to suspend control and giving over of oneself to the flow of the ongoing game. (Perhaps this is what organizations like Southwest Air are hoping to encourage when they declare having fun in the workplace as a core value). This suggests that we re-visit the conventional separation between work and play: legitimate play as a fruitful, meaningful activity, one that enhances the sheer joy of relational activity.

Conclusion and Discussion

The mechanistic, bureaucratic model for organizing—in which people do routine, repetitive tasks, in which rules and procedures are devised to handle contingencies, and in which managers are responsible for planning, monitoring and creating command and control systems to guarantee compliance—is no longer adequate. Managers will face more rather than less interactive complexity and uncertainty. This suggests that jazz improvisation is a useful metaphor for understanding organizations interested in learning and innovation. To be innovative, managers—like jazz musicians—must interpret vague cues, face unstructured tasks, process incomplete knowledge, and yet they must take action anyway. Managers, like jazz players, need to engage in dialogue and negotiation, the creation of shared spaces for decision making based on expertise rather than hierarchical position.

Although rich in implications, there are limits to the applicability of the improvisation metaphor. The discussion of jazz bands has held up jazz as an "ideal type." Most of the points discussed so far assume a base level of competence. In reality, not all players are equally competent. This is where the metaphor begins to break down for managerial purposes. No amount of listening, support, or "comping" can enhance a performance if the performer is not up to the task. If an interaction with competent players can enhance individual performance, there might also be an opposite effect: performers of lesser competence can have a debilitating effect on the overall group performance. Also while tolerance of errors is essential to enhance experimentation, there are cases where errors are intolerable: in high reliability organizations, for example. But even beyond high reliability organizations, the

consequences of small actions can have large consequences when the structure is loosely coupled (Weick 1991). Consider the collapse of Barring Bros., one of the most prestigious financial institutions in the world, due to the erroneous actions of one man.

By looking at the practices and structures associated with jazz playing, it is possible to see that successful jazz performances are not haphazard or accidental. Musicians prepare themselves to be spontaneous. Jazz improvisation has implications that would suggest ways that managers and executives can prepare organizations to learn while in the process of acting.

Finally, jazz improvisation can be seen as a hopeful activity. It models individual actors as protean agents capable of transforming the direction and flow of events. In that sense, jazz holds an appreciative view (Cooperrider and Srivastva 1987, Barrett 1995) of human potential: it represents the belief in the human capacity to think freshly, to generate novel solutions, to create something new and interesting, reminding us of John Dewey's contention that we are all natural learners. To quote the saxophonist Ornette Colman, "Jazz is the only music in which the same note can be played night after night but different each time."

Acknowledgments

The author would like to thank Kishore Sengupta, Reuben Harris, Mark Gridley, Ken Peplowski, Karl Weick, and two anonymous reviewers for their helpful comments and suggestions on earlier drafts.

Endnote

[1] Cognitive psychologists distinguish between "automatic" and "controlled" information processing. Automatic modes of processing are effortless, familiar, habitual, outside of conscious awareness. "Controlled" modes of processing are deliberate, effortful, active, strategic, directed, and intentional (Schneider and Shiffrin 1977, Shiffrin and Schneider 1977). Jazz improvising seems to employ a combination of modes of processing. When learning new phrases, or attempting challenging musical ideas, players employ controlled processing. Trumpeter Benny Bailey said, "You just have to keep on doing it (practicing phrases) over and over again until it comes automatically." (Berliner 1994, p. 165). Once learned, these become second nature, or learned habits that one can rely upon. Pianist Bill Evans (1991) explains "You take problems one by one and stay with it . . . until the process becomes secondary, or subconscious, then you take on the next problem until it becomes second nature, or subconscious." Pressing (1984, p. 139) describes the switch from controlled to automatic as one in which musicians "completely dispense with conscious monitoring of motor programmes, so that the hands appear to have a life of their own, driven by the musical constraints of the situation."

References

Abdel-Hamid, T., S. Madnick. 1990. The elusive silver lining: How we fail to learn from software development failures. *Sloan Management Review* 32 1 Fall 39–48.

FRANK J. BARRETT *Creativity and Improvisation in Jazz and Organizations*

Arendt, H. 1958. *The Human Condition.* Univ. of Chicago Press, Chicago, IL.

Argyris, C. 1990. *Overcoming Organizational Defenses.* Allyn-Bacon, Needham, MA.

Bailey, D. 1992. *Improvisation.* Da Capo Press, New York.

Barrett, F. J. 1995. Creating appreciative learning cultures. *Organization Dynamics* **24** 1 Fall 36–49.

——, D. Cooperrider. 1990. Generative metaphor intervention: A new approach to intergroup conflict. *J. Applied Behavioral Science* **26** 2 223–244.

Bastien, D., T. Hostagier. 1988. Jazz as a process of organizational innovation. *J. Communication Research* 15 5 October, 582–602.

Bell, D. 1976. *The Coming of the Post-Industrial Society.* Basic Books, New York.

Berliner, P. 1994. *Thinking in Jazz.* Univ. of Chicago Press, Chicago, IL.

Brown, J., P. Duguid. 1991. Organizational learning and communities of practice: Toward a unified view of working, learning, and innovation. *Organization Science* **2** 1 40–57.

Carr, D. 1991. *Keith Jarrett.* Da Capo Press, New York.

Cellar, D. F., G. V. Barrett. 1987. Script processing and intrinsic motivation: The cognitive sets underlying cognitive labels. *Organizational Behavior and Human Decision Processes* **40** 115–135.

Cohen, M. 1991. Individual learning and organizational routine: Emerging connections. *Organization Science* **2** 1 135–139.

Csikszentmihalyi, M. 1990. *Flow: The Psychology of Optimal Experience.* Harper, New York.

DeGeus, A. 1988. Planning as learning. *Harvard Business Review* **66** 2 70–74.

Delbecq, A. L., A. H. Van de Ven, D. Gustafson. 1975. *Group Techniques for Program Planning.* Scott-Foresman, Glenview, IL.

Drucker, P. 1989. *The New Realities.* Harper and Row, New York.

Edmonson, A. 1996. Learning from mistakes is easier said than done: Group and organizational influences on the detection and correction of human error. *J. Applied Behavioral Science* **32** 1 March 5–28.

Eisenberg, E. 1990. Jamming: Transcendence through organizing. *Communication Research* **17** 2 April, 139–164.

Evans, B. 1991. *The Universal Mind of Bill Evans.* Video. Rhapsody Films, New York.

Gioia, T. 1988. *The Imperfect Art.* Oxford Univ. Press, New York.

Gridley, M. 1991. *Jazz Styles.* Prentice-Hall, Englewood Cliffs, N.J.

Guzzo, R., ed. 1995. *Team Effectiveness and Decision Making in Organizations.* Jossey-Bass, San Francisco, CA.

Habermas, J. 1970. Toward a theory of communicative competence. *Inquiry* **13** 360–375.

Hampden-Turner, C. 1990. *Charting the Corporate Mind.* Free Press, New York.

Hargreaves, D. J., A. C. Cork, T. Setton. 1991. Cognitive strategies in jazz improvisation: An exploratory study. *Canadian J. Research in Music Education* **33** December 47–54.

Hedberg, B. 1981. How organizations learn and unlearn. N. Nystrom, W. Starbuck, eds. *Handbook of Organizational Design.* Oxford Univ. Press, Oxford, UK.

——, P. Nystrom, W. Starbuck. 1976. Camping on seesaws: Prescriptions for a self-designing organization. *Administrative Science Quarterly* **21** March 41–65.

Herrigel, E. 1989. *Zen in the Art of Archery.* Vintage Books, New York.

Hodgkinson, G. P., G. Johnson. 1994. Exploring the mental models of competitive strategists: The case for a processual approach. *J. Management Studies* **31** 525–551.

Lave, J., E. Wenger. 1991. *Situated Learning: Legitimate Peripheral Participation.* Cambridge Univ. Press, Cambridge, UK.

Levi-Strauss, C. 1966. *The Savage Mind.* Univ. of Chicago Press, Chicago, IL.

Levitt, B., J. March. 1988. Organizational learning. *Annual Review of Sociology* **14** 319–340.

Louis, M., R. Sutton. 1991. Switching cognitive gears: From habit of mind to active thinking. *Human Relations* **44** 1 55–76.

March, J. 1991. Exploration and exploitation in organizational learning. *Organization Science* **2** 1 71–87.

Marsalis, Wynton, Frank Stewart. 1995. *Sweet Swing Blues.* Norton and Company, New York.

Nasbitt, J. 1982. *Megatrends.* Warner Books, New York.

Novello, J. 1987. *Contemporary Keyboardist.* Source Productions, Toluea, CA.

Orr, J. 1990. Sharing knowledge, celebrating identity: War stories and community memory in a service culture. D. S. Middleton, D. Edwards, eds. *Collective Remembering: Memory in Society.* Sage, Beverly Hills, CA.

Peplowski, K. 1998. The process of improvisation. *Organization Science* **9** 5 560–561.

Pressing, J. 1984. Cognitive processes in improvisation. W. R. Crozier, A. J. Chapman, eds. *Cognitive Processes in the Perception of Art.* Elsevier, Amsterdam, The Netherlands.

Prokesch, S. 1993. Mastering chaos at the high-tech frontier: An interview with Silicon Graphics's Ed McCracken. *Harvard Business Review* November–December.

Purser, R., W. Pasmore. 1992. Organizing for learning. W. Pasmore, R. Woodman, eds. *Research in Organizational Change and Development* **6** 37–114.

Quinn, R. E. 1988. *Beyond Rational Management: Mastering the Paradoxes and Competing Demands of High Performance.* Jossey-Bass, San Francisco, CA.

Schneider, W., R. M. Shiffrin. 1977. Controlled and automatic human information processing: I. Detection, search, and attention. *Psychological Review* **84** 1–66.

Schuler, G. 1989. *The Swing Era.* Oxford Univ. Press, New York.

Seifert, C., E. Hutchins. 1992. Error as opportunity: Learning in a cooperative task. *Human-Computer Interaction* **7** 409–435.

Senge, P. 1990. *The Fifth Discipline.* Doubleday, New York.

Shiffrin, R. M., W. Schneider. 1977. Controlled and automatic human information processing: II. Perceptual learning, automatic attending, and a general theory. *Psychological Review* **84** 127–190.

Staw, B. 1980. Rationality and justification in organizational life. B. Staw, L. L. Cummings, eds. *Research in Organizational Behavior* **2** 45–80.

——, J. Ross. 1987. Behavior in escalation situations: Antecedents, prototypes and solutions. *Research in Organizational Behavior.* JAI Press, Greenwich, CT.

Takeuchi, H., I. Nonaka. 1986. The new product development game. *Harvard Business Review* January–February 137–146.

Toffler, A. 1981. *The Third Wave.* Bantam Books, New York.

FRANK J. BARRETT   *Creativity and Improvisation in Jazz and Organizations*

Vygotsky, L. 1987. *The Collected Works of Lev Vygotsky.* Plenum Press, New York.

Walsh, J. 1995. Managerial and organizational cognition: Notes from a trip down memory lane. *Organization Science* 6 3 280–321.

Weick, K. 1990. Managing as improvisation: Lessons from the world of jazz. Aubrey Fisher Memorial Lecture, Univ. of Utah, October 18.

——. 1991a. The nontraditional quality of organizational learning. *Organization Science* 2 1 116–124.

——. 1991b. The vulnerable system: An analysis of the Tenerife air disaster. P. Frost, L. Moore, M. Louis, C. Lundberg, J. Martin, eds. *Reframing Organizational Culture.* Sage Press, Newbury Park, CA. 117–130.

——. 1992. Agenda setting in organizational behavior. *J. Management Inquiry* 1 3 Sept. 171–182.

——. 1993. Organizational redesign as improvisation. G. Huber, W. Glick, eds. *Mastering Organizational Change.* Oxford Press, New York. 346–379.

——. 1995. Creativity and the aesthetics of imperfection. C. Ford, D. Gioia, eds. *Creative Action in Organizations.* Sage Press, Thousand Lakes, CA.

——, K. Roberts. 1993. Collective mind in organizations: Heedful interrelating on flight decks. *Administrative Science Quarterly* 38 357–381.

Zwerin, M. 1983. *Close Enough for Jazz.* Quartet Books, London, UK.

[21]

Towards a Theory of Organizational Improvisation: Looking Beyond the Jazz Metaphor

Ken Kamoche, Miguel Pina e Cunha and João Vieira da Cunha

City University of Hong Kong; Universidade Nova de Lisboa; MIT Sloan School of Management

ABSTRACT This paper calls for research on organizational improvisation to go beyond the currently dominant jazz metaphor in theory development. We recognize the important contribution that jazz improvisation has made and will no doubt continue to make in understanding the nature and complexity of organizational improvisation. This article therefore presents some key lessons from the jazz metaphor and then proceeds to identify the possible dangers of building scientific inquiry upon a single metaphor. We then present three alternative models – Indian music, music therapy and role theory. We explore their nature and seek to identify ways in which the insights they generate complement those from jazz. This leads us to a better understanding of the challenges of building a theory of organizational improvisation.

INTRODUCTION

Organizational theorists have continued to demonstrate a healthy concern for creativity as they approach organizational problems. This is evident in the unrelenting search for new ideas and metaphors from the most varied fields imaginable. The scope includes military imagery (Ries and Trout, 1986), orchestras (Voyer and Faulkner, 1989), political arenas (Pfeffer, 1992), complex responsive systems (Stacey et al., 2000), chimeras (Sewell, 1998) and so forth. In the more practitioner-orientated publications, lessons for managers are drawn from Star Trek: Next Generation (Roberts and Ross, 1996), Attila the Hun (Roberts, 1991) and quantum physics (Peters, 1992). This creativity is in large part motivated by the quest for organizational success in a time marked by turbulent and increasingly complex environments (Bettis and Hitt, 1995).

Address for reprints: Ken Kamoche, City University of Hong Kong, Dept of Management, Tat Chee Avenue, Kowloon, Hong Kong (mgnkk@cityu.edu.hk).

Improvisation has emerged as one of the most fascinating concepts in recent years. Improvisation can broadly be defined as the conception of action as it unfolds, drawing on available cognitive, affective, social and material resources (see also Crossan and Sorrenti, 1997; Kamoche et al., 2002). This concept appears to have substantial implications for a number of organizational phenomena, ranging from teamwork and creativity to product innovation and organizational adaptation and renewal. Current work focuses mainly on the quest for theoretical sophistication (e.g. Barrett, 1998; Hatch, 1999; Kamoche and Cunha, 2001; Moorman and Miner, 1998a; Weick, 1998; Zack, 2000), with a small but growing number of empirical investigations into the incidence and nature of improvisation (e.g. Brown and Eisenhardt, 1997; Kamoche et al., 2003; Moorman and Miner, 1998b; Miner et al., 2001; Orlikowski, 1996).

It is interesting to note that the pioneers in this discourse drew largely from jazz improvisation to sketch a theory of this phenomenon in organizational settings (for a review see Cunha et al., 1999). This appears to have been motivated by the fact that jazz is the one social phenomenon in which improvisation is more salient (Weick, 1999) – certainly in western societies and in particular amongst musical forms. It is also apparent that a number of the pioneers are either amateur jazz performers or know jazz musicians from whom they have learnt about jazz and subsequently made the connection to organizational analysis. We note, however, that improvisation is not exclusive to jazz. In fact, according to acclaimed guitarist and musical producer Derek Bailey (1992) there is scarcely any musical technique or form that did not originate in improvisation and scarcely any single field in music which has remained unaffected by improvisation. He cites examples from a wide range of music, from flamenco, baroque, to African music, Turkish music and some variations of rock music.

In spite of the contribution of jazz to organizational improvisation, there is a potential danger of jazz becoming what Weick (1980) calls a 'blinding spot', by obfuscating contributions from other areas of human endeavour and, most importantly, from grounded and empirical research. It is important not to be mesmerized by the jazz metaphor to the point of ignoring the potential contribution of alternative metaphors and other avenues of theory-development in organizational improvisation. There appears to be a need, therefore, to broaden the scope for theory-building by developing new insights from other relevant phenomena which contain interesting elements of improvisation. Similarly, even while drawing from jazz, it is worth bearing in mind that there are many forms of jazz, with concomitant degrees of improvisation, each providing different sets of implications for organizational improvisation. We discuss this further below.

This article thus aims to contribute toward the emergent yet currently amorphous theory of organizational improvisation by delving into other phenomena which exhibit improvisational elements/action and contrasting them with the insights generated by the jazz improvisation metaphor. To accomplish this purpose, we first present an integrative jazz-based model of organizational improvisation, and point out some dangers in relying on a single metaphor for theory development. We then contrast this model with three others which for our purposes are not necessarily meant to be 'alternative metaphors' but alternative ways of 'seeing' the dynamics of improvisation. In effect, these models serve as theoretical/analytical lenses which we believe can help us apprehend aspects of organizations which complement the insights generated by jazz. Finally, we bring together the contributions of the four models to demonstrate how they might lead to a more rigorous approach to theory-development in organizational improvisation. The definitive features of jazz and the three additional models are summarized in Table I.

A JAZZ-BASED THEORY OF ORGANIZATIONAL IMPROVISATION

In this section we discuss the characteristics of jazz improvisation that suggest its importance for the understanding of organizational improvisation. Music theorists have offered several broad categories of improvisation. Kernfeld (1995, pp. 131–58) discusses four: *paraphrase improvisation* (the 'recognizable ornamentation of an existing theme'); *formulaic improvisation* ('the artful weaving of formulas, through variation, into ever-changing, continuous lines'); *motivic improvisation* (where a motive forms the basis for a section of a piece); and *modal improvisation* (variation is achieved on the basis of pitch). Bailey (1992) makes a simple distinction between 'idiomatic' and 'non-idiomatic' improvisation. While the latter is mostly found in 'free' improvisation and does not represent any specific identity, the former is concerned with the expression of an idiom – e.g. jazz, flamenco, etc – and takes its identity and motivation from that particular idiom.

Others have identified 'degrees' of improvisation, e.g. a continuum that ranges from interpretation, minor deviation, embellishment, to full-fledged improvisation (e.g. Berliner, 1994; Moorman and Miner, 1998a; Weick, 1998). In a recent contribution, Zack (2000) has mapped these variations on four musical genres based on the extent of improvisation, from 'minimal to none' in classical, 'constrained within strong structure' in traditional jazz/swing, 'extensive' in bebop to 'maximal' in postbop. Zack (2000) argues that much of the current theorizing on organizational improvisation is based on the genre of jazz known as traditional jazz or swing, rather than 'free jazz'.[1]

According to Berliner (1994), improvisation involves reworking precomposed material in relation to unanticipated ideas that emerge and are conceived in the course of the performance. This observation has important implications for organizational improvisation because it implies the existence of a template upon which adaptation and deviation are realized. While such a template is most evident in swing jazz particularly in terms of rhythmic, melodic and harmonic structures, in bebop and postbop structure becomes progressing looser to the point that even

2026   K. Kamoche et al.

Table I. Antecedents, influencing factors and outcomes of improvisation

	Jazz	*Indian music*	*Music therapy*	*Role theory*
Antecedents				
Degree of deliberateness	High	High	High	Low (unintended deviation)
Social experience	Competition and Collaboration	Competition	Contact	Disclosure and meaning construction
Coordination	Organic solidarity	Mechanic solidarity	Explicit task rules	Social interaction
Minimal structure	Song (or riff, chords)	Musical formulas	Explicit social rules	Behavioural expectations and routines
Influencing factors				
Leadership style	Servant and rotating	Absent	Dual and directive	Balanced and dynamic
Individual characteristics	Virtuosity skills, trust, creativity	Virtuosity skills, competitiveness, creativity	No special skills required	Emphasis on role characteristics
Culture	Supportive	Adversarial	Supportive and nurturing	Supportive; continuity of membership
Memory	Declarative, procedural and situated	Procedural	None	Procedural
Group size	Small to medium	Small to medium	Medium or dyad	Dyad (may be within a network)
Outcomes				
Form of flexibility	Novelty	Novelty	Recovery	Adjustment
Nature of learning	Innovation	Innovation	Improving relationships	Local problem solving
Emotionality	Transcendence	Transcendence	Healing	Belonging
Further motivation	To compete and cooperate	To compete	To 'connect'	To continue

the basic harmonic structure is itself improvised (e.g. Zack, 2000). In assessing the robustness of the contribution of the jazz metaphor toward a theory of organizational improvisation, we find it helpful to characterize jazz improvisation under three headings: antecedents, influencing factors, and outcomes. We adopt this approach merely as an heuristic device to assist us achieve conceptual clarity in our analysis, rather than to imply a deterministic linear logic in the creation of jazz music. Within these general headings, we articulate a number of constructs based mainly on a careful reading of the emergent literature on organizational improvisation. This categorization is not exhaustive, but we believe it captures most of the key definitive features of jazz improvisation. It can be argued, however, that where antecedents, influences and outcomes interact simultaneously, as in free jazz, a structuration perspective (Ranson et al., 1980) might be more appropriate.[2] A structuration perspective focuses on the interpenetration of framework and interaction, with structures continually recreated.

Antecedents

The antecedents of jazz improvisation can be divided into two groups: the motivation to improvise and the potential to do so. The will to improvise comes from: a deliberate choice of improvisation as an action strategy and a culture that encourages experimentation and treats mistakes as learning opportunities (Crossan et al., 1996; Weick, 1999). The potential to improvise comes from: a task structure that reflects knowledge of musical norms and jazz standards (i.e. conventions as well as songs), a social structure based on implicit norms and the use of a song to drive task performance (see also Bastien and Hostager, 1991; Hatch, 1997, 1999).

The social experience of jazz improvisation is defined by both collaboration and competition. Collaboration exists because of the collective nature of the performance, and the fact that members are bound by the task in hand. Intense interaction includes both *comping* (i.e. lending harmonic and rhythmic support) and the partnering, risk-taking and mutual commitment found in creative collaboration (Kamoche and Cunha, 2001). This cooperative aspect is considered to be one of the major traits of jazz improvisation (e.g. Bastien and Hostager, 1988; Hatch, 1999; Weick, 1999). Competition is found in 'cutting sessions' where musicians try to outdo each other, and engage in brinkmanship behaviour. Achieving a meaningful performance requires a balance between collaboration and competition. Thus, without seeking to romanticize jazz, we would argue that egotistical behaviour must be situated within a context of a collaborative praxis.

Drawing from Durkheim (1933), Sharron (1983) argues that jazz is a *time biased* form of group interaction grounded in organic solidarity. A jazz band is coordinated by organic solidarity, in the sense that it benefits from a highly complex division of labour with every member playing several roles in sequence. In a single performance, one plays leader and follower, melody and rhythm. Moreover, harmony, melody and rhythm are the responsibility of the entire group and not of any individual musician (Berliner, 1994). This is a kind of 'all for one and one for all [music] and no instrument or section can be said to play exclusively one of these components' (Sharron, 1983, p. 228). This complexity is 'manageable' because of the existence of what can be called a 'minimal structure' (see below).

The motivation to improvise is not enough; the potential to do so must also be present, which is assured by the presence of a minimal structure (Eisenberg, 1990). This minimal structure refers to a shared knowledge among members of a community of practice that allows for members to depart from canonical practice, especially when acting together (Brown and Duguid, 1991). In jazz, we can identify three components of a minimal structure: the social structure, the technical structure and the 'jazz standards' – the shared repertoire of songs (Bastien and Hostager, 1988, 1995; Kamoche and Cunha, 1999, 2001; Weick, 1999). In their summary of minimal structures, Kamoche and Cunha (2001) include the following:

- Social structures: behavioural norms; communicative codes; partnering in an autonomous ensemble; soloing/comping; high trust and zones of manoeuvre; risk-taking attitudes; supportive culture.
- Technical structures: definition of key, chord progression and repertoire; template of a song, chorus or riff; wide stock of talent; knowledge of music technology and instrumentation.

This categorization of structure serves two important purposes: it characterizes the constitutive elements of the performance while at the same time denoting how the minimal structure guides rather than constrains action. We draw from this characterization of 'structure' to offer a more refined view of the nature of structure in jazz. For example, it is common for observers to argue that structure gets less and less as we move from swing to bebop and postpop (e.g. Zack, 2000). However, the notion of a *minimal structure* serves to signal some 'basic' conditions that must be satisfied for a performance to be accomplished. Once these are in place, the musicians can take the performance in any particular direction. Similarly, a riff or a song can serve as a basic template or frame of reference, allowing the performers to chart the course of the emergent performance, with improvisation proceeding according to any of the genres characterized by Zack (2000). Bastien and Hostager (1988) offer the concept of a 'centring strategy' whereby musicians start off with a shared sense of jazz music theory, behavioural norms and communicative codes, and then selectively invent ideas along some of the potential paths suggested by this centre. In our view, this minimal structure is not genre-specific, though we recognize that in freer jazz, the zones of manoevre are much wider since other aspects of structure, like harmony and tone are also subject to improvisation.

These characteristics of jazz improvisation have important implications for organizations, especially in fast-changing environments (Eisenhardt and Sull, 2001). For instance, managers often take decisions with little indication as to possible outcomes, staking their reputation in extremely demanding and anxiety-inducing tasks (Peters, 1994). Secondly, the professional culture of jazz musicians, when considered a community of practice, seems appropriate to tackle this set of challenges and seems somewhat more moderated than the 'all horizontal/no rules' organization that some prescribe (see Micklethwait and Wooldridge, 1996).

Influencing Factors

In this section we consider the factors that determine the sustainability and quality of the improvisational performance. For the purposes of capturing the dynamics and determinants of the improvisational action at the level of the team, we suggest they include but are not limited to leadership style, individual characteristics, culture, memory, and group size. Gioia (1988) argues that leadership factors can strongly influence the quality of a jazz band's performance. This form of leadership differs from that which we normally associate with organizations. For example, Greenleaf (1979) notes that a 'servant' leadership seems to be an important determinant of the quality and degree of an improvisation, helping to fight phenomena such as solipsism (Hatch, 1999). This in turn favours a rotating leadership style, in which each band member takes turns at deciding the direction and form of improvisation (Bastien and Hostager, 1991). Jazz is structured in such a way as to accommodate this form of soloing and 'comping'.

Individual characteristics include high levels of virtuosity skill, mutual trust and creativity. In addition to the requisite need for high degrees of performative competence (Crossan and Sorrenti, 1997; Kamoche and Cunha, 2001) jazz improvisers also need provocative competence: avoiding reliance on routines/past successes and exploring fresh alternatives thus testing the limits of their knowledge and comfort levels (Barrett, 1998). Trust should be seen alongside the need for a supportive culture in an activity defined by experimentation which requires some tolerance for mistakes, openness and faith in each other (Bastien and Hostager, 1991). Low creativity levels may limit the player's ability to imagine a rich set of variations, constraining his or her performance to a limited set of embellishments (Powers, 1981).

A final individual trait is the improviser's ability to deal with affective stress arising from dealing with the unknown. Musicians improvising in jazz and other genres, cited in Bailey (1992) and Gioia (1988) talk of the danger of 'crawling out on a limb', being on the 'edge', about facing a 'terrible moment', a 'dilemma', fearing to 'make a terrible fool' of themselves, and so forth. Others talk about the 'battle of getting up and playing,' and 'nervousness' (Peplowski, 1998). This clearly shows that improvising is a risky enterprise. Therefore, in order to deal effectively with these tensions it is necessary to have a culture that encourages experimentation and risk-taking. Within the organizational context, this poses a major challenge because managers tend to prefer familiar techniques, well-defined structures, and to avoid risk.

Memory, in various forms, plays an important role in improvisation. Situated, episodic memory generated from the 'structure of activity-in-setting' (Lave, 1988) is particularly crucial because it is grounded in the social context within which the musicians learn their trade and is enriched by social interaction, allowing individuals to learn from each other and to call on the benefit of shared experiences. Learning is thus *situated* and *distributed* in the processes of coparticipation, rather than in the heads of individuals (Lave and Wenger, 1991). Procedural memory – knowledge of repertoires and techniques – is important because it provides readily accessible material (Berliner, 1994), but can be a liability when musicians revert to familiar territory, which hampers innovativeness (see also Moorman and Miner, 1998a). Declarative memory refers to knowledge of musical theory, e.g. chord progressions, rhythmic patterns, and the disciplines of harmony and counterpoint, etc (Bailey, 1992; Kernfeld, 1995). It can be applied to different situations in countless ways, thus facilitating creativity (Moorman and Miner, 1998a). We concur with Moorman and Miner's (1998a) view that declarative and procedural memory are complementary competencies, and suggest further that this complementarity is situated and dynamic. Practice is also relevant to the quality of an improvisation (Crossan et al., 1996) because it strengthens both declarative (what?) and procedural (how to?) memory, and enhances the scope for learning in the context of interaction. A final condition affecting the quality and degree of improvisation is group size. Groups that are too large have lower levels of improvisation due to loss and distortion of communication, among other factors (Voyer and Faulkner, 1989).

Outcomes

We identify a number of outcomes from jazz improvisation. The most obvious one is the improvised performance which, if done well, is a triumph of competence, dynamic interaction and creativity over the competing pressures of chaos and routinization. Additional outcomes include: flexibility, learning, a personal feeling of transcendence, and an increasing motivation to improvise. Flexibility refers to members' ability to adapt to each other and to the situation. Mapped on to the organizational context, this is especially important in high-velocity environments, where pace, ambiguity and uncertainty are constant elements (Eisenhardt and Bhatia, 2002). Learning is about acquiring and expanding procedural, declarative and episodic memory. Improvisers can also attain a sense of personal transcendence (Barrett, 1998). In Eisenberg's words 'in these moments, participants experience something akin to the French *presque vu* – an unquestionable feeling of rightness. The relatedness problem is solved; through activity with others, people can transcend their separateness and live not only in themselves but also in community' (Eisenberg, 1990, p. 147). Flexibility, learning and transcendence, *inter alia*, in turn enhance the motivation to improvise. Successful improvisation ultimately engenders a constant sense of novelty and the promise of accomplished creativity. One negative outcome is 'trainwreck', where improvisers interfere with one another to the point that they fail to 'find themselves' on the music (Gioia, 1988; Hatch, 1999).

While the robustness of the jazz metaphor is not in question, earlier research on improvisation in fields other than music performance (including management) suggests there is more to improvisation than current research on jazz improvisation allows for. This implies a need for further theoretical elaboration by determining what we can learn from other models. Below we consider some limitations of relying on a single metaphor for theory development; then proceed to set out the basic features of three alternative models which might complement the insights generated by jazz.

LOOKING BEYOND JAZZ

Metaphor can be defined as '*a way of thinking* and *a way of seeing*' (Morgan, 1997, p. 4), an 'invitation to see the world' (Barrett and Cooperrider, 1990, p. 222), and according to Tsoukas (1993, p. 324) serve to 'generate alternative social realities' (for a detailed critique see Grant and Oswick, 1996, and McCourt, 1997). The metaphor of jazz improvisation has been mapped on to the organizational context in order to help us *see* organizations in a new light, thus generating useful insights into the phenomenon of 'organizational improvisation'. This activity has probably been stimulated by the observation that there seem to be remarkable similarities between what jazz improvisers do and what goes on in organizations with a predilection for action and continuous learning, and a culture of risk-taking and experimentation. Organization theorists who are very knowledgeable about jazz seem to have taken on board Grant and Oswick's (1996, p. 2) point that the use of metaphors enables 'the transfer of information about a relatively familiar subject (often referred to as the source or base domain), to a new and relatively unknown subject (often referred to as the target domain)' (see also Ortony, 1993; Tsoukas, 1991). Weick's (1999, p. 541) suggestion: 'if you want to study organizations, study something else', is also instructive in this enterprise.

However, there are some limitations in using metaphor, and in particular a single metaphor, for theory-building. Grant and Oswick (1996) provide an extensive summary. Some criticisms include the claim that metaphors, couched as they are in seductive figurative language, add little to scientific discourse; they reify and are ideologically questionable; they distort the object under investigation, thus potentially misleading managers. It is also worth noting that over time, metaphors 'die' by loosing their generative properties (Derrida, 1978). In fact, metaphors can gradually rigidify meaning and become more and more closed to empirical research (Letiche and Van Uden, 1998). Finally, from a socio-linguistic point of view, English (and most languages, for that matter) is not a *langue bien faite*; thus to the extent that a language does not posses a biunivocal relationship between signification and signifier, the same word/metaphor can have various meanings depending on its perceiver (Ricoeur, 1978). This potentially threatens theory diffusion, for example from academia to industry. *In extremis*, this could lead to the adoption of practices and behaviours not only different but even contrary to those intended by the proponents of the metaphor (Letiche and Van Uden, 1998).

In spite of the contribution that the analysis of jazz improvisation has made to our understanding of organizations, we urge caution in relying on a single analytical lens to develop theory, whether this be a metaphor or any other construct applied *metaphorically*. Clegg and Gray (1996) warn about the risk of getting 'locked in' to one way of thinking about an issue while applying a metaphor. Furthermore, due to the potential inherent dangers of inappropriately using one metaphor (e.g. jazz improvisation) to understand a phenomenon which is itself metaphorical (organizational improvisation), we use the terms 'analytical lens' or 'model', for the sake of argument.

Improvisation exists in many aspects of human behaviour. In the interest of parsimony we examine its incidence in three domains: Indian music, music therapy and role theory. These three appear appropriate for the following reasons: the first one retains our discussion within the field of music, thus offering some interesting contrasts with jazz. The second one goes even further to demonstrate the generative effects of simple rather than complex instruments/tools and the fact that virtuosity need not be an issue in improvisational ability. Finally, role theory brings the debate closer to the organizational context.

Improvisation in Indian Music

Improvisation in Indian music provides an interesting contrast to jazz music. Though coming from two very different musical traditions, they also share some remarkable similarities. Indian music is tied closely to the cultural and spiritual life of India, and according to Bailey (1992) is a catalogue of Hindu and Muslim saints, including their teachings and their deeds. Much has been written about the richness and diversity of Indian music, with some observers claiming that it is the most sophisticated musical culture outside the Western world (e.g. Sharron, 1983). While jazz can be represented by a system of notation, Indian music is unwritten, and is created and produced orally (Holroyde, 1972; Sharron, 1983). The basic components of Indian music are the *raga* and the *tala*. The *raga* is the framework within which the improvisation takes place (Bailey, 1992). It consists of two parts: the introductory out-of-tempo slow *alapa* in which the melodic patterns are first established, and the *gat* which sees an intensified pace, decorative pieces and a concentration on the rhythmic properties (Bailey, 1992). The ensuing rhythmic cycle permits variations which in turn constitute the basic rhythmic units – the *tala*. Indian music improvisers believe that the Indian scale system offers thousands of *ragas*, though only about 30–50 are in common use; as for *talas*, there are about

Organizational Improvisation   2033

120, with about 15–20 in popular use (e.g. Shankar, 1968; Sharron, 1983). Such routines are not unlike 'licks' applied by jazz improvisers over sets of chords.

Regarding antecedents, improvisation in Indian music is, as in jazz, triggered by the will to be experimental which, in Indian music, does not mean to depart from a given score but to build new music with a wide set of prescribed instrumental routines provided by the *talas*. Experimentation brings with it the risk of error, which requires an 'aesthetic of imperfection' (Weick, 1999) – a climate tolerant of mistakes. As in jazz, action/playing rather than planning/composing must be viewed as *the* way to create new music, demonstrating artistic accomplishment.

In a departure from jazz, the social experience in Indian music is defined by competitiveness rather than cooperation. While the jazz soloist is accompanied by others who provide harmonic and rhythmic support, Indian solos are an exchange of phrases between players who 'try to "outphrase" each other without diverting from the tonal order' (Sharron, 1983, p. 227). In terms of the coordination of social action, Indian music is *space biased* and is grounded in mechanical solidarity (Sharron, 1983). Without attributing simplicity or smallness of scale to his Durkheimian treatment of division of labour in Indian culture, Sharron (1983, p. 228) identifies a simplicity in the division of labour in Indian music where a soloist:

> [p]lays a time-free melodic line; an accompanist responds in melody and rhythm which are bound by the spatial notions of *raga* and *tala*, but not by any form or structure which are defined in measures; solos are juxtaposed, and they do not intermingle with one another, nor do they respond to one another simultaneously, as the case may be in jazz.

Indian music improvisation also relies on a minimal structure, albeit one that shares few traits with that of jazz. To be sure, Indian improvisers also come to the stage with a social structure and a task structure. However, they are permitted little tonal variation and melodic freedom, as opposed to jazz musicians who normally work around and ignore or violate the tonal/melodic/spatial structure (see also Hatch, 1999; Sharron, 1983). *Ragas* are the basic template for improvising. However, while jazz musicians can apply a 'centring strategy' to achieve variation with extensive harmonic zones of manouvre, the direction of the Indian music performance is stated during the introductory *alapa* and subsequent zones of manouvre are primarily rhythmic.

We now turn to the influencing factors affecting the degree and quality of improvisation in Indian music. Leadership, considered one of the cornerstones of jazz improvisation, is almost absent in Indian music. This is mainly explained by the fact that the latter is a competitive activity, and thus coordination mechanisms beyond those conveyed by the minimal structure we presented above, are seldom needed.

The individual characteristics of musicians performing either style of musical improvisation are in many ways similar. Instruments are basically complex, so skill in Indian music is as important as it is in jazz settings. Aspiring musicians spend years developing and polishing their competence either through practicing in jazz or working under a Guru in Indian music. Creativity is a vital ingredient in helping the musician create novelty with the musical procedures embodied in *ragas* and *talas*. Dealing with stress is also important, not only because of the simultaneity of planning and execution (as in jazz), but also because of the competitiveness embedded in Indian music improvisation.

The culture underlying the relationships among group members is as important in Indian music as in jazz. The only difference here is the purpose of that culture. In jazz it is aimed at achieving cooperation while accommodating degrees of competition but in Indian music it is targeted at achieving proficient levels of competition. Such a culture tends towards the adversarial as opposed to the cooperative in the execution of performance.

The difference in the task structure between these two genres of musical improvisation is notable. In jazz, as noted above, the task structure is mainly grounded in the complementarity of declarative memory and procedural memory *in situ*. In Indian music the task structure consists of the knowledge of *talas* and *ragas*, which are, respectively, formulas for melody and rhythm. Although these are also elements stored in memory, they are drawn upon largely in a procedural manner. This means that instead of knowing a set of scores *to improvise upon*, the Indian musician knows a set of musical 'procedures' *to improvise with* (Gosvami, 1957). According to Sharron (1983) the vast amount of ragas serve to compensate for the relative lack of melodic freedom and the heavy dependence on the tonal order. Finally, as in jazz, Indian improvisation works better with small sized groups, ranging from duo to quartet.

Regarding outcomes, Indian music is very similar to jazz in terms of creating a performance, and also in that it creates novelty, promotes learning and may foster feelings of transcendence. However, the sense of 'togetherness' found in jazz improvisation is absent in Indian music partly due to the competitiveness between performers and because the *talas* that constitute rhythmic patterns do not permit as much interpretation of a tune as the harmonic patterns in jazz, nor do they permit collaborative 'comping'.

Summary. This model highlights four major insights. Firstly, it illustrates how this phenomenon unfolds in competitive environments where the complementary forces of teamwork are counteracted by individual achievement. Secondly, it highlights the importance of procedural memory. Thirdly, it points to the significance of retaining a high degree of structure while permitting improvisation: this is achieved by setting out the melodic patterns (in the *alapa*) and working within a tonal structure. The organizational equivalent may be clear objectives and control mechanisms that do not constrain action. Finally, it shows how improvisation may happen in contexts where leadership is absent.

Music Therapy

Ever since its first recorded widespread use in American hospitals after the Second World War (Schullian and Schoen, 1948), music therapy is now regularly used in many aspects of psychiatric care, as well as among the physically disabled, developmentally disabled, sensory impaired, the elderly and in special education in many parts of the world (e.g. Benjamin, 1983; Plach, 1980). By allowing patients to sing or improvise on a variety of musical instruments, this practice applies music to group therapy as a stimulus for emotional and behavioural change. Music also becomes a vehicle for self-expression and a way to create a new identity. According to Aldridge (1996, p. 46) patients respond to music therapy because human beings 'are organized not in a mechanical way but in a musical form: i.e. a harmonic complex of intersecting rhythms and melodic contours'. This form of treatment has been shown to achieve communication with comatose patients and even to induce consciousness, whereby the coordination of impulses into a musical gestalt underlies recovery (Aldridge, 1996).

This practice is most often used as a treatment in *Gestalt* therapy, which differs from others in its existential and phenomenological perspective, hence experiential, rather than technical (Perls, 1969; Zinker, 1994). *Gestalt* therapists view the situated and immediate nature of improvisation in therapy as an opportunity to help their patients fully integrate the different features of their personality *in the present*, thus realizing healing through the client's actual experience and behaviour.

Regarding antecedents, therapy is a deliberate decision, something it shares with the two musical genres above. Nonetheless, therapy has no explicit ground upon which to improvise, so it cannot be considered a departure or a variation because it does not have anything to depart from or to vary upon (Southworth, 1983; Zinker, 1977). However, although the purpose is to heal a patient through a therapist/client relationship in the present, and although each session begins on a clean slate, so to speak, it could be argued that patients who are making progress might bring lessons from previous sessions to bear on future ones. Thus, in applying therapy to organizational analysis, it may be possible to view past dysfunctional behaviour as a basis upon which successful outcomes can be improvised.

This practice argues that the ability to improvise musically is present in every person and that that ability can be realized by relying on simple instruments such as drums and rattles. Drawing on this contention, therapy uses music improvisation to attain a moment of contact, defined in *gestalt* therapy as an experience that 'occurs when two people relate in a way that is fresh and new' (Southworth, 1983, p. 196), with the potential to contribute towards the patient's healing process or, at least, towards helping the patient express himself/herself in some way. Like

2036   K. Kamoche et al.

Indian music, therapy has no discrete degrees and can happen instantaneously, but unlike both musical forms, it requires no musical competence except in the therapist, the *de facto* leader.

The social experience of musical improvisation in the context of *gestalt* therapy is supposed to be a moderate one. Clinicians seldom let patients embark on highly affective states but they do make sure that they stay involved with the rest of the group. The notion of 'group' takes on a new meaning in therapy. Although patients are encouraged to follow the group, they are also allowed to play their own music, even if it is dissonant from that of the others (Southworth, 1983). Thus, a sense of involvement is not as relevant as in jazz or Indian music.

A minimal structure is also important here. In therapy, the task's minimal structure is composed of a 'theme' set by the therapist who then leads patients into improvisation by example (Southworth, 1983). Themes include music games like musical storytelling where the group listens to a musical selection and a storyline; the members then develop the story as they listen to intermittent selections. The level of structure depends heavily on the group's personal characteristics (see below). The leader therefore selects tasks and music that match the abilities, tastes and age of the clients. Depending on these characteristics, the therapist can determine the appropriate degree of task and social rules through which the activities are coordinated. The social structure is mainly drawn from social rules that can be embellished by minimal agreements prior to performance – a demanding task with mental patients (Forinash, 1992).

An important influencing factor for successful improvisation in therapy is the nature and role of leadership. The leader plays a pivotal role by generating all the initial ideas and facilitating participation. The leader should, for example, provide an atmosphere conducive to improvising and may encourage members to play music, either verbally or by handing them an instrument (Southworth, 1983). This differs from the case of jazz where the notional leader is essentially a first-among-equals. In some cases there may be dual leadership: one leader provides the theme and maintains the musical flow, while the other encourages members to follow suit, or deals with discipline problems from disruptive patients. The personal characteristics of the members differ markedly from the two musical forms. In this type of therapy, musical improvisation requires no special skill at all. The types of instruments used are also simple, as opposed to the more complex ones used in jazz and Indian music (Towse and Flower, 1993); the singing also requires no special skill and is fairly basic. Furthermore, in the case of patients with learning difficulties and similar disabilities any such skills might be totally absent.

Also, in music therapy, there is no need for the affective skills so important in the musical arena (Eisenberg, 1990). The more important 'skills' include attention span, reality orientation, level of verbal expressiveness, etc. (Plach, 1980). Though the absence of an audience may account for a low level of anxiety, participating in group activities with complete strangers, idealization or mistrust of the therapist, the use of strongly autistic attitudes etc can betray the evidence of 'persecutory anxiety' (Benenzon, 1997), especially in the early sessions. A culture that encourages mistakes as a source of aesthetics and learning is needed together with the belief that action is an important way to gain insight into the patient's behaviour and to foster healing.

Memory has several atypical traits. Improvisers do not share any kind of memory (procedural and declarative) and no practice is required. Some authors actually suggest that it is preferable for the patients not to have any profound knowledge of the instruments (e.g. Benenzon, 1997). The only participant who needs to draw on memory is the leader, in order to initiate or select appropriate music. In line with gestalt thinking, the challenge for the leader is 'to ensure that this musical memory works to add something to the present situation, not to trap people in the past' (Ansdell, 1995, p. 141). However, in applying this perspective to organizations, it could be argued that memory of past actions is an obstacle to be overcome, not just by the leader, but the organizational members. Thus, individuals will be trying to bring about change and generate new knowledge, by using past behaviours as a template upon which to improvise new behaviours. Regarding group size, Southworth (1983) proposes 8–10, arguing that size should neither hamper effective interaction nor result in muddy improvisation and loss of focus. Others recommend a group size of six (e.g. Benenzon, 1997). However, this approach is flexible enough to be used for a single client.

As far as outcomes are concerned, therapy grounded on improvisational music can result in (and aims at) improving the patient's mental condition, either by unearthing the underlying mental dynamics or by building the doctor/patient relationship (Forinash, 1992). However, improvisation in these settings can have just the opposite effect by fostering isolation through solipsism. In any case, some novelty emerges, often in the form of new behaviours and perceptions. This is especially driven by *gestalt* therapy's belief in self-reliance and by its situated nature. Learning, mostly in the shape of self-awareness, often results from this kind of exercise, as does an increased motivation to use it as a means of connecting with the others and the self.

Summary. From the foregoing we can articulate three key lessons from this model. Firstly, it requires no special skills and relies on simple tools, thus taking us closer to the art of bricolage, and within the scope of the ordinary person. Secondly, it requires no memory (except for the leader), and does not draw from a repertoire. Thirdly, leadership plays a more prominent integrative and decision-making role. Taken together, these contributions suggest that this approach is appropriate for dysfunctional groups with little performative competence, poor communication skills, and low self-confidence and initiative, thus requiring strong and directive leadership. This is an important critique of the orthodox view from the application of jazz that improvisation is something best done by highly skilled and self-

2038   K. Kamoche et al.

directed individuals who have absolute discretion over task, materials and tools. Similarly, while jazz and Indian music performers improvise to deliver a performance and thus derive intrinsic reward, music therapy is a problem-solving activity, with real practical implications for organizations.

Improvisation in Role Theory

Role theory is an area of social psychology concerned with the impact that socially constructed roles have on individual behaviour (Kahn, 1964). Role improvisation is the 'extent to which the organization and meaning of roles are invented by the people involved in a relationship' (Powers, 1981, p. 289). Researchers have been debating whether role-related behaviour is globally determined by an overarching social system or is locally improvised as relationships between actors unfold (Merton, 1957). Clearly, this debate is outside the scope of this article, but the nature of role-improvisation is not. Thus, while acknowledging the structuralist view that role-imposition is operative in some settings, we will focus attention on the interactionist view of the pervasiveness of improvisation (Blumer, 1969) in order to understand how this phenomenon works in role theory drawing on the work of Powers (1981). In pursuing this perspective, we are cognizant of Turner's (1985) argument that interactionists stressed that role playing and role taking processes are not merely about conforming to norms and expectations. Rather, they are ways of finding meaning, and are consistent with the gestalt approach, with particular regard to Lewin's (1948) view that human psychological processes are manifest through the discovery and creation of integrating patterns. Underpinning this approach is the assumption that creativity and a sense of discovery are tied in to the enactment of roles. Thus, even in the most rigid structures, interactionist processes which include improvisation can and do exist (Powers, 1981).

One notable feature of role improvisation is that it often results from an unintended deviation from a structure of prescribed roles (Banton, 1965). So, compared to the preceding models, the degree of deliberateness is lower. If one is unexpectedly called upon to lead a team but is unfamiliar with the standard, requisite norms of leadership, improvisation becomes inevitable. Such improvisation is not a deliberate departure from routinized action, nor necessarily an attempt to impress or entertain, but a matter of necessity. The social experience in role improvisation is one of disclosure and meaning-construction within the context of relationships. Therefore, it is about how people relate to each other in exchange relationships. In the course of their interaction, people continuously re-interpret their relationship through their actions. These re-interpretations arise not to demonstrate performance virtuosity as in jazz and Indian music but for the more mundane purpose of negotiating and sustaining the relationship or in response to changes in roles. Coordination comes about through social interaction while a set of socially constructed set of routines and behavioural expectations constitute the structure upon which role improvisation proceeds. An equally important aspect of structure is continuity of membership. Powers (1981) contends that role improvisation is enhanced the greater the continuity of personnel in role relationships.

Regarding the set of factors that impact upon the degree of role improvisation, we first consider leadership, drawing from Powers' (1981) treatment of the distribution of power. Power imbalance leads to the imposition of clearly defined role relationships, which are unlikely to change unless resources are modified or coalitions shifted (Emerson, 1972; Merton, 1957). Improvisation is unlikely to take place where an imbalance of power exists. If no one has a strong power advantage (leadership is balanced) then there is no authority to impose roles, and thus the degree of role improvisation is likely to be higher than in situations where that power exists (Weick, 1993). If the balance of power is dynamic rather than static, allowing leadership to rotate among group members, individuals will be motivated to vary the way they act because they may be called upon, at a given point in time, to perform a role with which they are unfamiliar. Depending on the configuration of roles, leadership might function in a way similar to jazz (where roles rotate), or may be absent (as in Indian music). We would expect little role improvisation in therapy where a power imbalance exists and directive leadership is necessary. This shows how different analytical lenses generate competing realities.

Individual characteristics have a very different treatment in role improvisation from that in the previous models. The focus is on the characteristics of a given role and not on the personal traits of its incumbent. Drawing from Powers (1981) we consider the following key characteristics: exposure and anonymity, transitory affect and routinization. The scope for role improvisation increases the less exposed a relationship is to observation by outsiders, which means that external scrutiny raises conformity and public accountability (see also Bott, 1957). The rationale behind this contention is that low exposure to outsiders relaxes the perception of 'panoptical surveillance' that tends to normalize behaviour and submit it to prescribed roles (Sewell, 1998). However, from a social network perspective whereby actor attributes and behaviours are explained in terms of the structure of relations in which they occur (e.g. Burt and Minor, 1983), improvisation may be facilitated or hindered by expectations from the social group/network within which one is embedded. It is also worth noting that a low level of exposure facilitates disclosure. The exposure scenario differs from musical performance where the presence of an audience is both unavoidable and a central feature of the performance. Similarly, a high degree of anonymity enhances the likelihood of role imposition, as people tend to resort to standard forms when their knowledge of another is limited (Powers, 1981; Turner, 1970). From this we can infer that relationships characterized by information-sharing and social familiarity can engender a higher propensity for role improvisation, with important implications for the organizational context in particular where teams are concerned.

People tend to develop their roles in a way that reduces concerns and augments benefits (Turner, 1980). However, performing imposed roles may lead to stressful relationships. Transitory affect is about the degree of fluctuating emotions, whereby emotionally trying relationships require 'cooling off' or 'exempting periods'. During such periods, imposed roles are changed in improvised ways, thus helping deal with stress and emotional costs. Such improvisations may be more marked when people collectively experience an 'uncommon fate' (Powers, 1981), such as environmental turbulence. This is borne out by the emergent organizational improvisation literature (e.g. Brown and Eisenhardt, 1997; Weick, 1993). Finally, routinization may cause some role-related activities to take on an imposed as opposed to an improvised form to the extent that it increases visibility and accountability. It may seem paradoxical that routinization diverts attention away from activities associated with the routinized behaviour, thus permitting scope for improvisation, as long as routinized tasks are executed properly. However, this view is consistent with the notion of minimal structures whereby guidelines at once specify and facilitate action – also analogous to the *alapa* in Indian music.

Apparently, both national and organizational cultures have an impact on role improvisation (e.g. Aram and Walochick, 1996). In keeping with our earlier observations, we argue that a culture in which experimentation is permitted will be conducive to role improvisation in the execution of role-based tasks and activities. An additional aspect of culture that we find relevant for role improvisation is continuity of membership. In this regard, Powers (1981, p. 289) contends that 'the human propensity to improvise increases with familiarity and with the amount of time spent interacting'.

In this type of culture the procedural memory that role improvisation draws upon (routines and role expectations) will most likely be treated as a grammar that can be used to build a number of variations in behaviour (Pentland and Reuter, 1994). Procedural grammar is similar to procedural memory in jazz (repertoires) and Indian music (*ragas*). As for group size, role improvisation mainly occurs in dyadic relationships because it is essentially a relational phenomenon, contingent on the specific nature of each interaction. In this regard it differs from the previous models (except one-to-one doctor–patient therapy).

Role improvisation has several outcomes. It increases flexibility via the incremental adjustment of roles. It fosters learning via local problem solving, as internal changes are incorporated into role expectations. The level of disclosure that this practice entails potentially creates an increasing sense of belonging between organizational members, motivating them to continue their association to the organization. Three additional characteristics of role improvisation are relevant. Firstly, the theory does not mention the existence of discrete degrees of improvisation. Furthermore, improvisation can take place immediately, without the need for social actors to use a 'centering strategy' to build confidence upon each other. Finally, there generally is no audience.

Summary. As a whole, this model offers three interesting insights for understanding improvisation in organizations. Firstly, unlike the previous ones, it focuses the analysis on roles and role expectations and not on individuals and individual characteristics. Secondly, it demonstrates that improvisation can be grounded on procedural, instead of declarative memory – a quality it shares with Indian music. Finally, it brings the level of analysis down to the dyad, thus extending the conceptual scope for theorizing organizational improvisation.

DISCUSSION

In the foregoing we have attempted to make the case for considering models other than jazz in developing a more robust theory of organizational improvisation. Although the alternative models we propose have the potential to yield new insights, the settings they derive from are sufficiently different from the organizational context (and from each other) as to require empirical research in order to better understand the dynamics of organizational improvisation.

The contrast between models is helpful for the purpose of raising questions like: can improvisation be planned or is it necessarily emergent (Miner et al., 2001)? Are improvisational variations blind or intentional (Aldrich, 1999)? Can improvisational knowledge be formalized and appropriated? Do minimal structures constrain (Moorman and Miner, 1998a), liberate, or constrain and liberate (Kamoche and Cunha, 2001)? Is the 'optimal amount of structure' (Eisenhardt and Martin, 2000, p. 1113) obtainable through different types of minimal structures? From our analysis, it is evident that the answers these various models provide can vary greatly. As such, the time seems opportune to study the diversity of improvisational behaviours, instead of implicitly assuming its unity under a jazz-based theory. The four models discussed here diverge in their antecedents, influencing factors and outcomes. This divergence may be a vital stimulus for theorizing organizational improvisation. In this section we piece together the various contributions of these models with reference to the structure set out in Table I.

The antecedents of *organizational* improvisation emerge as one of the major divergence points between improvisation in organizational settings and in the models above. In jazz and Indian music, improvisation is prompted by a *deliberate* attempt to deviate from what is perceived as 'standard' practice or rhythmic formula respectively. In therapy, improvisation is also emergent and exploratory, without the need to depart from a 'standard'. Although there is no deliberate will to improvise, role improvisation happens because of social factors that emerge from the broader social environment. In organizations, improvisation is generally not deliberate. It is mostly triggered by the perception of a problem that has to be tackled hastily.

This reveals a critical issue for building a theory of organizational improvisation. Firstly, managers tend to prefer planning and routinization to improvisa-

2042   K. Kamoche et al.

tional/emergent behaviour (Mintzberg and McHugh, 1985). Weick (1998, p. 552) contends that 'the intention of the jazz musician is to produce something that comes out *differently* than it did before, whereas organizations typically pride themselves on the opposite, namely, reliable performance that produces something that is standardized and that comes out the same way it did before. It is hard to imagine the typical manager feeling "guilty" when he or she plays things worked out before [whereas the typical jazz musician would]'. This means that they will tend to improvise when they do not have time to plan – thus, the problem to be tackled must demand fast action in order to trigger improvisational behaviour. Situations exist of course when managers talk of a 'bias for action', but even with empowerment, it is unusual to encourage people to work outside the management controls that define organizational structure.[3]

The representation of improvisation as a deliberate, collaborative, temporary effort is central to jazz. If one picks another model, however, improvisation may be represented quite differently. In role improvisation, for example, it may be a partly unintended variation, a process of 'muddling through' (Lindblom, 1959), taking place in an inductive and intuitive rather than methodical way. In this sense, improvisation evokes two different modes of learning: experimental and interactive (Miller, 1996). The possibility of introducing both purposeful and blind variations through improvisation, becomes more explicit if we consider role theory. The importance of blind variations has been stressed by several authors (e.g. Campbell, 1994; Weick, 1979) and would appear to be an important input in further research on organizational improvisation. The musical models may be appropriate when managers make deliberate efforts to improvise; when the external social (or competitive business) context imposes the need for improvisation, role theory becomes an important source of insights.

Cooperation has been emphasized in the empirical research on improvisation (e.g. Miner et al., 2001; Perry, 1991), although some competitiveness may be possible when the organization for example bets on competitive designs (Eisenhardt and Tabrizi, 1995). This suggests the complementary contributions from jazz and, at least, Indian music. The 'centrality' that cooperation and mutuality provide in jazz improvisation might be complemented by the definitive competitive ethos in Indian music. Organizations may need a good blend of internal competition and cooperation. The other models, however, illuminate additional features of the social experience of improvisation: achieving contact (therapy) and disclosure (role improvisation).

An essential aspect of organizational improvisation is alignment (Orlikowski and Hoffman, 1997). Since improvisation is not a common occurrence in many organizational settings, if any element of the organization's systems forfeits attempts to plan while acting, then the whole system is likely to fail (Johnson and Rice, 1987; Orlikowski, 1996). This requires some specific coordinating mechanisms which we have described here as a minimal structure. Where a tight structure is inevitable (as it often is, as manifest in management controls), members may be able to fall back on a range of flexible recipes of action, analogous to 'licks' and *ragas*. We refer to these as 'repertoires of innovative action'. 'Minimal' means general purpose/guidelines and basic rules. To improvise, individuals must possess general purpose plans which are like a map that offers various ways to get from one point to another. The tools that organizations use to produce their desired type of 'planning' include strategic intent (Hamel and Prahalad, 1994) and shared vision (Senge, 1990) – mechanisms that integrate individual actions by maintaining focus but that allow (and foster) diversity of action and thought. General purpose tools and technology are also necessary for real-time planning (Orlikowski, 1996). Thus, if one decides to change the nature of outputs instantaneously, then one's technology must be flexible enough to withstand that change.

This gives rise to the concept of 'radically tailorable tools' (Malone et al., 1992) that we find crucial for improvising organizations. Improvisational ability rests on having a multiple purpose structure (Ciborra, 1991), one that goes far in integrating but only partially constrains. This structure comprises an explicit and clear set of responsibilities and priorities (Hutchins, 1991); frequent milestones, to instill a sense of urgency (Eisenhardt and Tabrizi, 1995) and to provide the frequent feedback that fuels improvisers (Gardner and Rogoff, 1990); and choreographed transitions that purposefully introduce 'problems' (Brown and Eisenhardt, 1997). This 'generality' of organizational minimal structures shows the need to delineate explicitly, specific elements of the minimal structure whereas in some of our models, these are largely tacit and implicit. This serves to signify potential areas of difficulty in theorizing organizational improvisation on the basis of metaphors and related analytical lenses, while at the same time highlighting the need to pay more attention to the tacit side of human action in organizations.

'Minimality' defines three further dimensions for successful improvisation. First comes minimal agreement, meaning that some dissent of worldviews among members allows for a sharper scanning and thus to earlier and better detection of 'problems' that require fast action (Perry, 1991). Second, organizations need to maintain a minimal level of critical resources, bearing in mind the degree of slack necessary for innovative activity (Dougherty, 1996; Hedberg et al., 1976). Finally, minimal rationality helps keep action focused on ends, avoiding reification of means and concentrating on finding the questions the organization needs to ask. Minimal rationality also aims at keeping organizations from rationalizing all activity into procedures, thereby destroying adaptivity to both internal and external circumstances (Johnson and Rice, 1984). The differing degree of 'deliberateness' and concomitant zones of manouvre found in the various models are instructive in this regard.

We now consider those factors that influence improvisation. We begin with leadership. Apart from a certain degree of directivity, leaders must be proficient (and perceived as such by those they lead) in task performance (Johnson and Rice,

1987). In improvisational contexts, leaders may have to strike a balance between directive and participative styles (Cunha et al., 2003). Music therapy provides insights for directive leadership which is also facilitatory. This model is also appropriate for high power distance cultures. Insights from jazz are helpful for more democratic contexts where leadership is emergent and rotational. Indian music generates insights for task performance where leadership is apparently absent, and may be appropriate for self-directed, competitive and high-performing teams. Role improvisation introduces a new perspective because it explicitly addresses the significance of power.

We have noted that individual characteristics are theorized in different ways across the four models. In jazz and Indian music, virtuosity, competence and creativity are definitive features, implying that improvisation is a technically elitist undertaking. These models would suggest that managers should strive to cultivate highly technical skills combined with creativity. In therapy, on the other hand, no special skills are required. Anyone can improvise, and they can do so with simple tools. The challenge then becomes one of assuring quality, safety, efficiency etc. For the organization, the condition of technical ability in jazz and Indian music is thus complemented by the simplicity of music therapy to take account of the diversity of skill and technological capabilities in organizations. Evidence of the variation-generative power of play, errors, misunderstandings and human limitations (e.g. Aldrich and Kenworthy, 1999; Miner, 1994), is more accurately evoked in the case of therapy than in the musical models. In addition as we noted above, the therapy model is appropriate for dysfunctional organizations.

Role improvisation takes us even farther from the focus on individual abilities to the nature of the role itself. This suggests a need to examine the scope for improvisation and creativity at the level of social interaction amongst members, in addition to task performance. Furthermore, since the focus is on the characteristics of the role incumbent, managers would need to create circumstances that engender role improvisation, such as relaxing surveillance, teaching adaptability in anticipation of stressful/dangerous situations, and preventing routinization from taking root.

We now turn to culture. The culture in jazz is both supportive and competitive, in Indian music it tends to be competitive, while in music therapy it is supportive and nurturing. In music therapy, there is a much stronger emphasis on experimentation and bricolage than in the two musical forms. So, if patients do not feel comfortable with an instrument, they can easily switch to another at any time. A jazz improviser may switch between instruments in a performance for the purposes of exploring a new musical texture, not necessarily to feel more at ease, or because he suddenly discovers he cannot play it. In music therapy, the notion of 'aesthetics of imperfection' (Weick, 1999) takes on a new meaning because the objective of creating a musical product is even less important than achieving healing and contact. Common to all the models is the need to allow for risk-taking and learning.

The treatment of memory in the four models highlights different concerns for the organizational context. We noted that in jazz, declarative and procedural memory are complementary (Moorman and Miner, 1998a), and situated as well as episodic. This model appears to give the manager a fairly comprehensive ambit for striking a balance between *what* and *how*, and then locating sets of decisions in a context of *when*. However, it can be difficult to determine where relevant knowledge lies and how to access it in times of crisis (e.g. Goodhue et al., 1992). In this case, procedural memory as in Indian music (*ragas*) and role improvisation (scripts and grammar) becomes critical. Caution must be exercised because procedural memory might degenerate into routinization and hinder innovativeness. Both musical models are instructive for highly competent and self-motivated performers, as opposed to dysfunctional groups and low performers for whom the more appropriate model would be music therapy which invests memory (which could be declarative, procedural and situated) in the leader.

Regarding group size, empirical research has yet to reach consensus. Studies argue for both large (e.g. Brown and Eisenhardt, 1997; Ciborra, 1991) and small groups (Brown and Duguid, 1991; Hutchins, 1991), a decision that seems to depend on the specific format of both the supporting minimal structure and the pattern of communication among members. Regarding group composition it is difficult, again, to find common ground. Some studies support a 'mono-functional' view of groups (e.g. Hutchins, 1991; Orlikowski, 1996), while others argue for 'multi-functional' teams to produce the requisite variety that enables the attainment of higher levels of improvisation (Hedberg et al., 1976; Johnson and Rice, 1984). This has implications for the extent to which individuals are specialized or multi-skilled, as in the musical models and role theory, or where the task does not entail the possession of special skills as in music therapy.

In conclusion we argue that the sorts of outcomes the four models generate depict a fairly broad spectrum of the types of outcomes we might expect from real-life organizational improvisation. For example, the flexibility ascribed to jazz musicians (Eisenberg, 1990; Gioia, 1988) is an important quality/outcome for organizational improvisation. Such flexibility is taken to a higher level in models like improvisation-based therapy with an extremely low degree of formal structure. Further research would help clarify the suitability of such flexibility in activities such as teamwork in organizational settings. This would provide an interesting parallel with the organizational level, where flexibility has been shown to be particularly important in enabling organizations to respond to unexpected occurrences, either internally (Pearson et al., 1997) or externally (Ciborra, 1991; Moorman and Miner, 1995). Other outcomes like transcendence and achieving a sense of belonging allow us to theorize the social aspects in addition to the task-

2046   K. Kamoche et al.

related ones such as flexibility, innovation and learning. Achieving specific goals like healing (in therapy) is analogous to organizational problem-solving, where such problem-solving in undertaken through close interaction between the leader and subordinates. This highlights the potential contribution of little-explored models in this emergent discipline.

CONCLUSION

In the foregoing we sought to pinpoint various ways in which our models can be applied to organizational settings, suggesting which insights might be appropriate for what contexts. We now consider some additional implications for management practice. Given the differing perspectives these analytical lenses reveal, it would clearly be appropriate for managers to be eclectic in their choice of model. The jazz and Indian music models are appropriate for high-performing, self-directed workers, or for organizations that see themselves putting on a performance, e.g. providing a service for customers (the audience). However, given the relative significance of concepts like leadership and memory, a choice would have to be made about when to foster rotating leadership (jazz), or rely on procedural memory when time pressure requires a quick decision (Indian music). The Indian music model appears particularly relevant for managers who wish to set up explicit guidelines for action (as in the *alapa*), and subsequently permit improvisation within these constraints. It may also be appropriate when managers wish to foster a purely competitive atmosphere. The music therapy model is appropriate when managers want to create an innovative culture in dysfunctional organizations where the dysfunctionalism emanates for example from rigid bureaucracy that stifles initiative-taking and decision-making, and where skill levels are currently low. The role theory model can be applied where there is an interactional relationship, e.g. employees dealing with third parties like customers, or where organizational members are faced with little choice but to improvise, e.g. in highly interdependent or desperate situations. These suggestions are offered to managers who wish to foster improvisation through innovative action, rapid decision-making and adaptability amongst its workforce. There are situations where improvisation may not be necessary or desirable, e.g. where an uncalled for departure from routinized action in predictable circumstances might result in dire consequences, e.g. routine surgery. Therefore, every organization has to determine the objectives and degree of improvisation it requires, and secondly, the appropriate improvisational model or combination of models.

We now turn to the implications for research. When we say that a person is a lion, we are probably referring to his or her courage rather then to choice of food or facial hair. The use of metaphor in the emergent organizational improvisation literature is a powerful mechanism for generating insights into this phenomenon. This paper has characterized the most significant insights arising from the application of improvisational jazz, the predominant metaphor so far. Given the robustness of jazz improvisation, as well as its accessibility to theorists (many of whom seem to be jazz enthusiasts too), we expect this state of affairs to persist into the foreseeable future. However, organizations are not jazz combos, just like people are not lions. As such, we must not lose sight of the fact that there are several important differences between the forms of improvisation that occur within these two settings – differences that are not immediately evident if our theorizing is guided by a 'one-best-metaphor' approach.

Our purpose in this paper therefore is to broaden the theoretical spectrum upon which the study of organizational improvisation can be grounded, in order to uncover what other suitable models might offer, either in contrast with or in a complementary fashion to the jazz metaphor. The three additional models presented here have given us new ways of 'seeing' organizations and pointing to new directions in which research in organizational improvisation might develop. However as researchers we must keep an open mind about the opportunities and shortcomings of whatever analytical lenses we use to cast our gaze upon the organizational landscape. The foregoing will hopefully lead to further research to test the applicability of these models in organizational contexts. Within the models themselves, researchers could explore variations, e.g. the different genres of the musical forms, or proactive *vis-à-vis* reactive improvisation such as in role theory. Further research might also examine whether it is more appropriate to generate a synthesis of these seemingly divergent insights. As such, rather than pick one model for a particular context, would it be better to pick insights from these various models, and bring them together in an overarching model of organizational improvisation? Research might also explore other models like theatre, conversation, or genres of jazz where a wider range of structural aspects than the ones we have considered are suspended.[4] This would pave the way for a more incisive analysis of the structuration perspective. We hope that this discussion will spur further research into these challenging and exciting issues, bringing us to a better understanding of the nature and complexity of organizational improvisation.

NOTES

[1] The insights we generate here about the 'jazz metaphor' are drawn from the treatment of jazz improvisation in the emergent literature. This means that our discussion might seem to be too dependent on the 'swing/trad jazz' genre. This is not to deny the validity of 'free jazz'. In the conclusion we acknowledge the need for further research in this genre. We also hasten to add that our application of 'minimal structures' takes us beyond the orthodox definition of structure inherent in the organizational improvisation literature which appears limited to the rhythmic, melodic and harmonic aspects. It is also worth noting that even within postbop in which you can improvise the rules and also improvise *outside* as opposed to *within* or *with* forms (Zack, 2000), you still need a reference point – a song, a riff, a motif, or the elements of the minimal structure discussed here. As Moorman and Miner (1998a) point out, in free jazz the performers will ordinarily start with a 'head' then move on to melodic improvisations unrelated to any specific harmonic, rhythmic or melodic standards. The actual playing starts somewhere: in a particular

2048   K. Kamoche et al.

key. Since even the most innovative organizations have to have an initial goal, product concept or some form of management control, 'free' inevitably becomes a matter of interpretation. For our purposes, a reference point or structure is situated in the social and technical context of the performance. The initiators of free jazz like Ornette Coleman, retained episodic references, phrases, riffs and motifs that echoed previous compositions, drawing from episodic, situated memory, thus reminding us of Charles Mingus' famous retort: 'you can't improvise on nuthin'.

[2] We are grateful to a *JMS* reviewer for pointing this out.

[3] We must not romanticize any form of jazz. Operating outside controls, be they management, financial or cultural, may be very creative, but it often teeters dangerously on the edge of illegality and fraud. Examples of improvisation gone haywire (the fear of which leads managers to institute tight controls that in some contexts hamper innovativeness) include Barings Bank, Daiwa Bank, Sumitomo, and more recently Allied Irish and Enron.

[4] The challenge will be to find organizational alternatives to suspending harmonic and similar structures (i.e. those analogous to management controls and strategies), without inviting chaos. Our therapy metaphor offers a way forward because it does not treat confusion as chaos, but as uncharted territory. See also Zack (2000).

REFERENCES

Aldrich, H. (1999). *Organizations Evolving*. Thousand Oaks, CA: Sage.

Aldrich, H. and Kenworthy, A. L. (1999). 'The accidental entrepreneur. Campbellian antinomies and organizational foundings'. In Baum, J. A. C. and McKelvey, B. (Eds), *Variations in Organization Science: In Honor of Donald T. Campbell*. Thousand Oaks, CA: Sage, 19–33.

Aldridge, D. (1996). *Music Therapy and Practice in Medicine: From out of the Silence*. London: Jessica Kingsley.

Ansdell, G. (1995). *Music for Life: Aspects of Creative Music Therapy with Adult Clients*. London: Jessica Kingsley.

Aram, J. D. and Walochick, K. (1997). 'Improvisation and the Spanish manager'. *International Studies of Management and Organization*, **26**, 73–89.

Bailey, D. (1992). *Improvisation: Its Nature and Practice in Music*. New York: Da Capo Press.

Banton, M. (1965). *Roles: An Introduction to the Study of Social Relations*. Basic Books, New York.

Barrett, F. J. (1998). 'Creativity and improvisation in organizations: implications for organizational learning'. *Organization Science*, **9**, 5, 605–22.

Barrett, F. J. and Cooperrider, D. L. (1990). 'Generative metaphor intervention: a new behavioural approach for working with systems divided by conflict and caught in defensive perception'. *Journal of Behavioural Science*, **26**, 2, 219–39.

Bastien, D. T. and Hostager, T. J. (1988). 'Jazz as a process of organizational innovation'. *Communication Research*, **15**, 5, 582–602.

Bastien, D. T. and Hostager, T. J. (1991). 'Jazz as social structure, process and outcome'. In Buckner, R. T. and Weiland, S. (Eds), *Jazz in Mind: Essays on the History and Meanings of Jazz*. Detroit: Wayne State University Press, 148–65.

Bastien, D. T. and Hostager, T. J. (1995). 'On cooperation: a replication of an experiment in jazz and cooperation'. *Comportamento Organizacional e Gestão*, **2**, 1, 33–46.

Benenzon, R. O. (1997). *Music Therapy Theory and Manual: Contributions to the Knowledge of Nonverbal Contexts*. Springfield, IL: Charles C. Thomas.

Benjamin, B. (1983). 'The singing hospital – integrated group therapy in the Black mentally ill'. *South African Medical Journal*, **63**, 23, 897–9.

Berliner, P. F. (1994). *Thinking in Jazz: The Infinite Art of Improvisation*. Chicago: Chicago University Press.

Bettis, R. A. and Hitt, M. A. (1995). 'The new competitive landscape'. *Strategic Management Journal*, **16**, 7–19.

Blumer, H. (1969). *Symbolic Interaction*. Englewood Cliffs, NJ: Prentice-Hall.

Bott, E. (1957). *Family and Social Network: Roles, Norms and External Relationships in Ordinary Urban Families*. London: Tavistock.

Brown, J. S. and Duguid, P. (1991). 'Organizational learning and communities-of-practice: toward a unified view of working, learning and innovation'. *Organization Science*, **2**, 1, 40–57.

Organizational Improvisation   2049

Brown, S. L. and Eisenhardt, K. M. (1997). 'The art of continuous change: linking complexity theory and time-paced evolution in relentlessly shifting organizations'. *Administrative Science Quarterly*, **42**, 1, 1–34.

Burt, R. S. and Minor, M. J. (1983). *Applied Network Analysis*. London: Sage.

Campbell, D. T. (1994). 'How individual and face-to-face selection undermine firm selection in in organizational evolution'. In Baum, J. A. C. and Singh, J. V. (Eds), *Evolutionary Dynamics of Organizations*. New York: Oxford University Press, 23–38.

Ciborra, C. U. (1991). 'The platform organization: recombining strategies, structures and surprises'. *Organization Science*, **7**, 2, 103–18.

Clegg, S. R. and Gray, J. T. (1996). 'Metaphors in organizational research: of embedded embryos, paradigms and power people'. In Grant, D. and Oswick, C. (Eds), *Metaphor and Organizations*. London: Sage, 74–94.

Crossan, M. M. and Sorrenti, M. (1997). 'Making sense of improvisation'. *Advances in Strategic Management*, **14**, 155–80.

Crossan, M. M., White, R. E., Lane, H. and Klus, L. (1996). 'The improvising organization: where planning meets opportunity'. *Organizational Dynamics*, **24**, 4, 20–35.

Cunha, M. P., Cunha, J. V. and Kamoche, K. (1999). 'Organizational improvisation: what, when, how and why'. *International Journal of Management Reviews*, **1**, 3, 299–341.

Cunha, M. P., Kamoche, K. and Cunha, R. C. (2003). 'Organizational improvisation and leadership: a field study in two computer-mediated settings'. *International Studies of Management and Organization*, **33**, 1, 34–57.

Derrida, J. (1978). *Margins of Philosophy*. London: Harvester.

Dougherty, D. (1996). 'Organizing for innovation'. In Clegg, S. R., Hardy, C. and Nord, W. R. (Eds), *Handbook of Organization Studies*. Thousand Oaks, CA: Sage, 424–39.

Durkheim, E. (1933). *The Division of Labor in Society*. New York: Free Press.

Eisenberg, E. (1990). 'Jamming: transcendence through organizing'. *Communication Research*, **17**, 2, 139–64.

Eisenhardt, K. M. and Bhatia, M. M. (2002). 'Organizational complexity and computation'. In Baum, J. A. C. (Ed.), *Companion to Organizations*. Oxford: Blackwell, 442–66.

Eisenhardt, K. M. and Martin, J. A. (2000). 'Dynamic capabilities: what are they?'. *Strategic Management Journal*, **21**, 1105–21.

Eisenhardt, K. M. and Sull, D. N. (2001). 'Strategy as simple rules'. *Harvard Business Review*, **79**, 1, 107–16.

Eisenhardt, K. M. and Tabrizi, B. N. (1995). 'Accelerating adaptative processes: product innovation in the global computer industry'. *Administrative Science Quarterly*, **40**, 1, 84–110.

Emerson, R. (1972). 'Exchange theory. Part II: Exchange relations and network structures'. In Berger, J., Zelditch, M. and Anderson, B. (Eds), *Sociological Theories in Progress*. Boston: Houghton Mifflin, 58–87.

Forinash, M. (1992). 'A phenomenological analysis of Nordoff-Robbins approach to music therapy: the lived experience of clinical improvisation'. *Music Therapy*, **11**, 120–41.

Gardner, W. and Rogoff, B. (1990). 'Children's deliberateness of planning according to task circumstances'. *Developmental Psychology*, **26**, 3, 480–7.

Gioia, T. (1988). *The History of Jazz*. Oxford: Oxford University Press.

Goodhue, D. L., Wybo, M. D. and Kirsch, L. J. (1992). 'The impact of data integration on the costs and benefits of information systems'. *MIS Quarterly*, **16**, 293–311.

Gosvami, O. (1957). *The Story of Indian Music*. Bombay: Asia House.

Grant, D. and Oswick, C. (Eds) (1996). *Metaphor and Organizations*. London: Sage.

Greenleaf, R. K. (1979). *Servant Leadership: A Journey into the Nature of Legitimate Power and Greatness*. New York: Paulisi Press.

Hamel, G. and Prahalad, C. K. (1994). *Competing for the Future: Breakthrough Strategies for Seizing Control of your Industry and Controlling the Markets of Tomorrow*. Boston, MA: Harvard Business School Press.

Hatch, M. J. (1997). 'Jazzing up the theory of organizational improvisation'. *Advances in Strategic Management*, **14**, 181–91.

Hatch, M. J. (1999). 'Exploring the empty spaces of organizing: how improvisational jazz helps redescribe organizational structure'. *Organization Studies*, **20**, 1, 75–100.

Hedberg, B. L. T., Nystrom, P. C. and Starbuck, W. H. (1976). 'Camping on seesaws: prescriptions for self-designing organizations'. *Administrative Science Quarterly*, **21**, 41–65.

Holroyde, P. (1972). *The Music of India*. New York: Praeger.

Hutchins, E. (1991). 'Organizing work by adaptation'. *Organization Science*, **2**, 1, 14–39.

Johnson, B. M. and Rice, R. E. (1984). 'Reinvention in the innovation process: the case of word processing'. In Rice, R. E. (Ed.), *The New Media*. Beverly Hills, CA: Sage, 157–83.

Johnson, B. M. and Rice, R. E. (1987). *Managing Organizational Innovation: The Evolution from Word Processing to Office Information Systems*. New York: Columbia University Press.

Kahn, R. L. (1964). *Organizational Stress: Studies in Role Conflict and Ambiguity*. New York: Wiley.

Kamoche, K. and Cunha, M. P. (1999). 'Teamwork, knowledge-creation and improvisation'. *Readings in Organization Science*. Lisbon: ISPA, 435–52.

Kamoche, K. and Cunha, M. P. (2001). 'Minimal structures: from jazz improvisation to product innovation'. *Organization Studies*, **22**, 5, 733–64.

Kamoche, K., Cunha, M. P. and Cunha, J. V. (Eds) (2002). *Organizational Improvisation*. London: Routledge.

Kamoche, K., Cunha, M. P. and Cunha, R. C. (Eds) (2003). 'Improvisation in organizations.' *International Studies of Management and Organization*, **33**, 1.

Kernfeld, B. (1995). *What to Listen for in Jazz*. New Haven: Yale University Press.

Lave, J. (1988). *Cognition in Practice: Mind, Mathematics, and Culture in Everyday Life*. Cambridge: Cambridge University Press.

Lave, J. and Wenger, E. (1991). *Situated Learning: Legitimate Peripheral Participation*. Cambridge: Cambridge University Press.

Letiche, H. and Van Uden, J. (1998). 'Answers to a discussion note: on the "metaphor of the metaphor"'. *Organization Studies*, **19**, 6, 1029–33.

Lewin, K. (1948). *Resolving Social Conflicts*. New York: Harper and Brothers.

Lindblom, C. (1959). 'The science of "muddling through"'. *Public Administration Review*, **19**, 79–88.

Malone, T. W., Lai, K. Y. and Fry, C. (1992). 'Experiments with OVAL: a radically tailorable tool for cooperative work'. *Proceedings from the Conference on Computer Supported Cooperative Work*. ACM/SIGCHI & SIGOIS, 289–97.

McCourt, W. (1997). 'Discussion note: using metaphors to understand and to change organizations: a critique of Gareth Morgan's approach'. *Organization Studies*, **18**, 3, 511–22.

Merton, R. (1957). 'The role-set: problems in social theory'. *British Journal of Sociology*, **8**, 106–20.

Micklethwait, J. and Wooldridge, A. (1996). *The Witch Doctors: What the Management Gurus are Saying, Why it Matters and How to Make Sense of it*. London: Heinemann.

Miller, D. (1996). 'A preliminary typology of organizational learning: synthesizing the literature'. *Journal of Management*, **22**, 485–505.

Miner, A. S. (1994). 'Seeking adaptive advantage: evolutionary theory and managerial action'. In Baum, J. A. C. and Singh, J. V. (Eds), *Evolutionary Dynamics of Organizations*. New York: Oxford University Press, 76–89.

Miner, A., Bassoff, P. and Moorman, C. (2001). 'Organizational improvisation and learning: a field study'. *Administrative Science Quarterly*, **46**, 304–37.

Mintzberg, H. and McHugh, A. (1985). 'Strategy formation in an adhocracy'. *Administrative Science Quarterly*, **30**, 160–97.

Moorman, C. and Miner, A. (1995). *Walking the Tightrope: Improvisation and Information in New Product Development*. Report No. 95-101. Cambridge, MA: Marketing Science Institute.

Moorman, C. and Miner, A. (1998a). 'Organizational improvisation and organizational memory'. *Academy of Management Review*, **23**, 4, 698–723.

Moorman, C. and Miner, A. (1998b). 'The convergence between planning and execution: improvisation in new product development'. *Journal of Marketing*, **62**, 3, 1–20.

Morgan, G. (1997). *Images of Organization*, 2nd ed. Newbury Park, CA: Sage.

Orlikowski, W. J. (1996). 'Improvising organizational transformation over time: a situated change perspective'. *Information Systems Research*, **7**, 1, 63–92.

Orlikowski, W. J. and Hoffman, J. D. (1997). 'An improvisational model for change management: the case of groupware technologies'. *Sloan Management Review*, Winter, 11–21.

Ortony, A. (1993). *Metaphor and Thought*. Cambridge: Cambridge University Press.

Pearson, C. M., Clair, J. A., Misra, S. K. and Mitroff, I. I. (1997). 'Managing the unthinkable'. *Organizational Dynamics*, **25**, 2, 51–64.

Pentland, B. T. and Reuter, H. H. (1994). 'Organizational routines as grammars of action'. *Administrative Science Quarterly*, **39**, 484–510.

Peplowski, K. (1998). 'The process of improvising'. *Organization Science*, **9**, 5, 560–1.

Perls, F. S. (1969). *Ego, Hunger, and Aggression: The Beginning of Gestalt Therapy*. New York: Random House.

Perry, L. T. (1991). 'Strategic improvising: how to formulate and implement competitive strategies in concert'. *Organizational Dynamics*, **19**, 4, 51–64.

Peters, T. J. (1992). *Liberation Management: The Necessary Disorganization for the Nanosecond Nineties*. New York: Alfred A. Knopf.

Peters, T. J. (1994). *The Tom Peters Seminar*. New York: Vintage Books.

Pfeffer, J. (1992). *Managing with Power: Politics and Influence in Organizations*. Boston, MA: Harvard Business School Press.

Plach, T. (1980). *The Creative use of Music in Group Therapy*. Springfield, IL: Charles C. Thomas.

Powers, C. (1981). 'Role imposition or role improvisation: some theoretical principles'. *The Economic and Social Review*, **12**, 4, 287–99.

Ranson, S., Hinings, B. and Greenwood, R. (1980). 'The structuring of organizational structures'. *Administrative Science Quarterly*, **25**, 1–17.

Ricoeur, P. (1978). *The Philosophy of Paul Ricoeur: An Anthology of his Work*. Reagan, C. and Stewart, D. (Eds). Boston: Beacon Press.

Ries, A. and Trout, J. (1986). *Marketing Warfare*. New York: Pluve.

Roberts, W. (1991). *Leadership Secrets of Attila the Hun*. New York: Warner Books.

Roberts, W. and Ross, B. (1996). *Make it So: Leadership Lessons from Star Trek: The Next Generation*. New York: Pocket Books.

Schullian, D. and Schoen, M. (1948). *Music and Medicine*. New York: Henry Schuman.

Senge, P. M. (1990). *The Fifth Discipline: The Art and Practice of the Learning Organization*. London: Century Business.

Sewell, G. (1998). 'The discipline of teams: the control of team-based industrial work through electronic and peer surveillance'. *Administrative Science Quarterly*, **43**, 397–428.

Shankar, R. (1968). *My Music, My Life*. New York: Simon & Schuster.

Sharron, A. (1983). 'Time and space bias in group solidarity: action and process in musical improvisation'. *International Social Science Review*, **58**, 4, 222–30.

Southworth, J. S. (1983). 'Improvisation for nonmusicians: a workshop approach'. *Journal of Creative Behavior*, **17**, 3, 195–205.

Stacey, R. E., Griffin, D. and Shaw, P. (2000). *Complexity and Management: Fad or Radical Challenge to Systems Thinking?* London: Routledge.

Towse, E. and Flower, C. (1993). 'Levels of interaction in group improvisation'. In Heal, M. and Wigram, T. (Eds), *Music Therapy in Health and Education*. London: Kingsley, 73–81.

Tsoukas, H. (1991). 'The missing link: a transformational view of metaphors in organizational science'. *Academy of Management Review*, **16**, 3, 566–85.

Tsoukas, H. (1993). 'Analogical reasoning and knowledge generation in organizational theory'. *Organization Studies*, **14**, 3, 323–46.

Turner, R. (1970). *Family Interaction*. New York: Wiley.

Turner, R. (1980). 'Strategy for developing an integrated role theory'. *Humboldt Journal of Social Relations*, **7**.

Turner, R. (1985). 'Unanswered questions in the convergence between structuralist and interactionist role theories'. In Helle, H. J. and Eisenstadt, S. N. (Eds), *Micro-Sociological Theory: Perspectives on Sociological Theory*. London: Sage, 22–36.

Voyer, J. J. and Faulkner, R. R. (1989). 'Organizational cognition in a jazz ensemble'. *Empirical Studies of the Art*, **7**, 1, 57–77.

Weick, K. E. (1979). *The Social Psychology of Organizing*, 2nd ed. New York: McGraw-Hill.

Weick, K. E. (1980). 'Blind spots in organizational theorizing'. *Group and Organization Studies*, **5**, 2, 178–88.

Weick, K. E. (1993). 'Organizational redesign as improvisation'. In Huber, G. P. and Glick, W. H. (Eds), *Organizational Change and Redesign*. New York: Oxford University Press, 346–79.

Weick, K. E. (1998). 'Introductory essay: improvisation as a mindset for organizational analysis'. *Organization Science*, **9**, 5, 543–55.

Weick, K. E. (1999). 'The aesthetic of imperfection in organizations'. In Cunha, M. P. and Marques, C. A. (Eds), *Readings in Organization Science*. Lisbon: ISPA, 541–63.

Zack, M. (2000). 'Jazz improvisation and organizing: once more from the top'. *Organization Science*, **11**, 227–34.

Zinker, J. C. (1977). *The Creative Process in Gestalt Therapy*. New York: Brunner/Mazel.

Zinker, J. C. (1994). *In Search of Good Form*. San Francisco: Jossey-Bass.

[22]

The complexity of improvisation and the improvisation of complexity: Social science, art and creativity

Alfonso Montuori

ABSTRACT   The concept of improvisation has become increasingly popular in the discourse of organizational theory. This paper explores several aspects of improvisation, in the context of musical, organizational, and everyday activities, in order to address some of the philosophical and practical issues relevant to this emerging interest. Connections are made between the modernist concept of organization and scholarly inquiry, and post-modern or complexity-based approaches that stress creativity as an emergent property of the relationship between order and disorder. It concludes by suggesting that the study of improvisation demands a profound immersion in (inster-)subjectivity, emotions, time, aesthetics, performance, and social creativity, none of which have traditionally been the focus of organization and management studies, or the social sciences in general. It also suggests that the practice of social sciences itself should reflect upon, and attempt to incorporate these elements.

KEYWORDS   aesthetics ▪ complexity ▪ creativity ▪ disorder ▪ improvisation ▪ order organizational theory ▪ social science

We social scientists would do well to hold back our eagerness to control that world which we so imperfectly understand. The fact of our imperfect understanding should not be allowed to feed our anxiety and so increase the need to control. Rather, our studies could be inspired by a more ancient, but today less honored motive: a curiosity about the world of which we are part. The rewards of such work are not power but beauty.

(Bateson, 1972: 269)

Introduction

This article was sparked by my attendance at a conference in Rio de Janeiro. The location was obviously enticing, and even more important, perhaps, was the theme of the Rio conference: complexity, and in particular the epistemological and philosophical work on complexity found in the staggering, encyclopedic work of the French 'thinker' Edgar Morin. At the heart of this article is my belief that there is an important and potentially fruitful connection between improvisation and the lived experience of complexity, and that improvisation and creativity are capacities we would do well to develop in an increasingly unpredictable, complex, and at times chaotic existence. The writing style of this article is unusual for some academic publications, as it incorporates first-person narratives. It reflects my belief that in order to understand, and also live the phenomenon of improvisation, and in order to draw from the arts as a metaphor for both organization and for social science, it behooves us to incorporate 'performative' and other 'subjective' elements into our own scholarship. In that way, we may perhaps speak of the social arts and sciences, rather than simply the social sciences, heeding Bateson's (2002: 237) warning that 'rigor alone is paralytic death, but imagination alone is insanity' (Manghi, in press).

Despite the inroads of feminist and postmodern scholarship, the discourse of social science, and organization theory in particular, has historically privileged objective over subjective, rational over emotional, and theory over experience (Polkinghorne, 1983; Rosenau, 1992). Arguing for the relevance of psychoanalysis to organization studies, Gabriel (2001: 140) states that we still think of organizations as 'orderly places where people behave in a rational, business-like way.' This is particularly interesting when we consider our own lived experience of organizations. I suspect that most of us would admit that a rational and orderly view of organizations hardly does justice to the Byzantine complexities of life in academia or the private sector. In his valorization of aesthetics in organizations, Strati (1999) has similarly critiqued the discourse of organization theory and management studies as putting forth an ideal type that is fundamentally rational, logical, mental (perhaps in both senses of the term), and deeply disembodied. Anything (or anyone) emotional, subjective, or aesthetic was considered fundamentally unsuitable for organizations and for the study of organizations, according to Strati.

I believe that the concept and the practice of improvisation pose a clear challenge to traditional ways of thinking about social science, organization, and action. As I use it here, it is a musical metaphor, and therefore brings in all the elements from the arts that were successfully avoided by the social sciences. Jazz improvisation valorizes subjectivity, emotion, the aesthetic, but also the openness and uncertainty that go against the fundamental goals of prediction and control so highly valued by the traditional sciences. A defining quality of creative improvisation is precisely the generation of the unpredictable, the unusual, the unforeseen, within the pre-existing structures of the song form, navigating the edge between innovation and tradition (Berliner, 1994). In jazz improvisation, a commonly shared goal is to create within a musical and social context, requiring both control and spontaneity, constraints and possibilities, innovation and tradition, leading and supporting.

Improvisation and creativity are, as we shall see deeply paradoxical processes. Taking improvisation seriously arguably means addressing the very way we think. In Rio, Morin passionately articulates his vision of 'complex thought.' Critiquing the stress on reductionistic, decontextualizing, and disjunctive ways of thinking, he proposes the need for a thinking that recognizes both part and whole, contextualizes, and connects, as articulated in his magnum opus, the five-volume *La méthode* (Morin, 1977, 1980, 1984, 1991, 1992, 1994, 2001). He argues that in order to understand complexity we need to change the way we think: a thought that privileges simplicity and reduction and is predicated on the elimination of complexity is not suitable for addressing many complex phenomena because at the heart of their complexity lies precisely the irreducibility of that complexity. One key element is breaking down limiting hierarchical binary opposition such as science/art, innovation/tradition, serious/playful, order/disorder. In a similar vein, Beech and Cairns (2001) have critiqued dichotomous thinking in these pages and proposed postdichotomous ways of thinking that reflect the complexity of life, and do not attempt to reduce it to the mutilated simplicity and disjunction of binary oppositions. This project embarks on a similar journey and is sympathetic to the efforts of these fellow travelers. It is in the context of Morin's complex thought that I present the following ideas, and with a nod and a wink to my brothers in Strathclyde, Rio is my point of departure for this essay.

The soul of Rio

It's one o'clock in the morning, and we are walking back to the Hotel Gloria in Rio de Janeiro after a gargantuan dinner in a Churrascheria just off the beach at Copacabana. There's five of us here, part of a larger Italian contingent in Rio for an international conference. As with any conference, we are here also to enjoy each other's company, traveling thousands of miles to spend time with friends we rarely see, and certainly not in such a spectacular setting. Caught up in the legend of Brazilian football, and fueled by a few caipirinhas, a lovely and deceptively potent concoction of sugar cane firewater, sugar, and limes, we can't pass up the opportunity to head for the beach and look for a game. We find two local boys kicking a ball around, and before we know it we are playing football on the sand where so many legendary players enjoyed their first games. We are eager to show off to the boys and to each other, but we soon become aware of the very different conditions the sand creates. The ball reacts quirkily, unpredictably. Our balance is unsteady in the sand, the ground beneath our feet gives way. This is not grass, or any kind of turf we're used to. The skills that worked so well on grass, or on any hard field, somehow do not carry over to the sand of Copacabana. On top of that, our rusty skills are more than weighed down by staggering quantities of Brazilian meat, lubricated by numerous caipirinhas. It's almost as if we are playing a different game.

The conditions lead us to modify our game, to deal with unforeseen elements, with the complexity and uncertainty of a new and different environment. We begin to improvise. We explore the constraints created by the new conditions, but also the possibilities they offer. A breakdown in our normal way of practicing the game of football has elicited a renewed challenge to our capacities. It is inviting us to draw on our ability to go beyond the already known, and explore the possibilities of the present. We are improvising our game. We know the basic rules of football, but like so many before us, we improvise a goal with jackets instead of goalposts, and because we're not playing a game with 11 players on each side, we improvise a (tacit) set of 'rules.' These tell us when it is appropriate to shoot at goal, when we should pass the ball to someone else, and what constitutes annoyingly hogging the ball as opposed to simply clowning around. We improvise the way we handle the ball, we make up new ways of playing within the context of the skills and rules we already know through years of playing . . .

Life in a complex world, and a life which reflects and values the complexity of *both* self and world, requires the ability to improvise – to deal with, and indeed to create, the unforeseen, the *surprise*. Interestingly, the Latin root of improvisation is *improvisus*, or unforeseen. Increasingly, it seems, life in or out of organizations requires of us the ability to both *react* appropriately to unforeseen events, and actually *generate* those events – to act creatively and innovatively. Football players have to react to surprising moves from the opposition, and also generate moves that catch opposing players off guard.

They have to feed off the opposition's mistakes, the contingency of the bouncing ball, and the condition of the pitch. A jazz musician both generates novelty, by making rhythmic, harmonic, or melodic choices that are surprising, and reacts to the novelty generated by his or her fellow band-members. A piano player might place an unusual chord behind a soloist in what would normally be a predictable harmonic progression. This creates a slightly different context, a surprise, which can lead the experienced improvising soloist to find new ways to navigate a song. This kind of creative dialog is at the heart of much of what makes jazz a unique art form. It is an example of self-organizing social creativity in small groups (Bailey, 1993; Berliner, 1994; Hatch, 1999; Monson, 1996; Montuori & Purser, 1999). Creativity and improvisation might be said to serve at least a dual role, therefore. They allow us to adapt in our own way to complex environments, and they allow us to express our own (inner) complexity through the performance of our interaction with the world. The concept of improvisation is, I believe, crucial to the existential reality of complexity.

The challenge of complexity and creativity

In Rio, many speakers remind us of how our lives today are riddled with complexity, with the unforeseen, the ambiguous, the uncertain – in science, in the economy, in ethics, and indeed just about every aspect of life. Indeed, disorder, uncertainty, and individual subjectivity are increasingly being studied in the human and natural sciences (Morin, 1994; Ogilvy, 1989, 1992; Polkinghorne, 1983; Rosenau, 1992). Homogenizing, ordered and ordering visions of the universe, of human civilization, of nature and of progress are being dismantled (Bocchi & Ceruti, 2002; Morin & Kern, 1999). The sciences of chaos and complexity and the discourse of postmodernism show us the profound role of disorder, chance, uncertainty, and contingency in the world (Taylor, 2001).

In the traditional Newtonian scientific paradigm, order was king, privileged above disorder, chaos, and noise. Our understanding of the relationship between order and disorder was in terms of a binary opposition, and indeed a hierarchical opposition. One of the most interesting shifts in recent scientific thinking, in particular through the sciences of chaos and complexity, has been a deeper understanding of the mutually constitutive relationship between order and disorder, information and noise. This shift also reflects a transition from a fundamentally static worldview to one that is process oriented. Rather than seeing order as fundamental and unchanging, we are now seeing an ongoing process of order–disorder that is the hallmark of self-organization (Morin, 1992). As Taylor (2001: 121) writes, 'disorder does not simply destroy order, structure, and organization, but is also a condition of their formation and reformation.'

Self-organization has been defined variously as making meaning out of randomness (Atlan, 1986), or the spontaneous emergence of a coordinated and collective behavior in a population of elements (Gandolfi, 1999). One of the key aspects of self-organization is the creation of order out of chaos, the integration of elements perceived as disorder into a larger, more encompassing organization. We might think of Kuhnian paradigms as an analogy. What is inside the paradigm is considered order, what is outside is disorder. Anomalies on the edge of the paradigm, those things the paradigm cannot account for, may initially seem like noise, disorderly phenomena that cannot be accounted for. Indeed, the history of chaos theory itself (Gleick, 1987) shows how turbulent phenomena such as water flowing out of a faucet were rejected out of hand as subjects of study for the longest time because they seemed simply inexplicable. Yet it is the study of these anomalies that led to the development of the new science of dynamical systems, also known as chaos theory. In this sense, chaos theory as a field of study was itself a self-organizing process, the spontaneous emergence of a coordinated and collective behavior in a population of elements (researchers), making meaning out of (apparent) randomness.

Research on creativity has some very relevant things to say about this. It shows that 'creative individuals are more at home with complexity and disorder than most people' (Barron, 1958: 261). In fact, they have what is called a preference for complexity over simplicity – they are intrigued, puzzled, excited by complexity rather than afraid of it. Creative thought is marked by the active search for phenomena that destabilize order, that puzzle cognitive schemata and cannot be immediately understood. Creativity involves constant organizing, dis-organizing, and re-organizing. It involves actively breaking down assumptions, givens, traditions, pushing boundaries and moving out of comfort zones.

'At the very heart of the creative process,' writes Barron (1990: 249) 'is this ability to shatter the rule of law and regularity in the mind.' Creativity means shaking things up, both inside ourselves and in the world around us, and constant re-organizing of both cognitive schemata and, to a greater or lesser extent, the domain of the creative person's activity. The term 'ego-strength,' as used by Barron (1990), refers to the capacity to rally from setback, to learn from experience, to be a constantly dis-organizing and re-organizing system without falling apart completely. Creative thought seeks to make sense of phenomena that appear to be chaotic, and seeks to create a higher order simplicity – one that incorporates the complex, disorderly phenomena in a broader, more inclusive, more open perspective. Creative individuals, it seems, are ready to abandon old classifications, in an ongoing process of creation and re-creation. Self-organization in creative persons becomes what Morin (1994) calls self-eco-*re*-organization, suggesting that the nature of the organization changes as well, and that it is an ongoing process of self-renewal that always happens in a context, in an environment, never in isolation and abstraction (Montuori, 1992).

Following Morin, we can think of knowing as an ongoing process of *self-eco-re-organization*. Self-, because knowing involves a knower; Eco-, because a knower always exists in a context, in a given (but not necessarily 'known') world; Organization, because our knowledge is in fact organized, often with principles we are hardly aware of, because of history, habit, culture, reflection, and so on, but organized in some form or other; Re-, because knowing involves a constant active process of creative exploration and re-organization, and because our organization of knowledge is regularly re-organized through the process of existence and participation in the world. Knowing arises through the interplay of subject and object. Inquiry into the world and self-inquiry become interwoven in a process of self-eco-inquiry. In that case, if I accept that knowledge is always *my* knowing situated in a context, then the issue is not cleansing myself of exogenous elements to achieve pure, objective knowledge. Rather, the challenge becomes making my self more transparent in the process and acknowledging who I am in all of this.

Am I *observing* the universe, or am I *participating* in it (von Foerster, 1990)? Am I standing outside it, or am I in the middle of it? Am I watching the football game, or am I playing it? Am I listening to the music or am I performing it? If life is the game, or the song that we are playing, then, Von Foerster argues, we are also playing it, not only watching or listening.

A participatory view suggests that we are embodied and embedded in this world, not observing it dispassionately with a God's eye view from nowhere (Nagel, 1989). No self without an eco. No text without context. Even if I just observe life, it is always me observing it, with my history, my choices, my feelings, my relationships, my choices. In our everyday lives, we cannot eliminate exogenous variables, we cannot eliminate emotions, subjectivity, contingency, chance, we cannot replicate the pristine environment of the laboratory. To participate in life clearly does not mean that one cannot reflect on it. But one cannot reflect on it with a privileged view that transcends all contexts and all situatedness, or with the hope of being able to control and predict the way we might control and predict the behavior of machines. 'Life is not like that,' as Bateson (1972: 438) famously stated in reference to the dream of linear control (Manghi, in press).

Life is participation and participation is creation and improvisation, because life does not occur in a vacuum, it occurs always in a network of inter-retro-actions and of organization, in a constant play of order, disorder, and organization and ongoing learning. Improvisation and the creative process may be viewed as an ongoing process of learning and inquiry, learning-in-organizing, as Gherardi (1999) calls it, a distributed, provisional, embodied process.

Presenting Rio

Back at the Rio conference, our improvisations move into a new realm, as we participate in the presentations we have all come to attend. Many lengthy and fascinating papers have been read by the presenters while other presentations were extemporaneous. My friends and I have no intention of reading anything to our captive audience. There is something profoundly different about a paper that is read, and a presentation that emerges extemporaneously in the moment. We choose to improvise. But what does this mean? Surely it does not mean that we say just anything that comes into our mind, or that we choose to do a sloppy job, that we are not knowledgeable about our subjects, or that we have temporarily mislaid our papers. It does not mean that the written paper represents the culmination of our work, of which the extemporaneous presentation is merely a pale copy, an inferior derivative.

No, to improvise (or extemporize) here means something else. It means that we have chosen to think on our feet, to embody our presentation in the moment, including remarks which could only be made within the specific context of the conference, the previous speakers, with references to events, ideas, and moods that could simply not have been predicted when actually writing the paper. To improvise means to draw on all our knowledge and personal experience, and focus it on the very moment we are living in, in that very context. It requires a different discipline, a different way of organizing our thoughts and actions. It requires, and at its best elicits, a social virtuosity which reflects our state of mind, our perception of who and where we are, and a willingness to take risks, to let go of the safety of the ready-made, the already written, and to think, create, and 'write' on the spot. Is this an inferior form of intellectual 'production,' or is it in fact an alternative form, grounded in the existential, temporal, and contextual reality of human interaction?

I struggle to decide whether I really can improvise in French, one of the languages of the conferences along with Spanish and Portuguese. Italian, Dutch, and English, my main languages, are not an option. To improvise freely, I feel I need to be able to let go of worrying about syntax, about vocabulary. I must be able to let go of my language and not be constantly self-conscious about it, in the same way that a great jazz improviser does not continually have to think about the technical dimensions of his or her playing, and can thus simply create. Morin storms ahead in what he calls 'Fritagnol,' his all-purpose 'Mediterranean' language combining 'Fr–Français–ita–Italien–gnol–Espagnol.' Miraculously, he is understood not just by the French-, Spanish- and Italian-speaking contingent, but also the Portuguese speakers. I decide to go with my approximation of French, a language I read well but very rarely get the chance to speak.

Improvisation: A dance of constraints and possibilities

In the popular mind, improvisation is often misunderstood (Sawyer, 1999). When we say something is improvised we often mean something that was done to face some unforeseen circumstance, going back to the *improvisus* of the Latin etymology. It is not uncommon that the improvised is still seen as ultimately inferior. In some cases, the original program that was to be followed had to be deviated from, and the improvisation is seen as the next best thing. Improvisation can mean we had to do something for which there was no pre-established set of rules, no recipe, or that there was a breakdown in the correct procedure. The message is, things will be right again when the proper procedures are in place, when the order is restored.

One definition of the word extemporize – a synonym of improvise – in Webster's dictionary tells us it means to do something in a 'makeshift' manner. Makeshift, in turn, is defined as doing something in a crude and temporary manner. Improvisation is thought of as making the best of things, while awaiting a return to the way things should be done. Improvisation is an exception, something we can 'fall back on' when things don't go the way they should.

But can we really say that speaking without notes at a conference is somehow 'less' than the written word? That the presentation is inferior? Or does it show a different set of skills and capacities in the reader? The kind of thinking that relegates improvisation to a lesser status operates within a disjunctive paradigm in which order is privileged over disorder, a paradigm of either/or, dichotomous thinking. In a dialogical relationship of order–disorder improvisation takes on a whole new meaning. It shows the potentially generative function of disorder, and its continual presence in our world, not only in our need to react to external aleatory, chance events, but also in our need to create (Gabriel, 2002).

246   Human Relations 56(2)

Improvisers tell a story – they *are* a story (Kearney, 1988). They participate in the world, rather than simply observing it, and create a narrative that, interwoven with other narratives, develops a tapestry of stories. The improvisational process is one of laying a path down in walking, a co-evolutionary process that is not deterministic either because of 'laws of nature,' or because of the 'nature of laws' as outlined by some sociologists. But it is not random, either: the improvisational process occurs in a context, and it is performed by someone, with a history, with cultural, economic, political, and philosophical contexts, with perspectives, habits, and eccentricities, with the ability to make *choices* in context, which choices in turn affect the context.

Jazz musicians obviously improvise not because they cannot read music, or because they have temporarily mislaid the music. They have a completely different perspective and set of values. Their assumption is not that there is one correct way of doing things, one score, one right set of notes to play, one order, but rather that we can collaboratively create through the interaction of constraints and possibilities rather than *either* order *or* disorder (Ceruti, 1994). In their tradition, they go beyond the score, which is often minimal by the standards of western classical music, beyond interpretation of the notes to melodic and harmonic (re-)interpretation of the song itself. Improvisation involves a constant dialogic between order and disorder, tradition and innovation, security and risk, the individual and the group and the composition. In a jazz group, the degree of discretion for the individual musicians is considerable. The musician knows s/he has to get from A to Z, but how s/he does it, how a solo is performed, or even how a soloist is supported (by the rhythm section, the drummer's rhythmic accents, the piano player's choice of chords or 'comping'), is, within certain mutually agreed upon constraints (the group's aesthetic, mood of the piece, but also technical competence, etc.) wide open. And the creative ways in which the musician deviates from the expected are one of the main criteria for assessing mastery.

Within the context of a shared harmonic and social framework (in the sense of a community of practice), and certain well-developed personal and technical capacities, improvisation frees musicians to interpret and create together in a musical conversation. One need only listen to a jazz 'standard' like 'My Funny Valentine' in the interpretations of three different jazz musicians, say Billie Holiday, Miles Davis, and Coleman Hawkins, to see how the same basic song has been transformed into three totally different emotional, technical, and aesthetic performances while using fundamentally the same harmonic framework. The interpretations reflect the individual musician's, and the band's, aesthetic sense, subjectivity, and emotional, stylistic, and technical interpretation. A jazz musician must have a 'sound,' a 'personality,' to a far greater extent than a classical musician, because the latter has no choice about which notes to play. The musicians take a 'traditional' piece, a 'standard,' and re-interpret it, adding their own musical perspective by reharmonizing the chord changes, using new and different instrumentation, slowing the song down or speeding it up, and so on. This provides a context for their collective improvisation – a form of musical dialogue, requiring constant attention, negotiation, listening (Purser & Montuori, 1994). In creative improvised collaboration, both the creative process and the creative product are an emergent property of the interactions.

I find the same process in the long walks I take with my colleagues along the beaches of Rio. We have a shared background of knowledge – a horizon – and a personal knowledge base, and we are attentive to each other, spurring each other on in explorations and speculations, occasionally poking critically at some ideas, laughing, playing with ideas as we walk around the Jardim Botanico plotting books and other projects (Manghi, in press). It's clear to me that these are collective improvisations. Sometimes conversations sound great, other times the 'band' doesn't gel. Maybe somebody plays too loud or too long, or is just boring, or there isn't that shared rapport, or we're just tired. But the dialogue, the performance of our knowledge – and our friendship – is an art as well as a science. In the performing, the two are united.

The loss of improvisation – and more

How did improvisation get a bad name, and disappear from western music? Improvisation is central to most forms of music around the world (Bailey, 1993). It was standard practice in western music until about 1800, when it was displaced by two key events (Goehr, 1992). Before 1800, soloists improvised and embellished during their performance. Keyboard bass parts were largely improvised, and figured to suggest no more than a very basic chordal outline, in much the same way they are in jazz. Composers from Clementi to Mozart to Beethoven to Chopin were renowned improvisers, and even engaged in what jazz musicians call 'cutting contests': pitting the improvisational abilities of musicians against each other. The great Franz Liszt felt far too much time was devoted to the performance of notated music, and not nearly enough to virtuoso extemporization, at which he excelled.

After 1800 or so, with the birth of the concept of the 'genius composer' and of copyright, musicians began increasingly to perform scores strictly as written. Even cadenzas, historically an opportunity for the soloist to extemporize or improvise, began to be written out. The composer's musical vision became of paramount importance, and could be 'enforced' with copyrighted musical scores that ensured musicians performed the score as intended by the composer. The cult of the genius (Montuori & Purser, 1995) that arose along with copyright brought with it the desire to hear the score performed exactly as it was intended by the composer, without the interjections of the performers, whose role was subsequently redefined and reduced. Musical performance was now completely controlled, in order to ensure that it would reflect accurately the composer's intentions. What we gained in the correct performance of great works also entailed a concomitant loss in the value placed on improvisation, and the self-organization of performance by the performers.

A third, organizational factor comes into play. With a written score a musician can be monitored for the performance of every note. Symphonic music is performed by an orchestra with a clearly hierarchical organization. The composer is at the top, like the founder of a large corporation, viewed as the one source of creativity, the 'brains' of the organization. Then we move down to the conductor, the soloist, the first violin, the section leaders, and so on, who are literally the organization's 'hands.' Without in any way wishing to downplay the skill, creativity, and art involved in the production of symphonic music itself, the organization created to produce it is closely parallel what we typically think of as a bureaucratic hierarchy, and the historical parallels are considerable (Attali, 1985). The range and extent of contributions from individual performers is far more limited in symphonic music than in jazz: the degree of *discretion* is much more limited. The degree of *control* and *prediction* is much greater.

Higgins (1991) discusses the effects of the focus on performing scores on music and aesthetics in the West by pointing out that musical aestheticians began focusing on the musical score, and the correct performance of the musical score, at the expense of performance, emotion, context (where is the performance held), and subjectivity. She goes on to state that improvisation came to be viewed as an aberration, precisely because it reflected a lack of score, a valorization of subjectivity and emotionality which was, among other things, associated with more primitive and African elements. Improvisation became somewhat of a dirty word, referring to a less developed, preliterate form of music that had been superseded by the order and rationality of the western form (Goehr, 1992; Sawyer, 1999). This development parallels a trend in the West to focus on the objective, the measurable, the rational and the ordered, at the expense of that which appears subjective, qualitative, emotive, and disordered. It also reflects the privileging of certain special individuals as composers, others only as performers, and others as listeners, much the same way that social science has privileged the knowledge of expert researchers over those being researched. Much of social science thinking, and in consequence, much of the literature of management and organization theory, has been deeply influenced by this approach, although critiques have been emerging with increasing conviction over the past few decades.

The phenomenology of expertise and the experience of improvisation

The research of Dreyfus and Dreyfus (1986) into the phenomenology of expertise, developed specifically in reaction to the computer metaphor of expert systems, shows clearly that experts in any subject, whether chess players or racing car drivers or musicians, achieve a level of proficiency whereby they are constantly improvising. They know the rules, but do not have to think about them. They have developed the ability to act spontaneously and intuitively without needing to refer to rulebooks, without feeling they always have to stick to the rules (independence of judgment), and viewing mistakes as opportunities – tolerating, in other words, the ambiguity of unusual situations. The intuitive capacity Dreyfus and Dreyfus speak of is perhaps most apparent in chess masters who can play 15 or more games simultaneously, and spend only seconds looking at a board before they make a move and literally move on. There is little if any conscious reflection going on here. Rather, they respond in much the same pre-reflective way that a good driver would to a road hazard, a footballer to a scoring opportunity, or a musician to the context of his or her improvisation.

In musical improvisation, a genius like Miles Davis would utilize a 'mistake' (a note that from a certain perspective might be thought of as a mistake) of his, or of a fellow player, to explore different possibilities (Chambers, 1998). It's also apparent in games like football, where a bounce of the ball, or a mistake by an opposing player is utilized to create new possibilities, and in speaking a language, where grammatical constraints actually provide us with a set of possibilities for communication. Constraints themselves become avenues for possibilities (Ceruti, 1994).

Research into the phenomenology of jazz improvisation (Nardone, 1996) has stressed this ongoing dialogical nature of the process, this dance between two extremes. Jazz musicians immerse themselves in the technical aspects of the music only to let go of any conscious concern for them during performance. They stress the importance of being able to solo, but must also be capable side-persons, and support others. They respect – and indeed are in often in awe of – the tradition, and their forefathers and mothers – but are also looking to push the art forward. Indeed, Nardone's research suggests that the key element of the phenomenology of impro-visation is precisely a series of 'dialectical paradoxes,' between immersion in the tradition and taking risks, between standing out as an individual voice and being supportive of others' voices. This brings us to a key point in this article: in order to understand creativity and improvisation, it is necessary to develop a different way of thinking, one which might be described as post-formal, paradoxical, dialectical, post-dichotomous, or complex.

Complexity and going beyond binary opposition

Nardone's phenomenological research of the lived experience of improvisa-tion in jazz musicians found that 'dialectical paradoxes' were a central element. In other words, the musicians trust their own skills enough to take risks, they sustained, and were sustained by musical others, and explored musical territories that were both familiar and unfamiliar (because inter-preted anew during every performance). A recurring theme in the literature on creativity and improvisation is that the creative person and the creative process both have these seemingly paradoxical qualities. I want to suggest that one reason why improvisation and creativity have been so problematic in our society – mythologized, pathologized, misunderstood, glorified, and trivialized (Hampden-Turner, 1999; Montuori & Purser, 1995) – is that paradoxical phenomena are hard to understand because we are not used to 'thinking together' terms that we have, culturally and historically, come to view as oppositions. We have, following Morin's terms, thought about these phenomena in ways that are simplistic, disjunctive, and decontextualized. I have touched on many of these oppositions throughout this article, focusing for instance on the importance of a dialogical understanding of order–disorder to the new science of complexity and the phenomenon of self-organization. Other terms might include risk/security, discipline/spontaneity, individual/group. Traditionally, we think of them disjunctively as either/or (either you're secure or at risk, disciplined or spontaneous), when in fact in creative persons they might manifest as being secure enough (in one's musical capacities) to take risks, being disciplined enough to be spontaneous (walking the line between being rigid and chaotic). Order without any unpredictable, disordered elements is complete homogeneity. Disorder without any order is chaos, in the popular sense of the word. In his discussion of complexity theory, Kauffman (1995) echoes the earlier findings of creativity researchers (Barron, 1990) regarding order and disorder, and generalizes them to all complex systems. He writes that 'Networks near the edge of chaos – the compromise between order and surprise – appear best able to coordinate complex activities, and best able to evolve as well' (p. 26).

Hampden-Turner (1999) points to the recursive, cybernetic relationship between the characteristics associated with the creative person. He summarizes the research by writing that

> The creative person is by turns open and closed, tentative and certain, and flirting with disorder to create a better order. He or she is intuitive but then passes this over in favor of the rational mind for thorough assessment. The creative person scores higher on manifest anxiety, reporting more often despair, depression, anger, sorrow, and doubt; yet the creative person also recovers from these states far faster, showing ego-strength and reporting hope, elation, delight, happiness, and confidence. In other words, creatives rally more easily from setback, shift more readily between moods, and seem to destabilize more readily in order to reach higher equilibria. They are, from a mental health standpoint, both 'sicker' and 'healthier,' more vulnerable to what happens around them yet more able to solve the problems that arise.
>
> (p. 19)

According to the research, creative persons score higher both on measures of pathology and of psychological health. In other words, they have access to a much broader range of human experience. In the area of gender the research indicates that creative individuals are not limited by stereotypical gender behaviors. They do not have either stereotypically 'male' or 'female' personality characteristics. Rather, they move freely across a spectrum of possible 'human' behaviors.

Based on his extensive research, Barron (1964: 81) states that the creative process itself embodies an ongoing tension. Creative individuals 'exemplify vividly in their persons the incessant dialectic between integration and diffusion, convergence and divergence, thesis and antithesis.' The creative process can be likened to a dialectical process, in which in special moments common antinomies are resolved or synthesized.

The creative process seems to share many characteristics with so-called 'post-formal thought,' an advanced developmental stage of cognitive maturity (Kegan, 1982) beyond the generally accepted highest stage of cognitive development (formal). Koplowitz (1978: 32, in Kegan, 1982: 229) writes that

> Formal operational thought is dualistic. It draws sharp distinctions between the knower and the known, between one object (or variable)

and another, and between pairs of opposites (e.g., good and bad). In post-formal operational thought, the knower is seen as unified with the known, various objects (and variables) are seen as part of a continuum, and opposites are seen as poles of one concept.

Post-formal thought displays characteristics that involve openness, a dialectical process, contextualization, and ongoing reevaluation, characteristics that they share with the findings of creativity research, and with Morin's 'complex thought.' All of these perspectives point to the need to go beyond a certain kind of dichotomous, decontextualizing, and simplifying thinking and develop capacities for postdichotomous, dialogical, contextualizing, complex thought. As I suggested earlier, I believe one of the reasons creativity and improvisation have remained so mysterious is precisely because of their paradoxical qualities. Developing a better understanding of the paradoxical nature of creative thought may allow us to approach creativity and improvisation more creatively.

Farewell to Rio

The sun sets over Rio as I take my cab to the airport. I carry with me a few photos of my friends and I in Rio. I take with me memories of Corcovado, of the beaches at Ipanema, of the red beach of Praia Vermelha, a little jewel right under the startling Sugarloaf that seems like a tiny and remote fishing village in the heart of Rio, of discussions and friendships, of warm nights spent by the pool of the Hotel Gloria, of days watching and listening to the brilliant improvisations of Edgar Morin and my friends in the lecture hall of Candido Mendes University, and a CD of Brazilian music, rather appropriately titled *The heart of Rio*, a gift from a new Brazilian friend.

Brazil seems a like a good place to ponder the nature of complexity and improvisation – a country known for very improvisational forms of football and music. Brazilian music also captures *saudade*, a feeling that has no translation in the English language. Bittersweet, perhaps, or, as the Belgian jazz harmonica player Toots Thielemans put it, between a tear and smile. Brazil holds within itself shocking joy and joie de vivre, and shocking suffering and abject poverty. It is a country of great extremes, and experiencing them all at once certainly does give a hint of saudade, of gratitude and sorrow for all the beauty and the misery right there under the open arms of the huge statue of Jesus, on Corcovado overlooking the city. A complex feeling if ever there was one.

Ogilvy (1989: 9), has argued that 'The pressure toward postmodernism is building from our lack of ability to overcome certain dualisms that are built into modern ways of knowing.' In this article I have pointed to many of these dualisms or oppositions, and argued that, in many cases, they prevent us from understanding phenomena such as improvisation and creativity that according to the research are paradoxical, complex, and involve cybernetic, recursive relationships between order and disorder, health and pathology, constraints and possibilities, and so on. I have also attempted to sketch out why I think that in order to understand improvisation in jazz and in life it is important for researchers to address subjectivity, and specifically their own subjectivity, since they are participating in the research process and not standing outside it. Research is both discovery and creation, an ongoing dialogue between subject and object, with the researcher both subject and object of the process. I have gone further and suggested that there may be different ways of thinking – postdichotmous (Beech & Cairns, 2001), post-formal (Kegan, 1982), or, following Morin, complex – that allow us to view the recursive and interdependent nature of these apparent oppositions, situating them in a larger context, and viewing them as 'dilemmas' (Hampden-Turner, 1999) to be reconciled anew every day, opportunities for creativity and improvisation.

Coda

As I write these pages it becomes painfully clear to me that, on the one hand, the traditional academic writing style is useful but dreadfully limited and limiting since it leaves out so much of who we are, originating as it did in a time when for science to be science, the author's individuality and subjectivity had to be eliminated in favor of universality and objectivity. On the other hand, finding new ways to write that are both scholarly and personal, both 'science' and 'art,' if that's not too pretentious, is extremely difficult, as I've come to find out writing these pages. It's actually easier to leave all the personal, ambiguous, contextual material out. It is ultimately easier, I believe to present just the context of justification, and leave out the messy context of discovery – or creation. But it is also a tremendous creative challenge to be more transparent, to be more fully present in one's work, a challenge that is beginning to be tackled by some scholars, and particularly by anthropologists and feminist scholars. Perhaps one key challenge is to find, like jazz musicians, a voice, or voices, that incorporate both subjective and objective, rational and emotional, theory and experience, risk and trust. This makes the task of being a social scientist/artist also a task of self-development, of finding one's own identity in dialogue with and through the world one is studying. Then indeed our work can become an inquiry into the dialogical and

254   Human Relations 56(2)

recursive relationship between subject and object, self and other, head and heart, an ongoing invitation to, and navigation of, the paradoxical nature of the creative process.

References

Atlan, H. *Tra il cristallo e il fumo. Saggio sull'organizzazione del vivente.* [Between smoke and crystal. The self-organization of the living.] Firenze: Hopefulmonster, 1986.

Attali, J. *Noise: The political economy of music.* Minneapolis: University of Minnesota Press, 1985.

Bailey, D. *Improvisation: Its nature and practice in music.* New York: Da Capo Press, 1993.

Barron, F. The psychology of imagination. *Scientific American,* 1958, *199,* 255–61.

Barron, F. The relationship of ego diffusion to creative perception. In C.W. Taylor (Ed.), *Widening horizons in creativity: The proceedings of the Fifth Utah Creativity Conference.* New York: Wiley, 1964, pp. 80–7.

Barron, F. *Creativity and psychological health.* Buffalo, NY: Creative Education Foundation, 1990.

Bateson, G. *Steps to an ecology of mind.* New York: Ballantine, 1972.

Bateson, G. *Mind and nature: A necessary unity.* Cresskill, NJ: Hampton Press, 2002.

Beech, N. & Cairns, G. Coping with change: The contribution of postdichotomous ontologies. *Human Relations,* 2001, *54,* 1303–23.

Berliner, P.F. *Thinking in jazz: The infinite art of improvisation.* Chicago: University of Chicago Press, 1994.

Bocchi, G. & Ceruti, M. *The narrative universe.* Cresskill, NJ: Hampton Press, 2002.

Ceruti, M. *Constraints and possibilities: The evolution of knowledge and knowledge of evolution.* New York: Gordon & Breach, 1994.

Chambers, J. *Milestones. The life and times of Miles Davis.* New York: Da Capo, 1998.

Dreyfus, S. & Dreyfus, H. *Mind over machine.* New York: Free Press, 1986.

Gabriel, Y. Psychoanalysis, psychodynamics, and organizations. In J. Henry, *Creative management.* London: Sage, 2001.

Gabriel, Y. *Essai:* On paragrammatic uses of organizational theory: A provocation. *Organization Studies,* 2002, *23,* 133–51.

Gandolfi, A. *Formicai, imperi, cervelli.* [Ant-hills, empires, and brains.] Torino: Bollati Boringhieri, 1999.

Gherardi, S. Learning as problem-driven or learning in the face of mystery? *Organization Studies,* 1999, *20*(1), 101–24.

Gleick, J. *Chaos.* New York: Viking, 1987.

Goehr, L. *The imaginary museum of musical works.* New York: Oxford University Press, 1992.

Hampden-Turner, C. Control, chaos, control: A cybernetic view of creativity. In R. Purser & A. Montuori (Eds), *Social creativity, 2.* Cresskill, NJ: Hampton Press, 1999.

Hatch, M.J. Exploring the empty spaces of organizing: How improvisational jazz helps redescribe organizational structure. *Organizational Studies,* 1999, *20*(1), 75–100.

Higgins, K. *The music of our lives.* Philadelphia, PA: Temple University Press, 1991.

Kauffman, S. *At home in the Universe. The search for the laws of self-organization and complexity.* New York: Oxford University Press, 1995.

Kearney, R. *The wake of imagination: Toward a postmodern culture.* Minneapolis: University of Minnesota Press, 1988.

Kegan, R. *The evolving self.* Cambridge: Harvard University Press, 1982.

Manghi, S. *The cat with wings: Ecology of mind and social practices.* Cresskill, NJ: Hampton Press, in press.

Monson, I. *Saying something: Jazz improvisation and interaction.* Chicago: University of Chicago Press, 1996.

Montuori, A. Chaos, creativity, and self-renewal. *World Futures, The Journal of General Evolution,* 1992, *35,* 193–209.

Montuori, A. & Purser, R. Deconstructing the lone genius myth: Towards a contextual view of creativity. *Journal of Humanistic Psychology,* 1995, *35*(3), 69–112.

Montuori, A. & Purser, R. (Eds). *Social creativity, 1.* Cresskill, NJ: Hampton Press, 1999.

Morin, E. *La méthode. Vol. 1. La nature de la nature I.* Paris: Seuil, 1977.

Morin, E. *La méthode. Vol. 2. La vie de la vie.* Paris: Seuil, 1980.

Morin, E. *Science avec conscience.* Paris: Fayard, 1984.

Morin, E. *La méthode. Vol. 4. Les idées.* Paris: Seuil, 1991.

Morin, E. *Method: Towards a study of humankind: The nature of nature.* New York: Lang, 1992.

Morin, E. *La complexité humaine.* [Human complexity.] Paris: Flammarion, 1994.

Morin, E. *La méthode. Vol. 5. L'identité humaine.* Paris: Seuil, 2001.

Morin, E. & Kern, A.B. *Homeland earth: A manifesto for the new millennium.* Cresskill, NJ: Hampton Press, 1999.

Nagel, T. *The view from nowhere.* New York: Oxford University Press, 1989.

Nardone, P. The experience of improvisation in music: A phenomenological, psychological analysis. Unpublished doctoral dissertation, Saybrook Institute, 1996.

Ogilvy, J. This postmodern business. *The Deeper News,* 1989, *1*(5), 2–23.

Ogilvy, J. Future studies and the human sciences: The case for normative scenarios. *Futures Research Quarterly,* 1992, *8*(2), 5–65.

Polkinghorne, D. *Methodology for the human sciences.* New York: SUNY Press, 1983.

Purser, R. & Montuori, A. Miles Davis in the classroom: Using the jazz ensemble metaphor for enhancing team learning. *Journal of Management Education,* 1994, *18*(1), 21–31.

Rosenau, P.M. *Post-modernism and the social sciences: Insights, inroads, and intrusions.* Princeton, NJ: Princeton University Press, 1992.

Sawyer, R.K. Improvisation. In M. Runco & S. Pritzker (Eds), *Encyclopedia of creativity, Volume 2.* San Diego: Academic Press, 1999.

Strati, A. *Organization and aesthetics.* Thousand Oaks, CA: Sage, 1999.

Taylor, M. *The emergence of complexity.* Chicago: University of Chicago Press, 2001.

Von Foerster, H. Ethics and second order cybernetics. Paper presented at Systèmes & thérapie familiale. Ethique, Idéologie, Nouvelles Méthodes. Congrès International. Paris, 4–6 October 1990.

Alfonso Montuori, PhD, is Associate Professor at the California Institute of Integral Studies. His research has focused on creativity and innovation, improvisation, and the epistemology of complexity. A former professional musician, his most recent books are *Social creativity, Vols 1 & 2,* co-edited with Ron Purser. He is Associate Editor of *World Futures,* and Series Editor of *Advances in Systems Theory, Complexity, and the Human Sciences* at Hampton Press.

[E-mail: montuori@inreach.com]

Part VI
Crafting Management and Management Studies

[23]

Crafting strategy

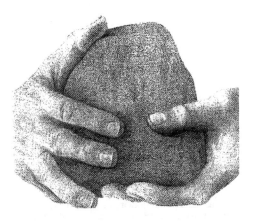

Henry Mintzberg

Imagine someone planning strategy. What likely springs to mind is an image of orderly thinking: a senior manager, or a group of them, sitting in an office formulating courses of action that everyone else will implement on schedule. The keynote is reason – rational control, the systematic analysis of competitors and markets, of company strengths and weaknesses, the combination of these analyses producing clear, explicit, full-blown strategies.

Now imagine someone *crafting* strategy. A wholly different image likely results, as different from planning as craft is from mechanization. Craft evokes traditional skill, dedication, perfection through the mastery of detail. What springs to mind is not so much thinking and reason as involvement, a feeling of intimacy and harmony with the materials at hand, developed through long experience and commitment. Formulation and implementation merge into a fluid process of learning through which creative strategies evolve.

My thesis is simple: the crafting image better captures the process by which effective strategies come to be. The planning image, long popular in the literature, distorts these processes and thereby misguides organizations that embrace it unreservedly.

In developing this thesis, I shall draw on the experiences of a single craftsman, a potter, and compare them with the results of a research project that tracked the strategies of a number of corporations across several decades. Because the two contexts are so obviously different, my metaphor, like my assertion, may seem farfetched at first. Yet if we think of a craftsman as an organization of one, we can see that he or she must also resolve one of the great challenges the corporate strategist faces: knowing the organization's capabilities well enough to think deeply enough about its strategic direction. By considering strategy making from the perspective of one person, free of all the paraphernalia of what has been called the strategy industry, we can learn something about the formation of strategy in the corporation. For much as our potter has to manage her craft, so too managers have to craft their strategy.

At work, the potter sits before a lump of clay on the wheel. Her mind is on the clay, but she is also aware of sitting between her past experiences and her future prospects. She knows exactly what has and has not worked for her in the past. She has an intimate knowledge of her work, her capabilities, and her markets. As a craftsman, she senses rather than analyzes these things; her knowledge is "tacit." All these things are working in her mind as her hands are working the clay. The product that emerges on the wheel is likely to be in the tradition of her past work, but she may break away and embark on a new direction. Even so, the past is no less present, projecting itself into the future.

In my metaphor, managers are craftsmen and strategy is their clay. Like the potter, they sit between a past of corporate capabilities and a future of market opportunities. And if they are truly craftsmen, they bring to their work an equally intimate knowledge of the materials at hand. That is the essence of crafting strategy.

Henry Mintzberg is Bronfman Professor of Management at McGill University. He has written three other HBR articles, including the McKinsey Award winner "The Manager's Job: Folklore and Fact" (July-August 1975), and is currently at work on a two-volume study of strategy formation.

Drawings by Anatoly.

not result from a plan. An organization can have a pattern (or realized strategy) without knowing it, let alone making it explicit.

Patterns, like beauty, are in the mind of the beholder, of course. But anyone reviewing a chronological lineup of our craftsman's work would have little trouble discerning clear patterns, at least in certain periods. Until 1974, for example, she made small, decorative ceramic animals and objects of various kinds. Then this "knickknack strategy" stopped abruptly, and eventually new patterns formed around waferlike sculptures and ceramic bowls, highly textured and unglazed.

Finding equivalent patterns in action for organizations isn't that much more difficult. Indeed, for such large companies as Volkswagenwerk and Air Canada, in our research, it proved simpler! (As well it should. A craftsman, after all, can change what she does in a studio a lot more easily than a Volkswagenwerk can retool its assembly lines.) Mapping the product models at Volkswagenwerk from the late 1940s to the late 1970s, for example, uncovers a clear pattern of concentration on the Beetle, followed in the late 1960s by a frantic search for replacements through acquisitions and internally developed new models, to a strategic reorientation around more stylish, water-cooled, front-wheel-drive vehicles in the mid-1970s.

But what about intended strategies, those formal plans and pronouncements we think of when we use the term *strategy*? Ironically, here we run into all kinds of problems. Even with a single craftsman, how can we know what her intended strategies really were? If we could go back, would we find expressions of intention? And if we could, would we be able to trust them? We often fool ourselves, as well as others, by denying our subconscious motives. And remember that intentions are cheap, at least when compared with realizations.

In the pages that follow, we will explore this metaphor by looking at how strategies get made as opposed to how they are supposed to get made. Throughout, I will be drawing on the two sets of experiences I've mentioned. One, described in the insert, is a research project on patterns in strategy formation that has been going on at McGill University under my direction since 1971. The second is the stream of work of a successful potter, my wife, who began her craft in 1967.

Strategies are both plans for the future and patterns from the past.

Ask almost anyone what strategy is, and they will define it as a plan of some sort, an explicit guide to future behavior. Then ask them what strategy a competitor or a government or even they themselves have actually pursued. Chances are they will describe consistency in *past* behavior—a pattern in action over time. Strategy, it turns out, is one of those words that people define in one way and often use in another, without realizing the difference.

The reason for this is simple. Strategy's formal definition and its Greek military origins notwithstanding, we need the word as much to explain past actions as to describe intended behavior. After all, if strategies can be planned and intended, they can also be pursued and realized (or not realized, as the case may be). And pattern in action, or what we call realized strategy, explains that pursuit. Moreover, just as a plan need not produce a pattern (some strategies that are intended are simply not realized), so too a pattern need

Reading the organization's mind

If you believe all this has more to do with the Freudian recesses of a craftsman's mind than with the practical realities of producing automobiles, then think again. For who knows what the intended strategies of a Volkswagenwerk really mean, let alone what they are? Can we simply assume in this collective context that the company's intended strategies are represented by its formal plans or by other statements emanating from the executive suite? Might these be just vain hopes or rationalizations or ploys to fool the competition? And even if expressed intentions exist, to what extent do others in the organization share them? How do we read the collective mind? Who is the strategist anyway?

The traditional view of strategic management resolves these problems quite simply, by what organizational theorists call attribution. You see it all the time in the business press. When General Motors

Harvard Business Review

July-August 1987

acts, it's because Roger Smith has made a strategy. Given realization, there must have been intention, and that is automatically attributed to the chief.

In a short magazine article, this assumption is understandable. Journalists don't have a lot of time to uncover the origins of strategy, and GM is a large, complicated organization. But just consider all the complexity and confusion that gets tucked under this assumption – all the meetings and debates, the many people, the dead ends, the folding and unfolding of ideas. Now imagine trying to build a formal strategy-making system around that assumption. Is it any wonder that formal strategic planning is often such a resounding failure?

To unravel some of the confusion – and move away from the artificial complexity we have piled around the strategy-making process – we need to get back to some basic concepts. The most basic of all is the intimate connection between thought and action. That is the key to craft, and so also to the crafting of strategy.

Strategies need not be deliberate—they can also emerge.

Virtually everything that has been written about strategy making depicts it as a deliberate process. First we think, then we act. We formulate, then we implement. The progression seems so perfectly sensible. Why would anybody want to proceed differently?

Our potter is in the studio, rolling the clay to make a waferlike sculpture. The clay sticks to the rolling pin, and a round form appears. Why not make a cylindrical vase? One idea leads to another, until a new pattern forms. Action has driven thinking: a strategy has emerged.

Out in the field, a salesman visits a customer. The product isn't quite right, and together they work out some modifications. The salesman returns to his company and puts the changes through; after two or three more rounds, they finally get it right. A new product emerges, which eventually opens up a new market. The company has changed strategic course.

In fact, most salespeople are less fortunate than this one or than our craftsman. In an organization of one, the implementor is the formulator, so innovations can be incorporated into strategy quickly and easily. In a large organization, the innovator may be ten levels removed from the leader who is supposed

to dictate strategy and may also have to sell the idea to dozens of peers doing the same job.

Some salespeople, of course, can proceed on their own, modifying products to suit their customers and convincing skunkworks in the factory to produce them. In effect, they pursue their own strategies. Maybe no one else notices or cares. Sometimes, however, their innovations do get noticed, perhaps years later, when the company's prevalent strategies have broken down and its leaders are groping for something new. Then the salesperson's strategy may be allowed to pervade the system, to become organizational.

Is this story farfetched? Certainly not. We've all heard stories like it. But since we tend to see only what we believe, if we believe that strategies have to be planned, we're unlikely to see the real meaning such stories hold.

Consider how the National Film Board of Canada (NFB) came to adopt a feature-film strategy. The NFB is a federal government agency, famous for its creativity and expert in the production of short documentaries. Some years back, it funded a filmmaker on a project that unexpectedly ran long. To distribute his film, the NFB turned to theaters and so inadvertently gained experience in marketing feature-length films. Other filmmakers caught onto the idea, and eventually the NFB found itself pursuing a feature-film strategy – a pattern of producing such films.

My point is simple, deceptively simple: strategies can *form* as well as be *formulated*. A realized strategy can emerge in response to an evolving situation, or it can be brought about deliberately, through a process of formulation followed by implementation. But when these planned intentions do not produce the desired actions, organizations are left with unrealized strategies.

Today we hear a great deal about unrealized strategies, almost always in concert with the claim that implementation has failed. Management has been lax, controls have been loose, people haven't been com-

happen way up there, far removed from the details of running an organization on a daily basis, is one of the great fallacies of conventional strategic management. And it explains a good many of the most dramatic failures in business and public policy today.

We at McGill call strategies like the NFB's that appear without clear intentions – or in spite of them – emergent strategies. Actions simply converge into patterns. They may become deliberate, of course, if the pattern is recognized and then legitimated by senior management. But that's after the fact.

All this may sound rather strange, I know. Strategies that emerge? Managers who acknowledge strategies already formed? Over the years, our research group at McGill has met with a good deal of resistance from people upset by what they perceive to be our passive definition of a word so bound up with proactive behavior and free will. After all, strategy means control – the ancient Greeks used it to describe the art of the army general.

Strategic learning

But we have persisted in this usage for one reason: learning. Purely deliberate strategy precludes learning once the strategy is formulated; emergent strategy fosters it. People take actions one by one and respond to them, so that patterns eventually form.

Our craftsman tries to make a freestanding sculptural form. It doesn't work, so she rounds it a bit here, flattens it a bit there. The result looks better, but still isn't quite right. She makes another and another and another. Eventually, after days or months or years, she finally has what she wants. She is off on a new strategy.

In practice, of course, all strategy making walks on two feet, one deliberate, the other emergent. For just as purely deliberate strategy making precludes learning, so purely emergent strategy making precludes control. Pushed to the limit, neither approach makes much sense. Learning must be coupled with control. That is why the McGill research group uses the word *strategy* for both emergent and deliberate behavior.

Likewise, there is no such thing as a purely deliberate strategy or a purely emergent one. No organization – not even the ones commanded by those ancient Greek generals – knows enough to work everything out in advance, to ignore learning en route. And no one – not even a solitary potter – can be flexible enough to leave everything to happenstance, to give up all control. Craft requires control just as it requires responsiveness to the material at hand. Thus deliberate and emergent strategy form the end points of a continuum along which the strategies that are crafted in the real world may be found. Some strategies may approach either end, but many more fall at intermediate points.

mitted. Excuses abound. At times, indeed, they may be valid. But often these explanations prove too easy. So some people look beyond implementation to formulation. The strategists haven't been smart enough.

While it is certainly true that many intended strategies are ill conceived, I believe that the problem often lies one step beyond, in the distinction we make between formulation and implementation, the common assumption that thought must be independent of (and precede) action. Sure, people could be smarter – but not only by conceiving more clever strategies. Sometimes they can be smarter by allowing their strategies to develop gradually, through the organization's actions and experiences. Smart strategists appreciate that they cannot always be smart enough to think through everything in advance.

Hands & minds

No craftsman thinks some days and works others. The craftsman's mind is going constantly, in tandem with her hands. Yet large organizations try to separate the work of minds and hands. In so doing, they often sever the vital feedback link between the two. The salesperson who finds a customer with an unmet need may possess the most strategic bit of information in the entire organization. But that information is useless if he or she cannot create a strategy in response to it or else convey the information to someone who can – because the channels are blocked or because the formulators have simply finished formulating. The notion that strategy is something that should

70   Harvard Business Review   July-August 1987

Effective strategies develop in all kinds of strange ways.

Effective strategies can show up in the strangest places and develop through the most unexpected means. There is no one best way to make strategy.

The form for a cat collapses on the wheel, and our potter sees a bull taking shape. Clay sticks to a rolling pin, and a line of cylinders results. Wafers come into being because of a shortage of clay and limited kiln space in a studio in France. Thus errors become opportunities, and limitations stimulate creativity. The natural propensity to experiment, even boredom, likewise stimulate strategic change.

Organizations that craft their strategies have similar experiences. Recall the National Film Board with its inadvertently long film. Or consider its experiences with experimental films, which made special use of animation and sound. For 20 years, the NFB produced a bare but steady trickle of such films. In fact, every film but one in that trickle was produced by a single person, Norman McLaren, the NFB's most celebrated filmmaker. McLaren pursued a *personal strategy* of experimentation, deliberate for him perhaps (though who can know whether he had the whole stream in mind or simply planned one film at a time?) but not for the organization. Then 20 years later, others followed his lead and the trickle widened, his personal strategy becoming more broadly organizational.

Conversely, in 1952, when television came to Canada, a *consensus strategy* quickly emerged at the NFB. Senior management was not keen on producing films for the new medium. But while the arguments raged, one filmmaker quietly went off and made a single series for TV. That precedent set, one by one his colleagues leapt in, and within months the NFB—and its management—found themselves committed for several years to a new strategy with an intensity unmatched before or since. This consensus strategy arose spontaneously, as a result of many independent decisions made by the filmmakers about the films they wished to make. Can we call this strategy deliberate? For the filmmakers perhaps; for senior management certainly not. But for the organization? It all depends on your perspective, on how you choose to read the organization's mind.

While the NFB may seem like an extreme case, it highlights behavior that can be found, albeit in muted form, in all organizations. Those who doubt this might read Richard Pascale's account of how Honda stumbled into its enormous success in the American motorcycle market. Brilliant as its strategy may have looked after the fact, Honda's managers

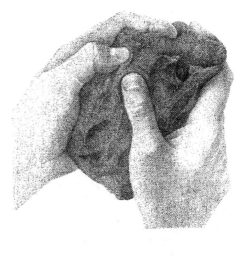

made almost every conceivable mistake until the market finally hit them over the head with the right formula. The Honda managers on site in America, driving their products themselves (and thus inadvertently picking up market reaction), did only one thing right: they learned, firsthand.[1]

Grass-roots strategy making

These strategies all reflect, in whole or part, what we like to call a grass-roots approach to strategic management. Strategies grow like weeds in a garden. They take root in all kinds of places, wherever people have the capacity to learn (because they are in touch with the situation) and the resources to support that capacity. These strategies become organizational when they become collective, that is, when they proliferate to guide the behavior of the organization at large.

Of course, this view is overstated. But it is no less extreme than the conventional view of strategic management, which might be labeled the hothouse approach. Neither is right. Reality falls between the two. Some of the most effective strategies we uncovered in our research combined deliberation and control with flexibility and organizational learning.

Consider first what we call the *umbrella strategy*. Here senior management sets out broad guidelines (say, to produce only high-margin products at the cutting edge of technology or to favor products using bonding technology) and leaves the specifics (such as what these products will be) to others lower down in the organization. This strategy is not only deliberate (in its clear, organizations pursue strategies to set direction, to lay out courses of action, and to elicit cooperation from their members around common, established guidelines. By any definition, strategy imposes stability on an organization. No stability means no strategy (no course to the future, no pattern from the past). Indeed, the very fact of having a strategy, and especially of making it explicit (as the conventional literature implores managers to do), creates resistance to strategic change!

What the conventional view fails to come to grips with, then, is how and when to promote change. A fundamental dilemma of strategy making is the need to reconcile the forces for stability and for change—to focus efforts and gain operating efficiencies on the one hand, yet adapt and maintain currency with a changing external environment on the other.

Quantum leaps

Our own research and that of colleagues suggest that organizations resolve these opposing forces by attending first to one and then to the other. Clear periods of stability and change can usually be distinguished in any organization: while it is true that particular strategies may always be changing marginally, it seems equally true that major shifts in strategic orientation occur only rarely.

In our study of Steinberg Inc., a large Quebec supermarket chain headquartered in Montreal, we found only two important reorientations in the 60 years from its founding to the mid-1970s: a shift to self-service in 1933 and the introduction of shopping centers and public financing in 1953. At Volkswagenwerk, we saw only one between the late 1940s and the 1970s, the tumultuous shift from the traditional Beetle to the Audi-type design mentioned earlier. And at Air Canada, we found none over the airline's first four decades, following its initial positioning.

Our colleagues at McGill, Danny Miller and Peter Friesen, found this pattern of change so common in their studies of large numbers of companies (especially the high-performance ones) that they built a theory around it, which they labeled the quantum theory of strategic change.[3] Their basic point is that organizations adopt two distinctly different modes of behavior at different times.

Most of the time they pursue a given strategic orientation. Change may seem continuous, but it occurs in the context of that orientation (perfecting a given retailing formula, for example) and usually

guidelines) and emergent (in its specifics), but it is also deliberately emergent in that the process is consciously managed to allow strategies to emerge en route. IBM used the umbrella strategy in the early 1960s with the impending 360 series, when its senior management approved a set of broad criteria for the design of a family of computers later developed in detail throughout the organization.[2]

Deliberately emergent, too, is what we call the *process strategy*. Here management controls the process of strategy formation—concerning itself with the design of the structure, its staffing, procedures, and so on—while leaving the actual content to others.

Both process and umbrella strategies seem to be especially prevalent in businesses that require great expertise and creativity—a 3M, a Hewlett-Packard, a National Film Board. Such organizations can be effective only if their implementors are allowed to be formulators because it is people way down in the hierarchy who are in touch with the situation at hand and have the requisite technical expertise. In a sense, these are organizations peopled with craftsmen, all of whom must be strategists.

Strategic reorientations happen in brief, quantum leaps.

The conventional view of strategic management, especially in the planning literature, claims that change must be continuous: the organization should be adapting all the time. Yet this view proves to be ironic because the very concept of strategy is rooted in stability, not change. As this same literature makes

1 Richard T. Pascale, "Perspective on Strategy: The Real Story Behind Honda's Success," *California Management Review,* May-June 1984, p. 47.

2 James Brian Quinn, IBM (A) case, in James Brian Quinn, Henry Mintzberg, and Robert M. James,

The Strategy Process: Concepts, Contexts, Cases (Englewood Cliffs, N.J.: Prentice-Hall, forthcoming).

3 See Danny Miller and Peter H. Friesen, *Organizations: A Quantum View* (Englewood Cliffs, N.J.: Prentice-Hall, 1984).

72   Harvard Business Review   July-August 1987

amounts to doing more of the same, perhaps better as well. Most organizations favor these periods of stability because they achieve success not by changing strategies but by exploiting the ones they have. They, like craftsmen, seek continuous improvement by using their distinctive competencies in established courses.

While this goes on, however, the world continues to change, sometimes slowly, occasionally in dramatic shifts. Thus gradually or suddenly, the organization's strategic orientation moves out of sync with its environment. Then what Miller and Friesen call a strategic revolution must take place. That long period of evolutionary change is suddenly punctuated by a brief bout of revolutionary turmoil in which the organization quickly alters many of its established patterns. In effect, it tries to leap to a new stability quickly to reestablish an integrated posture among a new set of strategies, structures, and culture.

But what about all those emergent strategies, growing like weeds around the organization? What the quantum theory suggests is that the really novel ones are generally held in check in some corner of the organization until a strategic revolution becomes necessary. Then as an alternative to having to develop new strategies from scratch or having to import generic strategies from competitors, the organization can turn to its own emerging patterns to find its new orientation. As the old, established strategy disintegrates, the seeds of the new one begin to spread.

This quantum theory of change seems to apply particularly well to large, established, mass-production companies. Because they are especially reliant on standardized procedures, their resistance to strategic reorientation tends to be especially fierce. So we find long periods of stability broken by short disruptive periods of revolutionary change.

Volkswagenwerk is a case in point. Long enamored of the Beetle and armed with a tightly integrated set of strategies, the company ignored fundamental changes in its markets throughout the late 1950s and 1960s. The bureaucratic momentum of its mass-production organization combined with the psychological momentum of its leader, who institutionalized the strategies in the first place. When change finally did come, it was tumultuous: the company groped its way through a hodgepodge of products before it settled on a new set of vehicles championed by a new leader. Strategic reorientations really are cultural revolutions.

Cycles of change

In more creative organizations, we see a somewhat different pattern of change and stability, one that's more balanced. Companies in the business of producing novel outputs apparently need to fly off in all directions from time to time to sustain their creativity. Yet they also need to settle down after such periods to find some order in the resulting chaos.

The National Film Board's tendency to move in and out of focus through remarkably balanced periods of convergence and divergence is a case in point. Concentrated production of films to aid the war effort in the 1940s gave way to great divergence after the war as the organization sought a new raison d'être. Then the advent of television brought back a very sharp focus in the early 1950s, as noted earlier. But in the late 1950s, this dissipated almost as quickly as it began, giving rise to another creative period of exploration. Then the social changes in the early 1960s evoked a new period of convergence around experimental films and social issues.

We use the label "adhocracy" for organizations, like the National Film Board, that produce individual, or custom-made, products (or designs) in an innovative way, on a project basis.[4] Our craftsman is an adhocracy of sorts too, since each of her ceramic sculptures is unique. And her pattern of strategic change was much like that of the NFB's, with evident cycles of convergence and divergence: a focus on knickknacks from 1967 to 1972; then a period of exploration to about 1976, which resulted in a refocus on ceramic sculptures; that continued to about 1981, to be followed by a period of searching for new directions. More recently, a focus on ceramic murals seems to be emerging.

Whether through quantum revolutions or cycles of convergence and divergence, however, organizations seem to need to separate in time the basic forces for change and stability, reconciling them by attending to each in turn. Many strategic failures can be attributed either to mixing the two or to an obsession with one of these forces at the expense of the other.

The problems are evident in the work of many craftsmen. On the one hand, there are those who seize on the perfection of a single theme and never change. Eventually the creativity disappears from their work and the world passes them by—much as it did Volkswagenwerk until the company was shocked into

if you will – who manages a process in which strategies (and visions) can emerge as well as be deliberately conceived. I also wish to redefine that strategist, to extend that someone into the collective entity made up of the many actors whose interplay speaks an organization's mind. This strategist *finds* strategies no less than creates them, often in patterns that form inadvertently in its own behavior.

What, then, does it mean to craft strategy? Let us return to the words associated with craft: dedication, experience, involvement with the material, the personal touch, mastery of detail, a sense of harmony and integration. Managers who craft strategy do not spend much time in executive suites reading MIS reports or industry analyses. They are involved, responsive to their materials, learning about their organizations and industries through personal touch. They are also sensitive to experience, recognizing that while individual vision may be important, other factors must help determine strategy as well.

Manage stability. Managing strategy is mostly managing stability, not change. Indeed, most of the time senior managers should not be formulating strategy at all; they should be getting on with making their organizations as effective as possible in pursuing the strategies they already have. Like distinguished craftsmen, organizations become distinguished because they master the details.

To manage strategy, then, at least in the first instance, is not so much to promote change as to know *when* to do so. Advocates of strategic planning often urge managers to plan for perpetual instability in the environment (for example, by rolling over five-year plans annually). But this obsession with change is dysfunctional. Organizations that reassess their strategies continuously are like individuals who reassess their jobs or their marriages continuously – in both cases, people will drive themselves crazy or else reduce themselves to inaction. The formal planning process repeats itself so often and so mechanically that it desensitizes the organization to real change, programs it more and more deeply into set patterns, and thereby encourages it to make only minor adaptations.

So-called strategic planning must be recognized for what it is: a means, not to create strategy, but to program a strategy already created – to work out its implications formally. It is essentially analytic in nature, based on decomposition, while strategy creation is essentially a process of synthesis. That is why

its strategic revolution. And then there are those who are always changing, who flit from one idea to another and never settle down. Because no theme or strategy ever emerges in their work, they cannot exploit or even develop any distinctive competence. And because their work lacks definition, identity crises are likely to develop, with neither the craftsmen nor their clientele knowing what to make of it. Miller and Friesen found this behavior in conventional business too; they label it "the impulsive firm running blind."[5] How often have we seen it in companies that go on acquisition sprees?

To manage strategy is to craft thought and action, control and learning, stability and change.

The popular view sees the strategist as a planner or as a visionary, someone sitting on a pedestal dictating brilliant strategies for everyone else to implement. While recognizing the importance of thinking ahead and especially of the need for creative vision in this pedantic world, I wish to propose an additional view of the strategist – as a pattern recognizer, a learner

4 See my article
"Organization Design: Fashion or Fit?"
HBR January-February 1981, p. 103;
also see my book *Structure in Fives:
Designing Effective Organizations*
(Englewood Cliffs, N.J.: Prentice-Hall, 1983).
The term *adhocracy* was coined by

Warren G. Bennis and Philip E. Slater in
The Temporary Society
(New York: Harper & Row, 1964).

5 Danny Miller and Peter H. Friesen,
"Archetypes of Strategy Formulation,"
Management Science, May 1978, p. 921.

trying to create strategies through formal planning most often leads to extrapolating existing ones or copying those of competitors.

This is not to say that planners have no role to play in strategy formation. In addition to programming strategies created by other means, they can feed ad hoc analyses into the strategy-making process at the front end to be sure that the hard data are taken into consideration. They can also stimulate others to think strategically. And of course people called planners can be strategists too, so long as they are creative thinkers who are in touch with what is relevant. But that has nothing to do with the technology of formal planning.

Detect discontinuity. Environments do not change on any regular or orderly basis. And they seldom undergo continuous dramatic change, claims about our "age of discontinuity" and environmental "turbulence" notwithstanding. (Go tell people who lived through the Great Depression or survivors of the siege of Leningrad during World War II that ours are turbulent times.) Much of the time, change is minor and even temporary and requires no strategic response. Once in a while there is a truly significant discontinuity or, even less often, a gestalt shift in the environment, where everything important seems to change at once. But these events, while critical, are also easy to recognize.

The real challenge in crafting strategy lies in detecting the subtle discontinuities that may undermine a business in the future. And for that, there is no technique, no program, just a sharp mind in touch with the situation. Such discontinuities are unexpected and irregular, essentially unprecedented. They can be dealt with only by minds that are attuned to existing patterns yet able to perceive important breaks in them. Unfortunately, this form of strategic thinking tends to atrophy during the long periods of stability that most organizations experience (just as it did at Volkswagenwerk during the 1950s and 1960s). So the trick is to manage within a given strategic orientation most of the time yet be able to pick out the occasional discontinuity that really matters.

The Steinberg chain was built and run for more than half a century by a man named Sam Steinberg. For 20 years, the company concentrated on perfecting a self-service retailing formula introduced in 1933. Installing fluorescent lighting and figuring out how to package meat in cellophane wrapping were the "strategic" issues of the day. Then in 1952, with the arrival of the first shopping center in Montreal, Steinberg realized he had to redefine his business almost overnight. He knew he needed to control those shopping centers and that control would require public financing and other major changes. So he reoriented his business. The ability to make that kind of switch in thinking is

the essence of strategic management. And it has more to do with vision and involvement than it does with analytic technique.

Know the business. Sam Steinberg was the epitome of the entrepreneur, a man intimately involved with all the details of his business, who spent Saturday mornings visiting his stores. As he told us in discussing his company's competitive advantage:

"Nobody knew the grocery business like we did. Everything has to do with your knowledge. I knew merchandise, I knew cost, I knew selling, I knew customers. I knew everything, and I passed on all my knowledge; I kept teaching my people. That's the advantage we had. Our competitors couldn't touch us."

Note the kind of knowledge involved: not intellectual knowledge, not analytical reports or abstracted facts and figures (though these can certainly help), but personal knowledge, intimate understanding, equivalent to the craftsman's feel for the clay. Facts are available to anyone; this kind of knowledge is not. Wisdom is the word that captures it best. But wisdom is a word that has been lost in the bureaucracies we have built for ourselves, systems designed to distance leaders from operating details. Show me managers who think they can rely on formal planning to create their strategies, and I'll show you managers who lack intimate knowledge of their businesses or the creativity to do something with it.

Craftsmen have to train themselves to see, to pick up things other people miss. The same holds true for managers of strategy. It is those with a kind of peripheral vision who are best able to detect and take advantage of events as they unfold.

Manage patterns. Whether in an executive suite in Manhattan or a pottery studio in Montreal, a key to managing strategy is the ability to detect emerging patterns and help them take shape. The job of the manager is not just to preconceive specific strategies but also to recognize their emergence elsewhere in the organization and intervene when appropriate.

Like weeds that appear unexpectedly in a garden, some emergent strategies may need to be uprooted immediately. But management cannot be too quick to cut off the unexpected, for tomorrow's vision may grow out of today's aberration. (Europeans, after all, enjoy salads made from the leaves of the dandelion, America's most notorious weed. Thus some patterns are worth watching until their effects have more clearly manifested themselves. Then those that prove useful can be made deliberate and be incorporated into the formal strategy, even if that means shifting the strategic umbrella to cover them.

To manage in this context, then, is to create the climate within which a wide variety of strategies can grow. In more complex organizations, this may mean building flexible structures, hiring creative people, defining broad umbrella strategies, and watching for the patterns that emerge.

Reconcile change and continuity. Finally, managers considering radical departures need to keep the quantum theory of change in mind. As Ecclesiastes reminds us, there is a time to sow and a time to reap. Some new patterns must be held in check until the organization is ready for a strategic revolution, or at least a period of divergence. Managers who are obsessed with either change or stability are bound eventually to harm their organizations. As pattern recognizer, the manager has to be able to sense when to exploit an established crop of strategies and when to encourage new strains to displace the old.

While strategy is a word that is usually associated with the future, its link to the past is no less central. As Kierkegaard once observed, life is lived forward but understood backward. Managers may have to live strategy in the future, but they must understand it through the past.

Like potters at the wheel, organizations must make sense of the past if they hope to manage the future. Only by coming to understand the patterns that form in their own behavior do they get to know their capabilities and their potential. Thus crafting strategy, like managing craft, requires a natural synthesis of the future, present, and past.

Tracking strategy

In 1971, I became intrigued by an unusual definition of strategy as a pattern in a stream of decisions (later changed to actions). I initiated a research project at McGill University, and over the next 13 years a team of us tracked the strategies of 11 organizations over several decades of their history. (Students at various levels also carried out about 20 other less comprehensive studies.) The organizations we studied were: Air Canada (1937-1976), Arcop, an architectural firm (1953-1978), Asbestos Corporation (1912-1975), Canadelle, a manufacturer of women's undergarments (1939-1976), McGill University (1829-1980), the National Film Board of Canada (1939-1976), Saturday Night Magazine (1928-1971), the Sherbrooke Record, a small daily newspaper (1946-1976), Steinberg Inc., a large supermarket chain (1917-1974), the U.S. military's strategy in Vietnam (1949-1973), and Volkswagenwerk (1934-1974).

As a first step, we developed chronological lists and graphs of the most important actions taken by each organization – such as store openings and closings, new flight destinations, and new product introductions. Second, we inferred patterns in these actions and labeled them as strategies.

Third, we represented graphically all the strategies we inferred in an organization so that we could line them up to see whether there were distinct periods in their development – for example, periods of stability, flux, or global change. Fourth, we used interviews and in-depth reports to study what appeared to be the key points of change in each organization's strategic history.

Finally, armed with all this strategic history, the research team studied each set of findings to develop conclusions about the process of strategy formation. Three themes guided us: the interplay of environment, leadership, and organization; the pattern of strategic change; and the processes by which strategies form. This article presents those conclusions.

Author's note: Readers interested in learning more about the results of the tracking strategy project have a wide range of studies to draw from. Works published to date can be found in Robert Lamb and Paul Shivastava, eds., *Advances in Strategic Management,* Vol. 4 (Greenwich, Conn.: Jai Press, 1986), pp. 3-41; *Management Science,* May 1978, p. 934; *Administrative Science Quarterly,* June 1985, p. 160; J. Grant, ed., *Strategic Management Frontiers* (Greenwich, Conn.: Jai Press, forthcoming); *Canadian Journal of Administrative Sciences,* June 1984, p. 1; *Academy of Management Journal,* September 1982, p. 465; Robert Lamb, ed., *Competitive Strategic Management* (Englewood Cliffs, N.J.: Prentice-Hall, 1984).

[24]

Crafting Organization

JULIE WOLFRAM COX[a,*] and STELLA MINAHAN[b,†]

[a]Department of Management, Monash University, P. O. Box 197, Caulfield East, Victoria 3145, Australia;
[b]Department of Marketing, Monash University, P. O. Box 197, Caulfield East, Victoria 3145, Australia

The recent shift in attention away from organization studies as science has allowed for consideration of new ways of thinking about both organization and organizing and has led to several recent attempts to 'bring down' organizational theorizing. In this paper, we extend calls for organization to be represented as a creative process by considering organization as craft. Organizational craft, we argue, is attractive, accessible, malleable,, reproducible, and marketable. It is also a tangible way of considering organization studies with irreverence. We draw on the hierarchy of distinctions among fine art, decorative art, and craft to suggest that understanding the organization of craft assists in complicating our understanding of marginality. We illustrate our argument by drawing on the case of a contemporary Australian craftworks and marketplace known initially as the Meat Market Craft Centre ('MMCC') and then, until its recent closure, as Metro![‡]

Key words: Organization Theory, Aesthetics, Marginality

Postmodern organizational analysis has seen a shift of emphasis from finding answers to 'problemizing' answers, and from considering formal organization as a bounded social system to questioning organizing as a local boundary process of formalization, suppression, and censoring (Chia, 1995; Cooper, 1986; Cooper and Burrell, 1988). Attention has been drawn not only to predicting and controlling what might be (for some) an optimistic future, but to re-introducing marginalized topics and voices and to paying attention to what/whom has been forgotten or bracketed out (Alvesson and Deetz, 1996; Calás and Smircich, 1991; Chia, 1996a; 1997; Ferguson, 1994; Kilduff, 1993; Mumby and Putnam, 1992).

In part influenced by the wider critique of reason and unity that has accompanied the growth of postmodernism, organization studies have, at least to some extent, been freed from the progressive assumptions of scientific development. Since Lyotard's (1984) *The Postmodern Condition*, such studies no longer necessarily mimic the disciplines of natural science and have been influenced by linguistic (Hall, 1980; cited in Baack and Prasch, 1997) and aesthetic turns (Gagliardi, 1996; Strati, 1999), and informed by discourse analysis (*e.g.*, Grant, Keenoy and Oswick, 1998), metaphor (*e.g.*, Grant and Oswick, 1996; Morgan, 1986; Oswick and Grant, 1996), theatre (Clark and Salaman, 1996; Mangham and Overington, 1987; *Studies in Cultures, Organizations, and Societies*, 1996), and jazz (*e.g.*, *Organization Science*, 1998; Weick and Westley, 1996).

Accompanying the growth of contemporary critical, postmodern and postcolonial organization and management studies (*e.g.*, Alvesson and Willmott, 1992; 1996; Calás and Smircich, 1999; Clegg, Hardy and Nord, 1996; Hassard and Parker, 1993; Kilduff and Mehra, 1997) is increasing attention to organizing and organization in the past. This attention has been reflected, for example, in interest in premodern narrative knowledge and in retro-organization theory's aim of reversing the marginalization and sanitation of the past (Burrell, 1996; 1997). Extending such recent attempts to 'bring down' organizational theorizing, we suggest that organization be considered as craft, an historically informed, marginal and processual enterprise.

Crafting can be considered as a provisional means of creating forms and their boundaries and as an aesthetic enterprise in which crafter and craft, human and non-human, are mutually entangled. Organisational craft, we argue, is also attractive, accessible, malleable, re-producible, and marketable (see, for example, Kieser, 1997). In the crafting process, as in organizational design, materials are used and re-used, skills are applied, and imagination and experimentation are encouraged. Structures are shaped, trimmed, resized, and sometimes even melted down. New pieces can be added, and offcuts are often saved for later.

Such language is certainly not alien to organization studies. For example, Chia and King discussed organization as a creative process rather than as a "bounded social entity" (Chia and King, 1998: 463). They emphasised "the perpetually perishing and perpetually reconstituting character of social reality" (Chia and King, 1998: 462), arguing that "reality comprises the continual building up and breaking down of actualized 'entities' through the assembling, dissembling and reassembling of past aggregations of events into ever newer and novel event-clusters in an interminable process of becoming" (Chia and King, 1998: 465–466). Both organizing and crafting are provisional and tentative processes, and while the language of crafting is implicit rather than explicit in Chia and King's (1998) analysis, it is everywhere. For example, like pottery at the wheel, organization is "a simultaneously ongoing compressive and extensive social process . . . involving the punctuating, arresting, simple locating and stabilizing of what is essentially an undifferentiated, fluxing and changeable reality" (Chia and King, 1998: 463).

Other, more literal efforts to understand organization as craft tend to present both in romantic or functionalist terms. In one example, Laubacher and Malone (1997) recently drew on some of the functions of premodern craft organizations to raise the idea that new workers' 'guilds' might assist workers working in decentralised networks and moving from job to job in the 21st century. In another, Knights and McCabe (1998) have commented on Mintzberg's (1987) discussion of the managerial crafting of organizational strategy, and his particular reference to the craft of pottery. They point out how this work has been criticised by Smircich (1983) in the following words:

> The metaphor of the craft potter reveals how Mintzberg's "thinking is shaped and constrained" (Smircich, 1983, p. 341) by a rationalist belief that management can control organizations for "craft requires control just as it requires responsiveness to the material at hand" (Mintzberg, 1987, p. 69). We are presented with a view of "organization's [sic] as purposeful instruments and adaptive mechanisms" (Smircich, 1983, p. 353) which are orchestrated and shaped by management. It is assumed that "power" rests with the "hands" of management. (Knights and McCabe, 1998: 770)

In a third example, Chia (1996b) cites Sandelands and Drazin's (1989) comments that crude attempts to include processual language within organizational analysis have been limited by an impoverished vocabulary of "achievement terms" such as *shape, determine* and *select*: instead of explaining how organization comes about, they tend to mystify the process "in a welter of misbegotten abstractions and unauthentic processes" (Sandelands and Drazin, 1989: 458; cited in Chia, 1996b: 157).

Thus, while the appropriation of craft within organization studies is not new, representations of *organization as craft* may be attractive but limited. In contrast, we suggest that the *crafting of organization* is more than a dualistic and distal process (cf. Cooper and Law, 1995); it is one that also draws meaning from the particular aesthetics and politics of art-craft relations. Indeed, it is noteworthy that while management has long been described as art (Conger, 1992; Strati, 1999: 174–178; Vaill, 1989) and while both art *and* craft have been invoked to describe the management of research (see, for example, Booth, Colomb and Wiliams 1995; Butler, 1997; Golden-Biddle and Locke, 1997; Neuman, 1994), craft is rarely used as a sole referent for titles on management practice or thought. In an effort to understand craft's marginality, we draw on the hierarchy of aesthetic distinctions among fine art, decorative art and craft. We then both illustrate and complicate this hierarchy, drawing on episodes from a case study of an Australian craft organization. We suggest that craft constitutes a tangible way of considering organization studies with irreverence and conclude by arguing for the potential contribution of craft in understanding organization as a provisional enterprise informed by an aesthetic that derives neither from science nor from fine art.

CRAFT AS A LOWLY PURSUIT

In part, craft's lowly status is informed by the devaluing of physical labour important since the classical Greeks privileged the mind over the body (Metcalf, 1993). What Alison Jaggar (1983) has termed *normative dualism*, or the privileging of things mental over things physical, has shaped not only morality, politics and gender but art, and "it is no accident that the work of marginalized groups often counts as craft" (Markowitz, 1994: 68; see also Browne, 1994; Marincola, 1995). This marginalisation was assisted by the rise of modernism, which is signified by the partition of 'the other'; of society from nature (Latour, 1993), of beauty from utility (Gagliardi, 1996), of production from craftsmanship (Boje, 1995), and of art from craft. Indeed, before the concept of fine art arose in the eighteenth century, craft and art were regarded as "inseparable" (Kuspit, 1996: 16). As explained by Kuspit (1996), there then grew an hierarchy of distinctions between art and craft, where art is fine and perceived to be at the 'high' end of the aesthetic ladder of preference and taste and craft is largely excluded "from the possibility of having an aesthetic component" (Metcalf, 1994: 16). Thus, it is probably not accidental that the writers of so many management texts have made references to art rather than to craft in their titles.

In what has become known as the "dreaded art versus craft debate" (Editor's introduction to Marincola, 1995), contemporary attempts to level and even remove aesthetic distinctions have been the subject of ongoing discussion but the debate remains strongly influenced by Kantian aesthetics. According to Kant, an aesthetic experience could be supported only by an autonomous art object, and the disinterested gaze of the art spectator is elicited only when art is removed from moral, social and religious values and from ordinary life (Metcalf, 1993). Indeed, the viewer of art experiences what Kant claimed to be a universal, *common sense* that ignores tradition and transcends material existence. This "tendency to value what is distinctive about paintings over what is distinctive about pots" (Markowitz, 1994: 67) means that fine art is distinguished from applied, more utilitarian art (see Osborne, 1970: 12), and that craft is regarded as a "lowly pursuit" (Ioannou, 1997/1998; Metcalf, 1994; Yanagi, 1989).

In addition, Metcalf (1993: 41) has suggested that the art-craft debate has been "infiltrated" by an ideology of modernism that constitutes the craft object as having a form that follows function, with no decoration or processing beyond functional requirements. As a consequence, it is often argued that "self-expression must not eclipse function" in craft objects (Markowitz, 1994: 63) which, however beautiful, "do not *require* an interpretation the way...paintings do" (Markowitz, 1994: 60–61; emphasis in original). While the supposed contextual autonomy of art and the claim for an ideal of disinterestedness have been debunked by the rise of Marxist, feminist and postmodern thought, the art-craft debate has remained the dominant rhetoric in all discourse on craft in the last couple of decades (Ioannou, 1997/1998).

The art-craft hierarchy also has institutional consequences. For example, Melbourne's Meat Market Craft Centre ('MMCC'), to be referred to in more detail below, was the city's largest craft centre. It was housed in a recycled meat market where the building has a cobbled floor, vaulted ceilings, and no environmental controls in an inner-city area separated from arts enterprises and on the 'wrong side of the river'. While the arts were located in an accessible, custom-built, prestige location, the crafts were hidden away in obsolete and recycled facilities and their geographical separation reproduced the art-craft hierarchy. Craft is represented in the Melbourne arts precinct, but only once a week (on Sundays) when crafts people are allowed to set up tables on the footpath, in front of the theatres, galleries and concert halls, to entertain those promenading on the boulevard. This presentation of craft in a temporary fashion, along the street and exposed to all weather, is opposed to the presentation of art only a few metres away in the controlled atmosphere of the National Gallery of Victoria.

In addition to this hierarchy between art and craft is a further hierarchy *within* the crafts, where those who work with precious metals are well regarded (see Tab. I), just as they were in the early craft guilds. Moving down this hierarchy, glass artists who use intense heat sources are seen as being more sophisticated, stronger and more technically skilled than glass artists who work in the safer, physically easier environment of kiln-formed slumped glass. Potters who throw using wheels are seen as much more technically competent, more engaged with their craft, than those who hand build. At the MMCC, for example, the potters in the ceramics workshop rejected a young hand builder. His space allocation was constantly reduced and invaded by the other potters as his work was seen as being simplistic and of little technical or aesthetic value.

Each craft discipline is defined by techniques from its history (Metcalf, 1993: 40, 44; see also Johnson, 1997; Markowitz, 1994), and where craft techniques have been retained, they are often retained in the home, involving textiles (knitting, weaving, stitchery, and crochet) and reproducing divisions between public/private, modern/premodern and male/female. It is notable that crafts with a majority of female participants are very low in terms of the hierarchy of craft and that the Textile Studio at the MMCC, like that at the German Bauhaus, was predominantly female. Yet even within textiles, embroidery and lace making are regarded more highly than spinning and weaving. Markowitz (1994) has argued that embroidery is often excluded from art not only because it is devalued as women's work, but because it more often concerns mottoes and motifs "to encourage girls and women to develop and display a domestic and submissive feminine character" rather than, like art, "to be about things pro-

TABLE I   Hierarchy of the Visual Arts and Crafts.

High end	Oil paintings, 'one-off/one-of' pieces
Middle point	Other paintings, porcelain, major sculptures, precious jewellery, short run production
Low end	Ceramics, glass, wood, furniture, functional objects such as vases and crockery; some textiles including American quilting and embroidery of historical significance, repetitious production work
Not on scale	Textiles including embroidery, quilting, wearable art, and weaving

found, personal, or original" (Markowitz, 1994: 61). Further, crochet is not only a domestic, feminine pursuit, but one that is further denigrated by its identification as an *old woman's craft* (Isaacs, 1987: 7), and since craft is gendered and seen as 'women's work', the notion of the *crafty woman* is often presented as a double pejorative (see Landay, 1998).

Thus, particular craft activities help to constitute and reproduce the discourses in which they are embedded, and the hierarchy of distinctions among and within arts and crafts can be examined and debated as an important intersection of aesthetic and social difference. However, we argue that understanding craft, and, by implication, other illustrations of organizational and disciplinary marginality, are also informed by looking beyond simple hierarchies and simple subordinations.

COMPLICATING THE MARGINALITY OF CRAFT

Local Enactments

First, it should be noted that such hierarchies are enacted (and inverted) in local ways and in local circumstances. For example, the techniques and language of craft had been well accepted in Australia in the 1960s, when some crafts were even seen as assisting the process of developing the national identity. Australia was seen as 'growing on the sheep's back', and craft activities that used Australian wool were well regarded by many sectors. At the same time, many espoused values of peace, care for the environment and personal freedom, and craft activities that combined Australiana and 'back to earth' products gained great popularity. Thus, while the MMCC was seen as a commercial low end venue appealing to hobbyists (see Tab. I), the context for low end Australian craft in the late 1960s and 1970s had been positive. For example, hand woven, hand dyed clothing and floor rugs were in great demand at both the low end and middle point and the convergence between the average Australian and the Hippie of the 1960s was fundamental to the early, nostalgia-driven success of the MMCC, which we now introduce in more detail.

The Meat Market Craft Centre: A craft organization. The Metropolitan Meat Market was built in 1879 and was located on a 2.5-hectare site close to the Queen Victoria retail meat and fresh produce markets in North Melbourne (see Johnson, 1988). The building was custom designed as a wholesale meat market, and the main hall of the building features 66-metre long clear span vaulted ceiling that replicates the Haymarket in London. Affected by changes in technology such as the introduction of the combustion engine and refrigeration, the rationalisation of the large number of small firms in the meat industry, an aspirational labour market, and increasing inner city property and rental costs, the property was put up for sale in 1973.

The major interest in the property was from developers who were looking for a large block of land close to the city. However, there were pressures to preserve the site. For example, the National Trust had already classified the buildings as worthy of preservation, and the radical left wing Meat Workers Union was committed to save the building as an important part of the history of the meat industry in Victoria – and determined to thwart the efforts of developers. The Historic Buildings Preservation Council registered the building shortly before the auction, meaning that it could not be demolished and was then no longer attractive to developers. The property was passed in at auction well below its expected price. Over a period of years it housed a warehouse, auction room, trash and treasure market, a car park and even a hellfire club (in the basement) until a group of crafts people came together to lobby the government to acquire the building and convert it to a craft centre.

The lobbying was successful, and the MMCC originally commenced in November 1979 as a non-government, not-for-profit organization and as the site for housing the government-owned Victorian State Crafts Collection. In the period from 1979–1984, the work at the MMCC was always identifiably Australian at a time when the arts industry in Australia was seen as having a strong identity that was separate from European and American models (Clark, 2000). The MMCC was recognised as a leader in its field and, occasionally, major commissions at the high end were awarded to crafts people for furniture and furnishings such as wall hangings and rugs for corporate, public and private domains.

By the mid 1990s, the Centre's facilities for craft production were ageing and, in some cases, obsolete. The Centre had spawned its own competition and modern facilities for crafts people were now available in universities, technical colleges and community centres. New facilities could not be fitted to the building without investing several millions of dollars. Sales income was decreasing, for the (mainly female, ageing) purchasers of larger, more expensive MMCC craft items were moving into smaller accommodations and divesting themselves of property rather than adding to their collections.

The Centre was seen as needing to be self-funding, but this was not possible when it had such low sales and was located in a poor position in a building that was very expensive to run. The costs of occupying and maintaining the historic building were becoming prohibitive and it was known that the Government wouldn't increase funding. A new board was appointed and decided to relaunch the MMCC as the Metro! Craft Centre since the abbreviation 'Metro!' was both a contemporary term and one that reflected the name of the Metropolitan Meat Market building.

In a strategic planning session in June 1998, the board stated that its vision was for Metro! to be recognised as Australia's premier showcase of excellence and innovation in craft. However, the Centre attracted limited government funding, and in its last years capital reserves were used to cover the gap between earned revenue and the costs of operating the facility. All activities that were not essential to craft were stopped or outsourced, and although Metro! generated nearly 90% of its annual $1.6 million turnover, it was put into voluntary administration on May 13, 1999. This was soon followed by liquidation when the State Government of Victoria withdrew funding and the licence to operate the Craft Centre. The local media published reports of the closure but there was very little public protest, and the company was wound up in May 2000. In summary, the centre's early success had facilitated its later decline, and a marginalisation or hardship narrative tells only part of the MMCC's local story.

The Organization of Craft

Second, and in addition to the potential for such local enactments, the art-craft hierarchy can be further complicated. In particular, we introduce seven different art-craft positions (see Tab. II) and provide illustrations of how some of those positions were embodied within the MMCC.

1. Art-envy. One consequence of the continuing distinction between art and craft has been the emergence of the (deliberately titled) phenomenon of *art-envy* (Metcalf, 1989), where crafts such as textiles "can cross over into the mainstream" (Ferris, 1996: 7) and where craft's emphasis on function is questioned and even debunked. For example, and with respect to ceramics:

Some work encourages an interpretation by being obviously if not belligerently nonutilitarian. Ceramicist Carl Borgeson, who started out making utilitarian objects, now makes deliberately nonfunctional teapots whose lids are glued on (Markowitz, 1994: 64).

TABLE II   Relationships Between Art and Craft.

Art-envy	Craft is art-like
Craft-in-art	Emphasis on residual craft skill and technique in art
Hybridity	Reflexive, often ironic mixing of art and craft genres
Nostalgia	Attempts to raise the status of craft relative to art by celebrating craft
Separation	Removes craft from comparison with art
Activism	Attempts to raise the status of craft relative to art by critique of the relative social marginalisation of craft workers
Romantic integration	Anti hierarchical, anti-dualistic integration of art and craft

Art-envy also includes the use of "common, even deliberately tacky materials...to de-heroicize the macho, superior notions of medium conventionally associated with painting and sculpture" (Marincola, 1995: 37). For example, Marincola (1995: 37) refers to Apfelbaum's use of crushed velvet to provide the ground for crumpled, collapsed 'paintings' presented on the floor rather than on the wall but points out that such attempts (still) use fine art as a referent.

Continuing with our case example, art-envy had material consequences at the MMCC, which adopted the rituals and artefacts of fine art from very early on. These included opening night functions, floor talks, expensive catalogues, and guest speakers. The arts community of Melbourne was attracted to the new venue in the historical building and opening nights would often attract many hundreds of visitors. The audience was willing and able to 'follow and support' a craft person, to attend the lectures by acknowledged experts, and 'to talk about the work' (Clark, 2000). Exhibitions would attract many thousands of people keen to see the crafts in action in this setting. In the early days, government funding was high and the Centre was able to attract additional patronage from companies associated with the crafts such as equipment suppliers. This allowed for the establishment of prize giving awards that attracted the best of the exhibitors and added significant prestige to MMCC activities.

In the 1980s, an 'A grade' gallery was installed within the MMCC. This gallery mimicked fine art galleries on the south side of the city, for its physical environment, name and location within the complex were all designed to separate it from ordinary craft. Within the building, it was a separate wing that could be closed off from the rest of the Craft Centre. From outside, the gallery even had a separate entrance. Its floor was timber, its walls were white, and the lighting was state of the art. It looked very different from the rest of the building as all historical references to the site's noisier, smellier, dirtier, more domestic and less erudite past were removed. "Craftsmen have long wished for the privileges of modern art: clean, white galleries, museum collections, [and] amazing prices" (Metcalf, 1993: 42), and in this case their wishes to be art-like were fulfilled.

However, such wishes were far from uniform among the MMCC's tenants, which included both the low end craft practitioners and, from 1979 until the late 1980s, the high end advocacy body, Craft Victoria. Their differences in preferred direction intensified over the years until there was a complete breakdown of communication during the 1980s that resulted in Craft Victoria moving out of the building to premises across the city. When Craft Victoria left the MMCC, it was seen as taking the high end of craft away, for the 'best' crafts people (the conceptual artists, the writers, and the critics) swore allegiance to Craft Victoria. Major craft awards and grant monies went with Craft Victoria, and Craft Victoria guarded this territory and actively excluded the MMCC from its domain.

The MMCC fought this change by holding high end expensive (and art-envious) exhibitions but, while these exhibitions attracted visitors to the Centre, they were expensive to mount and rarely attracted significant sales revenue. MMCC also launched touring shows and an acquisition program for the Victorian State Crafts Collection, and this expenditure, combined with high stock levels and low sales caused a financial crisis early in the 1990s. All staff were retrenched and it appeared as if the Centre would close. However, a group of community residents, artists and tenants came together as the 'Friends of the Meat Market Craft Centre' and staffed and ran the Centre as volunteers until the finances were restored by additional government grants. At this point, a General Manager was appointed and the Centre continued to function, but it can be seen that art-envy was both a cause and a consequence of crisis at the MMCC.

The emulation of art can also serve to suppress craft. For example, when the MMCC was renamed as Metro!, the Centre was no longer associated with the dirty, domestic craft of the building's past. Indeed, that past was now at best a quaint discussion point and at worst an aesthetic violation of Metro!'s contemporary and art-like orientation. In addition to this shift in overall identity, the workshops within the Centre were also re-named in 1998 and became known as *design studios*, which is a name that denies much of the craft*making* activity that took place there.

This is not surprising, for art-envy is often demonstrated in the language used by crafts people to describe their occupation. Terms such as *artisan* or *crafts/wo/man* are not used and are seen as 'down market' or unsophisticated. Crafts people will use many other words in an attempt to elevate their perceived status; spinners and weavers become *textile artists*, craftsmen become *designer/makers*, and potters become *ceramic artists* and craft makers want to exhibit their works in art galleries (Metcalf, 1993). For example, Australian craft became art-envious by the 1970s and 1980s, adopting the language of fine art (*craft artist, artist in wood, designer* etc.) in an effort to improve its status. However, the appropriation of such terms was not convincing for functional work in three dimensions, and craft lost not only its specific identity but much of its support from the arts.

2. Craft-in-art. In response both to art-envy and to conceptual art, which "privileged the idea to the point where process, materials, the production of any kind of object became irrelevant" (Johnson, 1997: 43), there has been increasing recognition of art skill and technique, and of the 'work' of craft-in-art. Whereas conceptual art was suspicious of materials and of skill, and art-envious crafts people may reject the craft in their work by not speaking of the materials or the technical issues resolved in the manufacture (Dormer, 1994), craft-in-art is "an attempt to return to the traditional conception of the artist as an expert in a particular medium" (Kuspit, 1996: 15; cf. Markowitz, 1994).

Kuspit suggests that two twentieth-century 'returns' to craft include the modernist Bauhaus movement's integration of art and craft through the attempt to popularise avant-garde art in "ordinary, useful objects" (Kuspit, 1996: 15; see also Browne, 1994; Kirkham, 1998), and the postmodernist "debunking or discrediting of the aesthetic as an elitist ideology" (Kuspit, 1996: 17).

With respect to the former, the Bauhaus school's emphasis on craft skills during the first year of study has had an extended influence on arts curricula. Indeed, the residue of the Bauhaus' organizational model could be seen at the MMCC where independent workshops were contemporary versions of craft guilds and where a senior crafts person was appointed as the supervisor (Master) of the workshops (Clark, 2000). The strength of the supervisors' identifications with low end crafts during the Craft Victoria dispute is, therefore, partly due to this heritage. In addition, their position was an attractive one as they had free use of new, well-equipped workshops and as they were also able to share in the profits of their teaching activities. As a result, many of these workshop supervisors saw the workshop as their personal fiefdom, and most of them remained long beyond their contracted three-year period. When, by the late 1980s, the outcomes of the dispute forced the MMCC Board to seek financial input from the workshops, this was met with great hostility.

In contrast, and with respect to the latter, Kuspit (1996: 17) has argued that:

> Postmodernism . . . involves the de-idealization of the artist as well as of the subjective mystery of art and the authenticity of the unique form. Feeling and form no longer being to the aesthetic point (sic.), art must only be significant as craft – no doubt by default' (cf. Markowitz, 1994).

Thus, and for two very different reasons, residual craft skills may be valued rather than dismissed.

3. Hybridity. Hybridization of art and craft is an interdisciplinary extension of the influence of postmodernism in art (see also Kallinikos, 1997), and ironic *hybrid* forms are art-like as a reflexive comment on the categorizations of *art* and *craft* rather than as a celebration or critique of one over the other. For example, exhibitions such as *Material Culture* have deliberately mixed genres (Johnson, 1997), and Marincola (1995) noted that an exhibition of fibre art by Alison Ferris combined both 'craft' and 'fine' artists in an effort to emphasise "both thematic and material connections" (p. 30).

4. Nostalgia. In contrast to such reflexivity, the fourth position adopts a "hopelessly uncritical" celebration of craft as a means for valuing the accessible and the familiar and for reinforcing personal identity and meaning (cf. Metcalf, 1993: 44). This nostalgic response to art-envy has been regarded as an attempt to "restor[e] the humble brown pot to a place of honor" (Metcalf, 1994: 15) and to celebrate its hand-made nature in the traditions of William Morris and of the art critic John Ruskin. Ruskin contrasted the "spiritual deadness" of machine-made goods with the craftsmanship of the Middle Ages, where goods may have been imperfect but where their makers were not reduced to "slavery" (Poulson, 1989: 35). Kuspit (1996: 19) comments that, for Ruskin and Morris, craft became a way of restoring the "lost utopia of unalienated work", and that their "craftsman ideal", where work was a means of individualization, was influential in America from around 1887 to 1915. This was the height of the American Arts and Crafts movement (Browne, 1994), whose legacies remain in organizations such as the Craft Centre (Osborne, 1970).

5 and 6. Separation and Activism. Craft is also potentially subversive to fine art because it is cheap (Metcalf, 1993; Yanagi, 1989) and is therefore accessible "to a wider range of the public" than fine art (Browne, 1994: 36). Indeed, two further art-craft positions include craft separation and activism, where craft either makes no attempt to be art-like or makes a critical statement on the social and institutional causes of its marginal status. For example, Johnson (1997) raises the importance of increased funding for craft in the United Kingdom, and suggests that there should be a Museum of British Craft, not so that craft can be art-like, but as institutional recognition of the need to break down aesthetic boundaries between art and craft through "positive restructuring rather than negative cost-cutting" (Johnson, 1997: 45).

Craft's activism is perhaps most evident in the use of the 'lowly, feminine' crafts such as embroidery as the medium for exhibitions such as *The Subversive Stitch* in 1991, *The Social Fabric* in 1993, and *Guys who Sew* in 1994, among many others (Marincola, 1995). Such exhibitions raise awareness of the institutions and artefacts of patriarchy. For example, one body of embroideries on domestic 'working textiles' textiles such as pot holders and aprons depicts women at home alone doing housework and shows a deliberate emphasis on feminine organization of a domestic sphere (Holloway, 1994; Peoples, 1994).

7. Romantic integration. A seventh position relating art and craft is the *romantic integrated* position, which sees no dualism or separation between the aesthetics of art and craft, and thus no need to describe one in terms of the other. Writing from a Buddhist perspective, Yanagi was an important contributor to the craft movement in Japan and he wrote many essays discussing the beauty and truth within craft that are relevant to this position. Yanagi (1989) is particularly critical of the social elitism of the art/craft debate and challenges the convention that art is available to an intellectual elite and protected from the working class or ignorant. There is even a sense of anti-intellectualism in Yanagi's writings, and he is scathing of those who know without seeing, arguing that beauty is a type of "mystery, which cannot be grasped adequately through the intellect" (Yanagi, 1989: 110). Not only does he break down the aesthetic duality of art/craft, but he also criticises the development of academies of art that, ironically, themselves developed from the sixteenth century in an effort to emancipate artists from control by the craft guilds (Osborne, 1970: 4; see also Krause, 1996).

In summary, *art-envy*, the residual *craft-in-art* position, and craft *activism* host definitions of craft that are dependent on or in reaction to a more primary concern with art, while the *hybrid* and *romantic integration* positions adopt a more equal positioning of the two, and the *nostalgic* and *separation* perspectives shift the balance toward craft as the dominant term. Although craft is usually the subordinate or marginalised term in art-craft discussions, attention to the art-craft dichotomy and to 'subordination-of-craft' discourse alone belies the heterogeneity of these various art-craft positions (cf. Chia and King, 1998; Knights, 1997). We now discuss the implications of this analysis, for such considerations of the organization of craft may also be of relevance to understanding mainstream-periphery dynamics in organization and management.

ORGANIZATION CRAFT

Drawing on Derrida's (1981) discussion of the play of opposites such as inside/outside, Cooper stresses the importance of such attention to the marginal:

> [T]he "outside" as the undesired supplement plays a necessary and constituting role in the formation of the "inside" and, far from being a mere accessory, is thus a central feature of the "inside". The supplement, therefore, acts as a frame or ground to the content of the inside to which it is marginal. In other words, the supplement supports the privileged "inside". (Cooper, 1986: 315)

Just as contingent workers support the definition of normal work, leisure time supports the notion of work time and as critical management studies may even reinforce the mainstream.

However, while craft may well be viewed as a supplement to art, we have shown that not all positions on craft view it in relation to art or even in separation from art. Thus craft, like postcolonial and some feminist analysis, allows attention to the margin for its own sake and legitimates the study of what might otherwise be ignored.

As an example, let us consider the MMCC case again, this time turning from its galleries to its basement. After Metro!'s closure, the building lay dormant for several months, although some sections of the basement are now leased to RMIT University for student workshops. Indeed, the cellars and basement area have perhaps been the site of the greatest variety of heterogeneous activities over the years, and just as the case study of the Centre is important because of its particular marginality as a craft organization, the cellars occupy a further periphery, a further margin *within* the Centre, each play of centre–margin and presence–absence contributing to understanding (cf. Cooper, 1986). For example, the sewers were essential to removing waste for the meat market above, the storage of the Victorian State Crafts Collection enabled the formation of the Craft Centre, the effects of the tactile extremities of the hellfire club disturbed and were in juxtaposition to the quiet, contemplative gentility of the galleries above, and the cellars allowed craft workers to forge, turn and weld away from the public's gaze. Just as the negative spaces of a William Morris pattern contribute both to its complexity and its beauty, the smells and sounds of these 'empty', 'other' areas (literally) cannot be ignored, cannot be suppressed or deferred in any aesthetic analysis of the Centre, for in and through these cellars has flowed a full sensory array of life and death. As the student workshops now operate not in relation to the space above but independent from it, it is only at its margin that the Centre now survives. However, while the cellars host what is the much of the only current life in the building, they are also the cause of the limitation of that life, for it is the cost of revisions to the cellars necessary for the meeting of occupational health and safety regulations that is one of the most important material barriers to the potential for re-opening of the building.

In summary, we suggest that the layering of meanings described here in terms of the relationships between art and craft, the particular and shifting textures of those relationships within Melbourne, within the Meat Market Craft Centre, and between the different parts of its building, all assist the appreciation of this case as an example of the play of various aesthetic, geographical and material centres and margins. First, we suggest that an understanding of both historical and contemporary art-craft dynamics helps to inform this organization's various and changing layers of activity and emphasis and of some of the events and associations from which mark its particular identities. In doing so, we avoid theorizing from a life cycle or institutional theory perspective, for our aim is to provide, instead, an aesthetic appreciation of this case, and "to concentrate on elements of distinction and difference in organizational life" (Strati, 1999: 80).

Second, and while we are conscious that Chia and King (1998) aimed to move organizational analysis away from the analysis of entities to the understanding of process, the choice of the craft centre as the subject for this case study is deliberate. This single case study is an extreme case (Yin, 1994) in that the Centre occupies a particularly marginal and subordinate space not only because of its own history and activities, but also because it has ceased operations. We suggest that reference to crafting may prove fruitful for others interested in further development of processual organizational theory and technique, for an imperative to attend to aesthetics is an imperative to attend not only to visual harmony but to broader sensory disharmony and to disorganization (cf. Cooper, 1986).

While we are aware that a margin-led/craft-led analysis holds within it the dangers of merely inverting rather than deconstructing the oppositional art-craft hierarchy (cf. Cooper, 1989; Knights, 1997; Linstead, 1993), the 'lesser' world of craft is worthy of contemplation. The particular combination of craft's provisionality and its subordination to art may help to inform organizational theorizing on topics such as "foolishness", "ambiguity" and "playfulness" (cf. Chia and King, 1998: 473–474), in line with other attempts both to 'bring down' and to 'lighten' organizational theorizing (*e.g.*, Gergen, 1992; Weick, 1979). For example, Clark (2000) sees the playful nature of craft in terms of Renaissance arts patronage where artists were encouraged by their patrons to be entertaining, provocative and to stay as children; the artist, like a child, is encouraged 'to go and play', 'to go out on a limb' and to enjoy creativity without having to worry about 'bread and butter items'. Craft and art, patronage and play, are mutually implicated and mutually dependent.

Further, Chia and King (1998) argue that "the substratum of flux, indeterminacy and openness which is frequently suppressed or denied" in mainstream organization theory is starting to receive some attention, but that this attention is often based on an impoverished conception of organization that privileges social entities rather than processual thinking. We suggest that research into the conceptual definitions and relationships of crafting may prove fruitful as a tangible way of considering organization studies with irreverence, for crafting is an activity and occupation of both movement and of marginalisation, in both a contemporary and historical context. In order to develop this proposition, we argue that the aesthetic turn in organization studies should be informed by craft, not art, and that the *organization of craft* and the *crafting of organization* are mutually informative.

Thus, crafting can inform organization not only because it is a provisional activity but also as a way of articulating various manifestations of *otherness* (Chia and King, 1998). It is by 'bringing down' the art-craft hierarchy to examine this heterogeneity from a craft-based rather than art-based perspective that we can begin to appreciate shades of meaning attached to the term *craft* that might elsewhere be deferred (cf. Derrida, 1981; cited in Cooper, 1986). Indeed, many of the references we have cited come from craft magazines such as *Ceramics Monthly, Fiberarts, Metalsmith,* and *Studio Potter* rather than art journals, for these magazines are the primary written outlets for discussion among craft workers and academics. Similarly, although craft may not be 'fine', it does not exclude hobbyists, 'coarse' materials, or workshops in which people experiment with new ideas, making many mistakes along the way. In this sense, the craft metaphor may have appeal both to those who advocate (often marginal) experimentation within organizational learning and innovation and to those who study the sites of experimentation, of subversion with humour, of breaking norms, and of suffering the consequences. Attention to craft, like attention to popular culture in organization studies, allows for the study of the raw, the accessible and the tacky and provides an additional vocabulary for such study.

In addition, it is also tempting to consider how the various positions relating art and craft may re-present existing debates and differences among organization and management theorists. In particular, art-craft relations can perhaps illustrate several positions of schools of organization studies in relation to science: the emulation of and nostalgia for science in positivist organization theory, the appropriation of science in research methodology curricula and in the 'strong programme' in the sociology of scientific knowledge (Woolgar, 1988), the rejection of empiricism by proponents of some postmodern studies, among many others. As art-craft relations have as much to do with legitimacy claims as aesthetic ones, we suggest that they may even be useful for consideration the aesthetics of organization metatheory. Here, debates over paradigm incommensurability and bridging have led to the use of epistemological crafting devices such as typology and triangulation (see, for recent examples and debates, Gioia and Pitre, 1990; Lewis and Grimes, 1999; *Organization,* 1998; Schultz and Hatch, 1996) in what can be seen as a romantic search for "higher vantage points" (Chia, 1996b: 79) or three-dimensional integrations.

ON WRITING CRAFT AND GUILDING ORGANIZATION STUDIES

In concluding our argument for attention to such craftings of organization, we also note the decorations or embellishments of our own organizational production (cf. Kirkham, 1998; Metcalf, 1993), for our choice of emphases in writing this paper may say more about ourselves than about organization, craft or the Craft Centre. For example, we have at times presented a linear sequence of events. At other times, we have shifted our emphasis, our subject, our stance. At others again we have discussed incidents or events that mark the flow of our discussion, that perhaps refer to earlier discussion. We have also made omissions, for we have relegated Stella Minahan's own participation in and moulding of Metro! to an authorship note and have remained observers of an art-like subject, hesitant to cause 'too much' offence or disruption to the sensibilities of our various colleagues by disrupting conventions of article form and content, by being too *craft-like.*

Further, and since "no amount of methodology . . . will ever bring 'representation' closer to 'reality'" (Chia, 1996b, p. 90), aesthetic criteria may also be relevant in assessing the contribution of research studies such as this one. Indeed, in assessing the writing of research, Cziarniawska–Joerges (1995: 26) has argued that "[t]he question is no longer 'Does it correspond to outside reality? Does it observe the rules of formal logic?', but 'Does it work? Is it beautiful? Who is it for?'". However, this is itself an art-like aesthetic, for the distinction of art from craft is usually made on the basis of an object's *formal aesthetic* qualities, such as its beauty, formal unity, or "evocativeness" (Markowitz, 1994: 57; see also Gagliardi, 1996: 576). While craft objects may "qualify as art objects" if they possess formal aesthetic qualities, Markowitz suggested an alternative criterion for the aesthetic assessment and contemplation of craft; one that includes rather than ignore's craft's utilitarian function:

[O]ne may insist that the utilitarian function of a craft object is neither in tension with nor even irrelevant to its aesthetic character, but rather essential to it. Indeed, we seem to have in mind here another sort of aesthetic quality, not a purely formal one, but one which involves fitness to form to some end. I shall call this a functional aesthetic quality...the craft object's functional aesthetic quality will rest on the fitness of its form for its utilitarian purpose (or even its looking as though its form were fit for its purpose)". (Markowitz, 1994: 58–59)

Under this *functional aesthetic*, material form does not necessarily follow function, but neither is it ignored. Form may not even be loosely coupled with function but may, instead, only refer to or *suggest* function, looking "as though" this is a possibility or deferred presence (cf. Cooper, 1986) rather than a necessity or actual correspondence. A less 'elevated', non-representational organization studies may therefore be informed by a similarly less elevated, non-representational aesthetic, and Czarniawska-Joerges' (1995) questions now become the more craft-like: *How and why does it seem as though it might work? What and for whom could it be? How else might it be used?* The functional aesthetic is therefore a relational and a tentative aesthetic, one that offers possibilities for the creative dissassembly and reassembly of ideas (cf. Chia and King, 1998). It also allows for investigations into the suggestion or semblance of functionality for its own sake in contrast to, for example, studies of processes of impression management, influence or enrolment as means either to 'misrepresent' or to 'create' the real. In studies of organizational design and technology, research informed by this aesthetic may be based on tentative questions such as *Does it look as though it might work?*, and in leadership *Does s/he seem to provide a vision?* rather than the more definitive *Does it work?* or *How are we convinced that it works?* or *Why does the vision not become reality?*

Thus, and at many levels, we argue for the study of craft. In its most literal sense, we call for consideration of craft in local, historical contexts such as in the case presented here. More generally, we call for greater reference to the legacies of craft in aesthetic studies and in the complicating of our understanding of marginality in organization theory. Craft, we suggest, is also worth considering in the writing of organization studies and as the basis for a criterion for their evaluation that is neither art- nor science-based. Finally, we hope that the particular convergence of craft and organization presented in this paper makes a contribution both to understanding Metro! and to the texture and g(u)i(l)ding of organization studies, and we encourage further analyses that complicate the crafting of organization and the taking of the aesthetic turn.

References

Alvesson, Mats and Deetz, Stanley (1996) Critical theory and postmodernism approaches to organization studies. In: Stewart R. Clegg, Cynthia Hardy and Walter R. Nord (Eds.), *Handbook of organization studies* (pp. 191–217), London: Sage.

Alvesson, Mats and Willmott, Hugh (Eds.) (1992) *Critical management studies*, London: Sage.

Alvesson, Mats and Willmott, Hugh (1996) *Making sense of management: A critical introduction*, London: Sage.

Baack, Donald and Prasch, Thomas (1997) The death of the subject and the life of the organization: Implications of new approaches to subjectivity for organizational analysis, *Journal of Management Inquiry*, 6(2), 131–141.

Black, Antony (1984) *Guilds and civil society in European political thought from the twelfth century to the present*, Ithaca: Cornell University Press.

Boje, David M. (1995) Stories of the storytelling organization: A postmodern analysis of Disney as *Tamara*-land, *Academy of Management Journal*, 38(4), 997–1035.

Booth, Wayne C., Colomb, Gregory G. and Williams, Joseph M. (1995) *The craft of research*, Chicago: University of Chicago Press.

Browne, Kathleen (1994) The future perfect: Activism and advocacy, *Metalsmith*, 14(Spring), 34–39.

Burrell, Gibson (1996) Normal science, paradigms, metaphors, discourses and genealogies of analysis, In: Stewart R. Clegg, Cynthia Hardy and Walter R. Nord (Eds.), *Handbook of organization studies* (pp. 642–658), London: Sage.

Burrell, Gibson (1997) *Pandemonium: Towards a retro-organization theory*, London: Sage.

Butler, Richard (1997) Stories and experiments in social inquiry, *Organization Studies*, 18(6), 927–948.

Calás, Marta B. and Smircich, Linda (1999) Past postmodernism? Reflections and tentative directions, *Academy of Management Review*, 24(4), 649–671.

Calás, Marta B. and Smircich, Linda (1991) Voicing seduction to silence leadership, *Organization Studies*, 12(4), 567–601.

Chia, Robert (1995) From modern to postmodern organizational analysis, *Organization Studies*, 16(4), 579–604.

Chia, Robert (1996a) Metaphors and metaphorization in organizational analysis: Thinking beyond the unthinkable. In: David Grant and Cliff Oswick (Eds.), *Metaphor and organizations* (pp. 127–145), London: Sage.

Chia, Robert (1996b) *Organizational analysis as deconstructive practice*, Berlin and New York: Walter de Gruyter.

Chia, Robert (1997) Essai: Thirty years on: From organizational structures to the organization of thought, *Organization Studies*, 18(4), 685–707.

Chia, Robert and King, Ian W. (1998) The organizational structuring of novelty, *Organization*, 5(4), 461–478.

Clark, Timothy and Salaman, Graeme (1996) The use of metaphor in the client-consultant relationship: a study of management consultants, In: Cliff Oswick and David Grant (Eds.), *Organisation development: Metaphorical explorations* (pp. 154–174), London: Pitman.

Clark, Sue (2000) Personal Communication, March 31.

Clegg, Stewart R., Hardy, Cynthia and Nord, Walter R. (Eds.) (1996) *Handbook of organization studies*, London: Sage.

Conger, Jay A. (1992) *Learning to lead: The art of transforming managers into leaders*, San Francisco: Jossey-Bass.

Cooper, Robert (1986) Organization/disorganization, *Social Science Information*, 25(2), 299–335.

Cooper, Robert (1989) Modernism, post modernism and organizational analysis 3: The contribution of Jacques Derrida, *Organization Studies*, 10(4), 479–502.

Cooper, Robert and Burrell, Gibson (1988) Modernism, postmodernism and organizational analysis: An introduction, *Organization Studies*, 9(1), 91–112.

Cooper, Robert and Law, John (1995) Organization: Distal and proximal views, *Research in the Sociology of Organizations*, 13, 237–274.

Czarniawska-Joerges, Barbara (1995) Narration or science? Collapsing the division in organization studies, *Organization*, 2(1), 11–33.

Derrida, Jacques (1981) *Dissemination*, London: Athlone Press.

Dormer, Peter (1994) *Art of the Maker*, London, Thames and Hudson

Ferguson, K. E. (1994) On bringing more theory, more voices and more politics to the study of organization, *Organization*, 1(1), 81–99.

Ferris, Alison (1996) Commentary, *Fiberarts*, 22(1), 7.

Frey, John P. (1945) *Craft unions of ancient and modern times*, Washington, D.C.: Randall, Inc.

Gagliardi, Pasquale (1996) Exploring the aesthetic side of organizational life. In: Stewart R. Clegg, Cynthia Hardy and Walter R. Nord (Eds.), *Handbook of Organization Studies* (pp. 565–580), London: Sage.

Gergen, Kenneth J. (1992) Organization theory in the postmodern era. In: Michael Reed and Michael Hughes (Eds.), *Rethinking organization: New directions in organization theory and analysis* (pp. 207–226), London: Sage.

Gioia, Dennis A. and Pitre, Evelyn (1990) Multiparadigm perspectives on theory building, *Academy of Management Review*, 15(4), 584–602.

Golden-Biddle, Karen and Locke, Karen D. (1997) *Composing qualitative research*, Thousand Oaks: Sage.

Grant, David, Keenoy, Tom and Oswick, Cliff (Eds.) (1988) *Discourse and organization*, London: Sage.

Grant, David and Oswick, Cliff (Eds.) (1996) *Metaphor and organizations*, London: Sage.

Hall, S. (1980) Cultural studies: Two paradigms, In: T. Bennett, G. Martin, C. Mercer and J. Woollacott (Eds.), *Culture, ideology and social process: A reader* (pp. 19–37), London: Open University Press.

Harrison, Michael I. and Shirom, Arie (1999) *Organizational diagnosis and assessment: Bridging theory and practice*, Thousand Oaks: Sage.

Hassard, John and Parker, Martin (1993) *Postmodernism and organizations*, London: Sage.

Holloway, Barbara (1994) *The great divide*, Unpublished catalogue essay, Australian National University, Canberra, Australia.

Ioannou, Noris (1997/1998) Collaboration in glass, *Craft Arts International*, 41, 61.

Jaggar, Alison M. (1983) *Feminist politics and human nature*, Totowak, NJ: Rowman and Allanheld.

Johnson, Pamela (1997) The right stuff, *Crafts*, 146(3), 42–45.

Johnson, M. (1988) History of the metropolitan meat market. In: *Victorian State Craft Collection: Catalogue of the Victorian State Craft Collection*, North Melbourne: The Meat Market Craft Centre.

Kallinikos, Jannis (1997) Classic Review: Science, knowledge and society: The postmodern condition revisited, *Organization*, 4(1), 114–129.

Kieser, Alfred (1997) Rhetoric and myth in management fashion, *Organization*, 4(1), 49–74.

Kilduff, Martin (1993) Deconstructing Organizations, *Academy of Management Review*, 18(1), 13–31.

Kilduff, Martin and Mehra, Ajay (1997) Postmodernism and organizational research, *Academy of Management Review*, 22(2), 453–481.

Kirkham, Pat (1998) Humanizing modernism: The crafts, 'functioning decoration' and the Eameses, *Journal of Design History*, 11(1), 15–29.

Knights, David (1997) Organization theory in the age of deconstruction: Dualism, gender and postmodernism revisited, *Organization Studies*, 18(1), 1–19.

Knights, David and McCabe, Darren (1998) When life is but a dream: Obliterating politics through business process reengineering, *Human Relations*, 51(6), 761–798.

Kuspit, Donald (1996) Craft in art, art as craft, *The New Art Examiner*, 23(April), 14–53.

Krause, Elliot A. (1996) *Death of the guilds. Professions, states, and the advance of capitalism, 1930 to the present*, New Haven and London: Yale University Press.

Landay, Lori (1998) *Madcaps, screwballs, and con women: The female trickster in American culture*, Philadelphia: University of Pennsylvania Press.

Latour, Bruno (1993) *We have never been modern*, translated by Catherine Porter, New York: Harvester Wheatsheaf.

Laubacher, Robert J. and Malone, Thomas W. (1997) Flexible work arrangements and 21st century workers' guilds, *Initiative on inventing the organizations of the 21st century*, Working paper 4, Sloan School of Management, Massachusetts Institute of Technology.

Law, John (1994) *Organizing modernity*, Oxford: Blackwell.

Lewis, Marianne W. and Grimes, Andrew J. (1999) Metatriangulation: Building theory from multiple paradigms, *Academy of Management Review*, 24(4), 672–690.

Linstead, Stephen (1993) From postmodern anthropology to deconstructive ethnography, *Human Relations*, 46(1), 97–120.

Lyotard, Jean-Francois (1984) *The postmodern condition: a report on knowledge*, Manchester: Manchester University Press.

Mangham, Iain L. and Overington, M. A. (1987) *Organizations as theatre: a social psychology of dramatic appearances*, Chichester: Wiley.

Marincola, Paula (1995) Fabric as fine art: Thinking across the divide, *Fiberarts*, 22(5), 34–39.

Markowitz, Sally J. (1994) *Journal of Aesthetic Education*, 28(1), 55–70.

Metcalf, Bruce (1989) Artlike, *Metalsmith*, 9(Winter), 10.

Metcalf, Bruce (1993) Replacing the myth of modernism, *American Craft*, 53(February–March), 40–47.

Metcalf, Bruce (1994) Toward an aesthetics of craft, *Studio Potter*, 22(June), 14–16.

Mintzberg, Henry (1987) Crafting strategy, *Harvard Business Review*, 65(4), 66–75.

Morgan, Gareth (1986) *Images of organization*, Newbury Park, CA: Sage.

Mumby, Dennis K. and Putnam, Linda (1992) The politics of emotion: A feminist reading of bounded rationality, *Academy of Management Review*, 17(3), 465–486.

Neuman, W. Lawrence (1994) *Social research methods: Qualitative and quantitative approaches*, Boston: Allyn and Bacon.

Organization (1998), 5(2), Special Issue.

Organization Science (1998), 9(5), Special Issue.

Osborne, Harold (Ed.) (1970) *The Oxford Companion to Art*, Oxford: Clarendon Press.

Oswick, Cliff and Grant, David (Eds.) (1996) *Organisation development: Metaphorical explorations*, London: Pitman.

Peoples, Sharon (1994) *Master of Arts (Visual Arts) thesis*, Institute of Arts, Australian National University, Canberra, Australia.

Poulson, Christine (1989) *William Morris*, London: New Burlington.

Sandelands, Lloyd and Drazin, Robert (1989) On the language of organization theory, *Organization Studies*, 10(4), 457–478.

Schultz, M. and Hatch, M. J. (1996) Living within multiple paradigms: The case of paradigm interplay in organizational culture studies, *Academy of Management Review*, 21(2), 529–557.

Slater, Hartley (1997) Art and aesthetics, *British Journal of Aesthetics*, 37(3), 226–231.

Smircich, Linda (1983) Concepts of culture and organizational analysis, *Administrative Science Quarterly*, 28(3), 339–358.

Strati, Antonio (1999) *Organization and aesthetics*, London: Sage.

Studies in Culture, Organizations and Societies (1996) Organizations and theatre: play and performance in the round, 2(1), Special Issue.

Vaill, Peter B. (1989) *Managing as a performing art: New ideas for a world of chaotic change*, San Francisco: Jossey-Bass

Weick, Karl E. (1979) *The social psychology of organizing* (2nd ed.), Reading, MA: Addison-Wesley.

Weick, Karl E. and Westley, F. (1996) Organizational learning: Affirming an oxymoron, In: Stewart R. Clegg, Cynthia Hardy and Walter R. Nord (Eds.), *Handbook of organization studies* (pp. 440–458), Sage: London.

Weltge, Sigrid Wortmann (1993) *Bauhaus textiles: Women artists and the weaving workshop*, London: Thames and Hudson.

Woolgar, Steve (1988) *Science: The very idea*, Chichester: Ellis Horwood.

Yanagi, Soetsu (1989) *The unknown craftsman: A Japanese insight into beauty*, London: Gillingham House.

Yin, Robert K. (1994) *Case study research: Design and methods* (2nd ed.), Thousand Oaks: Sage.

[25]

Organization, Decoration

Julie Wolfram Cox
RMIT University, Australia

Stella Minahan
Deakin University, Australia

Abstract. While organizational decoration has been of interest to those who study organizational artefacts, we suggest four ways in which decoration is worthy of fuller attention in organizational studies. First, decoration, ornament and embellishment are not only what we see, but also what we do as managers, consultants, writers and designers of both physical and project spaces. Second, and drawing on the art/craft debate, we note that decoration occupies contested and even liminal aesthetic position and that 'decorative art' lies betwixt and between fine art and craft. Neither fully accepted nor fully marginalized, decoration is 'only applied' and embodies shifting tensions between form and function. Third, we review the particular negotiations of these tensions at the Bauhaus, a controversial and highly influential aesthetic organization in early 20th century Germany. Fourth, we suggest that decoration, like disorganization, provides a source of complication for organizational studies that are neither pure nor parsimonious. **Key words.** *art/craft debate; aesthetics; Bauhaus; disorganization, mimesis*

In this paper, we examine the notion of decoration. Decoration is a subject that has been variously trivialized, discounted and admired, and we discuss its status, particularly in relation to craft activities which are themselves often marginalized within aesthetic debates. In contrast, we suggest that the decorative is worthy of attention in both aesthetic and organization theory. We propose that organization theorists should

Organization 12(4)
Articles

consider themselves as decorators working with peripheries, often violating contemporary standards of taste, repeating and elaborating the traditions of the past, causing much discussion and disagreement, and sometimes leaving material traces of their contributions.

Just Decoration?

For some, decoration should be celebrated. Drawing on the examples ranging from the decoration of a soldier to the 'strained relation' of ornament to the Christian spirit, the Australian commentator Robert Nelson has suggested that ornament is a metaphor for dignity and value (Nelson, 1993: 9). In his essay, Nelson (1993) discusses the Latin origins of the terms 'ornament' and 'decoration' and suggests that there are physical and moral associations for both. The latter are perhaps most evident in the noun *decus*:

> The term *decus* means ornament, grace, embellishment, splendour but also glory, honour, dignity and so on. The verb *decoro* means I adorn or decorate or beautify . . . But the adjectival form (*decorus*) is more exclusively moral, paralleling our contemporary 'decorous' and readily translating the Greek term for 'the appropriate' (*euprepês*). (Nelson, 1993: 8)

Nelson goes on to point out that this association means that decoration and ornament 'harbour not only an onus of conformity but institute an uncritical dictatorship of the appropriate' (Nelson, 1993: 13). Depending on the values of the time, the appropriateness of particular amounts and styles of decoration is, of course, a matter of aesthetic judgment. In one extreme, the Victorian era in arts and crafts had been known for its obsession with decoration, detail and excess ornament. From doileys to chair legs, the 'lace' on terraces, and to the finials of curtains, all items in the built environment displayed decoration.

For Nelson, ornament and decoration are both material manifestations of convention and indicators of value. Ornament can even be practical where decorations are applied to 'solve problems of finish and save the expense of perfection in fussy assemblies' (Nelson, 1993: 3). In addition, and rather than being merely 'unnecessary features in a design' (Nelson, 1993: 2) or a 'pure aesthetic' (Nelson, 1993: 6), decoration can also signify the necessary, the functional, and the stable in architectural construction as it 'celebrates the presence of things' (Nelson, 1993: 4). For example, Nelson discusses how wooden motifs on Greek stone temples helped the temple to 'look strong' and to 'argue its own structure' (Nelson, 1993: 2), and how brackets in Chinese temples celebrated their engineering even after the brackets were no longer structural requirements. Thus, ornament can be seen as 'an artifice for claiming space as meaningful' (Nelson, 1993: 5) and as 'a language of pattern which ritualizes function and structure within a design' (1993: 6).

The decorative can also fulfill a real structural role. For example, Japanese farmers' jackets are usually made of two layers of indigo-dyed

Organization, Decoration
Julie Wolfram Cox and Stella Minahan

cotton material, hemmed and bound together by stitching in very thick thread. This needlework looks like added decoration but it is nothing of the sort. Its charm is in its appropriateness to use and the strength of the stitching. The delightful patterning is incidental and utterly suitable. There is no concept of décor for its own sake (Yanagi, 1989).

In contrast to such celebration, and in a reference to the legacies of the Viennese architect, Adolf Loos, Nelson points out that ornament has also been derided as 'a device for soaking up meaningless space' (1993: 5). According to Kleinert (1992: 119), Loos 'suffered the modernist's usual aversion to decoration' and led a campaign against decoration that would influence architects for many years into the future. For Loos, decoration was 'a sign of degeneracy and immorality in a rational, civilized society' (Kleinert, 1992: 119). Only 'others'—children, criminals and primitives— would be interested in decoration and were denigrated for 'their obses- sive desire to in-fill space with decoration' (Kleinert, 1992: 119, with reference to Black, 1964: 49–50). Loos' (1908) paper titled 'Ornament and Crime' is also discussed by Fuller (1989), who comments that Loos' rejection of the decorative arts was based on arguments that they were not only erotic and regressive but also uneconomic (see also Pevsner, 1991: 30).

Nelson suggests that part of this disdain is due to ornament being 'paradigmatic of craft in general' (1993: 12) and to craft's association with traditions from the past which, under modernism, are identified with a backward commitment to outmoded precepts (Nelson, 1993: 12; cf. Metcalf, 1993: 40, 44). As a result:

> Ornament still finds itself oppressed by prejudices of the Modernist tradition. Never far from the opprobrium heaped upon it by Adolf Loos, ornament languishes under the doyley of quaintness and ineffectualness in all things emotional and spiritual. One speaks of 'surface decoration' as though superficial in the aesthetic sense, if not the moral sense as well. (Nelson, 1993: 4)

Similarly, Kleinert (1992: 116) cites Alberti's (1957: 230–231) view that:

> Ornament is painting and concealing anything that was deformed, trim- ming and polishing what was handsome; so that the unsightly parts might have given less offence . . .. A kind of auxiliary brightness and improve- ment to Beauty. So that then Beauty is somewhat lovely which is proper and innate, and diffused over the whole body, and Ornament somewhat added on or fastened on, rather than proper and innate.

Alberti argued that beauty conformed to the classical ideal of *decorum* where 'all parts fitted together with such proportion that nothing cou'd [sic] be added, diminished or altered but for the worse' (Alberti, 1957: 230; see also Pevsner, 1991: 28–32). As a result, this essentialism resulted in the association between decoration and decorum becoming inverted, and '[t]he concept of "decorative" still carries pejorative associations which relegate "the decorative" to a position of marginalization,

531

Organization 12(4)
Articles

spuriously associated with superficial ornamentation and the utilitarian'
(Kleinert, 1992:115).

Thus beauty became associated with an *absence* of decoration in
modern architecture and design. However, while modernism has been
regarded as 'a final nail in the coffin' for decoration (Collins, 1987: 6), it
was certainly not the first. For example, it is perhaps ironic that John
Ruskin's early rules for craft included: 'Never demand an exact finish for
its own sake, but only for some practical or noble end' (Lucie-Smith,
1981: 209). Decoration could, however, pursue such ends and mark the
importance of the individualism that Ruskin saw as so threatened by
the advance of industrial capitalism and the associated advance of
mechanized production. In this context, Fuller (1989: 133) discusses
Ruskin's admiration for Gothic ornament where 'every jot and tittle,
every point and niche affords room, fuel and focus for individual fire'.

In marked contrast to Ruskin and to the 'horror vacui' of William
Morris' densely decorated textiles (Collins, 1987), the 'chaste priests of
the Bauhaus . . . banish[ed] ornament from their credo' (Nelson, 1993: 3).
The Bauhaus' first director, Walter Gropius, sought a new society that
would embrace machine production and efficiency and would be 'ruth-
lessly modern' (Metcalf, 1993: 41). He contrasted the Bauhaus emphasis
on true form with the decadence and deceit of traditional style (Pier,
1999: 13, 15). Whereas Ruskin had stated in 1853 that '[o]rnament is the
origin of architecture' (Zerbst, 1988: 10), Gropius regarded decorated
buildings as 'lies' and derided those who disagreed with him (Pier, 1999:
16, 17). For example, the buildings he created for the new were of 'clear,
organic (form) whose inner logic (is) radiant, naked, unencumbered by
lying facades and trickeries' (Gropius, 1919, cited in Roper, 2000).
Bauhaus style was typified by machine technology, good design and
affordability (Greenberg, 1996), and the celebration of pure function even
became the 'new beauty':

> The Bauhaus attempts to find the functional form for the house, as well as
> for the simplest utensil. It wants things clearly constructed, it wants
> functional materials, it wants this new beauty. This new beauty is not a
> style, which matches one object with another aesthetically by using similar
> external forms (façade, motif, ornament). Today, something is beautiful if
> its form serves its function, if it is well made of chosen material. A good
> chair will then 'match' a good table. (Fleischmann, 1924, cited in Whitford,
> 1984: 210; cf. Strati, 2000a: 20)

Thus, 'Form without Ornament' was the name of a Bauhaus exhibition
that both heralded and embodied the era of modernism (Collins, 1987:
14), and the Bauhaus' Mies van der Rohe praised the decline in the
significance of the individual and the growing trend towards anonymity
(Fuller, 1989). Similarly, and in the context of his protest against the
elitism of Art Deco, the architect Le Corbusier intended to 'to "purify"
architecture of ornament to reveal the hidden structure and function'
(Roper, 2000) and to show that 'by virtue of . . . standardization . . .

Organization, Decoration
Julie Wolfram Cox and Stella Minahan

industry creates pure forms' (cited in Lucie-Smith 1981: 252; cf. Pevsner, 1991: 37).

Although decoration has since been celebrated under feminism and post modernism (Kleinert, 1992), its banishment had long-lasting effects. For example, Fuller (1989: 136) referred to the triumphant advance of 'the anaesthetic International Style' from the 1930s onwards and Greenberg (1996) suggested that the pervasive influence of the modern Bauhaus affected American resistance to decoration and ornament on design even until the 1980s. However, modernism is not *necessarily* associated with a lack of decoration. Powers (2000) has argued that modernism was both a rebellion against Art Nouveau and an extension of Art Nouveau and that modernism 'was deeply engaged in the issue of nature and was as much a return to ancient sources and standards as it was driven by progress and technology' (Powers, 2000: 28; see also Fuller, 1989). For example, while the growing emphasis on modernism in the works of the architect Charles Rennie Mackintosh has led Collins to the opinion that Mackintosh 'helped to cause the downfall of Art Nouveau simply by using an architectural style that was too rectilinear to accommodate it' (Collins, 1987: 48), Pevsner (1991) illustrates how Mackintosh's earlier Glasgow School of Art embodied a combination of Art Nouveau and modern styles, among others. Further, and in what might otherwise seem a rather unlikely combination, Ramirez (2000) has suggested that both Gaudí and Le Corbusier evoked images of bees and the beehive metaphor in their architecture, despite Le Corbusier's emphasis on the man-made and the machine aesthetic (Lucie-Smith, 1981).

More generally, art nouveau was even known as *modernisme* in Spain (Permanyer, 1999), and in Barcelona *modernista* architects, such as Gaudí, both embraced the new and drew on the city's craft tradition to display the 'characteristic aesthetic of restless movement' (Permanyer, 1999: 10) in their highly decorated facades:

> *Modernisme*'s movement is highlighted everywhere with the *fueteda* (*coup de fuet* or whiplash), that interminable stem-and-flower motif that meanders through and fills modernista spaces; it also appears in less descriptive form, such as in the triumph art curves of La Pedrera, the sinuous stone that dominates the whole façade. (Permanyer, 1999: 10; see also Howard, 1996)

Just as Ruskin had argued for the imitation of nature in decorative works, Gaudí's works were also imitative. For example, Sweeney and Sert (1960) comment that the glazed tile 'skins' of Gaudí's later buildings resembled the texture of local rock formations and that his use of colour was also inspired by nature. While decoration was supplemental to his interest in architectural structure, Sweeney and Sert (1960) suggest that Gaudí's naturalism was derivative of the Romantic movement in architecture.

In summary, while the worth and even existence of decoration is highly contested, even apparently strong positions on the subject belie

533

unexpected associations and contextual subtleties. We argue that attention to such (figurative) twists and turns is not only of relevance to the study of art, architecture and design, but also to organization studies, where decoration has received little attention.

Organizational Decoration

Within the arena of organizational culture studies, organizational decoration has perhaps been most closely associated with signification. For example, in one of the most influential popular texts on organizational culture, organizational artefacts are presented as superficial, material manifestations of 'deeper', more fundamental values and basic assumptions, or taken-for-granted beliefs about reality and human nature (Schein, 1985). Cultural artefacts such as interior design, artwork, office size and employee dress therefore give some indication of what is important to an organization, but because they occur only 'at the surface', they are not particularly important or reliable indicators of underlying meaning structures (Mohr, 1998).

Some attempts have been made to complicate the study of organizational artefacts. For example, Hatch (1993) introduced a variant of Schein's (1985) model of organizational culture that articulated particular cultural dynamics and gave greater attention to the importance of cultural artefacts in the constitution of organizational culture. Further, Gagliardi (1996: 568) presented a different view, suggesting that:

> Artefacts do not constitute secondary and superficial manifestations of deeper cultural phenomena . . ., but are themselves—so to speak—primary cultural phenomena which influence organizational life from two points of view: (a) artefacts make materially possible, help, hinder, or even prescribe organizational action; (b) more generally, artefacts influence our perception of reality, to the point of subtly shaping beliefs, norms, and cultural values.

For example, Munro (1999) has examined how organizational artefacts may be exhibited or 'managed' in order to present the semblance of a certain type of organization, or a certain type of manager. In addition, Strati (2000b) has argued that while artefacts, even photographic artefacts, may be limited in their ability to represent the real, their presence may create enjoyment and pleasure both for their viewers and for their creator(s), who may, in turn, be able to respond to the responses of the viewers.

Artefacts, therefore, are of interest not merely as decorative signifiers, but as aesthetic actants whose constitutive roles allow greater attention to the relevance of decoration for aesthetic organizational studies. In the following sections, we briefly outline some arenas for such attention. First, decoration, ornament and embellishment are not only what we see, but also what we do as managers, consultants, writers and as designers of both physical and project spaces. Second, and drawing on the art/craft debate, we note that decoration occupies contested and even liminal

Organization, Decoration
Julie Wolfram Cox and Stella Minahan

aesthetic position and that 'decorative art' lies betwixt and between fine art and craft. Neither fully accepted nor fully marginalized, decoration is 'only applied' and embodies shifting tensions between pure form and pure function. Third, we review the particular negotiations of these tensions at the Bauhaus, a controversial and highly influential aesthetic organization in early 20th century Germany. Fourth, we suggest that decoration, like disorganization, provides a source of complication for organizational studies that are neither pure nor parsimonious.

Organizational Decorators

Our first suggestion is far removed from the notion that organization theory can (or should) emulate some form of administrative science. If not lesser scientists, perhaps organization theorists can be considered as consultant designers and decorators of discursive space, reproducing, translating, extending and guiding the organizational tastes of (often) elite consumers. Their efforts in grouping and partitioning, including and excluding, smoothing or elaborating the contours of what is noticed, discussed and diffused as legitimate may be highly influential (cf. Clark and Salaman, 1996, 1998; Kieser, 1997).

This is not to suggest that such efforts do not have material effects and consequences, but to draw attention to the styling of organization within paradigmatic boundaries, narrative genres and feature themes, devices and topics. For example, and with respect to the latter, the diverse topics of empowerment, psychological contracts, benchmarking, emotional intelligence and the balanced scorecard are among many that the contemporary consumer of organizational knowledge would include within his or her discursive repertoire. And each of these has been embellished such that it can be applied at multiple levels of analysis. Empowerment, for example, is relevant to both individual and group applications; emotional intelligence has been deemed important for organizational leaders, individual managers, managerial groups and children; and benchmarking has been promoted for operations, human resource management and strategy. While the theoretical and empirical justifications for such extensions and embellishments are, of course, quite varied, our interest is in the nature of their enhancement and application. We suggest that such mimetic processes can be compared with the skill of patterning and repetition in craft where a finished design may be copied, altered, reformed and realigned in different media, with the surface creating effect rather than representing essence.

More generally, organizational decorators may well be informed by others who have worked with aesthetic peripheries rather than functional fundamentals of organizational life. In a book directed to what he has termed *paraesthetics*, Carroll (1987: xi) examines:

> art in terms of its relations with the extra-aesthetic in general. I am, for example, interested in the philosophical, historical, and political issues

Organization 12(4)
Articles

raised by the question of form or the problem of beauty rather than form and beauty as narrow aestheticist questions. (Carroll, 1987: xiv)

At its theoretical boundaries, Carroll sees paraesthetics as 'a faulty, irregular, disordered, improper aesthetics—one not content to remain within the area defined by the aesthetic' (1987: xiv). For example, he discusses Jacques Derrida's work on art and argues that it is paraesthetic in that it '"mobilizes" both theory and art by rethinking each in terms of the frames that both separate them and link them together, that both block and permit passage or movement between them' (1987: 144). In addition to Derrida, Carroll argues that Michel Foucault and Jean-Francois Lyotard have also been concerned 'with how art resists (even its own) theorization, and for this reason they attempt through various strategies to push the question of art beyond itself and its theoretical representation' (1987: xiv). As all of these theorists have had much influence on organization studies over the years since the publication of the series on Modernism, Postmodernism and Organizational Analysis in *Organization Studies* in the late 1980s (Burrell, 1988; Cooper and Burrell, 1988; Cooper, 1989), it is perhaps timely to remember that they shared a common concern with aesthetics. For Carroll (1987: xi), they are 'critical philosophers whose awareness of the limitations of theory has led them not to reject theory but rather to work at and on the borders of theory inorder to stretch, bend, or exceed its limitations.' For us, they are theoretical decorators.

Positioning Decoration

We now turn to a discussion of why such a categorization may be classed as superficial. Aside from the obvious limitations of any overly deliberate attempt to summarize the thesis of a major work in a few lines, it is worth noting that decoration itself occupies a borderline position within the art/craft debate. This debate concerns whether or not there remains a hierarchy of distinctions between art and craft, where art is fine and perceived to be at the 'high' end of the aesthetic ladder of preference and taste (Editor's introduction to Marincola, 1995; Kuspit, 1996; Ioannou, 1997/1998). Because of 'our tendency to value what is distinctive about paintings over what is distinctive about pots' (Markowitz, 1994: 67), *fine art* is distinguished from *applied*, more utilitarian art (see Osborne, 1970: 12), and art further marginalizes and excludes *craft* as a lowly pursuit (Metcalf, 1994; Ioannou, 1997/1998).

Drawing on Aristotle and Aquinas, Kuspit argued that before the concept of 'fine art' arose in the 18th century, craft and art were regarded as 'inseparable' (Kuspit, 1996: 16). However, and in contrast to craft, Kant claimed that the viewer of art experiences a universal, *common sense* that ignores tradition and transcends material existence. Thus, as Metcalf (1994: 16) has argued, 'Kantian notions of the aesthetic experience . . . exclude function—and thus much of craft—from the possibility of having an aesthetic component'. The art/craft debate stems from Kant's argument

Organization, Decoration
Julie Wolfram Cox and Stella Minahan

that an aesthetic experience could be supported only by an autonomous art object, and that the disinterested gaze of the art spectator is elicited only when art is removed from moral, social and religious values and from ordinary life (Metcalf, 1993).

While it is often argued that an object becomes *art* when decoration, special processing or the inclusion of precious materials takes place, decoration occupies contested and even liminal aesthetic position and *decorative art* lies betwixt and between craft and fine art. Kleinert (1992) has discussed the positioning of the decorative arts with particular reference to Australia and to the efforts of the artist, Lucien Henry, who wanted to improve the perception of decoration and went so far as to suggest that the decorative arts 'constitute the substrata of civilization; the rich soil from which the other arts draw their sap' (Smith, 1979: 242, cited in Kleinert, 1992: 123). Kleinert has presented arguments that Australian decorative art has legitimized space both for women and for Aboriginal culture, although that legitimation was only ever partial. For example, the superficial appropriation of Aboriginal motifs without reference to their symbolic value 'was closely linked to the widely held belief that the Aboriginal race was doomed to extinction' (Kleinert, 1992: 125) and assisted the status of neither Aborigines nor 'the decorative'. In addition:

> To be criticized as 'decorative' (as many women artists found) was to imply that one's work was superficially concerned with pattern, with a consequent disregard for structural form and content. (Kleinert, 1992: 125)

Decorative Debates

Thus, neither fully accepted nor fully marginalized, decoration is 'only applied'. Decoration also embodies shifting tensions between pure form and pure function. For example, one of the most well-known sites for the negotiation of such tensions was at the Bauhaus where, despite Gropius' distaste for architectural decoration, there was, supposedly, equal regard for fine, decorative and industrial arts (Greenberg, 1996: 69) and, despite the supposed emphasis on the new beauty and form following function, there were many instances of aesthetic debates.

Introduced briefly above, the Bauhaus was established by Walter Gropius in 1919 in the Weimar Republic when Van de Velde's School of Applied Art was amalgamated with the Academy of Fine Art (Rowland, 1997). After being given notice after a conservative local election win, the Bauhaus moved to Dessau and then to Berlin, where it was closed in 1933 (Greenberg, 1996). There were many differences and difficulties within the Bauhaus. Its predecessor organization, the Art Academy, had been a site for extensive debate on art and craft and the various stakeholders argued for four years 'over whether the Academy should be an art school that taught craft or one school that taught both' (Hochman, 1997: 31). Difficulties in finding any unity were apparent prior to the opening of the Bauhaus (see also Naylor, 1990), and only six weeks into its life the internal politics were described by Feininger (a staff member) as 'a hornets' nest' (Hochman, 1997: 86). Many students were angry with the notion that art was not a higher pursuit than craft and resented the attempt to transform what was an art academy into a craft school.

Walter Gropius was committed to the teaching and creation of craft as part of a broader social agenda to create a better world. He acknowledged Ruskin and Morris 'who consciously sought and found the first way to the reunification of the world of work with the creative artists' (Whitford, 1984: 23; see also Pevsner, 1991: 38–39). He argued:

> Let us create a new guild of craftsmen without the class distinctions which raise an arrogant barrier between craftsman and artist. (Gropius, 1919, cited in Lucie-Smith, 1981: 251–52; see also Whitford, 1984: 202).

Around 1921, Gropius became concerned with both the increased politicization in the Bauhaus workshops and with the sense that handcraft was being seen solely as art (Roper, 2000). His master Laszlo Moholy-Nagy moved the workshops away from self-expression, and traditional craft was superseded by modern geometric designs that used contemporary manufacturing techniques using accessible, manufactured materials such as tubular steel. A well-known example is the chair designed by Marcel Breuer (Collins, 1987: 69).

In 1923, the Bauhaus mounted an exhibition entitled 'Art and Technology: The New Unity'. This was designed to celebrate the work of the Bauhaus students and to explore opportunities for mass production of the prototypes on display. The exhibits were harshly criticized by some as 'misleading' as 'most of the objects were bulbously curved and harshly angled, more revealing of Expressionistic angst than the stark, geometric simplicities of machine technology' (Hochman, 1997: 160).

Gropius resigned as Director, tiring of the constant demands to protect the school and claiming 'that until now ninety percent of my work has been devoted to the defense of the school' (Ott, 2001: 2). His replacement, Meyer rejected any connection with art and was looking to mass produce domestic goods. However, the Bauhaus never managed to find an industrial manufacturer for its tableware (Rowland, 1997), and while the changing works of Marianne Brandt are often seen as an indication of the Weimar Bauhaus' transition from craft to industrial production (Lucie-Smith, 1981; Greenberg, 1996; Rowland, 1997), her hand-made tea sets, ashtrays and dishes include some that are decorated to look as if they were made by machine. Their smooth, apparently uniform finishes look undecorated and therefore 'modern', in contrast to their craft origins. Further, while the Bauhaus designs were supposedly based on function, the placing of the lids on tea and coffee pots drew comments as these lids were very close to the handles. Marianne Brandt even admitted that 'they were all obsessed with geometry' in the Bauhaus metal workshop (Rowland, 1997: 32).

At the Bauhaus building at Dessau, smoothness in appearance and absence of decoration became a material source of aesthetic disruption,

Organization, Decoration
Julie Wolfram Cox and Stella Minahan

for the 'new-style glass curtain wall' provided no insulation from heat or cold and it was claimed that no effort was made to respond to complaints and to solve this problem, or that of the building's poor acoustics. Indeed, Asendorf (1999: 80) argued that '[i]n the Dessau building practical efficiency was neglected in favor of the purity and smoothness of its technological appearance' and thus, at the Bauhaus, *absence* of decoration signified more an appeal to an aesthetics of function than any operational functionality. It was this *appearance* of functionality as signified by smoothness in form that was most important.

Decoration, Disorganization

Accordingly, we argue that the study of both decoration and absence of decoration is therefore the study of interdependence and of complication. Not only does decoration (at least in most cases) literally embellish what may otherwise be seen as plain, its discussion triggers a further play of positions and counter-positions. At the Bauhaus, this play was often located around particular material artefacts that ranged from buildings to paintings to tea sets, but we suggest that the serious plays of organization theory are, in both senses, highly decorative.

For example, Weick (1999: 797) has discussed recent efforts 'to make the tacit craft of theorizing more explicit', giving particular attention to recent manifestations of Thorngate's (1976) discussion of tradeoffs among theoretical generality, simplicity and accuracy. Weick has argued that one of these three dimensions is often omitted in discussions of theorizing in organizational studies:

> Carried to the extreme, accurate-simple explanations say everything about nothing, general-simple explanations say nothing about everything, and general-accurate explanations say everything about everything but are unintelligible ... Theorists may be better off trying to author relatively 'pure' exhibits of general or accurate or simple explanations and leave the readers to embellish the text in ways that add in the two dimensions. (Weick, 1999: 801)

Perhaps Weick's search for a 'useful starting point' (1999: 801) for theory development can be re-read as an articulation of theoretical styles. While his references to the 'craft of theorizing' and to reader 'embellishments' display aesthetic references quite different from the science-based comparisons in Fabian's (2000) discussion of the more specific arena of management studies, Fabian, too, can be read just as much as a style guide as a representation of debates over various disciplinary approaches. Fabian (2000: 353) presents a 'conceptual framework of the kinds of standards the discipline should use to adopt, accommodate or reject research as legitimate' and articulates a typology of nine disciplinary approaches that are differentiated in terms of their system of validation (universal or multiple standards), emphasis toward paradigm inclusion (solidarity, integration or segregation), and impetus for new

Organization 12(4)
Articles

research (knowledge development or knowledge breadth). Fabian's comparison of these centres on a distinction between scientific pressures for paradigm and theory proliferation and pragmatic pressures for consensus. While science rather than craft is her reference point, Thorngate's tradeoffs are clearly implicit in at least the first and third dimensions of her typology and, like Weick, she draws reference to the role of readers whom, 'it is hoped, will better discover their own predilections in these debates but also come to terms with why the discipline cannot move single-mindedly in their preferred direction' (Fabian, 2000: 366).

Within these debates on theory, readers, therefore, are presented variously as theoretical embellishers, theoretical consumers, and arbiters of taste. In this reading, theory is not necessarily a representation of the real, just as decoration is not necessarily imitative of nature. Generality, simplicity and accuracy are of no particular interest except as theoretical styles. Theorizing, then, can be thought of as a decorative or ornamental art, and as a means to complicate, attract attention and evoke response rather than to represent, control and predict.

However, this is not to suggest that the decorative is purely pleasurable or occasionally entertaining (cf. Weick, 1979: 264). First, it is never purely anything. As Nelson (1993) has argued:

> Ornament always assists another structure: it is never the total structure; there has to be a more fundamental structure which it does not circumscribe but which it inscribes with various intonations. Ornament presupposes a difference between itself and the design to which it is applied . . . .. The reason why ornament can never be the totality is because it expresses difference; it functions by contrasts and, as it goes distinguishing its support and its own motifs, it can never arrive at autonomy. (Nelson, 1993: 15)

Second, decoration, like disorganization, provides a source of complication for organizational studies that are neither pure nor parsimonious and that are also informed by attention to difference. For example, in his paper on the subject of 'Organization/disorganization', Cooper (1986) discusses the 'illusory edifice' of notions of structure and organization (Cooper, 1986: 317). Such notions represent the privileging of unity and order where 'what lies outside the system—or more accurately, what is said to lie outside the frame that creates the system—is viewed as less ordered and less unitary than what is included' (Cooper, 1986: 302). For example:

> Traditional conceptions of system are . . . structured so as to give preference to the idea of systemness, of articulated unity and order. The system (with its boundary) becomes conceptually detached from background or environment and this takes on a life of its own. This has the effect of diverting attention from the all-important function of the frame. (Cooper, 1986: 303)

Organization, Decoration
Julie Wolfram Cox and Stella Minahan

Cooper (1986: 303) conceives of the boundary or frame between the inside and outside of a system as 'an active process of differentiation,' and suggests that:

> attention to the divisionary nature of the boundary reveals that the work of organization is focused upon transforming an intrinsically ambiguous condition into one that is *ordered* so that organization as a process is constantly bound up with its contrary state of disorganization. (Cooper, 1986: 304–305; emphasis in original)

Cooper argues that the 'struggle for the "superior" position necessarily requires the "support" of an "inferior" position inasmuch as the latter is what defines the former' (1986: 328). Drawing on the work of Saussure, Bateson and Derrida, Cooper discusses 'the boundary concept as an active process of differentiation' (1986: 307). In the context of organization studies 'it becomes impossible to disentangle the "content" of organization studies from the theory or methodology that frames it' (Cooper, 1986: 331). In terms of this discussion, the boundary is more than 'purely ornamental' for it conducts a censuring function and requires '[a] certain force or violence . . . for the act of separating the decidable from the undecidable' (Cooper, 1986: 314). As ornament, it certainly assist structure. But as a frame, it may also direct attention, inhibit debate and artificially stabilize centre-periphery relations.

The Power of Decoration

In summary, our call for attention to organizational decoration is also a call for disorganization. It includes greater reflexive consideration of organizational decorators; their roles, their reception and, in a few cases, their legacies. It recognizes the liminal aesthetic position of decoration, and the associated placement of decoration as a highly contested site for aesthetic debates. It allows for the consideration of style in theoretical debates, and for the consideration of organization theory as an ornamental art. And it recognizes the power of decoration as a framing process where marking and boundary setting are not just 'purely decorative' but may be thought of as processes of violence.

Accordingly, this last emphasis draws our attention to the context for decoration, and to the impossibility of either organizational or aesthetic purity. With reference to the latter, it should be noted here that even Kant's (1952) requirement for the autonomy of fine art has been disputed by Slater (1997) who argued that:

> It is a matter of plain historic fact, however, that Kant held . . . that art involved the perfection of a concept, the achievement of a function, and so was a matter of what he called dependent beauty, not independent beauty, which was free of concepts, as with nature . . . .. Moreover it was free beauty which alone required abandonment of self-interest and attachment to objectivity. (Slater, 1997: 230; see also Wicks, 1995)

541

Organization 12(4)
Articles

In tracing the history of aesthetic thought, Kelly (2000), too, has questioned the possibility of art's autonomy, but from a different position and with particular attention to the thesis that 'the arts–politics choice is false' (Kelly, 2000: 223). For example, Kelly (2000: 225) argues that Kant's insistence on the autonomy of aesthetics 'was possible only in a social world in which autonomy of freedom was a prominent, if as yet largely unrealized, political (and moral) concept' and that Kantian autonomy 'does not separate art/aesthetics and politics, it actually unites them via a common philosophical presupposition and historical condition' (Kelly, 2000: 227).

Within a more contemporary context, the claim for the autonomy of art has itself been complicated in the work of the modern critical theorist Theodor Adorno. Adorno's (1997) *Aesthetic Theory* discusses the position and operation of autonomous works under advanced capitalist conditions. As interpreted by Zuidervaart (1991: 32), Adorno's position was that the autonomy of art 'can be equated . . . with freedom of art from religious, political and other social roles'. It is through art's very autonomy that art can be critical, for 'art criticizes society just by being there' (Adorno, 1984: 321):

> Indeed, [Adorno's] account of advanced capitalism as a function of exchange and domination leads him to attribute unusual social significance to autonomous art, a significance tied to the position and operation of autonomous works under advanced capitalist conditions. Where cultural commodity fetishism and domination in exchange prevail, autonomy enables art to mount critical resistance. Autonomous art is one part of the totality that challenges the totality from within. (Zuidervaart, 1991: 87)

Further, Adorno's reasoning was that:

> By appearing to be detached from the conditions of economic production, works of art acquire the ability to suggest changed conditions. And by appearing to be useless, works of art recall the human purposes of production that instrumental rationality forgets. (Zuidervaart, 1991: 89)

However, Adorno does not idealize art's autonomy, regarding it as 'illusory' (Zuidervaart, 1991: 182). His argument for autonomy is, instead, a resistance against simple historicist determination (Horowitz, 1997), a comment on the artwork as 'the literal embodiment of the distance between where we are and freedom' (Huhn, 1997: 249) and as afterimage, 'a response to socio-historical conditions that have since changed' (Harding, 1997: 12). Adorno has argued that while, 'every advance in political freedom is accompanied by repression', the dialectic of semblance allows for a possible reconciliation of reality with itself in a utopian future (Kelly, 2000: 232; see also Zuidervaart, 1997: 6). With reference to the particular importance of modern art:

> art's task (even its truth) is to sustain the dialectic of semblance: 'Through the irreconcilable renunciation of the semblance of reconciliation, art holds fast to the promise of reconciliation in the midst of the unreconciled'. Which in turn accounts for art's mimetic function; it 'imitates'

Organization, Decoration
Julie Wolfram Cox and Stella Minahan

reality's nonreconciliation while holding up a mirror to the possibility of reconciliation. (Kelly, 2000: 232–233, quoting Adorno, 1997: 33; see also Bernstein, 1997: 179; Huhn, 1997)

In Adorno's writings, the notion of mimesis means more than imitation. In contrast to the Platonic definition of mimesis as copy, Adorno's mimesis is not defined by reason and is 'a truly protean concept, refer[ing] to an archaic openness to the other' (Zuidervaart, 1997: 7; see also Schultz, 1990; Bubner, 1997: 175; Hansen, 1997). Art is mimetic but does not imitate. As explained by Jay (1997: 35):

by refusing to imitate, or be assimilated entirely to, a bad external reality ... works of art hold out the hope for a more benign version of mimesis in a future world beyond domination and reification.

While Adorno's praxis has drawn criticism from both Marxist and postmodern thinkers, it is perhaps surprising that his aesthetics has received such little discussion in organization and management studies. We suggest his discussions of mimesis and semblance could contribute to contemporary discussions on representation, on emancipatory potential, and on materiality (cf. Alvesson and Willmott, 1992, 1996; Alvesson and Deetz, 2000; Calás and Smircich, 1999). Of particular interest to us is his emphasis on the autonomy of art in contrast to recent calls for attention, instead, to craft as historically and culturally embedded and as a tangible way of considering marginality (see Wolfram Cox and Minahan, 2001; 2002). In this context, it is important to examine Zuidervaart's (1991) review of Bürger's (1984) criticisms of Adorno's autonomy of art, and Zuidervaart's own discussion of the distinction of autonomous art from 'heteronomous art'. The latter includes both traditional folk art and contemporary popular art and 'has not become relatively independent from other institutions of bourgeois society and whose products are produced and received to accomplish purposes that are directly served by other institutions' (Zuidervaart, 1991: 227). Zuidervaart discusses the proposition that autonomous art must be useless to be critical and the implication that 'major works' of autonomous art 'have greater social significance than any works of heteronomous art' (Zuidervaart, 1991: 233), suggesting that 'heteronomy need not keep a work from challenging the status quo and disclosing human aspirations' (1991: 231). Zuidervaart concludes that 'the criteria of truth and significance need not be restricted to autonomous art' (1991: 233), and that Adorno's aesthetics are 'inadequate with respect to popular art' (1991: 234).

In a world where the decorative can be both functional and violent, the autonomous is an illusion and not only the useless may be critical, we conclude that the search for organizational and representational purity therefore be abandoned on aesthetic as well as linguistic grounds (cf. Cooper, 1986). Disorganization and decoration have much greater appeal.

543

Organization 12(4)
Articles

Note

An earlier version of this paper was presented at the Negotiating Organizational Aesthetics Substream, 18th EGOS Colloquium, 4–6 July 2002, Barcelona, Spain.

References

Adorno, Theodor (1984) *Aesthetic Theory*, trans. C. Lenhardt. London: Routledge and Kegan Paul.

Adorno, Theodor (1997) *Aesthetic Theory*, trans. Robert Hullot-Kentor. Minneapolis, MN: Minnesota University Press.

Alberti, L. B. (1957) 'On Architecture', in E. G. Holt (ed.) *A Documentary History of Art, Volume 1*, revised edn, pp. 218–43. New York: Doubleday Anchor.

Alvesson, Mats and Deetz, Stanley (2000) *Doing Critical Management Research*. London: Sage.

Alvesson, Mats and Willmott, Hugh, eds (1992) *Critical Management Studies*. London: Sage.

Alvesson, Mats and Willmott, Hugh (1996) *Making Sense of Management: A Critical Introduction*. London: Sage.

Asendorf, Christoph (1999) 'The Bauhaus and the World of Technology—Work on Industrial Culture', in J. Fiedler and P. Feierabend (eds) *Bauhaus*, pp. 160–71. Cologne: Konemann.

Bernstein, J. M. (1997) 'Why Rescue Semblance? Metaphysical Experience and the Possibility of Ethics', in T. Huhn and L. Zuidervaart (eds) *The Semblance of Subjectivity: Essays in Adorno's Aesthetic Theory*, pp. 177–212. Cambridge, MA and London: MIT Press.

Black, Roman (1964) *Old and New Australian Aboriginal Art*. Sydney: Angus and Robertson.

Bubner, Rüdiger (1997) 'Concerning the Central Idea of Adorno's Philosophy', in T. Huhn and L. Zuidervaart (eds) *The Semblance of Subjectivity: Essays in Adorno's Aesthetic Theory*, pp. 147–75. Cambridge, MA and London: MIT Press.

Bürger, Peter (1984) *Theory of the Avant-Garde*, trans. Michael Shaw, foreward by Jochen Schulte-Sass. Minneapolis, MN: University of Minnesota Press.

Burrell, Gibson (1988) 'Modernism, Postmodernism and Organizational Analysis 2: The Contribution of Michel Foucault', *Organization Studies* 9(2): 221–35.

Calás, Marta B. and Smircich, Linda (1999) 'Past Postmodernism? Reflections and Tentative Directions', *Academy of Management Review* 24(4): 649–71.

Carroll, David (1987) *Paraesthetics: Foucault, Lyotard, Derrida*. New York and London: Methuen.

Clark, Timothy and Salaman, Graeme (1996) 'The Management Guru as Organizational Witchdoctor', *Organization* 3(2): 85–107.

Clark, Timothy and Salaman, Graeme (1998) 'Telling Tales: Management Gurus' Narratives and the Construction of Managerial Identity', *Journal of Management Studies* 35(2): 137–61.

Collins, M. (1987) *Towards Post-modernism: Design Since 1851*. London: British Museum Press.

Cooper, Robert (1986) 'Organization/Disorganization', *Social Science Information* 25(2): 299–335.

Organization, Decoration
Julie Wolfram Cox and Stella Minahan

Cooper, Robert (1989) 'Modernism, Post Modernism and Organizational Analysis 3: The Contribution of Jacques Derrida', *Organization Studies* 10(4): 479–502.

Cooper, Robert and Burrell, Gibson (1988) 'Modernism, Postmodernism and Organizational Analysis: An Introduction', *Organization Studies* 9(1): 91–112.

Fabian, Frances H. (2000) 'Keeping the Tension: Pressures to Keep the Controversy in the Management Discipline', *Academy of Management Review* 25(2): 350–71.

Fleischmann, A. (1924) 'Economic Living', *Neue Frauerkleidung und Frauenkultur* (supplement), Karlsruhe cited in Wortmann Weltge, S. (1993) *Bauhaus Textiles: Women Artists and the Weaving Workshop*. London: Thames and Hudson.

Fuller, Peter (1989) 'Aesthetics after Modernism', in P. Abbs (ed.) *The Symbolic Order: A Contemporary Reader on the Arts Debate*, pp. 126–42. London: The Falmer Press.

Gagliardi, Pasquale (1996) 'Exploring the Aesthetic Side of Organizational Life', in S. R. Clegg, C. Hardy and W. R. Nord (eds), *Handbook of Organization Studies*, pp. 565–80. London: Sage.

Greenberg, C. (1996) 'Bauhaus: A Look Back at the Future', *Art & Antiques*, October, 66–73.

Hansen, Miriam Bratu (1997) 'Mass Culture as Hieroglyphic Writing: Adorno, Derrida, Kracauer', in Max Pensky (ed.) *The Actuality of Adorno*, pp. 83–111. Albany, NY: State University of New York Press.

Harding, James Martin (1997) *Adorno and 'A Writing of the Ruins'*. Albany, NY: State University of New York Press.

Hatch, Mary Jo (1993) 'The Dynamics of Organizational Culture', *Academy of Management Review* 18(4): 657–93.

Hochman, Elaine S. (1997) *Bauhaus: Crucible of Modernism*. New York: Fromm International.

Horowitz, Gregg M. (1997) 'Art History and Autonomy', in T. Huhn and L. Zuidervaart (eds) *The Semblance of Subjectivity: Essays in Adorno's Aesthetic Theory*, pp. 177–212. Cambridge, MA and London: MIT Press.

Howard, Jeremy (1996) *Art Nouveau: International and National Styles in Europe*. Manchester and New York: Manchester University Press.

Huhn, Tom (1997) 'Kant, Adorno, and the Social Opacity of the Aesthetic', in T. Huhn and L. Zuidervaart (eds) *The Semblance of Subjectivity: Essays in Adorno's Aesthetic Theory*, pp. 238–57. Cambridge, MA and London: MIT Press.

Ioannou, Noris (1997/1998) 'Collaboration in Glass', *Craft Arts International* 41: 61.

Jay, Martin (1997) 'Mimesis and Mimetology: Adorno and Lacoue-Labarthe', in T. Huhn and L. Zuidervaart (eds) *The Semblance of Subjectivity: Essays in Adorno's Aesthetic Theory*, pp. 29–53. Cambridge, MA and London: MIT Press.

Kant, Immanuel (1952) *Critique of Judgment*, trans. J. C. Meredith. Oxford: Clarendon Press.

Kieser, Alfred (1997) 'Rhetoric and Myth in Management Fashion', *Organization* 4(1): 49–74.

Kelly, Michael (2000) 'The Political Autonomy of Contemporary Art: The Case of the 1993 Whitney Biennial' in S. Kemal and I. Gaskell (eds) *Politics and Aesthetics in the Arts*, pp. 221–63. Cambridge: Cambridge University Press.

Organization 12(4)
Articles

Kleinert, Sylvia (1992) 'Deconstructing "The Decorative": The Impact of Euro-American Artistic Traditions on the Reception of Aboriginal Art and Craft' in N. Ioannou (ed.) *Craft in Society*, pp. 115–30. South Fremantle, Western Australia: Freemantle Arts Centre Press.

Kuspit, Donald (1996) 'Craft in Art, Art as Craft', *The New Art Examiner* 23 (April): 14–53.

Lucie-Smith, Edward (1981) *The Story of Craft: The Craftsman's Role in Society.* Oxford: Phaidon.

Marincola, Paula (1995) 'Fabric as Fine Art: Thinking Across the Divide', *Fiberarts* 22(5): 34–9.

Markowitz, Sally J. (1994) 'The Distiction Between Art and Craft', *Journal of Aesthetic Education* 28(1): 55–70.

Metcalf, Bruce (1993) 'Replacing the Myth of Modernism', *American Craft* 53 (February–March): 40–7.

Metcalf, Bruce (1994) 'Toward an Aesthetics of Craft', *Studio Potter* 22 (June): 14–6.

Mohr, John W. (1998) 'Measuring Meaning Structures', *Annual Review of Sociology* 24: 345–70.

Munro, Rolland (1999) 'The Cultural Performance of Control', *Organization Studies* 20(4): 619–40.

Naylor, Gillian (1990) *The Arts and Crafts Movement: A Study of its Sources, Ideals and Influence on Design Theory.* London: Tefoil.

Nelson, Robert (1993) *Ornament: An Essay Concerning the Meaning of Decorative Design.* Fitzroy, Victoria: Craft Victoria.

Osborne, Harold, ed. (1970) *The Oxford Companion to Art.* Oxford: Clarendon Press.

Ott, Randall (2001) *Mies, Politics and the Bauhuas Closure: Polemics and Paradigms for Architectural Education.* University of Colorado, Denver, http://www.tulane.edu/swacasa/papers/7.html (accessed 19 August 2003).

Permanyer, Lluis (1999) *Barcelona Art Nouveau.* New York: Rizzoli.

Pevsner, Nikolaus (1991) *Pioneers of Modern Design: From William Morris to Walter Gropius.* London: Penguin.

Pier, A. S. (1999) 'Bauhaus: Walter Gropius and the Influence of the Bauhaus', *Sculpture Review*, 48(2): 13–7.

Powers, Alan (2000) 'A Natural Development', *Craft* 162(1): 26–31.

Ramirez, Juan Antonio (2000) *The Beehive Metaphor: From Gaudí to Le Corbusier.* London: Reaktion Books.

Roper, Q. (2000) 'Art Nouveau: the importance of decoration', http://www.qdesign.co.nz/designhist (accessed 13 July 2001).

Rowland, Anna (1997) *Bauhaus Source Book.* Leichardt: Quantum.

Schein, Edgar H. (1985) *Organizational Culture and Leadership.* San Francisco, CA: Jossey-Bass.

Schultz, Karla L. (1990) *Mimesis on the Move: Theodor Adorno's Concept of Imitation.* Berne: Peter Lang.

Slater, Hartley (1997) 'Art and Aesthetics', *British Journal of Aesthetics* 37(3): 226–31.

Smith, Bernard, ed. (1979) *Documents on Art and Taste in Australia.* Melbourne: Oxford University Press.

Organization, Decoration
Julie Wolfram Cox and Stella Minahan

Strati, Antonio (2000a) 'The Aesthetic Approach in Organization Studies', in S. Linstead and H. Höpfl (eds) *The Aesthetics of Organization*, pp. 13–34. London: Sage.

Strati, Antonio (2000b) 'Putting People in the Picture: Art and Aesthetics in Photography and in Understanding Organizational Life', *Organization Studies* 21: 53–69.

Sweeney, James J. and Sert, Jospe L. (1960) *Antoni Gaudí*. London: The Architectural Press.

Thorngate, W. (1976) 'Possible Limits on a Science of Social Behavior', in J. H. Strickland, F. E. Aboud and K. J. Gergen (eds), *Social Psychology in Transition*, pp. 121–39. New York: Plenum.

Weick, Karl E. (1979) *The Social Psychology of Organizing*, 2nd edn. New York: Random House.

Weick, Karl E. (1999) 'Theory Construction as Disciplined Reflexivity: Tradeoffs in the 90s', *Academy of Management Review* 24(4): 797–806.

Whitford, F. (1984) *Bauhaus*. London: Thames and Hudson.

Wicks, R. (1995) 'Kant on Fine Art: Artistic Sublimity Shaped by Beauty', *Journal of Aesthetics and Art Criticism* 53 (Spring): 189–93.

Wolfram Cox, Julie and Minahan, Stella (2001) 'Organizing the Aesthetic: Contestation and Craft', paper presented at APROS 2001: Asia-Pacific Researchers In Organisation Studies (December), Hong Kong.

Wolfram Cox, Julie and Minahan, Stella (2002) 'Crafting Organization', *Culture and Organization* 8(3): 209–24.

Yanagi, Soetsu (1989) *The Unknown Craftsman: A Japanese Insight into Beauty*. London: Gillingham House.

Zerbst, Rainer (1988) *Antoni Gaudí*. Cologne: Taschen.

Zuidervaart, Lambert (1991) *Adorno's Aesthetic Theory: The Redemption of Illusion*. Cambridge, MA and London: MIT Press.

Zuidervaart, Lambert (1997) 'Introduction', in T. Huhn and L. Zuidervaart (eds) *The Semblance of Subjectivity: Essays in Adorno's Aesthetic Theory*, pp. 1–28. Cambridge, MA and London: MIT Press.

Julie Wolfram Cox is Associate Professor of Organizational Analysis in the School of Management at RMIT University, Australia. Julie received BA (Honours) and MA (Research) degrees in psychology from the University of Melbourne and holds a PhD in organizational behaviour from Case Western Reserve University in Cleveland, USA. Her research interests include critical perspectives on emerging and established topics in management theory and research, craft, and healthcare, and her publications include articles in *Organization Studies*, *Organization*, *Journal of Management Studies*, *Culture and Organization*, *Journal of Organizational Change Management* and *Tamara*. She has recently co-edited a four-volume collection, *Fundamentals of Action Research* (Sage, 2005) with Bill Cooke, University of Manchester. **Address:** School of Management, RMIT University, GPO Box 2476V, Melbourne, Victoria 3001, Australia. [email: julie.wolfram-cox@rmit.edu.au]

Stella Minahan is the Senior Research Fellow in the Faculty of Business and Law at Deakin University. Her research interests include organizational theory, creativity, art and craft, and contemporary social anthropology. She has published in

Organization 12(4)
Articles

the *Journal of Organizational Change Management, Culture and Organization* and in the *International Journal of Diversity in Organizations, Communities and Nations.* Her work will appear soon in the *International Journal of Nonprofit and Voluntary Sector Marketing* and a book, *Why Women Shop* (Wiley Publishers with Michael Beverland) will be released in 2005. **Address:** Bowater School of Management and Marketing, Deakin University, 221 Burwood Highway, Burwood, Victoria 3125 Australia. [email: stella.minahan@deakin.edu.au]

[26]

Essai: On Paragrammatic Uses of Organizational Theory — A Provocation*

Yiannis Gabriel

Yiannis Gabriel
School of
Management,
Imperial College,
London, UK

Abstract

Having indicated some of the recurring difficulties in establishing a conceptual or philosophical link between theory and practice, the author examines the relation between organization theory and the practices of academics, managers and other organizational participants. He argues that this relation is shaped by the way organizational theories are disseminated in the face of an expanding hegemony of consumerization and consumerism. Like other commodities, organizational theories are not used passively, in general, but in a creative, opportunistic and individualistic way. In this, they resemble folk knowledge, such as cooking recipes and cookery books, which different users employ or experiment with in widely differing ways, for widely differing ends. In contrast to both programme and paradigm, the author uses the term 'paragramme' to indicate a shifting stock of ideas, routines, images and ingredients which invite improvization and elaboration, rather than copying or adherence.

Descriptors: programmes, paradigms, paragrammes, theory, practice, bricolage, consumption, recipes

The link between theory and practice has preoccupied many of the brightest intellects, and has generated one of the broadest discursive traditions in Western thought. Some theorists have looked at the precise ways in which theory influences practice, or *vice versa*, while others have theorized on how it *should* influence practice, or how it may be tested through practice. Some theorists have focused on moral action, others on political action, and yet others on aesthetic, technical or even entrepreneurial action. Yet, the link between theory and practice, while heavily theorized by most philosophical and scientific traditions, has remained problematic, provisional and ultimately unsatisfactory.

In the area of organizational studies, there is a pressing need to explore, understand and codify the relationship between theories, developed mostly by academics and popularized by consultants and gurus, and the actions of practicing managers. This is important because on it rests vital issues of management education and learning, and even more importantly, the basis on which business is conducted. Yet, the relationship between organizational theory and the practice of managers and other organizational participants has remained one of the most elusive and recalcitrant.

This paper indicates some of the recurring difficulties in establishing such a conceptual or philosophical link between theory and practice. It identifies some broad tendencies in the conceptualization of this link, before arguing that the link is not a conceptual, but practical. In particular, it proposes that the uses to which organizational theories are put are shaped by how they are disseminated in the face of an expanding hegemony of consumerization and consumerism, and in response to the needs of users. It will be argued that organizational theories, like other commodities, are not used in a passive way, in general, but creatively, opportunistically and individualistically. In this, they resemble cooking recipes and cookery books, which different users employ or experiment with in widely differing ways, for widely differing ends. The term 'paragramme', in contrast to both 'programme' and 'paradigm', is used to indicate a shifting stock of ideas, routines, images and ingredients which invite improvization and elaboration, rather than copying or adherence.

The problematic relationship between theory and practice can be encountered in every domain of human activity and endeavour. In the area of organizations, the issue is complicated by some particularities of organizational theory which set it apart from other human sciences, notably it's increasingly close alignment to the interests and concerns of practicing management, which often subsidizes it's production and dissemination. A number of theories in this field claim to be of practical use to managers, who claim to make use of (or at least to find usefulness in) some of them (not necessarily the same as those above) and for those theories which are meant to be effectively put into practice, practical successes are claimed. Thus, the impression is sometimes created that the different theories of organization amount to a toolkit for practicing managers. Summed up in Lewin's famous epigram 'there is nothing so practical as a good theory'. This view is in line with the positivist tradition pioneered in the social sciences by Auguste Comte: *'Voir pour prevoir, prevoir pour prevenir'*. The aim of social theory is to understand events in order to anticipate them, and to anticipate them in order to control them. Thus, in practice, control has undoubtedly been a central reason for the perceived value of organizational theory. In vastly different ways, the theories of Taylor, Weber and Peters and Waterman have, *willingly or unwillingly*, made their marks as ostensible instruments for a more efficient control of organizations and what goes on inside them from the point of view of people, information and resources. Much of what Burrell (1996) refers to as NATO (North American Theory of Organization), ranging from positivist research to guru theory, seeks to make itself useful to practitioners, offering them ways of achieving competitive advantage. Variants of vulgar Marxism — 'correct practice follows from correct theory' — aspired at using theory in similar ways, but to different ends.

This toolkit link of theory with practice has been challenged, and with good reasons, from several different quarters. Inspired by the work of Paulo Freire (1970/1996), some have sought to develop organizational theory as part of a humanist project in which theory is a force leading towards progressive learning, enlightenment and growth in the interest of material and spiritual amelioration of humanity. The aim here is to develop new forms of reflective management practice which are less deleterious to human growth and fulfilment and to generate less dysfunctional forms of organization.

Others have argued that organizational theories are essentially non-practical, because even if practitioners act under the illusion of putting into effect the latest theoretical findings, in practice, they use theory as a *post facto* rationalization for action. As such, theory then becomes part of a legitimating process, one that enhances the position of managers and bolsters their authority (MacIntyre 1981; Thomas 1993; Gabriel 1998). From a psychological point of view, theory, far from guiding action, is more akin to a transitional object, a soft blanket or teddy bear, that offers comfort and security to the perplexed and confused practitioner (Lawrence 1999; Obholzer 1999). Anti-performativity, i.e. a deep-seated aversion towards any type of theorizing which may directly or serendipitously find some practical implications in the hands of managers, is an important feature of many of those theories now referred to as critical management studies (Fournier and Grey 2000). This is consistent with an ironic postmodern twist, which seeks to denaturalize concepts and ideas and promote reflexivity through a deconstruction of managerial buzzwords and practice. The majority of theorists with this tendency have asserted the primacy of discourse, either viewing theory itself as practice (theoretical practice) or arguing for a total discontinuity between theory and action (Knights and Willmott 1989; Burrell 1990; Parker 1992; Carter 1995; Jackson 1995; Parker 1995).

The relation of theory and practice is frequently posed and debated in terms of the actions of practicing managers and the theoretical knowledge that mostly comes directly or indirectly out of business and management schools. (Sandelands 1990; Czarniawska 1999). Less developed is the link between theory and the actions of workers, unions activists and officials, environmental and other campaigners, equal opportunity officers, regulators, househusbands and housewives, TV viewers, and so forth. There is also a tendency to use 'knowledge' as a catch-all for all types of theory, treating different types of organizational theory, e.g. from the classical theories of Weber and Taylor to postmodern theorising and from positivist research to guru sermonizing, in similar ways. Commenting on different attempts, Czarniawska (1999: 8) argues that, in spite of attempts to bring them together, 'the chasm between theory and practice gapes as wide as ever', a view with which I am inclined to agree.

The basis on which these issues are addressed by different theorists involves, on the one hand, an analysis of the nature of management and the nature of its relation to knowledge, and, on the other, the nature of organizational theories and of their applications — in short, ontology and epistemology. What, however, if the determinant of whether these theories are actionable or not is not to be found in the ontology of management and the epistemology of management theory, but rather in the mode of the acquisition and dissemination of theories and the practical needs which they meet? A theory, a piece of information, an idea or even a story may become actionable because of the way it is disseminated, rather because of something ontologically or epistemologically intrinsic to it. For example, a piece of information that is stolen may be more actionable than one given away as a gift or as charity. A theory which is paid for and personally delivered may be actionable, whereas exactly the same theory being freely available and lying idle in the pages of a book may be less so. A theory that is packaged for dissemination to other academics in sober academic journals may be less actionable than a similar theory re-packaged, simplified and popularized for the practitioner. Moreover, a seemingly inconsequential theory or idea may shoot to prominence and be acted upon, because it appears to meet an urgent user-need at a particular moment in time. Thus, what I wish to explore is the view that organizational theories may be constructed as actionable knowledge due to the conditions of their dissemination and the needs of the users, rather than to any intrinsic properties or claims to truth (Jackson and Carter 1995).

It is apparent, even to a casual observer, that the dissemination of most organizational theories today is different in some important respects from that of 20 or 40 years ago. One only has to look at the books in airport lounges to realize that management literature has become part of popular culture. Armies of consultants are available to sell virtually every type of organizational theory to eager customers, and armies of academics are equally available to service the consultants. The nature of universities themselves is being revolutionized. From sober, utilitarian deliverers of services to elites, they are being rapidly transformed into businesses delivering outputs to customers, subject to commercial pressures and competition, and to regulation. Nowhere is this more evident than in business and management schools, which have been undergoing a palpable transformation in the twenty years that I have been part of them. Gone are the antiquated desks engraved with the initials of generations of suffering students; gone are the dusty blackboards of old; gone too are the linoleum floors. Paying customers could not be expected to put up with such shoddy environments.

Universities have not yet been transformed into theme parks, though there is little doubt that consumerism has penetrated deeply the world of academia. As Ritzer has argued:

'[University] administrators are coming to recognize that their educational campuses need to grow more like the other means of consumption to thrive. The high school has been described as resembling a shopping mall. The university, too, can be seen as a means of educational consumption. These days most campuses are dated, stodgy and ineffective compared to shopping malls, cruise ships, casinos and fast food restaurants. To compete, universities are trying to satisfy their students by offering, for example, 'theme housing' — dorms devoted to students with shared special interests. As universities learn more and more from the new means of consumption, it will be increasingly possible to refer to them as "McUniversities".' (Ritzer 1999: 24)

Can we take Ritzer's idea seriously and view the McUniversity as an ideal type of the kind of educational establishment that corresponds to a society of hyper-consumption? If we do so, we discover that the implications go considerably further than Ritzer himself realized. Quite apart from merchandizing t-shirts and track-suits with university logos, upgrading conference and catering facilities to match those of international hotels, and discovering a myriad of ways of creating spending opportunities, what goes on inside McUniversities becomes subject to the logic of McDonaldization. The subjects taught and researched, are McSociology, McManagement and McOB. If the students of such a university are customers, the subjects which they study are standard and uniform, and the workers delivering the service are dressed in a uniform (usually a suit and tie), homogenized and deskilled. The MBA in such an institution would be the ultimate in standardization, the McUniversity's 'Big Mac'. The service amounts to 'education' in exactly the same way as catering is the service of the fast-food output. In both cases, the mode of delivery hinges on the seduction of the customer — the customer who pays in order to receive a product or a service that represents, matches or stimulates a fantasy.

Ritzer uses the terms 'means of consumption' and 'cathedrals of consumption' to describe the organized settings that 'allow, encourage, and even compel us to consume so many of those goods and services' (p. 2). His central thesis is that contemporary management firmly sets its eyes not on the toiling and only intermittently recalcitrant worker, but on the fantasizing consumer. What management does is to furnish, in a highly rationalized manner, an endless stream of consumable fantasies inviting consumers to pick and choose, thus creating the possibility of re-enchanting a disenchanted world through mass festivals in the new cathedrals of consumption. Ritzer offers prodigious illustrations of the ways in which consumption is constantly promoted, enhanced and controlled in these new settings, not so much through direct advertising, as through indirect means, such as spatial arrangements, uses of language, festivals, simulations and extravaganzas, as well as the cross-fertilization ('implosion') of products and images. Above all, consumption gradually colonizes every public and private domain of social life, which become saturated with fantasizing, spending and discarding opportunities. Thus, along with other public spaces, schools, universities and hospitals, spearheaded by business schools, are converted into terrains of consumption, which treat their constituents as customers, offering them a profusion of merchandise, images, ideas and signs that indulge their fantasies and caprices.

In MBAs, the spirit of consumerism reigns supreme. The student is a customer and there is scarcely any pretence to the contrary (Sturdy and Gabriel 2000). Many of the theories to which s/he is exposed extol customer service, quality and consumer sovereignty (Du Gay and Salaman 1992; Knights and Morgan 1993; Gabriel and Lang 1995; Sturdy 1998), and s/he expects nothing less from those that deliver the service purchased. Thus, consumerism has forged a holy alliance of the manager and the consumer, an alliance that is now dominating culture, economy and politics, forged at the expense of the worker or employee. The manager has emerged as a cultural archetype in an age when the work ethic has been dislodged by a consumer ethic as the basis of each individual's moral and social outlook (Grey 1999). If Henry Ford was the manager who epitomized mass production, Walt Disney has posthumously become the emblematic figure of our time — the manager re-defined from agent of control to orchestrator of mass fantasies. The manager is lionized as indeed is the consumer. An 'enterprise culture', dynamic, self-confident, attractive and mostly spurious, has become a dominant feature of our cultural landscapes.

Thus, the cult of the consumer has now become a major feature of the ideological and political order of the business enterprise, legitimating, justifying and supporting a wide range of management practices that would be regarded as intolerable had it not been for the belief that the customer is sovereign (Du Gay and Salaman 1992; Sturdy 1998; Gabriel 1999; Long 1999). Consumption has become an ever more important sphere of human existence, one in which meanings and identities are forged and communicated, in which fantasies and desires are acted out, and in which group allegiances and antagonisms are fashioned. As Bauman (1988, 1992, 1998) has forcibly argued, in postmodernity, a consumer ethic dislodges the work ethic of past times, acting as the organizing principle for individual perceptions of self and other, restoring pleasure as the key objective of action and casting the freedom of the capitalist marketplace as the absolute guarantee of individual freedom, fulfilment and autonomy.

If organizational theories can be seen essentially through the prism of consumption, it may be that they too find applications in practice in ways not unlike those of other commodities. Consumers, ranging from students and participants in management-training workshops to readers of management manuals, conference participants and viewers of training videos, to academics, researchers and teachers who casually glance at each other's published work or listen to each other's presentations, they all appropriate and make use of theories in their day-to-day practice. They make use of them in a myriad of different ways, yet in ways which, in essence, are similar to the uses they make of other commodities, such as motor cars, blue-jeans, books and television shows. The use of the concept of consumption to describe the dissemination and utilization of organizational theories does not contradict the view of scholars constituting communities of practice (Brown and Duguid 1991; Lave and Wenger 1991; Gherardi et al. 1998), since consumers too can be thought of as communities of practice, in as much as they share the same tastes, lifestyles and aesthetics (Bourdieu 1984; Gabriel and Lang 1995). In this sense, communities of practice are not dissimilar 'imagined communities' (Anderson 1983; Hobsbawm 1983) or what Maffesoli (1995) describes as neo-tribes, using broadly similar theories, attributing broadly similar meanings to them, sharing totemic loves and hates and broadly recognizing themselves as communities.

Numerous theorists of contemporary consumption have taken an interest precisely in the ways consumers make use of the objects and services they buy or reject (de Certeau 1984; McCracken 1988; Campbell 1989; Fiske 1989; Bauman 1992; MacClancy 1992; Pandya and Venkatesh 1992; Hermann 1993; Abercrombie 1994; Gabriel and Lang 1995; Du Gay 1996;

Bauman 1998; Dobscha 1998; Sturdy 1998). One of the most significant contributions made in this area lies in the argument that consumers do not generally respond to commodities like Pavlov's dogs, passively salivating after them, wanting them and getting them. Instead, they often explore, experiment, day-dream, critique, toy with them in their minds, and, when they acquire them, they tend to recreate them actively, customize them, adapt them to their needs and incorporate them in their repertoire of actions. They frequently use the things and services that they buy in unorthodox ways; in ways that are very different from those imagined by the providers, marketers and sellers — in short, they turn commodities into raw materials for a kind of creative bricolage.

Bricolage — an everyday French term describing the activity of the handyman or woman who makes do with whatever materials and tools are at hand to accomplish a task — was used by Lévi-Strauss (1966) to contrast the analytic methodology of Western science with what he called the 'science of the concrete' of pre-literate societies. Mythical thought, he argued, is a form of 'intellectual bricolage' (Lévi-Strauss 1966: 21). While at pains to emphasize that there is no superiority or primacy of the one over the other (thus, neolithic people, he argues, made remarkable scientific breakthroughs), Lévi-Strauss insisted that they represent radically different forms of thinking.

'The "bricoleur" is adept at performing a large number of diverse tasks; but, unlike the engineer, he does not subordinate each of them to the availability of raw materials and tools conceived and procured for the purpose of the project. His universe of instruments is closed and the rules of his game are always to make do with "whatever is at hand", that is to say with a set of tools and materials which is always finite and is also heterogeneous, because what it contains bears no relation to the current project, or indeed to any particular project, but is the contingent result of all the occasions there have been to renew or enrich the stock or to maintain it with the remains of previous constructions of destructions.' (Lévi-Strauss 1966: 17)

A fundamental feature of bricolage is that it does not worry about 'proper' and 'improper' uses of objects. It makes do with whatever is available, whether perfect or imperfect, cheap or expensive, simple or elaborate. It is no respecter of conventional definitions of value — under certain circumstances a discarded soup tin may be more valuable than a diamond. An expensive piece of furniture and a rotting log may double up as a stool, under different circumstances, and perform the task equally effectively. Thus, bricolage is opportunistic, *ad hoc*, devious, creative and original, constantly re-defining tools into materials and materials into tools, while, at the same time, re-defining the task at hand in the light of the meanings attributed to the available resources. As a form of work, Lévi-Strauss argues that the preferred materials of bricolage are not concepts (the materials of scientific theories), but signs (p.20ff) — the bricoleur has the privilege over the scientist of being able to define a block of wood alternately as material, support, extension, chopping board, hammer, and so forth — each potential use representing a distinct signification. In this sense, the bricoleur 'interrogates all the heterogeneous objects of which his treasury is composed to discover what each of them could "signify" and so contribute to the definition of a set which has yet to materialize, but which will ultimately differ from the instrumental set only in the internal disposition of parts.' (Lévi-Strauss 1966: 18)

Bricolage has become a fairly popular term in organizational theory, capturing the makeshift, improvisatory and creative qualities of cultural life in organizations (Grafton-Small and Linstead 1989; Linstead and Grafton-Small 1990b; Linstead and Grafton-Small 1992). Weick (1993) has used bricolage as the basis for a radical new understanding of organizational redesign; Rynes and Trank (1999) have used it to describe the activities of creative teaching; while Knorr Cetina (1981) has used the related term of 'tinkering' to capture the opportunism inherent in much research activity. In all of these instances, bricolage has become a way of describing modes of *use* rather than *thought*. It has also lost its initial juxtaposition to its original opposite, scientific methodology and thought. In fact, this latter is frequently shown to possess the same opportunistic, *ad hoc*, improvisatory qualities that are the essence of bricolage. However, in spite of this ever-widening range of applications, it is in consumer studies that the concept of bricolage has come into its own, opening up great possibilities for understanding the relationship between commodities and consumers.

Thus, De Certeau (1984) views consumption (whether the consumption of ideas and theories or the consumption of clothing brands) as an area of fragmentation, instability and heterogeneity in sharp contrast to production, which he views as managed, planned and controlled. In this, he pre-figures Ritzer's view that management seeks to enchant the world by carefully controlled and planned routines. While the producer may control the spaces and circumstances where enchantment takes place, the nature of the enchantment experience itself entails unpredictability and instability. Consumption is tactical, opportunistic and *ad hoc*, whereas production is strategic, planned and rational:

'In reality, a rationalized, expansionist, centralist, spectacular and clamorous production is confronted by an entirely different kind of production, called "consumption" and characterized by its ruses, its fragmentation ... its poaching, its clandestine nature, its tireless but quiet activity, in short, its quasi-invisibility, since it shows itself not in its own products ... but in an art of using products imposed on it.' (1984: 31)

Consumption then is viewed as a process of bricolage, characterized by improvization, tinkering and makeshift in contrast to rational procedures and plans of production. From this perspective, commodities offer consumers something akin to "recipe books" on which they draw to make their own dishes. Consumers are active, but can also be critically resistant. They do not passively follow the recipe books but select some of the recipes, discard others and combine yet others. They adapt the recipes to local conditions; they creatively introduce new ingredients in the dishes they prepare; and they substitute recipe ingredients for acceptable of desirable alternatives. At times, they lose faith in a particular recipe or in an entire recipe book, and get rid of it. In all these instances, consumers adapt objects to highly specific, often *ad hoc* uses, devising unique combinations and variations. If organizational theories are approached in this manner, as consumer goods whose uses are often eclectic and detached from those envisaged by their producers and merchandisers, would it not be possible to argue that managers, as well as other users, use them in roughly similar ways to those in which sophisticated cooks may use recipe books?

Thus, different consumers make different uses of theories, and, in particular, organizational theories. A student may use a theory to fashion an essay which ensures success in his course; a researcher may use another theory to develop a questionnaire or a plan for field research; an academic may use it as a stalking horse against which her own theory can be pitched. A consultant may use it to impress a client. A client may use it to impress her superiors or to dazzle her peers. In all these instances, a theory may be used in a way which bears the hallmark of the user's appropriation. For academics, I would venture to suggest that the three commonest uses to which theories are put are critique, source of authority and source of ideas. Given the time pressures under which most academics work, it is likely that many spend more time writing than reading — hence, they 'use' theories not in 'reading' them, reproducing or criticising them, but rather in cutting and trimming them to fit selective parts into their writing practices. Managers, too, may, and often do, use theories in ways particular to their own preoccupations, but, in a similar manner, they incorporate them into their own creative bricolage, using them to achieve diverse ends in more or less effective ways.

There may be those who do not view managers as the agents of 'rationalized, expansionist, centralist, spectacular and clamorous production', because their thinking is essentially strategic, and hence ill-suited to clandestine, opportunistic tactics of consumption. There may also be objections to De Certeau's strictures being taken as applying to the underdog, rather than the top dog, the position of management. De Certeau maintains, after all, that consumers use creative tactics to evade the power of business and capital, to reclaim spaces, discourses and meanings *from management*. For the past hundred years or more, management (and not only in the catering industry) has been seen as desperately trying to 'stop cooks from messing up the recipes' — whether 'cooks' are recalcitrant workers, temperamental employees or unpredictable customers.

Yet, I would contend that what may be true of management is not necessarily true of managers. Managers may harbour the illusion of being in control, but such control is, at best, precarious, fragile and iconic. Organizations have unmanaged spaces which managers themselves help to create and maintain (de Certeau 1984; Watson 1994; Gabriel 1995; Gabriel and Lang 1995). Within these unmanaged spaces, the practices of every-day life are tactical, not strategic. As de Certeau (1984: 35–37) recognizes, 'strategy is the calculation of power relationships that becomes possible as soon as a subject with a will to power (an army, a business, etc.) can be isolated. It postulates a place from which targets and threats can be managed.' By contrast, a tactic is 'a calculated action determined by the absence of proper locus. ... It is a manoeuvre "within the enemy's field of vision", as von Bulow put it, "and within enemy territory". It does not, therefore, have the options of planning general strategy and viewing the adversary as a whole within a distinct, visible, and objectifiable space. It operates in the form of isolated actions, blow by blow. It takes advantage of "opportunities" and depends on them, being without any base to stockpile its winnings, to build up its own position, and to plan raids. What it wins it cannot keep. ... It must vigilantly make use of the cracks that particular conjunctions open in the surveillance of proprietary powers. It poaches in them. It creates surprises in them. It can be where it is least expected. It is a guileful ruse. In short, a tactic is an art of the weak.' (de Certeau 1984: 37)

Our argument, then, is that the uses to which organizational theory is put by managers, academics and others is essentially tactical rather than strategic. This use of organizational theories by managers is consistent with views that see contemporary management itself as being subject to flexibility, short-termism and opportunism (Maccoby 1976; Sennett 1998) as well as those who systematically seek to demolish the myth of strategic planning in times of complexity and chaos (Cohen et al. 1972; MacIntyre 1981; Stacey 1992; Thomas 1993; Watson 1994; Stacey 1996; Gabriel 1998). Managers use theories in a short-term, opportunistic, flexible way, just as they use other resources in the organization, including each other. Displaying loyalty or uncritical faith in any one theory makes one a hostage to fate, just as one would by putting blind commitment in a single organization, recipe or recipe book. Using organizational theory tactically means being selective, eclectic and flexible in one's uses of recipe books from which to draw ideas for creative bricolage. At times, managers may use recipes as they find them in the book, but more often they modify, adapt, combine, simplify or disregard them. They often display their recipe books as a means of earning themselves status and prestige, not unlike the kitchens of middle-class homes, that bulge with alluringly illustrated cookery books. At other times, they may simply enjoy leafing through the recipes, relishing the pictures and fantasizing about tastes. Occasionally, a recipe will come in handy, when bereft of ideas and faced with an unexpected problem, such as having to cook for a formal visitor. Very frequently, the mere existence of the book will act as adequate support and comfort, even though it is hardly ever consulted — it is a placebo effect which, far from representing deception, has a valid and openly acknowledged therapeutic use. In different circumstances, if one is suddenly presented with a large and unexpected quantity of ripe blueberries or unripe tomatoes, the book may prove useful in offering tips on how to use them. All in all then, organizational theory may be put to a myriad of uses in the hands of different practitioners, as objects of improvisation and experimentation, few of which were ever dreamed of by their disseminators or inventors. Throughout this argument, I refuse to acknowledge a difference between good and bad, appropriate and inappropriate uses of theories. To be sure, as Watson has eloquently argued, some users make very superficial use of an idea 'Motivation: that's Maslow, isn't it?'. Such users may be said to be as inept bricoleurs as theoreticians, though the simple link between Maslow and motivation may be the perfect key for answering a question in a multiple-choice test.

To the question of whether organizational theories are made use of, the answer is 'Of course they are, in exactly the same way as commodities, religious ideas, and recipe books'. They lend themselves to as many different types of action and justification as there are limits to the ingenuity of users. Users incorporate endless and often idiosyncratic variations of organizational theories in their actions. Organizational theories can be instruments of praxis through which a hero confronts his or her predicament and achieves glory or doom; equally, they can be poetic material which a craftsman fashions in order to generate something uniquely novel and personal. In this sense, even fantastic, simplistic, naïve, mystical and self-contradictory theories can function perfectly well as recipes.

In concluding I would like to reflect on the nature of recipe books as prototypes of the ways in which consumers relate to commodities, including theories of organizations. A recipe book appears to be highly precise, well planned and rationally arranged. unless rabbit is lumped with farmed animals and hare with game, all recipes for rabbit will be conveniently grouped together in close proximity to recipes for hare. The ingredients are clearly stipulated and the quantities are fixed. Above all, recipe books appear to be *programmatic* — sets of instructions to be faithfully executed, in a precise sequence, exactly as digital computers execute long algorithms of logically inter-connected instructions. One may rightly imagine that one only needs to follow a recipe to produce the culinary masterpieces of its frequently illustrious author. If you use the recipe book faithfully, the temptation is to believe that success is inevitable. Yet modest familiarity with recipe books indicates this to be far from the case. 'Feather, bone and clean a brace of pheasants' is the type of instruction which, if taken in a programmatic sense, will leave amateur cooks perplexed, angry and covered in feathers. One can imagine the organizational theory equivalent — 'Identify the core competences of your organization, and eliminate all else, the feathers, the bones and the guts'. Yet, consumers know well that the programmatic quality of the recipe book is there to be subverted, abused, dismissed or modified. Instead of a programme, sophisticated consumers see in a recipe a set of ideas which may stimulate them into certain actions. Just as in *commedia del' arte*, the audience know the basic plot, but are waiting to see how the actors will improvise around it. In much the same way, the recipes in a recipe book invite improvisation and elaboration rather than copying and imitation. Instead of programmes, they provide recipes or 'flexible routines', which I prefer to call *'paragrammes'* — basic stocks of ideas, routines, images and ingredients which may be selectively trawled, lifted and adapted to the situation at hand. Paragrammes can also be said to underlie the skill of the jazz musician and the storyteller, both of whom seek to discover new and original ways of recreating something established.

Paragramme is a neologism condensing programme and paradigm into a new concept which entails something written down ('gramme') but not used as written ('para' as in paraphrase, parody and paradox). It is not an exemplar, a model or a set of instructions, but a set of ideas which acts as a prompt and guide for action. In this way, its closeness to 'pragmatic' is serendipitous. ('Paragrammatic' has a totally different etymology from 'pragmatic' which belongs to the cluster of words that share a root with 'praxis' and 'practice'.) Programmes, as epitomized by computer software, are digital arrangements. In other words, they are grids of slots that may be full or empty, whose relations are determined by certain rules of operation, whereby certain patterns in some grid areas affect patterns in other areas, in a highly orderly manner. Slots can either be full or empty, occupied or vacant, electrically charged or not. In short, they must be reducible to immense sequences of zeros and ones. Paragrammes, on the other hand, are profoundly undigital, involving no distinctions of right and wrong, black and white, and so forth. They have a wealth of rules-of-thumb, where quality may not be reduced to quantity, where 'a little bit more' of this or a 'little bit less' of that can make all the difference, yet without anybody being able to specify how much this 'little bit' is. Their complexity is of a non-algorithmic type, stubbornly refusing to be tamed within clearly specified sequences of zeros and ones.

The argument here is that organizational theory is used by its consumers as a set of paragrammes addressing organizations, management, innovation, leadership, etc. Occasionally, a user may be inspired, seduced or deceived sufficiently by one such paragramme to seek in it the solution to current problems and difficulties, although I suspect that even the most impressionable consumers will not seek directly to apply in their actions the theories to which they were exposed in books, journals or business programmes. Instead, they will seek to try out some of these ideas after suitable modification, combination, critique, ridicule, experiment and to ignore others, in short, to appropriate them tactically. Many users (academic users too) treat organizational theory or theories as paragrammes rather than paradigms.

Is it legitimate to group together as paragrammes different forms of organizational theorizing? Clearly some of the more practical accounts, such as *The One Minute Manager* (Blanchard 2000) or *How to Make Millions With Your Ideas : An Entrepreneur's Guide* (Kennedy 1996) lend themselves readily to such treatment. It may be countered that theoretical statements, such as *Sociological Paradigms and Organizational Analysis* (Burrell and Morgan 1979), belong to a different type of discourse, the uses of which are quite distinct from those of populist literature. Yet, I would argue that under the influence of consumerism, academic consumers of books, researchers, teachers, writers and theorists, display opportunistic, short-term, flexible, idiosyncratic, experimental and unorthodox proclivities similar to those displayed by practitioners. They too are engaged in bricolage, albeit of a different genre from that practised by managers (Knorr Cetina 1981; Linstead and Grafton-Small 1990a). Bricolage is no respecter of distinctions between high and low, appropriate and inappropriate; its criteria are essentially pragmatic — if 'Burrell and Morgan' can be used to lend support to an idea, to act as suitable target for criticism or to be framed as precursors of some discursive trend, they serve their purpose every bit as well as 'Aristotle', 'Lévi-Strauss', 'Peters and Waterman' or the latest guru and popularizer. Most hard-pressed academics, like bricoleurs working under tight deadlines and publication pressures, will use any resources readily available to them, stretching them to fit the job at hand, irrespective of whether they are perfect for the occasion or not. Bricolage is the enemy of perfectionism or optimization, in every way, and the champion of 'good enough' pragmatism. Good and bad theories can become useful, once framed in a suitable way, just as 'beautiful' and 'grotesque' objects can become features of aesthetic display, once suitably crafted.

Paragrammatic users of theories, ideas or concepts do not merely re-define them in novel ways — they are also apt to 'lift' them out of different contexts and discourses, with little concern for their original articulations and qualities — as Mary Klages (1997) argues:

'Bricolage doesn't worry about the coherence of the words or ideas it uses. For example, you are a bricoleur if you talk about penis envy or the *oedipus* complex and you don't know anything about psychoanalysis; you use the terms without having to acknowledge that the whole system of thought that produced these terms and ideas, i.e. Freudian psychoanalysis, is valid and "true". In fact, you don't care if psychoanalysis is true or not (since, at heart, you don't really believe in "truth" as an absolute, but only as something that emerges from a coherent system, as a kind of illusion) as long as the terms and ideas are useful to you.'

In this way, most contemporary theoreticians, no less than consultants, teachers and practicing managers are engaged in creative bricolage, using theories, concepts and ideas *paragrammatically* — the very concept of bricolage is used paragrammatically, in discourses which feel neither obliged to accept nor even to acknowledge Lévi-Strauss's key distinction between mythical and scientific thought, on which it was originally founded.

What then is the relationship between bricolage and paragramme? I would suggest that bricolage represents a particular type of activity or practice, whereas paragramme refers to the *modus operandi* of the bricoleur in relation to the materials, tools and knowledge at his/ her disposal. Thus the bricoleur does not use resources paradigmatically (as examples forming the basis for generalizations) or programmatically (as detailed plans for action), but paragrammatically, in a flexible and opportunistic way. Materials, tools and knowledge are continuously defined through the task at hand, thereby, at the same time, helping to define this task. Using a mathematical analogy, if paradigms are examples of how problems may be solved and programmes are detailed sets of instructions on how to solve problems, paragrammes are solutions, free-floating and looking for problems on which to attach themselves.

One of the benefits of looking at theories of organization, high and low, popular and sophisticated, abstract and applied, partial and total, as paragrammes for action concerns management learning and pedagogy. As a teacher, one is often asked the unsettling question of what one should teach management students who come from very different cultures, with different traditions and different organizations from the ones on which most theories are based. For many years, I found this question quite awkward. The concept of paragramme, however, enables us to explain rather convincingly the value of the ideas, theories and concepts to which students are introduced. Theories are not programmes of action or solutions to problems, but may become such through creative improvization and bricolage. They represent a stock of potential solutions to future problems and a source of confidence once used in a free and flexible manner. The analogy of cooking strengthens the argument. Teaching French cuisine to Mexican or Chinese students may seem pointless or perverse, since the ingredients, tools and even tastes in their own cultures are quite different. Yet, the bricoleur cook, using recipes as paragrammes, can discover no end of creative possibilities, by modifying and adapting ingredients, engaging in creative substitution, and translating ideas from one context to another.

*   *   *   *

As I have argued elsewhere (Gabriel 1998), the image of practitioners using theories to tame irregularity and achieve control is severely at odds with the precarious qualities of life in contemporary organizations. Those managers who suffer from the delusion that the answer to their prayers lies in the latest guru's wisdom or the latest buzz-word out of business schools are rapidly disabused of such notions. Some of them may be tempted to embrace new fads and new gods to replace yesterday's fallen idols, but the sensible ones learn that organizational theories are not to be used as scientific absolutes, but more as provisional and contingent rules-of-thumb, at times offering clever short-cuts, at times offering temporary solutions to problems and at times generating results which run contrary to expectations. The practical intelligence (akin to Aristotle's 1983 *phronesis*) lies not in the recipe or the rule-of-thumb itself, but in the ability to identify when and how to invoke them. The same applies to proverbs; while commonly regarded as a distillation of popular wisdom, they defy the rationality of the scientific thinker by frequently contradicting themselves. Yet, true practical wisdom lies in a user's ability to invoke the appropriate one in different circumstances, rather than in the proverb itself. Proverbs and maxims may sometimes appear weak and ineffectual when contrasted to the gleaming towers of science. Yet, when confronted with the unpredictable and transitory qualities of human affairs, as MacIntyre (1981: 105) has argued: 'we should not be surprised or disappointed that the generalizations and maxims of the best social science share certain characteristics of their predecessors — the proverbs of folk societies, the generalizations of jurists, the maxims of Machiavelli'. The same can be said to apply to the famous Chinese War Manual by Sun Tzu (1963: 100), which includes numerous mutually contradictory maxims. The wise general is one who knows under what conditions to use specific instructions and does not seek to repeat a 'winning formula': 'When I have won a victory I do not repeat my tactics, but respond to circumstance in an infinite variety of ways'.

At the cost of appearing to proffer a programmatic rather than a paragrammatic account myself, I shall conclude by identifying some common features of paragrammatic uses of organizational theories by different practitioners. As I have already indicated, paragrammatic users *improvise*, and, in so doing, they continuously seek to adapt the general to the particular, by diagnosing situations where particular theories or ideas may yield productive results. In doing so, they constantly observe, compare and adjust the consequences of their actions, rather than adhere to any specific plan. Second, paragrammatic users *combine*, not merely different elements from different theories, but also theories with other discursive devices, including platitudes, labels, acronyms, and any kind of idea that is deemed promising by their reading of the situation. They constantly look for combinations that are infinitely superior to the sum of their parts and appreciate the power of synergy.

Third, in combining such ingredients, paragrammatic users are careful about *details*. A single detail, if overlooked, may irreparably damage a combination (just as a single infected ingredient may contaminate the entire combination). At the same time, in combining ingredients or ideas, paragrammatic users constantly make use of creative substitution, where specific ingredients may be replaced by others to generate marginal improvements.

Fourth, paragrammatic users pay great attention to *timing*. A winning recipe can easily be ruined by a single lapse in timing, for instance in the introduction of a particular innovation or ingredient. Paragrammatic users recognise the necessity of feverish action at certain times, and patient inactivity at others. Like sensible cooks who resist the temptation to keep opening the oven in order to check the state of their soufflé, paragrammatic users resist the temptation of constant interference which undermines an unfolding process.

Fifth, paragrammatic users draw a distinction between winning recipes which may be relied upon to produce consistent results, and recipes which call for creative experimentation and improvement. They apply the former with *consistency* while seeking to *experiment* with the latter. While looking for short-cuts in certain situations, they will lavish time and resources in others. In a paradoxical way, paragrammatic users combine a deep conservatism with an obsession for innovation and experimentation.

Sixth, paragrammatic users *avoid waste*; they preserve ideas, recipes and materials for future uses or as potential substitutes of those in actual use. They try to recycle and retrieve. They insist on treating waste and junk as a potential resource. At the same time, they recognize non-recoverable situations and are prepared to cut their losses.

Seventh, paragrammatic users rummage for resources, ideas and materials, without any specific task in mind, but in the belief that these may sometime *come in handy*. They rarely complain about shortage of resources,

148   Yiannis Gabriel

since they continuously redefine the task at hand to fit the resources available and they define the resources to meet the task.

Eighth, paragrammatic users engage in *multi-tasking*, in that they are able to pursue several objectives at once. Time itself becomes a malleable resource and interruptions are used to advantage. Instead of waiting in frustration for a missing ingredient, paragrammatic users will readily swap tasks, taking advantage of existing opportunities.

Finally, paragrammatic users do not become obsessed with perfection, but look for good enough practical solutions. While capable of great originality, creativity and innovation, they maintain a *practical interest* to the end and do not pursue dream-like chimeras. They are pragmatic rather than dogmatic, constantly concerned with results rather that with the ideas *per se*.

If we accept the main argument of this paper, that organizational theories are mostly paragrammes rather than programmes of action, it follows that their quality is viewed differently from the perspective of different users. A theory that strikes a researcher as naïve or untenable may be stimulating and imaginative to a manager, handy to a team-leader, amusing to a lecturer, status reinforcing to a trainee and comforting to a student before an examination. Each will find distinct ways of incorporating such a theory into their practice; other organizational theories may be used in different ways, there being no one appropriate or standard way for doing so. The fact that different organizational theories are despised with passion by some, espoused with verve by others, while remaining stubbornly ignored by yet others, indicates that, like so many things in our time, they too have been drawn into the whirlpools of fashion. The same with this essay — it can only become useful or even actionable, if it is appreciated as a paragramme in its own right.

Note

* An early version of this paper was presented to Sub-theme 1 of the 16th EGOS Colloquium, Helsinki, 2-4 July 2000.

References

Abercrombie, Nicholas
1994 'Authority and consumer society' in *The authority of the consumer.* Russel Keat, Nigel Whiteley and Nicholas Abercrombie (eds.), 47–53. London: Routledge.

Anderson, Benedict
1983 *Imagined communities.* London: Verso.

Aristotle
1983 'The Nicomachean ethics' in *A new Aristotle reader.* J. L. Ackrill (ed.), 363–478. Princeton, NJ: Princeton University Press.

Bauman, Zygmunt
1988 *Freedom.* Milton Keynes: Open University Press.

Bauman, Zygmunt
1992 *Intimations of postmodernity.* London: Routledge.

Bauman, Zygmunt
1998 *Work, consumerism and the new poor.* Buckingham: Open University Press.

Blanchard, Keith
2000 *One minute manager.* New York: HarperCollins.

Bourdieu, Pierre
1984 *Distinction: A social critique of the judgement of taste.* London: Routledge.

Brown, John S., and Paul Duguid
1991 'Organizational learning and communities of practice: Toward a unified view of working, learning and innovation'. *Organization Science* 2/1: 40–57.

Burrell, Gibson
1990 'Fragmented labours' in *Labour process theory.* D. Knights and H. Willmott (eds.), 274–296. London: Macmillan.

Burrell, Gibson
1996 'Normal science, paradigms, metaphors, discourses and genealogies of analysis' in *Handbook of organization studies.* S. Clegg, C. Hardy and W. Nord (eds.), 642–658. London: Sage.

Burrell, Gibson, and Gareth Morgan
1979 *Sociological paradigms and organizational analysis.* London: Heinemann.

Campbell, Colin
1989 *The romantic ethic and the spirit of modern consumerism.* Oxford: Macmillan.

Carter, Pippa
1995 'Writing the wrongs'. *Organization Studies* 16/4: 573–575.

Cohen, M. D., J. G. March, and J. P. Olsen
1972 'A garbage can model of organizational choice'. *Administrative Science Quarterly* 17: 1–25.

Czarniawska, Barbara
1999 *Writing management: Organization theory as a literary genre.* Oxford: Oxford University Press.

de Certeau, Michel
1984 *The practice of everyday life.* Berkeley, CA: University of California Press.

Dobscha, Susan
1998 'The lived experience of consumer rebellion against marketing'. *Advances in Consumer Research* 25: 91–97.

Du Gay, Paul
1996 *Consumption and identity at work.* London: Sage.

Du Gay, Paul, and Graeme Salaman
1992 'The cult(ure) of the customer'. *Journal of Management Studies* 29/5: 615–633.

Fiske, John
1989 *Understanding popular culture.* London: Unwin Hyman.

Fournier, Valerie, and Christopher Grey
2000 'At the critical moment: Conditions and prospects for critical management studies'. *Human Relations* 53/1: 7–32.

Freire, Paulo
1996 *Pedagogy of the oppressed.* Harmondsworth: Penguin.

Gabriel, Yiannis
1995 'The unmanaged organization: Stories, fantasies, subjectivity'. *Organization Studies* 16/3: 477–501.

Gabriel, Yiannis
1998 'The hubris of management'. *Administrative Theory and Praxis* 20/3: 257–273.

Gabriel, Yiannis
1999 'Beyond happy families: A critical re-evaluation of the control-resistance-identity triangle'. *Human Relations* 52/2: 179–203.

Gabriel, Yiannis
2000 *Organizational storytelling: Facts, fictions, fantasies.* Oxford: Oxford University Press.

Gabriel, Yiannis, and Tim Lang
1995 *The unmanageable consumer: Contemporary consumption and its fragmentation.* London: Sage.

Gherardi, Silvia, Davide Nicolini, and Francesca Odella
1998 'Toward a social understanding of how people learn in organizations: The notion of the situated curriculum'. *Management Learning* 29/3: 273–297.

Grafton-Small, Robert, and Stephen A. Linstead
1989 'Advertisements as artefacts: Everyday understanding and the creative consumer'. *International Journal of Advertising* 8/3: 205–218.

Grey, Christopher
1999 '"We are all managers now"; "We always were": on the development and demise of management'. *Journal of Management Studies* 36/5: 561–585.

Hatch, Mary Jo
1999 'Exploring the empty spaces of organizing: How improvisational jazz helps redescribe organizational structure'. *Organization Studies* 20/1: 75–100.

Hermann, Robert O.
1993 'The tactics of consumer resistance: Group action and marketplace exit'. *Advances in Consumer Research* 20: 130–134.

Hobsbawm, Eric
1983 'Inventing traditions' in *The invention of tradition*. E. Hobsbawm (ed.), 263–607. Cambridge: Cambridge University Press.

Jackson, Norman
1995 'To write, or not to write? ...' *Organization Studies* 16/4: 571–573.

Jackson, Norman, and Pippa Carter
1995 'The fact of management'. *Scandinavian Journal of Management* 11/3: 197–208.

Kennedy, Dan S.
1996 *How to make millions with your ideas: An entrepreneur's guide*. London: Plume.

Klages, Mary
1997 Notes on Derrida. http://www.colorado.edu/English/ENGL2012Klages/2derrida.html

Knights, David, and Glenn Morgan
1993 'Organization theory and consumption in a post-modern era.' *Organization Studies* 14/2: 211–234.

Knights, David, and Hugh Willmott
1989 'Power and subjectivity at work: From degradation to subjugation'. *Sociology* 23/4: 535–558.

Knorr Cetina, Karin D.
1981 *The manufacture of knowledge: An essay on the constructivist and contextual nature of science*. Oxford: Pergamon.

Lave, J., and E. Wenger
1991 *Situated learning: Legitimate peripheral participation*. Cambridge: Cambridge University Press.

Lawrence, W. Gordon
1999 'A mind for business' in *Group relations, management, and organization*. R. French and R. Vince (eds.), 40–53. Oxford: Oxford University Press.

Lévi-Strauss, Claude
1966 *The savage mind*. Oxford: Oxford University Press.

Linstead, Stephen A., and Robert Grafton-Small
1990a 'Organizational bricolage' *in Organizational symbolism*. B. A. Turner (ed.), 291–309. Berlin: Walter de Gruyter.

Linstead, Stephen A., and Robert Grafton-Small
1990b 'Theory as artefact: Artefact as theory' in *The symbolism of artefacts*. P. Gagliardi (ed.), 387–419. Berlin: Walter de Gruyter.

Linstead, Stephen A., and Robert Grafton-Small
1992 'On reading organizational culture'. *Organization Studies* 13/3: 331–355.

Long, Susan
1999 'The tyranny of the customer and the cost of consumerism: An analysis using systems and psychoanalytic approaches to groups and society'. *Human Relations* 52/6: 723–743.

MacClancy, Jeremy
1992 *Consuming culture*. London: Chapman.

Maccoby, Michael
1976 *The gamesman: New corporate leaders*. New York: Simon and Shuster.

MacIntyre, Alasdair
1981 *After virtue*. London: Duckworth.

Maffesoli, Michel
1995 *The time of tribes: The decline of individualism in mass society.* London: Sage.

McCracken, Grant
1988 *Culture and consumpton: New approaches to the symbolic character of consumer goods and activities.* Bloomington: Indiana University Press.

Obholzer, Anton
1999 'Managing the unconscious at work' in *Group relations, management, and organization.* R. French and R. Vince (eds.), 87–97. Oxford: Oxford University Press.

Pandya, Anil, and A. Venkatesh
1992 'Symbolic communication among consumers in self-consumption and gift-giving: A semiotic approach'. *Advances in Consumer Research* 19: 147–154.

Parker, Martin
1992 'Post-modern organizations or postmodern theory?' *Organization Studies* 13/1: 1–17.

Parker, Martin
1995 'Critique in the name of what? Postmodernism and critical approaches to organization'. *Organization Studies* 16/4: 553–564.

Ritzer, George
1999 *Enchanting a disenchanted world: Revolutionizing the means of consumption.* Thousand Oaks, CA: Pine Forge Press.

Rynes, Sara L., and Christine Quinn Trank
1999 'Behavioral science in the business school curriculum: Teaching in a changing institutional environment'. *Academy of Management Review* 24/4: 808–824.

Sandelands, Lloyd E.
1990 'What is so practical about theory? Lewin revisited'. *Journal for the Theory of Social Behavior* 20/3: 235–262.

Sennett, Richard
1998 *The corrosion of character: The personal consequences of work in the new capitalism.* New York: Norton.

Stacey, Ralph D.
1992 *Managing chaos: Dynamic business strategies in an unpredictable world.* London: Kegan Page.

Stacey, Ralph D.
1996 *Strategic management and organizational dynamics.* London: Pitman.

Sturdy, Andrew
1998 'Customer care in a consumer society: Smiling and sometimes meaning it?' *Organization* 5/1: 27–53.

Sturdy, Andrew, and Yiannis Gabriel
2000 'Missionaries, mercenaries or used car salesmen? Teaching MBA in Malaysia'. *Journal of Management Studies* 37/4: 979–1002.

Thomas, Alan B.
1993 *Controversies in management.* London: Routledge.

Tzu, Sun
1963 *The art of war.* Oxford: Oxford University Press.

Watson, Tony J.
1994 *In search of management: Culture, chaos and control in managerial work.* London: Routledge.

Watson, Tony J.
1996 'Motivation: that's Maslow, isn't it?' *Management Learning* 27/4: 447–464.

Weick, Karl E.
1993 'Organizational redesign as improvisation' in *Organizational change and redesign: Ideas and insights for improving performance.* G. P. Huber and W. H. Glick (eds.), 346–379. New York: Oxford University Press.

Name Index